INSTRUCTOR'S GUIDE TO TEXT AND MEDIA FOR
Biology

Campbell • Reece

Sixth Edition

Benjamin
Cummings

San Francisco   Boston   New York
Cape Town   Hong Kong   London   Madrid   Mexico City
Montreal   Munich   Paris   Singapore   Sydney   Tokyo   Toronto

Development Manager: Pat Burner
Project Editor: Evelyn Dahlgren
Production Editor: Steven Anderson
Production Service: Matrix Productions
Compositor: GTS Graphics, Inc.
Cover Designer: Roy Neuhaus

On the cover: Photograph of an agave plant, Hawaii, © 1991 by Brett Weston.
Courtesy of the Brett Weston Archive.

The objectives in this guide were written by Edward Zalisko, Blackburn College.
The references were compiled by David Reid, also of Blackburn College.

ISBN 0-8053-6635-0

Benjamin
Cummings

2 3 4 5 6 7 8 9 10—VG—06 05 04 03 02

www.aw.com/bc

About This Book

This *Instructor's Guide to Text and Media* is designed to help you organize and integrate the many different student and instructor resources that are available with Campbell/Reece *Biology*, Sixth Edition. The following sections are included for each chapter:

- The **Chapter Outline** provides a list of the main headings of the chapter with the key concepts under each heading.

- **Transparency Acetates,** which include all the art and tables from the book, are listed to help you prepare for lecture.

- The **Media for Instructors** section provides a quick reference to all of the digital instructor's resources available in the different components of the supplements package: The Campbell Image Presentation Library, PowerPoint Lectures, Instructor Resources on the Campbell Biology Website (**www.campbellbiology.com**), and course management systems (CourseCompass™, Blackboard, and WebCT).

- **Media for Students** includes a list of the various resources for students on the Campbell Biology CD-ROM and Website. Following this is a list of the individual student media Activities and the Case Studies in the Process of Science for each chapter.

- The **Objectives** list the key teaching and learning goals for each main section of the chapter. The objectives are also on the Campbell Biology CD-ROM and Website at the beginning of each chapter to guide student learning.

- **Key Terms** includes a convenient list of all boldfaced terms that appear in the text. The key terms are also on the Campbell Biology CD-ROM and Website in the Chapter Review section, where they are linked to the glossary.

- **Word Roots** includes key word roots for each chapter, giving the meaning of each root and an example of a term from the text. The Word Roots are also on the Campbell Biology CD-ROM and Website in the Chapter Review section.

- **References** provide a list of books and journal articles appropriate for the chapter.

- In each chapter, the **Visual Guide to the Image Library** shows thumbnail versions of every image on the Campbell Image Presentation Library: photos, art with labels, art without labels, layered art, tables, animations, and videos. This printed reference guide allows you to plan lecture presentations even when away from your computer.

Supplements for Instructors

New! Campbell Image Presentation Library (ISBN 0-8053-6632-6)

The new Campbell Image Presentation Library is a chapter-by-chapter visual archive that includes over 1600 photos from the text plus additional sources, all text art with and without labels in several convenient formats (jpeg, gif, pdf), selected figures layered for step-by-step presentation, all text tables, over 100 animations, and over 80 video clips. All of the diverse images—photos, art, tables, animations, and videos—are organized by chapter. The art, photos, and tables are also provided as PowerPoint slides. These assets are provided on CD-ROMs and in the Instructor Resources section of the Campbell Biology Website.

New! Campbell Biology Website www.campbellbiology.com

The Instructor Resources section of the Campbell Biology Website includes the Campbell Image Presentation Library (see above), Lecture Outlines in Word, suggested answers to Lab Report questions from the Case Studies in the Process of Science, and links to free Internet photo resources. Instructors may also participate in the Forum for Great Teaching Ideas to share tips for teaching introductory biology. The website also includes a Syllabus Manager for instructors who wish to post their syllabus to a website without creating their own website or using a complete course management system. For access to the website, refer to the insert in the Professional copy of Campbell/Reece *Biology* Sixth Edition.

Transparency Acetates (ISBN 0-8053-6636-9)

Over 1,000 full-color acetates include all illustrations and tables from the text, many of which incorporate photographs. New to this edition are selected figures illustrating key concepts broken down into a series of images for step-by-step lecture presentation. Brightened colors in the transparencies provide excellent viewing in the classroom or lecture hall.

Test Bank (ISBN 0-8053-6637-7)
Computerized Test Bank (ISBN 0-8053-6748-9)

Edited by William Barstow, University of Georgia

Thoroughly revised and updated. Includes new media Activity test questions and many of the Self-Quiz questions from the text, which can be used on tests to encourage students to use these resources. Available in print and on a cross-platform CD-ROM. Also included in the instructor section of the course management systems (CourseCompass™, Blackboard, and WebCT).

New! PowerPoint Lectures (ISBN 0-8053-6756-X)

Steve Norton, East Carolina University

Prepared PowerPoint lectures integrate the art, photos, tables, and lecture outline for each chapter. These PowerPoint Lectures can be used as is, or customized for your course with your own images and text and/or additional images from the Campbell Image Presentation Library.

New! Course Management Systems

The content from the Campbell Biology Website and Computerized Test Bank is available in these popular course management systems: CourseCompass™, Blackboard, and WebCT. Visit http://cms.aw.com for more information.

Investigating Biology, Annotated Instructor's Edition, Fourth Edition (ISBN 0-8053-7366-7)

Judith Giles Morgan, Emory University, and M. Eloise Brown Carter, Oxford College of Emory University

Teaching information, added to the original Student Edition text, includes margin notes with hints on lab procedures, additional art, and answers to in-text and end-of-chapter questions from the Student Edition. A detailed Teaching Plan at the end of each lab features specific suggestions for organizing labs, including estimated time allotments for each part of the lab, and suggestions for encouraging independent thinking and collaborative discussion.

Preparation Guide for Investigating Biology, Fourth Edition (ISBN 0-8053-7367-5)

Judith Giles Morgan, Emory University, and M. Eloise Brown Carter, Oxford College of Emory University

Guides lab coordinators in ordering materials as well as in planning, setting up, and running labs.

New! Symbiosis Book Building Kit—Customized Lab Manuals (ISBN 0-201-72142-2)

Build a customized lab manual, choosing the labs you want, importing artwork from our graphics library, and even adding your own notes, syllabi, or other material. Visit http://www.pearsoncustom.com/database/symbiosis.html for more information.

Supplements for Students

New! Campbell Biology CD-ROM and Website
www.campbellbiology.com

The student CD-ROM and website included with each book contain over 230 Activities, over 55 Case Studies in the Process of Science, Objectives, Word Roots, Key Terms linked to the glossary, several forms of assessment for each chapter (Pre-Test, Activities Quiz, Chapter Quiz), News Articles, a Glossary with pronunciations, and the Campbell Biology Interviews from all six editions of the book. In addition, the website provides access to an E-Book, all the art from the book with labels and without labels, over 80 Videos, the Biology Tutor Center, interactive Chapter Reviews, Essay Questions, Web Links, News Links, Further Readings, and Syllabus Manager. The CD-ROM and website are included with new books. Students who buy a used book may purchase a subscription to the website at www.campbellbiology.com.

Student Study Guide (ISBN 0-8053-6634-2)

Martha R. Taylor

This printed learning aid provides a concept map of each chapter, chapter summaries, word roots, chapter tests, and a variety of interactive questions, including multiple choice, short-answer essay, labeling art, and interpreting graphs.

Biology Tutor Center www.aw.com/tutorcenter

This center provides one-to-one tutoring for college students four ways—phone, fax, e-mail, and the Internet—during evening hours and on weekends. Qualified college instructors are available to answer questions and provide instruction regarding self-quizzes and other content found in *Biology*, Sixth Edition. Visit **www.aw.com/tutorcenter** for more information. The Biology Tutor Center is free when packaged with a new book; contact your sales representative for the correct ISBN.

Investigating Biology, Fourth Edition (ISBN 0-8053-7365-9)

Judith Giles Morgan, Emory University, and M. Eloise Brown Carter, Oxford College of Emory University

With its distinctive investigative approach to learning, this laboratory manual encourages students to practice science. Students are invited to pose hypotheses, make predictions, conduct open-ended experiments, collect data, and then apply the results to new problems.

Biology Labs On-Line www.biologylabsonline.com

Enables students to expand their scientific horizons beyond the traditional wet lab setting and perform potentially dangerous, lengthy, or expensive experiments in a safe electronic environment. Visit **www.biologylabsonline.com** for more information.

New! The Benjamin Cummings Special Topics Series

A series of brief 32-page booklets that explain in accessible language what students need to know about these special topics, presenting background, basic findings, and social and ethical implications. They are free when packaged with a new book, and also available for sale when ordered separately. To package with the book, contact your sales representative for the correct ISBN.

Understanding the Human Genome Project (ISBN 0-8053-6774-8)
  Michael Palladino, Monmouth University

Stem Cells and Cloning (ISBN 0-8053-4864-6)
  David Prentice, Indiana State University, Terre Haute

The Chemistry of Life CD-ROM (ISBN 0-8053-8150-3)

Robert M. Thornton, University of California, Davis

This CD-ROM teaches the essentials of chemistry to biology students by presenting them with interactive animations and multimedia tutorials, and then testing their grasp of the material.

An Introduction to Chemistry for Biology Students, Seventh Edition (ISBN 0-8053-3075-5)

George I. Sackheim, University of Illinois, Chicago

Using a programmed approach, this printed workbook takes students step-by-step through the chemistry necessary for success in life sciences courses.

Biomath: Problem Solving for Biology Students
(ISBN 0-8053-6524-9)

Robert W. Keck, Indiana University, Purdue University at Indianapolis and Richard R. Patterson, Indiana University, Purdue University at Indianapolis

This problem-solving supplement teaches biology students the mathematical concepts they need to succeed in their introductory biology courses. Problems, 250 in all, are organized according to topics in a typical biology course.

A Short Guide to Writing about Biology, Fourth Edition
(ISBN 0-321-07843-8)

Jan A. Pechenik, Tufts University

This book teaches students to think as biologists and to then express that thinking clearly and concisely through their writing and speaking.

The Scientific Endeavor: A Primer on Scientific Principles and Practice (ISBN 0-8053-4596-5)

Jeffrey A. Lee, Texas Tech University

The Scientific Endeavor creates a framework for students' future coursework in the sciences by discussing what science is and how it is done.

Doing Biology (ISBN 0-673-99638-7)

Joel B. Hagen, Radford University, Douglas Allchin, University of Texas, El Paso, and Fred Singer, Radford University

This book teaches problem solving through exercises with actual data, real problems, and alternative explanations to examine, criticize, or defend.

Studying for Biology (ISBN 0-06-500650-X)

Anton E. Lawson, Arizona State University

This supplemental guide offers insights not only into what biologists think, but how they think, by discussing the nature of scientific thinking and the primary thinking patterns that biologists use to generate and test alternative hypotheses.

Contents

Effective Uses of Instructional Technologies in Teaching Introductory Biology

By Eric J. Simon
Fordham College
at Lincoln Center

Technology is a funny thing. During the last decade, methods of teaching and learning have changed faster than during any time in the history of organized education. What is responsible for this rapid reformulation? Technology, of course. As educators, we hear about it all the time. The myriad benefits of instructional technologies have been stated and restated so many times that they are approaching mantra, if not dogma.

Yet, almost every educator has a favorite story about how technology can be overemphasized, inappropriately glorified, or just plain misused. Here is mine. A few years ago, my wife and I were in Hawaii (she on business, me as the grateful spouse). We decided to visit the observatories at the top of Mauna Kea, nearly 14,000 feet above the sea. The trip to the top is precarious enough to require a 4-wheel-drive jeep, so we rented one for the occasion. On our way down the mountain, when we returned to paved road, I needed to take the jeep out of 4-wheel drive and back into 2-wheel drive for the highway. My efforts failed and caused a terrible grinding of the gears. In a flash of inspiration, I decided to check the driver's manual. I opened the glove compartment, smiling at my cleverness. Inside, however, I found no driver's manual. What I found was an instructional video.

I could just imagine a committee patting each other on the back for the excellent way they had used technology to help jeep drivers. But at the top of a Hawaiian mountain, I was less impressed. The point was clearly noted: technology should not be haphazardly applied across the whole spectrum of educational situations, but should be used in a thoughtful manner that always supports pre-established learning objectives.

Biology Sixth Edition by Neil Campbell and Jane Reece has a number of technology supplements for students and instructors. First, every new copy of the book includes a student CD-ROM and an access code to the Campbell Biology Website (www.campbellbiology.com). The website includes the same materials that are on the CD-ROM plus additional web-only content. Instructors also have the option of establishing an online course website for their students using Campbell/Reece-specific content in a course management system. CourseCompass, provided by Pearson Education, is a nationally-hosted course management system. Alternatively, instructors can download a Campbell/Reece Blackboard course or WebCT course for local hosting. All of these websites are password-protected and contain the same content that is on the Campbell Biology Website.

Students who purchase a new copy of the textbook receive an access code card for the online course with their textbook. Students who buy a used book can purchase access to a website separately.

The purpose of this introduction is to present ways that these instructional technology tools for students can be used to enhance teaching and learning in introductory biology courses that use *Biology* Sixth Edition. I will present issues to consider and ideas gained from my own experience. In keeping with the lesson cited above, this introduction also discusses the possible pitfalls of technology use. Most importantly, this guide to technology is firmly grounded in one fundamental learning objective: teaching introductory biology using *Biology* Sixth Edition.

A quick word on what this introduction does *not* cover. This introduction will not discuss details of implementation. Visit **http://cms.aw.com** for information on specific course management systems (CourseCompass, Blackboard, and WebCT). The ideas presented in this introduction are general enough to apply to multiple course management systems and related technologies such as CD-ROMs, the Campbell Biology Website, and e-books. The purpose of this introduction is to stimulate thought and provide ideas on how any instructor might gain the advantages of technology use in the classroom while, hopefully, avoiding the types of inappropriate uses that form the basis of so many apocryphal tales.

General Considerations

This section will discuss some general issues related to the use of instructional technologies in the introductory biology classroom.

The most important general point to be made about using technology tools is the one already stated: don't let the technology tail wag the learning dog. Before implementing any specific technology, make sure to pause and ask yourself a few questions: Is this technology appropriate for my classroom? Is the proposed use firmly grounded in one or more of my course objectives? Will the technology under consideration enhance my ability to teach and/or the students' ability to learn? If the answer to any of these questions is "no," then perhaps using the new technologies under consideration should be reconsidered or saved for another course or semester.

Today's students are fairly technology literate. We've all heard the cliché of a young child teaching his/her parents how to use a VCR or computer, and many classroom instructors may feel that the students are as comfortable (or more) with particular technologies than they are. While this may often be true, instructors need to acknowledge that some students may be very uncomfortable, perhaps even functionally illiterate, with certain technological learning aids. In particular, adults or returning students and economically disadvantaged students might be behind their peers in experience with new technologies. In addition, no matter how good they are at certain specific uses of the Internet, nearly every student needs guidance on the proper use of technology as an educational tool.

Thus, it is important for the instructor to introduce technology to the students and to carefully evaluate if it is serving all students. This introduction and evaluation can be accomplished in several ways. First, circulate a questionnaire to determine the level of computer literacy and comfort among your students. If you plan to make heavy use of instructional technologies during your course, poll your students on the first day of class to determine their comfort level. These polls and questionnaires can help guide the instructor regarding the pace of introducing new technologies, indicating which technologies the students are very comfortable with (e.g., e-mail) and which might require more training or supervision (e.g., presentation software). The polls can also be used to establish teams of students by pairing less savvy students with those who are more competent. Figure I-1 (page I-15) contains a sample technology questionnaire that can serve as the basis for your own.

A similar poll can be used at the end of the course (or at the end of the first semester of a two-semester course) to evaluate the technology experience of your students. This poll can provide helpful information to the instructor regarding adapting the technologies for future courses or semesters. I have often found the students' comments to be insightful with respect to how the technologies were used and any perceived benefits and drawbacks. Figure I-2 (page I-16) contains a sample end-of-semester technology questionnaire.

A useful method for introducing students to the technologies you plan to use is to create assignments that combine course material with technology usage. For example, ask students to track down certain specific information on the Internet (e.g., "How many organisms have had their genomes sequenced?" or "How many different species of mammal have been cloned?"). Require students to provide both the answer and a proper citation for their source. This assignment will help to familiarize students with Web-based biology resources and can also turn into a sophisticated lesson on how to critically evaluate Internet sources, a crucial skill as the Internet gains prominence as a scholarly tool. Other possible assignments can be based on the content provided on the *Biology* Sixth Edition CD-ROM and website. In each case, the assignment serves a dual purpose: to guide the students in a biology-related inquiry, and to ensure their proper use of the technology involved.

Many students, particularly those less familiar with technology, will experience two learning curves in a technology-heavy course: one for the curricular material itself and another for the technologies. Students can thus benefit from the stepwise introduction of instructional technologies into the classroom. A recommended approach is to use a series of assignments that gradually introduce the different instructional technologies. The first technology-related assignment should use an easy and familiar resource, such as e-mail. Future assignments should build upon each other with respect to the technologies required. A second assignment, for example, might involve e-mailing a report, thus combining e-mail and word processing skills. Future assignments can involve the course bulletin board, Internet, CD-ROMs, websites, and other resources. A capstone assignment for the course might involve creating a multimedia presentation on some relevant subject, requiring skills in presentation software, word processing, graphics, Internet searches, etc. The important point is to make sure that no particular assignment introduces more than one new technology component at a time and that the assignments build upon each other with respect to both curricular and technology content.

A final general piece of advice is to use both incentives ("carrots") and requirements ("sticks") to encourage students to participate in the technology components of the course. Assignments are a great way to ensure that every student is benefiting from the technologies, but remember to toss out some carrots as well. I have found that the prompt posting of grades to an online gradebook provides incentive for students to access the course website, particularly for once-a-week courses or at the end of the semester. Providing hints for an exam (through, for example, a virtual chat study session or postings to a bulletin board) is an excellent way of increasing participation. Providing fun links to multimedia such as videos, cartoons, and songs is another way to capture student interest. For example, point students toward content-related songs (such as Weird Al Yankovic's "I Think I'm a Clone Now" or Pearl Jam's "Do the Evolution") available as free samples on some retail websites (e.g., **http://cdnow.com**). Or provide links to movie websites that connect to the curriculum, such as those for the *Jurassic Park* movies or *GATTACA.* I often allow students to earn extra credit by completing small technology projects, such as creating a slide for my in-class PowerPoint presentations or taking a quiz on the book's website. Remember that to be used to its maximum potential, the technology, like the material itself, must be both informative and interesting to the students.

Technology alternatives to standard media have many potential benefits to the teaching and learning processes. Some of these benefits include:

- Multimedia capabilities
- Improved assessment
- Ability to present timely material
- Improved communication
- Customization of curriculum
- Portability

The following sections will discuss each of these advantages in detail. Specific suggestions will be made on using course management systems and related technologies to gain each advantage. In addition, tips on avoiding certain pitfalls of technology use will also be discussed.

Multimedia

One of the most obvious and powerful advantages that technology offers over the printed medium is the ability to display multimedia such as video, animation, hyperlinks, and sound. Movement is one of the characteristics of life, and explaining certain complex biological processes using only static visuals often proves difficult. Metabolic pathways, anatomical configurations, ecological systems, pronunciations of difficult words, and cell cycles are just a few of the topics that benefit from multimedia exposition.

Biology Sixth Edition comes loaded with multimedia supplements. They fall into two general categories: those for the students and those for the instructor. Each chapter in this *Instructor's Guide to Text and Media* includes a list of the media assets available for that chapter.

Student Media

Multimedia student materials can be found on the CD-ROM, Campbell Biology Website, and Campbell course management websites. Every student media chapter includes the following sections:

- Each chapter starts with **Objectives** to guide student learning.
- A **Chapter Review** includes the summary from the book with links to Activities and Case Studies in the Process of Science; the book's Self-Quiz with

immediate feedback; Essay Questions from the book so students can e-mail their answers to TAs or instructors; Word Roots to help students decipher new terminology; and Key Terms linked to the Glossary.

- The **Activities** section contains over 230 tutorials on chapter content that use animations, interactive exercises, audio, and digital video to convey key concepts.

- More than 55 **Case Studies in the Process of Science** involve students in interactive laboratory activities that teach them to follow the scientific method by making observations, formulating a hypothesis, designing and performing an experiment, collecting data, and drawing conclusions. Each Case Study includes a Lab Notebook for recording data and a Lab Report that can be e-mailed to instructors. Students can also link to Biology Labs On-Line, 12 extensive virtual labs. (For more information, see **www.biologylabsonline.com**.) Assignments for Biology Labs On-Line can also be e-mailed.

- The **Quizzes** section includes a Pre-Test, Activities Quiz, Chapter Quiz, and Essay Questions.

- An **E-Book** gives students quick access to the book while they are using the Campbell website. The E-Book includes text, art, tables, and photos organized by the key concepts within each chapter with links to Activities, Case Studies in the Process of Science, and glossary terms.

- Chapter **Web Links** connect students to further Internet resources.

- The **News and References** section includes links to news stories that present recent developments related to the chapter content, longer news articles, and further readings.

- **Art** from the book and over 80 **Videos** are available for student viewing. The art is provided both with labels and without labels. Students can print out the art to take to class for note-taking and they can use the version without labels as a self-quiz.

- **The Campbell Biology Interviews** section contains discussions with specialists from a variety of fields, including many well-known scientists. This section includes all of the interviews in the current print edition of the textbook as well as all those from previous editions. Every interview includes text and photos. The interviews can help students personalize the curriculum and research experience.

- The **Glossary** includes every boldface term from Campbell/Reece *Biology* Sixth Edition with audio pronunciations of selected terms. Terms in the Activities and E-Book are linked to the glossary and students can also access the glossary independently.

- A **Syllabus Manager** is available on the Campbell website for instructors who wish to post their syllabus to the website without using a full course management system.

- **About the Book** provides more information about *Biology* Sixth Edition, the authors, and the supplements.

Instructor Media

Nothing captures student interest during lengthy lectures more than lively presentations with informative multimedia elements. The **Campbell Image Presentation Library**, available via instructor CD-ROMs and the Instructor

Resources section of the Biology Sixth Edition Website and course management systems, aids the instructor in improving classroom lectures and presentations. This chapter-by-chapter visual archive of over 2700 images is for the exclusive use of adopters of Campbell/Reece *Biology,* Sixth Edition. All of the diverse images—art and tables, photos, videos, and animations—are organized by chapter. All file formats have been thoroughly tested in large lecture halls. The Image Library includes:

- **1600 photos,** including the photos from the text, plus additional photos collected from a variety of sources that have been especially chosen to match the content of each chapter. Photo captions are provided as background information for lectures.

- **All the art and tables from the text.** Art figures are provided in several convenient formats (jpg, gif, pdf). Art figures are provided both with and without labels for maximum flexibility in lecture presentations. The version without labels can be customized for lecture, used to create a quiz, or used to create step-by-step presentations. All of the art and tables have been reformatted to be larger and clearer when used for lecture presentation.

- **Selected art figures are layered** for step-by-step presentation.

- **PowerPoint Slides.** All of the photos, art, and tables have been imported into PowerPoint. (For more information about getting started with PowerPoint, visit **www.microsoft.com/office/powerpoint**.)

- **More than 80 video clips.** Instructors can enhance their lectures with QuickTime videos on a variety of biological concepts. Scripts are provided for background information. The videos are available in large (640x480) and small (320x240) formats.

- **Over 100 animations.** Animations can be used in lecture to help students understand key biological concepts.

- **All assets in an easy-to-use HTML viewer.** Thumbnails and enlarged images can be easily viewed on-line so instructors can decide which images to use in lecture.

- **Thumbnails** are also available in this *Instructor's Guide to Text and Media* in the "Visual Guide to the Image Library" section of each chapter.

Fully prepared PowerPoint Lectures with lecture outlines, art, tables, and photos are also available. The PowerPoint Slides or Lectures can be customized for an instructor's course. If desired, the PowerPoint files can be printed out and duplicated for students to use for taking notes during lecture. Customized lecture notes can be published through Pearson Custom Publishing. (See **www.pearsoncustom.com** for more information.)

Other Instructor Resources available on the Campbell Website include an electronic version of the Lecture Outlines (in Word), suggested answers to Lab Report questions from the Case Studies in the Process of Science, and links to free Internet photo resources. Instructors may also participate in the Forum for Great Teaching Ideas, where they can read teaching tips from other instructors, respond with feedback, and/or submit their own teaching ideas.

Assessment

One of the most tedious and time-consuming aspects of teaching is creating and grading tests and quizzes. Many teachers find it to be the most frustrating aspect of the job, from keeping track of old exam questions to calculating and recording grades. Technology can alleviate some of this frustration by doing what computers do best: repetitive tasks. There are also, however, some interesting problems that arise when using technology-based assessment tools.

The assessment tools available with *Biology* Sixth Edition fall into two basic categories: those intended to help the student test their knowledge of the material, and those intended to aid the instructor in the assessment process. For the students, the CD-ROM and the Campbell Biology Website include multiple self-assessment aids organized by chapter. In the Chapter Review section of the student media, the Self-Quiz from the book (ten multiple choice questions and five short answer essay questions) is included on-line so students can easily check their answers. The Chapter Review also includes the book's essay questions— Evolution Connection; The Process of Science; and Science, Technology, and Society—so that student responses to these questions can be submitted by e-mail. Every chapter includes a Pre-Test of ten multiple choice questions which can be used by the instructor to gauge student understanding before lecture. A Chapter Quiz of 30–50 multiple choice questions helps students test their new knowledge. Each quiz has hints and feedback for students, and answers can be e-mailed.

Several of the features included on the Campbell CD-ROM and Website have their own internal assessment tools. The multimedia Activities section associated with each chapter, for example, includes a multiple-choice quiz of 15–25 questions, many of which include graphics from the activities themselves. This quiz reinforces the materials presented in that chapter's Activities, thereby reinforcing important curricular concepts. Assigning the Activities Quiz is a good way to ensure that students successfully complete the Activities section. Also, student understanding of the Case Studies in the Process of Science can be measured by requiring students to e-mail their responses to the Lab Report. Suggested answers to the Lab Report questions can be found in the Instructor Resources section of the Campbell Website. For instructors who assign any of the Biology Labs On-Line (**www.biologylabsonline.com**), students can e-mail responses to assignments from within the Campbell Biology Website.

The Computerized Test Bank for instructors includes 50–60 multiple-choice questions per chapter that students do not have access to. In addition, the Test Bank includes the book's multiple-choice Self-Quiz questions and five multiple-choice questions on the Media Activities so that instructors can encourage students to use these features by including questions on tests if they would like to.

All of these same assessment tools from the *Biology* Sixth Edition Website are included in the CourseCompass, Blackboard, and WebCT course management systems, giving the instructor great flexibility in preparing and presenting quizzes and tests. The Assessment Manager tools (in CourseCompass/Blackboard) control the pre-written quizzes for each chapter: Self-Quiz, Essay Questions, Pre-Test, Activities Quiz, and Chapter Quiz (all taken from the Campbell Biology Website) and Test Bank questions (taken from the Instructor's Computerized Test Bank). In each case, the instructor has the ability to preview, modify, or remove the pre-loaded question set. The modifications that an instructor can make are quite extensive. Every question can be altered to include text, images, or links. The number of answer choices can be set and the text and image for each answer modified. The specific feedback given upon a correct or incorrect answer can be changed for each question. The questions can be grouped into categories for easier selection. The instructor can use all of the questions provided or a subset of them, and the instructor can add original questions and answers.

Once a quiz/test has been created, the instructor has many options for making the quiz available to the students. The instructor controls when to make the quiz/test available to students. The correct answer can be revealed or not, depending on whether the instructor wishes the students to take a quiz multiple times. The customized feedback can be displayed or not. Students may be permitted multiple attempts at each question. A time limit can be set for the quiz, and it can be password-protected. All of these options allow the instructor to tailor each quiz to a particular learning goal. Taken together, these assessment tools provide great convenience in managing the creation and distribution of quizzes and tests while also providing great flexibility.

Once quizzes are made available to students, the Assessment Manager (in CourseCompass/Blackboard) makes grading very convenient for the instructor. The students submit their answers electronically. The quizzes can be automatically graded, with grades sent to the instructor and/or recorded in the online gradebook. The instructor has the ability to view each student's quiz results from anywhere with Internet access, removing the requirement of physical proximity to the office. The online gradebook can calculate averages, create a variety of reports, and is exportable to spreadsheet programs. Students also have access to their own grades on the website so that they can easily keep track of their standing in the course.

No matter which quiz format is being used, online assessment always involves issues of security. Secure online testing is one of the most vexing problems currently facing instructors who deliver courses electronically and I know of no solution that is fully satisfactory for every teaching situation. The course management Assessment Manager (in CourseCompass/Blackboard) does include some security features. A timer can be set to limit the amount of time a student has to complete a quiz. Setting the timer to a sufficiently low value can reduce the chances that a student can consult non-permitted materials (i.e., the book) but obviously does not eliminate that possibility. A password can be associated with each quiz, thereby controlling access starting from the time the instructor makes that password available and ending when the instructor removes access to the quiz. Neither of these features allows for total confidence, however. Probably the most secure method of online testing can be found in schools with a testing center, i.e., a computer facility with a proctor. Such a facility gives students great flexibility of when to take their quiz while also ensuring a high level of security. Some distance learning formats allow students to visit a testing center at a local institution, or with a previously established proctor. Some day, I can imagine secure online testing being achieved through the use of Web cameras that will allow students to take a quiz at home under the scrutiny of an electronic eye that keeps them honest.

Timeliness

No subject in the curriculum is more affected by recent advances than biology. We live in a time when biology seems to be in the news every day. Recent advances in cloning, genetically engineered foods, stem cells, genomes, fertility, and DNA technologies easily capture student attention. In addition to being very interesting, students see the relevance of these topics to their lives. Students, particularly introductory students, always appreciate when connections are made between the subject matter at hand, current events, and popular culture. Biology instructors are uniquely positioned to take advantage of our current biology-centric society to improve the climate of learning in their classrooms.

Several technology resources available with *Biology* Sixth Edition allow for the introduction of timely material. The Campbell Biology Website contains several timely content areas, and nearly identical materials are also built into the pre-loaded online course for *Biology* Sixth Edition in the three course management systems. Even better, the timely materials available on each of these resources (the Website and course management system offerings) are pre-sorted by the relevant *Biology* Sixth Edition textbook chapter, making it easy for the instructor to incorporate current events into classroom activities.

The website that comes with the printed text and the course management websites contain three sets of particularly timely materials: News Links that cover recent advances, News Articles written for introductory biology students, and Web Links that point to timely Internet resources. Between News Links and News Articles, there is at least one relevant article associated with every chapter. On the average, each chapter has about ten Web Links with descriptions of the sites. In the course management systems, instructors can also add their own News Links and Web Links.

An advantage of using the online resources for recent news is that it avoids any copyright conflict. Most instructors know that photocopying articles and handing them out in class raises issues of copyright violation. Reprinting an article electronically on a course website raises identical issues. The Internet offers a way to avoid this potential problem through News Links and Web Links. A local link to a remote article that has been publicly posted by the producer poses no risk of copyright violation. Instructors can thus provide access to online versions of recent news articles without the possibility of recrimination.

Communication

Effective communication is important in every classroom. There are several avenues of communication that must be maintained: professor to student, student to student, and student to teaching assistant. Many introductory biology courses have large enrollments, thus making effective communication simultaneously more important and more difficult.

Computer resources have the potential to vastly improve communication between all participants. Many instructors have found that the nature of the electronic medium encourages some students to speak up who otherwise might not. Students who may be intimidated to participate during lecture are often more comfortable participating via e-mail and online discussions wherein they can compose and edit their comments before submitting them. The asynchronous nature of these forms of electronic communication (e-mail and bulletin boards) provides greater access for all students but is particularly helpful for part-time or non-traditional students who are not on campus as often as their traditional peers. Multiple forms of electronic communication can also be used to create a sense of community and overcome the somewhat impersonal nature of the electronic medium. Creating a learning community is particularly helpful when teaching distance learning courses that lack the close in-person contact of the classroom environment. Students and instructors also benefit from the more global nature of electronic communication. Outside experts, colleagues, and other students can join in the forum, providing resources that are generally not available in a traditional classroom setting.

Within the course management systems, there are seven major communication vehicles: announcements, e-mail, bulletin boards, live chat, home pages, digital drop box, and online gradebook. All of these resources will be discussed below.

Announcements

The most immediate way to communicate with students is through the Announcements feature. All students see announcements from their instructor as soon as they log into the course website. Announcements can include text, images, and links. I usually post at least one announcement per week. A typical announcement will remind students about upcoming assignments, lab activities, study sessions, or quizzes/exams. They can also be more whimsical, such as mentioning important dates in the history of science as they occur, or displaying digital photos taken during recent class activities. It is important to check your particular course management system to find out if announcements disappear from the front page after a certain amount of time and are then only visible if the student clicks on a tab to show older messages. I have found it useful to include a permanent announcement reminding students to look for older announcements.

E-mail

E-mail is the most widely used form of electronic communication. It is effective because it is asynchronous, thereby allowing students to read your comments whenever they have time (often, it seems, late at night). E-mail also allows students and instructors to archive conversations and exchange documents. Personally, I prefer to receive electronic files from my students via e-mail because it is easier to detect and avoid viruses; floppy disks from college students are notoriously prone to invisible viruses. E-mail makes for a good first technology assignment because most students are very comfortable with it. During the first week of the semester, have every student e-mail you with a simple hello message, or perhaps answers to a questionnaire that you have sent them. The successful completion of this simple assignment ensures that every student has access to a working computer and an e-mail account, and that every student knows how to contact the instructor via e-mail. The instructor can then check the e-mail addresses received against the e-mail database maintained by the course management software to make sure they match. This step is important because some students maintain multiple accounts and the course management software may use their school account or an internal e-mail address as default. Within the course management system, it is easy to send e-mail to an individual, the entire class, or any subset thereof. This feature is available to all users so that students can easily e-mail each other. Informing students that they should expect regular e-mail from you will ensure effective communication in most cases.

Bulletin Boards

While e-mail simulates a private office meeting, bulletin boards offer a reasonable simulation of classroom question-and-answer sessions. The bulletin board allows everyone in the class to "hear" the question and answer. I typically expect every student to participate verbally at least once during each in-class lecture. Similarly, I expect every student to participate at least once a week in the class bulletin board, either by posting a question/comment or by responding to a classmate's question/comment. Some instructors require students to post a number of questions and a number of answers in a given time period. In a typical bulletin board assignment, I will bring up an important biological issue (such as the use of DNA forensic evidence to examine old criminal cases or the ethics of reproductive technologies) and assign half the class to each side of that issue. I am often impressed with the enthusiasm and sophistication with which students participate in these discussions. The course management systems include a good threaded discussion system in their bulletin boards. Students can start new discussion topics and can include Internet links in their postings. The instructor can create new threads and has the option of allowing students to create them. I usually create a new thread for each week, so that the topmost level of the bulletin board has a link to each week and subject (such as "Week #3: The cell"). Within each week, I then create some standard subthreads that appear every week: questions/comments, homework assignments, and extra credit. Students are also free to create their own additional subthreads to raise issues of importance to them. The instructor can monitor the discussion and remove repeated, blank, erroneous, or inappropriate postings. I try to read the bulletin board every day during the school week so that I can answer questions, correct misconceptions, and keep the discussion focused on the subject. I find the bulletin board is used most heavily during the weeks before exams. This electronic forum can stimulate interesting questions, debates, and discussions among the students. The class bulletin board is particularly important when teaching distance learning courses because it can go a long way towards supplying interaction among the participants that might otherwise be absent. It also provides a good forum for working on group projects where progress can be monitored in real time.

Live Chat

In-class study sessions can be supplemented or replaced by a virtual discussion held in an online chat room. Such virtual chats have the additional benefit of being logged and archived for students who could not participate. The course management software includes an easy-to-use but sophisticated virtual chat room. The instructor can monitor who is present and everyone can read everyone else's comments. I have found that students often need to "warm up" and be encouraged to participate, so I always have several practice questions prepared, just as I would for an in-person study session. The virtual chat forum is particularly handy before an exam and can also be used to facilitate virtual office hours. I always schedule two virtual chats during the week before an exam to accommodate a wide range of schedules. Classes comprised largely of traditional on-campus students probably fare better with live meetings. In classes with significant numbers of non-traditional, part-time, or off-campus students, however, the virtual meetings are often much more convenient for the students and may significantly increase participation levels.

Home Pages

Home pages offer a good way for members of the class to get to know each other. The course management systems provide an easy-to-use tool that guides even the most novice users to create a home page in a few minutes. For the more sophisticated, home pages can include images, links, or any other HTML code. Having every student create their own home page with answers to standard questions ("What is your major?" "What are your hobbies and interests?") is a good early technology assignment. Students always appreciate a detailed home page from the instructor and teaching assistants. I have found that students truly enjoy the chance to get to know me better, both personally and professionally, through my home page.

Digital Drop Box

Much communication within a class, particularly a large class, centers on the receipt and acknowledgement of assignments. The course management systems offer a "Digital Drop Box" feature that allows students to submit assignments electronically. The students submit their assignments as electronic files into the drop box and receive a receipt. The instructor can remove assignments at any time, from any location with Internet access. This method is much more convenient for both parties than having a fixed location for students to turn in their assignments. Materials placed in the drop box have an attached link that allows an instructor to send an e-mail to the student with one click. I usually send a quick e-mail note to let the student know that their materials have been successfully received.

Online Gradebook

While an online gradebook may not seem like a form of communication, it is, and it can have a great impact. The course management systems offer an online gradebook with many organizational features. Only the instructor can view the entire set of results and modify them, but each student can see their own grades. Instructors can add, edit, or remove gradebook entries at will. Online grade posting allows for rapid communication of grades, and students can track their progress during the course. By viewing the gradebook as a spreadsheet, exporting the grade database to an external tool, or using various analysis tools included in the course management software, instructors can view trends, compare students, and search for weaknesses and strengths within the class.

Customization of the Curriculum

There is probably no introductory biology course that teaches the entire curriculum covered in *Biology* Sixth Edition. Printed textbooks are, by necessity, designed to carry the superset of possible materials covered in any individual course. Different courses will cover only a subset of these materials based on the interests of the students, the instructor, and the program. One advantage of technology is that it can help focus the curriculum from the full range of possible subject matter to just the subset covered in any particular course.

Students appreciate when their study materials are concise and focused. The recent popularity of custom printed texts that incorporate just a portion of the possible materials confirms this need. Some instructors prepare their own self-written materials in order to make them more focused, but this approach requires a large start-up cost and will usually not reach the quality of professionally prepared learning aids.

Course management software provides an opportunity to have the best of both worlds: to pick and choose appropriate high quality pre-written materials for your course from among a large set prepared by the publisher. The ability to customize curricular materials lies within the course management systems. When instructors copy the *Biology* Sixth Edition CourseCompass Course, building upon it to create their own course website, or when they download the *Biology* Sixth Edition Blackboard or WebCT courses, they will find courses pre-loaded with the content of the Campbell/Reece Biology Website, such as Internet links, quizzes, and interactive activities as well as the entire computerized test bank. An optional e-book is available.

Instructors have the ability to customize these pre-loaded materials in several ways. First, any unwanted materials (i.e., those that cover chapters not included in the course) can be deleted from the course website. Students will thus be assured that all of the material on the course website is directly applicable to their particular course, as opposed to the CD-ROM or Campbell Biology Website that contains the full set of materials. The instructor can also modify some of the default material; for example, the instructor can change quiz questions or answers. Finally, instructors always have the ability to create new materials to upload to the site, either from scratch or by using external utilities such as Word or the TestGen software to prepare new quizzes. Instructors can thus simply and effectively customize the instructional materials available to students in ways that are impossible with the standard printed medium.

Portability

Students appreciate the ability to access their study materials from multiple locations, and Internet-based materials offer this convenience. Students can view the summaries, practice tests, news articles, etc. from their dorm, the library, work, and home during vacation. Several students have told me that they like to access the multimedia elements from work because of the higher available bandwidth. Students can leave their book in their primary study location and then use the Internet in several satellite locations. For students who travel, CD-ROMs are also considerably more portable and therefore more convenient than the book. Commuting students appreciate that the CD-ROM can turn travel time into productive study time. I have also heard stories from several students of sharing their class materials from home with family and friends, thereby connecting their academic interests to the larger world.

The ultimate portability is achieved through the use of an electronic version of the text. E-books free students from the physical book in the printed medium all together, providing the full text in a lighter weight format. The Campbell Biology Website includes an e-book for students who buy a new book. The website plus e-book can also be purchased separately. The course management systems (CourseCompass, Blackboard, and WebCT) are available with or without an e-book.

Conclusions

As technology plays an increasingly larger role in the modern biology classroom, two general types of features are emerging. The first are those that simply increase convenience for the student and/or the instructor. Examples include being able to access learning materials from multiple locations, the online gradebook, and the ability to customize a set of learning materials for a particular course. The second category of technology features includes those technologies that actually increase the potential for teaching and learning. Examples include the ability to provide access to very timely materials (i.e., News Links), multimedia explanations of important concepts, and access to outside resources via the Internet.

The instructional technologies included with *Biology* Sixth Edition address both categories described above. Through proper implementation of the CD-ROM, the Campbell Biology Website, and/or the course management systems, a lively and informative learning atmosphere can be created that benefits all students and the instructor.

About the Author

Eric J. Simon, Ph.D., is an assistant professor of biology in the Department of Natural Sciences at Fordham College at Lincoln Center in New York City. He teaches introductory biology and chemistry as well as upper-division biology majors' courses. In all of his classes, Dr. Simon makes heavy use of technology as teaching and learning supplements. His research interests involve investigating innovative uses of technology in the science classroom. His first book, *Teachers Using Technology: Practical Ideas From the Classroom,* will be published in 2002.

Name _____ Course _____ Section _____

1. How comfortable are you with each of the following? (circle one)

    1 = not at all comfortable → 5 = extremely comfortable

A. Computers in general	1	2	3	4	5
B. E-mail	1	2	3	4	5
C. Word processing	1	2	3	4	5
D. Bulletin boards	1	2	3	4	5
E. CD-ROMs	1	2	3	4	5
F. Internet searches	1	2	3	4	5
G. Presentation software (e.g., PowerPoint)	1	2	3	4	5
H. Chat rooms	1	2	3	4	5

2. How comfortable are you using computers as an educational tool?

                               1   2   3   4   5

3. How would you rate your computer literacy compared to your peers? (circle one)

way below average   below average   average   above average   way above average

4. Are there any computer technologies that give you particular difficulties?

5. Do you think you need training in the use of any of the computer technologies listed above? If so, which ones?

Figure I-1 A sample questionnaire that can be distributed at the start of a course to determine the level of computer literacy among students. The results can be used to guide the pace of technology usage, determine necessary levels of training and supervision, and guide in the creation of teams of students.

Course _____   Section _____

1. Please rate your overall level of satisfaction with the instructional technologies used in this course.

      1 = not at all satisfied   → 5 = extremely satisfied

            (circle one)   1   2   3   4   5

2. Please rate your level of satisfaction with each of the following specific technologies used in this course:

A. E-mail	1	2	3	4	5
B. Word processing	1	2	3	4	5
C. Bulletin boards	1	2	3	4	5
D. CD-ROMs	1	2	3	4	5
E. Internet	1	2	3	4	5
F. Presentation software (e.g., PowerPoint)	1	2	3	4	5
G. Chat rooms	1	2	3	4	5

3. What were the advantages of using technology in this course?

4. What were the disadvantages of using technology in this course?

5. Which technologies would you like to see emphasized more in this course? Less?

6. Please make specific suggestions for how technology usage in this course can be improved.

7. Did you feel unprepared for any of the technologies used?

Figure I-2 A sample questionnaire that can be distributed at the end of a semester or course to determine the level of satisfaction with instructional technologies.

CHAPTER 1

Introduction: Ten Themes in the Study of Life

Chapter Outline

Exploring Life on Its Many Levels

Each level of biological organization has emergent properties

Cells are an organism's basic units of structure and function

The continuity of life is based on heritable information in the form of DNA

Structure and function are correlated at all levels of biological organization

Organisms are open systems that interact continuously with their environments

Regulatory mechanisms ensure a dynamic balance in living systems

Evolution, Unity, and Diversity

Diversity and unity are the dual faces of life on Earth

Evolution is the core theme of biology

The Process of Science

Science is a process of inquiry that includes repeatable observations and testable hypotheses

Science and technology are functions of society

Review: Using Themes to Connect the Concepts of Biology

Transparency Acetates

The Transparency Acetates for *Biology*, Sixth Edition, include the following images:

Media for Instructors

Campbell Image Presentation Library

The Campbell Image Presentation Library CD-ROM set includes the following for your use:

- All art (available in pdf and jpeg or gif formats), photos (from the text and outside sources), and tables. Art images are also available without callouts. See the Visual Guide to the Image Library section at the end of this chapter for thumbnail versions of every image.
- A PowerPoint™ slide show of the art (with callouts), photos (both text and outside sources), and tables.
- The following video clip:

    01-16-SeaHorses-B.mov   Sea Horses

PowerPoint Lectures CD-ROM

The PowerPoint Lectures CD-ROM contains slides that integrate the art, photos, tables, and lecture outline from this chapter.

Campbell Biology Website (Instructor Resources)

See the insert in your copy of Campbell/Reece *Biology,* Sixth Edition, for instructions on how to access the Campbell Biology Website. The Instructor Resources section of the website includes the following:

- The art, photos, tables, PowerPoint slide shows, videos, and animations from the Campbell Image Presentation Library
- Suggested answers to the Lab Report questions from the Case Studies in the Process of Science
- The PowerPoint Lecture for this chapter
- Word files of the lecture outline for this chapter
- Photo links

Course Management Systems

The media content for this chapter is available in three course management systems: CourseCompass™, Blackboard, and WebCT. For more information, go to http://cms.aw.com. For the latest pdf instructions on how to use CourseCompass, go to www.coursecompass.com. In addition, a Syllabus Manager is offered on the Campbell Biology Website.

Media for Students

The Campbell Biology Website and CD-ROM include the following for your students:

- Objectives
- Chapter Review (Summary, Self-Quiz, and Essay Questions from the book)
- Quizzes (Pre-test, Activities Quiz, Chapter Quiz, Essay Questions)
- Web Links
- News and References
- Art and videos from the Campbell Image Presentation Library
- The Campbell *Biology* Interviews (from all editions)
- Glossary with audio pronunciations
- Syllabus Manager

Objectives

1. Briefly describe the unifying themes that pervade the biological sciences.

Exploring Life on Its Many Levels

2. Diagram the hierarchy of structural levels in biology.
3. Explain how the properties of life emerge from complex organization.
4. Describe the seven properties of life.
5. Describe the dilemma of reductionism.
6. Explain how technological breakthroughs contributed to the formulation of the cell theory and our current knowledge of the cell.
7. Distinguish between prokaryotic and eukaryotic cells.
8. Describe the structure and function of DNA.
9. Explain what is meant by "form fits function."
10. Explain how an organism is a type of open system.
11. Describe the two major dynamic processes of any ecosystem.
12. Explain how regulatory mechanisms control reactions in organisms.

Evolution, Unity, and Diversity

13. Distinguish among the three domains of life. List and distinguish among the kingdoms of eukaryotic life.

14. Briefly describe how Charles Darwin's ideas contributed to the conceptual framework of biology.

The Process of Science

15. Outline the scientific method.

16. Distinguish between inductive and deductive reasoning.

17. Distinguish between a scientific hypothesis and a scientific theory.

18. Explain how science is influenced by social and cultural factors.

19. Explain how science and technology are interdependent.

References

Becker, W. M., L. J. Kleinsmith, and J. Hardin. *The World of the Cell.* 4th ed. San Francisco, California: Benjamin Cummings, 2000.

Gilbert, S. F. *Developmental Biology.* 6th ed. Sunderland, Massachusetts: Sinauer Associates, Inc. 2000.

Hickman, C. P., L. S. Roberts and A. Larson. *Integrated Principles of Zoology.* 11th ed. New York, McGraw-Hill Company, 2001.

Moore, J. A. "Science as a Way of Knowing-Evolutionary Biology." *American Zoologist,* 24(2): 470–475, 1980.

Visual Guide to the Image Library

01-01-ScientistsCollage.jpg

01-01a-Sereno.jpg

01-01b-Chory.jpg

01-01c-WongStaal.jpg

01-01d-Langford.jpg

01-01x-MaryClaireKing.jpg

01-02-HierarchyCollage.jpg

01-02a-MoleculeChlorophyll.jpg

01-02b-OrganelleChloroplast.jpg

01-02c-CellsPlant.jpg

01-02d-TissueLeafXSextion.jpg

01-02e-OrganLeaf.jpg

01-02f-OrganismTree.jpg

01-03-LifeCollage.jpg

01-03a-OrderSunflower.jpg

01-03ax-OrderCollage.jpg

01-03ax1-OrderButterfly.jpg

01-03ax2-OrderNautilus.jpg

01-03ax3-OrderGaillardia.jpg

01-03ax4-OrderXylem.jpg

01-03b-ReproductionMacaques.jpg

01-03bx-ReproductionCollage.jpg

01-03bx1-ReproBeetles.jpg

01-03bx2-ReproductionHumans.jpg

01-03bx3-ReproBacteria.jpg

01-03bx4-ReproductionLily.jpg

01-03c-DevelopmentTadpole.jpg

01-03cx-DevelopmentCollage.jpg

01-03cx1-DevelopmentSnake.jpg

01-03cx2-DevelopFrogEggs.jpg

01-03cx3-DevelopSeedling.jpg

01-03cx4-DevelopmentDeer.jpg

01-03d-EnergyHummingbird.jpg

01-03dx-EnergyCollage.jpg

01-03dx1-EnergySunlight.jpg

01-03dx2-EnergyMosquito.jpg

01-03dx3-EnergyLeopard.jpg

01-03dx4-EnergyKoala.jpg

01-03e-ResponseVenusFlytrap.jpg

01-03f-HomeostasisRabbit.jpg

01-03g-AdaptationPtarmigan.jpg

01-04-EukaryoticProkary-L.jpg

01-04-EukaryoticProkary-NL.jpg

01-05-DNA-L.gif

01-05-DNA-NL.gif

01-05x-DNAModel.jpg

01-06-FormFunctionCollage.jpg

01-06a-Gulls.jpg

01-06b-Bone.jpg

01-06c-Neurons.jpg

01-06d-Mitochondrion.jpg

01-07-EcosystemEnergyFl-L.gif

01-07-EcosystemEnergyFl-NL.jpg

01-08-NegAndPosFeedback-L.gif

01-08-NegAndPosFeedback-NL.gif

01-09-BioDiversity.jpg

01-10-TaxonomicScheme-L.gif

01-10-TaxonomicScheme-NL.gif

01-11-DomainsCollage.jpg

01-11a-Bacteria.jpg

01-11b-Archaea.jpg

01-11c-Protista.jpg

01-11d-Plantae.jpg

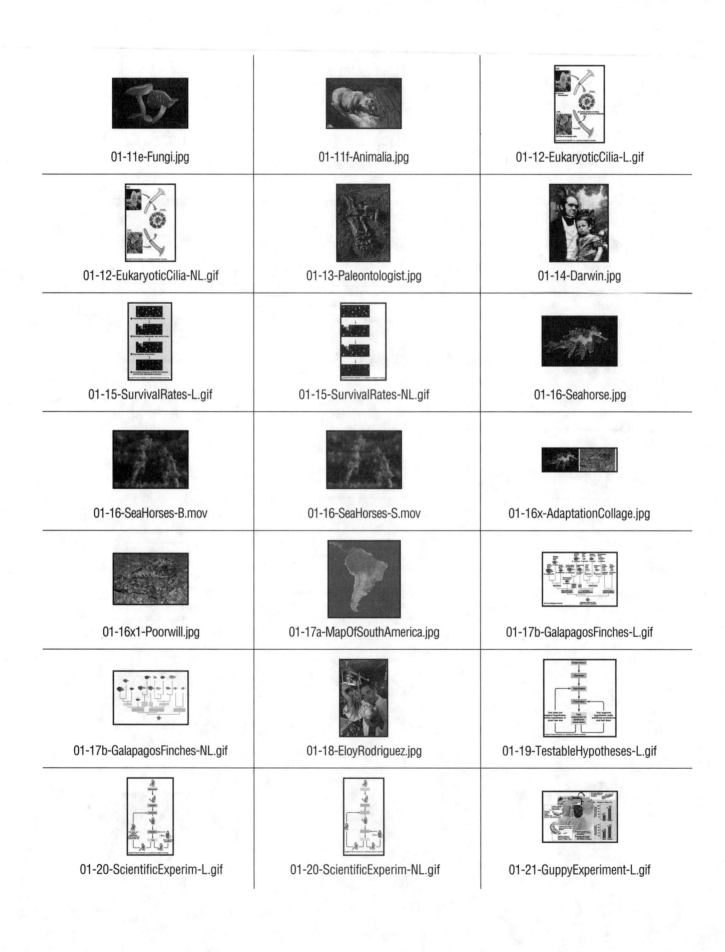

01-11e-Fungi.jpg

01-11f-Animalia.jpg

01-12-EukaryoticCilia-L.gif

01-12-EukaryoticCilia-NL.gif

01-13-Paleontologist.jpg

01-14-Darwin.jpg

01-15-SurvivalRates-L.gif

01-15-SurvivalRates-NL.gif

01-16-Seahorse.jpg

01-16-SeaHorses-B.mov

01-16-SeaHorses-S.mov

01-16x-AdaptationCollage.jpg

01-16x1-Poorwill.jpg

01-17a-MapOfSouthAmerica.jpg

01-17b-GalapagosFinches-L.gif

01-17b-GalapagosFinches-NL.gif

01-18-EloyRodriguez.jpg

01-19-TestableHypotheses-L.gif

01-20-ScientificExperim-L.gif

01-20-ScientificExperim-NL.gif

01-21-GuppyExperiment-L.gif

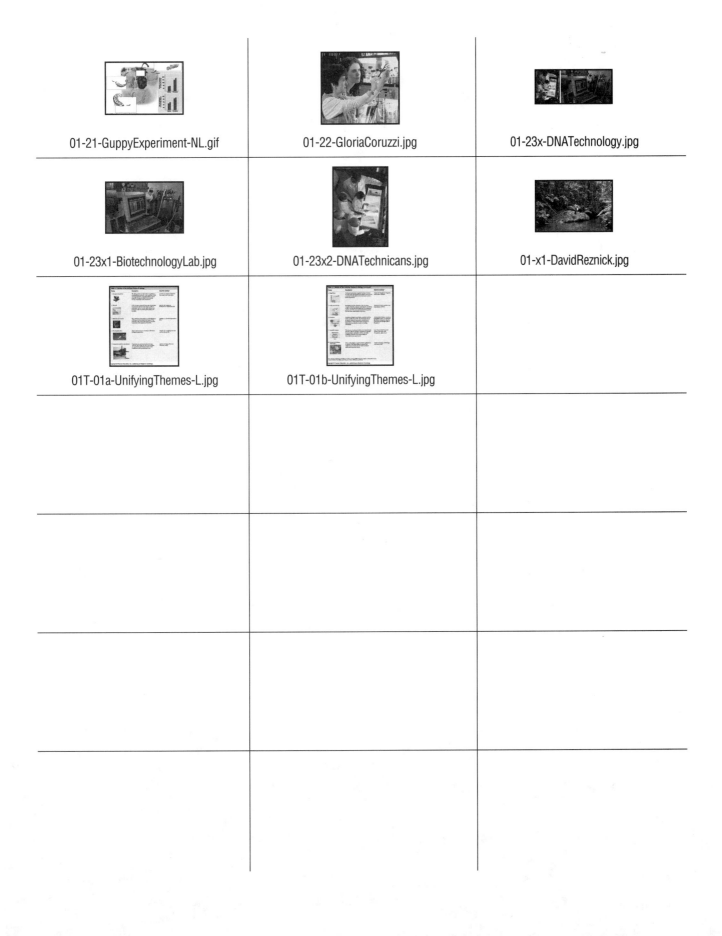

01-21-GuppyExperiment-NL.gif

01-22-GloriaCoruzzi.jpg

01-23x-DNATechnology.jpg

01-23x1-BiotechnologyLab.jpg

01-23x2-DNATechnicans.jpg

01-x1-DavidReznick.jpg

01T-01a-UnifyingThemes-L.jpg

01T-01b-UnifyingThemes-L.jpg

CHAPTER 2

The Chemical Context of Life

Chapter Outline

Chemical Elements and Compounds

Matter consists of chemical elements in pure form and in combinations called compounds

Life requires about 25 chemical elements

Atoms and Molecules

Atomic structure determines the behavior of an element

Atoms combine by chemical bonding to form molecules

Weak chemical bonds play important roles in the chemistry of life

A molecule's biological function is related to its shape

Chemical reactions make and break chemical bonds

Transparency Acetates

Media for Instructors

Campbell Image Presentation Library

The Campbell Image Presentation Library CD-ROM set includes the following for your use:

- All art (available in pdf and jpeg or gif formats), photos (from the text and outside sources), and tables. Art images are also available without callouts. See the Visual Guide to the Image Library section at the end of this chapter for thumbnail versions of every image.
- A PowerPoint™ slideshow of the art (with callouts), photos (both text and outside sources), and tables.
- The following animations, adapted from student media activities (available in QuickTime and Flash file formats):

  02-12-CovalentBonds.mov

  02-14-IonicBonds.mov

PowerPoint Lectures CD-ROM

The PowerPoint Lectures CD-ROM contains slides that integrate the art, photos, tables, and lecture outline from this chapter.

Campbell Biology Website (Instructor Resources)

See the insert in your copy of Campbell/Reece *Biology*, Sixth Edition, for instructions on how to access the Campbell Biology Website. The Instructor Resources section of the website includes the following:

- The art, photos, tables, PowerPoint slide shows, videos, and animations from the Campbell Image Presentation Library
- Suggested answers to the Lab Report questions from the Case Studies in the Process of Science
- The PowerPoint Lecture for this chapter
- Word files of the lecture outline for this chapter
- Photo links

Course Management Systems

The media content for this chapter is available in three course management systems: CourseCompass™, Blackboard, and WebCT. For more information, go to http://cms.aw.com. For the latest pdf instructions on how to use CourseCompass, go to www.coursecompass.com. In addition, a Syllabus Manager is offered on the Campbell Biology Website.

Media for Students

The Campbell Biology Website and CD-ROM include the following for your students:

- Objectives
- Chapter Review (Summary, Self-Quiz, and Essay Questions from the book; Word Roots; Key Terms linked to the Glossary)
- Activities (see list below)
- Case Studies in the Process of Science (see list below)
- Quizzes (Pre-test, Activities Quiz, Chapter Quiz, Essay Questions)
- Web Links
- News and References
- Art and videos from the Campbell Image Presentation Library
- The Campbell *Biology* Interviews (from all editions)
- Glossary with audio pronunciations
- Syllabus Manager

Student Media Activities and Case Studies in The Process of Science

Web/CD Activity 2A: *The Levels of Life Card Game*

Web/CD Case Study in the Process of Science: *How Are Space Rocks Analyzed for Signs of Life?*

Web/CD Activity 2B: *Structure of the Atomic Nucleus*

Web/CD Activity 2C: *Electron Arrangement*

Web/CD Activity 2D: *Build an Atom*

Web/CD Activity 2E: *Covalent Bonds*

Web/CD Activity 2F: *Nonpolar and Polar Molecules*

Web/CD Activity 2G: *Ionic Bonds*

Web/CD Activity 2H: *Hydrogen Bonds*

Objectives

Chemical Elements and Compounds

1. Distinguish between an element and a compound.
2. Identify the four elements that make up 96% of living matter.

Atoms and Molecules

3. Describe the structure of an atom.
4. Define and distinguish among atomic number, mass number, atomic weight, and valence.
5. Given the atomic number and mass number of an atom, how do you determine the number of its neutrons?
6. Explain why radioactive isotopes are important to biologists.
7. Explain how its electron configuration influences the chemical behavior of an atom.
8. Distinguish among nonpolar covalent, polar covalent, and ionic bonds.
9. Explain why weak bonds are important to living organisms.
10. Describe and compare hydrogen bonds and van der Waals interactions.
11. Explain how a molecule's shape influences its biological function.
12. Write the chemical equation that summarizes the process of photosynthesis, noting the reactants and products.
13. Describe how the relative concentrations of reactants and products affect a chemical reaction.

Key Terms

matter	potential energy	nonpolar covalent
element	energy level	bond
compound	electron shell	polar covalent bond
trace element	valence electron	ion
atom	valence shell	cation
neutron	orbital	anion
proton	chemical bond	ionic bond
electron	covalent bond	ionic compound
atomic nucleus	molecule	salt
dalton	structural formula	hydrogen bond
atomic number	molecular formula	van der Waals
mass number	double covalent bond	interactions
atomic weight	(double bond in	chemical reaction
isotope	glossary)	reactant
radioactive isotope	valence	product
energy	electronegativity	chemical equilibrium

Word Roots

an- = not (*anion*: a negatively charged ion)

co- = together; **-valent** = strength (*covalent bond*: an attraction between atoms that share one or more pairs of outer-shell electrons)

electro- = electricity (*electronegativity:* the tendency for an atom to pull electrons towards itself)

iso- = equal (*isotope*: an element having the same number of protons and electrons but a different number of neutrons)

neutr- = neither (*neutron*: a subatomic particle with a neutral electrical charge)

pro- = before (*proton*: a subatomic particle with a single positive electrical charge)

References

Brown, T. L., H. E. LeMay, Jr., and B. Bursten. *Chemistry: The Central Science.* 7th ed. Upper Saddle River, New Jersey: Prentice Hall, 1997.

Campbell, M. *Biochemistry.* 3rd ed. Orlando, Florida: Harcourt, Inc, 1999.

Visual Guide to the Image Library

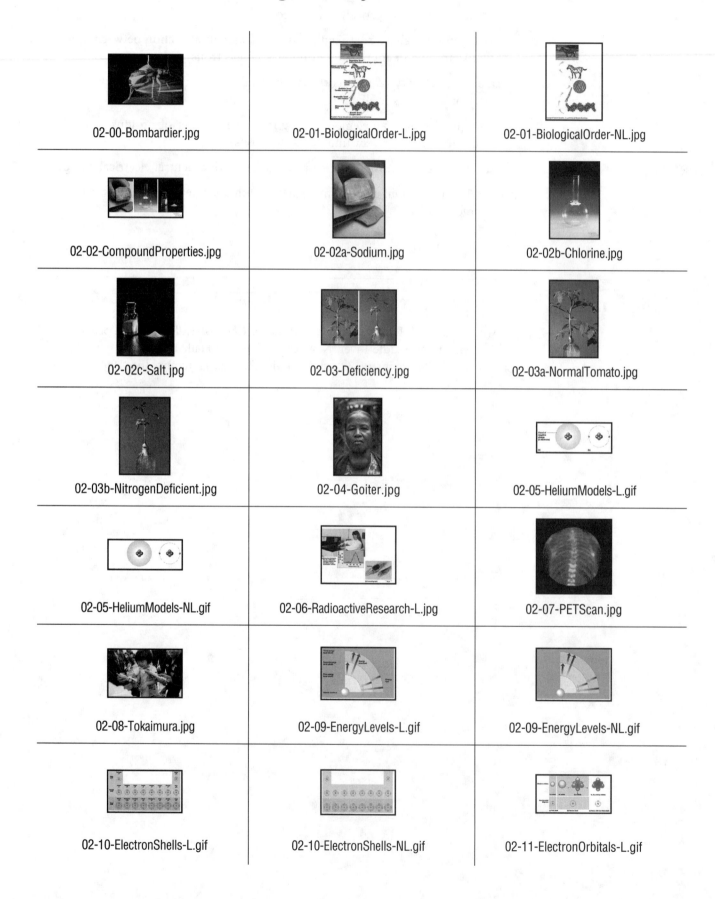

02-00-Bombardier.jpg

02-01-BiologicalOrder-L.jpg

02-01-BiologicalOrder-NL.jpg

02-02-CompoundProperties.jpg

02-02a-Sodium.jpg

02-02b-Chlorine.jpg

02-02c-Salt.jpg

02-03-Deficiency.jpg

02-03a-NormalTomato.jpg

02-03b-NitrogenDeficient.jpg

02-04-Goiter.jpg

02-05-HeliumModels-L.gif

02-05-HeliumModels-NL.gif

02-06-RadioactiveResearch-L.jpg

02-07-PETScan.jpg

02-08-Tokaimura.jpg

02-09-EnergyLevels-L.gif

02-09-EnergyLevels-NL.gif

02-10-ElectronShells-L.gif

02-10-ElectronShells-NL.gif

02-11-ElectronOrbitals-L.gif

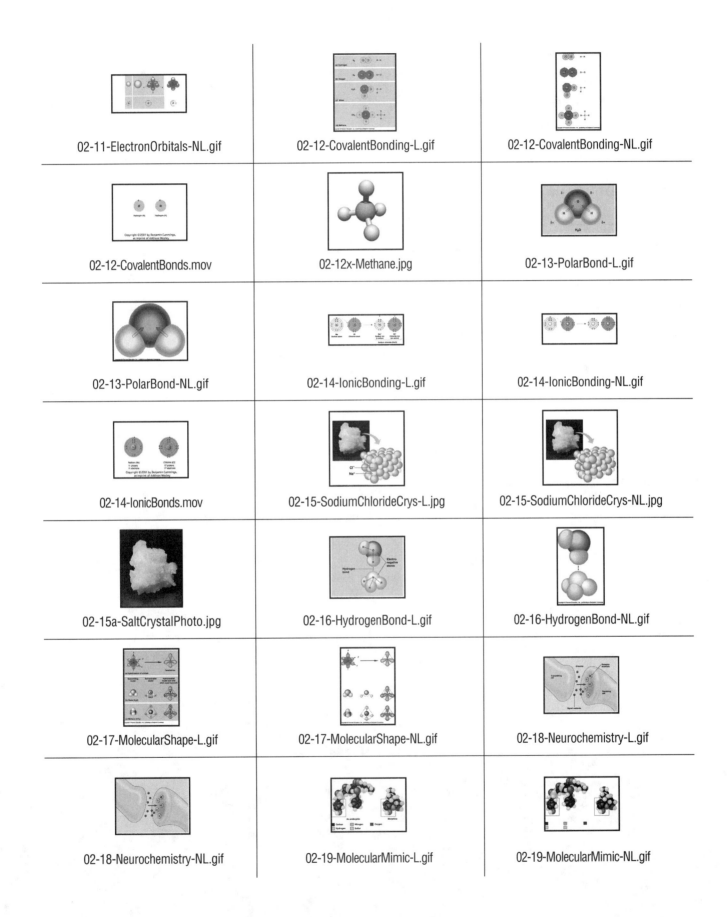

02-11-ElectronOrbitals-NL.gif

02-12-CovalentBonding-L.gif

02-12-CovalentBonding-NL.gif

02-12-CovalentBonds.mov

02-12x-Methane.jpg

02-13-PolarBond-L.gif

02-13-PolarBond-NL.gif

02-14-IonicBonding-L.gif

02-14-IonicBonding-NL.gif

02-14-IonicBonds.mov

02-15-SodiumChlorideCrys-L.jpg

02-15-SodiumChlorideCrys-NL.jpg

02-15a-SaltCrystalPhoto.jpg

02-16-HydrogenBond-L.gif

02-16-HydrogenBond-NL.gif

02-17-MolecularShape-L.gif

02-17-MolecularShape-NL.gif

02-18-Neurochemistry-L.gif

02-18-Neurochemistry-NL.gif

02-19-MolecularMimic-L.gif

02-19-MolecularMimic-NL.gif

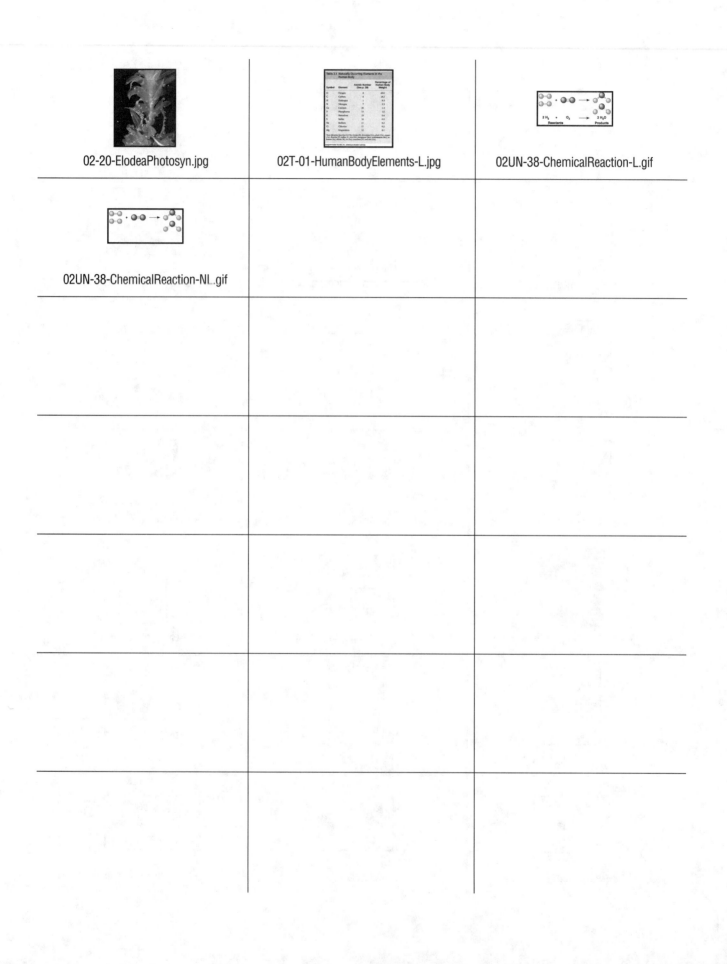

02-20-ElodeaPhotosyn.jpg

02T-01-HumanBodyElements-L.jpg

02UN-38-ChemicalReaction-L.gif

02UN-38-ChemicalReaction-NL.gif

CHAPTER 3

Water and the Fitness of the Environment

Chapter Outline

The Effects of Water's Polarity

The polarity of water molecules results in hydrogen bonding

Organisms depend on the cohesion of water molecules

Water moderates temperatures on Earth

Oceans and lakes don't freeze solid because ice floats

Water is the solvent of life

The Dissociation of Water Molecules

Organisms are sensitive to changes in pH

Acid precipitation threatens the fitness of the environment

Transparency Acetates

The Transparency Acetates for *Biology*, Sixth Edition, include the following images:

Figure 3.1	Hydrogen bonds between water molecules
Figure 3.2	Water transport in plants
Figure 3.5	The structure of ice (Layer 1)
Figure 3.5	The structure of ice (Layer 2)
Figure 3.7	A crystal of table salt dissolving in water
Figure 3.8	A water-soluble protein
Figure 3.UN1	Chemical reaction: hydrogen bond shift
Figure 3.9	The pH of some aqueous solutions

Media for Instructors

Campbell Image Presentation Library

The Campbell Image Presentation Library CD-ROM set includes the following for your use:

- All art (available in pdf and jpeg or gif formats), photos (from the text and outside sources), and tables. Art images are also available without callouts. See the Visual Guide to the Image Library section at the end of this chapter for thumbnail versions of every image.
- A PowerPoint™ slideshow of the art (with callouts), photos (both text and outside sources), and tables.
- The following QuickTime animation, adapted from student media activities (also available as Shockwave Flash .swf files):

  03-02-WaterTransport.mov

PowerPoint Lectures CD-ROM

The PowerPoint Lectures CD-ROM contains slides that integrate the art, photos, tables, and lecture outline from this chapter.

Campbell Biology Website (Instructor Resources)

See the insert in your copy of Campbell/Reece *Biology,* Sixth Edition, for instructions on how to access the Campbell Biology Website. The Instructor Resources section of the website includes the following:

- The art, photos, tables, PowerPoint slide shows, videos, and animations from the Campbell Image Presentation Library
- Suggested answers to the Lab Report questions from the Case Studies in the Process of Science
- The PowerPoint Lecture for this chapter
- Word files of the lecture outline for this chapter
- Photo links

Course Management Systems

The media content for this chapter is available in three course management systems: CourseCompass™, Blackboard, and WebCT. For more information, go to http://cms.aw.com. For the latest pdf instructions on how to use CourseCompass, go to www.coursecompass.com. In addition, a Syllabus Manager is offered on the Campbell Biology Website.

Media for Students

The Campbell Biology Website and CD-ROM include the following for your students:

- Objectives
- Chapter Review (Summary, Self-Quiz, and Essay Questions from the book; Word Roots; Key Terms linked to the Glossary)
- Activities (see list below)
- Case Studies in the Process of Science (see list below)
- Quizzes (Pre-test, Activities Quiz, Chapter Quiz, Essay Questions)
- Web Links
- News and 7
- Art and videos from the Campbell Image Presentation Library
- The Campbell *Biology* Interviews (from all editions)
- Glossary with audio pronunciations
- Syllabus Manager

Student Media Activities and Case Studies in The Process of Science

Web/CD Activity 3A: *The Polarity of Water*

Web/CD Activity 3B: *Cohesion of Water*

Web/CD Activity 3C: *Dissociation of Water Molecules*

Web/CD Activity 3D: *Acids, Bases, and pH*

Web/CD Case Study in the Process of Science: *How Does Acid Rain Affect Trees?*

Objectives

The Effects of Water's Polarity

1. Describe how water contributes to the fitness of the environment to support life.
2. Describe the structure and geometry of a water molecule, and explain what properties emerge as a result of this structure.
3. Explain the relationship between the polar nature of water and its ability to form hydrogen bonds.
4. List four characteristics of water that are emergent properties resulting from hydrogen bonding.
5. Describe the biological significance of the cohesiveness of water.
6. Distinguish between heat and temperature.

7. Explain how water's high specific heat, high heat of vaporization, and expansion upon freezing affect both aquatic and terrestrial ecosystems.
8. Distinguish among a solute, a solvent, and a solution.
9. Explain how the polarity of the water molecule makes it a versatile solvent.
10. Distinguish between hydrophilic and hydrophobic substances.
11. Distinguish between a mole and the molecular weight of a substance.

The Dissociation of Water Molecules

12. Write the equation for the dissociation and re-formation of water.
13. Explain the basis for the pH scale.
14. Explain how acids and bases directly or indirectly affect the hydrogen ion concentration of a solution.
15. Using the bicarbonate buffer system as an example, explain how buffers work.
16. Describe the causes of acid precipitation and explain how it harms the environment.

Key Terms

polar molecule	specific heat	molecular weight
cohesion	heat of vaporization	molarity
adhesion	evaporative cooling	hydrogen ion
surface tension	solution	hydroxide ion
kinetic energy	solvent	acid
heat	solute	base
temperature	aqueous solution	pH
Celsius scale	hydration shell	buffer
calorie (cal)	hydrophilic	acid precipitation
kilocalorie (kcal)	hydrophobic	
joule (J)	mole (mol)	

Word Roots

kilo- = a thousand (*kilocalorie:* a thousand calories)

hydro- = water; **-philos** = loving; **-phobos** = fearing (*hydrophilic:* having an affinity for water; hydrophobic: having an aversion to water)

References

Campbell, M. *Biochemistry.* 3rd ed. Orlando, Florida: Harcourt, Inc, 1999.
Enger, E. D. and B. F. Smith. *Environmental Science: A Study of Interrelationships.* 7th ed. Boston, Massachusetts, McGraw-Hill, 2000.

Visual Guide to the Image Library

03-00-Earth.gif

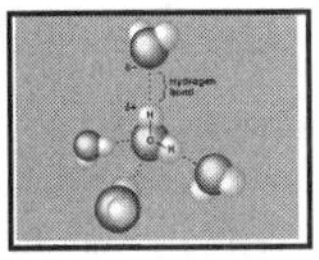

03-01-WaterMolecules-L.gif

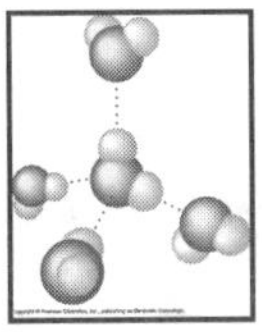

03-01-WaterMolecules-NL.gif

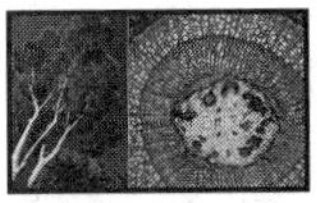

03-02-WaterTransport.jpg

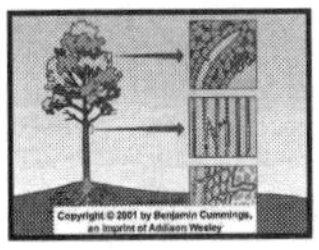

03-02-WaterTransport.mov

03-02x-Trees.jpg

03-03-WaterStrider.jpg

03-04-EvaporativeCooling.jpg

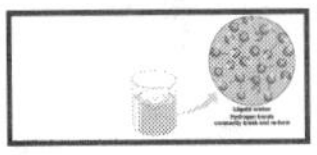

03-05-IceStructure-L1.gif

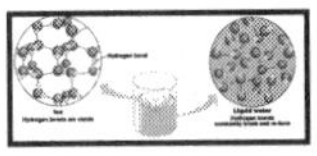

03-05-IceStructure-L2.gif

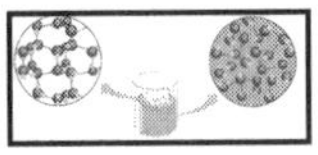

03-05-IceStructure-NL.gif

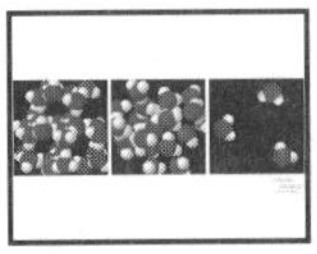

03-05x1-IceWaterSteam.gif

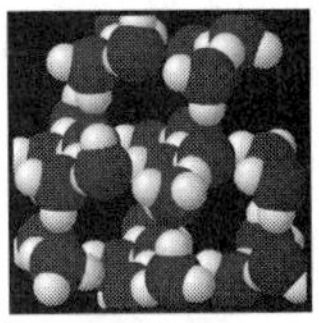

03-05x1a-Ice.gif

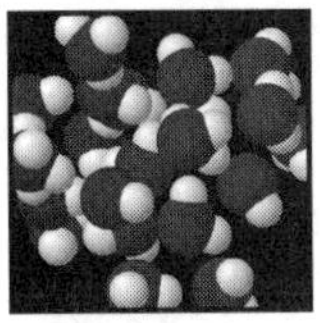

03-05x1b-Water.gif

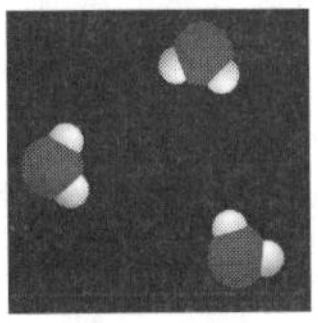

03-05x1c-Steam.gif

03-06-Krill.jpg

03-06x1-IceFishing.jpg

03-06x2-FrozenWaterBenzene.jpg

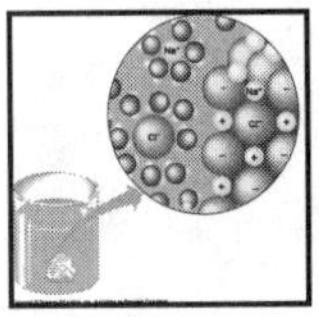

03-07-DissolvedSalt-L.gif

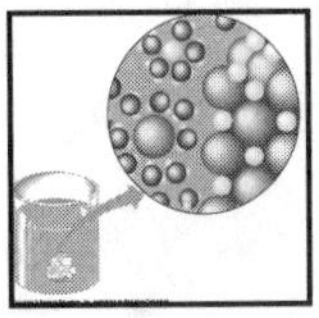

03-07-DissolvedSalt-NL.gif

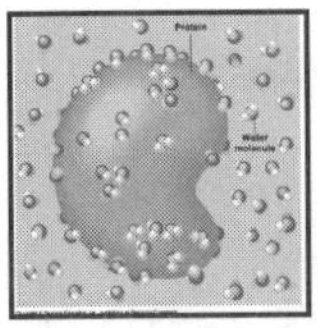

03-08-WatrSolubleProtein-L.gif

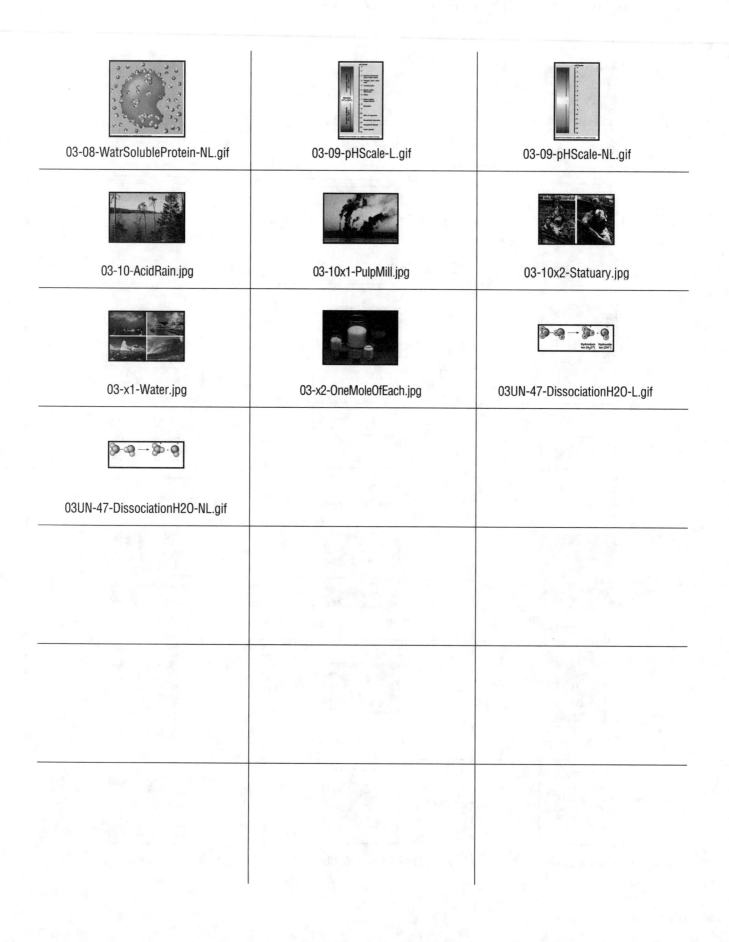

03-08-WatrSolubleProtein-NL.gif

03-09-pHScale-L.gif

03-09-pHScale-NL.gif

03-10-AcidRain.jpg

03-10x1-PulpMill.jpg

03-10x2-Statuary.jpg

03-x1-Water.jpg

03-x2-OneMoleOfEach.jpg

03UN-47-DissociationH2O-L.gif

03UN-47-DissociationH2O-NL.gif

CHAPTER 4

Carbon and the Molecular Diversity of Life

Chapter Outline

The Importance of Carbon
Organic chemistry is the study of carbon compounds
Carbon atoms are the most versatile building blocks of molecules
Variation in carbon skeletons contributes to the diversity of organic molecules

Functional Groups
Functional groups contribute to the molecular diversity of life
The chemical elements of life: *a review*

Transparency Acetates

The Transparency Acetates for *Biology*, Sixth Edition, include the following images:

Media for Instructors

Campbell Image Presentation Library

The Campbell Image Presentation Library CD-ROM set includes the following for your use:

- All art (available in pdf and jpeg or gif formats), photos (from the text and outside sources), and tables. Art images are also available without callouts. See the Visual Guide to the Image Library section at the end of this chapter for thumbnail versions of every image.
- A PowerPoint™ slideshow of the art (with callouts), photos (both text and outside sources), and tables.

PowerPoint Lectures CD-ROM

The PowerPoint Lectures CD-ROM contains slides that integrate the art, photos, tables, and lecture outline from this chapter.

Campbell Biology Website (Instructor Resources)

See the insert in your copy of Campbell/Reece *Biology*, Sixth Edition, for instructions on how to access the Campbell Biology Website. The Instructor Resources section of the website includes the following:

- The art, photos, tables, PowerPoint slide shows, videos, and animations from the Campbell Image Presentation Library
- Suggested answers to the Lab Report questions from the Case Studies in the Process of Science
- The PowerPoint Lecture for this chapter
- Word files of the lecture outline for this chapter
- Photo links

Course Management Systems

The media content for this chapter is available in three course management systems: CourseCompass™, Blackboard, and WebCT. For more information, go to http://cms.aw.com. For the latest pdf instructions on how to use CourseCompass, go to www.coursecompass.com. In addition, a Syllabus Manager is offered on the Campbell Biology Website.

Media for Students

The Campbell Biology Website and CD-ROM include the following for your students:

- Objectives
- Chapter Review (Summary, Self-Quiz, and Essay Questions from the book; Word Roots; Key Terms linked to the Glossary)

- Activities (see list below)
- Case Studies in the Process of Science (see list below)
- Quizzes (Pre-test, Activities Quiz, Chapter Quiz, Essay Questions)
- Web Links
- News and References
- Art and videos from the Campbell Image Presentation Library
- The Campbell *Biology* Interviews (from all editions)
- Glossary with audio pronunciations
- Syllabus Manager

Student Media Activities and Case Studies in The Process of Science

Web/CD Activity 4A: *Diversity of Carbon-Based Molecules*

Web/CD Activity 4B: *Isomers*

Web/CD Case Study in the Process of Science: *What Factors Determine the Effectiveness of Drugs?*

Web/CD Activity 4C: *Functional Groups*

Objectives

The Importance of Carbon

1. Summarize the philosophies of vitalism and mechanism and explain how they influenced the development of organic chemistry and mainstream biological thought.
2. Explain how carbon's electron configuration determines the kinds and numbers of bonds that carbon will form.
3. Describe how carbon skeletons may vary, and explain how this variation contributes to the diversity and complexity of organic molecules.
4. Distinguish among the three types of isomers: structural, geometric, and enantiomer.

Functional Groups

5. Name the major functional groups and describe the chemical properties of the organic molecules in which they occur.

Key Terms

organic chemistry	hydroxyl group	amino group
hydrocarbon	alcohol	amine
isomer	carbonyl group	sulfhydryl group
structural isomer	aldehyde	thiol
geometric isomer	ketone	phosphate group
enantiomer	carboxyl group	
functional group	carboxylic acid	

Word Roots

hydro- = water (*hydrocarbon*: an organic molecule consisting only of carbon and hydrogen)

iso- = equal (*isomer*: one of several organic compounds with the same molecular formula but different structures and therefore different properties)

enanti- = opposite (*enantiomer*: molecules that are mirror images of each other)

carb- = coal (*carboxyl group*: a functional group present in organic acids, consisting of a carbon atom double-bonded to an oxygen atom)

sulf- = sulfur (*sulfhydryl group*: a functional group which consists of a sulfur atom bonded to an atom of hydrogen)

thio- = sulfur (*thiol*: organic compounds containing sulfhydryl groups)

References

Becker, W. M., L. J. Kleinsmith, and J. Hardin. *The World of the Cell*. 4th ed. San Francisco, California: Benjamin Cummings, 2000.

Campbell, M. *Biochemistry*. 3rd ed. Orlando, Florida: Harcourt, Inc, 1999.

Visual Guide to the Image Library

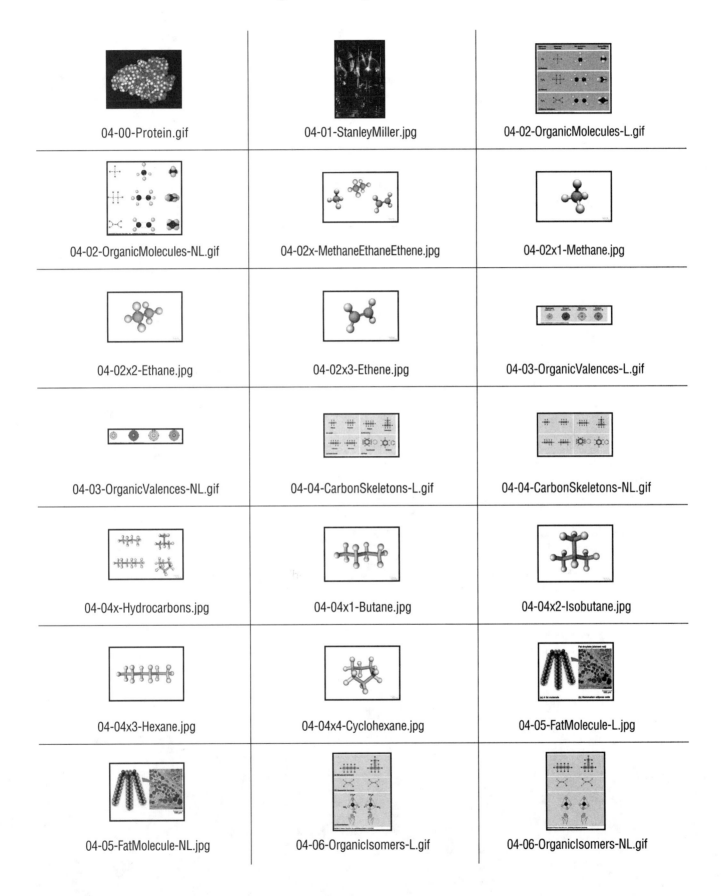

04-00-Protein.gif

04-01-StanleyMiller.jpg

04-02-OrganicMolecules-L.gif

04-02-OrganicMolecules-NL.gif

04-02x-MethaneEthaneEthene.jpg

04-02x1-Methane.jpg

04-02x2-Ethane.jpg

04-02x3-Ethene.jpg

04-03-OrganicValences-L.gif

04-03-OrganicValences-NL.gif

04-04-CarbonSkeletons-L.gif

04-04-CarbonSkeletons-NL.gif

04-04x-Hydrocarbons.jpg

04-04x1-Butane.jpg

04-04x2-Isobutane.jpg

04-04x3-Hexane.jpg

04-04x4-Cyclohexane.jpg

04-05-FatMolecule-L.jpg

04-05-FatMolecule-NL.jpg

04-06-OrganicIsomers-L.gif

04-06-OrganicIsomers-NL.gif

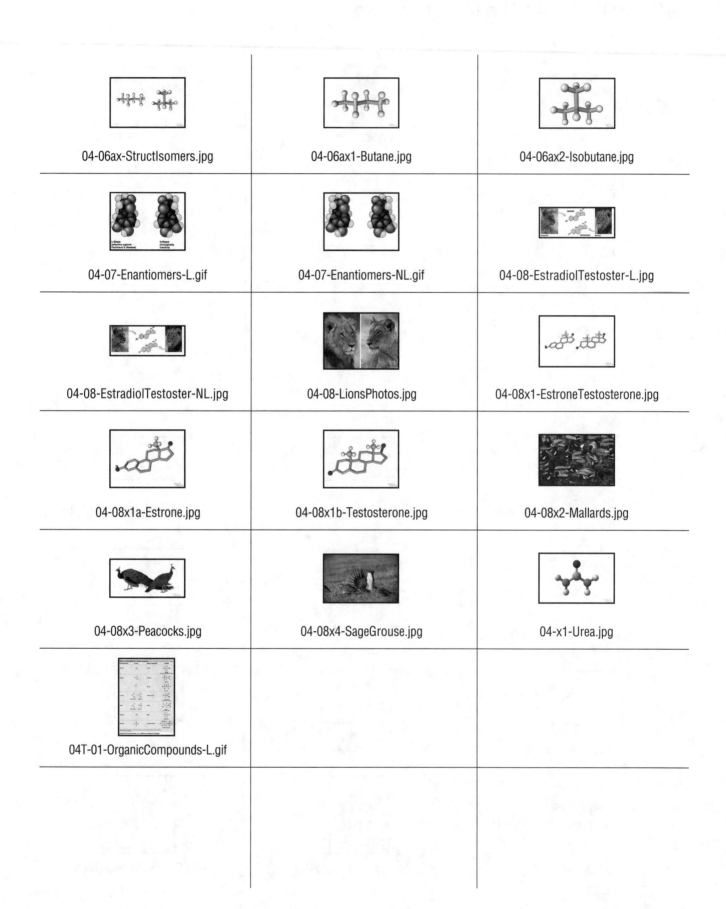

04-06ax-StructIsomers.jpg

04-06ax1-Butane.jpg

04-06ax2-Isobutane.jpg

04-07-Enantiomers-L.gif

04-07-Enantiomers-NL.gif

04-08-EstradiolTestoster-L.jpg

04-08-EstradiolTestoster-NL.jpg

04-08-LionsPhotos.jpg

04-08x1-EstroneTestosterone.jpg

04-08x1a-Estrone.jpg

04-08x1b-Testosterone.jpg

04-08x2-Mallards.jpg

04-08x3-Peacocks.jpg

04-08x4-SageGrouse.jpg

04-x1-Urea.jpg

04T-01-OrganicCompounds-L.gif

CHAPTER 5

The Structure and Function of Macromolecules

Chapter Outline

Transparency Acetates

The Transparency Acetates for *Biology*, Sixth Edition, include the following images:

Figure 5.2	The synthesis and breakdown of polymers
Figure 5.3	The structure and classification of some monosaccharides
Figure 5.4	Linear and ring forms of glucose
Figure 5.5	Examples of disaccharide synthesis
Figure 5.6	Storage polysaccharides
Figure 5.7	Starch and cellulose structures
Figure 5.8	The arrangement of cellulose in plant cell walls
Figure 5.UN1	Glucose monomer of chitin
Figure 5.10	The synthesis and structure of a fat, or triacylglycerol
Figure 5.11	Examples of saturated and unsaturated fats and fatty acids
Figure 5.12	The structure of a phospholipid
Figure 5.13	Two structures formed by self-assembly of phospholipids in aqueous environments
Figure 5.14	Cholesterol, a steroid
Table 5.1	An Overview of Protein Functions
Figure 5.15	The 20 amino acids of proteins: nonpolar
Figure 5.15	The 20 amino acids of proteins: polar and electrically charged
Figure 5.16	Making a polypeptide chain
Figure 5.18	The primary structure of a protein
Figure 5.19	A single amino acid substitution in a protein causes sickle-cell disease
Figure 5.20	The secondary structure of a protein
Figure 5.22	Examples of interactions contributing to the tertiary structure of a protein
Figure 5.23	The quaternary structure of proteins
Figure 5.24	Review: the four levels of protein structure
Figure 5.25	Denaturation and renaturation of a protein
Figure 5.26	A chaperonin in action
Figure 5.27	X-ray crystallography
Figure 5.28	DNA→RNA→protein: a diagrammatic overview of information flow in a cell
Figure 5.29	The components of nucleic acids
Figure 5.30	The DNA double helix and its replication
Table 5.2	Polypeptide Sequence as Evidence for Evolutionary Relationships

Media for Instructors

Campbell Image Presentation Library

The Campbell Image Presentation Library CD-ROM set includes the following for your use:

- All art (available in pdf and jpeg or gif formats), photos (from the text and outside sources), and tables. Art images are also available without callouts. See the Visual Guide to the Image Library section at the end of this chapter for thumbnail versions of every image.

- A PowerPoint™ slideshow of the art (with callouts), photos (both text and outside sources), and tables.

- The following QuickTime animations, adapted from student media activities (also available as Shockwave Flash .swf files):

  05-02-Macromolecules.mov

  05-05-Disaccharides.mov

  05-07-Polysaccharides.mov

  05-10-Fats.mov

  05-24-ProteinStructureIntro.mov

  05-24a-PrimaryStructure.mov

  05-24b-SecondaryStructure.mov

  05-24c-TertiaryStructure.mov

  05-24d-QuarternaryStructure.mov

  05T-01a-StructuralProteins.mov

  05T-01b-StorageProteins.mov

  05T-01c-TransportProteins.mov

  05T-01d-ReceptorProteins.mov

  05T-01e-ContractileProteins.mov

  05T-01f-DefensiveProteins.mov

  05T-01g-Enzymes.mov

  05T-01h-SignalProteins.mov

  05T-01i-SensoryProteins.mov

  05T-01j-GeneRegulatoryProt.mov

PowerPoint Lectures CD-ROM

The PowerPoint Lectures CD-ROM contains slides that integrate the art, photos, tables, and lecture outline from this chapter.

Campbell Biology Website (Instructor Resources)

See the insert in your copy of Campbell/Reece *Biology*, Sixth Edition, for instructions on how to access the Campbell Biology Website. The Instructor Resources section of the website includes the following:

- The art, photos, tables, PowerPoint slide shows, videos, and animations from the Campbell Image Presentation Library

- Suggested answers to the Lab Report questions from the Case Studies in the Process of Science

- The PowerPoint Lecture for this chapter
- Word files of the lecture outline for this chapter
- Photo links

Course Management Systems

The media content for this chapter is available in three course management systems: CourseCompass™, Blackboard, and WebCT. For more information, go to http://cms.aw.com. For the latest pdf instructions on how to use CourseCompass, go to **www.coursecompass.com**. In addition, a Syllabus Manager is offered on the Campbell Biolog*y* Website.

Media for Students

The Campbell Biology Website and CD-ROM include the following for your students:

- Objectives
- Chapter Review (Summary, Self-Quiz, and Essay Questions from the book; Word Roots; Key Terms linked to the Glossary)
- Activities (see list below)
- Case Studies in the Process of Science (see list below)
- Quizzes (Pre-test, Activities Quiz, Chapter Quiz, Essay Questions)
- Web Links
- News and References
- Art and videos from the Campbell Image Presentation Library
- The Campbell *Biology* Interviews (from all editions)
- Glossary with audio pronunciations
- Syllabus Manager

Student Media Activities and Case Studies in The Process of Science

Web/CD Activity 5A: *Making and Breaking Polymers*

Web/CD Activity 5B: *Models of Glucose*

Web/CD Activity 5C: *Carbohydrates*

Web/CD Activity 5D: *Lipids*

Web/CD Activity 5E: *Protein Functions*

Web/CD Activity 5F: *Protein Structure*

Biology Labs On-Line: *HemoglobinLab*

Web/CD Activity 5G: *Nucleic Acid Functions*

Web/CD Activity 5H: *Nucleic Acid Structure*

Objectives

Polymer Principles

1. Explain how monomers are used to build polymers.
2. List the four major classes of macromolecules.
3. Compare condensation and hydrolysis.
4. Explain how organic polymers contribute to biological diversity.

Carbohydrates—Fuel and Building Material

5. Describe the distinguishing characteristics of carbohydrates and explain how they are classified.
6. Distinguish between monosaccharides and disaccharides.
7. Identify a glycosidic linkage and describe how it is formed.
8. Describe the structure and functions of polysaccharides.
9. Distinguish between the glycosidic linkages found in starch and cellulose and explain why the difference is biologically important.

Lipids—Diverse Hydrophobic Molecules

10. Explain what distinguishes lipids from other major classes of macromolecules.
11. Describe the unique properties, building-block molecules, and biological importance of the three important groups of lipids: fats, phospholipids, and steroids.
12. Identify an ester linkage and describe how it is formed.
13. Distinguish between a saturated and an unsaturated fat and list some unique emergent properties that are a consequence of these structural differences.

Proteins—Many Structures, Many Functions

14. Describe the characteristics that distinguish proteins from the other major classes of macromolecules and explain the biologically important functions of this group.
15. List and describe the four major components of an amino acid. Explain how amino acids may be grouped according to the physical and chemical properties of the side chains.
16. Identify a peptide bond and explain how it is formed.
17. Distinguish between a polypeptide and a protein.
18. Explain what determines protein conformation and why it is important.
19. Define primary structure and describe how it may be deduced in the laboratory.
20. Describe the two types of secondary protein structure. Explain the role of hydrogen bonds in maintaining the structure.
21. Explain how weak interactions and disulfide bridges contribute to tertiary protein structure.
22. Using collagen and hemoglobin as examples, describe quaternary protein structure.
23. Define denaturation and explain how proteins may be denatured.

Nucleic Acids—Informational Polymers

24. Describe the characteristics that distinguish nucleic acids from the other major groups of macromolecules.

25. Summarize the functions of nucleic acids.

26. List the major components of a nucleotide, and describe how these monomers are linked to form a nucleic acid.

27. Distinguish between a pyrimidine and a purine.

28. Briefly describe the three-dimensional structure of DNA.

29. Explain how the structure of DNA and proteins can be used to document the hereditary background of an organism.

Key Terms

macromolecule	triacylglycerol	quaternary structure
polymer	saturated fatty acid	denaturation
monomer	unsaturated fatty acid	chaperonin
condensation reaction	phospholipids	x-ray crystallography
dehydration reaction	steroids	gene
hydrolysis	cholesterol	nucleic acid
carbohydrate	polypeptide	deoxyribonucleic acid
monosaccharide	proteins	(DNA)
disaccharide	amino acid	ribonucleic acid
glycosidic linkage	peptide bond	(RNA)
polysaccharide	primary structure	nucleotide
starch	secondary structure	pyrimidine
glycogen	α helix	purine
cellulose	β pleated sheet	ribose
chitin	tertiary structure	deoxyribose
lipid	hydrophobic	polynucleotide
fat	interaction	double helix
fatty acid	disulfide bridge	

Word Roots

con- = together (*condensation reaction*: a reaction in which two molecules become covalently bonded to each other through the loss of a small molecule, usually water)

di- = two (*disaccharide*: two monosaccharides joined together)

glyco- = sweet (*glycogen*: a polysaccharide sugar used to store energy in animals)

hydro- = water; **-lyse** = break (*hydrolysis*: breaking chemical bonds by adding water)

macro- = large (*macromolecule*: a large molecule)

meros- = part (*polymer*: a chain made from smaller organic molecules)

mono- = single; **-sacchar** = sugar (*monosaccharide*: simplest type of sugar)

poly- = many (*polysaccharide*: many monosaccharides joined together)

tri- = three (*triacylglycerol*: three fatty acids linked to one glycerol molecule)

References

Becker, W. M., L. J. Kleinsmith, and J. Hardin. *The World of the Cell.* 4th ed. San Francisco, California: Benjamin Cummings, 2000.

Campbell, M. *Biochemistry.* 3rd ed. Orlando, Florida: Harcourt, Inc, 1999.

Gerstein, M. and M. Levitt. "H$_2$O and Macromolecules." *Scientific American,* November 1998.

Visual Guide to the Image Library

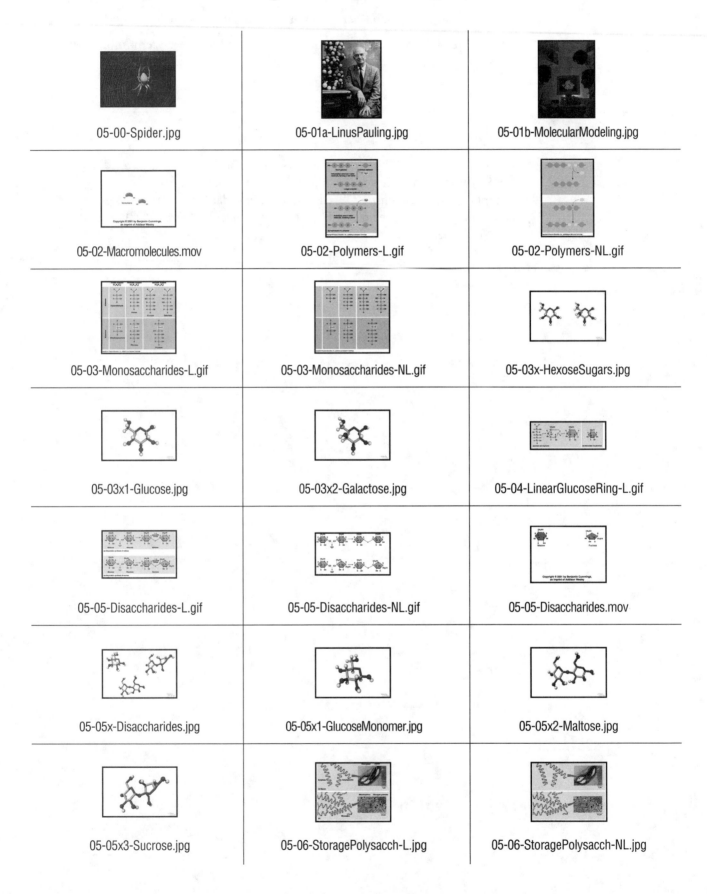

05-00-Spider.jpg

05-01a-LinusPauling.jpg

05-01b-MolecularModeling.jpg

05-02-Macromolecules.mov

05-02-Polymers-L.gif

05-02-Polymers-NL.gif

05-03-Monosaccharides-L.gif

05-03-Monosaccharides-NL.gif

05-03x-HexoseSugars.jpg

05-03x1-Glucose.jpg

05-03x2-Galactose.jpg

05-04-LinearGlucoseRing-L.gif

05-05-Disaccharides-L.gif

05-05-Disaccharides-NL.gif

05-05-Disaccharides.mov

05-05x-Disaccharides.jpg

05-05x1-GlucoseMonomer.jpg

05-05x2-Maltose.jpg

05-05x3-Sucrose.jpg

05-06-StoragePolysacch-L.jpg

05-06-StoragePolysacch-NL.jpg

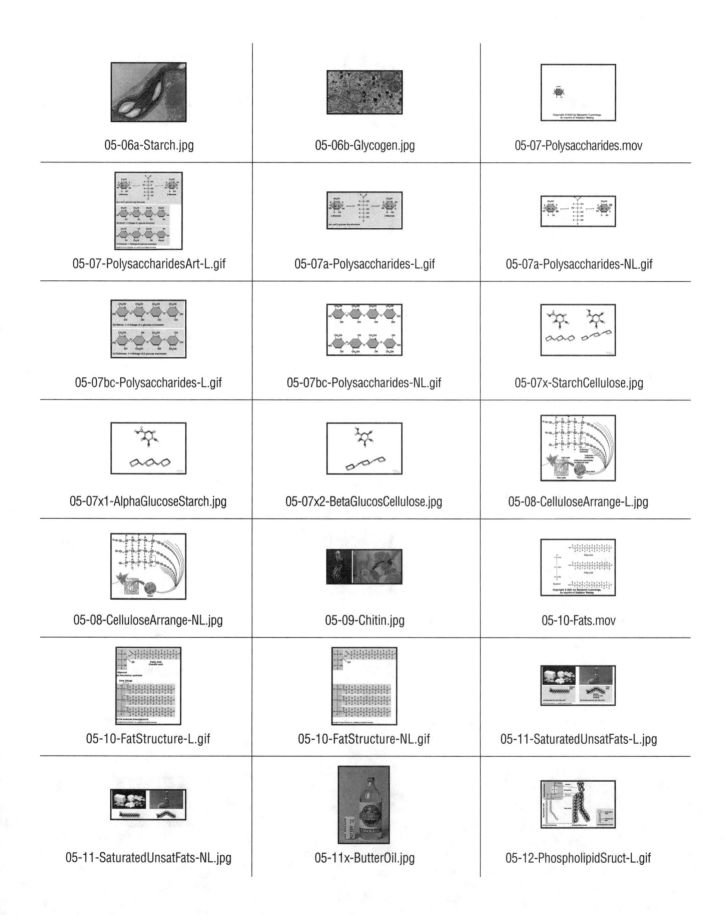

05-06a-Starch.jpg

05-06b-Glycogen.jpg

05-07-Polysaccharides.mov

05-07-PolysaccharidesArt-L.gif

05-07a-Polysaccharides-L.gif

05-07a-Polysaccharides-NL.gif

05-07bc-Polysaccharides-L.gif

05-07bc-Polysaccharides-NL.gif

05-07x-StarchCellulose.jpg

05-07x1-AlphaGlucoseStarch.jpg

05-07x2-BetaGlucosCellulose.jpg

05-08-CelluloseArrange-L.jpg

05-08-CelluloseArrange-NL.jpg

05-09-Chitin.jpg

05-10-Fats.mov

05-10-FatStructure-L.gif

05-10-FatStructure-NL.gif

05-11-SaturatedUnsatFats-L.jpg

05-11-SaturatedUnsatFats-NL.jpg

05-11x-ButterOil.jpg

05-12-PhospholipidSruct-L.gif

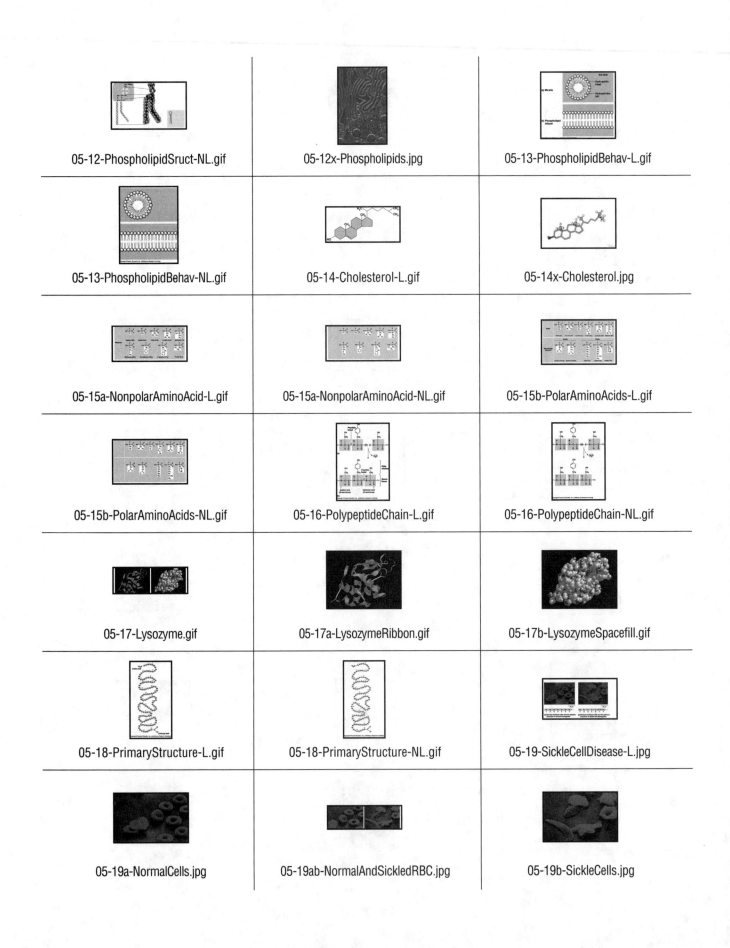

05-12-PhospholipidSruct-NL.gif

05-12x-Phospholipids.jpg

05-13-PhospholipidBehav-L.gif

05-13-PhospholipidBehav-NL.gif

05-14-Cholesterol-L.gif

05-14x-Cholesterol.jpg

05-15a-NonpolarAminoAcid-L.gif

05-15a-NonpolarAminoAcid-NL.gif

05-15b-PolarAminoAcids-L.gif

05-15b-PolarAminoAcids-NL.gif

05-16-PolypeptideChain-L.gif

05-16-PolypeptideChain-NL.gif

05-17-Lysozyme.gif

05-17a-LysozymeRibbon.gif

05-17b-LysozymeSpacefill.gif

05-18-PrimaryStructure-L.gif

05-18-PrimaryStructure-NL.gif

05-19-SickleCellDisease-L.jpg

05-19a-NormalCells.jpg

05-19ab-NormalAndSickledRBC.jpg

05-19b-SickleCells.jpg

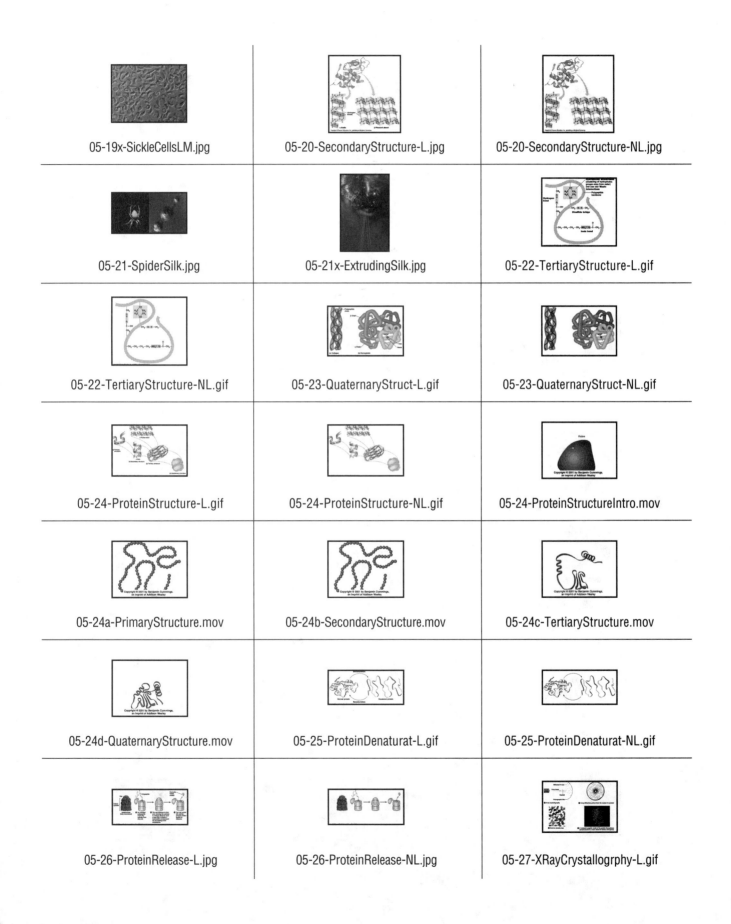

05-19x-SickleCellsLM.jpg

05-20-SecondaryStructure-L.jpg

05-20-SecondaryStructure-NL.jpg

05-21-SpiderSilk.jpg

05-21x-ExtrudingSilk.jpg

05-22-TertiaryStructure-L.gif

05-22-TertiaryStructure-NL.gif

05-23-QuaternaryStruct-L.gif

05-23-QuaternaryStruct-NL.gif

05-24-ProteinStructure-L.gif

05-24-ProteinStructure-NL.gif

05-24-ProteinStructureIntro.mov

05-24a-PrimaryStructure.mov

05-24b-SecondaryStructure.mov

05-24c-TertiaryStructure.mov

05-24d-QuaternaryStructure.mov

05-25-ProteinDenaturat-L.gif

05-25-ProteinDenaturat-NL.gif

05-26-ProteinRelease-L.jpg

05-26-ProteinRelease-NL.jpg

05-27-XRayCrystallogrphy-L.gif

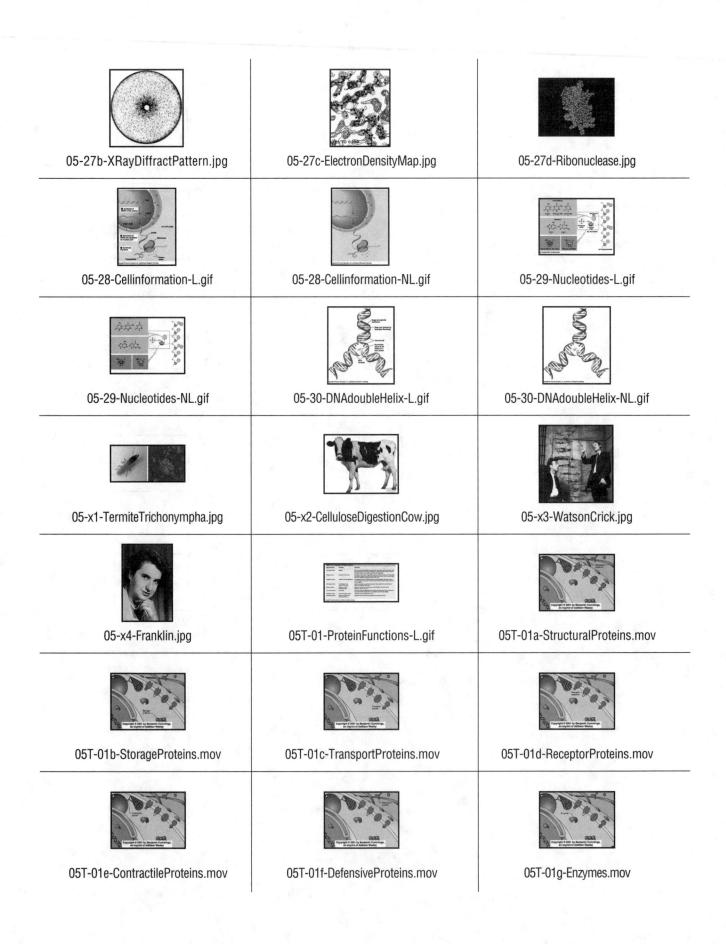

05-27b-XRayDiffractPattern.jpg

05-27c-ElectronDensityMap.jpg

05-27d-Ribonuclease.jpg

05-28-Cellinformation-L.gif

05-28-Cellinformation-NL.gif

05-29-Nucleotides-L.gif

05-29-Nucleotides-NL.gif

05-30-DNAdoubleHelix-L.gif

05-30-DNAdoubleHelix-NL.gif

05-x1-TermiteTrichonympha.jpg

05-x2-CelluloseDigestionCow.jpg

05-x3-WatsonCrick.jpg

05-x4-Franklin.jpg

05T-01-ProteinFunctions-L.gif

05T-01a-StructuralProteins.mov

05T-01b-StorageProteins.mov

05T-01c-TransportProteins.mov

05T-01d-ReceptorProteins.mov

05T-01e-ContractileProteins.mov

05T-01f-DefensiveProteins.mov

05T-01g-Enzymes.mov

05T-01h-SignalProteins.mov

05T-01i-SensoryProteins.mov

05T-01j-GeneRegulatoryProt.mov

05T-02-PolypeptideSequenc-L.gif

05UN-68-ChitinMonomer-L.gif

Chapter 6

An Introduction to Metabolism

Chapter Outline

Metabolism, Energy, and Life

The chemistry of life is organized into metabolic pathways

Organisms transform energy

The energy transformations of life are subject to two laws of thermodynamics

Organisms live at the expense of free energy

ATP powers cellular work by coupling exergonic reactions to endergonic reactions

Enzymes

Enzymes speed up metabolic reactions by lowering energy barriers

Enzymes are substrate specific

The active site is an enzyme's catalytic center

A cell's physical and chemical environment affects enzyme activity

The Control of Metabolism

Metabolic control often depends on allosteric regulation

The localization of enzymes within a cell helps order metabolism

The theme of emergent properties is manifest in the chemistry of life: *a review*

Transparency Acetates

The Transparency Acetates for *Biology*, Sixth Edition, include the following images:

Figure 6.1	The complexity of metabolism
Figure 6.5	The relationship of free energy to stability, work capacity, and spontaneous change
Figure 6.6	Energy changes in exergonic and endergonic reactions
Figure 6.7	Disequilibrium and work in closed and open systems
Figure 6.8	The structure and hydrolysis of ATP
Figure 6.9	Energy coupling by phosphate transfer
Figure 6.10	The ATP cycle

Figure 6.11 Example of an enzyme-catalyzed reaction: Hydrolysis of sucrose
Figure 6.12 Energy profile of an exergonic reaction
Figure 6.13 Enzymes lower the barrier of activation energy
Figure 6.15 The catalytic cycle of an enzyme
Figure 6.16 Environmental factors affecting enzyme activity
Figure 6.17 Inhibition of enzyme activity
Figure 6.18 Allosteric regulation of enzyme activity
Figure 6.19 Feedback inhibition
Figure 6.20 Cooperativity
Figure 6.21 Organelles and structural order in metabolism

Media for Instructors

Campbell Image Presentation Library

The Campbell Image Presentation Library CD-ROM set includes the following for your use:

- All art (available in pdf and jpeg or gif formats), photos (from the text and outside sources), and tables. Art images are also available without callouts. See the Visual Guide to the Image Library section at the end of this chapter for thumbnail versions of every image.
- A PowerPoint™ slideshow of the art (with callouts), photos (both text and outside sources), and tables.
- The following QuickTime animations, adapted from student media activities (also available as Shockwave Flash .swf files):

  06-02-EnergyConcepts.mov

  06-14-HowEnzymesWork.mov

PowerPoint Lectures CD-ROM

The PowerPoint Lectures CD-ROM contains slides that integrate the art, photos, tables, and lecture outline from this chapter.

Campbell Biology Website (Instructor Resources)

See the insert in your copy of Campbell/Reece *Biology*, Sixth Edition, for instructions on how to access the Campbell Biology Website. The Instructor Resources section of the website includes the following:

- The art, photos, tables, PowerPoint slide shows, videos, and animations from the Campbell Image Presentation Library
- Suggested answers to the Lab Report questions from the Case Studies in the Process of Science
- The PowerPoint Lecture for this chapter
- Word files of the lecture outline for this chapter
- Photo links

Course Management Systems

The media content for this chapter is available in three course management systems: CourseCompass™, Blackboard, and WebCT. For more information, go to http://cms.aw.com. For the latest pdf instructions on how to use CourseCompass, go to **www.coursecompass.com**. In addition, a Syllabus Manager is offered on the Campbell Biolog*y* Website.

Media for Students

The Campbell Biology Website and CD-ROM include the following for your students:

- Objectives
- Chapter Review (Summary, Self-Quiz, and Essay Questions from the book; Word Roots; Key Terms linked to the Glossary)
- Activities (see list below)
- Case Studies in the Process of Science (see list below)
- Quizzes (Pre-test, Activities Quiz, Chapter Quiz, Essay Questions)
- Web Links
- News and References
- Art and videos from the Campbell Image Presentation Library
- The Campbell *Biology* Interviews (from all editions)
- Glossary with audio pronunciations
- Syllabus Manager

Student Media Activities and Case Studies in The Process of Science

Web/CD Activity 6A: *Energy Transformations*

Web/CD Activity 6B: *The Structure of ATP*

Web/CD Activity 6C: *Chemical Reactions and ATP*

Web/CD Activity 6D: *How Enzymes Work*

Web/CD Case Study in the Process of Science: *How Is the Rate of Enzyme Catalysis Measured?*

Biology Labs On-Line: *EnzymeLab*

Objectives

Metabolism, Energy, and Life

1. Explain the role of catabolic and anabolic pathways in the energy exchanges of cellular metabolism.
2. Distinguish between kinetic and potential energy.
3. Distinguish between open and closed systems.
4. Explain, in your own words, the first and second laws of thermodynamics.
5. Explain why highly ordered living organisms do not violate the second law of thermodynamics.
6. Write and define each component of the equation for free-energy change.
7. Explain how changes in temperature influence the maximum amount of usable energy that can be harvested from a reaction.
8. Describe the relationship between free energy and equilibrium.
9. Distinguish between exergonic and endergonic reactions.
10. Explain why metabolic disequilibrium is one of the defining features of life.
11. Describe the three main kinds of cellular work.
12. Describe the function of ATP in a cell.
13. List the three components of ATP and identify the major class of macromolecules to which ATP belongs.
14. Explain how ATP performs cellular work.

Enzymes

15. Describe the function of enzymes in biological systems.
16. Explain the relationship between enzyme structure and enzyme specificity.
17. Explain the induced-fit model of enzyme function and describe the catalytic cycle of an enzyme.
18. Describe several mechanisms by which enzymes lower activation energy.
19. Explain how substrate concentration affects the rate of an enzyme-controlled reaction.
20. Explain how enzyme activity can be regulated or controlled by environmental factors, co-factors, and enzyme inhibitors.

The Control of Metabolism: *a review*

21. Explain how metabolic pathways are regulated.
22. Explain how the location of enzymes in a cell influences metabolism.

Key Terms

metabolism	entropy	substrate
catabolic pathway	free energy	active site
anabolic pathway	exergonic reaction	induced fit
bioenergetics	endergonic reaction	cofactor
energy	energy coupling	coenzyme
kinetic energy	ATP (adenosine	competitive inhibitor
potential energy	triphosphate)	noncompetitive
chemical energy	phosphorylated	inhibitor
thermodynamics	catalyst	allosteric site
first law of	enzyme	feedback inhibition
thermodynamics	free energy of	cooperativity
second law of	activation	
thermodynamics	activation energy	

Word Roots

cata- = down (*catabolic pathway*: a metabolic pathway that releases energy by breaking down complex molecules into simpler ones)

ana- = up (*anabolic pathway*: a metabolic pathway that consumes energy to build complex molecules from simpler ones)

bio- = life (*bioenergetics*: the study of how organisms manage their energy resources)

kinet- = movement (*kinetic energy*: the energy of motion)

therm- = heat (*thermodynamics*: the study of the energy transformations that occur in a collection of matter)

ex- = out (*exergonic reaction*: a reaction that proceeds with a net release of free energy)

endo- = within (*endergonic reaction*: a reaction that absorbs free energy from its surroundings)

allo- = different (*allosteric site*: a specific receptor site on some part of an enzyme molecule remote from the active site)

References

Atkins, P. W. *The Second Law*. New York, Oxford: W. H. Freeman and Company, 1984. A beautifully written, understandable description of the second Law of Thermodynamics; addresses the role of the Second Law in life processes.

Becker, W. M., L. J. Kleinsmith, and J. Hardin. *The World of the Cell*. 4th ed. San Francisco, California: Benjamin Cummings, 2000.

Campbell, M. *Biochemistry*. 3rd ed. Orlando, Florida: Harcourt, Inc, 1999.

Visual Guide to the Image Library

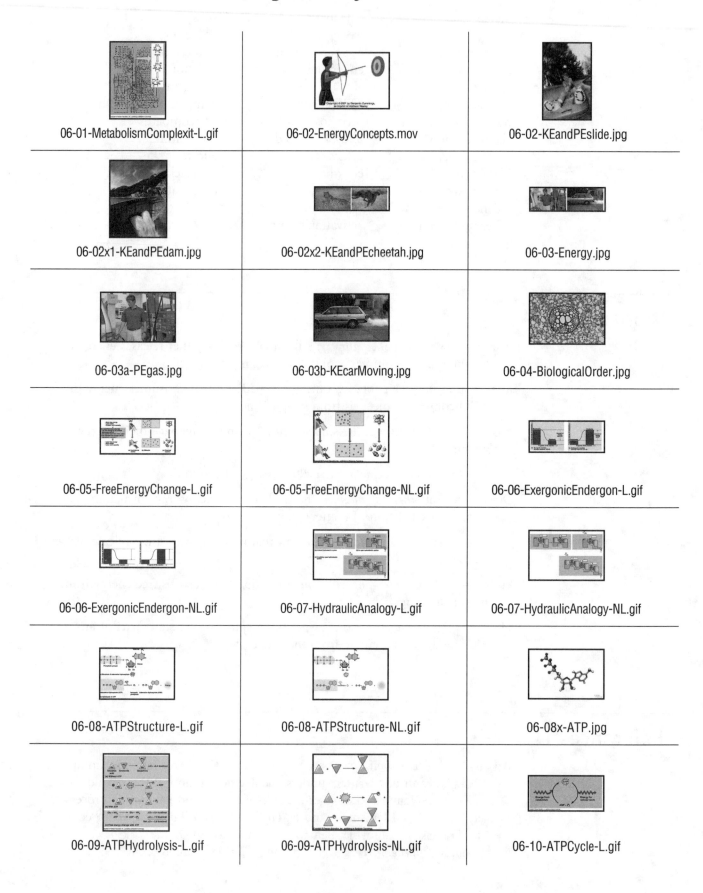

06-01-MetabolismComplexit-L.gif

06-02-EnergyConcepts.mov

06-02-KEandPEslide.jpg

06-02x1-KEandPEdam.jpg

06-02x2-KEandPEcheetah.jpg

06-03-Energy.jpg

06-03a-PEgas.jpg

06-03b-KEcarMoving.jpg

06-04-BiologicalOrder.jpg

06-05-FreeEnergyChange-L.gif

06-05-FreeEnergyChange-NL.gif

06-06-ExergonicEndergon-L.gif

06-06-ExergonicEndergon-NL.gif

06-07-HydraulicAnalogy-L.gif

06-07-HydraulicAnalogy-NL.gif

06-08-ATPStructure-L.gif

06-08-ATPStructure-NL.gif

06-08x-ATP.jpg

06-09-ATPHydrolysis-L.gif

06-09-ATPHydrolysis-NL.gif

06-10-ATPCycle-L.gif

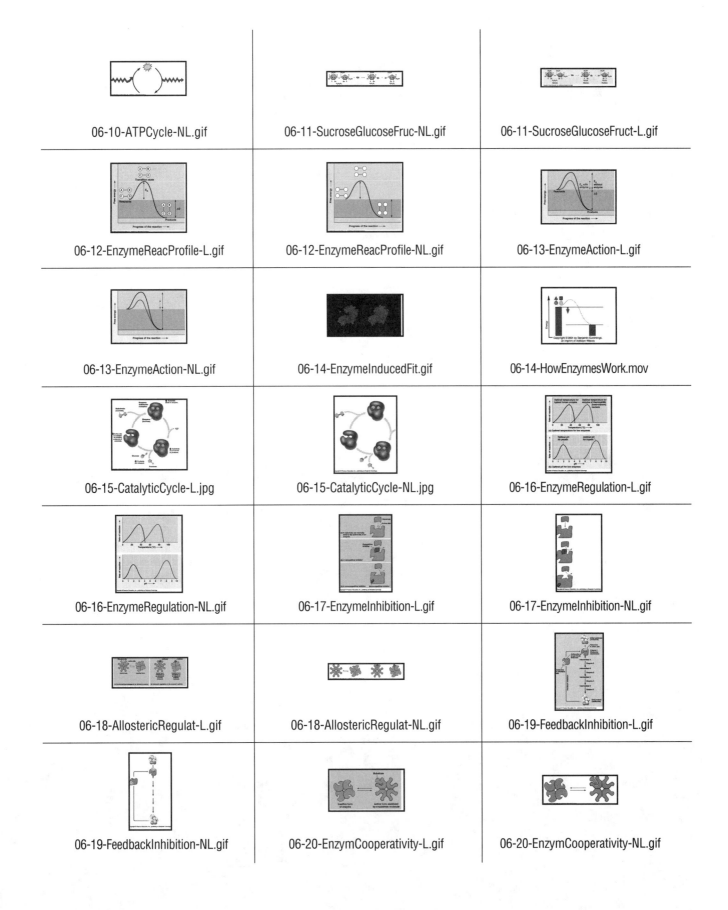

06-10-ATPCycle-NL.gif

06-11-SucroseGlucoseFruc-NL.gif

06-11-SucroseGlucoseFruct-L.gif

06-12-EnzymeReacProfile-L.gif

06-12-EnzymeReacProfile-NL.gif

06-13-EnzymeAction-L.gif

06-13-EnzymeAction-NL.gif

06-14-EnzymeInducedFit.gif

06-14-HowEnzymesWork.mov

06-15-CatalyticCycle-L.jpg

06-15-CatalyticCycle-NL.jpg

06-16-EnzymeRegulation-L.gif

06-16-EnzymeRegulation-NL.gif

06-17-EnzymeInhibition-L.gif

06-17-EnzymeInhibition-NL.gif

06-18-AllostericRegulat-L.gif

06-18-AllostericRegulat-NL.gif

06-19-FeedbackInhibition-L.gif

06-19-FeedbackInhibition-NL.gif

06-20-EnzymCooperativity-L.gif

06-20-EnzymCooperativity-NL.gif

06-21-Mitochondria-L.jpg

06-21-Mitochondria-NL.jpg

A Tour of the Cell

Chapter Outline

Transparency Acetates

The Transparency Acetates for *Biology*, Sixth Edition, include the following images:

Figure 7.1	The size range of cells
Table 7.1	Different Types of Light Microscopy: A Comparison
Figure 7.3	Cell fractionation
Figure 7.4	A prokaryotic cell
Figure 7.5	Geometric relationships explain why most cells are microscopic
Figure 7.6	The plasma membrane
Figure 7.7	Overview of an animal cell
Figure 7.8	Overview of a plant cell
Figure 7.9	The nucleus and its envelope
Figure 7.10	Ribosomes
Figure 7.11	Endoplasmic reticulum (ER)
Figure 7.12	The Golgi apparatus
Figure 7.13	Lysosomes
Figure 7.14	The formation and functions of lysosomes (Layer 1)
Figure 7.14	The formation and functions of lysosomes (Layer 2)
Figure 7.14	The formation and functions of lysosomes (Layer 3)
Figure 7.15	The plant cell vacuole
Figure 7.16	Review: relationships among organelles of the endomembrane system
Figure 7.17	The mitochondrion, site of cellular respiration
Figure 7.18	The chloroplast, site of photosynthesis
Figure 7.19	Peroxisomes
Figure 7.20	The cytoskeleton
Figure 7.21	Motor molecules and the cytoskeleton
Table 7.2	The structure and function of the cytoskeleton
Figure 7.22	Centrosome containing a pair of centrioles
Figure 7.23	A comparison of the beating of flagella and cilia
Figure 7.24	Ultrastructure of a eukaryotic flagellum or cilium
Figure 7.25	How dynein "walking" moves cilia and flagella
Figure 7.26	A structural role of microfilaments
Figure 7.27	Microfilaments and motility
Figure 7.28	Plant cell walls
Figure 7.29	Extracellular matrix (ECM) of an animal cell
Figure 7.30	Intercellular junctions in animal tissues

Media for Instructors

Campbell Image Presentation Library

The Campbell Image Presentation Library CD-ROM set includes the following for your use:

- All art (available in pdf and jpeg or gif formats), photos (from the text and outside sources), and tables. Art images are also available without callouts. See the Visual Guide to the Image Library at the end of this chapter for thumbnail versions of every image.

- A PowerPoint™ slide show of the art (with callouts), photos (both text and outside sources), and tables.

- The following video clips:

  07-15-ParameciumVacuole-B.mov   *Paramecium* with contractile vacuole

  07-23b-ParameciumCilia-B.mov   *Paramecium* with beating cilia

  07-27c-CytoplasmicStream-B.mov   Cytoplasmic streaming in *Elodea*

  See also

  28-03-Euglena_B.mov   *Euglena acus* (two swimming cells, 400x)

- The following QuickTime animations, adapted from student media activities (also available as Shockwave Flash .swf files):

  07-14-LysosomeFormation.mov

  07-16-EndomembraneSystem.mov

  07-24-CiliaFlagella.mov

  07-30a-TightJunctions.mov

  07-30b-AnchoringJunctions.mov

  07-30c-CommunicatingJunct.mov

PowerPoint Lectures CD-ROM

The PowerPoint Lectures CD-ROM contains slides that integrate the art, photos, tables, and lecture outline from this chapter.

Campbell Biology Website (Instructor Resources)

See the insert in your copy of Campbell/Reece *Biology*, Sixth Edition, for instructions on how to access the Cambell Biology Website. The Instructor Resources section of the website includes the following:

- The art, photos, tables, PowerPoint slide shows, videos, and animations from the Campbell Image Presentation Library

- Suggested answers to the Lab Report questions from the Case Studies in the Process of Science

- The PowerPoint Lecture for this chapter

- Word files of the lecture outline for this chapter

- Photo links

Course Management Systems

The media content for this chapter is available in three course management systems: CourseCompass™, Blackboard, and WebCT. For more information, go to http://cms.aw.com. For the latest pdf instructions on how to use CourseCompass, go to **www.coursecompass.com**. In addition, a Syllabus Manager is offered on the Campbell Biolog*y* Website.

Media for Students

The Campbell Biology Website and CD-ROM include the following for your students:

- Objectives
- Chapter Review (Summary, Self-Quiz, and Essay Questions from the book; Word Roots; Key Terms linked to the Glossary)
- Activities (see list below)
- Case Studies in the Process of Science (see list below)
- Quizzes (Pre-test, Activities Quiz, Chapter Quiz, Essay Questions)
- Web Links
- News and References
- Art and videos from the Campbell Image Presentation Library
- The Campbell *Biology* Interviews (from all editions)
- Glossary with audio pronunciations
- Syllabus Manager

Student Media Activities and Case Studies in The Process of Science

Web/CD Activity 7A: *Metric System Review*

Web/CD Case Study in the Process of Science: *What is the Size and Scale of Our World?*

Web/CD Activity 7B: *Prokaryotic Cell Structure and Function*

Web/CD Activity 7C: *Comparing Prokaryotic and Eukaryotic Cells*

Web/CD Activity 7D: *Build an Animal Cell and a Plant Cell*

Web/CD Activity 7E: *Role of the Nucleus and Ribosomes in Protein Synthesis*

Web/CD Activity 7F: *The Endomembrane System*

Web/CD Activity 7G: *Build a Chloroplast and a Mitochondrion*

Web/CD Activity 7H: *Cilia and Flagella*

Web/CD Activity 7I: *Cell Junctions*

Web/CD Activity 7J: *Review: Animal Cell Structure and Function*

Web/CD Activity 7K: *Review: Plant Cell Structure and Function*

Objectives

How We Study Cells

1. Distinguish between magnification and resolving power.

2. Describe the principles, advantages, and limitations of the light microscope, transmission electron microscope, and scanning electron microscope.

3. Describe the major steps of cell fractionation and explain why it is a useful technique.

A Panoramic View of the Cell

4. Distinguish between prokaryotic and eukaryotic cells.

5. Explain why there are both upper and lower limits to cell size.

6. Explain why compartmentalization is important in eukaryotic cells.

The Nucleus and Ribosomes

7. Describe the structure and function of the nucleus and briefly explain how the nucleus controls protein synthesis in the cytoplasm.

8. Describe the structure and function of a eukaryotic ribosome.

The Endomembrane System

9. List the components of the endomembrane system, describe their structures and functions, and summarize the relationships among them.

10. Explain how impaired lysosomal function can cause the symptoms of storage diseases.

11. Describe the different structures and functions of vacuoles.

12. Describe the structure of a mitochondrion and explain the importance of compartmentalization in mitochondrial function.

13. Distinguish among amyloplasts, chromoplasts, and chloroplasts.

14. Identify the three functional compartments of a chloroplast. Explain the importance of compartmentalization in chloroplast function.

Other Membranous Organelles

15. Explain the roles of mitochondria and chloroplasts.

16. Explain the role of peroxisomes in eukaryotic cells.

The Cytoskeleton

17. Describe the functions of the cytoskeleton.

18. Describe the structure, monomers, and functions of microtubules, microfilaments, and intermediate filaments.

19. Explain how the ultrastructure of cilia and flagella relate to their functions.

Cell Surfaces and Junctions

20. Describe the development of plant cell walls.

21. Describe the structure and list four functions of the extracellular matrix in animal cells.

22. Describe the structures of intercellular junctions found in plant and animal cells and relate those structures to their functions.

Key Terms

light microscope (LM)
resolving power
organelle
electron microscope
transmission electron
  microscope (TEM)
scanning electron
  microscope (SEM)
cell fractionation
ultracentrifuge
cytosol
prokaryotic cell
nucleoid
cytoplasm
plasma membrane
nucleus
nuclear lamina
chromatin
chromosome
nucleolus
ribosome
endomembrane system
vesicle
endoplasmic reticulum
  (ER)

smooth ER
rough ER
glycoprotein
transport vesicle
Golgi apparatus
lysosome
phagocytosis
food vacuole
contractile vacuole
central vacuole
tonoplast
mitochondrion
chloroplast
crista
mitochondrial matrix
plastid
thylakoid
granum
stroma
peroxisome
cytoskeleton
microtubule
microfilament
intermediate filament
centrosome

centriole
flagellum
cilium
basal body
dynein
actin
myosin
pseudopodium
cytoplasmic streaming
cell wall
primary cell wall
middle lamella
secondary cell wall
extracellular matrix
collagen
proteoglycan
fibronectin
integrin
plasmodesma
tight junction
desmosome
gap junction

Word Roots

centro- = the center; **-soma** = a body (*centrosome*: material present in the cytoplasm of all eukaryotic cells and important during cell division)

chloro- = green (*chloroplast*: the site of photosynthesis in plants and eukaryotic algae)

cili- = hair (*cilium*: a short hair-like cellular appendage with a microtubule core)

cyto- = cell (*cytosol*: a semifluid medium in a cell in which are located organelles)

-ell = small (*organelle*: a small formed body with a specialized function found in the cytoplasm of eukaryotic cells)

endo- = inner (*endomembrane system*: the system of membranes within a cell that include the nuclear envelope, endoplasmic reticulum, Golgi apparatus, lysosomes, vacuoles, and the plasma membrane)

eu- = true (*eukaryotic cell*: a cell that has a true nucleus)

extra- = outside (*extracellular matrix*: the substance in which animal tissue cells are embedded)

flagell- = whip (*flagellum*: a long whip-like cellular appendage that moves cells)

glyco- = sweet (*glycoprotein*: a protein covalently bonded to a carbohydrate)

lamin- = sheet / layer (*nuclear lamina*: a netlike array of protein filaments that maintains the shape of the nucleus)

lyso- = loosen (*lysosome*: a membrane-bounded sac of hydrolytic enzymes that a cell uses to digest macromolecules)

micro- = small; **-tubul** = a little pipe (*mirotubule*: a hollow rod of tubulin protein in the cytoplasm of almost all eukaryotic cells)

nucle- = nucleus; **-oid** = like (*nucleoid*: the region where the genetic material is concentrated in prokaryotic cells)

phago- = to eat; **-kytos** = vessel (*phagocytosis*: a form of cell eating in which a cell engulfs a smaller organism or food particle)

plasm- = molded; **-desma** = a band or bond (*plasmodesmata*: an open channel in a plant cell wall)

pro- = before; **karyo-** = nucleus (*prokaryotic cell*: a cell that has no nucleus)

pseudo- = false; **-pod** = foot (*pseudopodium*: a cellular extension of amoeboid cells used in moving and feeding)

thylaco- = sac or pouch (*thylakoid*: a series of flattened sacs within chloroplasts)

tono- = stretched; **-plast** = molded (*tonoplast*: the membrane that encloses a large central vacuole in a mature plant cell)

trans- = across; **-port** = a harbor (*transport vesicle*: a membranous compartment used to enclose and transport materials from one part of a cell to another)

ultra- = beyond (*ultracentrifuge*: a machine that spins test tubes at the fastest speeds to separate liquids and particles of different densities)

vacu- = empty (*vacuole*: sac that buds from the ER, Golgi, or plasma membrane)

References

Becker, W. M., L. J. Kleinsmith, and J. Hardin. *The World of the Cell*. 4th ed. San Francisco, California: Benjamin Cummings, 2000.

deDuve, C. *A Guided Tour of the Living Cell*. Volumes I and II. New York: Scientific American Books, 1984. Literally, a guided tour of the cell with the reader as "cytonaut." This is an excellent resource for lecture material and enjoyable reading.

Goldberg, A., et al. "The Cellular Chamber of Doom." *Scientific American*, January 2001.

Visual Guide to the Image Library

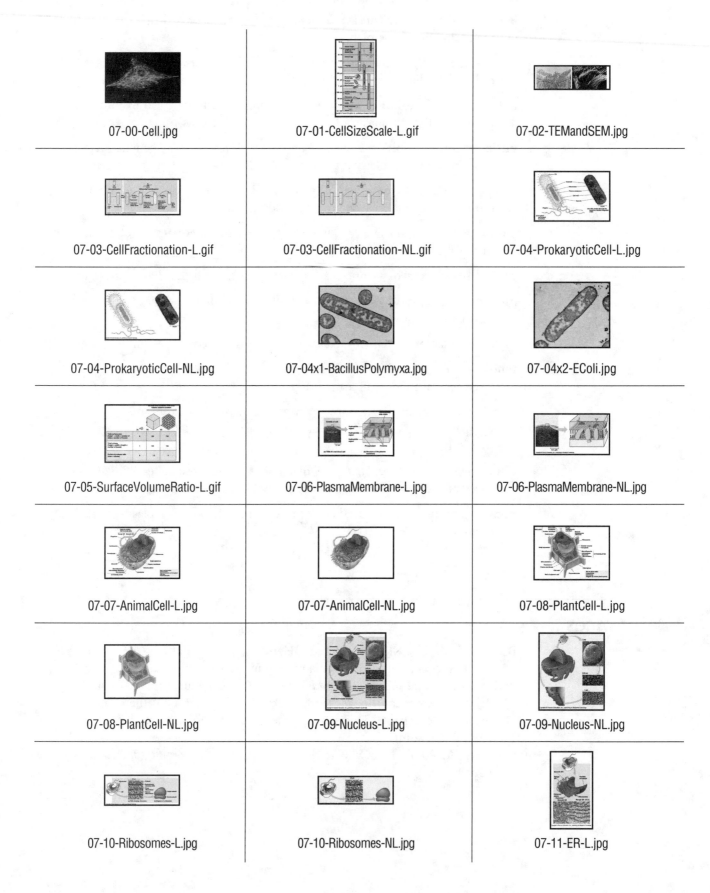

07-00-Cell.jpg

07-01-CellSizeScale-L.gif

07-02-TEMandSEM.jpg

07-03-CellFractionation-L.gif

07-03-CellFractionation-NL.gif

07-04-ProkaryoticCell-L.jpg

07-04-ProkaryoticCell-NL.jpg

07-04x1-BacillusPolymyxa.jpg

07-04x2-EColi.jpg

07-05-SurfaceVolumeRatio-L.gif

07-06-PlasmaMembrane-L.jpg

07-06-PlasmaMembrane-NL.jpg

07-07-AnimalCell-L.jpg

07-07-AnimalCell-NL.jpg

07-08-PlantCell-L.jpg

07-08-PlantCell-NL.jpg

07-09-Nucleus-L.jpg

07-09-Nucleus-NL.jpg

07-10-Ribosomes-L.jpg

07-10-Ribosomes-NL.jpg

07-11-ER-L.jpg

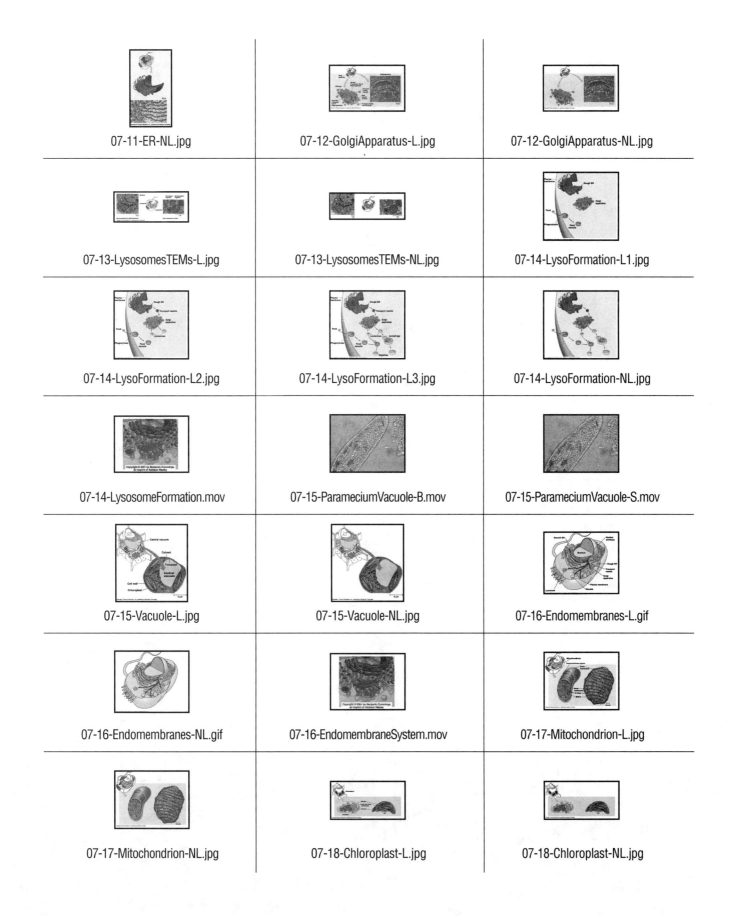

07-11-ER-NL.jpg

07-12-GolgiApparatus-L.jpg

07-12-GolgiApparatus-NL.jpg

07-13-LysosomesTEMs-L.jpg

07-13-LysosomesTEMs-NL.jpg

07-14-LysoFormation-L1.jpg

07-14-LysoFormation-L2.jpg

07-14-LysoFormation-L3.jpg

07-14-LysoFormation-NL.jpg

07-14-LysosomeFormation.mov

07-15-ParameciumVacuole-B.mov

07-15-ParameciumVacuole-S.mov

07-15-Vacuole-L.jpg

07-15-Vacuole-NL.jpg

07-16-Endomembranes-L.gif

07-16-Endomembranes-NL.gif

07-16-EndomembraneSystem.mov

07-17-Mitochondrion-L.jpg

07-17-Mitochondrion-NL.jpg

07-18-Chloroplast-L.jpg

07-18-Chloroplast-NL.jpg

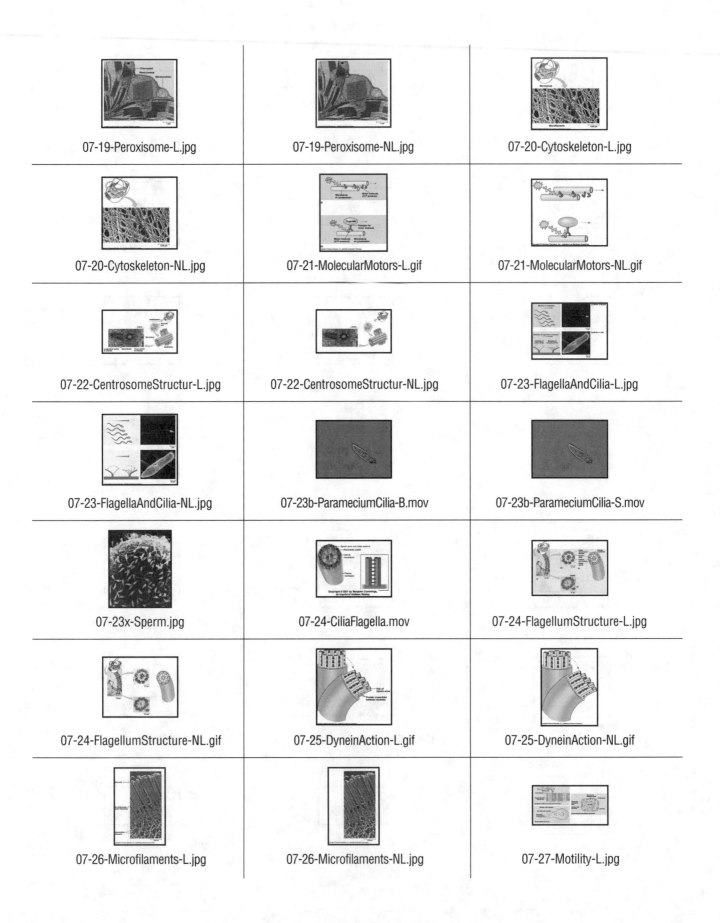

07-19-Peroxisome-L.jpg

07-19-Peroxisome-NL.jpg

07-20-Cytoskeleton-L.jpg

07-20-Cytoskeleton-NL.jpg

07-21-MolecularMotors-L.gif

07-21-MolecularMotors-NL.gif

07-22-CentrosomeStructur-L.jpg

07-22-CentrosomeStructur-NL.jpg

07-23-FlagellaAndCilia-L.jpg

07-23-FlagellaAndCilia-NL.jpg

07-23b-ParameciumCilia-B.mov

07-23b-ParameciumCilia-S.mov

07-23x-Sperm.jpg

07-24-CiliaFlagella.mov

07-24-FlagellumStructure-L.jpg

07-24-FlagellumStructure-NL.gif

07-25-DyneinAction-L.gif

07-25-DyneinAction-NL.gif

07-26-Microfilaments-L.jpg

07-26-Microfilaments-NL.jpg

07-27-Motility-L.jpg

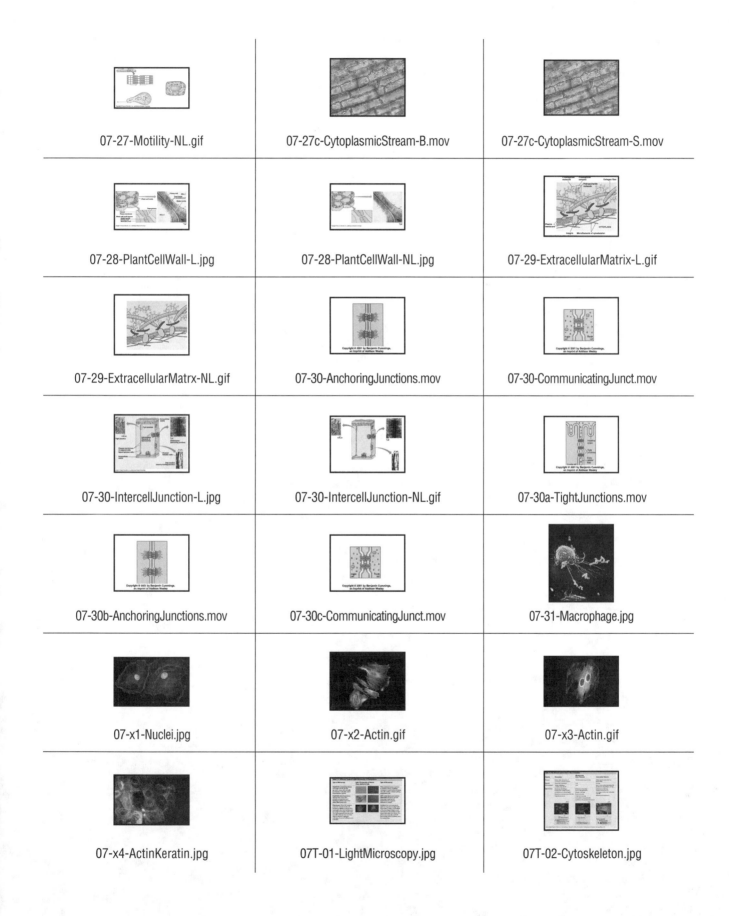

07-27-Motility-NL.gif

07-27c-CytoplasmicStream-B.mov

07-27c-CytoplasmicStream-S.mov

07-28-PlantCellWall-L.jpg

07-28-PlantCellWall-NL.jpg

07-29-ExtracellularMatrix-L.gif

07-29-ExtracellularMatrx-NL.gif

07-30-AnchoringJunctions.mov

07-30-CommunicatingJunct.mov

07-30-IntercellJunction-L.jpg

07-30-IntercellJunction-NL.gif

07-30a-TightJunctions.mov

07-30b-AnchoringJunctions.mov

07-30c-CommunicatingJunct.mov

07-31-Macrophage.jpg

07-x1-Nuclei.jpg

07-x2-Actin.gif

07-x3-Actin.gif

07-x4-ActinKeratin.jpg

07T-01-LightMicroscopy.jpg

07T-02-Cytoskeleton.jpg

CHAPTER 8

Membrane Structure and Function

Chapter Outline

Membrane Structure

Membrane models have evolved to fit new data

Membranes are fluid

Membranes are mosaics of structure and function

Membrane carbohydrates are important for cell-cell recognition

Traffic across Membranes

A membrane's molecular organization results in selective permeability

Passive transport is diffusion across a membrane

Osmosis is the passive transport of water

Cell survival depends on balancing water uptake and loss

Specific proteins facilitate the passive transport of selected solutes: *a closer look*

Active transport is the pumping of solutes against their gradients

Some ion pumps generate voltage across membranes

In cotransport, a membrane protein couples the transport of two solutes

Exocytosis and endocytosis transport large molecules

Transparency Acetates

The Transparency Acetates for *Biology*, Sixth Edition, include the following images:

Figure 8.1	Artificial membranes (cross sections)
Figure 8.2	Two generations of membrane models
Figure 8.3	Freeze-fracture and freeze-etch
Figure 8.4	The fluidity of membranes
Figure 8.5	Evidence for the drifting of membrane proteins
Figure 8.6	The detailed structure of an animal cell's plasma membrane, in cross section
Figure 8.7	The structure of a transmembrane protein
Figure 8.8	Sidedness of the plasma membrane

Media for Instructors

Campbell Image Presentation Library

The Campbell Image Presentation Library CD-ROM set includes the following for your use:

- All art (available in pdf and jpeg or gif formats), photos (from the text and outside sources), and tables. Art images are also available without callouts. See the Visual Guide to the Image Library section at the end of this chapter for thumbnail versions of every image.

- A PowerPoint™ slideshow of the art (with callouts), photos (both text and outside sources), and tables.

- The following video clips:

  08-12-PlasmolyzingElodea-B.mov   *Elodea* in process of plasmolyzing

  08-12-TurgidElodea-B.mov

  See also

  07-15-ParameciumVacuole-B.mov   *Paramecium* contracting vacuole

- The following QuickTime animations, adapted from student media activities (also available as Shockwave Flash .swf files):

  08-02-MembraneStructure.mov

  08-10-Diffusion.mov

  08-11-Osmosis.mov

  08-15-ActiveTransport.mov

  08-19-ExocytEndoIntroAnim.mov

  08-19-ExocytosisAnim.mov

  08-19a-PhagocytosisAnim.mov

  08-19b-PinocytosisAnim.mov

  08-19c-ReceptMedEndoAnim.mov

PowerPoint Lectures CD-ROM

The PowerPoint Lectures CD-ROM contains slides that integrate the art, photos, tables, and lecture outline from this chapter.

Campbell Biology Website (Instructor Resources)

See the insert in your copy of Campbell/Reece *Biology*, Sixth Edition, for instructions on how to access the Campbell Biology Website. The Instructor Resources section of the website includes the following:

- The art, photos, tables, PowerPoint slide shows, videos, and animations from the Campbell Image Presentation Library
- Suggested answers to the Lab Report questions from the Case Studies in the Process of Science
- The PowerPoint Lecture for this chapter
- Word files of the lecture outline for this chapter
- Photo links

Course Management Systems

The media content for this chapter is available in three course management systems: CourseCompass™, Blackboard, and WebCT. For more information, go to http://cms.aw.com. For the latest pdf instructions on how to use CourseCompass, go to www.coursecompass.com. In addition, a Syllabus Manager is offered on the Campbell Biolog*y* Website.

Media for Students

The Campbell Biology Website and CD-ROM include the following for your students:

- Objectives
- Chapter Review (Summary, Self-Quiz, and Essay Questions from the book; Word Roots; Key Terms linked to the Glossary)
- Activities (see list below)
- Case Studies in the Process of Science (see list below)
- Quizzes (Pre-test, Activities Quiz, Chapter Quiz, Essay Questions)
- Web Links
- News and References
- Art and videos from the Campbell Image Presentation Library
- The Campbell *Biology* Interviews (from all editions)
- Glossary with audio pronunciations
- Syllabus Manager

Student Media Activities and Case Studies in The Process of Science

Web/CD Activity 8A: *Membrane Structure*

Web/CD Activity 8B: *Selective Permeability of Membranes*

Web/CD Activity 8C: *Diffusion*

Web/CD Activity 8D: *Osmosis and Water Balance in Cells*

Web/CD Case Study in the Process of Science: *How Does Osmosis Affect Cells?*

Web/CD Activity 8E: *Facilitated Diffusion*

Web/CD Activity 8F: *Active Transport*

Web/CD Activity 8G: *Exocytosis and Endocytosis*

Objectives

Membrane Structure

1. Describe the properties of phospholipids and their arrangement in cellular membranes.
2. Explain what freeze-fracture techniques reveal about the involvement of proteins in membranes.
3. Describe the fluid properties of the cell membrane and explain how membrane fluidity is influenced by membrane composition.
4. Describe how proteins and carbohydrates are spatially arranged in cell membranes and how they contribute to membrane function.

Traffic across Membranes

5. Describe factors that affect the selective permeability of membranes.
6. Describe the locations and functions of transport proteins.
7. Define diffusion. Explain what causes diffusion and why it is a spontaneous process.
8. Explain what regulates the rate of passive transport.
9. Explain why a concentration gradient across a membrane represents potential energy.
10. Distinguish between hypertonic, hypotonic, and isotonic solutions.
11. Define osmosis and predict the direction of water movement based on differences in solute concentrations.
12. Describe how living cells with and without walls regulate the balance of water content.
13. Explain how transport proteins are similar to enzymes.
14. Explain how transport proteins facilitate diffusion.
15. Explain how active transport differs from diffusion.

16. Explain what mechanism can generate a membrane potential or electrochemical gradient.
17. Describe the process of co-transport.
18. Explain how large molecules are transported across the cell membrane.
19. Compare pinocytosis and receptor-mediated endocytosis.

Key Terms

selective permeability
amphipathic molecule
fluid mosaic model
integral protein
peripheral protein
transport protein
diffusion
concentration gradient
passive transport
hypertonic solution
hypotonic solution
isotonic solutions

osmosis
osmoregulation
turgid
flaccid
plasmolysis
facilitated diffusion
aquaporin
gated channel
active transport
sodium-potassium
  pump
membrane potential

electrochemical
  gradient
electrogenic pump
proton pump
cotransport
exocytosis
endocytosis
phagocytosis
pinocytosis
receptor-mediated
  endocytosis
ligand

Word Roots

amphi- = dual (*amphipathic molecule*: a molecule that has both a hydrophobic and a hydrophilic region)

aqua- = water; **-pori** = a small opening (*aquaporin*: a transport protein in the plasma membrane of a plant or animal cell that specifically facilitates the diffusion of water across the membrane)

co- = together; **trans-** = across (*cotransport*: the coupling of the "downhill" diffusion of one substance to the "uphill" transport of another against its own concentration gradient)

electro- = electricity; **-genic** = producing (*electrogenic pump*: an ion transport protein generating voltage across a membrane)

endo- = inner; **cyto-** = cell (*endocytosis*: the movement of materials into a cell. Cell-eating)

exo- = outer (*exocytosis*: the movement of materials out of a cell)

hyper- = exceeding; **-tonus** = tension (*hypertonic*: a solution with a higher concentration of solutes)

hypo- = lower (*hypotonic*: a solution with a lower concentration of solutes)

iso- = same (*isotonic*: solutions with equal concentrations of solutes)

phago- = eat (*phagocytosis*: cell eating)

pino- = drink (*pinocytosis*: cell drinking)

plasm- = molded; **-lyso** = loosen (*plasmolysis*: a phenomenon in walled cells in which the cytoplasm shrivels and the plasma membrane pulls away from the cell wall when the cell loses water to a hypertonic environment)

References

Becker, W. M., L. J. Kleinsmith, and J. Hardin. *The World of the Cell.* 4th ed. San Francisco, California: Benjamin Cummings, 2000.

deDuve, C. *A Guided Tour of the Living Cell.* Volumes I and II. New York: Scientific American Books, 1984. Literally, a guided tour of the cell with the reader as "cytonaut." This is an excellent resource for lecture material and enjoyable reading.

Mellman, I., and G. Warren. "The Road Taken: Past and Future Foundations of Membrane Traffic." *Cell,* January 2000.

Visual Guide to the Image Library

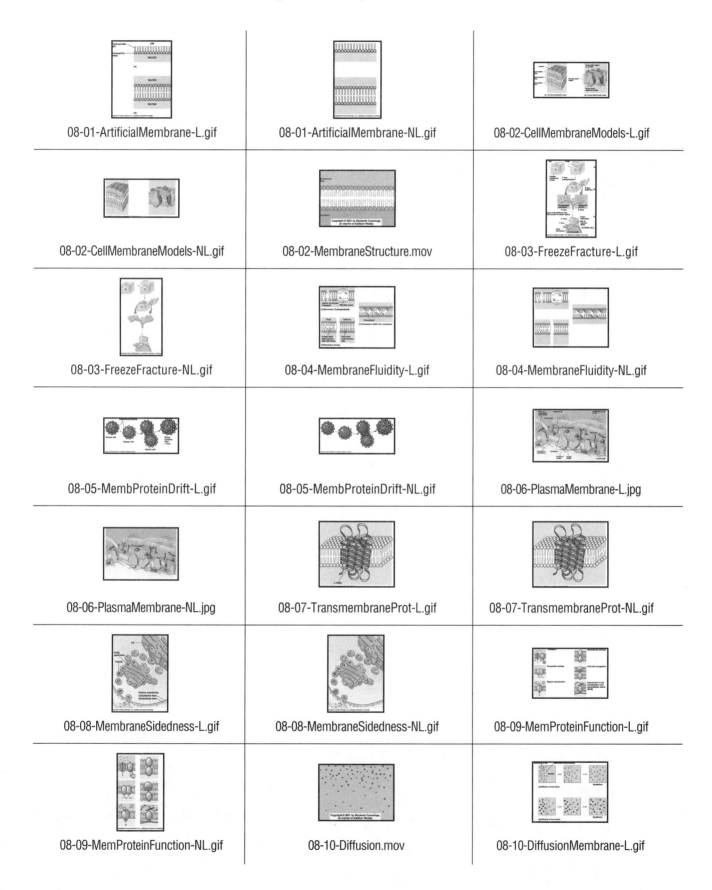

08-01-ArtificialMembrane-L.gif

08-01-ArtificialMembrane-NL.gif

08-02-CellMembraneModels-L.gif

08-02-CellMembraneModels-NL.gif

08-02-MembraneStructure.mov

08-03-FreezeFracture-L.gif

08-03-FreezeFracture-NL.gif

08-04-MembraneFluidity-L.gif

08-04-MembraneFluidity-NL.gif

08-05-MembProteinDrift-L.gif

08-05-MembProteinDrift-NL.gif

08-06-PlasmaMembrane-L.jpg

08-06-PlasmaMembrane-NL.jpg

08-07-TransmembraneProt-L.gif

08-07-TransmembraneProt-NL.gif

08-08-MembraneSidedness-L.gif

08-08-MembraneSidedness-NL.gif

08-09-MemProteinFunction-L.gif

08-09-MemProteinFunction-NL.gif

08-10-Diffusion.mov

08-10-DiffusionMembrane-L.gif

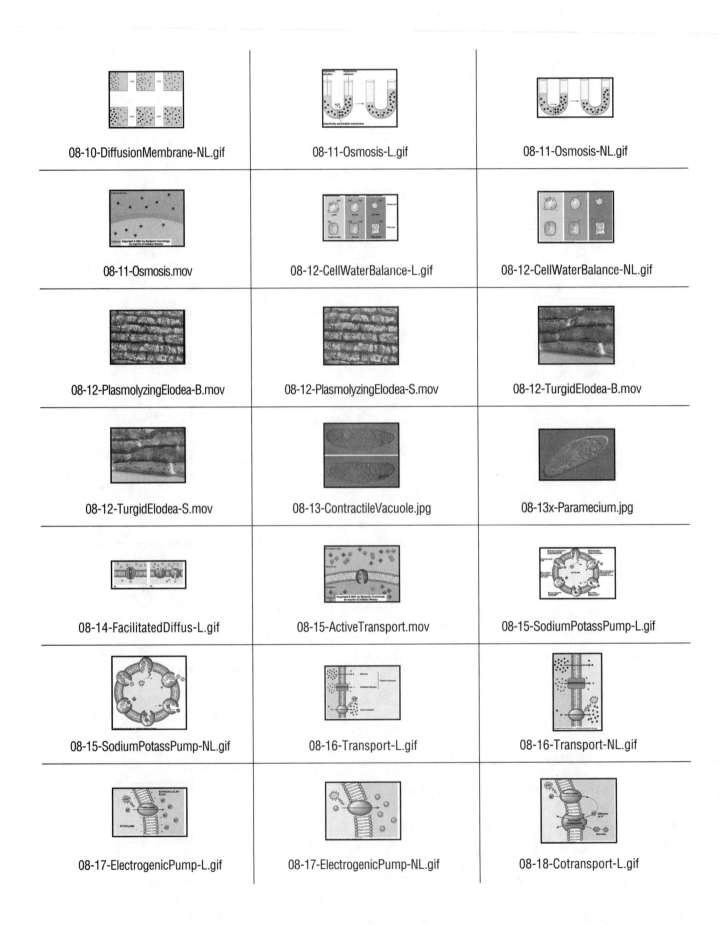

08-10-DiffusionMembrane-NL.gif

08-11-Osmosis-L.gif

08-11-Osmosis-NL.gif

08-11-Osmosis.mov

08-12-CellWaterBalance-L.gif

08-12-CellWaterBalance-NL.gif

08-12-PlasmolyzingElodea-B.mov

08-12-PlasmolyzingElodea-S.mov

08-12-TurgidElodea-B.mov

08-12-TurgidElodea-S.mov

08-13-ContractileVacuole.jpg

08-13x-Paramecium.jpg

08-14-FacilitatedDiffus-L.gif

08-15-ActiveTransport.mov

08-15-SodiumPotassPump-L.gif

08-15-SodiumPotassPump-NL.gif

08-16-Transport-L.gif

08-16-Transport-NL.gif

08-17-ElectrogenicPump-L.gif

08-17-ElectrogenicPump-NL.gif

08-18-Cotransport-L.gif

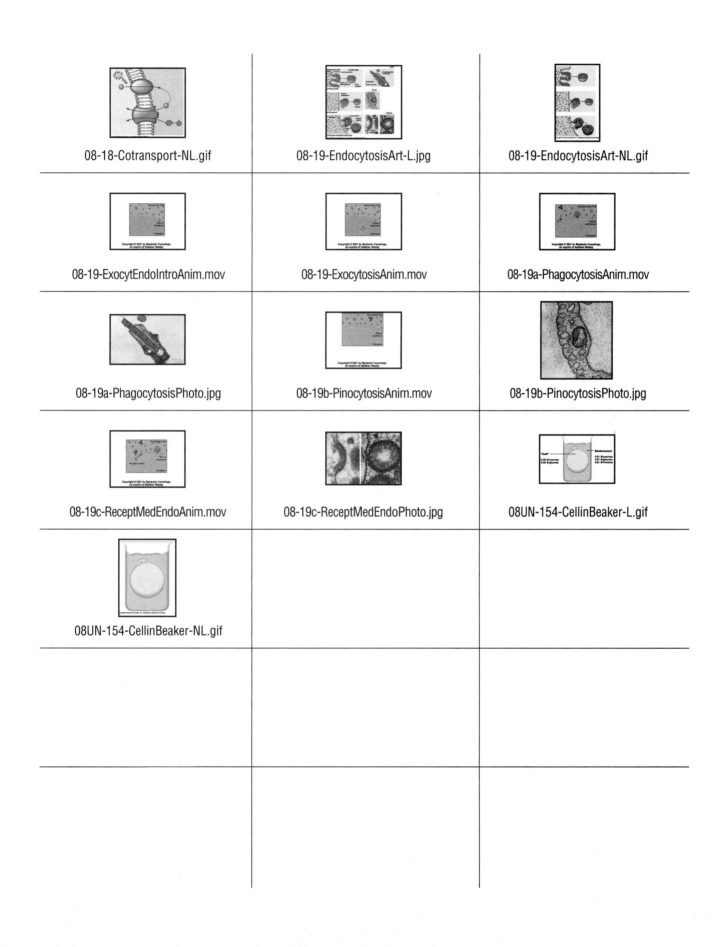

08-18-Cotransport-NL.gif

08-19-EndocytosisArt-L.jpg

08-19-EndocytosisArt-NL.gif

08-19-ExocytEndoIntroAnim.mov

08-19-ExocytosisAnim.mov

08-19a-PhagocytosisAnim.mov

08-19a-PhagocytosisPhoto.jpg

08-19b-PinocytosisAnim.mov

08-19b-PinocytosisPhoto.jpg

08-19c-ReceptMedEndoAnim.mov

08-19c-ReceptMedEndoPhoto.jpg

08UN-154-CellinBeaker-L.gif

08UN-154-CellinBeaker-NL.gif

CHAPTER 9

Cellular Respiration: Harvesting Chemical Energy

Chapter Outline

Transparency Acetates

The Transparency Acetates for *Biology*, Sixth Edition, include the following images:

Figure 9.1	Energy flow and chemical recycling in ecosystems
Figure 9.2	A review of how ATP drives cellular work
Figure 9.3	Methane combustion as an energy-yielding redox reaction
Figure 9.4	NAD^+ as an electron shuttle
Figure 9.5	An introduction to electron transport chains
Figure 9.6	An overview of cellular respiration (Layer 1)
Figure 9.6	An overview of cellular respiration (Layer 2)
Figure 9.6	An overview of cellular respiration (Layer 3)
Figure 9.7	Substrate-level phosphorylation
Figure 9.8	The energy input and output of glycolysis
Figure 9.9	A closer look at glycolysis: energy investment phase (Layer 1)
Figure 9.9	A closer look at glycolysis: energy investment phase (Layer 2)
Figure 9.9	A closer look at glycolysis: energy payoff phase (Layer 3)
Figure 9.9	A closer look at glycolysis: energy payoff phase (Layer 4)
Figure 9.10	Conversion of pyruvate to acetyl CoA, the junction between glycolysis and the Krebs cycle
Figure 9.11	A closer look at the Krebs cycle (Layer 1)
Figure 9.11	A closer look at the Krebs cycle (Layer 2)
Figure 9.11	A closer look at the Krebs cycle (Layer 3)
Figure 9.11	A closer look at the Krebs cycle (Layer 4)
Figure 9.12	A summary of the Krebs cycle
Figure 9.13	Free-energy change during electron transport
Figure 9.14	ATP synthase, a molecular mill
Figure 9.15	Chemiosmosis couples the electron transport chain to ATP synthesis
Figure 9.16	Review: how each molecule of glucose yields many ATP molecules during cellular respiration
Figure 9.17	Fermentation
Figure 9.18	Pyruvate as a key juncture in catabolism
Figure 9.19	The catabolism of various food molecules
Figure 9.20	The control of cellular respiration

Media for Instructors

Campbell Image Presentation Library

The Campbell Image Presentation Library CD-ROM set includes the following for your use:

- All art (available in pdf and jpeg or gif formats), photos (from the text and outside sources), and tables. Art images are also available without callouts. See the Visual Guide to the Image Library section at the end of this chapter for thumbnail versions of every image.
- A PowerPoint™ slide show of the art (with callouts), photos (both text and outside sources), and tables.
- The following QuickTime animations, adapted from student media activities (also available as Shockwave Flash .swf files):

  09-09-Glycolysis.mov

  09-12-KrebsCycle.mov

  09-15-ElectronTransport.mov

  09-17a-AlcoholFermentation.mov

  09-17b-LacticAcidFerment.mov

PowerPoint Lectures CD-ROM

The PowerPoint Lectures CD-ROM contains slides that integrate the art, photos, tables, and lecture outline from this chapter.

Campbell Biology Website (Instructor Resources)

See the insert in your copy of Campbell/Reece *Biology*, Sixth Edition, for instructions on how to access the Campbell Biology Website. The Instructor Resources section of the website includes the following:

- The art, photos, tables, PowerPoint slide shows, videos, and animations from the Campbell Image Presentation Library
- Suggested answers to the Lab Report questions from the Case Studies in the Process of Science
- The PowerPoint Lecture for this chapter
- Word files of the lecture outline for this chapter
- Photo links

Course Management Systems

The media content for this chapter is available in three course management systems: CourseCompass™, Blackboard, and WebCT. For more information, go to http://cms.aw.com. For the latest pdf instructions on how to use CourseCompass, go to www.coursecompass.com. In addition, a Syllabus Manager is offered on the Campbell Biology Website.

Media for Students

The Campbell Biology Website and CD-ROM include the following for your students:

- Objectives
- Chapter Review (Summary, Self-Quiz, and Essay Questions from the book; Word Roots; Key Terms linked to the Glossary)
- Activities (see list below)
- Case Studies in the Process of Science (see list below)
- Quizzes (Pre-test, Activities Quiz, Chapter Quiz, Essay Questions)
- Web Links
- News and References
- Art and videos from the Campbell Image Presentation Library
- The Campbell *Biology* Interviews (from all editions)
- Glossary with audio pronunciations
- Syllabus Manager

Student Media Activities and Case Studies in The Process of Science

Web/CD Activity 9A: *Build a Chemical Cycling System*

Web/CD Activity 9B: *Overview of Cellular Respiration*

Web/CD Activity 9C: *Glycolysis*

Web/CD Activity 9D: *The Krebs Cycle*

Web/CD Activity 9E: *Electron Transport*

Biology Labs On-Line: *MitochondriaLab*

Web/CD Activity 9F: *Fermentation*

Web/CD Case Study in the Process of Science: *How is the Rate of Cellular Respiration Measured?*

Objectives

The Principles of Energy Harvest

1. Distinguish between fermentation and cellular respiration.
2. Describe the summary equation for cellular respiration. Also note the specific chemical equation for the degradation of glucose.
3. Explain how ATP is recycled in cells.
4. Define oxidation and reduction.
5. Explain how redox reactions are involved in energy exchanges.

6. Explain why organic molecules that have an abundance of hydrogen are excellent cellular fuels.
7. Describe the role of NAD^+ and the electron transport chain during respiration.

The Process of Cellular Respiration

8. Describe the cellular regions where glycolysis, the Krebs cycle, and the electron transport chain occur.
9. Describe how the carbon skeleton of glucose changes as it proceeds through glycolysis.
10. Explain why ATP is required for the preparatory steps of glycolysis.
11. Identify where sugar oxidation, substrate-level phosphorylation, and the reduction of NAD^+ occur in glycolysis.
12. Describe where pyruvate is oxidized to acetyl CoA, what molecules are produced, and how this process links glycolysis to the Krebs cycle.
13. Describe the form and fate of the carbons in the Krebs cycle. Note the role of oxaloacetate in this cycle.
14. Describe the point at which glucose is completely oxidized during cellular respiration.
15. Explain how the exergonic "slide" of electrons down the electron transport chain is coupled to the endergonic production of ATP by chemiosmosis.
16. Describe the process of chemiosmosis.
17. Explain how membrane structure is related to membrane function in chemiosmosis.
18. Summarize the net ATP yield from the oxidation of a glucose molecule by constructing an ATP ledger that includes coenzyme production during the different stages of glycolysis and cellular respiration.

Related Metabolic Processes

19. Explain why fermentation is necessary.
20. Compare the fate of pyruvate in alcohol fermentation and lactic acid fermentation.
21. Compare the processes of fermentation and cellular respiration.
22. Describe evidence that the first prokaryotes produced ATP by glycolysis.
23. Describe how food molecules other than glucose can be oxidized to make ATP.
24. Explain how glycolysis and the Krebs cycle can contribute to anabolic pathways.
25. Explain how ATP production is controlled by the cell and what role the allosteric enzyme, phosphofructokinase, plays in the process.

Key Terms

fermentation	glycolysis	proton-motive force
cellular respiration	Krebs cycle	aerobic
redox reaction	oxidative	anaerobic
oxidation	phosphorylation	alcohol fermentation
reduction	substrate-level	lactid acid
reducing agent	phosphorylation	fermentation
oxidizing agent	acetyl CoA	facultative anaerobe
NAD^+	cytochromes (cyt)	beta oxidation
electron transport	ATP synthase	
chain	chemiosmosis	

Word Roots

aero- = air (*aerobic*: chemical reaction using oxygen)

an- = not (*anaerobic*: chemical reaction not using oxygen)

chemi- = chemical (*chemiosmosis*: the production of ATP using the energy of hydrogen ion gradients across membranes to phosphorylate ADP)

glyco- = sweet; **-lysis** = split (*glycolysis*: the splitting of glucose into pyruvate)

References

Becker, W. M., L. J. Kleinsmith, and J. Hardin. *The World of the Cell.* 4th ed. San Francisco, California: Benjamin Cummings, 2000.

Campbell, M. *Biochemistry.* 3rd ed. Orlando, Florida: Harcourt, Inc, 1999.

Visual Guide to the Image Library

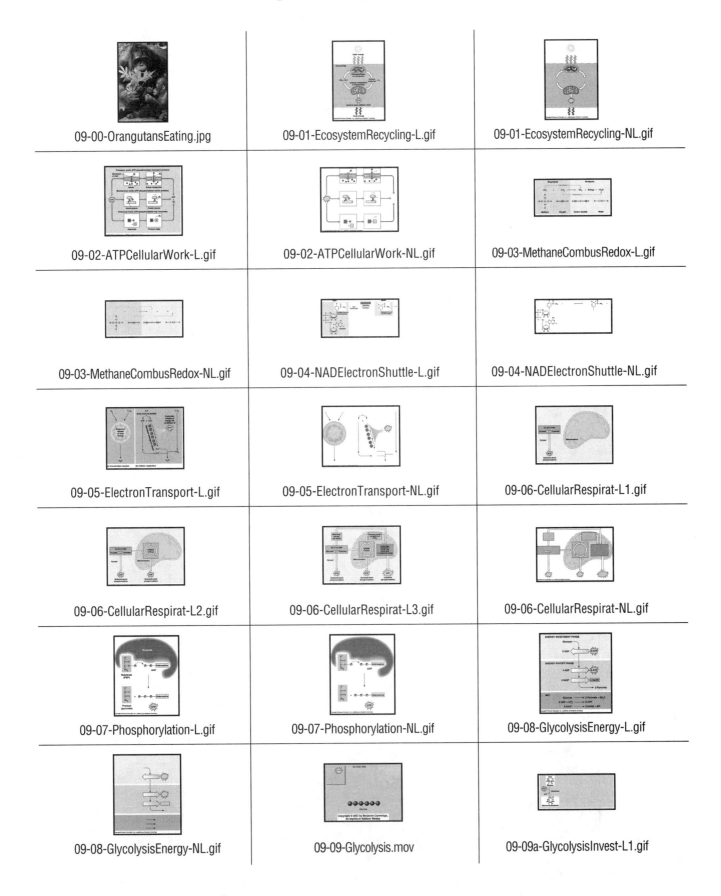

09-00-OrangutansEating.jpg

09-01-EcosystemRecycling-L.gif

09-01-EcosystemRecycling-NL.gif

09-02-ATPCellularWork-L.gif

09-02-ATPCellularWork-NL.gif

09-03-MethaneCombusRedox-L.gif

09-03-MethaneCombusRedox-NL.gif

09-04-NADElectronShuttle-L.gif

09-04-NADElectronShuttle-NL.gif

09-05-ElectronTransport-L.gif

09-05-ElectronTransport-NL.gif

09-06-CellularRespirat-L1.gif

09-06-CellularRespirat-L2.gif

09-06-CellularRespirat-L3.gif

09-06-CellularRespirat-NL.gif

09-07-Phosphorylation-L.gif

09-07-Phosphorylation-NL.gif

09-08-GlycolysisEnergy-L.gif

09-08-GlycolysisEnergy-NL.gif

09-09-Glycolysis.mov

09-09a-GlycolysisInvest-L1.gif

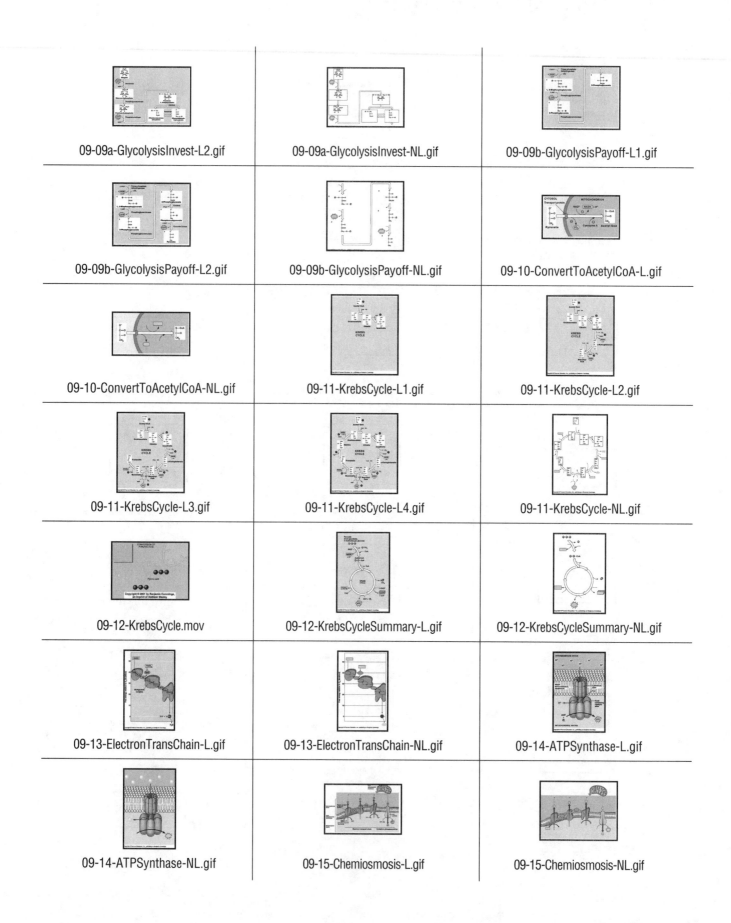

09-09a-GlycolysisInvest-L2.gif

09-09a-GlycolysisInvest-NL.gif

09-09b-GlycolysisPayoff-L1.gif

09-09b-GlycolysisPayoff-L2.gif

09-09b-GlycolysisPayoff-NL.gif

09-10-ConvertToAcetylCoA-L.gif

09-10-ConvertToAcetylCoA-NL.gif

09-11-KrebsCycle-L1.gif

09-11-KrebsCycle-L2.gif

09-11-KrebsCycle-L3.gif

09-11-KrebsCycle-L4.gif

09-11-KrebsCycle-NL.gif

09-12-KrebsCycle.mov

09-12-KrebsCycleSummary-L.gif

09-12-KrebsCycleSummary-NL.gif

09-13-ElectronTransChain-L.gif

09-13-ElectronTransChain-NL.gif

09-14-ATPSynthase-L.gif

09-14-ATPSynthase-NL.gif

09-15-Chemiosmosis-L.gif

09-15-Chemiosmosis-NL.gif

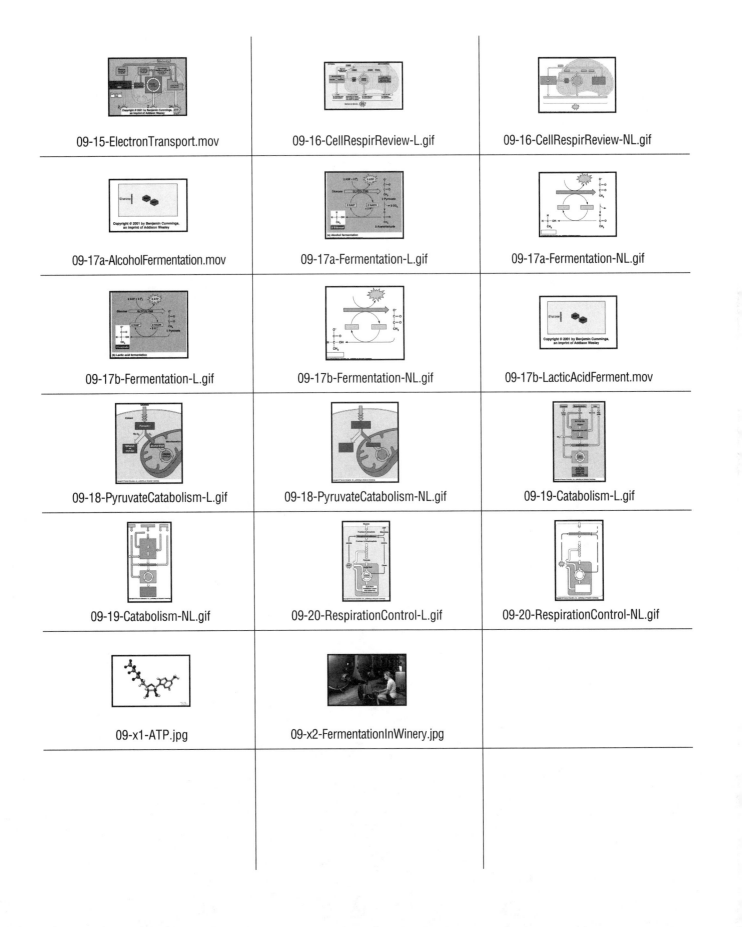

09-15-ElectronTransport.mov

09-16-CellRespirReview-L.gif

09-16-CellRespirReview-NL.gif

09-17a-AlcoholFermentation.mov

09-17a-Fermentation-L.gif

09-17a-Fermentation-NL.gif

09-17b-Fermentation-L.gif

09-17b-Fermentation-NL.gif

09-17b-LacticAcidFerment.mov

09-18-PyruvateCatabolism-L.gif

09-18-PyruvateCatabolism-NL.gif

09-19-Catabolism-L.gif

09-19-Catabolism-NL.gif

09-20-RespirationControl-L.gif

09-20-RespirationControl-NL.gif

09-x1-ATP.jpg

09-x2-FermentationInWinery.jpg

CHAPTER 10

Photosynthesis

Chapter Outline

Photosynthesis in Nature

Plants and other autotrophs are the producers of the biosphere

Chloroplasts are the sites of photosynthesis in plants

The Pathways of Photosynthesis

Evidence that chloroplasts split water molecules enabled researchers to track atoms through photosynthesis: *the process of science*

The light reactions and the Calvin cycle cooperate in converting light energy to the chemical energy of food: *an overview*

The light reactions convert solar energy to the chemical energy of ATP and NADPH: *a closer look*

The Calvin cycle uses ATP and NADPH to convert CO_2 to sugar: *a closer look*

Alternative mechanisms of carbon fixation have evolved in hot, arid climates

Photosynthesis is the biosphere's metabolic foundation: *a review*

Transparency Acetates

The Transparency Acetates for *Biology*, Sixth Edition, include the following images:

Media for Instructors

Campbell Image Presentation Library

The Campbell Image Presentation Library CD-ROM set includes the following for your use:

- All art (available in pdf and jpeg or gif formats), photos (from the text and outside sources), and tables. Art images are also available without callouts. See the Visual Guide to the Image Library section at the end of this chapter for thumbnail versions of every image.

- A PowerPoint™ slide show of the art (with callouts), photos (both text and outside sources), and tables.

- The following QuickTime animations, adapted from student media activities (also available as Shockwave Flash .swf files):

  10-16-CalvinCycle.mov

  10-17-LightReactions.mov

PowerPoint Lectures CD-ROM

The PowerPoint Lectures CD-ROM contains slides that integrate the art, photos, tables, and lecture outline from this chapter.

Campbell Biology Website (Instructor Resources)

See the insert in your copy of Campbell/Reece *Biology*, Sixth Edition, for instructions on how to access the Campbell Biology Website. The Instructor Resources section of the website includes the following:

- The art, photos, tables, PowerPoint slide shows, videos, and animations from the Campbell Image Presentation Library
- Suggested answers to the Lab Report questions from the Case Studies in the Process of Science
- The PowerPoint Lecture for this chapter
- Word files of the lecture outline for this chapter
- Photo links

Course Management Systems

The media content for this chapter is available in three course management systems: CourseCompass^{TM}, Blackboard, and WebCT. For more information, go to http://cms.aw.com. For the latest pdf instructions on how to use CourseCompass, go to **www.coursecompass.com**. In addition, a Syllabus Manager is offered on the Campbell Biology Website.

Media for Students

The Campbell Biology Website and CD-ROM include the following for your students:

- Objectives
- Chapter Review (Summary, Self-Quiz, and Essay Questions from the book; Word Roots; Key Terms linked to the Glossary)
- Activities (see list below)
- Case Studies in the Process of Science (see list below)
- Quizzes (Pre-test, Activities Quiz, Chapter Quiz, Essay Questions)
- Web Links
- News and References
- Art and videos from the Campbell Image Presentation Library
- The Campbell *Biology* Interviews (from all editions)
- Glossary with audio pronunciations
- Syllabus Manager

Student Media Activities and Case Studies in The Process of Science

Web/CD Activity 10A: *The Sites of Photosynthesis*

Web/CD Activity 10B: *Overview of Photosynthesis*

Web/CD Activity 10C: *Light Energy and Pigments*

Web/CD Case Study in the Process of Science: *How Does Paper Chromatography Separate Plant Pigments?*

Web/CD Activity 10D: *The Light Reactions*

Web/CD Activity 10E: *The Calvin Cycle*

Web/CD Case Study in the Process of Science: *How Is the Rate of Photosynthesis Measured?*

Biology Labs On-Line: *LeafLab*

Web/CD Activity 10F: *Photosynthesis in Dry Climates*

Objectives

Photosynthesis in Nature

1. Distinguish between autotrophic and heterotrophic nutrition.

2. Distinguish between photoautotrophs and chemoautotrophs.

3. Describe the structure of chloroplasts and indicate their locations within plant cells. Describe where most chloroplasts are located in a leaf.

4. Explain how chloroplast structure relates to its function.

5. Write a summary equation for photosynthesis.

The Pathways of Photosynthesis

6. Explain van Niel's hypothesis and describe how it contributed to our current understanding of photosynthesis.

7. Explain the role of redox reactions in photosynthesis.

8. Describe in general the two main stages of photosynthesis.

9. Describe the wavelike and particle-like behaviors of light.

10. Describe the relationship between an action spectrum and an absorption spectrum.

11. Explain why the absorption spectrum for chlorophyll differs from the action spectrum for photosynthesis.

12. List the wavelengths of light that are most effective for photosynthesis.

13. Explain what happens when chlorophyll or accessory pigments absorb photons.

14. List the components of a photosystem and explain their functions.

15. Trace electron flow through photosystems II and I.

16. Compare cyclic and noncyclic electron flow and explain the relationship between these components of the light reactions.

17. Describe important differences in chemiosmosis between oxidative phosphorylation in mitochondria and photophosphorylation in chloroplasts.

18. Summarize the carbon-fixing reactions of the Calvin cycle and describe changes that occur in the carbon skeletons of intermediates.

19. Describe the role of ATP and NADPH in the Calvin cycle.

20. Describe what happens to rubisco when the O_2 concentration is much higher than CO_2.

21. Describe the major consequences of photorespiration.

22. Describe two important photosynthetic adaptations that minimize photorespiration.

23. Describe the fate of photosynthetic products.

Key Terms

photosynthesis
autotroph
heterotroph
chlorophyll
mesophyll
stomata
light reactions
Calvin cycle
$NADP^+$
photophosphorylation
carbon fixation
wavelength
electromagnetic
  spectrum
visible light
photon

spectrophotometer
absorption spectrum
chlorophyll *a*
action spectrum
chlorophyll *b*
carotenoids
photosystems
reaction center
primary electron
  acceptor
photosystem I
photosystem II
noncyclic electron flow
noncyclic
  photophosphorylation
cyclic electron flow

cyclic
  photophosphorylation
glyceraldehyde-3-
  phosphate (G3P)
rubisco
C_3 plant
photorespiration
C_4 plant
bundle-sheath cell
mesophyll cell
PEP carboxylase
crassulacean acid
  metabolism (CAM)
CAM plant

Word Roots

auto- = self; **-troph** = food (*autotroph*: an organism that obtains organic food molecules without eating other organisms)

chloro- = green; **-phyll** = leaf (*chlorophyll*: photosynthetic pigment in chloroplasts)

electro- = electricity; **magnet-** = magnetic (*electromagnetic spectrum*: the entire spectrum of radiation)

hetero- = other (*heterotroph*: an organism that obtains organic food molecules by eating other organisms or their by-products)

meso- = middle (*mesophyll*: the green tissue in the middle, inside of a leaf)

photo- = light (*photosystem*: cluster of pigment molecules)

References

Atkins, P. W. *Atoms, Electrons, and Change.* New York, Oxford: W. H. Freeman and Company, 1991. Chapter 9, "Light and Life" is a witty, imaginative description of photosynthesis. Though written for a lay audience, it is probably best appreciated by someone already familiar with photosynthesis.

Campbell, M. *Biochemistry.* 3rd ed. Orlando, Florida: Harcourt, Inc, 1999.

Hopkins, W. G. *Introduction to Plant Physiology.* New York: John Wiley & Sons, Inc. 1995.

Visual Guide to the Image Library

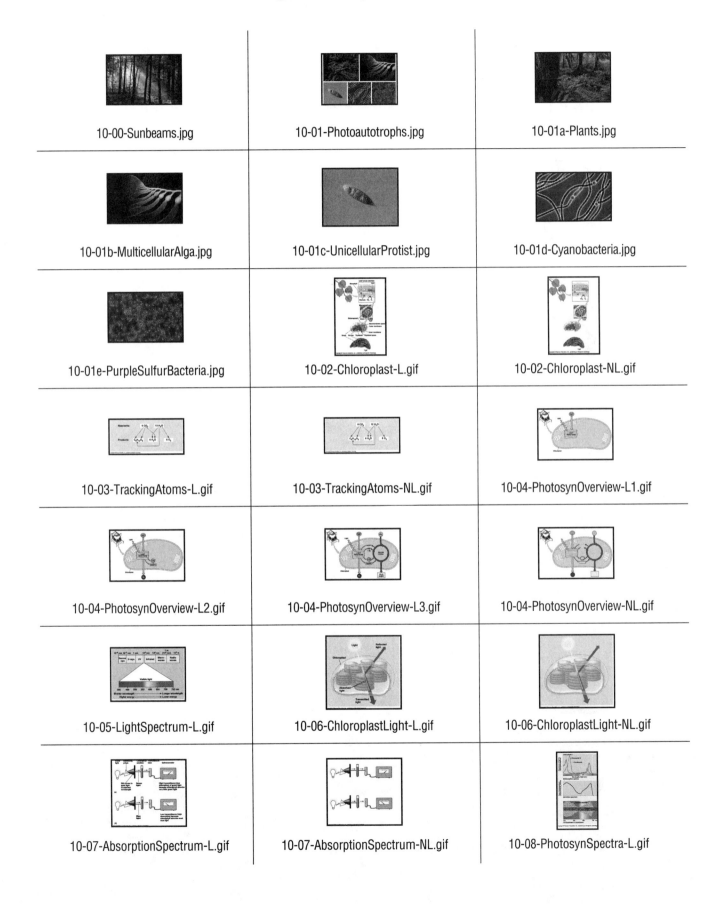

10-00-Sunbeams.jpg

10-01-Photoautotrophs.jpg

10-01a-Plants.jpg

10-01b-MulticellularAlga.jpg

10-01c-UnicellularProtist.jpg

10-01d-Cyanobacteria.jpg

10-01e-PurpleSulfurBacteria.jpg

10-02-Chloroplast-L.gif

10-02-Chloroplast-NL.gif

10-03-TrackingAtoms-L.gif

10-03-TrackingAtoms-NL.gif

10-04-PhotosynOverview-L1.gif

10-04-PhotosynOverview-L2.gif

10-04-PhotosynOverview-L3.gif

10-04-PhotosynOverview-NL.gif

10-05-LightSpectrum-L.gif

10-06-ChloroplastLight-L.gif

10-06-ChloroplastLight-NL.gif

10-07-AbsorptionSpectrum-L.gif

10-07-AbsorptionSpectrum-NL.gif

10-08-PhotosynSpectra-L.gif

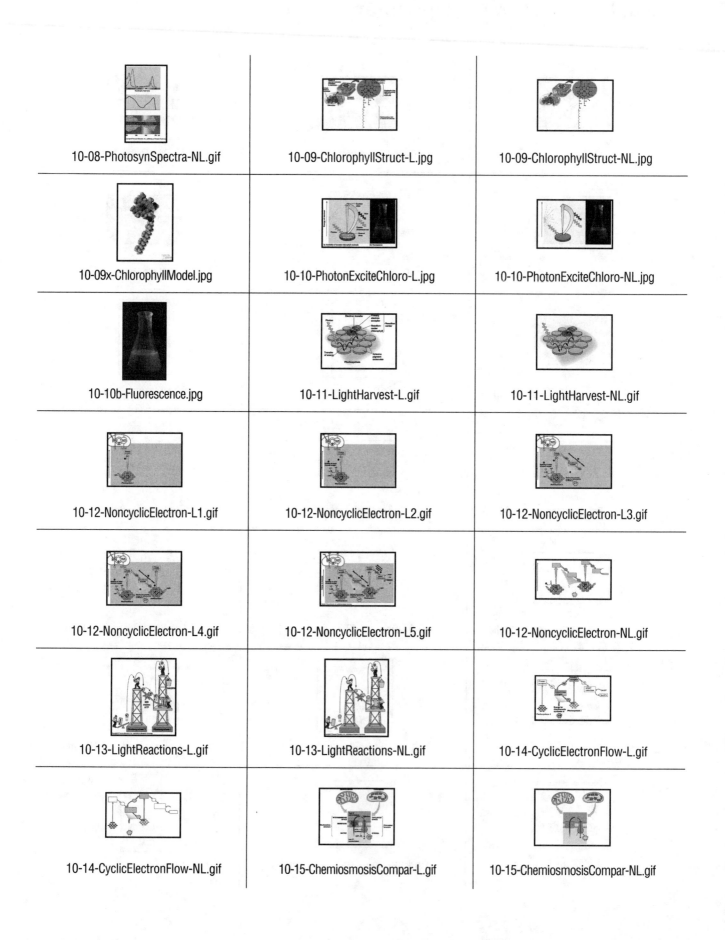

10-08-PhotosynSpectra-NL.gif

10-09-ChlorophyllStruct-L.jpg

10-09-ChlorophyllStruct-NL.jpg

10-09x-ChlorophyllModel.jpg

10-10-PhotonExciteChloro-L.jpg

10-10-PhotonExciteChloro-NL.jpg

10-10b-Fluorescence.jpg

10-11-LightHarvest-L.gif

10-11-LightHarvest-NL.gif

10-12-NoncyclicElectron-L1.gif

10-12-NoncyclicElectron-L2.gif

10-12-NoncyclicElectron-L3.gif

10-12-NoncyclicElectron-L4.gif

10-12-NoncyclicElectron-L5.gif

10-12-NoncyclicElectron-NL.gif

10-13-LightReactions-L.gif

10-13-LightReactions-NL.gif

10-14-CyclicElectronFlow-L.gif

10-14-CyclicElectronFlow-NL.gif

10-15-ChemiosmosisCompar-L.gif

10-15-ChemiosmosisCompar-NL.gif

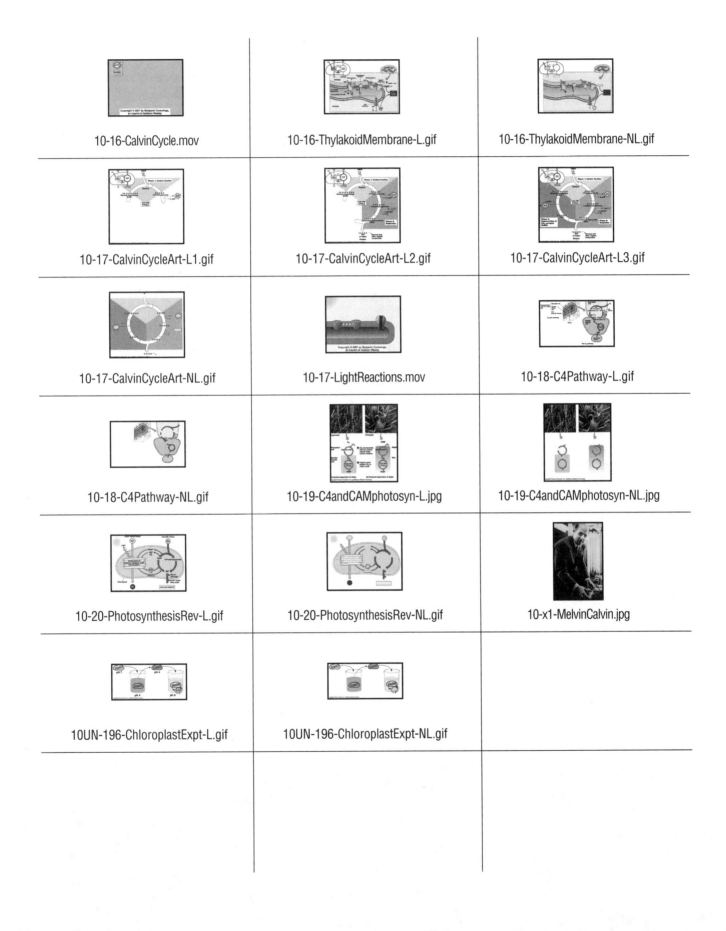

10-16-CalvinCycle.mov

10-16-ThylakoidMembrane-L.gif

10-16-ThylakoidMembrane-NL.gif

10-17-CalvinCycleArt-L1.gif

10-17-CalvinCycleArt-L2.gif

10-17-CalvinCycleArt-L3.gif

10-17-CalvinCycleArt-NL.gif

10-17-LightReactions.mov

10-18-C4Pathway-L.gif

10-18-C4Pathway-NL.gif

10-19-C4andCAMphotosyn-L.jpg

10-19-C4andCAMphotosyn-NL.jpg

10-20-PhotosynthesisRev-L.gif

10-20-PhotosynthesisRev-NL.gif

10-x1-MelvinCalvin.jpg

10UN-196-ChloroplastExpt-L.gif

10UN-196-ChloroplastExpt-NL.gif

CHAPTER 11

Cell Communication

Chapter Outline

An Overview of Cell Signaling

Cell signaling evolved early in the history of life

Communicating cells may be close together or far apart

The three stages of cell signaling are reception, transduction, and response

Signal Reception and the Initiation of Transduction

A signal molecule binds to a receptor protein, causing the protein to change shape

Most signal receptors are plasma membrane proteins

Signal-Transduction Pathways

Pathways relay signals from receptors to cellular responses

Protein phosphorylation, a common mode of regulation in cells, is a major mechanism of signal transduction

Certain small molecules and ions are key components of signaling pathways (second messengers)

Cellular Responses to Signals

In response to a signal, a cell may regulate activities in the cytoplasm or transcription in the nucleus

Elaborate pathways amplify and specify the cell's response to signals

---

Transparency Acetates

The Transparency Acetates for *Biology*, Sixth Edition, include the following images:

Figure 11.5	Overview of cell signaling (Layer 3)
Figure 11.6	The structure of a G-protein-linked receptor
Figure 11.7	The functioning of a G-protein-linked receptor
Figure 11.8	The structure and function of a tyrosine-kinase receptor
Figure 11.9	A ligand-gated ion-channel receptor
Figure 11.10	Steroid hormone interacting with an intracellular receptor
Figure 11.11	A phosphorylation cascade
Figure 11.12	Cyclic AMP
Figure 11.13	cAMP as a second messenger
Figure 11.14	The maintenance of calcium ion concentrations in an animal cell
Figure 11.15	Calcium and inositol triphosphate in signaling pathways (Layer 1)
Figure 11.15	Calcium and inositol triphosphate in signaling pathways (Layer 2)
Figure 11.15	Calcium and inositol triphosphate in signaling pathways (Layer 3)
Figure 11.16	Cytoplasmic response to a signal: the stimulation of glycogen breakdown by epinephrine
Figure 11.17	Nuclear response to a signal: the activation of a specific gene by a growth factor
Figure 11.18	The specificity of cell signaling
Figure 11.19	A scaffolding protein

Media for Instructors

Campbell Image Presentation Library

The Campbell Image Presentation Library CD-ROM set includes the following for your use:

- All art (available in pdf and jpeg or gif formats), photos (from the text and outside sources), and tables. Art images are also available without callouts. See the Visual Guide to the Image Library section at the end of this chapter for thumbnail versions of every image.
- A PowerPoint™ slide show of the art (with callouts), photos (both text and outside sources), and tables.
- The following QuickTime animations, adapted from student media activities (also available as Shockwave Flash .swf files):

  11-05-CellSignaling.mov

  11-17-SignalTransduction.mov

PowerPoint Lectures CD-ROM

The PowerPoint Lectures CD-ROM contains slides that integrate the art, photos, tables, and lecture outline from this chapter.

Campbell Biology Website (Instructor Resources)

See the insert in your copy of Campbell/Reece *Biology*, Sixth Edition, for instructions on how to access the Campbell Biology Website. The Instructor Resources section of the website includes the following:

- The art, photos, tables, PowerPoint slide shows, videos, and animations from the Campbell Image Presentation Library
- Suggested answers to the Lab Report questions from the Case Studies in the Process of Science
- The PowerPoint Lecture for this chapter
- Word files of the lecture outline for this chapter
- Photo links

Course Management Systems

The media content for this chapter is available in three course management systems: CourseCompass™, Blackboard, and WebCT. For more information, go to http://cms.aw.com. For the latest pdf instructions on how to use CourseCompass, go to www.coursecompass.com. In addition, a Syllabus Manager is offered on the Campbell Biology Website.

Media for Students

The Campbell Biology Website and CD-ROM include the following for your students:

- Objectives
- Chapter Review (Summary, Self-Quiz, and Essay Questions from the book; Word Roots; Key Terms linked to the Glossary)
- Activities (see list below)
- Case Studies in the Process of Science (see list below)
- Quizzes (Pre-test, Activities Quiz, Chapter Quiz, Essay Questions)
- Web Links
- News and References
- Art and videos from the Campbell Image Presentation Library
- The Campbell *Biology* Interviews (from all editions)
- Glossary with audio pronunciations
- Syllabus Manager

Student Media Activities and Case Studies in The Process of Science

Web/CD Case Study in the Process of Science:*How Do Cells Communicate with Each Other?*

Web/CD Activity 11A: *Overview of Cell Signaling*

Web/CD Activity 11B: *Reception*

Web/CD Activity 11C: *Signal-Transduction Pathways*

Web/CD Activity 11D: *Cellular Responses*

Web/CD Activity 11E: *Build a Signaling Pathway*

Objectives

An Overview of Cell Signaling

1. Describe the basic signal-transduction pathway of yeast. Explain why we believe these pathways in yeast, mammals, and plants evolved before the first multicellular organisms appeared on Earth.

2. Categorize chemical signals in terms of the proximity of the communicating cells.

3. Describe the three main stages of cell signaling.

Signal Reception and the Initiation of Transduction

4. Describe the nature of a ligand-receptor interaction and state how such interactions initiate a signal-transduction system.

5. Compare and contrast G-protein-linked receptors, tyrosine-kinase receptors, and ligand-gated ion channels.

Signal-Transduction Pathways

6. Describe several advantages of using a multistep pathway in the transduction stage of cell signaling.

7. Explain what is usually passed along in a signal-transduction pathway.

8. Describe how phosphorylation propagates signal information.

9. Describe how cyclic AMP is formed and how it propagates signal information.

10. Describe how the cytoplasmic concentration of Ca^{2+} can be altered and how this increased pool of Ca^{2+} is involved with signal transduction.

Cellular Responses to Signals

11. Describe how signal information is transduced into cellular responses in the cytoplasm and in the nucleus.

12. Describe how signal amplification is accomplished in target cells.

13. Describe how target cells discriminate among signals and how the same signal can elicit multiple cellular responses.

14. Explain how scaffolding proteins help to increase the efficiency of signal transduction.

Key Terms

signal-transduction pathway	tyrosine kinase	cyclic AMP (cAMP)
local regulator	tyrosine-kinase receptor	adenylyl cyclase
hormone	ligand-gated ion channel	diacylglycerol (DAG)
ligand	protein kinase	inositol trisphosphate (IP3)
G-protein-linked receptor	protein phosphatase	calmodulin
G protein	second messenger	scaffolding protein

Word Roots

liga- = bound or tied (*ligand*: a small molecule that specifically binds to a larger one)

trans- = across (*signal-transduction pathway*: the process by which a signal on a cell's surface is converted into a specific cellular response inside the cell)

-yl = substance or matter (*adenylyl cyclase*: an enzyme built into the plasma membrane that converts ATP to cAMP)

References

Aldrich, R. W. "Fifty Years of Inactivation." *Nature*, June 7, 2001.

Becker, W. M., L. J. Kleinsmith, and J. Hardin. *The World of the Cell.* 4th ed. San Francisco, California: Benjamin Cummings, 2000.

Hunter, T. "Signaling–2000 and Beyond." *Cell*, January 2000.

Norman A. and G. Litwack. *Hormones*, 2nd ed. New York: Academic Press, 1997.

Norris, D. *Vertebrate Endocrinology*, 3rd ed. New York: Academic Press, 1997.

Visual Guide to the Image Library

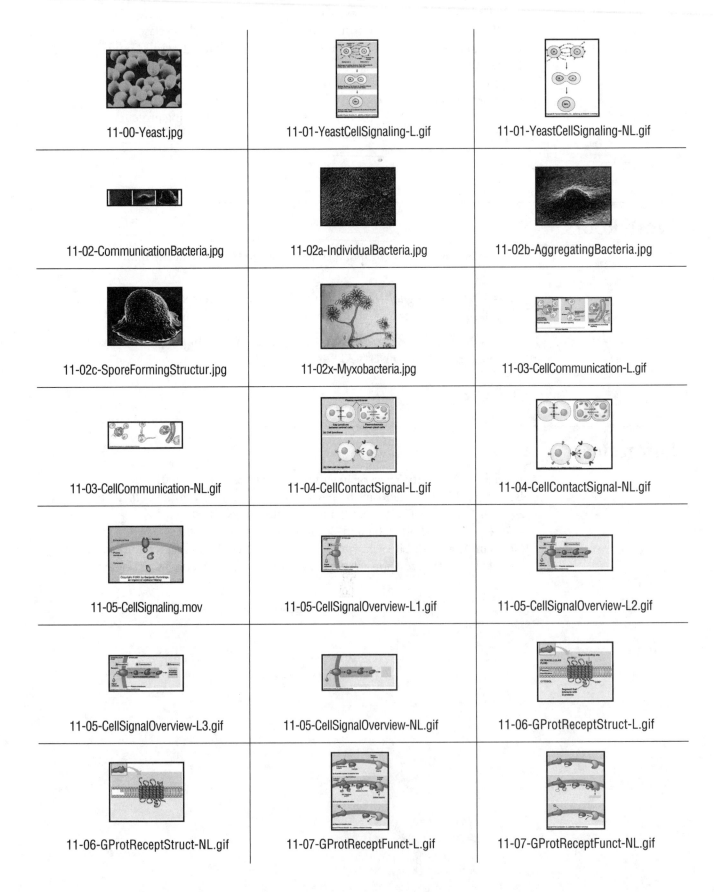

11-00-Yeast.jpg

11-01-YeastCellSignaling-L.gif

11-01-YeastCellSignaling-NL.gif

11-02-CommunicationBacteria.jpg

11-02a-IndividualBacteria.jpg

11-02b-AggregatingBacteria.jpg

11-02c-SporeFormingStructur.jpg

11-02x-Myxobacteria.jpg

11-03-CellCommunication-L.gif

11-03-CellCommunication-NL.gif

11-04-CellContactSignal-L.gif

11-04-CellContactSignal-NL.gif

11-05-CellSignaling.mov

11-05-CellSignalOverview-L1.gif

11-05-CellSignalOverview-L2.gif

11-05-CellSignalOverview-L3.gif

11-05-CellSignalOverview-NL.gif

11-06-GProtReceptStruct-L.gif

11-06-GProtReceptStruct-NL.gif

11-07-GProtReceptFunct-L.gif

11-07-GProtReceptFunct-NL.gif

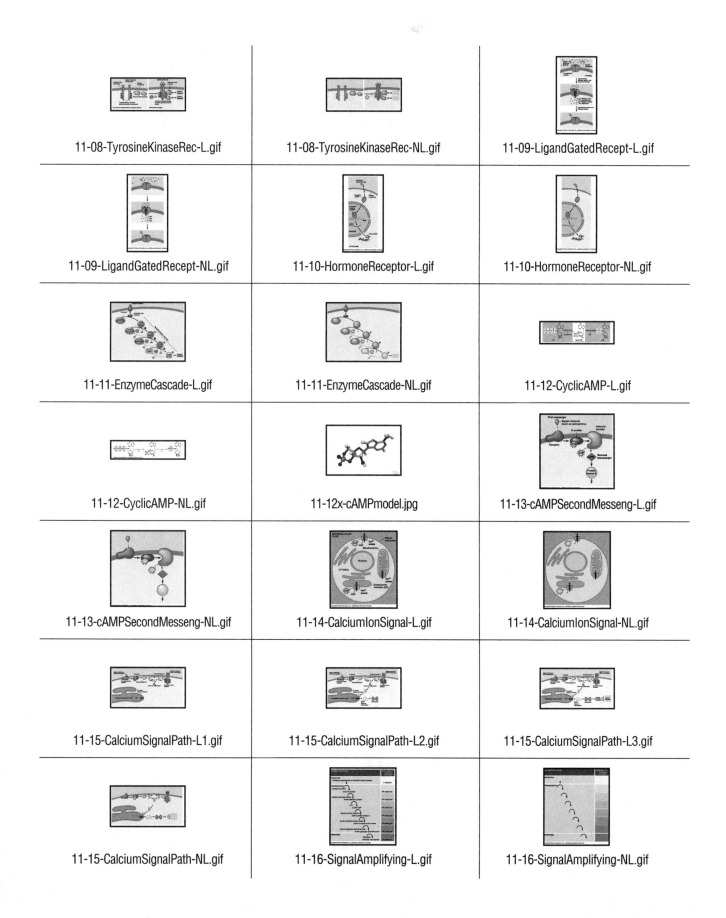

11-08-TyrosineKinaseRec-L.gif

11-08-TyrosineKinaseRec-NL.gif

11-09-LigandGatedRecept-L.gif

11-09-LigandGatedRecept-NL.gif

11-10-HormoneReceptor-L.gif

11-10-HormoneReceptor-NL.gif

11-11-EnzymeCascade-L.gif

11-11-EnzymeCascade-NL.gif

11-12-CyclicAMP-L.gif

11-12-CyclicAMP-NL.gif

11-12x-cAMPmodel.jpg

11-13-cAMPSecondMesseng-L.gif

11-13-cAMPSecondMesseng-NL.gif

11-14-CalciumIonSignal-L.gif

11-14-CalciumIonSignal-NL.gif

11-15-CalciumSignalPath-L1.gif

11-15-CalciumSignalPath-L2.gif

11-15-CalciumSignalPath-L3.gif

11-15-CalciumSignalPath-NL.gif

11-16-SignalAmplifying-L.gif

11-16-SignalAmplifying-NL.gif

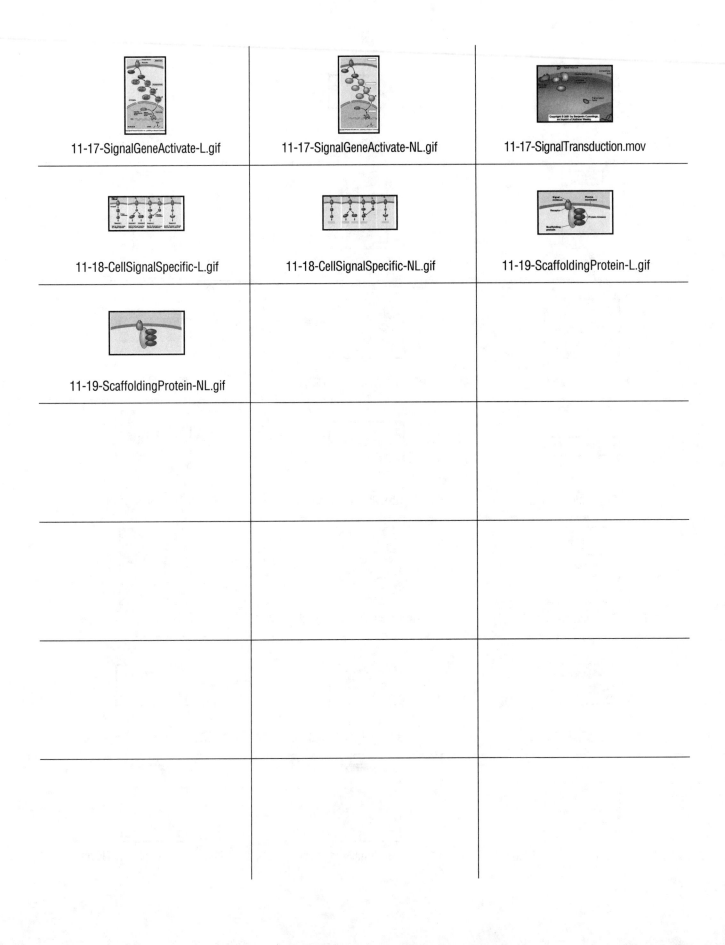

11-17-SignalGeneActivate-L.gif

11-17-SignalGeneActivate-NL.gif

11-17-SignalTransduction.mov

11-18-CellSignalSpecific-L.gif

11-18-CellSignalSpecific-NL.gif

11-19-ScaffoldingProtein-L.gif

11-19-ScaffoldingProtein-NL.gif

CHAPTER 12

The Cell Cycle

Chapter Outline

The Key Roles of Cell Division

Cell division functions in reproduction, growth, and repair

Cell division distributes identical sets of chromosomes to daughter cells

The Mitotic Cell Cycle

The mitotic phase alternates with interphase in the cell cycle: *an overview*

The mitotic spindle distributes chromosomes to daughter cells: *a closer look*

Cytokinesis divides the cytoplasm: *a closer look*

Mitosis in eukaryotes may have evolved from binary fission in bacteria

Regulation of the Cell Cycle

A molecular control system drives the cell cycle

Internal and external cues help regulate the cell cycle

Cancer cells have escaped from cell cycle controls

Transparency Acetates

The Transparency Acetates for *Biology*, Sixth Edition, include the following images:

Figure 12.3	Chromosome duplication and distribution during mitosis
Figure 12.4	The cell cycle
Figure 12.5	The stages of mitotic cell division in an animal cell: G_2 phase; prophase; prometaphase
Figure 12.5	The stages of mitotic cell division in an animal cell: metaphase; anaphase; telophase and cytokinesis
Figure 12.6	The mitotic spindle at metaphase
Figure 12.7	Testing a hypothesis for chromosome migration during anaphase
Figure 12.8	Cytokinesis in animal and plant cells
Figure 12.10	Bacterial cell division (binary fission) (Layer 1)
Figure 12.10	Bacterial cell division (binary fission) (Layer 2)

Media for Instructors

Campbell Image Presentation Library

The Campbell Image Presentation Library CD-ROM set includes the following for your use:

- All art (available in pdf and jpeg or gif formats), photos (from the text and outside sources), and tables. Art images are also available without callouts. See the Visual Guide to the Image Library section at the end of this chapter for thumbnail versions of every image.

- A PowerPoint^{TM} slide show of the art (with callouts), photos (both text and outside sources), and tables.

- The following video clip:

  12-05-AnimalMitosisVideo-B.mov Time-lapse video of mitosis (animal)

- The following QuickTime animations, adapted from student media activities (also available as Shockwave Flash .swf files):

  12-05-MitosisOverviewAnimat.mov

  12-05a-LateInterphaseAnimat.mov

  12-05b-ProphaseAnimation.mov

  12-05c-PrometaphaseAnimat.mov

  12-05d-MetaphaseAnimation.mov

  12-05e-AnaphaseAnimation.mov

  12-05f-TelophaseAnimation.mov

  12-05g-CytokinesisAnimation.mov

PowerPoint Lectures CD-ROM

The PowerPoint Lectures CD-ROM contains slides that integrate the art, photos, tables, and lecture outline from this chapter.

Campbell Biology Website (Instructor Resources)

See the insert in your copy of Campbell/Reece *Biology*, Sixth Edition, for instructions on how to access the Campbell Biology Website. The Instructor Resources section of the website includes the following:

- The art, photos, tables, PowerPoint slide shows, videos, and animations from the Campbell Image Presentation Library
- Suggested answers to the Lab Report questions from the Case Studies in the Process of Science
- The PowerPoint Lecture for this chapter
- Word files of the lecture outline for this chapter
- Photo links

Course Management Systems

The media content for this chapter is available in three course management systems: CourseCompass™, Blackboard, and WebCT. For more information, go to http://cms.aw.com. For the latest pdf instructions on how to use CourseCompass, go to **www.coursecompass.com**. In addition, a Syllabus Manager is offered on the Campbell Biolog*y* Website.

Media for Students

The Campbell Biology Website and CD-ROM include the following for your students:

- Objectives
- Chapter Review (Summary, Self-Quiz, and Essay Questions from the book; Word Roots; Key Terms linked to the Glossary)
- Activities (see list below)
- Case Studies in the Process of Science (see list below)
- Quizzes (Pre-test, Activities Quiz, Chapter Quiz, Essay Questions)
- Web Links
- News and References
- Art and videos from the Campbell Image Presentation Library
- The Campbell *Biology* Interviews (from all editions)
- Glossary with audio pronunciations
- Syllabus Manager

Student Media Activities and Case Studies in The Process of Science

Web/CD Activity 12A: *Roles of Cell Division*

Web/CD Activity 12B: *The Cell Cycle*

Web/CD Activity 12C: *Mitosis and Cytokinesis Animation*

Web/CD Activity 12D: *Mitosis and Cytokinesis Video*

Web/CD Case Study in The Process of Science: *How Do Cells Divide by Mitosis?*

Web/CD Activity 12E: *Causes of Cancer*

Objectives

The Key Roles of Cell Division

1. Explain how cell division functions in reproduction, growth, and repair.
2. Describe the structural organization of the genome.
3. Describe the major events of cell division that enable the genome of one cell to be passed on to two daughter cells.
4. Describe how the chromosome number changes throughout the human life cycle.

The Mitotic Cell Cycle

5. List the phases of the cell cycle and describe the sequence of events that occurs during each phase.
6. List the phases of mitosis and describe the events characteristic of each phase.
7. Recognize the phases of mitosis from diagrams and micrographs.
8. Draw or describe the spindle apparatus, including centrosomes, kinetochore microtubules, nonkinetochore microtubules, asters, and centrioles (in animal cells).
9. Describe what characteristic changes occur in the spindle apparatus during each phase of mitosis.
10. Explain the current models for poleward chromosomal movement and elongation of the cell's polar axis.
11. Compare cytokinesis in animals and plants.
12. Describe the process of binary fission in bacteria and how this process may have evolved in eukaryotic mitosis.

Regulation of the Cell Cycle

13. Describe the roles of checkpoints, cyclin, Cdk, and MPF in the cell cycle control system.
14. Describe the internal and external factors that influence the cell cycle control system.
15. Explain how the abnormal cell division of cancerous cells differs from normal cell division.

Key Terms

cell division	G₂ phase	checkpoint
cell cycle	prophase	G₀ phase
genome	prometaphase	cyclin
chromosome	metaphase	cyclin-dependent
somatic cell	anaphase	kinase (Cdk)
gamete	telophase	MPF
chromatin	mitotic spindle	growth factor
sister chromatids	centrosome	density-dependent
centromere	kinetochore	inhibition
mitosis	metaphase plate	anchorage dependence
cytokinesis	cleavage	transformation
meiosis	cleavage furrow	tumor
mitotic (M) phase	cell plate	benign tumor
interphase	binary fission	malignant tumor
G₁ phase	origin of replication	metastasis
S phase	cell cycle control system	

Word Roots

ana- = up, throughout, again (*anaphase*: the mitotic stage in which the chromatids of each chromosome have separated and the daughter chromosomes are moving to the poles of the cell)

bi- = two (*binary fission*: a type of cell division in which a cell divides in half)

centro- = the center; **-mere** = a part (*centromere*: the narrow "waist" of a condensed chromosome)

chroma- = colored (*chromatin*: DNA and the various associated proteins that form eukaryotic chromosomes)

cyclo- = a circle (*cyclin*: a regulatory protein whose concentration fluctuates cyclically)

cyto- = cell; **kinet-** = move (*cytokinesis*: division of the cytoplasm)

gamet- = a wife or husband (*gamete*: a haploid egg or sperm cell)

gen- = produce (*genome*: a cell's endowment of DNA)

inter- = between (*interphase*: time when a cell metabolizes and performs its various functions)

mal- = bad or evil (*malignant tumor*: a cancerous tumor that is invasive enough to impair functions of one or more organs)

meio- = less (*meiosis*: a variation of cell division that yields daughter cells with half as many chromosomes as the parent cell)

meta- = between (*metaphase*: the mitotic stage in which the chromosomes are aligned in the middle of the cell, at the metaphase plate)

mito- = a thread (*mitosis*: the division of the nucleus)

pro- = before (*prophase*: the first mitotic stage in which the chromatin is condensing)

soma- = body (*centrosome*: a nonmembranous organelle that functions throughout the cell cycle to organize the cell's microtubules)

telos- = an end (*telophase*: the final stage of mitosis in which daughter nuclei are forming and cytokinesis has typically begun)

trans- = across; **-form** = shape (*transformation*: the process that converts a normal cell into a cancer cell)

References

Becker, W. M., L. J. Kleinsmith, and J. Hardin. *The World of the Cell.* 4th ed. San Francisco, California: Benjamin Cummings, 2000.

Karp, G. *Cell and Molecular Biology: Concepts and Experiments.* 3rd ed. New York, New York, John Wiley & Sons, Inc. 2002.

Nurse, P. "A Long Twentieth Century of the Cell Cycle and Beyond." *Cell,* January 2000.

Visual Guide to the Image Library

12-00-MitosisPhoto.jpg

12-01a-FunctionsRepro.jpg

12-01b-FunctionsGrowthDevel.jpg

12-01c-FunctionsRenewal.jpg

12-02-EukChromosomes.jpg

12-03-ChromosomeDupe-L.jpg

12-03-ChromosomeDupe-NL.jpg

12-04-CellCycle-L.gif

12-04-CellCycle-NL.gif

12-05-AnimalMitosisVideo-B.mov

12-05-AnimalMitosisVideo-S.mov

12-05-MitosisArtLeft-L.jpg

12-05-MitosisArtLeft-NL.jpg

12-05-MitosisArtRight-L.jpg

12-05-MitosisArtRight-NL.jpg

12-05-MitosisOverviewAnimat.mov

12-05-MitosisPhotoCollage.jpg

12-05a-InterphasePhoto.jpg

12-05a-LateInterphaseAnimat.mov

12-05b-ProphaseAnimation.mov

12-05b-ProphasePhoto.jpg

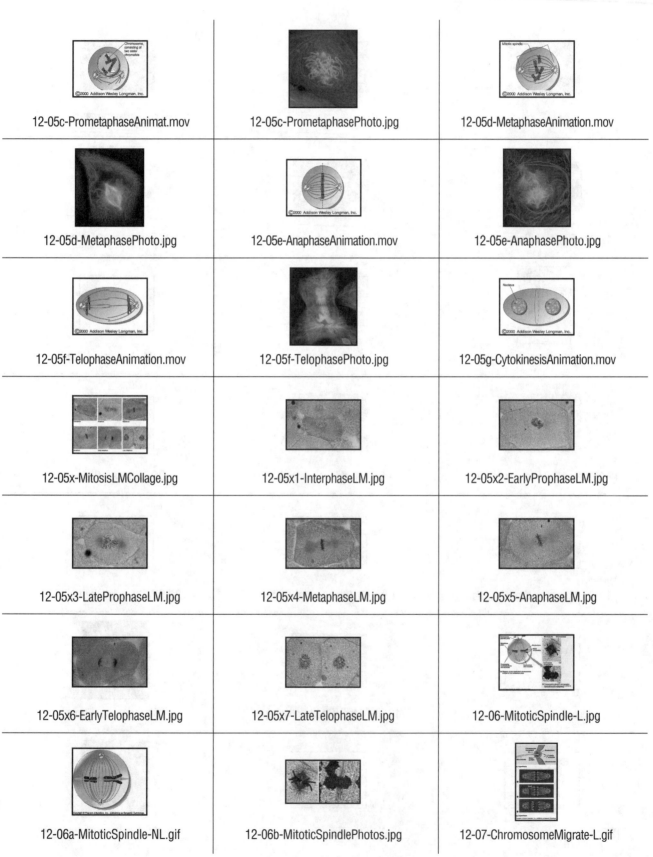

12-05c-PrometaphaseAnimat.mov

12-05c-PrometaphasePhoto.jpg

12-05d-MetaphaseAnimation.mov

12-05d-MetaphasePhoto.jpg

12-05e-AnaphaseAnimation.mov

12-05e-AnaphasePhoto.jpg

12-05f-TelophaseAnimation.mov

12-05f-TelophasePhoto.jpg

12-05g-CytokinesisAnimation.mov

12-05x-MitosisLMCollage.jpg

12-05x1-InterphaseLM.jpg

12-05x2-EarlyProphaseLM.jpg

12-05x3-LateProphaseLM.jpg

12-05x4-MetaphaseLM.jpg

12-05x5-AnaphaseLM.jpg

12-05x6-EarlyTelophaseLM.jpg

12-05x7-LateTelophaseLM.jpg

12-06-MitoticSpindle-L.jpg

12-06a-MitoticSpindle-NL.gif

12-06b-MitoticSpindlePhotos.jpg

12-07-ChromosomeMigrate-L.gif

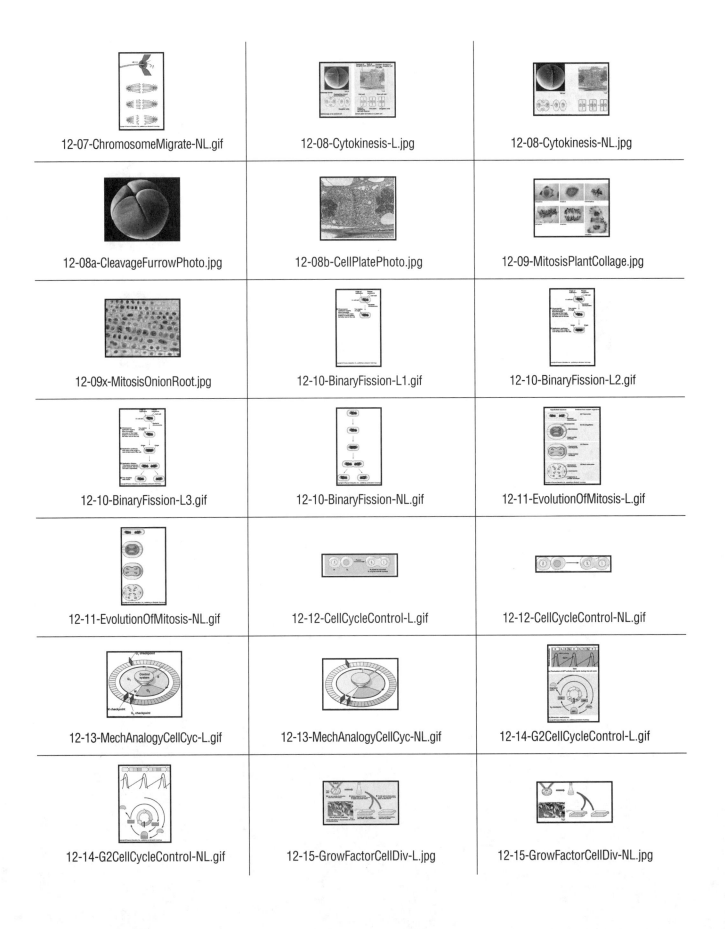

12-07-ChromosomeMigrate-NL.gif

12-08-Cytokinesis-L.jpg

12-08-Cytokinesis-NL.jpg

12-08a-CleavageFurrowPhoto.jpg

12-08b-CellPlatePhoto.jpg

12-09-MitosisPlantCollage.jpg

12-09x-MitosisOnionRoot.jpg

12-10-BinaryFission-L1.gif

12-10-BinaryFission-L2.gif

12-10-BinaryFission-L3.gif

12-10-BinaryFission-NL.gif

12-11-EvolutionOfMitosis-L.gif

12-11-EvolutionOfMitosis-NL.gif

12-12-CellCycleControl-L.gif

12-12-CellCycleControl-NL.gif

12-13-MechAnalogyCellCyc-L.gif

12-13-MechAnalogyCellCyc-NL.gif

12-14-G2CellCycleControl-L.gif

12-14-G2CellCycleControl-NL.gif

12-15-GrowFactorCellDiv-L.jpg

12-15-GrowFactorCellDiv-NL.jpg

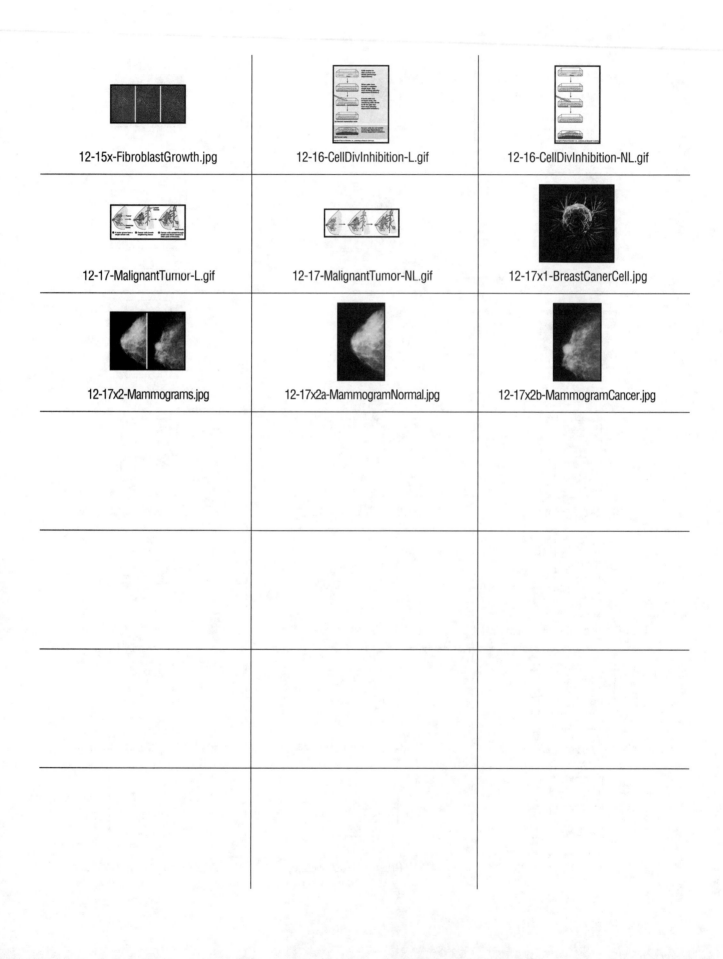

12-15x-FibroblastGrowth.jpg

12-16-CellDivInhibition-L.gif

12-16-CellDivInhibition-NL.gif

12-17-MalignantTumor-L.gif

12-17-MalignantTumor-NL.gif

12-17x1-BreastCanerCell.jpg

12-17x2-Mammograms.jpg

12-17x2a-MammogramNormal.jpg

12-17x2b-MammogramCancer.jpg

CHAPTER 13

Meiosis and Sexual Life Cycles

Chapter Outline

An Introduction to Heredity
Offspring acquire genes from parents by inheriting chromosomes
Like begets like, more or less: a comparison of asexual and sexual reproduction

The Role of Meiosis in Sexual Life Cycles
Fertilization and meiosis alternate in sexual life cycles
Meiosis reduces chromosome number from diploid to haploid: *a closer look*

Origins of Genetic Variation
Sexual life cycles produce genetic variation among offspring
Evolutionary adaptation depends on a population's genetic variation

Transparency Acetates

The Transparency Acetates for *Biology*, Sixth Edition, include the following images:

Media for Instructors

Campbell Image Presentation Library

The Campbell Image Presentation Library CD-ROM set includes the following for your use:

- All art (available in pdf and jpeg or gif formats), photos (from the text and outside sources), and tables. Art images are also available without callouts. See the Visual Guide to the Image Library section at the end of this chapter for thumbnail versions of every image.
- A PowerPoint™ slide show of the art (with callouts), photos (both text and outside sources), and tables.
- The following video clip:

    13-01-HydraBudding-B.mov   Time-lapse of budding in hydra

- The following QuickTime animations, adapted from student media activities (also available as Shockwave Flash .swf files):

    13-07a-InterphaseI.mov

    13-07b-ProphaseI.mov

    13-07c-MetaphaseI.mov

    13-07d-AnaphaseI.mov

    13-07e-TelophaseICytokin.mov

    13-07f-MeiosisIICytokin.mov

    13-10-CrossingOver.mov

PowerPoint Lectures CD-ROM

The PowerPoint Lectures CD-ROM contains slides that integrate the art, photos, tables, and lecture outline from this chapter.

Campbell Biology Website (Instructor Resources)

See the insert in your copy of Campbell/Reece *Biology,* Sixth Edition, for instructions on how to access the Campbell Biology Website. The Instructor Resources section of the website includes the following:

- The art, photos, tables, PowerPoint slide shows, videos, and animations from the Campbell Image Presentation Library
- Suggested answers to the Lab Report questions from the Case Studies in the Process of Science
- The PowerPoint Lecture for this chapter
- Word files of the lecture outline for this chapter
- Photo links

Course Management Systems

The media content for this chapter is available in three course management systems: CourseCompass™, Blackboard, and WebCT. For more information, go to http://cms.aw.com. For the latest pdf instructions on how to use CourseCompass, go to **www.coursecompass.com**. In addition, a Syllabus Manager is offered on the Campbell Biology Website.

Media for Students

The Campbell Biology Website and CD-ROM include the following for your students:

- Objectives
- Chapter Review (Summary, Self-Quiz, and Essay Questions from the book; Word Roots; Key Terms linked to the Glossary)
- Activities (see list below)
- Case Studies in the Process of Science (see list below)
- Quizzes (Pre-test, Activities Quiz, Chapter Quiz, Essay Questions)
- Web Links
- News and References
- Art and videos from the Campbell Image Presentation Library
- The Campbell *Biology* Interviews (from all editions)
- Glossary with audio pronunciations
- Syllabus Manager

Student Media Activities and Case Studies in The Process of Science

Web/CD Activity 13A: *Asexual and Sexual Life Cycles*

Web/CD Activity 13B: *Meiosis Animation*

Web/CD Activity 13C: *Origins of Genetic Variation*

Web/CD Case Study in the Process of Science: *How Does Meiosis Occur in the Fungus* Sordaria?

Objectives

An Introduction to Heredity

1. Explain why organisms reproduce only their own kind and why offspring more closely resemble their parents than unrelated individuals of the same species.
2. Explain what makes heredity possible.
3. Distinguish between asexual and sexual reproduction.

The Role of Meiosis in Sexual Life Cycles

4. Diagram the human life cycle and indicate where in the human body that mitosis and meiosis occur; which cells are the result of meiosis and mitosis; and which cells are haploid.
5. Distinguish among the life cycle patterns of animals, fungi, and plants.

6. List the phases of meiosis I and meiosis II and describe the events characteristic of each phase. Recognize the phases of meiosis from diagrams or micrographs.

7. Describe the process of synapsis during prophase I and explain how genetic recombination occurs.

8. Describe the key differences between mitosis and meiosis. Explain how the end result of meiosis differs from that of mitosis.

Origins of Genetic Variation

9. Explain how independent assortment, crossing over, and random fertilization contribute to genetic variation in sexually reproducing organisms.

10. Explain why inheritable variation was crucial to Darwin's theory of evolution.

Key Terms

heredity	sex chromosomes	gametophyte
variation	autosome	meiosis I
genetics	gamete	meiosis II
gene	haploid cell	synapsis
asexual reproduction	fertilization	tetrad
locus	syngamy	chiasmata
clone	zygote	crossing over
sexual reproduction	diploid cell	recombinant
life cycle	meiosis	chromosomes
somatic cell	alternation of	
karyotype	generations	
homologous	sporophyte	
chromosome	spore	

Word Roots

-apsis = juncture (*synapsis*: the pairing of replicated homologous chromosomes during prophase I of meiosis)

a- = not or without (*asexual*: type of reproduction not involving fertilization)

auto- = self (*autosome*: the chromosomes that do not determine gender)

chiasm- = marked crosswise (*chiasma*: the X-shaped microscopically visible region representing homologous chromosomes that have exchanged genetic material through crossing over during meiosis)

di- = two (*diploid*: cells that contain two homologous sets of chromosomes)

fertil- = fruitful (*fertilization*: process of fusion of a haploid sperm and a haploid egg cell)

haplo- = single (*haploid*: cells that contain only one chromosome of each homologous pair)

homo- = like (*homologous*: like chromosomes that form a pair)

karyo- = nucleus (*karyotype*: a display of the chromosomes of a cell)

meio- = less (*meiosis*: a variation of cell division which yields daughter cells with half as many chromosomes as the parent cell)

soma- = body (*somatic*: body cells with 46 chromosomes in humans)

sporo- = a seed; **-phyt** = a plant (*sporophyte*: the multicellular diploid form in organisms undergoing alternation of generations that results from a union of gametes and that meiotically produces haploid spores that grow into the gametophyte generation)

syn- = together; **gam-** = marriage (*syngamy*: the process of cellular union during fertilization)

tetra- = four (*tetrad*: the four closely associated chromatids of a homologous pair of chromosomes)

References

Becker, W. M., L. J. Kleinsmith, and J. Hardin. *The World of the Cell.* 4th ed. San Francisco, California: Benjamin Cummings, 2000

Karp, G. *Cell and Molecular Biology: Concepts and Experiments.* 3rd ed. New York, New York, John Wiley & Sons, Inc. 2002.

Sluder, G. and D. McCollum. "The Mad Ways of Meiosis." *Science,* 289, 2000.

Visual Guide to the Image Library

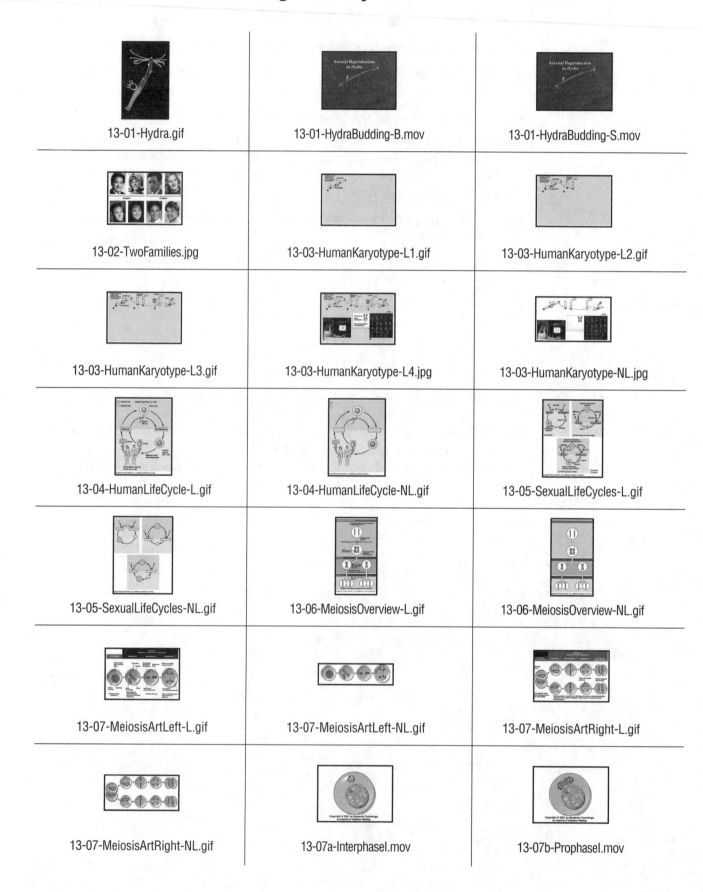

13-01-Hydra.gif

13-01-HydraBudding-B.mov

13-01-HydraBudding-S.mov

13-02-TwoFamilies.jpg

13-03-HumanKaryotype-L1.gif

13-03-HumanKaryotype-L2.gif

13-03-HumanKaryotype-L3.gif

13-03-HumanKaryotype-L4.jpg

13-03-HumanKaryotype-NL.jpg

13-04-HumanLifeCycle-L.gif

13-04-HumanLifeCycle-NL.gif

13-05-SexualLifeCycles-L.gif

13-05-SexualLifeCycles-NL.gif

13-06-MeiosisOverview-L.gif

13-06-MeiosisOverview-NL.gif

13-07-MeiosisArtLeft-L.gif

13-07-MeiosisArtLeft-NL.gif

13-07-MeiosisArtRight-L.gif

13-07-MeiosisArtRight-NL.gif

13-07a-InterphaseI.mov

13-07b-ProphaseI.mov

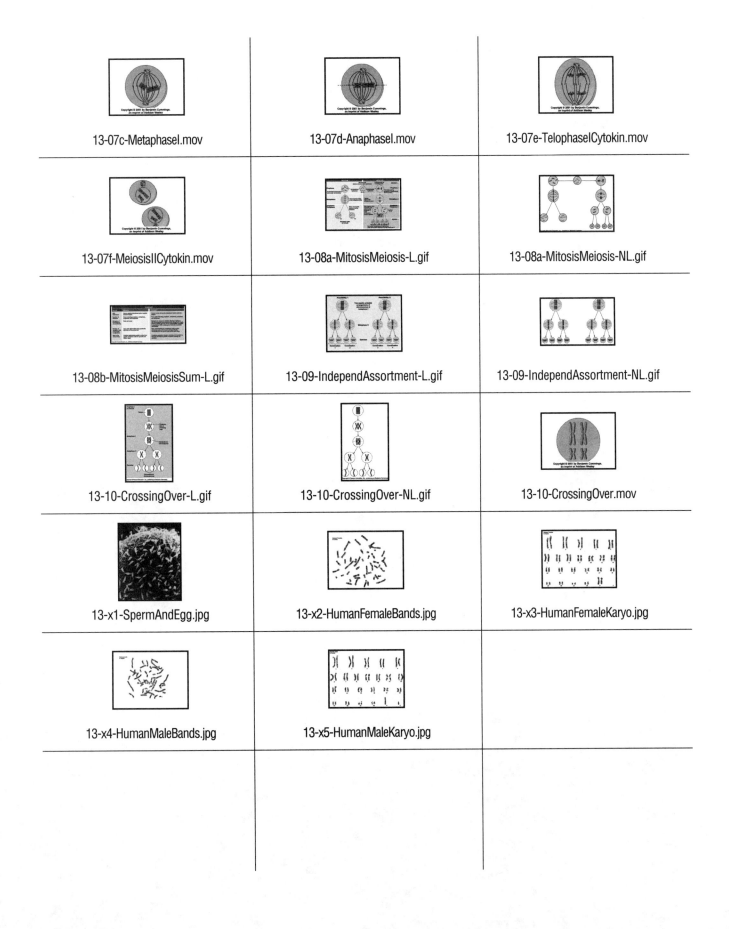

13-07c-MetaphaseI.mov

13-07d-AnaphaseI.mov

13-07e-TelophaseICytokin.mov

13-07f-MeiosisIICytokin.mov

13-08a-MitosisMeiosis-L.gif

13-08a-MitosisMeiosis-NL.gif

13-08b-MitosisMeiosisSum-L.gif

13-09-IndependAssortment-L.gif

13-09-IndependAssortment-NL.gif

13-10-CrossingOver-L.gif

13-10-CrossingOver-NL.gif

13-10-CrossingOver.mov

13-x1-SpermAndEgg.jpg

13-x2-HumanFemaleBands.jpg

13-x3-HumanFemaleKaryo.jpg

13-x4-HumanMaleBands.jpg

13-x5-HumanMaleKaryo.jpg

CHAPTER 14

Mendel and the Gene Idea

Chapter Outline

Gregor Mendel's Discoveries

Mendel brought an experimental and quantitative approach to genetics: *the process of science*

By the law of segregation, the two alleles for a character are packaged into separate gametes

By the law of independent assortment, each pair of alleles segregates into gametes independently

Mendelian inheritance reflects rules of probability

Mendel discovered the particulate behavior of genes: *a review*

Extending Mendelian Genetics

The relationship between genotype and phenotype is rarely simple

Mendelian Inheritance in Humans

Pedigree analysis reveals Mendelian patterns in human inheritance

Many human disorders follow Mendelian patterns of inheritance

Technology is providing new tools for genetic testing and counseling

Transparency Acetates

The Transparency Acetates for *Biology*, Sixth Edition, include the following images:

Media for Instructors

Campbell Image Presentation Library

The Campbell Image Presentation Library CD-ROM set includes the following for your use:

- All art (available in pdf and jpeg or gif formats), photos (from the text and outside sources), and tables. Art images are also available without callouts. See the Visual Guide to the Image Library section at the end of this chapter for thumbnail versions of every image.

- A PowerPoint™ slide show of the art (with callouts), photos (both text and outside sources), and tables.

PowerPoint Lectures CD-ROM

The PowerPoint Lectures CD-ROM contains slides that integrate the art, photos, tables, and lecture outline from this chapter.

Campbell Biology Website (Instructor Resources)

See the insert in your copy of Campbell/Reece *Biology*, Sixth Edition, for instructions on how to access the Campbell Biology Website. The Instructor Resources section of the website includes the following:

- The art, photos, tables, PowerPoint slide shows, videos, and animations from the Campbell Image Presentation Library

- Suggested answers to the Lab Report questions from the Case Studies in the Process of Science

- The PowerPoint Lecture for this chapter

- Word files of the lecture outline for this chapter

- Photo links

Course Management Systems

The media content for this chapter is available in three course management systems: CourseCompass™, Blackboard, and WebCT. For more information, go to http://cms.aw.com. For the latest pdf instructions on how to use CourseCompass, go to **www.coursecompass.com**. In addition, a Syllabus Manager is offered on the Campbell Biology Website.

Media for Students

The Campbell Biology Website and CD-ROM include the following for your students:

- Objectives
- Chapter Review (Summary, Self-Quiz, and Essay Questions from the book; Word Roots; Key Terms linked to the Glossary)
- Activities (see list below)
- Case Studies in the Process of Science (see list below)
- Quizzes (Pre-test, Activities Quiz, Chapter Quiz, Essay Questions)
- Web Links
- News and References
- Art and videos from the Campbell Image Presentation Library
- The Campbell *Biology* Interviews (from all editions)
- Glossary with audio pronunciations
- Syllabus Manager

Student Media Activities and Case Studies in The Process of Science

Web/CD Activity 14A: *Monohybrid Cross*

Web/CD Activity 14B: *Dihybrid Cross*

Web/CD Activity 14C: *Gregor's Garden*

Web/CD Activity14D: *Incomplete Dominance*

Web/CD Case Study in the Process of Science: *How Do You Diagnose a Genetic Disorder?*

Objectives

Gregor Mendel's Discoveries

1. Describe the favored model of heredity in the 19th century prior to Mendel.

2. Explain how observations by Mendel and others and Mendel's hypothesis of inheritance differed from the blending theory of inheritance.

3. List several features of Mendel's methods that contributed to his success.

4. Define true breeding, hybridization, monohybrid cross, P generation, F_1 generation, and F_2 generation.

5. List and explain the four components of Mendel's hypothesis that led him to deduce the law of segregation.

6. Explain how Mendel's law of segregation got its name.

7. Use a Punnett square to predict the results of a monohybrid cross and state the phenotypic and genotypic ratios of the F_2 generation.

8. Distinguish between the following pairs of terms: dominant and recessive; heterozygous and homozygous; genotype and phenotype.

9. Explain how a testcross can be used to determine if a dominant phenotype is homozygous or heterozygous.

10. Use a Punnett square to predict the results of a dihybrid cross and state the phenotypic and genotypic ratios of the F_2 generation.

11. Define Mendel's law of independent assortment.

12. Use the rule of multiplication to calculate the probability that a particular F_2 individual will be homozygous recessive or dominant.

13. Given a Mendelian cross, use the rule of addition to calculate the probability that a particular F_2 individual will be heterozygous.

14. Use the laws of probability to predict from a trihybrid cross between two individuals that are heterozygous for all three traits, what expected proportion of the offspring would be:

    a. homozygous for the three dominant traits

    b. heterozygous for all three traits

    c. homozygous recessive for two specific traits and heterozygous for the third

15. Explain why Mendel was wise to use large sample sizes in his studies.

Extending Mendelian Genetics

16. Give an example of incomplete dominance and explain why it is not evidence for the blending theory of inheritance.

17. Explain how the phenotypic expression of the heterozygote is affected by complete dominance, incomplete dominance, and co-dominance.

18. Explain why Tay-Sachs is considered recessive at the organismic level but co-dominant at the molecular level.

19. Explain why genetic dominance does not mean that the dominant allele subdues a recessive allele. Illustrate your explanation with the use of the round versus wrinkled pea seed shape.

20. Explain why dominant alleles do not necessarily mean that the allele is more common in a population. Illustrate your explanation with the character polydactyly.

21. Describe the inheritance of the ABO blood system and explain why the I^A and I^B alleles are said to be co-dominant.

22. Define and give examples of pleiotropy and epistasis.

23. Describe a simple model for polygenic inheritance and explain why most polygenic characters are described in quantitative terms.

24. Describe how environmental conditions can influence the phenotypic expression of a character. Explain what is meant by "a norm of reaction."

25. Distinguish between the specific and broad interpretations of the terms "phenotype" and "genotype."

Mendelian Inheritance in Humans

26. Explain why studies of human inheritance are not as easily conducted as Mendel's work with his peas.

27. Given a simple family pedigree, deduce the genotypes for some of the family members.

28. Explain how a lethal recessive gene can be maintained in a population.

29. Describe the inheritance and expression of cystic fibrosis, Tay-Sachs disease, and sickle-cell disease.

30. Explain why consanguinity increases the probability of homozygosity in offspring.

31. Explain why lethal dominant genes are much rarer than lethal recessive genes.

32. Give an example of a late-acting lethal dominant in humans and explain how it can escape elimination.

33. Define and give examples of multifactorial disorders in humans. Explain what can currently be done to reduce the frequency of these diseases.

34. Explain how carrier recognition, fetal testing, and newborn screening can be used in genetic screening and counseling.

Key Terms

character	heterozygous	quantitative characters
trait	phenotype	polygenic inheritance
true-breeding	genotype	norm of reaction
hybridization	testcross	multifactorial
P generation	monohybrid	pedigree
F_1 generation	dihybrid	carrier
F_2 generation	law of independent	cystic fibrosis
alleles	assortment	Tay-Sachs disease
dominant allele	incomplete dominance	sickle-cell disease
recessive allele	complete dominance	Huntington's disease
law of segregation	codominance	amniocentesis
Punnett square	pleiotropy	chorionic villus
homozygous	epistasis	sampling (CVS)

Word Roots

co- = together (*codominance*: phenotype in which both dominant alleles are expressed in the heterozygote)

-centesis = a puncture (*amniocentesis*: a technique for determining genetic abnormalities in a fetus by the presence of certain chemicals or defective fetal cells in the amniotic fluid, obtained by aspiration from a needle inserted into the uterus)

di- = two (*dihybrid cross*: a breeding experiment in which parental varieties differing in two traits are mated)

epi- = beside; **-stasis** = standing (*epistasis*: a phenomenon in which one gene alters the expression of another gene that is independently inherited)

geno- = offspring (*genotype*: the genetic makeup of an organism)

hetero- = different (*heterozygous*: having two different alleles for a trait)

homo- = alike (*homozygous*: having two identical alleles for a trait)

mono- = one (*monohybrid cross*: a breeding experiment that uses parental varieties differing in a single character)

pedi- = a child (*pedigree*: a family tree describing the occurrence of heritable characters in parents and offspring across as many generations as possible)

pheno- = appear (*phenotype*: the physical and physiological traits of an organism)

pleio- = more (*pleiotropy*: when a single gene impacts more than one characteristic)

poly- = many; **gen-** = produce (*polygenic*: an additive effect of two or more gene loci on a single phenotypic character)

References

Futuyma, D. J. *Evolutionary Biology*, Sunderland, Massachusetts, Sinauer Associates, Inc. 1998.

Hartwell, L. H., et. al. *Genetics: From Genes to Genomes*. New York: McGraw-Hill, 2000.

Karp, G. *Cell and Molecular Biology: Concepts and Experiments*. 3rd ed. New York: John Wiley & Sons, Inc., 2002.

Visual Guide to the Image Library

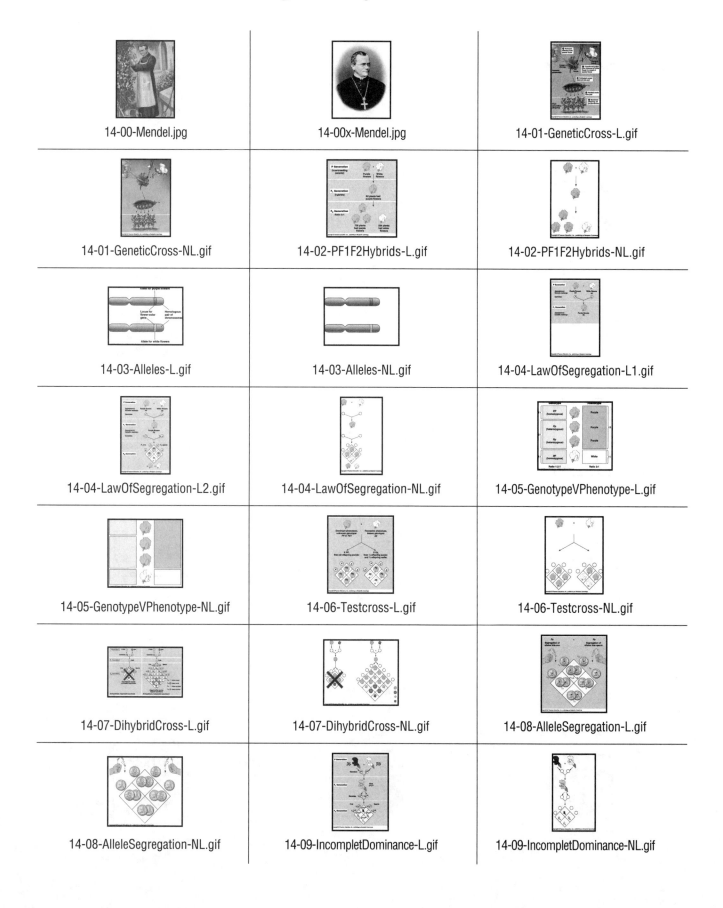

14-00-Mendel.jpg

14-00x-Mendel.jpg

14-01-GeneticCross-L.gif

14-01-GeneticCross-NL.gif

14-02-PF1F2Hybrids-L.gif

14-02-PF1F2Hybrids-NL.gif

14-03-Alleles-L.gif

14-03-Alleles-NL.gif

14-04-LawOfSegregation-L1.gif

14-04-LawOfSegregation-L2.gif

14-04-LawOfSegregation-NL.gif

14-05-GenotypeVPhenotype-L.gif

14-05-GenotypeVPhenotype-NL.gif

14-06-Testcross-L.gif

14-06-Testcross-NL.gif

14-07-DihybridCross-L.gif

14-07-DihybridCross-NL.gif

14-08-AlleleSegregation-L.gif

14-08-AlleleSegregation-NL.gif

14-09-IncompletDominance-L.gif

14-09-IncompletDominance-NL.gif

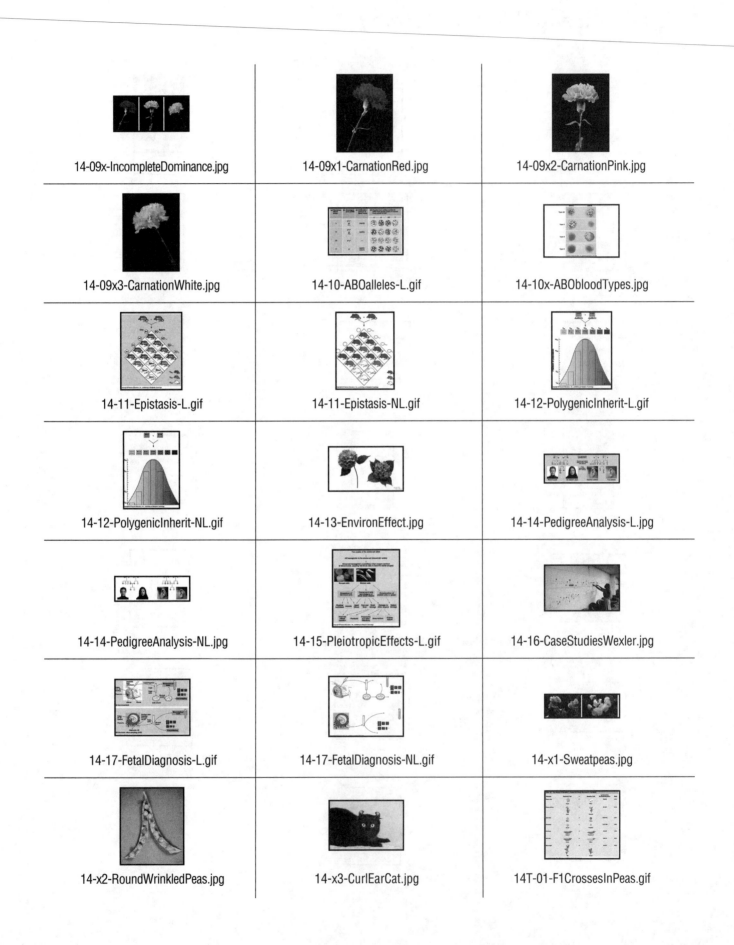

14-09x-IncompleteDominance.jpg

14-09x1-CarnationRed.jpg

14-09x2-CarnationPink.jpg

14-09x3-CarnationWhite.jpg

14-10-ABOalleles-L.gif

14-10x-ABObloodTypes.jpg

14-11-Epistasis-L.gif

14-11-Epistasis-NL.gif

14-12-PolygenicInherit-L.gif

14-12-PolygenicInherit-NL.gif

14-13-EnvironEffect.jpg

14-14-PedigreeAnalysis-L.jpg

14-14-PedigreeAnalysis-NL.jpg

14-15-PleiotropicEffects-L.gif

14-16-CaseStudiesWexler.jpg

14-17-FetalDiagnosis-L.gif

14-17-FetalDiagnosis-NL.gif

14-x1-Sweatpeas.jpg

14-x2-RoundWrinkledPeas.jpg

14-x3-CurlEarCat.jpg

14T-01-F1CrossesInPeas.gif

14UN-268-Pedigree-L.gif

CHAPTER 15

The Chromosomal Basis of Inheritance

Chapter Outline

Relating Mendelism to Chromosomes

Mendelian inheritance has its physical basis in the behavior of chromosomes during sexual life cycles

Morgan traced a gene to a specific chromosome: *the process of science*

Linked genes tend to be inherited together because they are located on the same chromosome

Independent assortment of chromosomes and crossing over produce genetic recombinants

Geneticists can use recombination data to map a chromosome's genetic loci: *the process of science*

Sex Chromosomes

The chromosomal basis of sex varies with the organism

Sex-linked genes have unique patterns of inheritance

Errors and Exceptions in Chromosomal Inheritance

Alterations of chromosome number or structure cause some genetic disorders

The phenotypic effects of some mammalian genes depend on whether they were inherited from the mother or the father (imprinting)

Extranuclear genes exhibit a non-Mendelian pattern of inheritance

---

Transparency Acetates

The Transparency Acetates for *Biology*, Sixth Edition, include the following images:

Media for Instructors

Campbell Image Presentation Library

The Campbell Image Presentation Library CD-ROM set includes the following for your use:

- All art (available in pdf and jpeg or gif formats), photos (from the text and outside sources), and tables. Art images are also available without callouts. See the Visual Guide to the Image Library section at the end of this chapter for thumbnail versions of every image.

- A PowerPoint^{TM} slide show of the art (with callouts), photos (both text and outside sources), and tables.

PowerPoint Lectures CD-ROM

The PowerPoint Lectures CD-ROM contains slides that integrate the art, photos, tables, and lecture outline from this chapter.

Campbell Biology Website (Instructor Resources)

See the insert in your copy of Campbell/Reece *Biology,* Sixth Edition, for instructions on how to access the Campbell Biology Website. The Instructor Resources section of the website includes the following:

- The art, photos, tables, PowerPoint slide shows, videos, and animations from the Campbell Image Presentation Library

- Suggested answers to the Lab Report questions from the Case Studies in the Process of Science

- The PowerPoint Lecture for this chapter

- Word files of the lecture outline for this chapter

- Photo links

Course Management Systems

The media content for this chapter is available in three course management systems: CourseCompass™, Blackboard, and WebCT. For more information, go to http://cms.aw.com. For the latest pdf instructions on how to use CourseCompass, go to www.coursecompass.com. In addition, a Syllabus Manager is offered on the Campbell Biology Website.

Media for Students

The Campbell Biology Website and CD-ROM include the following for your students:

- Objectives
- Chapter Review (Summary, Self-Quiz, and Essay Questions from the book; Word Roots; Key Terms linked to the Glossary)
- Activities (see list below)
- Case Studies in the Process of Science (see list below)
- Quizzes (Pre-test, Activities Quiz, Chapter Quiz, Essay Questions)
- Web Links
- News and References
- Art and videos from the Campbell Image Presentation Library
- The Campbell *Biology* Interviews (from all editions)
- Glossary with audio pronunciations
- Syllabus Manager

Student Media Activities and Case Studies in The Process of Science

Web/CD Activity 15A: *Linked Genes and Crossing Over*

Web/CD Activity 15B: *Sex-Linked Genes*

Web/CD Case Study in the Process of Science: *How Is the Chi-Square Test Used in Genetic Analysis?*

Biology Labs On-Line: *FlyLab*

Biology Labs On-Line: *PedigreeLab*

Web/CD Activity 15C: *Polyploid Plants*

Objectives

Relating Mendelism to Chromosomes

1. Explain how the observations of cytologists and geneticists provided the basis for the chromosome theory of inheritance.

2. Describe the contributions that Walter Sutton, Theodor Boveri, and Thomas Hunt Morgan made to current understanding of chromosomal inheritance.

3. Explain why Drosophila melanogaster is a good experimental organism.

4. Define and compare linked genes and sex-linked genes. Explain why the inheritance of linked genes is different from independent assortment.

5. Distinguish between parental and recombinant phenotypes.

6. Explain why linked genes do not assort independently.

7. Explain how crossing over can unlink genes.

8. Explain how Sturtevant created linkage maps.

9. Define a map unit.

10. Explain why Mendel did not find linkage between seed color and flower color.

11. Explain how genetic maps are constructed for genes located far apart on a chromosome.

12. Explain the impact of multiple crossovers between loci.

13. Explain what additional information cytological maps provide over linkage maps.

Sex Chromosomes

14. Explain how sex is genetically determined in humans and the significance of the SRY gene.

15. Explain why sex-linked diseases are more common in human males.

16. Describe the inheritance patterns and symptoms of color blindness, Duchenne muscular dystrophy, and hemophilia.

17. Describe the process of X inactivation in female mammals. Explain how this phenomenon produces the tortoiseshell coloration in cats.

Errors and Exceptions in Chromosomal Inheritance

18. Distinguish among nondisjunction, aneuploidy, trisomy, triploidy, and polyploidy. Explain how these major chromosomal changes occur and describe the consequences.

19. Distinguish among deletions, duplications, inversions, and translocations.

20. Describe the type of chromosomal alterations implicated in the following human disorders: Down syndrome, Klinefelter's syndrome, extra Y, triple-X syndrome, Turner's syndrome, cri du chat syndrome, and chronic myelogenous leukemia.

21. Define genomic imprinting and provide evidence to support this model.

22. Give some exceptions to the chromosome theory of inheritance. Explain why extranuclear genes are not inherited in a Mendelian fashion and how they can contribute to disease.

Key Terms

chromosome theory
  of inheritance
wild type
sex-linked gene
linked gene
genetic recombination
parental types
recombinant
genetic map
linkage map

map units
cytological maps
Duchenne muscular
  dystrophy
hemophilia
Barr body
nondisjunction
aneuploidy
trisomic
monosomic

polyploidy
deletion
duplication
inversion
translocation
Down syndrome
genomic imprinting
fragile X syndrome

Word Roots

aneu- = without (*aneuploidy*: a chromosomal aberration in which certain chromosomes are present in extra copies or are deficient in number)

cyto- = cell (*cytological maps*: charts of chromosomes that locate genes with respect to chromosomal features)

hemo- = blood (*hemophilia*: a human genetic disease caused by a sex-linked recessive allele, characterized by excessive bleeding following injury)

mono- = one (*monosomic*: a chromosomal condition in which a particular cell has only one copy of a chromosome, instead of the normal two; the cell is said to be monosomic for that chromosome)

non- = not; **dis-** = separate (*nondisjunction*: an accident of meiosis or mitosis, in which both members of a pair of homologous chromosomes or both sister chromatids fail to move apart properly)

poly- = many (*polyploidy*: a chromosomal alteration in which the organism possesses more than two complete chromosome sets)

re- = again; **com-** = together; **-bin** = two at a time (*recombinant*: an offspring whose phenotype differs from that of the parents)

trans- = across (*translocation*: attachment of a chromosomal fragment to a nonhomologous chromosome)

tri- = three; **soma-** = body (*trisomic*: a chromosomal condition in which a particular cell has an extra copy of one chromosome, instead of the normal two; the cell is said to be trisomic for that chromosome)

References

Collins, F. S. and K. G. Jegalian. "Deciphering the Code of Life." *Scientific American,* December 1999.

Hartwell, L. H., et. al. *Genetics: From Genes to Genomes.* New York: McGraw-Hill, 2000.

Visual Guide to the Image Library

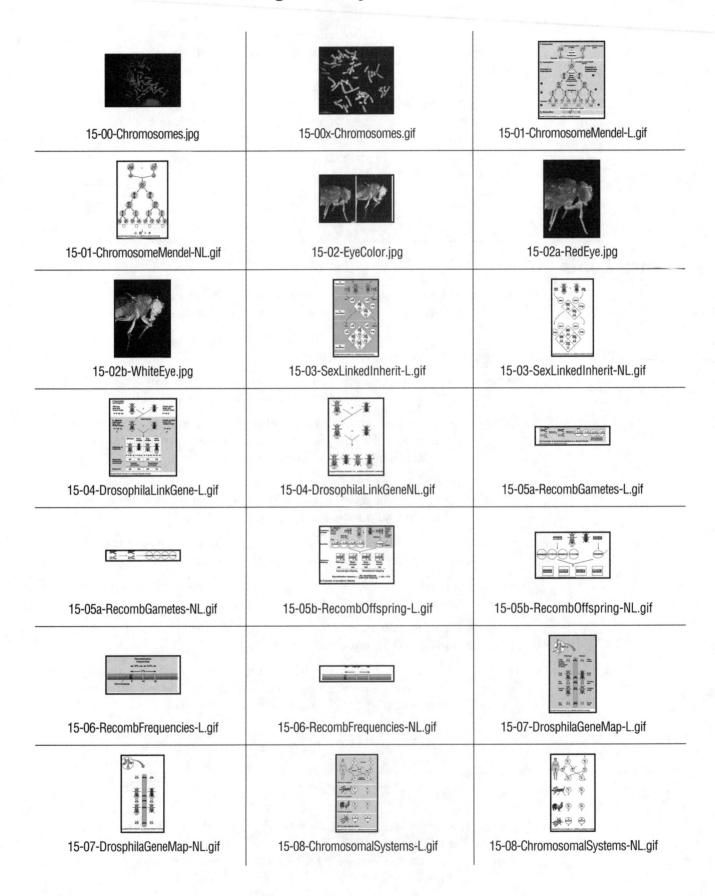

15-00-Chromosomes.jpg

15-00x-Chromosomes.gif

15-01-ChromosomeMendel-L.gif

15-01-ChromosomeMendel-NL.gif

15-02-EyeColor.jpg

15-02a-RedEye.jpg

15-02b-WhiteEye.jpg

15-03-SexLinkedInherit-L.gif

15-03-SexLinkedInherit-NL.gif

15-04-DrosophilaLinkGene-L.gif

15-04-DrosophilaLinkGeneNL.gif

15-05a-RecombGametes-L.gif

15-05a-RecombGametes-NL.gif

15-05b-RecombOffspring-L.gif

15-05b-RecombOffspring-NL.gif

15-06-RecombFrequencies-L.gif

15-06-RecombFrequencies-NL.gif

15-07-DrosphilaGeneMap-L.gif

15-07-DrosphilaGeneMap-NL.gif

15-08-ChromosomalSystems-L.gif

15-08-ChromosomalSystems-NL.gif

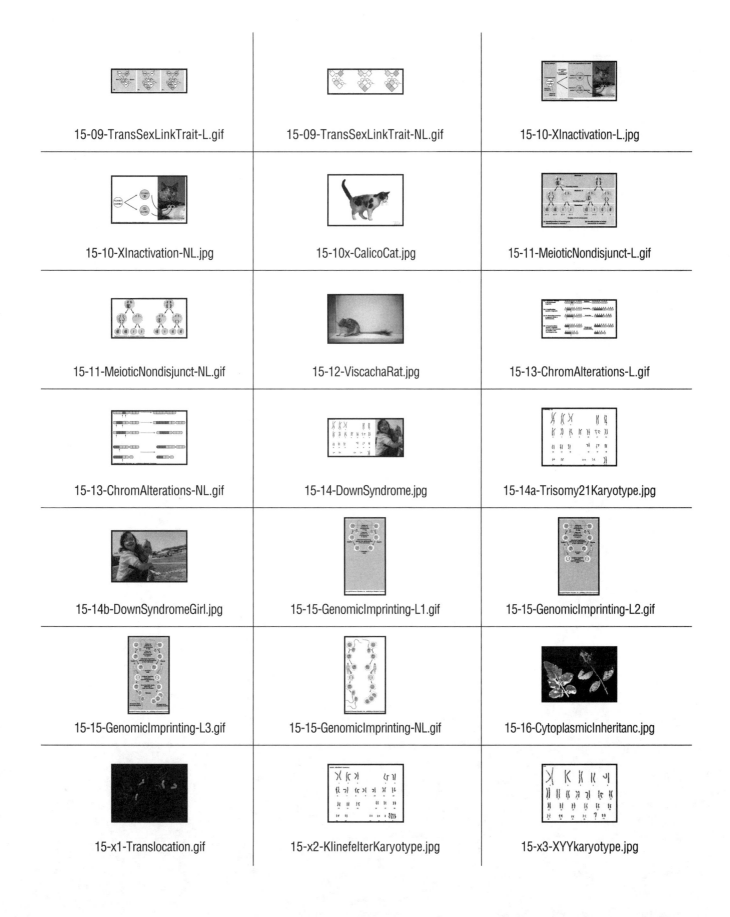

15-09-TransSexLinkTrait-L.gif

15-09-TransSexLinkTrait-NL.gif

15-10-XInactivation-L.jpg

15-10-XInactivation-NL.jpg

15-10x-CalicoCat.jpg

15-11-MeioticNondisjunct-L.gif

15-11-MeioticNondisjunct-NL.gif

15-12-ViscachaRat.jpg

15-13-ChromAlterations-L.gif

15-13-ChromAlterations-NL.gif

15-14-DownSyndrome.jpg

15-14a-Trisomy21Karyotype.jpg

15-14b-DownSyndromeGirl.jpg

15-15-GenomicImprinting-L1.gif

15-15-GenomicImprinting-L2.gif

15-15-GenomicImprinting-L3.gif

15-15-GenomicImprinting-NL.gif

15-16-CytoplasmicInheritanc.jpg

15-x1-Translocation.gif

15-x2-KlinefelterKaryotype.jpg

15-x3-XYYkaryotype.jpg

15UN-272-DrosphiliaCross-L.gif

15UN-272-DrosphiliaCross-NL.gif

CHAPTER 16

The Molecular Basis of Inheritance

Chapter Outline

DNA as the Genetic Material

The search for the genetic material led to DNA: *the process of science*

Watson and Crick discovered the double helix by building models to conform to X-ray data: *the process of science*

DNA Replication and Repair

During DNA replication, base pairing enables existing DNA strands to serve as templates for new complementary strands: *the process of science*

A large team of enzymes and other proteins carries out DNA replication

Enzymes proofread DNA during its replication and repair damage in existing DNA

The ends of DNA molecules are replicated by a special mechanism

Transparency Acetates

The Transparency Acetates for *Biology*, Sixth Edition, include the following images:

Media for Instructors

Campbell Image Presentation Library

The Campbell Image Presentation Library CD-ROM set includes the following for your use:

- All art (available in pdf and jpeg or gif formats), photos (from the text and outside sources), and tables. Art images are also available without callouts. See the Visual Guide to the Image Library section at the end of this chapter for thumbnail versions of every image.

- A PowerPoint^{TM} slide show of the art (with callouts), photos (both text and outside sources), and tables.

- The following QuickTime animations, adapted from student media activities (also available as Shockwave Flash .swf files):

  16-02-PhageT2Reproduction.mov

  16-05-DNAstructNarrAnim_S.mov

  16-05-DNAstructureAnim_B.mov

  16-10-DNAReplicatAnim_B.mov

  16-10-DNAReplication.mov

  16-10-DNAReplicatNarrAnim_S.mov

  16-13-LaggingStrandAnim_B.mov

  16-13-LeadingStndNarrAnim_S.mov

  16-13-LeadingStrandAnim_B.mov

  16-16-DNAreplicReviewAnim_B.mov

PowerPoint Lectures CD-ROM

The PowerPoint Lectures CD-ROM contains slides that integrate the art, photos, tables, and lecture outline from this chapter.

Campbell Biology Website (Instructor Resources)

See the insert in your copy of Campbell/Reece *Biology*, Sixth Edition, for instructions on how to access the Campbell Biology Website. The Instructor Resources section of the website includes the following:

- The art, photos, tables, PowerPoint slide shows, videos, and animations from the Campbell Image Presentation Library
- Suggested answers to the Lab Report questions from the Case Studies in the Process of Science
- The PowerPoint Lecture for this chapter
- Word files of the lecture outline for this chapter
- Photo links

Course Management Systems

The media content for this chapter is available in three course management systems: CourseCompass™, Blackboard, and WebCT. For more information, go to http://cms.aw.com. For the latest pdf instructions on how to use CourseCompass, go to **www.coursecompass.com**. In addition, a Syllabus Manager is offered on the Campbell Biology Website.

Media for Students

The Campbell Biology Website and CD-ROM include the following for your students:

- Objectives
- Chapter Review (Summary, Self-Quiz, and Essay Questions from the book; Word Roots; Key Terms linked to the Glossary)
- Activities (see list below)
- Case Studies in the Process of Science (see list below)
- Quizzes (Pre-test, Activities Quiz, Chapter Quiz, Essay Questions)
- Web Links
- News and References
- Art and videos from the Campbell Image Presentation Library
- The Campbell *Biology* Interviews (from all editions)
- Glossary with audio pronunciations
- Syllabus Manager

Student Media Activities and Case Studies in The Process of Science

Web/CD Activity 16A: *The Hershey-Chase Experiment*

Web/CD Activity 16B: *DNA and RNA Structure*

Web/CD Activity 16C: *DNA Double Helix*

Web/CD Activity 16D: *DNA Replication: An Overview*

Web/CD Case Study in the Process of Science: *What Is the Correct Model for DNA Replication?*

Web/CD Activity 16E: *DNA Replication: A Closer Look*

Web/CD Activity 16F: *DNA Replication Review*

Objectives

DNA as the Genetic Material

1. Explain why researchers originally thought protein was the genetic material.

2. Summarize the experiments performed by the following scientists that provided evidence that DNA is the genetic material:
   a. Frederick Griffith
   b. Oswald Avery, Maclyn McCarty, and Colin MacLeod
   c. Alfred Hershey and Martha Chase
   d. Erwin Chargaff

3. Explain how Watson and Crick deduced the structure of DNA and describe the evidence they used. Explain the significance of the research of Rosalind Franklin.

4. Describe the structure of DNA. Explain the "base-pairing rule" and describe its significance.

DNA Replication and Repair

5. Describe the semiconservative model of replication and the significance of the experiments by Matthew Meselson and Franklin Stahl.

6. Describe the process of DNA replication. Note the structure of the many origins of replication and replication forks and explain the role of DNA polymerase.

7. Explain what energy source drives the polymerization of DNA.

8. Define "antiparallel" and explain why continuous synthesis of both DNA strands is not possible.

9. Distinguish between the leading strand and the lagging strand.

10. Explain how the lagging strand is synthesized even though DNA polymerase can add nucleotides only to the 3' end.

11. Explain the roles of DNA ligase, primer, primase, helicase, and the single-strand binding protein.

12. Explain why an analogy can be made comparing DNA replication to a locomotive made of DNA polymerase moving along a railroad track of DNA.

13. Explain the roles of DNA polymerase, mismatch repair enzymes, and nuclease in DNA proofreading and repair.

14. Describe the structure and functions of telomeres. Explain the significance of telomerase to healthy and cancerous cells

Key Terms

transformation
bacteriophages
phage
double helix
semiconservative
 model
origins of replication
replication fork
DNA polymerase

leading strand
lagging strand
DNA ligase
primer
primase
helicase
single-strand binding
 protein
mismatch repair

nuclease
nucleotide excision
 repair
telomere
telomerase

Word Roots

helic- = a spiral (*helicase*: an enzyme that untwists the double helix of DNA at the replication forks)

liga- = bound or tied (*DNA ligase*: a linking enzyme for DNA replication)

-phage = to eat (*bacteriophages*: viruses that infect bacteria)

semi- = half (*semiconservative model*: type of DNA replication in which the replicated double helix consists of one old strand, derived from the old molecule, and one newly made strand)

telos- = an end (*telomere*: the protective structure at each end of a eukaryotic chromosome)

trans- = across (*transformation*: a phenomenon in which external DNA is assimilated by a cell)

References

Becker, W. M., L. J. Kleinsmith, and J. Hardin. *The World of the Cell.* 4th ed. San Francisco, California: Benjamin Cummings, 2000.

Campbell, M. *Biochemistry.* 3rd ed. Orlando, Florida: Harcourt, Inc, 1999.

Hartwell, L. H., et. al. *Genetics: From Genes to Genomes.* New York: McGraw-Hill, 2000.

Visual Guide to the Image Library

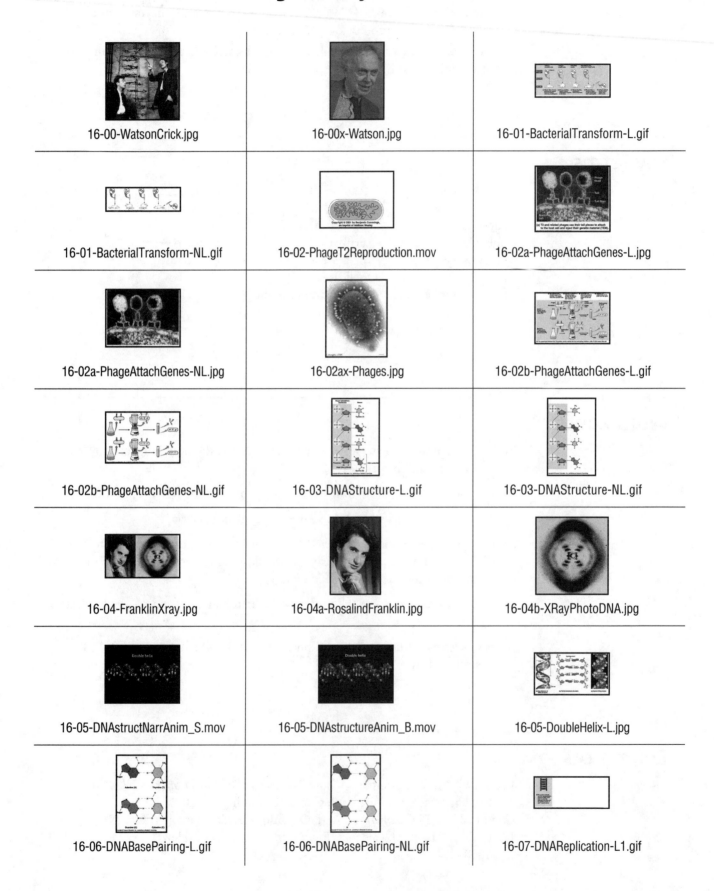

16-00-WatsonCrick.jpg

16-00x-Watson.jpg

16-01-BacterialTransform-L.gif

16-01-BacterialTransform-NL.gif

16-02-PhageT2Reproduction.mov

16-02a-PhageAttachGenes-L.jpg

16-02a-PhageAttachGenes-NL.jpg

16-02ax-Phages.jpg

16-02b-PhageAttachGenes-L.gif

16-02b-PhageAttachGenes-NL.gif

16-03-DNAStructure-L.gif

16-03-DNAStructure-NL.gif

16-04-FranklinXray.jpg

16-04a-RosalindFranklin.jpg

16-04b-XRayPhotoDNA.jpg

16-05-DNAstructNarrAnim_S.mov

16-05-DNAstructureAnim_B.mov

16-05-DoubleHelix-L.jpg

16-06-DNABasePairing-L.gif

16-06-DNABasePairing-NL.gif

16-07-DNAReplication-L1.gif

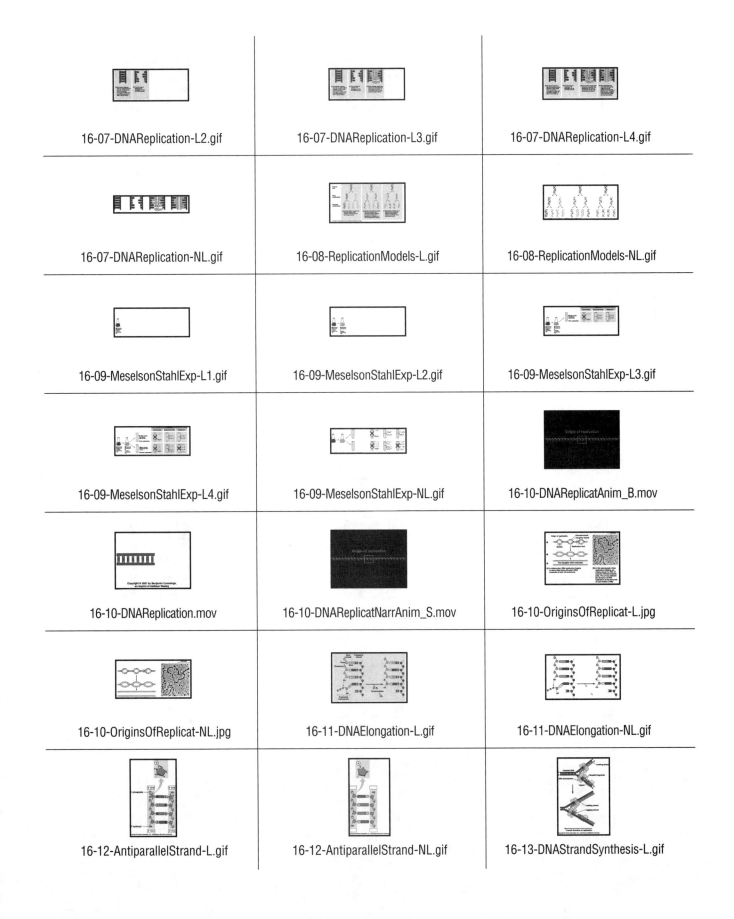

16-07-DNAReplication-L2.gif	16-07-DNAReplication-L3.gif	16-07-DNAReplication-L4.gif
16-07-DNAReplication-NL.gif	16-08-ReplicationModels-L.gif	16-08-ReplicationModels-NL.gif
16-09-MeselsonStahlExp-L1.gif	16-09-MeselsonStahlExp-L2.gif	16-09-MeselsonStahlExp-L3.gif
16-09-MeselsonStahlExp-L4.gif	16-09-MeselsonStahlExp-NL.gif	16-10-DNAReplicatAnim_B.mov
16-10-DNAReplication.mov	16-10-DNAReplicatNarrAnim_S.mov	16-10-OriginsOfReplicat-L.jpg
16-10-OriginsOfReplicat-NL.jpg	16-11-DNAElongation-L.gif	16-11-DNAElongation-NL.gif
16-12-AntiparallelStrand-L.gif	16-12-AntiparallelStrand-NL.gif	16-13-DNAStrandSynthesis-L.gif

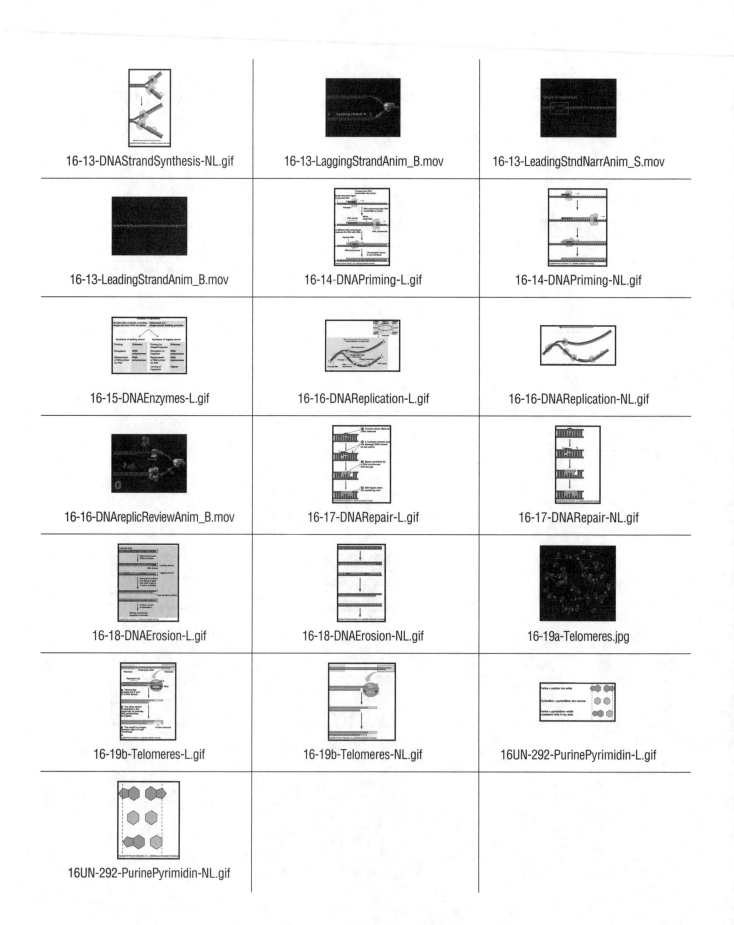

16-13-DNAStrandSynthesis-NL.gif

16-13-LaggingStrandAnim_B.mov

16-13-LeadingStndNarrAnim_S.mov

16-13-LeadingStrandAnim_B.mov

16-14-DNAPriming-L.gif

16-14-DNAPriming-NL.gif

16-15-DNAEnzymes-L.gif

16-16-DNAReplication-L.gif

16-16-DNAReplication-NL.gif

16-16-DNAreplicReviewAnim_B.mov

16-17-DNARepair-L.gif

16-17-DNARepair-NL.gif

16-18-DNAErosion-L.gif

16-18-DNAErosion-NL.gif

16-19a-Telomeres.jpg

16-19b-Telomeres-L.gif

16-19b-Telomeres-NL.gif

16UN-292-PurinePyrimidin-L.gif

16UN-292-PurinePyrimidin-NL.gif

CHAPTER 17

From Gene to Protein

Chapter Outline

The Connection between Genes and Proteins

The study of metabolic defects provided evidence that genes specify proteins: *the process of science*

Transcription and translation are the two main processes linking gene to protein: *an overview*

In the genetic code, nucleotide triplets specify amino acids

The genetic code must have evolved very early in the history of life

The Synthesis and Processing of RNA

Transcription is the DNA-directed synthesis of RNA: *a closer look*

Eukaryotic cells modify RNA after transcription

The Synthesis of Protein

Translation is the RNA-directed synthesis of a polypeptide: *a closer look*

Signal peptides target some eukaryotic polypeptides to specific destinations in the cell

RNA plays multiple roles in the cell: *a review*

Comparing protein synthesis in prokaryotes and eukaryotes: *a review*

Point mutations can affect protein structure and function

What is a gene? *revisiting the question*

Transparency Acetates

The Transparency Acetates for *Biology*, Sixth Edition, include the following images:

Media for Instructors

Campbell Image Presentation Library

The Campbell Image Presentation Library CD-ROM set includes the following for your use:

- All art (available in pdf and jpeg or gif formats), photos (from the text and outside sources), and tables. Art images are also available without callouts. See the Visual Guide to the Image Library section at the end of this chapter for thumbnail versions of every image.
- A PowerPoint™ slide show of the art (with callouts), photos (both text and outside sources), and tables.
- The following QuickTime animations, adapted from student media activities (also available as Shockwave Flash .swf files):

  17-06-Transcription.mov

  17-17-Translation.mov

PowerPoint Lectures CD-ROM

The PowerPoint Lectures CD-ROM contains slides that integrate the art, photos, tables, and lecture outline from this chapter.

Campbell Biology Website (Instructor Resources)

See the insert in your copy of Campbell/Reece *Biology*, Sixth Edition, for instructions on how to access the Campbell Biology Website. The Instructor Resources section of the website includes the following:

- The art, photos, tables, PowerPoint slide shows, videos, and animations from the Campbell Image Presentation Library
- Suggested answers to the Lab Report questions from the Case Studies in the Process of Science
- The PowerPoint Lecture for this chapter
- Word files of the lecture outline for this chapter
- Photo links

Course Management Systems

The media content for this chapter is available in three course management systems: CourseCompass™, Blackboard, and WebCT. For more information, go to http://cms.aw.com. For the latest pdf instructions on how to use CourseCompass, go to www.coursecompass.com. In addition, a Syllabus Manager is offered on the Campbell Biology Website.

Media for Students

The Campbell Biology Website and CD-ROM include the following for your students:

- Objectives
- Chapter Review (Summary, Self-Quiz, and Essay Questions from the book; Word Roots; Key Terms linked to the Glossary)
- Activities (see list below)
- Case Studies in the Process of Science (see list below)
- Quizzes (Pre-test, Activities Quiz, Chapter Quiz, Essay Questions)
- Web Links
- News and References
- Art and videos from the Campbell Image Presentation Library
- The Campbell *Biology* Interviews (from all editions)
- Glossary with audio pronunciations
- Syllabus Manager

Student Media Activities and Case Studies in The Process of Science

Web/CD Case Study in the Process of Science: *How Is a Metabolic Pathway Analyzed?*

Web/CD Activity 17A: *Overview of Protein Synthesis*

Web/CD Activity 17B: *Transcription*

Web/CD Activity 17C: *RNA Processing*

Web/CD Activity 17D: *Translation*

Biology Labs On-Line: *TranslationLab*

Objectives

The Connection between Genes and Proteins

1. Explain why dwarf peas have shorter stems than tall varieties.
2. Explain the reasoning that led Archibald Garrod to first suggest that genes dictate phenotypes through enzymes.
3. Describe Beadle and Tatum's experiments with Neurospora and explain the contribution they made to our understanding of how genes control metabolism.
4. Distinguish between the "one gene–one enzyme" hypothesis and the "one gene–one polypeptide" hypothesis and explain why the original hypothesis was changed.

5. Explain how RNA differs from DNA.

6. Briefly explain how information flows from gene to protein.

7. Distinguish between transcription and translation.

8. Compare where transcription and translation occur in prokaryotes and in eukaryotes.

9. Define "codon" and explain the relationship between the linear sequence of codons on mRNA and the linear sequence of amino acids in a polypeptide.

10. Explain the early techniques used to identify what amino acids are specified by the triplets UUU, AAA, GGG, and CCC.

11. Explain why polypeptides begin with methionine when they are synthesized.

12. Explain in what way the genetic code is redundant and unambiguous.

13. Explain the significance of the reading frame during translation.

14. Explain the evolutionary significance of a nearly universal genetic code.

The Synthesis and Processing of RNA

15. Explain how RNA polymerase recognizes where transcription should begin. Describe the promoter, the terminator, and the transcription unit.

16. Explain the general process of transcription, including the three major steps of initiation, elongation, and termination.

17. Explain how RNA is modified after transcription in eukaryotic cells.

18. Define and explain the role of ribozymes.

19. Describe the functional and evolutionary significance of introns.

The Synthesis of Protein

20. Describe the structure and functions of tRNA.

21. Describe the structure and functions of ribosomes.

22. Describe the process of translation (including initiation, elongation, and termination) and explain which enzymes, protein factors, and energy sources are needed for each stage.

23. Describe the significance of polyribosomes.

24. Explain what determines the primary structure of a protein and describe how a polypeptide must be modified before it becomes fully functional.

25. Describe what determines whether a ribosome will be free in the cytosol or attached to the rough endoplasmic reticulum.

26. Describe two properties of RNA that allow it to perform so many different functions.

27. Compare protein synthesis in prokaryotes and eukaryotes.

28. Define "point mutations." Distinguish between base-pair substitutions and base-pair insertions. Give examples of each and note the significance of such changes.

29. Describe several examples of mutagens and explain how they cause mutations.

30. Describe the historical evolution of the concept of a gene.

Key Terms

one gene-one polypeptide hypothesis	transcription initiation complex	ribosomal RNA (rRNA)
transcription	TATA box	P site
messenger RNA (mRNA)	5′ cap	A site
translation	poly(A) tail	E site
RNA processing	RNA splicing	polyribosome
primary transcript	intron	signal peptide
triplet code	exon	signal-recognition
template strand	spliceosome	particle (SRP)
codon	ribozymes	mutation
reading frame	alternative RNA splicing	point mutation
RNA polymerase	domain	base-pair substitution
promoter	transfer RNA (tRNA)	missense mutation
terminator	anticodon	nonsense mutation
transcription unit	wobble	insertion
transcription factor	aminoacyl-tRNA synthetase	deletion
		frameshift mutation
		mutagen

Word Roots

anti- = opposite (*anticodon*: a specialized base triplet on one end of a tRNA molecule that recognizes a particular complimentary codon on an mRNA molecule)

exo- = out, outside, without (*exon*: a coding region of a eukaryotic gene that is expressed)

intro- = within (*intron*: a noncoding, intervening sequence within a eukaryotic gene)

muta- = change; **-gen** = producing (*mutagen*: a physical or chemical agent that causes mutations)

poly- = many (*poly A tail*: the modified end of the 3' end of an mRNA molecule consisting of the addition of some 50 to 250 adenine nucleotides)

trans- = across; **-script** = write (*transcription*: the synthesis of RNA on a DNA template)

References

Becker, W. M., L. J. Kleinsmith, and J. Hardin. *The World of the Cell.* 4th ed. San Francisco, California: Benjamin Cummings, 2000.

Campbell, M. *Biochemistry.* 3rd ed. Orlando, Florida: Harcourt, Inc, 1999.

Hartwell, L. H., et. al. *Genetics: From Genes to Genomes.* New York: McGraw-Hill, 2000.

Scott, M. P. "Development: The Natural History of Genes." *Cell,* January 2000.

Visual Guide to the Image Library

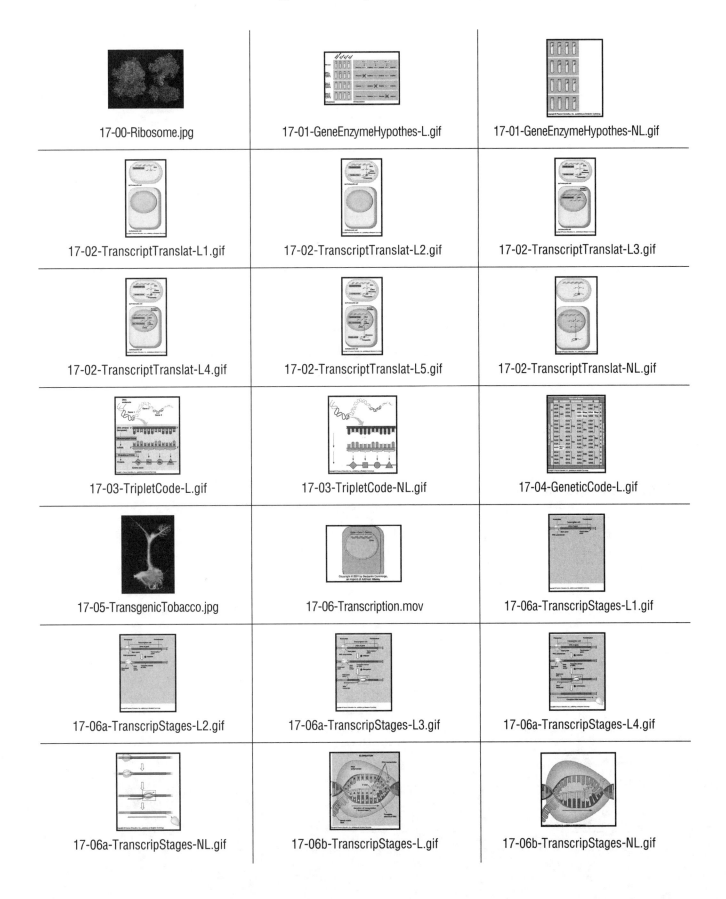

17-00-Ribosome.jpg

17-01-GeneEnzymeHypothes-L.gif

17-01-GeneEnzymeHypothes-NL.gif

17-02-TranscriptTranslat-L1.gif

17-02-TranscriptTranslat-L2.gif

17-02-TranscriptTranslat-L3.gif

17-02-TranscriptTranslat-L4.gif

17-02-TranscriptTranslat-L5.gif

17-02-TranscriptTranslat-NL.gif

17-03-TripletCode-L.gif

17-03-TripletCode-NL.gif

17-04-GeneticCode-L.gif

17-05-TransgenicTobacco.jpg

17-06-Transcription.mov

17-06a-TranscripStages-L1.gif

17-06a-TranscripStages-L2.gif

17-06a-TranscripStages-L3.gif

17-06a-TranscripStages-L4.gif

17-06a-TranscripStages-NL.gif

17-06b-TranscripStages-L.gif

17-06b-TranscripStages-NL.gif

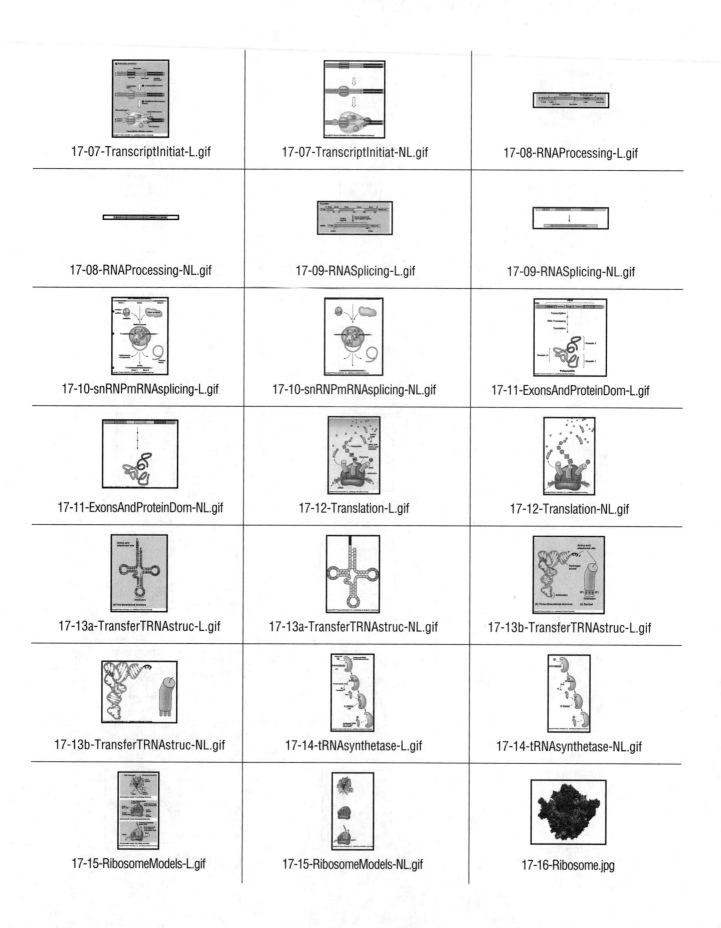

17-07-TranscriptInitiat-L.gif	17-07-TranscriptInitiat-NL.gif	17-08-RNAProcessing-L.gif
17-08-RNAProcessing-NL.gif	17-09-RNASplicing-L.gif	17-09-RNASplicing-NL.gif
17-10-snRNPmRNAsplicing-L.gif	17-10-snRNPmRNAsplicing-NL.gif	17-11-ExonsAndProteinDom-L.gif
17-11-ExonsAndProteinDom-NL.gif	17-12-Translation-L.gif	17-12-Translation-NL.gif
17-13a-TransferTRNAstruc-L.gif	17-13a-TransferTRNAstruc-NL.gif	17-13b-TransferTRNAstruc-L.gif
17-13b-TransferTRNAstruc-NL.gif	17-14-tRNAsynthetase-L.gif	17-14-tRNAsynthetase-NL.gif
17-15-RibosomeModels-L.gif	17-15-RibosomeModels-NL.gif	17-16-Ribosome.jpg

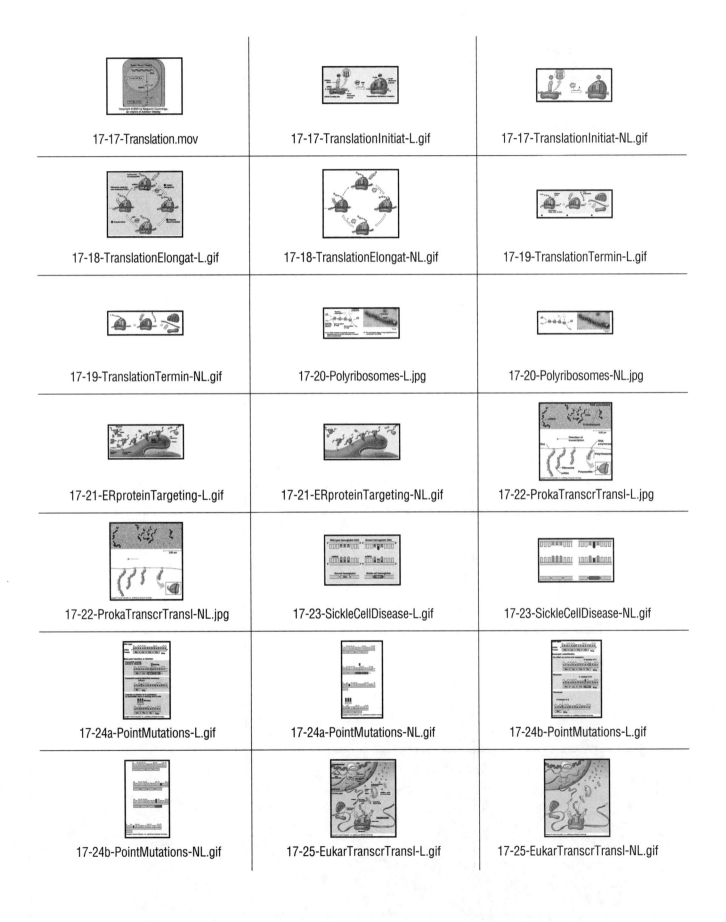

17-17-Translation.mov

17-17-TranslationInitiat-L.gif

17-17-TranslationInitiat-NL.gif

17-18-TranslationElongat-L.gif

17-18-TranslationElongat-NL.gif

17-19-TranslationTermin-L.gif

17-19-TranslationTermin-NL.gif

17-20-Polyribosomes-L.jpg

17-20-Polyribosomes-NL.jpg

17-21-ERproteinTargeting-L.gif

17-21-ERproteinTargeting-NL.gif

17-22-ProkaTranscrTransl-L.jpg

17-22-ProkaTranscrTransl-NL.jpg

17-23-SickleCellDisease-L.gif

17-23-SickleCellDisease-NL.gif

17-24a-PointMutations-L.gif

17-24a-PointMutations-NL.gif

17-24b-PointMutations-L.gif

17-24b-PointMutations-NL.gif

17-25-EukarTranscrTransl-L.gif

17-25-EukarTranscrTransl-NL.gif

17T-01-RNAinEukaryCell-L.gif

CHAPTER 18

Microbial Models:
The Genetics of Viruses and Bacteria

Chapter Outline

The Genetics of Viruses

Researchers discovered viruses by studying a plant disease: *the process of science*

A virus is a genome enclosed in a protective coat

Viruses can reproduce only within a host cell: *an overview*

Phages reproduce using lytic or lysogenic cycles

Animal viruses are diverse in their modes of infection and replication

Plant viruses are serious agricultural pests

Viroids and prions are infectious agents even simpler than viruses

Viruses may have evolved from other mobile genetic elements

The Genetics of Bacteria

The short generation span of bacteria helps them adapt to changing environments

Genetic recombination produces new bacterial strains

The control of gene expression enables individual bacteria to adjust their metabolism to environmental change

Transparency Acetates

The Transparency Acetates for *Biology*, Sixth Edition, include the following images:

Media for Instructors

Campbell Image Presentation Library

The Campbell Image Presentation Library CD-ROM set includes the following for your use:

- All art (available in pdf and jpeg or gif formats), photos (from the text and outside sources), and tables. Art images are also available without callouts. See the Visual Guide to the Image Library section at the end of this chapter for thumbnail versions of every image.

- A PowerPoint™ slide show of the art (with callouts), photos (both text and outside sources), and tables.

- The following QuickTime animations, adapted from student media activities (also available as Shockwave Flash .swf files):

  18-05-PhageLambdaReproduct.mov

  18-07-HIVreproduction.mov

PowerPoint Lectures CD-ROM

The PowerPoint Lectures CD-ROM contains slides that integrate the art, photos, tables, and lecture outline from this chapter.

Campbell Biology Website (Instructor Resources)

See the insert in your copy of Campbell/Reece *Biology*, Sixth Edition, for instructions on how to access the Campbell Biology Website. The Instructor Resources section of the website includes the following:

- The art, photos, tables, PowerPoint slide shows, videos, and animations from the Campbell Image Presentation Library
- Suggested answers to the Lab Report questions from the Case Studies in the Process of Science
- The PowerPoint Lecture for this chapter
- Word files of the lecture outline for this chapter
- Photo links

Course Management Systems

The media content for this chapter is available in three course management systems: CourseCompass™, Blackboard, and WebCT. For more information, go to http://cms.aw.com. For the latest pdf instructions on how to use CourseCompass, go to www.coursecompass.com. In addition, a Syllabus Manager is offered on the Campbell Biology Website.

Media for Students

The Campbell Biology Website and CD-ROM include the following for your students:

- Objectives
- Chapter Review (Summary, Self-Quiz, and Essay Questions from the book; Word Roots; Key Terms linked to the Glossary)
- Activities (see list below)
- Case Studies in the Process of Science (see list below)
- Quizzes (Pre-test, Activities Quiz, Chapter Quiz, Essay Questions)
- Web Links
- News and References
- Art and videos from the Campbell Image Presentation Library
- The Campbell *Biology* Interviews (from all editions)
- Glossary with audio pronunciations
- Syllabus Manager

Student Media Activities and Case Studies in The Process of Science

Web/CD Activity 18A: *Simplified Viral Reproductive Cycle*

Web/CD Activity 18B: *Phage Lytic Cycle*

Web/CD Activity 18C: *Phage Lysogenic and Lytic Cycles*

Web/CD Activity 18D: *Retrovirus (HIV) Reproductive Cycle*

Web/CD Case Study in the Process of Science: *What Causes Infections in AIDS Patients?*

Web/CD Case Study in the Process of Science: *Why Do AIDS Rates Differ Across the U.S.?*

Web/CD Case Study in the Process of Science: *What Are the Patterns of Antibiotic Resistance?*

Web/CD Activity 18E: *The* lac *Operon in* E. coli

Objectives

The Genetics of Viruses

1. Recount the history leading up to the discovery of viruses. Include the contributions of Adolf Mayer, D. Ivanowsky, Martinus Beijerinck, and Wendell Stanley.

2. List and describe the structural components of viruses.

3. Explain why viruses are obligate parasites.

4. Distinguish between the lytic and lysogenic reproductive cycles, using phage T4 and phage lambda as examples.

5. Describe the reproductive cycle of an enveloped virus. Explain how the reproductive cycle of herpes viruses is different.

6. Describe the reproductive cycle of retroviruses.

7. Explain how viral infections in animals cause disease.

8. Define "vaccine" and describe the research of Jenner that led to the development of the smallpox vaccine.

9. Describe the best current medical defenses against viruses. Explain how AZT helps to fight HIV infections.

10. Describe the mechanisms by which new viral diseases emerge.

11. List some viruses that have been implicated in human cancers and explain how tumor viruses transform cells.

12. Distinguish between the horizontal and vertical routes of viral transmission in plants.

13. Describe the structures and replication cycles of viroids and prions.

14. List some characteristics that viruses share with living organisms and explain why viruses do not fit our usual definition of life.

15. Describe the evidence that viruses probably evolved from fragments of cellular nucleic acid.

The Genetics of Bacteria

16. Describe the structure of a bacterial chromosome.

17. Describe the process of binary fission in bacteria.

18. Compare the sources of genetic variation in bacteria and humans.

19. Compare the processes of transformation, transduction, and conjugation.

20. Distinguish between plasmids and viruses. Define an episome.

21. Explain how the F plasmid controls conjugation in bacteria.

22. Describe the significance of R plasmids. Explain how the widespread use of antibiotics contributes to R-plasmid-related disease.

23. Define transposon and describe two types of transposition.

24. Distinguish between an insertion sequence and a complex transposon.

25. Describe the role of transposase and DNA polymerase in the process of transposition.

26. Briefly describe two main strategies that cells use to control metabolism.

27. Explain the adaptive advantage of genes grouped into an operon.

28. Using the trp operon as an example, explain the concept of an operon and the function of the operator, repressor, and co-repressor.

29. Distinguish between structural and regulatory genes.

30. Describe how the lac operon functions and explain the role of the inducer, allolactose.

31. Explain how repressible and inducible enzymes differ and how those differences reflect differences in the pathways they control.

32. Distinguish between positive and negative control and give examples of each from the lac operon.

33. Explain how cyclic AMP and the cyclic AMP receptor protein are affected by glucose concentration.

Key Terms

capsid	AIDS (acquired	episome
viral envelopes	immunodeficiency	F plasmid
bacteriophages	syndrome)	R plasmid
phages	vaccine	transposon
host range	viroid	insertion sequence
lytic cycle	prions	operator
virulent phage	nucleoid	operon
lysogenic cycle	transformation	repressor
temperate phages	transduction	regulatory gene
prophage	generalized	corepressor
provirus	transduction	inducer
retrovirus	specialized	cyclic AMP (cAMP)
reverse transcriptase	transduction	cAMP receptor protein
HIV (human	conjugation	(CRP)
immunodeficiency	F factor	
virus)	plasmid	

Word Roots

capsa- = a box (*capsid*: the protein shell that encloses the viral genome)

conjug- = together (*conjugation*: in bacteria, the transfer of DNA between two cells that are temporarily joined)

lyto- = loosen (*lytic cycle*: a type of viral replication cycle resulting in the release of new phages by death or lysis of the host cell)

-oid = like, form (*nucleoid*: a dense region of DNA in a prokaryotic cell)

-phage = to eat (*bacteriophages*: viruses that infect bacteria)

pro- = before (*provirus*: viral DNA that inserts into a host genome)

retro- = backward (*retrovirus*: an RNA virus that reproduces by transcribing its RNA into DNA and then inserting the DNA into a cellular chromosome)

trans- = across (*transformation*: a phenomenon in which external DNA is assimilated by a cell)

virul- = poisonous (*virulent virus*: a virus that reproduces only by a lytic cycle)

References

Becker, W. M., L. J. Kleinsmith, and J. Hardin. *The World of the Cell.* 4th ed. San Francisco, California: Benjamin Cummings, 2000.

Prescott, L. M., J. P. Harley and D. A. Klein. *Microbiology.* 5th ed. Boston, Massachusetts: McGraw-Hill, 2002.

Visual Guide to the Image Library

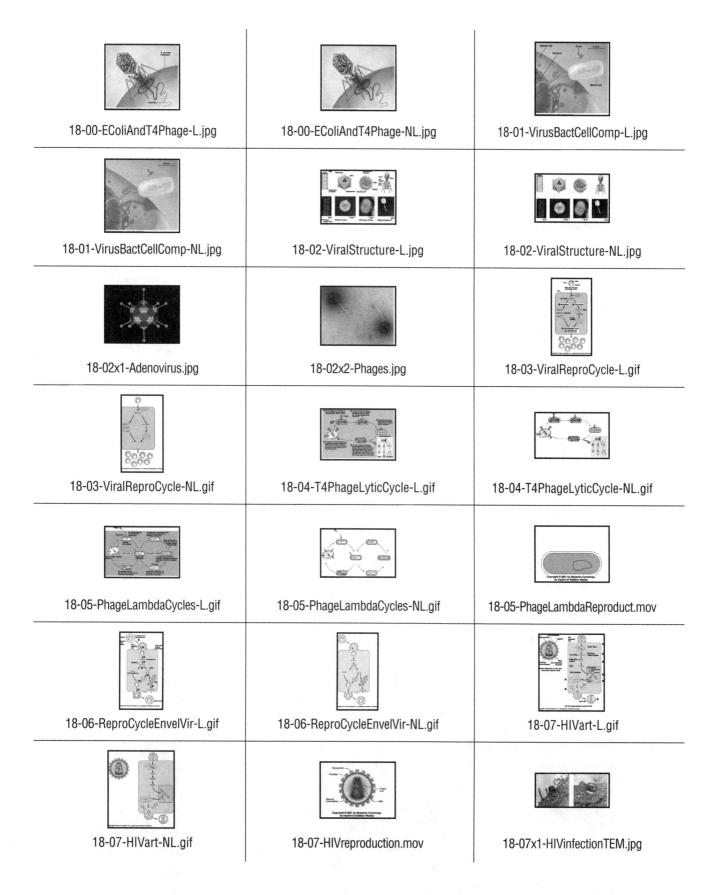

18-00-EColiAndT4Phage-L.jpg

18-00-EColiAndT4Phage-NL.jpg

18-01-VirusBactCellComp-L.jpg

18-01-VirusBactCellComp-NL.jpg

18-02-ViralStructure-L.jpg

18-02-ViralStructure-NL.jpg

18-02x1-Adenovirus.jpg

18-02x2-Phages.jpg

18-03-ViralReproCycle-L.gif

18-03-ViralReproCycle-NL.gif

18-04-T4PhageLyticCycle-L.gif

18-04-T4PhageLyticCycle-NL.gif

18-05-PhageLambdaCycles-L.gif

18-05-PhageLambdaCycles-NL.gif

18-05-PhageLambdaReproduct.mov

18-06-ReproCycleEnvelVir-L.gif

18-06-ReproCycleEnvelVir-NL.gif

18-07-HIVart-L.gif

18-07-HIVart-NL.gif

18-07-HIVreproduction.mov

18-07x1-HIVinfectionTEM.jpg

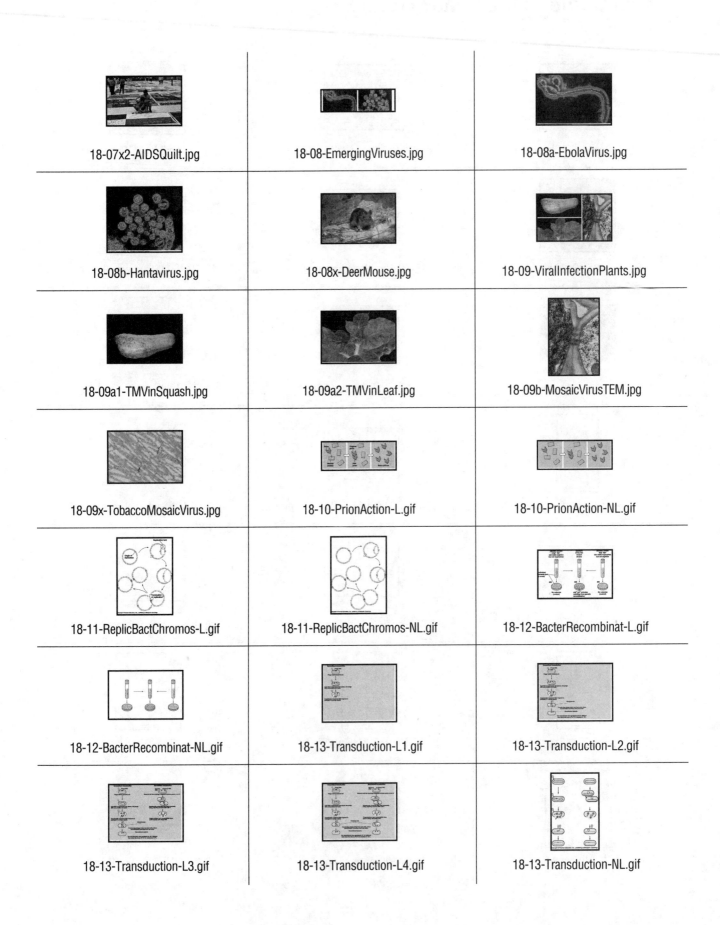

18-07x2-AIDSQuilt.jpg

18-08-EmergingViruses.jpg

18-08a-EbolaVirus.jpg

18-08b-Hantavirus.jpg

18-08x-DeerMouse.jpg

18-09-ViralInfectionPlants.jpg

18-09a1-TMVinSquash.jpg

18-09a2-TMVinLeaf.jpg

18-09b-MosaicVirusTEM.jpg

18-09x-TobaccoMosaicVirus.jpg

18-10-PrionAction-L.gif

18-10-PrionAction-NL.gif

18-11-ReplicBactChromos-L.gif

18-11-ReplicBactChromos-NL.gif

18-12-BacterRecombinat-L.gif

18-12-BacterRecombinat-NL.gif

18-13-Transduction-L1.gif

18-13-Transduction-L2.gif

18-13-Transduction-L3.gif

18-13-Transduction-L4.gif

18-13-Transduction-NL.gif

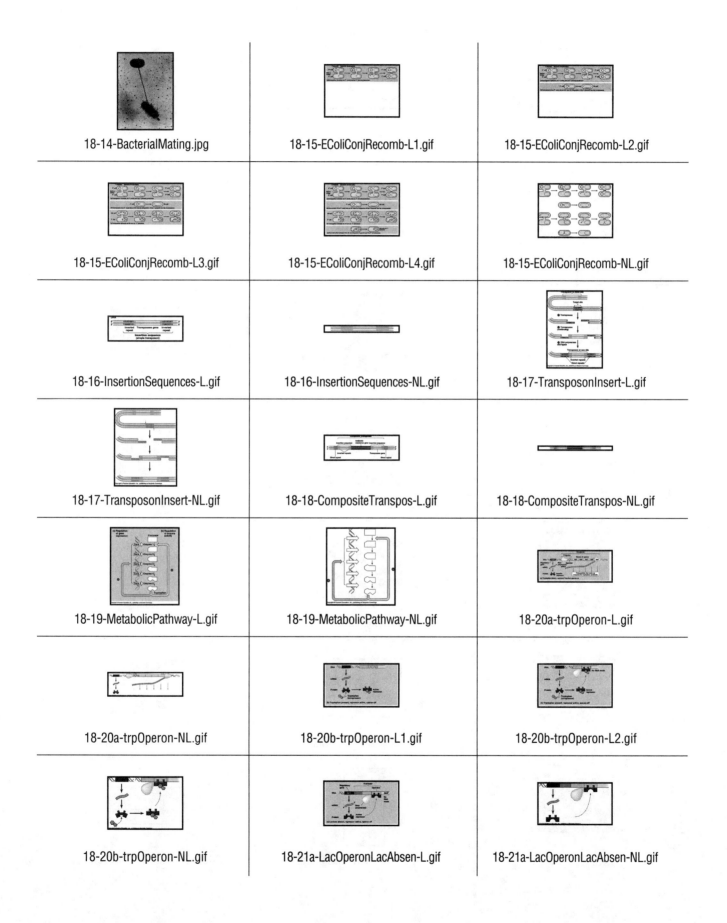

18-14-BacterialMating.jpg

18-15-EColiConjRecomb-L1.gif

18-15-EColiConjRecomb-L2.gif

18-15-EColiConjRecomb-L3.gif

18-15-EColiConjRecomb-L4.gif

18-15-EColiConjRecomb-NL.gif

18-16-InsertionSequences-L.gif

18-16-InsertionSequences-NL.gif

18-17-TransposonInsert-L.gif

18-17-TransposonInsert-NL.gif

18-18-CompositeTranspos-L.gif

18-18-CompositeTranspos-NL.gif

18-19-MetabolicPathway-L.gif

18-19-MetabolicPathway-NL.gif

18-20a-trpOperon-L.gif

18-20a-trpOperon-NL.gif

18-20b-trpOperon-L1.gif

18-20b-trpOperon-L2.gif

18-20b-trpOperon-NL.gif

18-21a-LacOperonLacAbsen-L.gif

18-21a-LacOperonLacAbsen-NL.gif

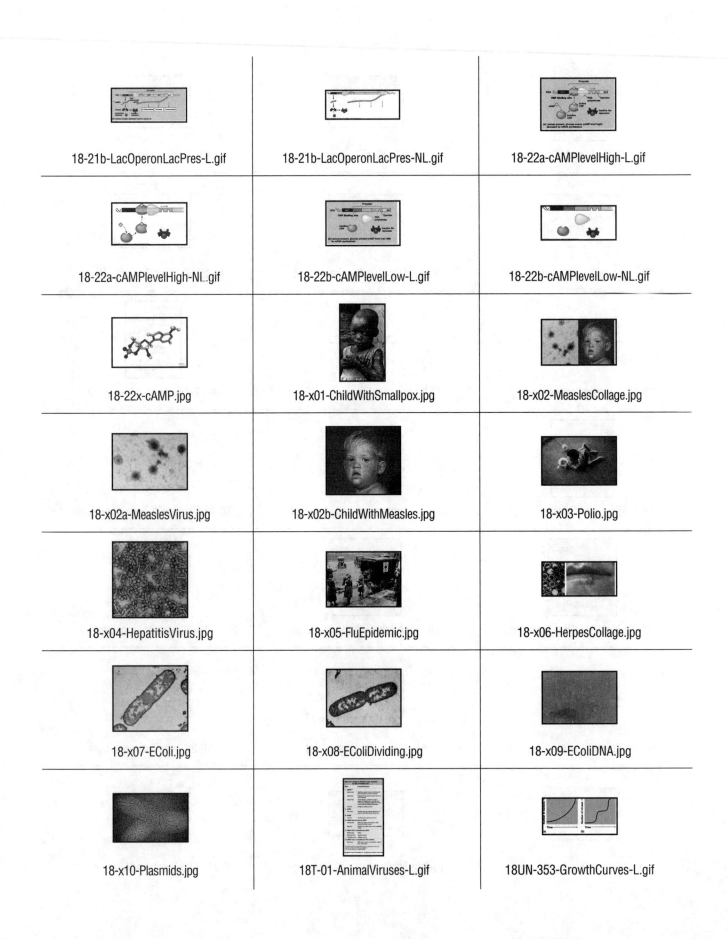

18-21b-LacOperonLacPres-L.gif

18-21b-LacOperonLacPres-NL.gif

18-22a-cAMPlevelHigh-L.gif

18-22a-cAMPlevelHigh-NL.gif

18-22b-cAMPlevelLow-L.gif

18-22b-cAMPlevelLow-NL.gif

18-22x-cAMP.jpg

18-x01-ChildWithSmallpox.jpg

18-x02-MeaslesCollage.jpg

18-x02a-MeaslesVirus.jpg

18-x02b-ChildWithMeasles.jpg

18-x03-Polio.jpg

18-x04-HepatitisVirus.jpg

18-x05-FluEpidemic.jpg

18-x06-HerpesCollage.jpg

18-x07-EColi.jpg

18-x08-EColiDividing.jpg

18-x09-EColiDNA.jpg

18-x10-Plasmids.jpg

18T-01-AnimalViruses-L.gif

18UN-353-GrowthCurves-L.gif

CHAPTER 19

The Organization and Control of Eukaryotic Genomes

Chapter Outline

Transparency Acetates

The Transparency Acetates for *Biology*, Sixth Edition, include the following images:

Figure 19.1	Levels of chromatin packing
Table 19.1	Types of Repetitive DNA
Figure 19.2	Part of a family of identical genes for ribosomal RNA
Figure 19.3	The evolution of human α-globin and β-globin gene families
Figure 19.5	Retrotransposon movement
Figure 19.6	DNA rearrangement in the maturation of an immunoglobulin (antibody) gene
Figure 19.7	Opportunities for the control of gene expression in eukaryotic cells
Figure 19.8	A eukaryotic gene and its transcript
Figure 19.9	A model for enhancer action
Figure 19.10	Three of the major types of DNA-binding domains in transcription factors
Figure 19.11	Alternative RNA splicing
Figure 19.12	Degradation of a protein by a proteasome
Figure 19.13	Genetic changes that can turn proto-ocogenes into oncogenes
Figure 19.14	Signaling pathways that regulate cell growth (Layer 1)
Figure 19.14	Signaling pathways that regulate cell growth (Layer 2)
Figure 19.14	Signaling pathways that regulate cell growth (Layer 3)
Figure 19.15	A multi-step model for the development of colorectal cancer

Media for Instructors

Campbell Image Presentation Library

The Campbell Image Presentation Library CD-ROM set includes the following for your use:

- All art (available in pdf and jpeg or gif formats), photos (from the text and outside sources), and tables. Art images are also available without callouts. See the Visual Guide to the Image Library section at the end of this chapter for thumbnail versions of every image.
- A PowerPoint™ slide show of the art (with callouts), photos (both text and outside sources), and tables.
- The following QuickTime animations, adapted from student media activities (also available as Shockwave Flash .swf files):

  19-01-DNAPacking.mov

  19-08-RNAprocessing.mov

  19-09-TurningOnAGene.mov

  19-10-ControlOfTranslation.mov

  19-12-ProteinProcessing.mov

PowerPoint Lectures CD-ROM

The PowerPoint Lectures CD-ROM contains slides that integrate the art, photos, tables, and lecture outline from this chapter.

Campbell Biology Website (Instructor Resources)

See the insert in your copy of Campbell/Reece *Biology*, Sixth Edition, for instructions on how to access the Campbell Biology Website. The Instructor Resources section of the website includes the following:

- The art, photos, tables, PowerPoint slide shows, videos, and animations from the Campbell Image Presentation Library
- Suggested answers to the Lab Report questions from the Case Studies in the Process of Science
- The PowerPoint Lecture for this chapter
- Word files of the lecture outline for this chapter
- Photo links

Course Management Systems

The media content for this chapter is available in three course management systems: CourseCompass^{TM}, Blackboard, and WebCT. For more information, go to http://cms.aw.com. For the latest pdf instructions on how to use CourseCompass, go to **www.coursecompass.com**. In addition, a Syllabus Manager is offered on the Campbell *Biology* Website.

Media for Students

The Campbell Biology Website and CD-ROM include the following for your students:

- Objectives
- Chapter Review (Summary, Self-Quiz, and Essay Questions from the book; Word Roots; Key Terms linked to the Glossary)
- Activities (see list below)
- Case Studies in the Process of Science (see list below)
- Quizzes (Pre-test, Activities Quiz, Chapter Quiz, Essay Questions)
- Web Links
- News and References
- Art and videos from the Campbell Image Presentation Library
- The Campbell *Biology* Interviews (from all editions)
- Glossary with audio pronunciations
- Syllabus Manager

Student Media Activities and Case Studies in The Process of Science

Web/CD Activity 19A: *DNA Packing*

Web/CD Activity 19B: *Gene Amplification, Loss, and Rearrangement*

Web/CD Activity 19C: *Overview: Control of Gene Expression*

Web/CD Activity 19D: *Control of Transcription*

Web/CD Case Study in the Process of Science: *How Do You Design a Gene Expression System?*

Web/CD Activity 19E: *Post-Transcriptional Control Mechanisms*

Web/CD Activity 19F: *Review: Control of Gene Expression*

Web/CD Activity 19G: *Causes of Cancer*

Objectives

Eukaryotic Chromatin Structure

1. Compare the structure and organization of prokaryotic and eukaryotic genomes.
2. Describe the current model for progressive levels of DNA packing.
3. Explain how histones influence folding in eukaryotic DNA.
4. Distinguish between heterochromatin and euchromatin.

Genome Organization at the DNA Level

5. Describe the structure and functions of the portions of eukaryotic DNA that do not encode protein or RNA.
6. Define and distinguish between the three types of satellite DNA.
7. Explain how tandemly repeated nucleotide triplets can lead to human disease.
8. Describe the role of telomeres and centromeres.
9. Describe the structure and proportion of interspersed repetitive DNA.
10. Using the genes for rRNA as an example, explain how multigene families of identical genes can be advantageous for a cell.
11. Using alpha-globin and beta-globin genes as examples, describe how multigene families of nonidentical genes probably evolve; include the role of transposition in your description.
12. Define pseudogenes.
13. Describe the process and significance of gene amplification.
14. Define and explain the significance of transposons and retrotransposons.
15. Explain how genetic recombination during development results in millions of different kinds of antibody molecules.

The Control of Gene Expression

16. Define differentiation and describe at what level gene expression is generally controlled.

17. Explain how DNA methylation and histone acetylation affects chromatin structure and the regulation of transcription.

18. Describe the eukaryotic processing of pre-mRNA.

19. Define control elements and explain how they influence transcription.

20. Explain the potential role that promoters, enhancers, activators, and repressors play in transcriptional control.

21. Describe the two basic structural domains of transcription factors.

22. Explain how eukaryotic genes can be coordinately expressed and give some examples of coordinate gene expression in eukaryotes.

23. Describe the process of alternative splicing.

24. Describe factors that influence the lifetime of mRNA in the cytoplasm. Compare the longevity of mRNA in prokaryotes and eukaryotes.

25. Explain how gene expression may be controlled at the translational and post-translational level.

The Molecular Biology of Cancer

26. Distinguish between proto-oncogenes and oncogenes. Describe three genetic changes that can convert proto-oncogenes to oncogenes.

27. Explain how mutations in tumor-suppressor genes can contribute to cancer.

28. Explain how excessive cell division can result from mutations in the *ras* oncogenes.

29. Explain why a mutation knocking out the p53 gene can lead to excessive cell growth and cancer. Describe three ways that p53 prevents a cell from passing on mutations caused by DNA damage.

30. Describe the set of genetic factors typically associated with the development of cancer.

31. Explain how viruses can cause cancer. Describe several examples.

32. Explain how inherited cancer alleles can lead to a predisposition to certain cancers.

Key Terms

histone	gene amplification	DNA-binding domain
nucleosome	retrotransposons	alternative RNA
heterochromatin	immunoglobulins	splicing
euchromatin ("true	cellular differentiation	proteasome
chromatin")	DNA methylation	oncogene
repetitive DNA	genomic imprinting	proto-oncogene
satellite DNA	histone acetylation	tumor-suppressor gene
Alu element	control elements	ras gene
multigene family	enhancer	*p53* gene
pseudogenes	activator	

Word Roots

eu- = true (*euchromatin*: the more open, unraveled form of eukaryotic chromatin)

hetero- = different (*heterochromatin*: nontranscribed eukaryotic chromatin that is so highly compacted that it is visible with a light microscope during interphase)

immuno- = safe, free (*immunoglobulin*: one of the class of proteins comprising the antibodies)

nucleo- = the nucleus; **-soma** = body (*nucleosome*: the basic beadlike unit of DNA packaging in eukaryotes)

proto- = first, original; **onco-** = tumor (*proto-oncogene*: a normal cellular gene corresponding to an oncogene)

pseudo- = false (*pseudogenes*: DNA segments very similar to real genes but which do not yield functional products)

retro- = backward (*retrotransposons*: transposable elements that move within a genome by means of an RNA intermediate, a transcript of the retrotransposon DNA)

References

Becker, W. M., L. J. Kleinsmith, and J. Hardin. *The World of the Cell.* 4th ed. San Francisco, California: Benjamin Cummings, 2000.

Brent, R. "Genomic Biology." *Cell*, January 2000.

Hanahan, D., and R. A. Weinberg. "The Hallmarks of Cancer." *Cell*, January 2000.

Karp, G. *Cell and Molecular Biology: Concepts and Experiments.* 3rd ed. New York: John Wiley & Sons, Inc., 2002.

Visual Guide to the Image Library

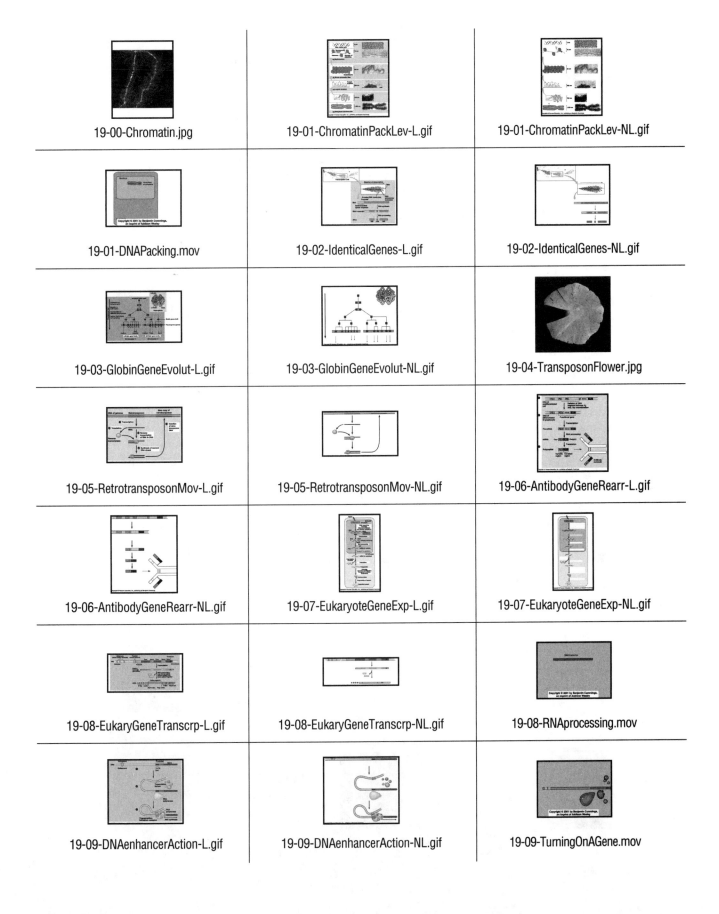

19-00-Chromatin.jpg

19-01-ChromatinPackLev-L.gif

19-01-ChromatinPackLev-NL.gif

19-01-DNAPacking.mov

19-02-IdenticalGenes-L.gif

19-02-IdenticalGenes-NL.gif

19-03-GlobinGeneEvolut-L.gif

19-03-GlobinGeneEvolut-NL.gif

19-04-TransposonFlower.jpg

19-05-RetrotransposonMov-L.gif

19-05-RetrotransposonMov-NL.gif

19-06-AntibodyGeneRearr-L.gif

19-06-AntibodyGeneRearr-NL.gif

19-07-EukaryoteGeneExp-L.gif

19-07-EukaryoteGeneExp-NL.gif

19-08-EukaryGeneTranscrp-L.gif

19-08-EukaryGeneTranscrp-NL.gif

19-08-RNAprocessing.mov

19-09-DNAenhancerAction-L.gif

19-09-DNAenhancerAction-NL.gif

19-09-TurningOnAGene.mov

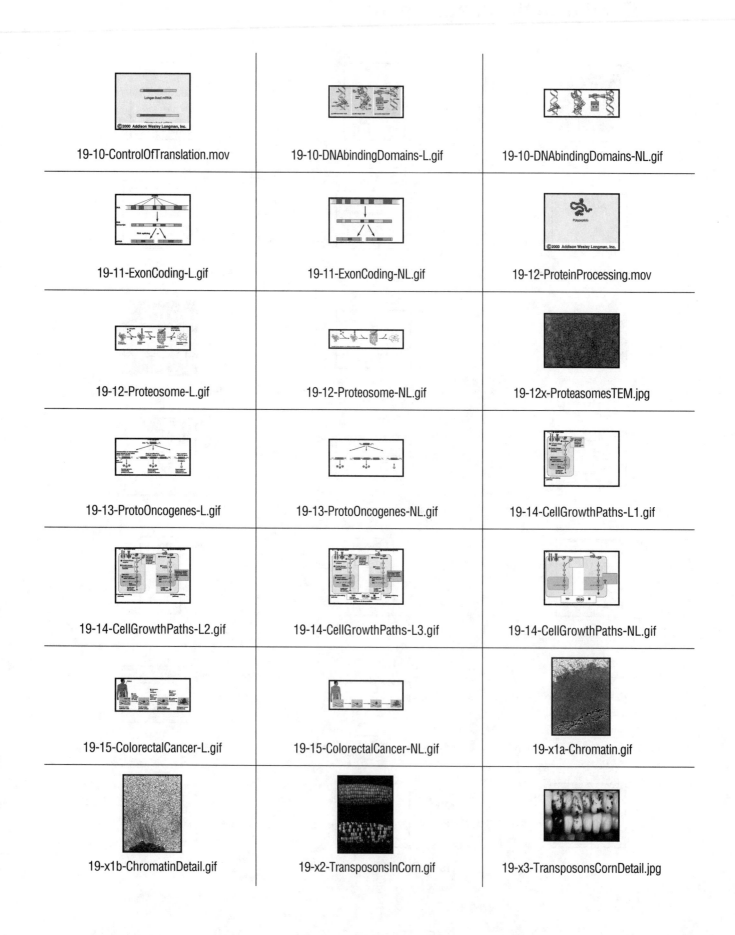

19-10-ControlOfTranslation.mov

19-10-DNAbindingDomains-L.gif

19-10-DNAbindingDomains-NL.gif

19-11-ExonCoding-L.gif

19-11-ExonCoding-NL.gif

19-12-ProteinProcessing.mov

19-12-Proteosome-L.gif

19-12-Proteosome-NL.gif

19-12x-ProteasomesTEM.jpg

19-13-ProtoOncogenes-L.gif

19-13-ProtoOncogenes-NL.gif

19-14-CellGrowthPaths-L1.gif

19-14-CellGrowthPaths-L2.gif

19-14-CellGrowthPaths-L3.gif

19-14-CellGrowthPaths-NL.gif

19-15-ColorectalCancer-L.gif

19-15-ColorectalCancer-NL.gif

19-x1a-Chromatin.gif

19-x1b-ChromatinDetail.gif

19-x2-TransposonsInCorn.gif

19-x3-TransposonsCornDetail.jpg

Table 19.1 Types of Repetitive DNA
Tandemly Repetitive DNA (Satellite DNA)
Repeated units at a site are usually identical
Proportion of mammalian DNA: 10–15%
Length of each repeated unit: 1–10 base pairs
Total length of repetitive DNA per site, in base pairs:
Regular satellite DNA: 100,000–10 million
Minisatellite DNA: 100–100,000
Microsatellite DNA: 10–100
Interspersed Repetitive DNA
"Copies" are very similar but not identical
Proportion of mammalian DNA: 25–40%
Length of each repeated unit: 100–10,000 base pairs
Number of repetitions per genome: 10–1 million

19T-01-RepetitiveDNA-L.gif

CHAPTER 20

DNA Technology and Genomics

Chapter Outline

DNA Cloning

DNA technology makes it possible to clone genes for basic research and commercial applications: *an overview*

Restriction enzymes are used to make recombinant DNA: *the process of science*

Genes can be cloned in recombinant DNA vectors: *a closer look*

Cloned genes are stored in DNA libraries

The polymerase chain reaction (PCR) clones DNA entirely *in vitro*

DNA Analysis and Genomics

Restriction fragment analysis detects DNA differences that affect restriction sites

Entire genomes can be mapped at the DNA level: *the process of science*

Genome sequences provide clues to important biological questions

Practical Applications of DNA Technology

DNA technology is reshaping medicine and the pharmaceutical industry

DNA technology offers forensic, environmental, and agricultural applications

DNA technology raises important safety and ethical questions

Transparency Acetates

The Transparency Acetates for *Biology*, Sixth Edition, include the following images:

Figure 20.1	An overview of how bacterial plasmids are used to clone genes
Figure 20.2	Using a restriction enzyme and DNA ligase to make recombinant DNA
Figure 20.3	Cloning a human gene in a bacterial plasmid: a closer look (Layer 1)
Figure 20.3	Cloning a human gene in a bacterial plasmid: a closer look (Layer 2)
Figure 20.3	Cloning a human gene in a bacterial plasmid: a closer look (Layer 3)

Figure 20.4   Using a nucleic acid probe to identify a cloned gene

Figure 20.5   Making complementary DNA (cDNA) for a eukaryotic gene

Figure 20.6   Genomic libraries

Figure 20.7   The polymerase chain on reaction (PCR)

Figure 20.8   Gel electrophoresis of macromolecules

Figure 20.9   Using restriction fragment patterns to distinguish DNA from different alleles

Figure 20.10   Restriction fragment analysis by Southern blotting

Figure 20.11   Chromosome walking

Figure 20.12   Sequencing of DNA by the Sanger method (Layer 1)

Figure 20.12   Sequencing of DNA by the Sanger method (Layer 2)

Figure 20.12   Sequencing of DNA by the Sanger method (Layer 3)

Figure 20.12   Sequencing of DNA by the Sanger method (Layer 4)

Figure 20.13   Alternative strategies for sequencing an entire genome

Table 20.1   Genome Sizes and Numbers of Genes

Figure 20.14a   DNA microarray assay for gene expression

Figure 20.15   RFLP makers close to a gene

Figure 20.16   One type of gene therapy procedure

Figure 20.17   DNA fingerprints from a murder case

Figure 20.19   Using the Ti plasmid as a vector for genetic engineering in plants

---

Media for Instructors

Campbell Image Presentation Library

The Campbell Image Presentation Library CD-ROM set includes the following for your use:

- All art (available in pdf and jpeg or gif formats), photos (from the text and outside sources), and tables. Art images are also available without callouts. See the Visual Guide to the Image Library section at the end of this chapter for thumbnail versions of every image.

- A PowerPoint™ slide show of the art (with callouts), photos (both text and outside sources), and tables.

- The following video clip:

    20-14-ScientistsWorking-B.mov   Scientists performing steps in DNA technology

- The following QuickTime animations, adapted from student media activities (also available as Shockwave Flash .swf files):

    20-02-RestrictionEnzymes.mov

    20-03-CloningAGene.mov

PowerPoint Lectures CD-ROM

The PowerPoint Lectures CD-ROM contains slides that integrate the art, photos, tables, and lecture outline from this chapter.

Campbell Biology Website (Instructor Resources)

See the insert in your copy of Campbell/Reece *Biology*, Sixth Edition, for instructions on how to access the Campbell Biology Website. The Instructor Resources section of the website includes the following:

- The art, photos, tables, PowerPoint slide shows, videos, and animations from the Campbell Image Presentation Library
- Suggested answers to the Lab Report questions from the Case Studies in the Process of Science
- The PowerPoint Lecture for this chapter
- Word files of the lecture outline for this chapter
- Photo links

Course Management Systems

The media content for this chapter is available in three course management systems: CourseCompass™, Blackboard, and WebCT. For more information, go to http://cms.aw.com. For the latest pdf instructions on how to use CourseCompass, go to **www.coursecompass.com**. In addition, a Syllabus Manager is offered on the Campbell Biology Website.

Media for Students

The Campbell Biology Website and CD-ROM include the following for your students:

- Objectives
- Chapter Review (Summary, Self-Quiz, and Essay Questions from the book; Word Roots; Key Terms linked to the Glossary)
- Activities (see list below)
- Case Studies in the Process of Science (see list below)
- Quizzes (Pre-test, Activities Quiz, Chapter Quiz, Essay Questions)
- Web Links
- News and References
- Art and videos from the Campbell Image Presentation Library
- The Campbell *Biology* Interviews (from all editions)
- Glossary with audio pronunciations
- Syllabus Manager

Student Media Activities and Case Studies in The Process of Science

Web/CD Activity 20A: *Applications of DNA Technology*

Web/CD Activity 20B: *Restriction Enzymes*

Web/CD Activity 20C: *Cloning a Gene in Bacteria*

Web/CD Case Study in the Process of Science: *How Can Antibiotic-Resistant Plasmids Transform* E.coli?

Web/CD Activity 20D: *Gel Electrophoresis of DNA*

Web/CD Activity 20E: *Analyzing DNA Fragments Using Gel Electrophoresis*

Web/CD Case Study in the Process of Science: *How Can Gel Electrophoresis Be Used to Analyze DNA?*

Web/CD Activity 20F: *The Human Genome Project: Genes on Human Chromosome 17*

Web/CD Activity 20G: *DNA Fingerprinting*

Web/CD Activity 20H: Making Decisions About DNA Technology: Golden Rice

Objectives

DNA Cloning

1. Explain how advances in recombinant DNA technology have helped scientists study the eukaryotic genome.

2. Describe the natural function of restriction enzymes.

3. Explain how the creation of sticky ends by restriction enzymes is useful in producing a recombinant DNA molecule.

4. Outline the procedures for cloning a eukaryotic gene in a bacterial plasmid.

5. Describe the role of an expression vector.

6. Explain how eukaryotic genes are cloned to avoid the problems associated with introns.

7. Describe two advantages of using yeast cells instead of bacteria as hosts for cloning or expressing eukaryotic genes.

8. Describe three techniques to aggressively introduce recombinant DNA into eukaryotic cells.

9. Define and distinguish between genomic libraries using plasmids, phages, and cDNA.

10. Describe the polymerase chain reaction (PCR) and explain the advantages and limitations of this procedure.

DNA Analysis and Genomics

11. Explain how gel electrophoresis is used to analyze nucleic acids and proteins and to distinguish between two alleles of a gene.

12. Describe the process of nucleic acid hybridization.

13. Describe the Southern blotting procedure and explain how it can be used to detect and analyze instances of restriction fragment length polymorphism (RFLP).

14. Explain how RFLP analysis facilitated the process of genomic mapping.

15. List the goals of the Human Genome Project.

16. Explain how linkage mapping, physical mapping, and DNA sequencing each contributed to the genome mapping project.

17. Describe the alternate approach to whole-genome sequencing pursued by J. Craig Venter and the Celera Genomics company. Describe the advantages and disadvantages of public and private efforts.

18. Describe the surprising results of the Human Genome Project.

19. Explain how the vertebrate genome, including that of humans, generates greater diversity than the genomes of invertebrate organisms.

20. Describe what we have learned by comparing the human genome to that of other organisms.

21. Explain the purposes of gene expression studies. Describe the use of DNA microarray assays and explain how they facilitate such studies.

22. Explain how in vitro mutagenesis and RNA interference help to discover the functions of some genes.

23. Define and compare the fields of proteomics and genomics.

24. Explain the significance of single nucleotide polymorphisms in the study of the human genome.

Practical Applications of DNA Technology

25. Describe how DNA technology can have medical applications in such areas as the diagnosis of genetic disease, the development of gene therapy, vaccine production, and the development of pharmaceutical products.

26. Explain how DNA technology is used in the forensic sciences.

27. Describe how gene manipulation has practical applications for environmental and agricultural work.

28. Describe how plant genes can be manipulated using the Ti plasmid carried by Agrobacterium as a vector.

29. Explain how DNA technology can be used to improve the nutritional value of crops and to develop plants that can produce pharmaceutical products.

30. Describe the safety and ethical questions related to recombinant DNA studies and the biotechnology industry.

Key Terms

recombinant DNA
genetic engineering
biotechnology
gene cloning
restriction enzyme
restriction site
restriction fragments
sticky end
DNA ligase
cloning vector
nucleic acid hybridization
nucleic acid probe
denaturation
expression vector
complementary DNA (cDNA)
yeast artificial chromosomes (YACs)

electroporation
genomic library
cDNA library
polymerase chain reaction (PCR)
genomics
gel electrophoresis
Southern blotting
restriction fragment length polymorphisms (RFLPs)
Human Genome Project
chromosome walking
bacterial artificial chomosome (BAC)
DNA microarray assays

in vitro mutagenesis
RNA interference (RNAi)
proteomics
bioinformatics
single nucleotide polymorphisms (SNPs)
gene therapy
DNA fingerprint
simple tandem repeats (STRs)
transgenic organisms
Ti plasmid
genetically modified (GM) organisms

Word Roots

liga- = bound, tied (*DNA ligase*: a linking enzyme essential for DNA replication)

electro- = electricity (*electroporation*: a technique to introduce recombinant DNA into cells by applying a brief electrical pulse to a solution containing cells)

muta- = change; **-genesis** = origin, birth (*in vitro mutagenesis*: a technique to discover the function of a gene by introducing specific changes into the sequence of a cloned gene, reinserting the mutated gene into a cell, and studying the phenotype of the mutant)

poly- = many; **morph-** = form (*Single nucleotide polymorphisms*: one base-pair variations in the genome sequence)

References

Brent, R. "Genomic Biology." *Cell,* January 2000.
Campbell, M. *Biochemistry.* 3rd ed. Orlando, Florida: Harcourt, Inc, 1999.
Ezzell, C. "The Business of the Human Genome." *Scientific American,* July 2000.

Visual Guide to the Image Library

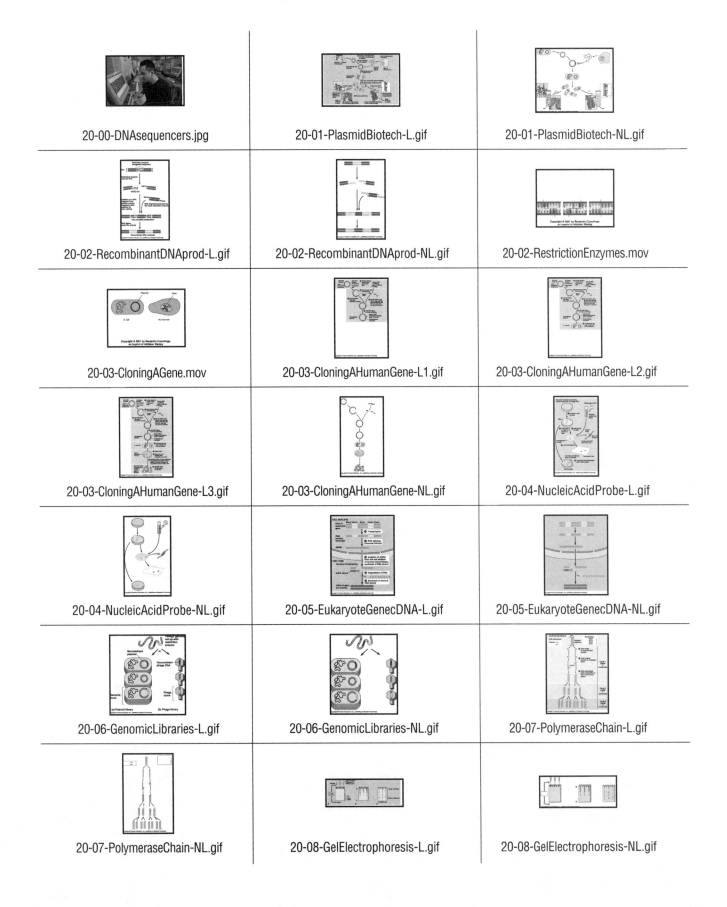

20-00-DNAsequencers.jpg

20-01-PlasmidBiotech-L.gif

20-01-PlasmidBiotech-NL.gif

20-02-RecombinantDNAprod-L.gif

20-02-RecombinantDNAprod-NL.gif

20-02-RestrictionEnzymes.mov

20-03-CloningAGene.mov

20-03-CloningAHumanGene-L1.gif

20-03-CloningAHumanGene-L2.gif

20-03-CloningAHumanGene-L3.gif

20-03-CloningAHumanGene-NL.gif

20-04-NucleicAcidProbe-L.gif

20-04-NucleicAcidProbe-NL.gif

20-05-EukaryoteGenecDNA-L.gif

20-05-EukaryoteGenecDNA-NL.gif

20-06-GenomicLibraries-L.gif

20-06-GenomicLibraries-NL.gif

20-07-PolymeraseChain-L.gif

20-07-PolymeraseChain-NL.gif

20-08-GelElectrophoresis-L.gif

20-08-GelElectrophoresis-NL.gif

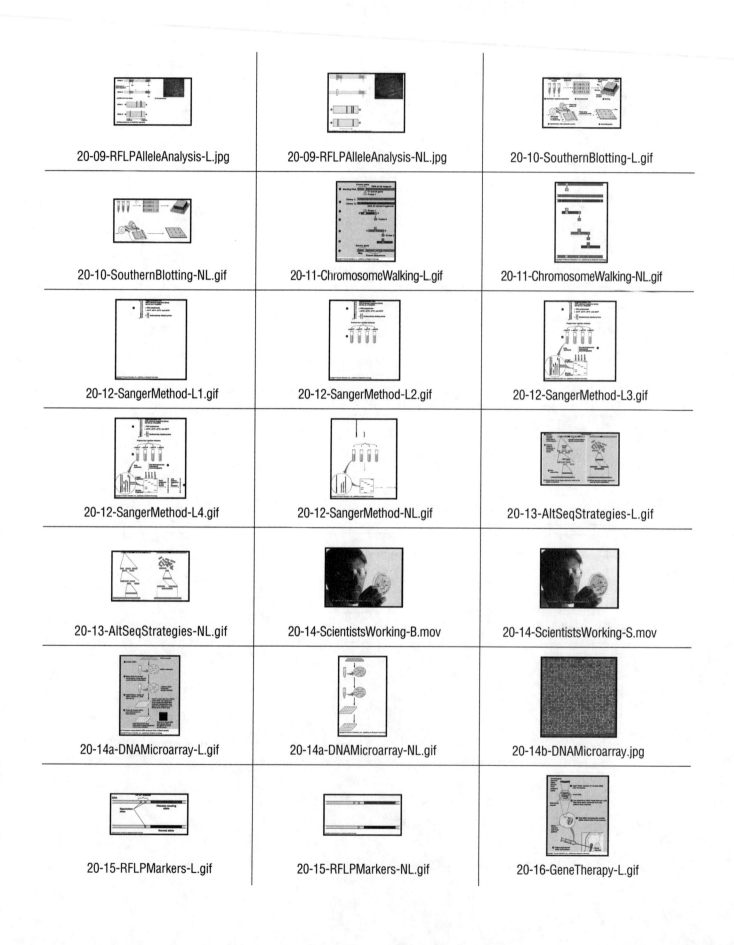

20-09-RFLPAlleleAnalysis-L.jpg

20-09-RFLPAlleleAnalysis-NL.jpg

20-10-SouthernBlotting-L.gif

20-10-SouthernBlotting-NL.gif

20-11-ChromosomeWalking-L.gif

20-11-ChromosomeWalking-NL.gif

20-12-SangerMethod-L1.gif

20-12-SangerMethod-L2.gif

20-12-SangerMethod-L3.gif

20-12-SangerMethod-L4.gif

20-12-SangerMethod-NL.gif

20-13-AltSeqStrategies-L.gif

20-13-AltSeqStrategies-NL.gif

20-14-ScientistsWorking-B.mov

20-14-ScientistsWorking-S.mov

20-14a-DNAMicroarray-L.gif

20-14a-DNAMicroarray-NL.gif

20-14b-DNAMicroarray.jpg

20-15-RFLPMarkers-L.gif

20-15-RFLPMarkers-NL.gif

20-16-GeneTherapy-L.gif

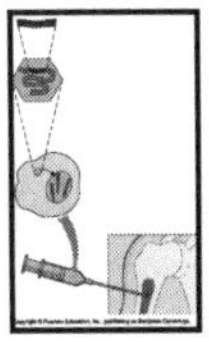

20-16-GeneTherapy-NL.gif

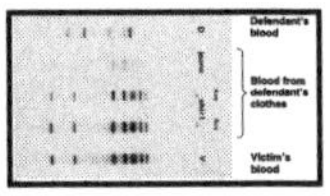

20-17-DNAFingerprints-L.gif

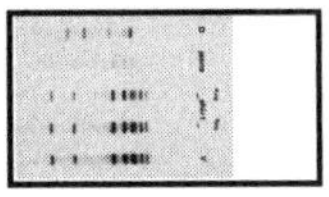

20-17-DNAFingerprints-NL.gif

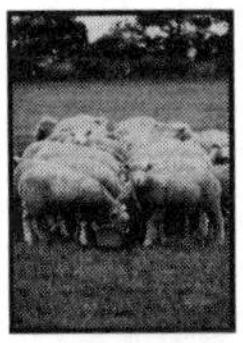

20-18-PharmAnimals.jpg

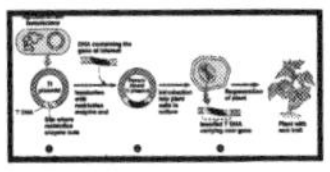

20-19-TiPlasmidVector-L.gif

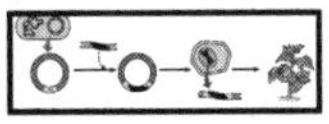

20-19-TiPlasmidVector-NL.gif

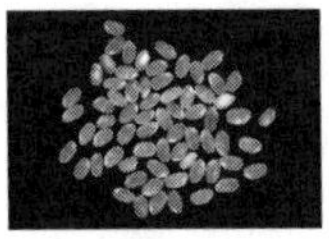

20-20-GoldenRice.jpg

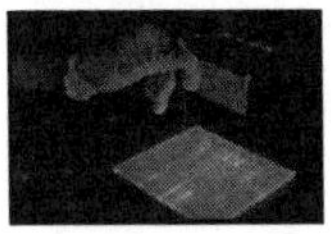

20-x1a-DNABandPattern.jpg

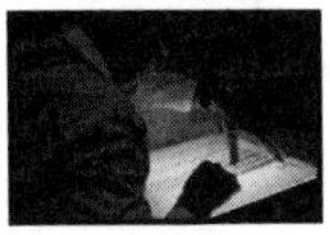

20-x1b-DNAAnalysisInCDCLab.jpg

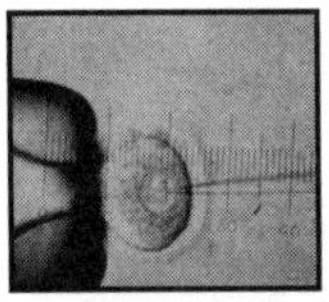

20-x2-InjectingDNA.jpg

Table 20.1 Genome Sizes and Numbers of Genes

Organism	Genome Size	Estimated Number of Genes	Genes per Mb*
H. influenzae (bacterium)	1.8 Mb*	1,700	950
S. cerevisiae (yeast)	12 Mb	6,000	500
C. elegans (nematode)	97 Mb	19,000	200
A. thaliana (plant)	100 Mb	25,000	200
D. melanogaster (fruit fly)	180 Mb	13,000	100
H. sapiens (human)	3,200 Mb	30,000–40,000	10

*Mb = million base pairs

20T-01-GenomeSizesNumbers-L.gif

CHAPTER 21

The Genetic Basis of Development

Chapter Outline

From Single Cell to Multicellular Organism

Embryonic development involves cell division, cell differentiation, and morphogenesis

Researchers study development in model organisms to identify general principles: *the process of science*

Differential Gene Expression

Different types of cells in an organism have the same DNA: *the process of science*

Different cell types make different proteins, usually as a result of transcriptional regulation

Transcriptional regulation is directed by maternal molecules in the cytoplasm and signals from other cells

Genetic and Cellular Mechanisms of Pattern Formation

Genetic analysis of *Drosophila* reveals how genes control development: *an overview*

Gradients of maternal molecules in the early embryo control axis formation

A cascade of gene activations sets up the segmentation pattern in *Drosophila: a closer look*

Homeotic genes direct the identity of body parts

Homeobox genes have been highly conserved in evolution

Neighboring cells instruct other cells to form particular

structures: cell signaling and induction in the nematode

Plant development depends on cell signaling and transcriptional regulation: *the process of science*

Transparency Acetates

The Transparency Acetates for *Biology,* Sixth Edition, include the following images:

Figure 21.2 Some key stages of development in animals and plants

Figure 21.4 Cell lineage in *C. elegans*

Media for Instructors

Campbell Image Presentation Library

The Campbell Image Presentation Library CD-ROM set includes the following for your use:

- All art (available in pdf and jpeg or gif formats), photos (from the text and outside sources), and tables. Art images are also available without callouts. See the Visual Guide to the Image Library section at the end of this chapter for thumbnail versions of every image.
- A PowerPoint™ slide show of the art (with callouts), photos (both text and outside sources), and tables.
- The following video clips:

  21-04-CElegansCrawl-B.mov   Close-up video of *C. elegans* crawling

  21-04-CElegansEmbryo-B.mov   Time-lapse *C. elegans* embryo development

- The following QuickTime animation, adapted from student media activities (also available as a Shockwave Flash .swf file):

  21-11-HeadTailAxisFruitFly.mov

PowerPoint Lectures CD-ROM

The PowerPoint Lectures CD-ROM contains slides that integrate the art, photos, tables, and lecture outline from this chapter.

Campbell Biology Website (Instructor Resources)

See the insert in your copy of Campbell/Reece *Biology*, Sixth Edition, for instructions on how to access the Campbell Biology Website. The Instructor Resources section of the website includes the following:

- The art, photos, tables, PowerPoint slide shows, videos, and animations from the Campbell Image Presentation Library
- Suggested answers to the Lab Report questions from the Case Studies in the Process of Science
- The PowerPoint Lecture for this chapter
- Word files of the lecture outline for this chapter
- Photo links

Course Management Systems

The media content for this chapter is available in three course management systems: CourseCompass™, Blackboard, and WebCT. For more information, go to http://cms.aw.com. For the latest pdf instructions on how to use CourseCompass, go to **www.coursecompass.com**. In addition, a Syllabus Manager is offered on the Campbell Biology Website.

Media for Students

The Campbell Biology Website and CD-ROM include the following for your students:

- Objectives
- Chapter Review (Summary, Self-Quiz, and Essay Questions from the book; Word Roots; Key Terms linked to the Glossary)
- Activities (see list below)
- Case Studies in the Process of Science (see list below)
- Quizzes (Pre-test, Activities Quiz, Chapter Quiz, Essay Questions)
- Web Links
- News and References
- Art and videos from the Campbell Image Presentation Library
- The Campbell *Biology* Interviews (from all editions)
- Glossary with audio pronunciations
- Syllabus Manager

Student Media Activities and Case Studies in The Process of Science

Web/CD Activity 21A: C. elegans *Development Video*

Web/CD Activity 21B: *Adult* C. elegans *Video*

Web/CD Activity 21C: *Signal-Transduction Pathways*

Web/CD Activity 21D: *Role of* bicoid *Gene in* Drosophila *Development*

Web/CD Case Study in the Process of Science: *How Do* bicoid *Mutations Alter Development?*

Objectives

From Single Cell to Multicellular Organism

1. Distinguish between the patterns of morphogenesis in plants and in animals.

2. List the animals used as models for developmental biology research and provide a rationale for their choice.

Differential Gene Expression

3. Describe how genomic equivalence was determined for plants and animals.

4. Describe what kinds of changes occur to the genome during differentiation.

5. Describe the general process by which the ewe Dolly and the first mice were cloned.

6. Describe the two important properties of stem cells. Explain their significance to medicine.

7. Describe the molecular basis of determination.

8. Describe the two sources of information that instruct a cell to express genes at the appropriate time.

Genetic and Cellular Mechanisms of Pattern Formation

9. Describe how *Drosophila* were used to explain the basic aspects of pattern formation (axis formation and segmentation).

10. Describe how homeotic genes serve to identify parts of the developing organism.

11. Provide evidence of the conservation of homeobox patterns.

12. Describe how the study of nematodes contributed to the general understanding of embryonic formation.

13. Describe how apoptosis functions in normal and abnormal development.

14. Describe how the study of tomatoes has contributed to the understanding of flower development.

15. Describe how the study of *Arabidopsis* has contributed to the understanding of organ identity in plants.

Key Terms

differentiation	cytoplasmic	gap genes
morphogenesis	determinants	pair-rule genes
apical meristem	induction	segment-polarity genes
model organism	pattern formation	homeotic genes
cell lineage	positional information	homeobox
cloning	embryonic lethals	apoptosis
clone	maternal effect genes	chimeras
totipotent	egg-polarity genes	organ identity gene
stem cell	morphogens	
determination	segmentation genes	

Word Roots

apic- = tip (*apical meristem*: embryonic plant tissue in the tips of roots and in the buds of shoots that supplies cells for the plant to grow in length)

morph- = form; **-gen** = produce (*morphogens*: a substance that provides positional information in the form of a concentration gradient along an embryonic axis)

toti- = all; **-potent** = powerful (*totipotent*: the ability of a cell to form all parts of the mature organism)

References

Futuyma, D. J. *Evolutionary Biology*, Sunderland, Massachusetts: Sinauer Associates, Inc. 1998.

Gilbert, S. F. *Developmental Biology*. 6th ed. Sunderland, Massachusetts: Sinauer Associates, Inc. 2000.

Visual Guide to the Image Library

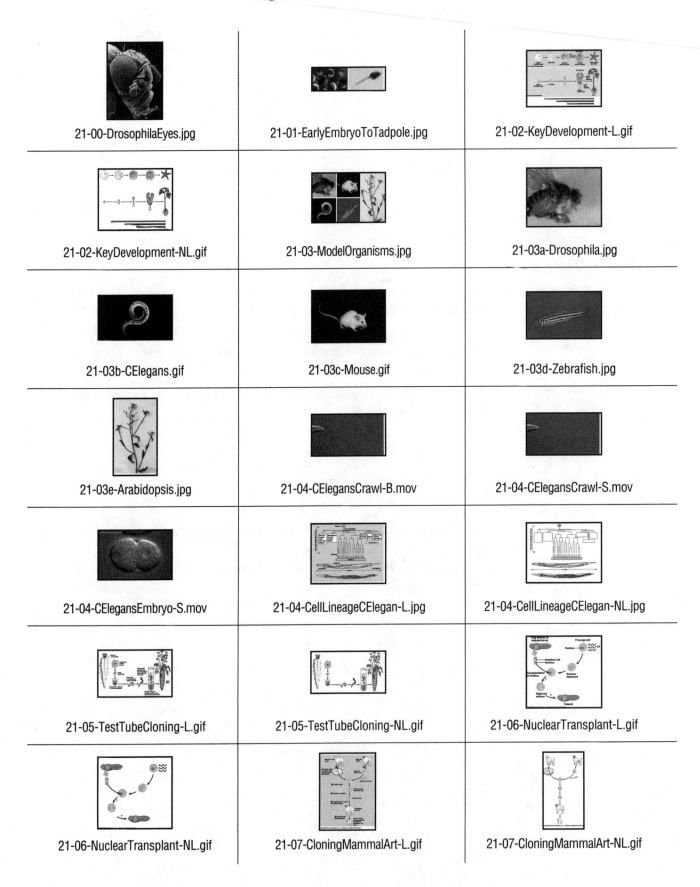

21-00-DrosophilaEyes.jpg

21-01-EarlyEmbryoToTadpole.jpg

21-02-KeyDevelopment-L.gif

21-02-KeyDevelopment-NL.gif

21-03-ModelOrganisms.jpg

21-03a-Drosophila.jpg

21-03b-CElegans.gif

21-03c-Mouse.gif

21-03d-Zebrafish.jpg

21-03e-Arabidopsis.jpg

21-04-CElegansCrawl-B.mov

21-04-CElegansCrawl-S.mov

21-04-CElegansEmbryo-S.mov

21-04-CellLineageCElegan-L.jpg

21-04-CellLineageCElegan-NL.jpg

21-05-TestTubeCloning-L.gif

21-05-TestTubeCloning-NL.gif

21-06-NuclearTransplant-L.gif

21-06-NuclearTransplant-NL.gif

21-07-CloningMammalArt-L.gif

21-07-CloningMammalArt-NL.gif

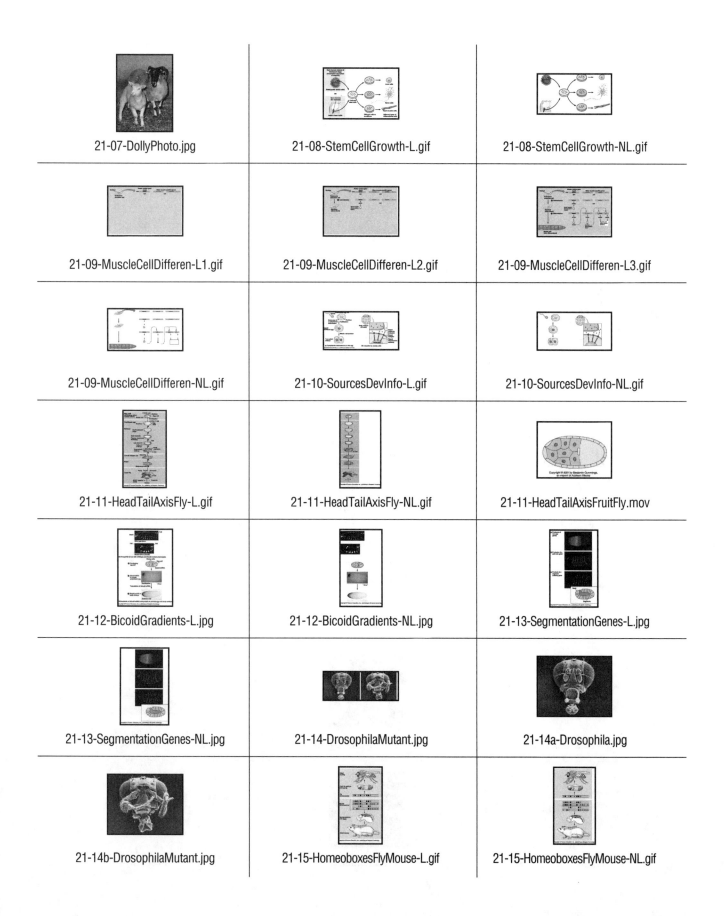

21-07-DollyPhoto.jpg

21-08-StemCellGrowth-L.gif

21-08-StemCellGrowth-NL.gif

21-09-MuscleCellDifferen-L1.gif

21-09-MuscleCellDifferen-L2.gif

21-09-MuscleCellDifferen-L3.gif

21-09-MuscleCellDifferen-NL.gif

21-10-SourcesDevInfo-L.gif

21-10-SourcesDevInfo-NL.gif

21-11-HeadTailAxisFly-L.gif

21-11-HeadTailAxisFly-NL.gif

21-11-HeadTailAxisFruitFly.mov

21-12-BicoidGradients-L.jpg

21-12-BicoidGradients-NL.jpg

21-13-SegmentationGenes-L.jpg

21-13-SegmentationGenes-NL.jpg

21-14-DrosophilaMutant.jpg

21-14a-Drosophila.jpg

21-14b-DrosophilaMutant.jpg

21-15-HomeoboxesFlyMouse-L.gif

21-15-HomeoboxesFlyMouse-NL.gif

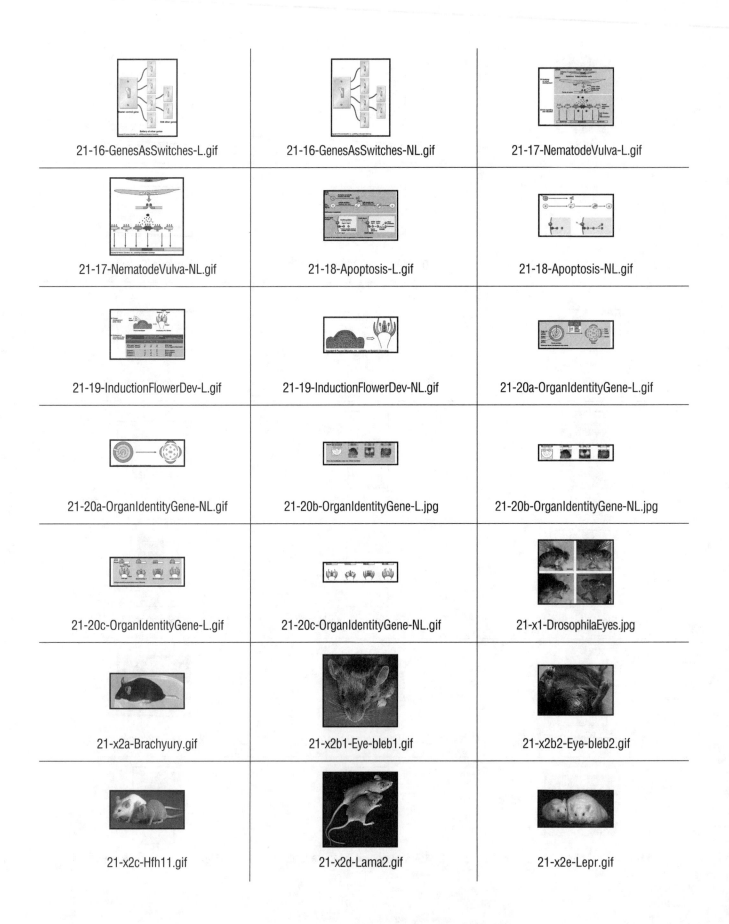

21-16-GenesAsSwitches-L.gif

21-16-GenesAsSwitches-NL.gif

21-17-NematodeVulva-L.gif

21-17-NematodeVulva-NL.gif

21-18-Apoptosis-L.gif

21-18-Apoptosis-NL.gif

21-19-InductionFlowerDev-L.gif

21-19-InductionFlowerDev-NL.gif

21-20a-OrganIdentityGene-L.gif

21-20a-OrganIdentityGene-NL.gif

21-20b-OrganIdentityGene-L.jpg

21-20b-OrganIdentityGene-NL.jpg

21-20c-OrganIdentityGene-L.gif

21-20c-OrganIdentityGene-NL.gif

21-x1-DrosophilaEyes.jpg

21-x2a-Brachyury.gif

21-x2b1-Eye-bleb1.gif

21-x2b2-Eye-bleb2.gif

21-x2c-Hfh11.gif

21-x2d-Lama2.gif

21-x2e-Lepr.gif

21-x2f1-Mgf.gif

21-x2f2-Pax3.gif

21-x2g-Otc.gif

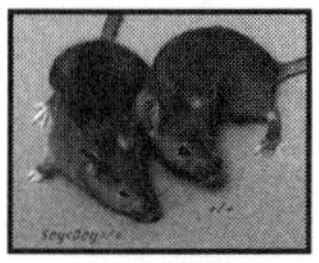

21-x2h-Pax6.gif

21-x2i-Pit1.gif

21-x2j-Pudgy.gif

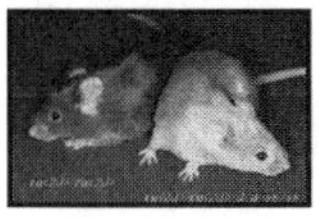

21-x2k-Ruby-eye.gif

21-x2l-Stargazer.gif

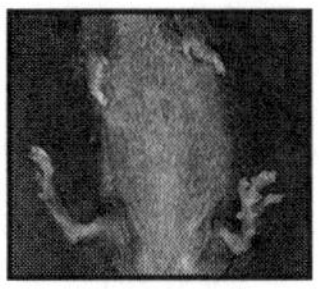

21-x2m1-Ulnaless1.gif

21-x2m2-Ulnaless2.gif

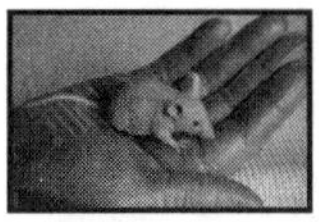

21-x3-NudeMouse.jpg

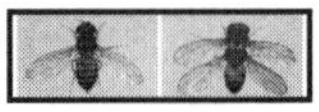

21-x4-DrosoNormalDoubleWing.jpg

21-x4a-DrosophilaNormalWing.jpg

21-x4b-DrosophilaDoubleWing.jpg

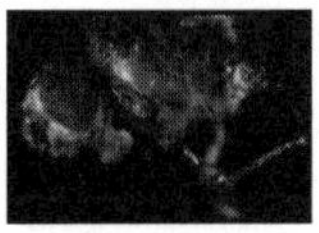

21-x5-DrosophilaEyeLM.jpg

CHAPTER 22

Descent with Modification: A Darwinian View of Life

Chapter Outline

The Historical Context for Evolutionary Theory

Western culture resisted evolutionary views of life

Theories of geological gradualism helped clear the path for evolutionary biologists

Lamarck placed fossils in an evolutionary context

The Darwinian Revolution

Field research helped Darwin frame his view of life: *the process of science*

The Origin of Species developed two main points: the occurrence of evolution and natural selection as its mechanism

Examples of natural selection provide evidence of evolution

Other evidence of evolution pervades biology

What is theoretical about the Darwinian view of life?

Transparency Acetates

The Transparency Acetates for *Biology*, Sixth Edition, include the following images:

Figure 22.1	The historical context of Darwin's life and ideas
Figure 22.3	Formation of sedimentary rock and deposition of fossils from different time periods
Figure 22.5	The Voyage of HMS *Beagle*
Figure 22.7	Descent with modification
Figure 22.12	Evolution of insecticide resistance in insect populations
Figure 22.13	Evolution of drug resistance in HIV
Figure 22.14	Homologous structures: anatomical signs of descent with modification

Media for Instructors

Campbell Image Presentation Library

The Campbell Image Presentation Library CD-ROM set includes the following for your use:

- All art (available in pdf and jpeg or gif formats), photos (from the text and outside sources), and tables. Art images are also available without callouts. See the Visual Guide to the Image Library section at the end of this chapter for thumbnail versions of every image.
- A PowerPoint™ slide show of the art (with callouts), photos (both text and outside sources), and tables.
- The following video clips:

22-04-GrandCanyon-B.mov	Grand Canyon fly over
22-05-GalapagosIslands-B.mov	Overview of Islands
22-05-MarineIguana-B.mov	Galapagos: Iguana
22-05-SeaLion-B.mov	Galapagos: Sea Lion
22-05-Tortoise-B.mov	Galapagos: Tortoise

See also

01-16-SeaHorses-B.mov	Sea Horses
51-19-SnakesWrestle-B.mov	Diamondback rattlesnakes

PowerPoint Lectures CD-ROM

The PowerPoint Lectures CD-ROM contains slides that integrate the art, photos, tables, and lecture outline from this chapter.

Campbell Biology Website (Instructor Resources)

See the insert in your copy of Campbell/Reece *Biology,* Sixth Edition, for instructions on how to access the Campbell Biology Website. The Instructor Resources section of the website includes the following:

- The art, photos, tables, PowerPoint slide shows, videos, and animations from the Campbell Image Presentation Library
- Suggested answers to the Lab Report questions from the Case Studies in the Process of Science
- The PowerPoint Lecture for this chapter
- Word files of the lecture outline for this chapter
- Photo links

Course Management Systems

The media content for this chapter is available in three course management systems: CourseCompass™, Blackboard, and WebCT. For more information, go to http://cms.aw.com. For the latest pdf instructions on how to use CourseCompass, go to **www.coursecompass.com**. In addition, a Syllabus Manager is offered on the Campbell Biology Website.

Media for Students

The Campbell Biology Website and CD-ROM include the following for your students:

- Objectives
- Chapter Review (Summary, Self-Quiz, and Essay Questions from the book; Word Roots; Key Terms linked to the Glossary)
- Activities (see list below)
- Case Studies in the Process of Science (see list below)
- Quizzes (Pre-test, Activities Quiz, Chapter Quiz, Essay Questions)
- Web Links
- News and References
- Art and videos from the Campbell Image Presentation Library
- The Campbell *Biology* Interviews (from all editions)
- Glossary with audio pronunciations
- Syllabus Manager

Student Media Activities and Case Studies in The Process of Science

Web/CD Activity 22A: *Grand Canyon Video*

Web/CD Activity 22B: *Darwin and the Galapagos Islands*

Web/CD Activity 22C: *Videos of the Galapagos Islands*

Biology Labs On-Line: *EvolutionLab*

Web/CD Activity 22D: *The Voyage of the* Beagle: *Darwin's Trip Around the World*

Web/CD Activity 22E: *Evolutionary Adaptation: Seahorse Camouflage Video*

Web/CD Case Study in the Process of Science: *How Do Environmental Changes Affect A Population?*

Web/CD Case Study in the Process of Science: *What Are the Patterns of Antibiotic Resistance?*

Web/CD Activity 22F: *Reconstructing Forelimbs*

Objectives

The Historical Context for Evolutionary Theory

1. State the two major points that Charles Darwin made in The Origin of Species concerning Earth's biota.

2. Compare and contrast Plato's philosophy of idealism and Aristotle's scala naturae.

3. Describe Carolus Linnaeus's contribution to Darwin's theory of evolution.

4. Describe Georges Cuvier's contribution to paleontology.

5. Explain how Cuvier and his followers used the concept of catastrophism to oppose the theory of evolution.

6. Explain how the principle of gradualism and Charles Lyell's theory of uniformitarianism influenced Darwin's ideas about evolution.

7. Describe Jean Baptiste Lamarck's model for how adaptations evolve. Explain the challenges to Lamarck's ideas with respect to current understandings of biology.

The Darwinian Revolution

8. Describe how Darwin used his observations from the voyage of the HMS Beagle to formulate and support his theory of evolution.

9. Describe how Lyell and Alfred Russel Wallace influenced Darwin.

10. Explain what Darwin meant by "descent with modification."

11. Explain what evidence convinced Darwin that species change over time.

12. Describe the three inferences Darwin made from his observations that led him to propose natural selection as a mechanism for evolutionary change.

13. Explain how an essay by the Rev. Thomas Malthus influenced Charles Darwin.

14. Distinguish between artificial selection and natural selection.

15. Explain why the population is the smallest unit that can evolve.

16. Using some contemporary examples, explain how natural selection results in evolutionary change.

17. Describe the research that suggested to David Reznick and John Endler that the life-history traits among guppy populations are correlated with the main type of predator in a stream pool.

18. Explain how homologous structures support Darwin's theory of natural selection. Explain how biogeography and the fossil record support the evolutionary deductions based on homologies.

19. Explain the problem with the statement that Darwinism is "just a theory." Distinguish between the scientific and colloquial use of the word "theory."

Key Terms

natural selection
evolutionary
  adaptation
evolution
natural theology
taxonomy
fossil

sedimentary rock
paleontology
catastrophism
gradualism
uniformitarianism
descent with
  modification

artificial selection
homology
homologous structures
vestigial organs
biogeography
endemic

Word Roots

bio- = life; **geo-** the Earth (*biogeography*: the study of the past and present distribution of species)

end- = within (*endemic*: a type of species that is found only in one region and nowhere else in the world.)

homo- = like, resembling (*homology*: Similarity in characteristics resulting from a shared ancestry)

paleo- = ancient (*paleontology*: the scientific study of fossils)

taxo- = arrange (*taxonomy*: the branch of biology concerned with naming and classifying the diverse forms of life)

vestigi- = trace (*vestigial organs*: structures of marginal, if any, importance to an organism; they are historical remnants of structures that had important functions in ancestors)

References

Futuyma, D. J. *Evolutionary Biology*, Sunderland, Massachusetts, Sinaur Associates, Inc. 1998.

Mayr, E. *The Growth of Biological Thought: Diversity, Evolution and Inheritance.* Cambridge, Massachusetts: Harvard University Press, 1982. This is an excellent reference for historical perspective and could be a useful companion to the text for supplementing lecture material on many topics.

Jones, S. Darwin's Ghost: The Origin of Species Updated. New York: Random House, 2000.

Visual Guide to the Image Library

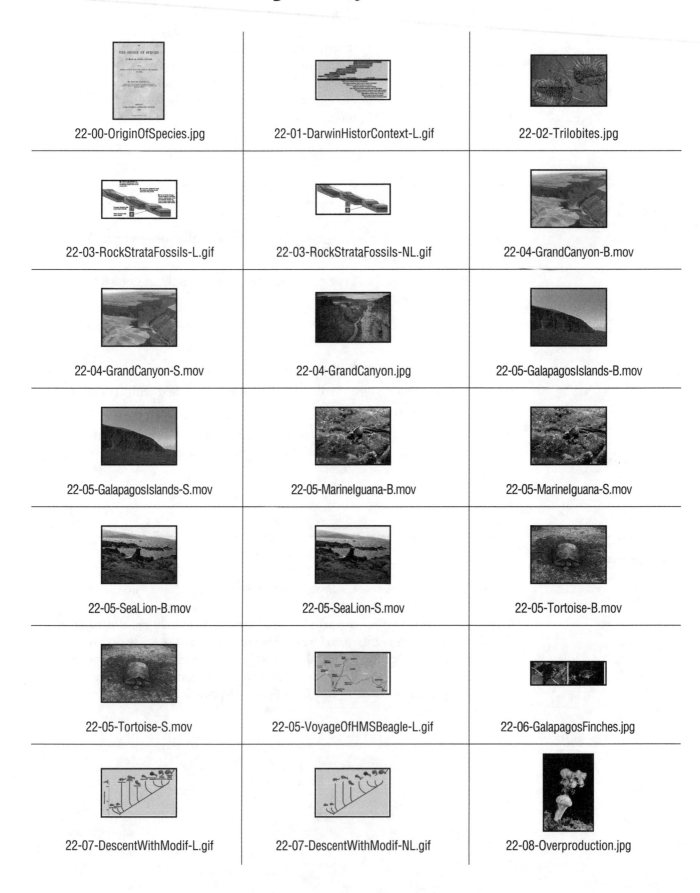

22-00-OriginOfSpecies.jpg

22-01-DarwinHistorContext-L.gif

22-02-Trilobites.jpg

22-03-RockStrataFossils-L.gif

22-03-RockStrataFossils-NL.gif

22-04-GrandCanyon-B.mov

22-04-GrandCanyon-S.mov

22-04-GrandCanyon.jpg

22-05-GalapagosIslands-B.mov

22-05-GalapagosIslands-S.mov

22-05-MarineIguana-B.mov

22-05-MarineIguana-S.mov

22-05-SeaLion-B.mov

22-05-SeaLion-S.mov

22-05-Tortoise-B.mov

22-05-Tortoise-S.mov

22-05-VoyageOfHMSBeagle-L.gif

22-06-GalapagosFinches.jpg

22-07-DescentWithModif-L.gif

22-07-DescentWithModif-NL.gif

22-08-Overproduction.jpg

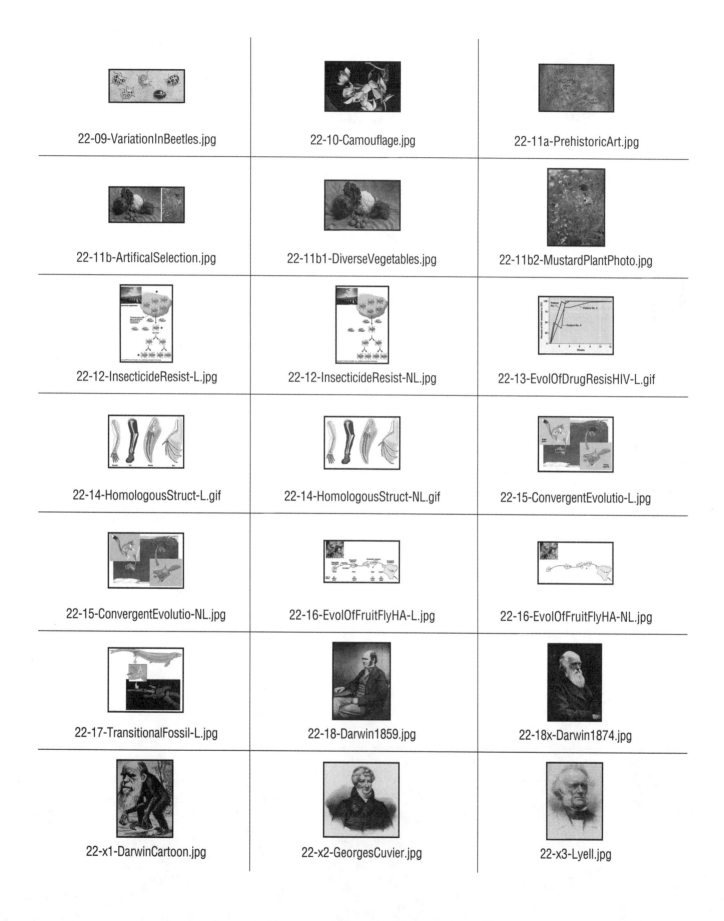

22-09-VariationInBeetles.jpg

22-10-Camouflage.jpg

22-11a-PrehistoricArt.jpg

22-11b-ArtificalSelection.jpg

22-11b1-DiverseVegetables.jpg

22-11b2-MustardPlantPhoto.jpg

22-12-InsecticideResist-L.jpg

22-12-InsecticideResist-NL.jpg

22-13-EvolOfDrugResisHIV-L.gif

22-14-HomologousStruct-L.gif

22-14-HomologousStruct-NL.gif

22-15-ConvergentEvolutio-L.jpg

22-15-ConvergentEvolutio-NL.jpg

22-16-EvolOfFruitFlyHA-L.jpg

22-16-EvolOfFruitFlyHA-NL.jpg

22-17-TransitionalFossil-L.jpg

22-18-Darwin1859.jpg

22-18x-Darwin1874.jpg

22-x1-DarwinCartoon.jpg

22-x2-GeorgesCuvier.jpg

22-x3-Lyell.jpg

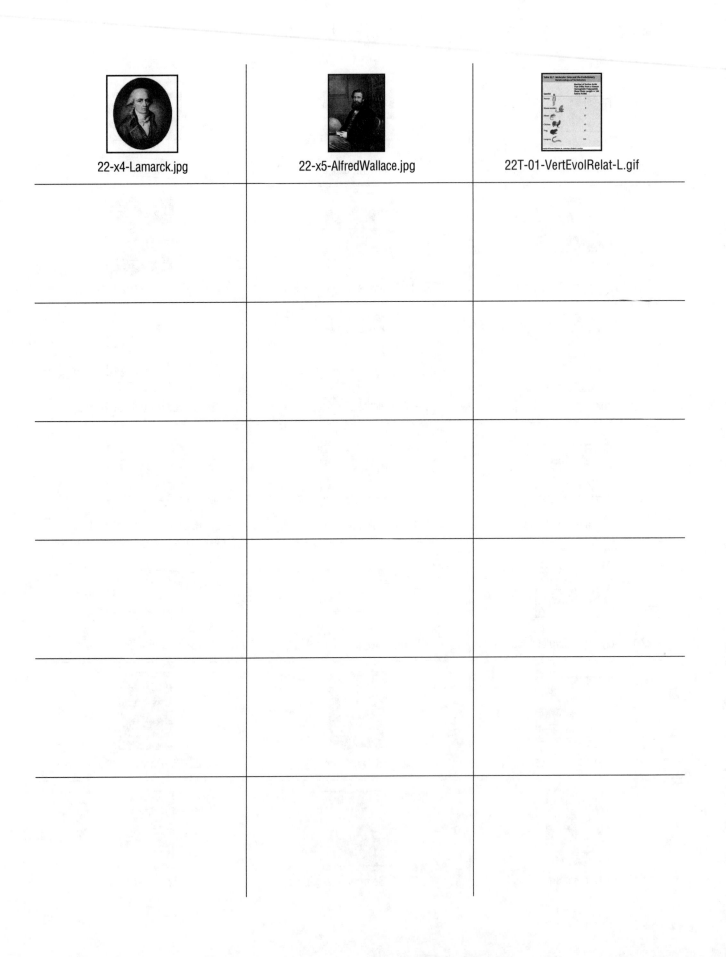

22-x4-Lamarck.jpg

22-x5-AlfredWallace.jpg

22T-01-VertEvolRelat-L.gif

The Evolution of Populations

Chapter Outline

Transparency Acetates

The Transparency Acetates for *Biology*, Sixth Edition, include the following images:

Figure 23.3a   The Hardy-Weinberg theorem

Figure 23.3b   The Hardy-Weinberg theorem

Figure 23.4   Genetic drift

Figure 23.5   The bottleneck effect: an analogy

Figure 23.8   Clinal variation in a plant

Figure 23.10   Mapping malaria and the sickle-cell allele

Figure 23.11   Frequency-dependent selection in a host-parasite relationship

Figure 23.12   Modes of selection

Figure 23.13   Directional selection for beak size in a Galápagos population of the medium ground finch

Figure 23.15   The two-fold disadvantage of sex

Media for Instructors

Campbell Image Presentation Library

The Campbell Image Presentation Library CD-ROM set includes the following for your use:

- All art (available in pdf and jpeg or gif formats), photos (from the text and outside sources), and tables. Art images are also available without callouts. See the Visual Guide to the Image Library section at the end of this chapter for thumbnail versions of every image.

- A PowerPoint™ slide show of the art (with callouts), photos (both text and outside sources), and tables.

PowerPoint Lectures CD-ROM

The PowerPoint Lectures CD-ROM contains slides that integrate the art, photos, tables, and lecture outline from this chapter.

Campbell Biology Website (Instructor Resources)

See the insert in your copy of Campbell/Reece *Biology*, Sixth Edition, for instructions on how to access the Campbell Biology Website. The Instructor Resources section of the website includes the following:

- The art, photos, tables, PowerPoint slide shows, videos, and animations from the Campbell Image Presentation Library

- Suggested answers to the Lab Report questions from the Case Studies in the Process of Science

- The PowerPoint Lecture for this chapter

- Word files of the lecture outline for this chapter

- Photo links

Course Management Systems

The media content for this chapter is available in three course management systems: CourseCompass™, Blackboard, and WebCT. For more information, go to http://cms.aw.com. For the latest pdf instructions on how to use CourseCompass, go to www.coursecompass.com. In addition, a Syllabus Manager is offered on the Campbell Biology Website.

Media for Students

The Campbell Biology Website and CD-ROM include the following for your students:

- Objectives
- Chapter Review (Summary, Self-Quiz, and Essay Questions from the book; Word Roots; Key Terms linked to the Glossary)
- Activities (see list below)
- Case Studies in the Process of Science (see list below)
- Quizzes (Pre-test, Activities Quiz, Chapter Quiz, Essay Questions)
- Web Links
- News and References
- Art and videos from the Campbell Image Presentation Library
- The Campbell *Biology* Interviews (from all editions)
- Glossary with audio pronunciations
- Syllabus Manager

Student Media Activities and Case Studies in The Process of Science

Web/CD Case Study in the Process of Science: *How Can Frequency of Alleles Be Calculated?*

Biology Labs On-Line: *PopulationGeneticsLab*

Web/CD Activity 23A: *Causes of Microevolution*

Biology Labs On-Line: *EvolutionLab*

Web/CD Activity 23B: *Genetic Variation from Sexual Recombination*

Objectives

Population Genetics

1. Explain why it is incorrect to say that individual organisms evolve.
2. Explain what is meant by "the modern synthesis."
3. Define a population; define a species.
4. Explain how microevolutionary change can affect a gene pool.

5. State the Hardy-Weinberg theorem.

6. Write the general Hardy-Weinberg equation and use it to calculate allele and genotype frequencies.

7. Explain why the Hardy-Weinberg theorem is important conceptually and historically.

8. List the conditions a population must meet to maintain Hardy-Weinberg equilibrium.

Causes of Microevolution

9. Define microevolution.

10. Define evolution at the population level.

11. Explain how genetic drift, gene flow, mutation, nonrandom mating, and natural selection can cause microevolution.

12. Explain the role of population size in genetic drift.

13. Distinguish between the bottleneck effect and the founder effect.

14. Explain why mutation has little quantitative effect on a large population.

Genetic Variation, the Substrate for Natural Selection

15. Explain how quantitative and discrete characters contribute to variation within a population.

16. Define polymorphism and morphs. Describe an example of polymorphism within the human population.

17. Distinguish between gene diversity and nucleotide diversity. Describe examples of each in humans.

18. List some factors that can produce geographic variation among closely related populations. Define a cline.

19. Explain why even though mutation can be a source of genetic variability, it contributes a negligible amount to genetic variation in a population.

20. Describe the cause of nearly all genetic variation in a population.

21. Explain how genetic variation may be preserved in a natural population.

22. Briefly describe the neutral theory of molecular evolution and explain how changes in gene frequency may be nonadaptive.

A Closer Look at Natural Selection as the Mechanism of Adaptive Evolution

23. Distinguish between Darwinian fitness and relative fitness.

24. Describe what selection acts on and what factors contribute to the overall fitness of a genotype.

25. Describe examples of how an organism's phenotype may be influenced by the environment.

26. Distinguish among stabilizing selection, directional selection, and diversifying selection.

27. Describe the advantages and disadvantages of sexual reproduction.

28. Define sexual dimorphism and explain how it can influence evolutionary change.

29. Distinguish between intrasexual selection and intersexual selection.

30. Describe at least four reasons why natural selection cannot breed perfect organisms.

Key Terms

population genetics
modern synthesis
population
species
gene pool
Hardy-Weinberg
  theorem
Hardy-Weinberg
  equilibrium
Hardy-Weinberg
  equation
microevolution
genetic drift

bottleneck effect
founder effect
natural selection
gene flow
mutation
polymorphic
gene diversity
nucleotide diversity
geographic variation
cline
balanced
  polymorphism
heterozygote advantage

frequency-dependent
  selection
neutral variation
Darwinian fitness
relative fitness
directional selection
diversifying selection
stabilizing selection
sexual dimorphism
intrasexual selection
intersexual selection

Word Roots

inter- = between (*intersexual selection*: individuals of one sex are choosy in selecting their mates from individuals of the other sex, also called mate choice)

intra- = within (*intrasexual selection*: a direct competition among individuals of one sex for mates of the opposite sex)

micro- = small (*microevolution*: a change in the gene pool of a population over a succession of generations)

muta- = change (*mutation*: a change in the DNA of genes that ultimately creates genetic diversity)

poly- = many; **morph-** = form (*polymorphism*: the coexistence of two or more distinct forms of individuals in the same population)

References

Barlow, G. W. *The Cichlid Fishes: Nature's Grand Experiment in Evolution.* Cambridge MA: Perseus, 2000.

Futuyma, D. J. Evolutionary Biology. Sunderland, Massachusetts: Sinauer, 1998.

Losos, J. B. "Evolution: A Lizard's Tale." *Scientific American*, March 2001.

Moxon, E. R. and C. Wills. "DNA Microsatellites: Agents of Evolution." *Scientific American*, January 1999.

Visual Guide to the Image Library

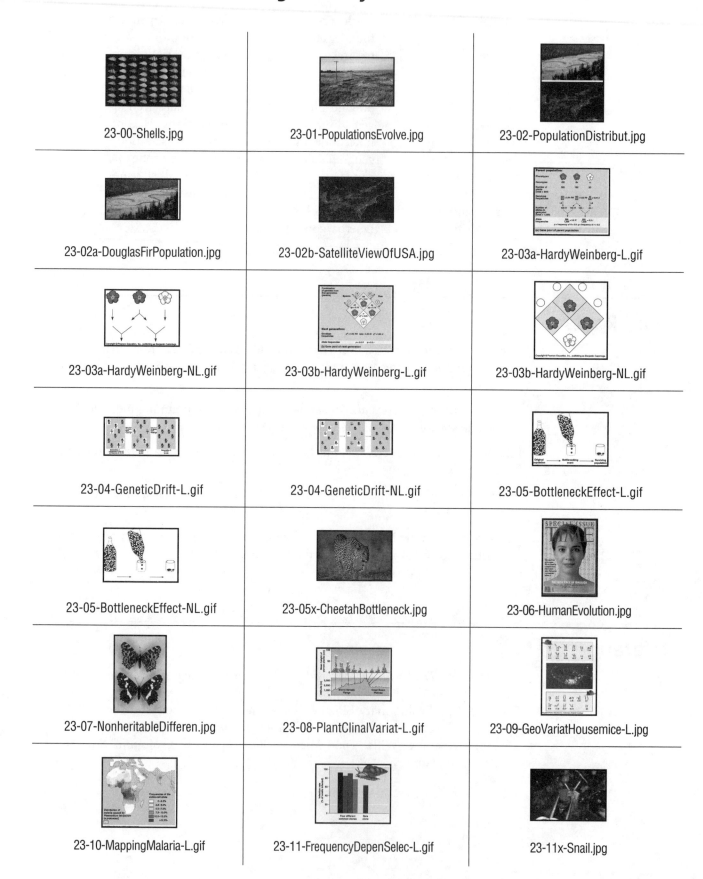

23-00-Shells.jpg

23-01-PopulationsEvolve.jpg

23-02-PopulationDistribut.jpg

23-02a-DouglasFirPopulation.jpg

23-02b-SatelliteViewOfUSA.jpg

23-03a-HardyWeinberg-L.gif

23-03a-HardyWeinberg-NL.gif

23-03b-HardyWeinberg-L.gif

23-03b-HardyWeinberg-NL.gif

23-04-GeneticDrift-L.gif

23-04-GeneticDrift-NL.gif

23-05-BottleneckEffect-L.gif

23-05-BottleneckEffect-NL.gif

23-05x-CheetahBottleneck.jpg

23-06-HumanEvolution.jpg

23-07-NonheritableDifferen.jpg

23-08-PlantClinalVariat-L.gif

23-09-GeoVariatHousemice-L.jpg

23-10-MappingMalaria-L.gif

23-11-FrequencyDepenSelec-L.gif

23-11x-Snail.jpg

23-12-ModesOfSelection-L.gif	23-12-ModesOfSelection-NL.gif	23-12x-NormalAndSickled.jpg
23-13-DirectionalSelect-L.jpg	23-13-DirectionalSelect-NL.jpg	23-14-DiversifyingSelect.jpg
23-15-DisadvantageOfSex-L.gif	23-15-DisadvantageOfSex-NL.gif	23-16x1-SexualDimorphism.jpg
23-16x2-MalePeacock.jpg	23-x1-Gaillardia.jpg	23-x2-Polymorphism.jpg

CHAPTER 24

The Origin of Species

Chapter Outline

What Is a Species?

The biological species concept emphasizes reproductive isolation

Prezygotic and postzygotic barriers isolate the gene pools of biological species

The biological species concept has some major limitations

Evolutionary biologists have proposed several alternative concepts of species

Modes of Speciation

Allopatric speciation: Geographic barriers can lead to the origin of species

Sympatric speciation: A new species can originate in the geographic midst of the parent species

The punctuated equilibrium model has stimulated research on the tempo of speciation

From Speciation to Macroevolution

Most evolutionary novelties are modified versions of older structures

"Evo-devo": Genes that control development play a major role in evolution

An evolutionary trend does not mean that evolution is goal oriented

Transparency Acetates

The Transparency Acetates for *Biology*, Sixth Edition, include the following images:

Figure 24.1	Two patterns of speciation
Figure 24.5	A summary of reproductive barriers between closely related species
Figure 24.6	Two modes of speciation
Figure 24.8	Has speciation occurred during geographic isolation?
Figure 24.9	*Ensatina eschscholtzii,* a ring species
Figure 24.11	A model for adaptive radiation on island chains
Figure 24.12	Evolution of reproductive isolation in lab populations of *Drosophila*

Media for Instructors

Campbell Image Presentation Library

The Campbell Image Presentation Library CD-ROM set includes the following for your use:

- All art (available in pdf and jpeg or gif formats), photos (from the text and outside sources), and tables. Art images are also available without callouts. See the Visual Guide to the Image Library section at the end of this chapter for thumbnail versions of every image.

- A PowerPoint™ slide show of the art (with callouts), photos (both text and outside sources), and tables.

- The following QuickTime animations, adapted from student media activities (also available as Shockwave Flash .swf files):

    24-01-Macroevolution.mov

    24-21-Paedomorphosis.mov

PowerPoint Lectures CD-ROM

The PowerPoint Lectures CD-ROM contains slides that integrate the art, photos, tables, and lecture outline from this chapter.

Campbell Biology Website (Instructor Resources)

See the insert in your copy of Campbell/Reece *Biology*, Sixth Edition, for instructions on how to access the Campbell Biology Website. The Instructor Resources section of the website includes the following:

- The art, photos, tables, PowerPoint slide shows, videos, and animations from the Campbell Image Presentation Library

- Suggested answers to the Lab Report questions from the Case Studies in the Process of Science

- The PowerPoint Lecture for this chapter

- Word files of the lecture outline for this chapter

- Photo links

Course Management Systems

The media content for this chapter is available in three course management systems: CourseCompass™, Blackboard, and WebCT. For more information, go to http://cms.aw.com. For the latest pdf instructions on how to use CourseCompass, go to www.coursecompass.com. In addition, a Syllabus Manager is offered on the Campbell Biology Website.

Media for Students

The Campbell Biology Website and CD-ROM include the following for your students:

- Objectives
- Chapter Review (Summary, Self-Quiz, and Essay Questions from the book; Word Roots; Key Terms linked to the Glossary)
- Activities (see list below)
- Case Studies in the Process of Science (see list below)
- Quizzes (Pre-test, Activities Quiz, Chapter Quiz, Essay Questions)
- Web Links
- News and References
- Art and videos from the Campbell Image Presentation Library
- The Campbell *Biology* Interviews (from all editions)
- Glossary with audio pronunciations
- Syllabus Manager

Student Media Activities and Case Studies in The Process of Science

Web/CD Activity 24A: *Overview of Macroevolution*

Web/CD Case Study in the Process of Science: *How Do New Species Arise by Genetic Isolation?*

Web/CD Activity 24B: *Allometric Growth*

Objectives

What Is a Species?

1. Distinguish between anagenesis and cladogenesis.
2. Define biological species according to Ernst Mayr.
3. Distinguish between prezygotic and postzygotic isolating mechanisms.
4. Describe five prezygotic isolating mechanisms and give an example of each.
5. Explain why many hybrids are sterile.
6. Explain how hybrid breakdown maintains separate species even if gene flow occurs.
7. Describe some limitations of the biological species concept.
8. Define and distinguish among each of the following: ecological species concept, pluralistic species concept, morphological species concept, and genealogical species concept.

Modes of Speciation

9. Distinguish between allopatric and sympatric speciation.
10. Explain the allopatric speciation model and describe the role of intraspecific variation and geographic isolation.
11. Define a ring species and describe an example found in salamanders.
12. Describe examples of adaptive radiation in the Galápagos and Hawaiian archipelagoes.
13. Explain how reproductive barriers evolve. Describe an example of the evolution of a prezygotic barrier and the evolution of a postzygotic barrier.
14. Define sympatric speciation and explain how polyploidy can cause reproductive isolation.
15. Distinguish between an autopolyploid and an allopolyploid species and describe examples of each.
16. Describe an example of sympatric speciation in fish.
17. List some points of agreement and disagreement between the two schools of thought about the tempo of speciation (gradualism versus punctuated equilibrium).

From Speciation to Macroevolution

18. Explain why speciation is at the boundary between microevolution and macroevolution.
19. Define exaptation and illustrate this concept with an example.
20. Explain how the evolution of changes in temporal and spatial developmental dynamics can result in evolutionary novelties. Define evo-devo, allometric growth, heterochrony, and paedomorphosis.
21. Explain why extracting a single evolutionary progression from a fossil record can be misleading.
22. Define and illustrate the concept of species selection. Explain why evolutionary trends are not directional.

Key Terms

macroevolution
speciation
species
biological species
   concept
prezygotic barrier
postzygotic barrier
ecological species
   concept
pluralistic species
   concept

morphological species
   concept
genealogical species
   concept
allopatric speciation
sympatric speciation
adaptive radiation
polyploidy
autopolyploid
allopolyploid

punctuated
   equilibrium
exaptations
allometric growth
heterochrony
paedomorphosis
homeotic
species selection

Word Roots

allo- = other; **-metron** = measure (*allometric growth*: the variation in the relative rates of growth of various parts of the body, which helps shape the organism)

ana- = up; **-genesis** = origin, birth (*anagenesis*: a pattern of evolutionary change involving the transformation of an entire population, sometimes to a state different enough from the ancestral population to justify renaming it as a separate species)

auto- = self; **poly-** = many (*autopolyploid*: a type of polyploid species resulting from one species doubling its chromosome number to become tretraploid)

clado- = branch (*cladogenesis*: a pattern of evolutionary change that produces biological diversity by budding one or more new species from a parent species that continues to exist)

hetero- = different (*heterochrony*: evolutionary changes in the timing or rate of development)

macro- = large (*macroevolution*: evolutionary change on a grand scale, encompassing the origin of novel designs, evolutionary trends, adaptive radiation, and mass extinction)

paedo- = child (*paedomorphosis*: the retention in the adult organism of the juvenile features of its evolutionary ancestors)

post- = after (*postzygotic barrier*: any of several species-isolating mechanisms that prevent hybrids produced by two different species from developing into viable, fertile adults)

sym- = together; **-patri** = father (*sympatric speciation*: a mode of speciation occurring as a result of a radical change in the genome that produces a reproductively isolated subpopulation in the midst of its parent population)

References

Futuyma, D. J. *Evolutionary Biology*. 3rd ed. Sunderland, Massachusetts: Sinauer, 1998.

Schilthuizen, M. *Frogs, Flies and Dandelions: The Making of Species.* New York: Oxford University Press, 2001.

Visual Guide to the Image Library

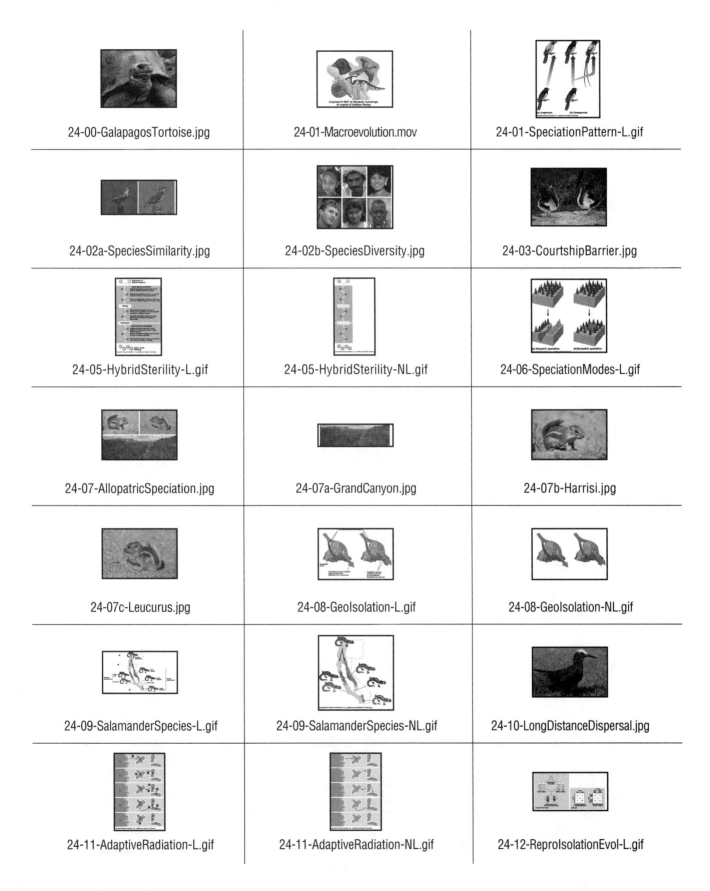

24-00-GalapagosTortoise.jpg

24-01-Macroevolution.mov

24-01-SpeciationPattern-L.gif

24-02a-SpeciesSimilarity.jpg

24-02b-SpeciesDiversity.jpg

24-03-CourtshipBarrier.jpg

24-05-HybridSterility-L.gif

24-05-HybridSterility-NL.gif

24-06-SpeciationModes-L.gif

24-07-AllopatricSpeciation.jpg

24-07a-GrandCanyon.jpg

24-07b-Harrisi.jpg

24-07c-Leucurus.jpg

24-08-GeoIsolation-L.gif

24-08-GeoIsolation-NL.gif

24-09-SalamanderSpecies-L.gif

24-09-SalamanderSpecies-NL.gif

24-10-LongDistanceDispersal.jpg

24-11-AdaptiveRadiation-L.gif

24-11-AdaptiveRadiation-NL.gif

24-12-ReproIsolationEvol-L.gif

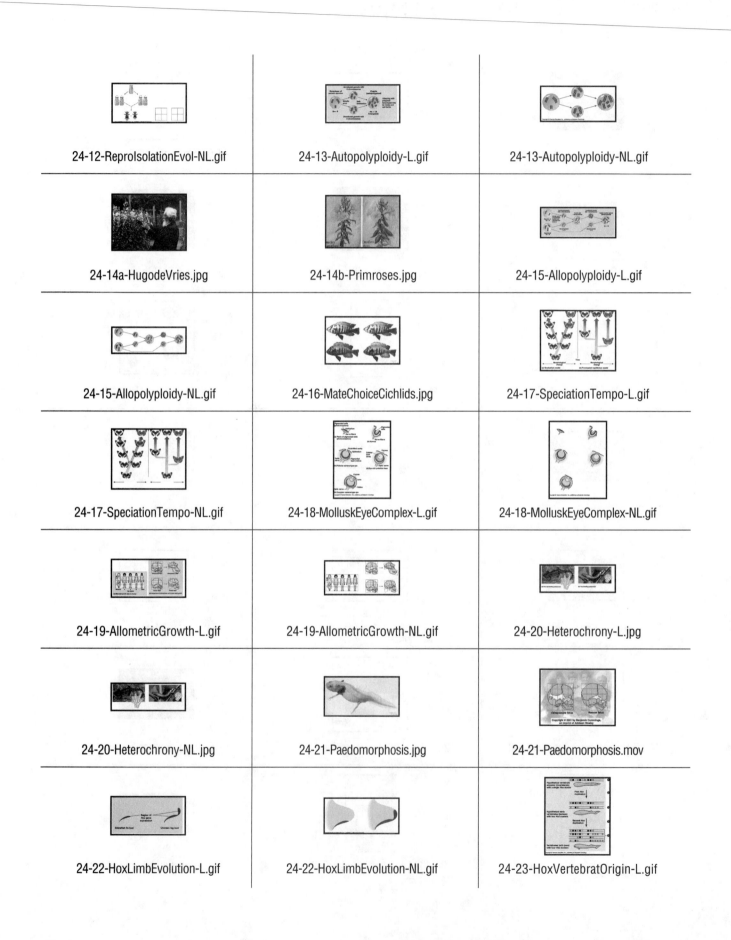

24-12-ReproIsolationEvol-NL.gif

24-13-Autopolyploidy-L.gif

24-13-Autopolyploidy-NL.gif

24-14a-HugodeVries.jpg

24-14b-Primroses.jpg

24-15-Allopolyploidy-L.gif

24-15-Allopolyploidy-NL.gif

24-16-MateChoiceCichlids.jpg

24-17-SpeciationTempo-L.gif

24-17-SpeciationTempo-NL.gif

24-18-MolluskEyeComplex-L.gif

24-18-MolluskEyeComplex-NL.gif

24-19-AllometricGrowth-L.gif

24-19-AllometricGrowth-NL.gif

24-20-Heterochrony-L.jpg

24-20-Heterochrony-NL.jpg

24-21-Paedomorphosis.jpg

24-21-Paedomorphosis.mov

24-22-HoxLimbEvolution-L.gif

24-22-HoxLimbEvolution-NL.gif

24-23-HoxVertebratOrigin-L.gif

24-23-HoxVertebratOrigin-NL.gif	24-24-HorseEvolution-L.jpg	24-24-HorseEvolution-NL.jpg

CHAPTER 25

Phylogeny and Systematics

Chapter Outline

The Fossil Record and Geological Time

Sedimentary rocks are the richest sources of fossils

Paleontologists use a variety of methods to date fossils: *the process of science*

The fossil record is a substantial, but incomplete, chronicle of evolutionary history

Phylogeny has a biogeographic basis in continental drift

The history of life is punctuated by mass extinctions

Systematics: Connecting Classification to Phylogeny

Taxonomy employs a hierarchical system of classification

Modern phylogenetic systematics is based on cladistic analysis: *the process of science*

Systematics can infer phylogeny from molecular evidence: *the process of science*

The principle of parsimony helps systematists reconstruct phylogeny: *the process of science*

Phylogenetic trees are hypotheses

Molecular clocks may keep track of evolutionary time: *the process of science*

Modern systematics is flourishing with lively debate: *the process of science*

Transparency Acetates

The Transparency Acetates for *Biology*, Sixth Edition, include the following images:

Media for Instructors

Campbell Image Presentation Library

The Campbell Image Presentation Library CD-ROM set includes the following for your use:

- All art (available in pdf and jpeg or gif formats), photos (from the text and outside sources), and tables. Art images are also available without callouts. See the Visual Guide to the Image Library section at the end of this chapter for thumbnail versions of every image.

- A PowerPoint™ slide show of the art (with callouts), photos (both text and outside sources), and tables.

- The following video clips:

  25-03-LavaFlow-B.mov   Volcanic eruption

  25-03-VolcanicEruption-B.mov

  See also

  22-04-GrandCanyon-B.mov   Grand Canyon fly over

- The following QuickTime animation, adapted from student media activities (also available as a Shockwave Flash .swf file):

  25T-01-GeologicTimeScale.mov

PowerPoint Lectures CD-ROM

The PowerPoint Lectures CD-ROM contains slides that integrate the art, photos, tables, and lecture outline from this chapter.

Campbell Biology Website (Instructor Resources)

See the insert in your copy of Campbell/Reece *Biology*, Sixth Edition, for instructions on how to access the Campbell Biology Website. The Instructor Resources section of the website includes the following:

- The art, photos, tables, PowerPoint slide shows, videos, and animations from the Campbell Image Presentation Library
- Suggested answers to the Lab Report questions from the Case Studies in the Process of Science
- The PowerPoint Lecture for this chapter
- Word files of the lecture outline for this chapter
- Photo links

Course Management Systems

The media content for this chapter is available in three course management systems: CourseCompass™, Blackboard, and WebCT. For more information, go to http://cms.aw.com. For the latest pdf instructions on how to use CourseCompass, go to www.coursecompass.com. In addition, a Syllabus Manager is offered on the Campbell Biolog*y* Website.

Media for Students

The Campbell Biology Website and CD-ROM include the following for your students:

- Objectives
- Chapter Review (Summary, Self-Quiz, and Essay Questions from the book; Word Roots; Key Terms linked to the Glossary)
- Activities (see list below)
- Case Studies in the Process of Science (see list below)
- Quizzes (Pre-test, Activities Quiz, Chapter Quiz, Essay Questions)
- Web Links
- News and References
- Art and videos from the Campbell Image Presentation Library
- The Campbell *Biology* Interviews (from all editions)
- Glossary with audio pronunciations
- Syllabus Manager

Student Media Activities and Case Studies in The Process of Science

Web/CD Activity 25A: *Grand Canyon Video*

Web/CD Activity 25B: *A Scrolling Geologic Time Scale*

Web/CD Case Study in the Process of Science: *How Is Phylogeny Determined by Comparing Proteins?*

Objectives

The Fossil Record and Geologic Time

1. Distinguish between phylogeny and systematics.

2. Describe the process of sedimentation and the formation of fossils. Explain what portions of organisms mostly fossilize and why.

3. Distinguish between relative dating and absolute dating.

4. Explain how isotopes can be used in absolute dating.

5. Explain why the fossil record is incomplete.

6. Describe two dramatic chapters in the history of continental drift. Explain how those movements affected biological evolution.

7. Explain how mass extinctions have occurred and how they affected the evolution of surviving forms.

8. Describe the evidence related to the impact hypothesis associated with the Cretaceous extinctions. Describe the hypothesized consequences of such an impact.

Systematics: Connecting Classification to Phylogeny

9. Distinguish between systematics and taxonomy.

10. Explain how species are named and categorized into a hierarchy of groups.

11. List the major taxonomic categories from the most to least inclusive.

12. Define the parts and describe the interrelationships within a cladogram. Explain how a cladogram is constructed.

13. Distinguish between homologous and analogous structures. Explain why the similarity of complex systems implies a more recent common ancestor.

14. Distinguish between shared primitive characters and shared derived characters. Compare the definitions of an ingroup and outgroup.

15. Compare the cladistic and phylocode classification systems.

16. Explain how nucleotide sequences and amino acid sequences can be used to help classify organisms. Explain the advantages that molecular methods have over other forms of classification.

17. Explain the principle of parsimony. Explain why any phylogenetic diagram is viewed as a hypothesis.

18. Explain how molecular clocks are used to determine the approximate time of key evolutionary events. Explain how molecular clocks are calibrated in actual time.

19. Explain how scientists determined the approximate time when HIV first infected humans.

20. Describe an example of a conflict between molecular data and other evidence, such as the fossil record. Explain how these differences can be addressed.

Key Terms

phylogeny
fossil record
geologic time scale
radiometric dating
half-life
Pangaea
systematics
binomial
genus
specific epithet
species
family

order
class
phyla (singular, phylum)
kingdoms
domain
taxon (plural, taxa)
phylogenetic tree
cladogram
clade
monophyletic
homology

convergent evolution
analogy
shared primitive character
shared derived character
outgroup
ingroup
phylocode
parsimony
molecular clocks
phylogenetic fuse

Word Roots

analog- = proportion (*analogy*: similarity due to convergence)

bi- = two; **nom-** = name (*binomial*: a two-part latinized name of a species)

clado- = branch (*cladogram*: a dichotomous phylogenetic tree that branches repeatedly)

homo- = like, resembling (*homology*: similarity in characteristics resulting from a shared ancestry)

mono- = one (*monophyletic*: pertaining to a taxon derived from a single ancestral species that gave rise to no species in any other taxa)

parsi- = few (*principle of parsimony*: the premise that a theory about nature should be the simplest explanation that is consistent with the facts)

phylo- = tribe; **-geny** = origin (*phylogeny*: the evolutionary history of a taxon)

References

Doolittle, W. F. "Uprooting the Tree of Life." *Scientific American*, February 2000.
Futuyma, D. J. *Evolutionary Biology*. 3rd ed. Sunderland, Massachusetts: Sinauer, 1998.
Morris, S. C. "Evolution: Bringing Molecules into the Fold." *Cell*, January 2000.
Wroe, S. "Killer Kangaroos and Other Murderous Marsupials." *Scientific American*, May 1999.

Visual Guide to the Image Library

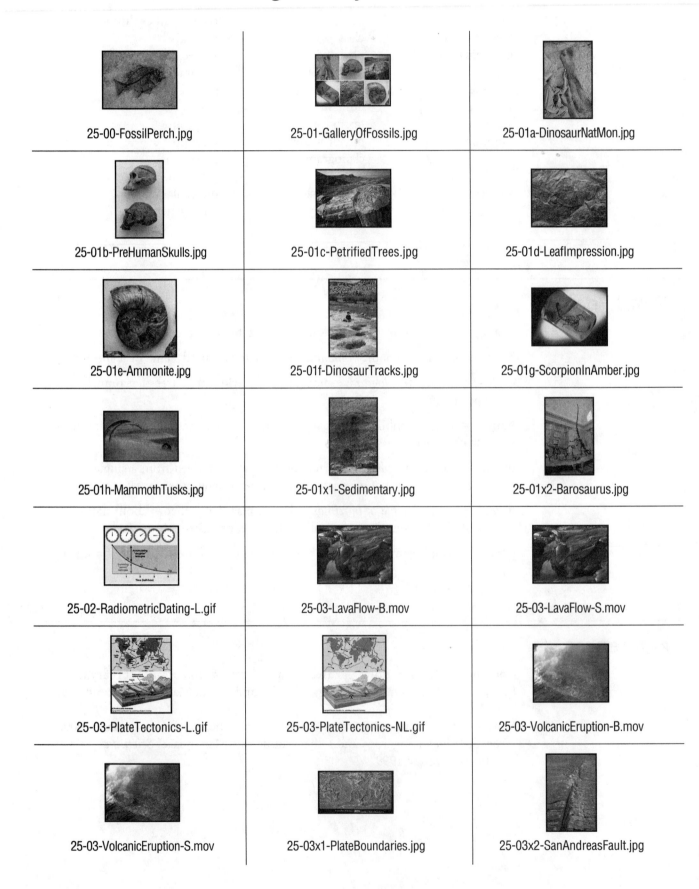

25-00-FossilPerch.jpg

25-01-GalleryOfFossils.jpg

25-01a-DinosaurNatMon.jpg

25-01b-PreHumanSkulls.jpg

25-01c-PetrifiedTrees.jpg

25-01d-LeafImpression.jpg

25-01e-Ammonite.jpg

25-01f-DinosaurTracks.jpg

25-01g-ScorpionInAmber.jpg

25-01h-MammothTusks.jpg

25-01x1-Sedimentary.jpg

25-01x2-Barosaurus.jpg

25-02-RadiometricDating-L.gif

25-03-LavaFlow-B.mov

25-03-LavaFlow-S.mov

25-03-PlateTectonics-L.gif

25-03-PlateTectonics-NL.gif

25-03-VolcanicEruption-B.mov

25-03-VolcanicEruption-S.mov

25-03x1-PlateBoundaries.jpg

25-03x2-SanAndreasFault.jpg

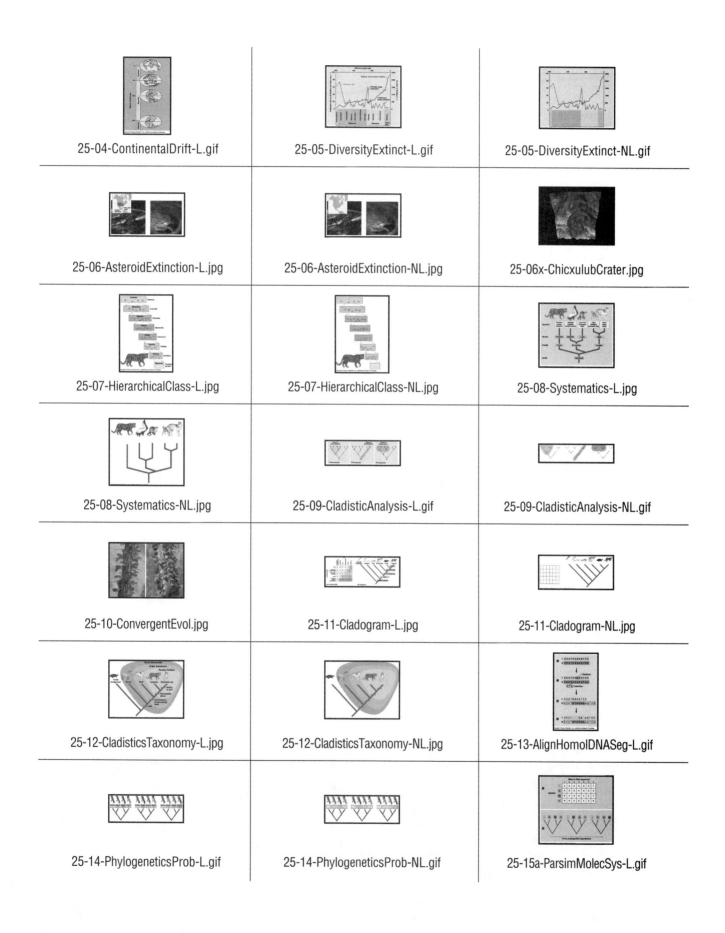

25-04-ContinentalDrift-L.gif

25-05-DiversityExtinct-L.gif

25-05-DiversityExtinct-NL.gif

25-06-AsteroidExtinction-L.jpg

25-06-AsteroidExtinction-NL.jpg

25-06x-ChicxulubCrater.jpg

25-07-HierarchicalClass-L.jpg

25-07-HierarchicalClass-NL.jpg

25-08-Systematics-L.jpg

25-08-Systematics-NL.jpg

25-09-CladisticAnalysis-L.gif

25-09-CladisticAnalysis-NL.gif

25-10-ConvergentEvol.jpg

25-11-Cladogram-L.jpg

25-11-Cladogram-NL.jpg

25-12-CladisticsTaxonomy-L.jpg

25-12-CladisticsTaxonomy-NL.jpg

25-13-AlignHomolDNASeg-L.gif

25-14-PhylogeneticsProb-L.gif

25-14-PhylogeneticsProb-NL.gif

25-15a-ParsimMolecSys-L.gif

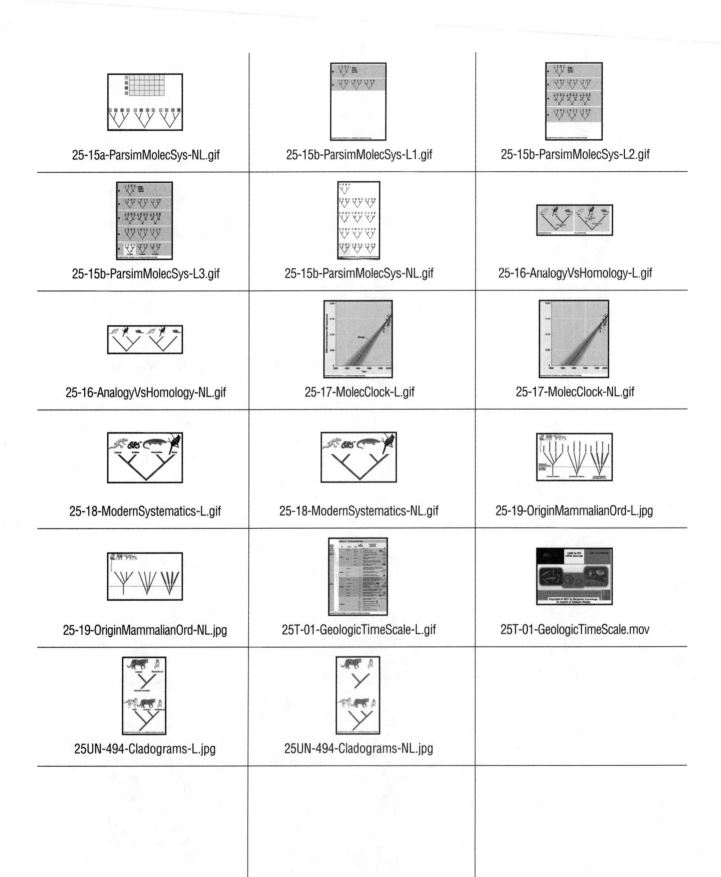

25-15a-ParsimMolecSys-NL.gif

25-15b-ParsimMolecSys-L1.gif

25-15b-ParsimMolecSys-L2.gif

25-15b-ParsimMolecSys-L3.gif

25-15b-ParsimMolecSys-NL.gif

25-16-AnalogyVsHomology-L.gif

25-16-AnalogyVsHomology-NL.gif

25-17-MolecClock-L.gif

25-17-MolecClock-NL.gif

25-18-ModernSystematics-L.gif

25-18-ModernSystematics-NL.gif

25-19-OriginMammalianOrd-L.jpg

25-19-OriginMammalianOrd-NL.jpg

25T-01-GeologicTimeScale-L.gif

25T-01-GeologicTimeScale.mov

25UN-494-Cladograms-L.jpg

25UN-494-Cladograms-NL.jpg

CHAPTER 26

Early Earth and the Origin of Life

Chapter Outline

Introduction to the History of Life

Life on Earth originated between 3.5 and 4.0 billion years ago

Prokaryotes dominated evolutionary history from 3.5 to 2.0 billion years ago

Oxygen began accumulating in the atmosphere about 2.7 billion years ago

Eukaryotic life began by 2.1 billion years ago

Multicellular eukaryotes evolved by 1.2 billion years ago

Animal diversity exploded during the early Cambrian period

Plants, fungi, and animals colonized the land about 500 million years ago

The Origin of Life

The first cells may have originated by chemical evolution on a young Earth: *an overview*

Abiotic synthesis of organic monomers is a testable hypothesis

Laboratory simulations of early-Earth conditions have produced organic polymers

RNA may have been the first genetic material

Protobionts can form by self-assembly

Natural selection could refine protobionts containing hereditary information

Debate about the origin of life abounds

The Major Lineages of Life

The five-kingdom system reflected increased knowledge of life's diversity

Arranging the diversity of life into the highest taxa is a work in progress

Transparency Acetates

The Transparency Acetates for *Biology*, Sixth Edition, include the following images:

Figure 26.1	Some major episodes in the history of life
Figure 26.2	Clock analogy for some key events in evolutionary history
Figure 26.8	The Cambrian radiation of animals

Media for Instructors

Campbell Image Presentation Library

The Campbell Image Presentation Library CD-ROM set includes the following for your use:

- All art (available in pdf and jpeg or gif formats), photos (from the text and outside sources), and tables. Art images are also available without callouts. See the Visual Guide to the Image Library section at the end of this chapter for thumbnail versions of every image.

- A PowerPoint^{TM} slide show of the art (with callouts), photos (both text and outside sources), and tables.

- The following video clips:

  26-14-DeepSeaVent-B.mov   Deep-sea vent

  See also

  25-03-VolcanicEruption-B.mov

  25-03-LavaFlow-B.mov   Volcanic eruption—Hawaii

- The following QuickTime animation, adapted from student media activities (also available as a Shockwave Flash .swf file):

  26-16-ClassificationSchemes.mov

PowerPoint Lectures CD-ROM

The PowerPoint Lectures CD-ROM contains slides that integrate the art, photos, tables, and lecture outline from this chapter.

Campbell Biology Website (Instructor Resources)

See the insert in your copy of Campbell/Reece *Biology*, Sixth Edition, for instructions on how to access the Campbell Biology Website. The Instructor Resources section of the website includes the following:

- The art, photos, tables, PowerPoint slide shows, videos, and animations from the Campbell Image Presentation Library

- Suggested answers to the Lab Report questions from the Case Studies in the Process of Science

- The PowerPoint Lecture for this chapter
- Word files of the lecture outline for this chapter
- Photo links

Course Management Systems

The media content for this chapter is available in three course management systems: CourseCompass™, Blackboard, and WebCT. For more information, go to http://cms.aw.com. For the latest pdf instructions on how to use CourseCompass, go to **www.coursecompass.com**. In addition, a Syllabus Manager is offered on the Campbell Biology Website.

Media for Students

The Campbell Biology Website and CD-ROM include the following for your students:

- Objectives
- Chapter Review (Summary, Self-Quiz, and Essay Questions from the book; Word Roots; Key Terms linked to the Glossary)
- Activities (see list below)
- Case Studies in the Process of Science (see list below)
- Quizzes (Pre-test, Activities Quiz, Chapter Quiz, Essay Questions)
- Web Links
- News and References
- Art and videos from the Campbell Image Presentation Library
- The Campbell *Biology* Interviews (from all editions)
- Glossary with audio pronunciations
- Syllabus Manager

Student Media Activities and Case Studies in The Process of Science

Web/CD Activity 26A: *The History of Life*

Web/CD Case Study in the Process of Science: *How Did Life Begin on Early Earth?*

Web/CD Activity 26B: *Tubeworm Video*

Web/CD Activity 26C: *Classification Schemes*

Objectives

Introduction to the History of Life

1. Explain how the histories of Earth and life are inseparable.

2. Describe the major events in Earth's history from its origin up to about 2 billion years ago. In particular, note when Earth first formed, when life first evolved, and what forms of life existed up until about 2 billion years ago.

3. Describe the timing and significance of the evolution of photosynthesis.

4. Describe the timing of key events in the evolution of the first eukaryotes and later multicellular eukaryotes. Describe the snowball-Earth hypothesis.

5. Describe the timing of key evolutionary adaptations as life colonized land.

The Origin of Life

6. Contrast the concept of spontaneous generation and the principle of biogenesis. Describe the biogenesis paradox and suggest a solution.

7. Describe the four stages of the hypothesis for the origin of life on Earth.

8. Describe the contributions that A. I. Oparin, J. B. S. Haldane, and Stanley Miller made toward developing a model for the abiotic synthesis of organic molecules. Describe the conditions and locations where most of these early organic reactions probably occurred on Earth.

9. Describe the evidence that suggests that RNA was the first genetic material. Explain the significance of the discovery of ribozymes.

10. Describe how natural selection would have worked in an early RNA world.

11. Describe the key properties of protobionts in the evolution of the first cells.

12. Describe the evidence that suggests that life first evolved on the sea floor near deep-sea vents.

The Major Lineages of Life

13. Describe the basis for R. H. Whittaker's five-kingdom system.

14. List, distinguish among, and describe examples from each of the five kingdoms.

15. Compare the three-domain system and R. H. Whittaker's five-kingdom system of classification.

Key Terms

stromatolite	biogenesis
snowball Earth	ribozyme
spontaneous	protobionts
generation	three-domain system

Word Roots

bio- = life; **-genesis** = origin, birth (*biogenesis*: the principle that "life comes from life")

proto- = first (*protobionts*: aggregates of abiotically produced molecules)

stromato- = something spread out; **-lite** = a stone (*stromatolite*: rocks made of banded domes of sediment in which are found the most ancient forms of life)

References

Futuyma, D. J. *Evolutionary Biology*, Sunderland, Massachusetts: Sinauer Associates, Inc. 1998.

Hazen, R. M. "Life's Rocky Start." *Scientific American*, April 2001.

Hoffman, P. F. and D. P. Schrag. "Snowball Earth." *Scientific American*, January 2000.

Visual Guide to the Image Library

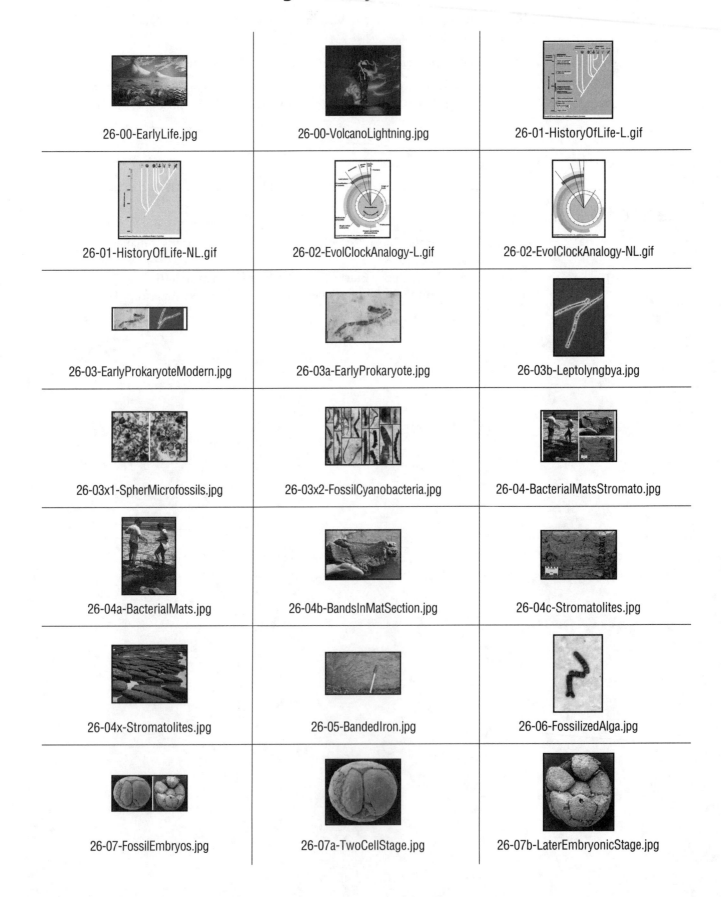

26-00-EarlyLife.jpg

26-00-VolcanoLightning.jpg

26-01-HistoryOfLife-L.gif

26-01-HistoryOfLife-NL.gif

26-02-EvolClockAnalogy-L.gif

26-02-EvolClockAnalogy-NL.gif

26-03-EarlyProkaryoteModern.jpg

26-03a-EarlyProkaryote.jpg

26-03b-Leptolyngbya.jpg

26-03x1-SpherMicrofossils.jpg

26-03x2-FossilCyanobacteria.jpg

26-04-BacterialMatsStromato.jpg

26-04a-BacterialMats.jpg

26-04b-BandsInMatSection.jpg

26-04c-Stromatolites.jpg

26-04x-Stromatolites.jpg

26-05-BandedIron.jpg

26-06-FossilizedAlga.jpg

26-07-FossilEmbryos.jpg

26-07a-TwoCellStage.jpg

26-07b-LaterEmbryonicStage.jpg

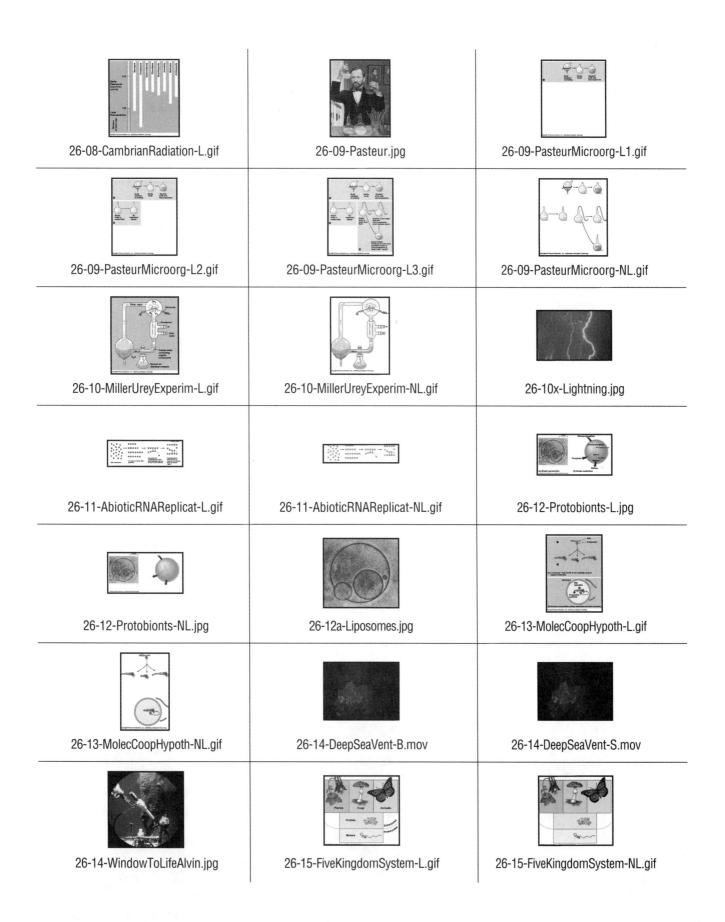

26-08-CambrianRadiation-L.gif

26-09-Pasteur.jpg

26-09-PasteurMicroorg-L1.gif

26-09-PasteurMicroorg-L2.gif

26-09-PasteurMicroorg-L3.gif

26-09-PasteurMicroorg-NL.gif

26-10-MillerUreyExperim-L.gif

26-10-MillerUreyExperim-NL.gif

26-10x-Lightning.jpg

26-11-AbioticRNAReplicat-L.gif

26-11-AbioticRNAReplicat-NL.gif

26-12-Protobionts-L.jpg

26-12-Protobionts-NL.jpg

26-12a-Liposomes.jpg

26-13-MolecCoopHypoth-L.gif

26-13-MolecCoopHypoth-NL.gif

26-14-DeepSeaVent-B.mov

26-14-DeepSeaVent-S.mov

26-14-WindowToLifeAlvin.jpg

26-15-FiveKingdomSystem-L.gif

26-15-FiveKingdomSystem-NL.gif

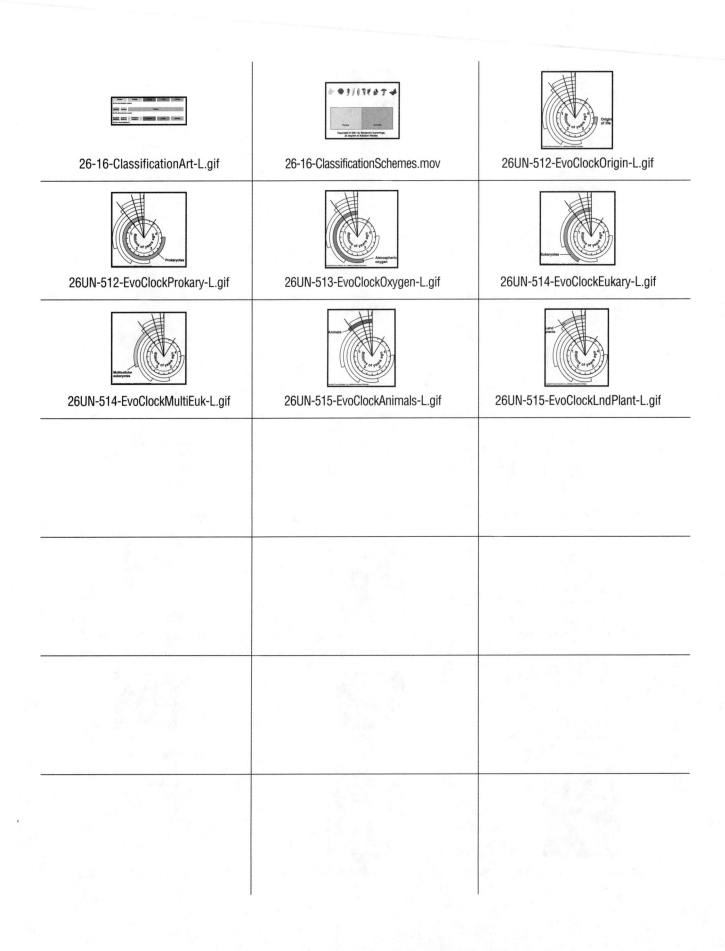

26-16-ClassificationArt-L.gif

26-16-ClassificationSchemes.mov

26UN-512-EvoClockOrigin-L.gif

26UN-512-EvoClockProkary-L.gif

26UN-513-EvoClockOxygen-L.gif

26UN-514-EvoClockEukary-L.gif

26UN-514-EvoClockMultiEuk-L.gif

26UN-515-EvoClockAnimals-L.gif

26UN-515-EvoClockLndPlant-L.gif

CHAPTER 27

Prokaryotes and the Origins of Metabolic Diversity

Chapter Outline

The World of Prokaryotes

They're (almost) everywhere! An overview of prokaryotic life

Bacteria and archaea are the two main branches of prokaryote evolution

The Structure, Function, and Reproduction of Prokaryotes

Nearly all prokaryotes have cell walls external to their plasma membranes

Many prokaryotes are motile

The cellular and genomic organization of prokaryotes is fundamentally different from that of eukaryotes

Populations of prokaryotes grow and adapt rapidly

Nutritional and Metabolic Diversity

Prokaryotes can be grouped into four categories according to how they obtain energy and carbon

Photosynthesis evolved early in prokaryotic life

A Survey of Prokaryotic Diversity

Molecular systematics is leading to a phylogenetic classification of prokaryotes: *the process of science*

Researchers are identifying a great diversity of archaea in extreme environments and in the oceans

Most known prokaryotes are bacteria

The Ecological Impact of Prokaryotes

Prokaryotes are indispensable links in the recycling of chemical elements in ecosystems

Many prokaryotes are symbiotic

Pathogenic prokaryotes cause many human diseases

Humans use prokaryotes in research and technology

Transparency Acetates

The Transparency Acetates for *Biology*, Sixth Edition, include the following images:

Figure 27.2	The three domains of life
Figure 27.5	Gram-positive and gram-negative bacteria
Figure 27.7	Form and function of prokaryotic flagella
Table 27.1	Major nutritional modes
Figure 27.12	Contrasting hypotheses for the taxonomic distribution of photosynthesis among prokaryotes
Figure 27.13	Some major groups of prokaryotes
Table 27.2	A Comparison of the three domains of life
Table 27.3	Five of the major clades of bacteria
Figure 27.18	Putting prokaryotes to work in sewage treatment

Media for Instructors

Campbell Image Presentation Library

The Campbell Image Presentation Library CD-ROM set includes the following for your use:

- All art (available in pdf and jpeg or gif formats), photos (from the text and outside sources), and tables. Art images are also available without callouts. See the Visual Guide to the Image Library section at the end of this chapter for thumbnail versions of every image.
- A PowerPoint™ slide show of the art (with callouts), photos (both text and outside sources), and tables.
- The following video clips:

  27-07-SalmonellaFlagella-S.mov

  27-11-Oscillatoria-B.mov

PowerPoint Lectures CD-ROM

The PowerPoint Lectures CD-ROM contains slides that integrate the art, photos, tables, and lecture outline from this chapter.

Campbell Biology Website (Instructor Resources)

See the insert in your copy of Campbell/Reece *Biology*, Sixth Edition, for instructions on how to access the Campbell Biology Website. The Instructor Resources section of the website includes the following:

- The art, photos, tables, PowerPoint slide shows, videos, and animations from the Campbell Image Presentation Library
- Suggested answers to the Lab Report questions from the Case Studies in the Process of Science

- The PowerPoint Lecture for this chapter
- Word files of the lecture outline for this chapter
- Photo links

Course Management Systems

The media content for this chapter is available in three course management systems: CourseCompass™, Blackboard, and WebCT. For more information, go to http://cms.aw.com. For the latest pdf instructions on how to use CourseCompass, go to www.coursecompass.com. In addition, a Syllabus Manager is offered on the Campbell Biology Website.

Media for Students

The Campbell Biology Website and CD-ROM include the following for your students:

- Objectives
- Chapter Review (Summary, Self-Quiz, and Essay Questions from the book; Word Roots; Key Terms linked to the Glossary)
- Activities (see list below)
- Case Studies in the Process of Science (see list below)
- Quizzes (Pre-test, Activities Quiz, Chapter Quiz, Essay Questions)
- Web Links
- News and References
- Art and videos from the Campbell Image Presentation Library
- The Campbell *Biology* Interviews (from all editions)
- Glossary with audio pronunciations
- Syllabus Manager

Student Media Activities and Case Studies in The Process of Science

Web/CD Activity 27A: *Prokaryotic Cell Structure and Function*

Web/CD Case Study in the Process of Science: *What Are the Modes of Nutrition in Prokaryotes?*

Web/CD Activity 27B: *Classification of Prokaryotes*

Objectives

The World of Prokaryotes

1. Describe the many unique characteristics of prokaryotes. Explain why it might be said that prokaryotes are the most successful organisms ever to live.

2. Describe the impact of prokaryotes on humans and biological ecosystems.

3. Describe the classification of the archaea and the bacteria in the three-domain system.

The Structure, Function, and Reproduction of Prokaryotes

4. Describe the general size, organization, and specialization of prokaryotic organisms.

5. Describe the structure, composition, and functions of prokaryotic cell walls.

6. Distinguish between the structure and staining properties of gram-positive and gram-negative bacteria. Explain why disease-causing gram-negative bacterial species are generally more pathogenic than disease-causing gram-positive bacteria.

7. Describe three mechanisms that motile bacteria use to move. Explain how prokaryotic flagella work and why they are not considered to be homologous to eukaryotic flagella.

8. Explain how the organization of the prokaryotic genome differs from that in eukaryotic cells.

9. List the mechanisms that are sources of genetic variation in prokaryotes and indicate which one is the major source.

10. Describe growth as it applies to prokaryotes. Explain what is meant by geometric growth.

11. Describe the functions of endospores.

12. Describe the natural adaptive advantage of antibiotics.

Nutritional and Metabolic Diversity

13. Distinguish between photoautotrophs, chemoautotrophs, photoheterotrophs, chemoheterotrophs, saprobes, and parasites. Give examples of each.

14. Describe the process and explain the significance of nitrogen fixation.

15. Distinguish among obligate aerobes, facultative anaerobes, and obligate anaerobes.

16. Describe, with supporting evidence, plausible scenarios for the evolution of metabolic diversity, including the
    a. nutrition of early prokaryotes
    b. origin of electron transport chains
    c. origin of photosynthesis
    d. origin of aerobic respiration

A Survey of Prokaryotic Diversity

17. Explain how molecular systematics has been used in developing a moneran classification. Explain why clinical phenotypes are a poor guide to phylogeny.

18. Describe the distinguishing features and give examples of the methanogens, extreme halophiles, and extreme thermophiles. Explain why these groups are collectively known as extremeophiles.

The Ecological Impact of Prokaryotes

19. Describe the role of prokaryotes in recycling within ecosystems.
20. Distinguish among mutualism, commensalism, and parasitism. Describe examples of prokaryotes in each of these relationships.
21. List Koch's postulates, which are used to substantiate a specific pathogen as the cause of a disease.
22. Distinguish between exotoxins and endotoxins and describe examples of each.
23. Describe how *Streptomyces* can be used commercially.
24. Describe the limitations of antibiotics in combating bacterial diseases.
25. Describe how humans exploit the metabolic diversity of prokaryotes for scientific and commercial purposes.

Key Terms

domain	photoautotroph	extreme thermophiles
peptidoglycan	chemoautotroph	Euryarchaeota
Gram stain	photoheterotroph	Crenarchaeota
gram-positive	chemoheterotroph	decomposers
gram-negative	saprobe	symbiosis
capsule	parasite	host
pili (singular, pilus)	nitrogen fixation	mutualism
taxis	obligate aerobe	commensalism
nucleoid region	facultative anaerobe	parasitism
plasmids	obligate anaerobe	parasite
binary fission	anaerobic respiration	opportunistic
transformation	signature sequences	Koch's postulates
conjugation	extremeophile	exotoxin
transduction	methanogen	endotoxin
endospore	extreme halophile	bioremediation
antibiotic	bacteriorhodopsin	

Word Roots

-gen = produce (*methanogen*: microorganisms which obtain energy by using carbon dioxide to oxidize hydrogen, producing methane as a waste product)

-oid = like, form (*nucleoid*: a dense region of DNA in a prokaryotic cell)

an- = without, not; **aero-** = the air (*anaerobic*: lacking oxygen; referring to an organism, environment, or cellular process that lacks oxygen and may be poisoned by it)

anti- = against; **-biot** = life (*antibiotic*: a chemical that kills bacteria or inhibits their growth)

bi- = two (*binary fission*: the type of cell division by which prokaryotes reproduce; each dividing daughter cell receives a copy of the single parental chromosome)

chemo- = chemical; **hetero-** = different (*chemoheterotroph*: an organism that must consume organic molecules for both energy and carbon)

endo- = inner, within (*endotoxin*: a component of the outer membranes of certain gram-negative bacteria responsible for generalized symptoms of fever and ache)

exo- = outside (*exotoxin*: a toxic protein secreted by a bacterial cell that produces specific symptoms even in the absence of the bacterium)

halo- = salt; **-philos** = loving (*halophile*: microorganisms which live in unusually highly saline environments such as the Great Salt Lake or the Dead Sea)

mutu- = reciprocal (*mutualism*: a symbiotic relationship in which both the host and the symbiont benefit)

photo- = light; **auto-** = self; **-troph** = food, nourish (*photoautotroph*: an organism that harnesses light energy to drive the synthesis of organic compounds from carbon dioxide)

sapro- = rotten (*saprobe*: an organism that acts as a decomposer by absorbing nutrients from dead organic matter)

sym- = with, together; **-bios** = life (*symbiosis*: an ecological relationship between organisms of two different species that live together in direct contact)

thermo- = temperature (*thermophiles*: microorganisms which thrive in hot environments, often 60–80°C)

trans- = across (*transformation*: a phenomenon in which external DNA is assimilated by a cell)

References

Doolittle, W. F. "Uprooting the Tree of Life." *Scientific American*, February 2000.

Futuyma, D. J. *Evolutionary Biology*, Sunderland, Massachusetts: Sinauer Associates, Inc. 1998.

Hoppert, M. and F. Mayer "Prokaryotes" *American Scientist*, May–June 1999.

Visual Guide to the Image Library

27-00-BacteriaOnPin.jpg

27-01-HeatLovingProkaryotes.jpg

27-02-ThreeDomains-L.gif

27-02-ThreeDomains-NL.gif

27-03-ProkaryoteShapes.jpg

27-03a-SphericalProkaryotes.jpg

27-03b-RodShapedProkaryotes.jpg

27-03c-HelicalProkaryote.jpg

27-04-LargestProkaryote.jpg

27-04x1-LargeProkaryote.jpg

27-04x2-ProkaryotesAndEukar.jpg

27-05-GramPosGramNegBact-L.jpg

27-05-GramPosGramNegBact-NL.jpg

27-05x-GramPositiveNegative.jpg

27-06-Pili.jpg

27-07-ProkaryoteFlagella-L.jpg

27-07-ProkaryoteFlagella-NL.jpg

27-07-SalmonellaFlagella-S.mov

27-07x1-Flagella.jpg

27-07x1a-Flagella.jpg

27-07x1b-Flagella.jpg

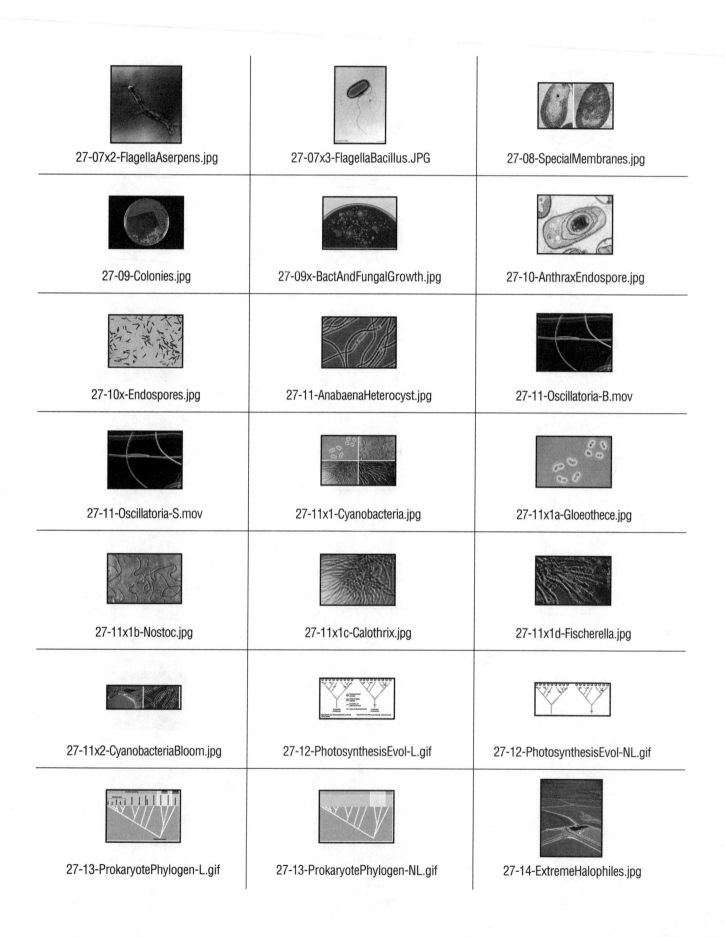

27-07x2-FlagellaAserpens.jpg

27-07x3-FlagellaBacillus.JPG

27-08-SpecialMembranes.jpg

27-09-Colonies.jpg

27-09x-BactAndFungalGrowth.jpg

27-10-AnthraxEndospore.jpg

27-10x-Endospores.jpg

27-11-AnabaenaHeterocyst.jpg

27-11-Oscillatoria-B.mov

27-11-Oscillatoria-S.mov

27-11x1-Cyanobacteria.jpg

27-11x1a-Gloeothece.jpg

27-11x1b-Nostoc.jpg

27-11x1c-Calothrix.jpg

27-11x1d-Fischerella.jpg

27-11x2-CyanobacteriaBloom.jpg

27-12-PhotosynthesisEvol-L.gif

27-12-PhotosynthesisEvol-NL.gif

27-13-ProkaryotePhylogen-L.gif

27-13-ProkaryotePhylogen-NL.gif

27-14-ExtremeHalophiles.jpg

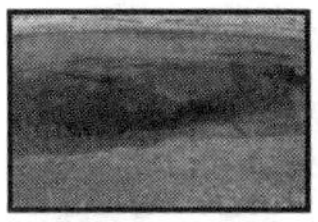

27-14x1-HotSprings.jpg

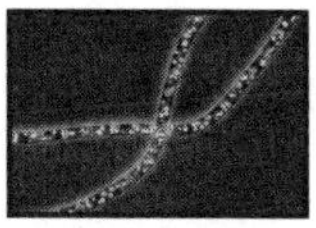

27-14x2-BeggiatoaSulfurEat.jpg

27-15-BacterialHeadlights.jpg

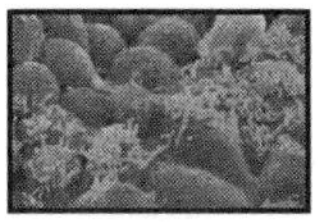

27-16-Hinfluenzae.jpg

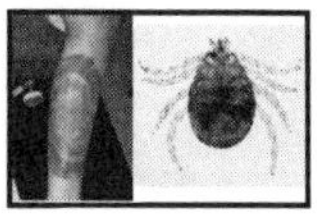

27-17-LymeDiseaseCollage.jpg

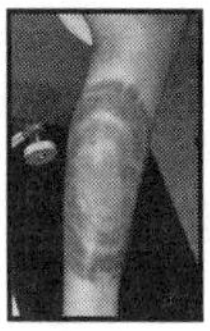

27-17a-LymeDisease.jpg

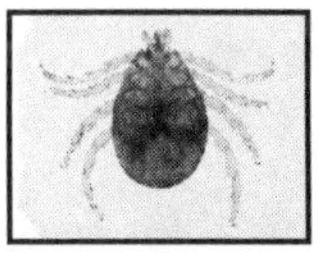

27-17b-LymeTick.jpg

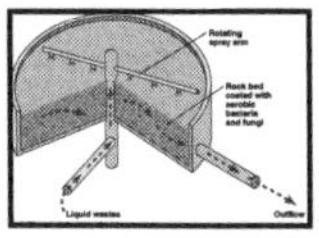

27-18-SewageTreatment-L.gif

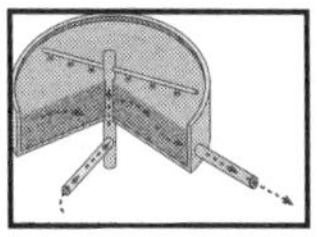

27-18-SewageTreatment-NL.gif

27-18-SewageTreatment.jpg

27-19-OilSpillTreatment.jpg

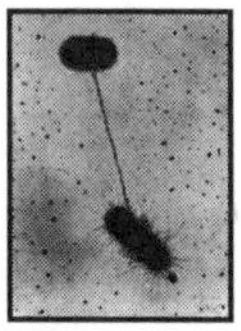

27-x1-ProkaryoteConjugation.jpg

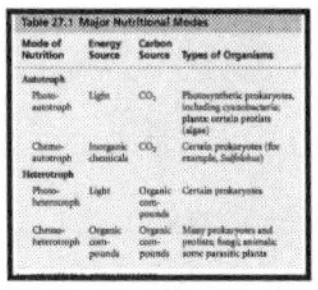

27T-01-NutritionalModes-L.gif

27T-02-ThreeDomainsofLife-L.gif

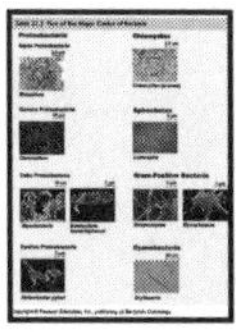

27T-03-BacteriaClades-L.jpg

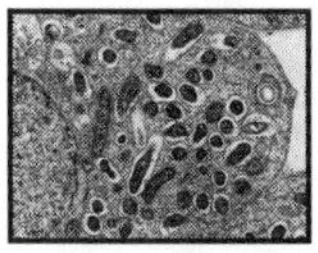

27T-03a-Rhizobium.jpg

27T-03b-Chromatium.jpg

27T-03c-Myxobacteria.jpg

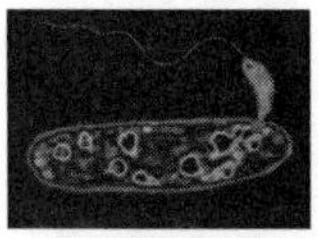

27T-03d-Bdellovibrio.jpg

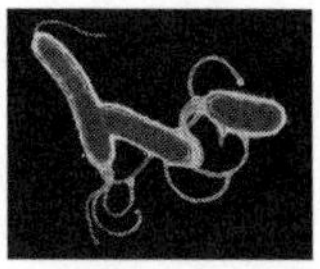

27T-03e-Helicobacter.jpg

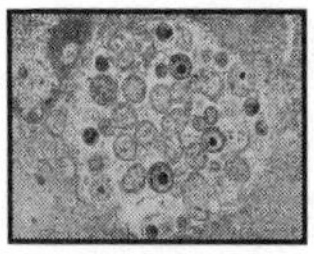

27T-03f-Chlamydias.jpg

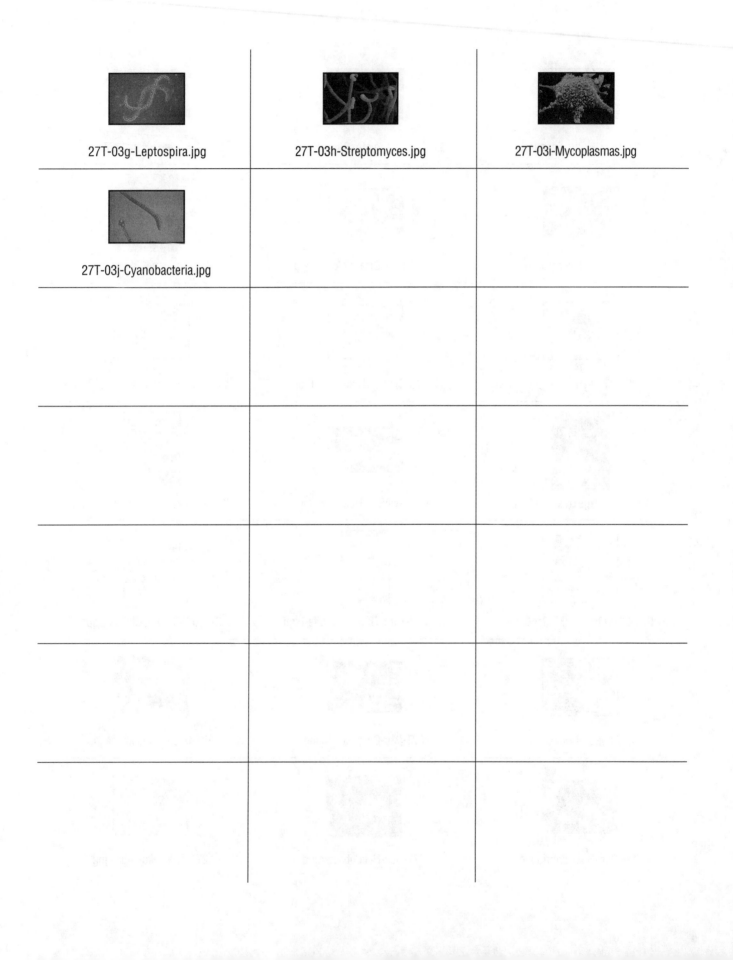

27T-03g-Leptospira.jpg

27T-03h-Streptomyces.jpg

27T-03i-Mycoplasmas.jpg

27T-03j-Cyanobacteria.jpg

CHAPTER 28

The Origins of Eukaryotic Diversity

Chapter Outline

Transparency Acetates

The Transparency Acetates for *Biology*, Sixth Edition, include the following images:

Figure 28.2	The kingdom Protista problem
Figure 28.3	*Euglena*: an example of a single-celled protist
Figure 28.4	A model of the origin of eukaryotes
Figure 28.5	Secondary endosymbiosis and the origin of algal diversity
Figure 28.6	Traditional hypothesis for how the three domains of life are related
Figure 28.7	An alternative hypothesis for how the three domains of life are related
Figure 28.8	A tentative phylogeny of eukaryotes
Figure 28.13	The two-host life history of *Plasmodium*, the apicomplexan that causes malaria
Figure 28.14c	Ciliates: *Paramecium*
Figure 28.15	Conjugation and genetic recombination in *Paramecium caudatum*
Figure 28.16	The life cycle of a water mold (Layer 1)
Figure 28.16	The life cycle of a water mold (Layer 2)
Figure 28.16	The life cycle of a water mold (Layer 3)
Figure 28.21	The life cycle of *Laminaria:* and example of alternation of generations
Figure 28.24	The life cycle of *Chlamydomonas*
Figure 28.25	A simplified history of plastids in the photosynthetic eukaryotes
Figure 28.29	The life cycle of a plasmodial slime mold, such as *Physarum*
Figure 28.30	The life cycle of a cellular slime mold (*Dictyostelium*)
Table 28.1	A sample of protistan diversity

Media for Instructors

Campbell Image Presentation Library

The Campbell Image Presentation Library CD-ROM set includes the following for your use:

- All art (available in pdf and jpeg or gif formats), photos (from the text and outside sources), and tables. Art images are also available without callouts. See the Visual Guide to the Image Library section at the end of this chapter for thumbnail versions of every image.
- A PowerPoint™ slide show of the art (with callouts), photos (both text and outside sources), and tables.
- The following video clips:

28-01a-Amoeba-B.mov	Amoeboid movement
28-03-Euglena-B.mov	*Euglena acus* (two swimming cells, 400x)
28-03-EuglenaMotion-B.mov	Euglenoid Motion (one cell treated with NiSO4)

28-12-Dinoflagellate-B.mov	Dinoflagellate showing whirling motion
28-14-VorticellaCilia-B.mov	Vorticella cilia
28-14-VorticellaDetail-B.mov	Vorticella detailed view
28-14-VorticellaHabitat-B.mov	Vorticella in its environment
28-14a-Stentor-B.mov	Vortical beating of cilia
28-14a-Stentor2-B.mov	Stentor
28-16-SaprolegniaOogonium-B.mov	Through-focus Saprolegnia containing zygotes
28-16-ZoosporeRelease-B.mov	Zoosporangium release in Saprolegnia
28-17-DiatomsMoving-B.mov	Diatoms—Navicula moving around
28-17-VariousDiatoms-B.mov	Diatoms, cyanobacteria, spyrogyra
28-23a-VolvoxColony-B.mov	Through-focus Volvox, 200x
28-23a-VolvoxDaughter-B.mov	Through-focus Volvox, 100x daughter colony
28-23a-VolvoxFlagella-B.mov	Through-focus Volvox, 600x
28-24-Chlamydomonas-B.mov	Unicellular algae—anterior flagella and contractile vacuole
28-26-AmoebaPseudopodia-B.mov	Amoeba pseudopod
28-29-SlimeMoldStreaming-B.mov	Slime mold cytoplasmic streaming
28-29-SlimeMoldZoom-B.mov	Slime mold zoom

PowerPoint Lectures CD-ROM

The PowerPoint Lectures CD-ROM contains slides that integrate the art, photos, tables, and lecture outline from this chapter.

Campbell Biology Website (Instructor Resources)

See the insert in your copy of Campbell/Reece *Biology*, Sixth Edition, for instructions on how to access the Campbell Biology Website. The Instructor Resources section of the website includes the following:

- The art, photos, tables, PowerPoint slide shows, videos, and animations from the Campbell Image Presentation Library
- Suggested answers to the Lab Report questions from the Case Studies in the Process of Science
- The PowerPoint Lecture for this chapter
- Word files of the lecture outline for this chapter
- Photo links

Course Management Systems

The media content for this chapter is available in three course management systems: CourseCompass™, Blackboard, and WebCT. For more information, go to http://cms.aw.com. For the latest pdf instructions on how to use CourseCompass, go to www.coursecompass.com. In addition, a Syllabus Manager is offered on the Campbell Biology Website.

Media for Students

The Campbell Biology Website and CD-ROM include the following for your students:

- Objectives
- Chapter Review (Summary, Self-Quiz, and Essay Questions from the book; Word Roots; Key Terms linked to the Glossary)
- Activities (see list below)
- Case Studies in the Process of Science (see list below)
- Quizzes (Pre-test, Activities Quiz, Chapter Quiz, Essay Questions)
- Web Links
- News and References
- Art and videos from the Campbell Image Presentation Library
- The Campbell *Biology* Interviews (from all editions)
- Glossary with audio pronunciations
- Syllabus Manager

Student Media Activities and Case Studies in The Process of Science

Web/CD Activity 28A: *Tentative Phylogeny of Eukaryotes*

Web/CD Case Study in the Process of Science: *What Kinds of Protists Do Various Habitats Support?*

Objectives

Introduction to the Protists

1. Explain the historical and current difficulties in classifying members of the kingdom Protista.
2. Explain why protistan cells are not analogous to a single cell from a multicellular organism.
3. Describe the different nutritional strategies of protists.
4. Describe the three ecological categories of protists. Explain why the terms "protozoa" and "algae" have little usefulness.
5. Distinguish between prokaryotic and eukaryotic flagella.
6. Describe the general protistan life cycles and habitats.

The Origin and Early Diversification of Eukaryotes

7. Describe three evolutionary trends that occurred as some prokaryotic groups became increasingly complex.
8. Describe the evidence that supports the theory that mitochondria and plastids evolved by serial endosymbiosis. Explain what living organisms are the likely relatives of the prokaryotes that gave rise to mitochondria and plastids.

9. Given the endosymbiosis theory, explain the modern collaboration between the genome of the organelles and nucleus.

10. Explain the diversity of plastids and the phylogenetic discontinuity of photosynthesis among protists.

11. Explain why the evolutionary origin of the eukaryotic cell doesn't easily fit within the traditional model of an evolutionary tree. Describe the reasons for the new weblike phylogeny and the problem of assigning groups to kingdoms and phyla.

A Sample of Protistan Diversity

12. Describe the current hypothesis for the lack of mitochondria in diplomonads and parabasalids.

13. Describe the structure, ecology, and human impact of diplomonads, parabasalids, euglenoids, kinetoplastids, dinoflagellates, apicomplexans, ciliates, stramenopiles, heterokont algae, oomycotes, bacillariophytes, chrysophytes, phaeophytes, rhodophytes, and chlorophytes.

14. Describe the similarities and distinct characteristics of the rhizopods, actinopods, and foraminifera.

15. Describe the adaptations of Mycetozoa that facilitate their role as decomposers.

16. Compare the life cycles and ecology of plasmodial and cellular slime molds.

Key Terms

mixotrophs
protozoa (singular, protozoan)
algae (singular, alga)
syngamy
cysts
plankton
phytoplankton
plastid
serial endosymbiosis
secondary endosymbiosis
diplomonads
parabasalids
kinetoplastids
euglenoid
Alveolata
dinoflagellate

apicomplexan
sporozoites
ciliate
conjugation
Stramenopila
Oomycotes
water molds
white rusts
downy mildews
diatom
golden algae
thallus (plural, thalli)
holdfast
stipe
blades
alternation of generations

sporophyte
gametophyte
heteromorphic
isomorphic
red algae
green algae
lichen
pseudopodium
amoeba
heliozoan
radiolarian
foram
Mycetozoa
plasmoidal slime mold
plasmodium
cellular slime mold

Word Roots

-phyte = plant (*gametophyte*: the multicellular haploid form in organisms undergoing alternation of generations)

con- = with, together (*conjugation*: in bacteria, the transfer of DNA between two cells that are temporarily joined)

helio- = sun; **-zoan** = animal (*heliozoan*: sun animals that live in fresh water. They have skeletons made of siliceous or chitinous unfused plates)

hetero- = different; **-morph** = form (*heteromorphic*: a condition in the life cycle of all modern plants in which the sporophyte and gametophyte generations differ in morphology)

iso- = same (*isomorphic*: alternating generations in which the sporophytes and gametophytes look alike, although they differ in chromosome number)

pseudo- = false; **-podium** = foot (*pseudopodium*: a cellular extension of amoeboid cells used in moving and feeding)

thallos- = sprout (*thallus*: a seaweed body that is plantlike but lacks true roots, stems, and leaves)

References

Bold, H. C. and M. J. Wynne. *Introduction to the Algae: Structure and Reproduction*. 2nd ed. Englewood Cliffs, New Jersey: Prentice-Hall, Inc., 1985.

Doolittle, W. F. "Uprooting the Tree of Life." *Scientific American*, February 2000.

Lee, J. J., S. H. Hutner and E. C. Bovee. *An Illustrated Guide to the Protozoa*. Lawrence, Kansas: Allen Press, Inc., 1985.

Visual Guide to the Image Library

28-00-Protozoan.jpg

28-01a-Amoeba-B.mov

28-01a-Amoeba-S.mov

28-01a-AmoebaProteus.jpg

28-01b-Diatom.jpg

28-01c-SlimeMold.jpg

28-01d-Kelp.jpg

28-02-ProtistaProblem-L.gif

28-02-ProtistaProblem-NL.gif

28-03-Euglena-B.mov

28-03-Euglena-S.mov

28-03-EuglenaArt-L.jpg

28-03-EuglenaArt-NL.jpg

28-03-EuglenaMotion-B.mov

28-03-EuglenaMotion-S.mov

28-03x-EuglenaPhoto.jpg

28-04-EukaryoteOrigin-L.gif

28-04-EukaryoteOrigin-NL.gif

28-05-OriginAlgalDivers-L.gif

28-05-OriginAlgalDivers-NL.gif

28-06-LUCAhypothesis-L.gif

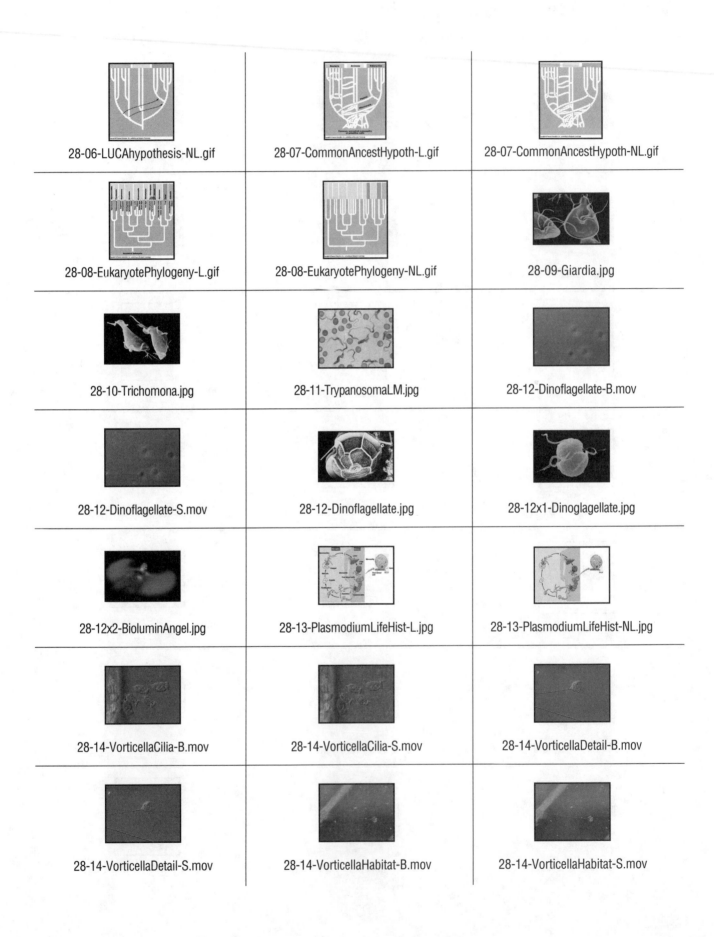

28-06-LUCAhypothesis-NL.gif

28-07-CommonAncestHypoth-L.gif

28-07-CommonAncestHypoth-NL.gif

28-08-EukaryotePhylogeny-L.gif

28-08-EukaryotePhylogeny-NL.gif

28-09-Giardia.jpg

28-10-Trichomona.jpg

28-11-TrypanosomaLM.jpg

28-12-Dinoflagellate-B.mov

28-12-Dinoflagellate-S.mov

28-12-Dinoflagellate.jpg

28-12x1-Dinoglagellate.jpg

28-12x2-BioluminAngel.jpg

28-13-PlasmodiumLifeHist-L.jpg

28-13-PlasmodiumLifeHist-NL.jpg

28-14-VorticellaCilia-B.mov

28-14-VorticellaCilia-S.mov

28-14-VorticellaDetail-B.mov

28-14-VorticellaDetail-S.mov

28-14-VorticellaHabitat-B.mov

28-14-VorticellaHabitat-S.mov

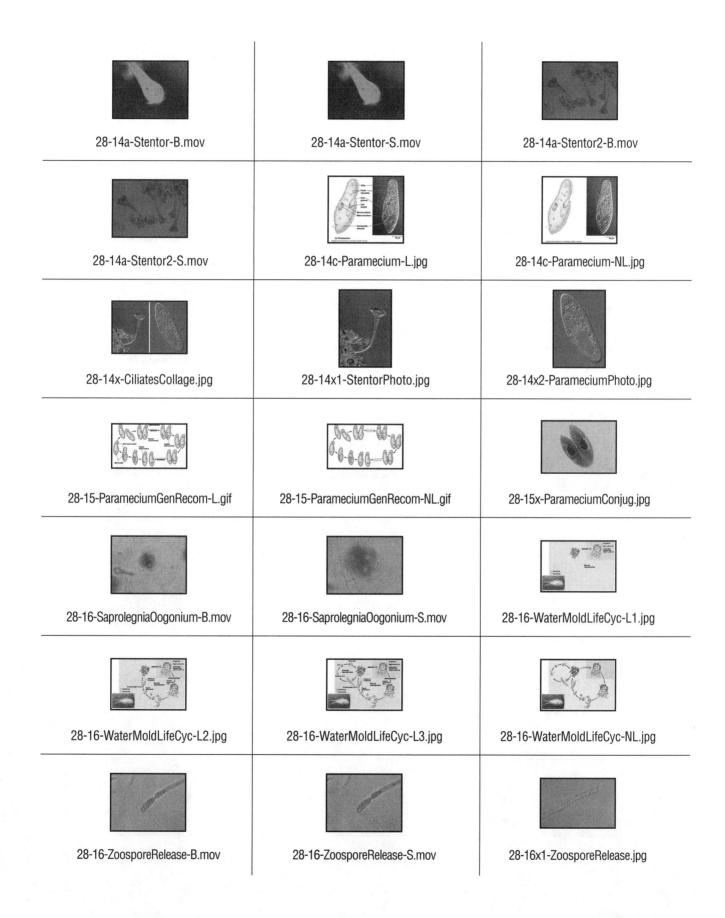

28-14a-Stentor-B.mov

28-14a-Stentor-S.mov

28-14a-Stentor2-B.mov

28-14a-Stentor2-S.mov

28-14c-Paramecium-L.jpg

28-14c-Paramecium-NL.jpg

28-14x-CiliatesCollage.jpg

28-14x1-StentorPhoto.jpg

28-14x2-ParameciumPhoto.jpg

28-15-ParameciumGenRecom-L.gif

28-15-ParameciumGenRecom-NL.gif

28-15x-ParameciumConjug.jpg

28-16-SaprolegniaOogonium-B.mov

28-16-SaprolegniaOogonium-S.mov

28-16-WaterMoldLifeCyc-L1.jpg

28-16-WaterMoldLifeCyc-L2.jpg

28-16-WaterMoldLifeCyc-L3.jpg

28-16-WaterMoldLifeCyc-NL.jpg

28-16-ZoosporeRelease-B.mov

28-16-ZoosporeRelease-S.mov

28-16x1-ZoosporeRelease.jpg

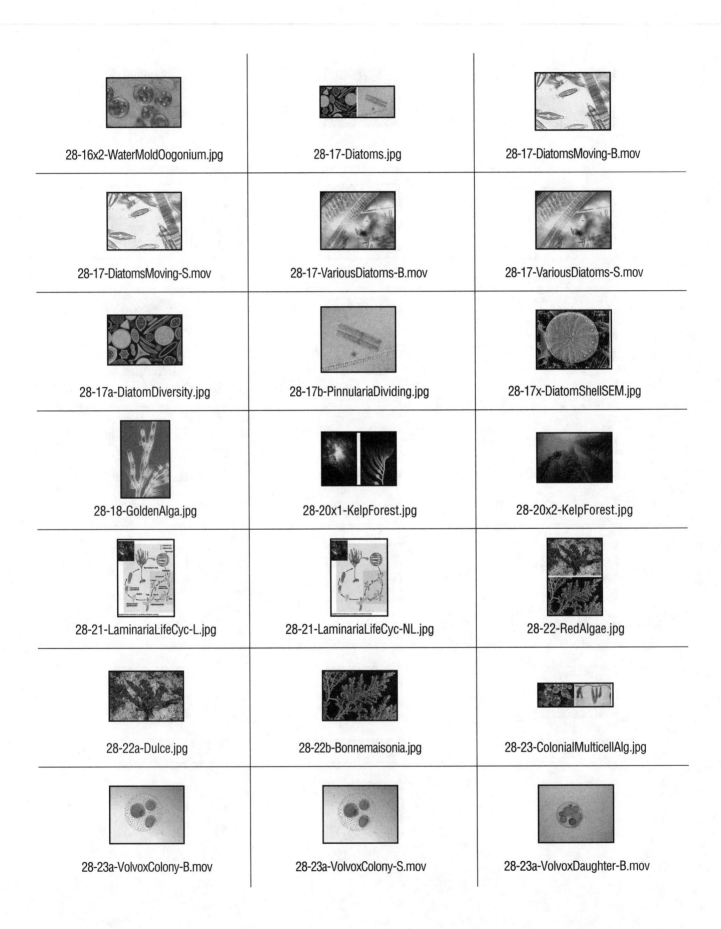

28-16x2-WaterMoldOogonium.jpg

28-17-Diatoms.jpg

28-17-DiatomsMoving-B.mov

28-17-DiatomsMoving-S.mov

28-17-VariousDiatoms-B.mov

28-17-VariousDiatoms-S.mov

28-17a-DiatomDiversity.jpg

28-17b-PinnulariaDividing.jpg

28-17x-DiatomShellSEM.jpg

28-18-GoldenAlga.jpg

28-20x1-KelpForest.jpg

28-20x2-KelpForest.jpg

28-21-LaminariaLifeCyc-L.jpg

28-21-LaminariaLifeCyc-NL.jpg

28-22-RedAlgae.jpg

28-22a-Dulce.jpg

28-22b-Bonnemaisonia.jpg

28-23-ColonialMulticellAlg.jpg

28-23a-VolvoxColony-B.mov

28-23a-VolvoxColony-S.mov

28-23a-VolvoxDaughter-B.mov

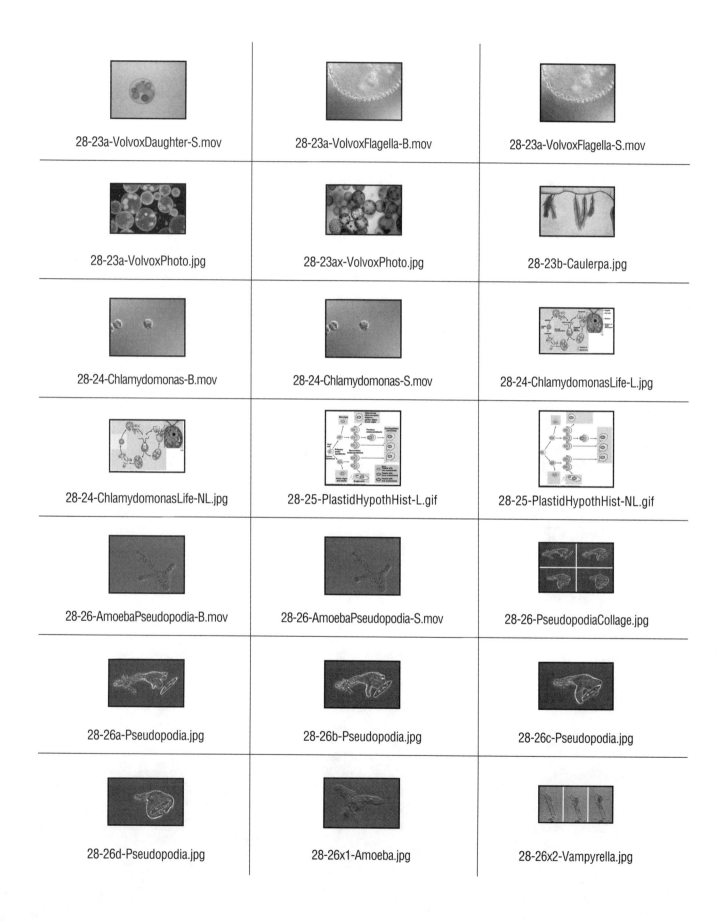

28-23a-VolvoxDaughter-S.mov

28-23a-VolvoxFlagella-B.mov

28-23a-VolvoxFlagella-S.mov

28-23a-VolvoxPhoto.jpg

28-23ax-VolvoxPhoto.jpg

28-23b-Caulerpa.jpg

28-24-Chlamydomonas-B.mov

28-24-Chlamydomonas-S.mov

28-24-ChlamydomonasLife-L.jpg

28-24-ChlamydomonasLife-NL.jpg

28-25-PlastidHypothHist-L.gif

28-25-PlastidHypothHist-NL.gif

28-26-AmoebaPseudopodia-B.mov

28-26-AmoebaPseudopodia-S.mov

28-26-PseudopodiaCollage.jpg

28-26a-Pseudopodia.jpg

28-26b-Pseudopodia.jpg

28-26c-Pseudopodia.jpg

28-26d-Pseudopodia.jpg

28-26x1-Amoeba.jpg

28-26x2-Vampyrella.jpg

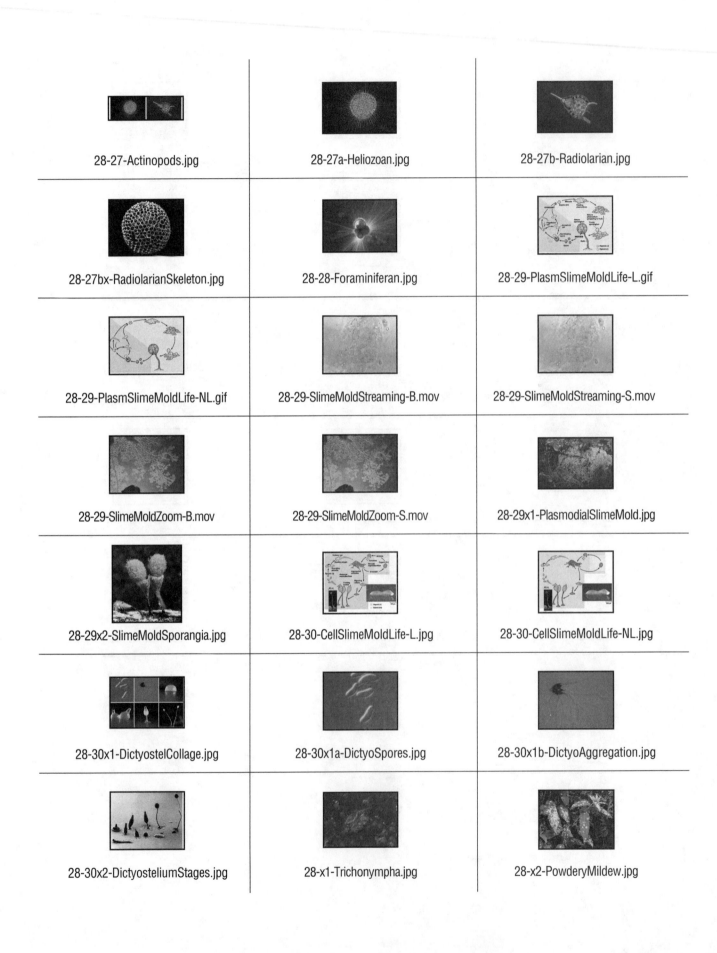

28-27-Actinopods.jpg

28-27a-Heliozoan.jpg

28-27b-Radiolarian.jpg

28-27bx-RadiolarianSkeleton.jpg

28-28-Foraminiferan.jpg

28-29-PlasmSlimeMoldLife-L.gif

28-29-PlasmSlimeMoldLife-NL.gif

28-29-SlimeMoldStreaming-B.mov

28-29-SlimeMoldStreaming-S.mov

28-29-SlimeMoldZoom-B.mov

28-29-SlimeMoldZoom-S.mov

28-29x1-PlasmodialSlimeMold.jpg

28-29x2-SlimeMoldSporangia.jpg

28-30-CellSlimeMoldLife-L.jpg

28-30-CellSlimeMoldLife-NL.jpg

28-30x1-DictyostelCollage.jpg

28-30x1a-DictyoSpores.jpg

28-30x1b-DictyoAggregation.jpg

28-30x2-DictyosteliumStages.jpg

28-x1-Trichonympha.jpg

28-x2-PowderyMildew.jpg

28-x3-SpirogyraConjugation.jpg

28T-01-ProtistanDiversity-L.gif

28UN-555-DiplomonadParab-L.gif

28UN-555-Euglenozoa-L.gif

28UN-556-Alveolata-L.gif

28UN-560-Stramenopila-L.gif

28UN-565-Cholorophyta-L.gif

28UN-565-Rhodophyta-L.gif

28UN-570-Mycetozoa-L.gif

CHAPTER 29

Plant Diversity I: How Plants Colonized Land

Chapter Outline

Transparency Acetates

The Transparency Acetates for *Biology,* Sixth Edition, include the following images:

Table 29.1	Ten Phyla of Extant Plants
Figure 29.1	Some highlights of plant evolution
Figure 29.6	Alternation of generations: a generalized scheme
Figure 29.13	A hypothetical mechanism for the origin of alternation of generations in the ancestor of plants
Figure 29.14	Three clades competing for designation as the plant kingdom
Figure 29.16	The life cycle of *Polytrichum,* a moss (Layer 1)
Figure 29.16	The life cycle of *Polytrichum,* a moss (Layer 2)
Figure 29.16	The life cycle of *Polytrichum,* a moss (Layer 3)
Figure 29.20	*Cooksonia,* a vascular plant of the Siluria
Figure 29.22	Hypotheses for the evolution of leaves
Figure 29.23	The life cycle of a fern

Media for Instructors

Campbell Image Presentation Library

The Campbell Image Presentation Library CD-ROM set includes the following for your use:

- All art (available in pdf and jpeg or gif formats), photos (from the text and outside sources), and tables. Art images are also available without callouts. See the Visual Guide to the Image Library section at the end of this chapter for thumbnail versions of every image.
- A PowerPoint™ slide show of the art (with callouts), photos (both text and outside sources), and tables.
- The following QuickTime animations, adapted from student media activities (also available as Shockwave Flash .swf files):

  29-16-MossLifeCycle.mov

  29-23-FernLifeCycle.mov

PowerPoint Lectures CD-ROM

The PowerPoint Lectures CD-ROM contains slides that integrate the art, photos, tables, and lecture outline from this chapter.

Campbell Biology Website (Instructor Resources)

See the insert in your copy of Campbell/Reece *Biology,* Sixth Edition, for instructions on how to access the Campbell Biology Website. The Instructor Resources section of the website includes the following:

- The art, photos, tables, PowerPoint slide shows, videos, and animations from the Campbell Image Presentation Library

- Suggested answers to the Lab Report questions from the Case Studies in the Process of Science
- The PowerPoint Lecture for this chapter
- Word files of the lecture outline for this chapter
- Photo links

Course Management Systems

The media content for this chapter is available in three course management systems: CourseCompass™, Blackboard, and WebCT. For more information, go to http://cms.aw.com. For the latest pdf instructions on how to use CourseCompass, go to **www.coursecompass.com**. In addition, a Syllabus Manager is offered on the Campbell Biology Website.

Media for Students

The Campbell Biology Website and CD-ROM include the following for your students:

- Objectives
- Chapter Review (Summary, Self-Quiz, and Essay Questions from the book; Word Roots; Key Terms linked to the Glossary)
- Activities (see list below)
- Case Studies in the Process of Science (see list below)
- Quizzes (Pre-test, Activities Quiz, Chapter Quiz, Essay Questions)
- Web Links
- News and References
- Art and videos from the Campbell Image Presentation Library
- The Campbell *Biology* Interviews (from all editions)
- Glossary with audio pronunciations
- Syllabus Manager

Student Media Activities and Case Studies in The Process of Science

Web/CD Activity 29A: *Highlights of Plant Phylogeny*

Web/CD Activity 29B: *Terrestrial Adaptations of Plants*

Web/CD Activity 29C: *Moss Life Cycle*

Web/CD Activity 29D: *Fern Life Cycle*

Web/CD Case Study in the Process of Science: *What Are the Different Stages of a Fern Life Cycle?*

Objectives

An Overview of Land Plant Evolution

1. Distinguish between the four main groups of land plants.

2. Describe the four great evolutionary episodes in the history of land plants.

3. Describe four shared derived homologies that link charophyceans and land plants.

4. Describe eight characteristics that distinguish land plants from charophycean algae. Explain how these features facilitate life on land.

5. Define and distinguish between the stages of the alternation of generations reproductive cycle. Compare the life cycle of humans with alternation of generations.

The Origin of Land Plants

6. Describe the evidence for a phylogenetic connection between land plants and green algae.

7. Describe the fossil record of the early land plants 550 to 425 million years ago.

8. Describe a likely hypothesis for the origin of alternation of generations in plants.

9. Explain how adaptations of charophycean algae to shallow water preadapted plants for life on land.

10. Distinguish between the kingdoms Plantae, Streptophyta, and Viridiplantae. Note which of these is used in the textbook.

Bryophytes

11. List and distinguish between the three phyla of bryophytes. Briefly describe the members of each group, note their common names, and indicate which phylum represented the earliest plants.

12. Describe the structure of the sporophyte and gametophyte stages of bryophytes. Explain why most bryophytes grow close to the ground.

13. Describe the stemlike and leaflike structures that occur in mosses.

14. Diagram the life cycle of a bryophyte. Label the gametophyte and sporophyte stages and the locations of gamete production, fertilization, and spore production.

15. Describe the ecological and economic benefits of bryophytes.

The Origin of Vascular Plants

16. List and distinguish between the groups of modern vascular plants. Explain how they are different from bryophytes.

17. Describe the adaptations of vascular plants, including modifications of the life cycle and modifications of the sporophyte, that have contributed to their success on land.

Pteridophytes: Seedless Vascular Plants

18. Compare the structure of pteridophytes and lycophytes.

19. Distinguish between homosporous and heterosporous conditions.

20. Explain why seedless vascular plants are most commonly found in damp habitats.

21. Describe the structure and habitats of giant and small lycophytes.

22. Compare the typical structure of ferns, sphenophytes, and psilophytes.

23. Describe the production and dispersal of fern spores.

24. Describe the major life cycle differences between mosses and ferns.

25. Explain how coal is formed and note during which geologic period the most extensive coal beds were produced.

Key Terms

bryophytes	sporangia	rhizoids
vascular plants	spore mother cells	foot
vascular tissue	gametangia	seta
pteridophytes	archegonia	sporangium
seed	antheridia	capsule
gymnosperm	cuticle	calyptra
angiosperm	stomata	peristome
charophyceans	xylem	peat
rosette cellulose-synthesizing complexes	phloem	branched sporophytes
	deep green	seedless vascular plants
peroxisome	kingdom Streptophyta	protracheophyte
phragmoplast	kingdom Viridiplantae	polysporangiophytes
apical meristem	kingdom Plantae	microphylls
placental transfer cells	phylum Hepatophyta	megaphylls
embryophyte	liverworts	homosporous
alternation of generations	phylum Anthocerophyta (hornworts)	heterosporous
gametophyte		megaspores
sporophyte	phylum Bryophyta (mosses)	microspores
spore	protonema	sporophylls
sporopollenin	gametophore	sori

Word Roots

-angio = vessel (*gametangia*: the reproductive organ of bryophytes, consisting of the male antheridium and female archegonium; a multichambered jacket of sterile cells in which gametes are formed)

-phore - bearer (*gametophore*: the mature gamete-producing structure of a gametophyte body of a moss)

bryo- = moss; **-phyte** = plant (*bryophytes*: the mosses, liverworts, and hornworts; a group of nonvascular plants that inhabit the land but lack many of the terrestrial adaptations of vascular plants)

gymno- = naked; **-sperm** = seed (*gymnosperm*: a vascular plant that bears naked seeds not enclosed in any specialized chambers)

hetero- = different; **-sporo** = a seed (*heterosporous*: referring to plants in which the sporophyte produces two kinds of spores that develop into unisexual gametophytes, either female or male)

homo- = like (*homosporous*: referring to plants in which a single type of spore develops into a bisexual gametophyte having both male and female sex organs)

mega- = large (*megaspores*: a spore from a heterosporous plant that develops into a female gametophyte bearing archegonia)

micro- = small; **-phyll** = leaf (*microphylls*: the small leaves of lycophytes that have only a single, unbranched vein)

peri- = around; **-stoma** = mouth (*peristome*: the upper part of the moss capsule often specialized for gradual spore discharge)

phragmo- = a partition; **-plast** = formed, molded (*phragmoplast*: an alignment of cytoskeletal elements and Golgi-derived vesicles across the mid-line of a dividing plant cell)

pro- = before; **poly-** = many (*protracheophytepolysporangiophytes*: a group of Silurian moss-like ancestors that were like bryophytes in lacking lignified vascular tissue but were different in having independent, branched, sporophytes that were not dependent on gametophytes for their growth)

proto- = first; **-nema** = thread (*protonema*: a mass of green, branched, one-cell thick filaments produced by germinating moss spores)

pterido- = fern (*pteridophytes*: seedless plants with true roots with lignified vascular tissue; the group includes ferns, whisk ferns, and horsetails)

rhizo- = root; **-oid** = like, form (*rhizoids*: long tubular single cells or filaments of cells that anchor bryophytes to the ground)

References

Raven, P. H., R. F. Evert and S. E. Eichhorn. *Biology of Plants*. 6th ed. New York: Worth Publishers, Inc., 1998.

Visual Guide to the Image Library

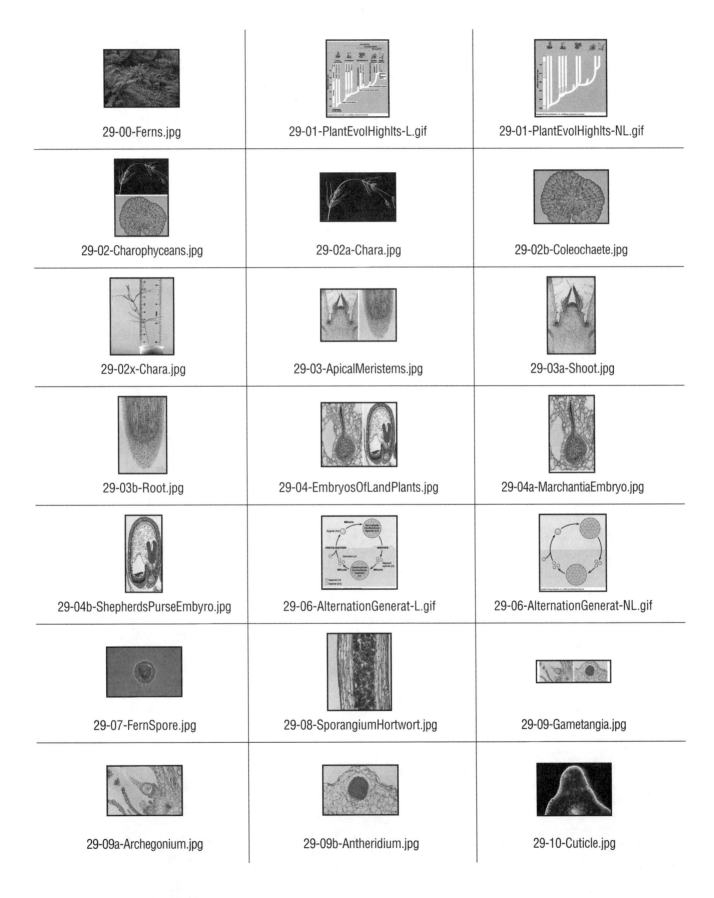

29-00-Ferns.jpg

29-01-PlantEvolHighlts-L.gif

29-01-PlantEvolHighlts-NL.gif

29-02-Charophyceans.jpg

29-02a-Chara.jpg

29-02b-Coleochaete.jpg

29-02x-Chara.jpg

29-03-ApicalMeristems.jpg

29-03a-Shoot.jpg

29-03b-Root.jpg

29-04-EmbryosOfLandPlants.jpg

29-04a-MarchantiaEmbryo.jpg

29-04b-ShepherdsPurseEmbyro.jpg

29-06-AlternationGenerat-L.gif

29-06-AlternationGenerat-NL.gif

29-07-FernSpore.jpg

29-08-SporangiumHortwort.jpg

29-09-Gametangia.jpg

29-09a-Archegonium.jpg

29-09b-Antheridium.jpg

29-10-Cuticle.jpg

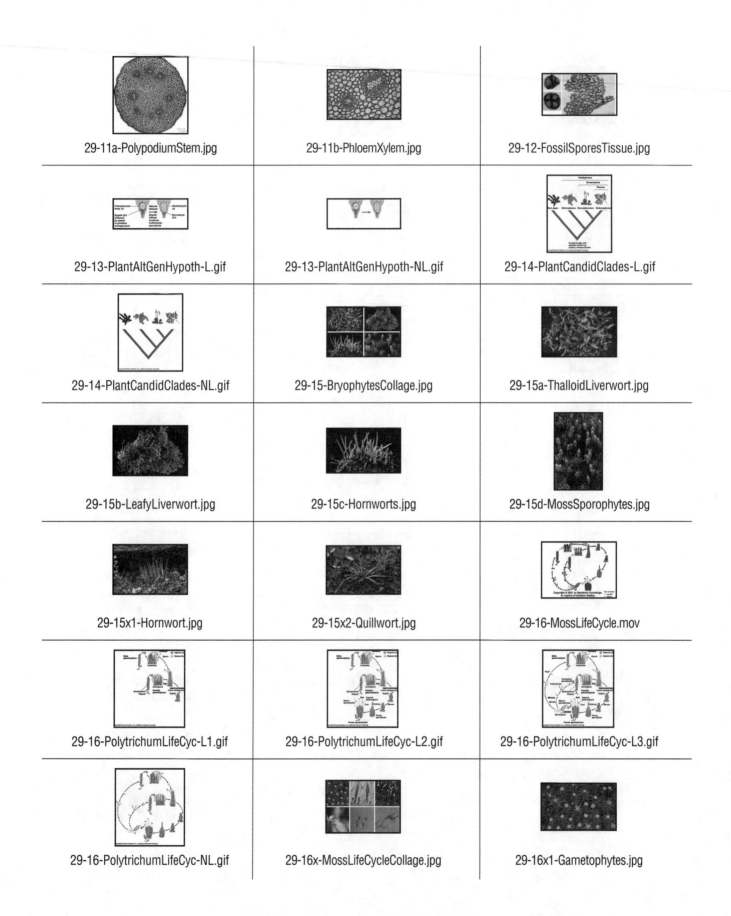

29-11a-PolypodiumStem.jpg

29-11b-PhloemXylem.jpg

29-12-FossilSporesTissue.jpg

29-13-PlantAltGenHypoth-L.gif

29-13-PlantAltGenHypoth-NL.gif

29-14-PlantCandidClades-L.gif

29-14-PlantCandidClades-NL.gif

29-15-BryophytesCollage.jpg

29-15a-ThalloidLiverwort.jpg

29-15b-LeafyLiverwort.jpg

29-15c-Hornworts.jpg

29-15d-MossSporophytes.jpg

29-15x1-Hornwort.jpg

29-15x2-Quillwort.jpg

29-16-MossLifeCycle.mov

29-16-PolytrichumLifeCyc-L1.gif

29-16-PolytrichumLifeCyc-L2.gif

29-16-PolytrichumLifeCyc-L3.gif

29-16-PolytrichumLifeCyc-NL.gif

29-16x-MossLifeCycleCollage.jpg

29-16x1-Gametophytes.jpg

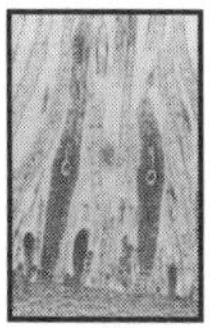

29-16x2-Archegonium.jpg

29-16x3-Sporophytes.jpg

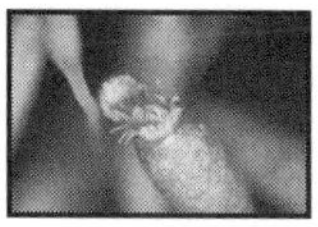

29-16x4-Sporangium.jpg

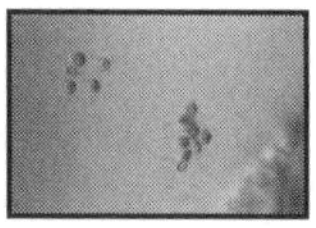

29-16x5-Spores.jpg

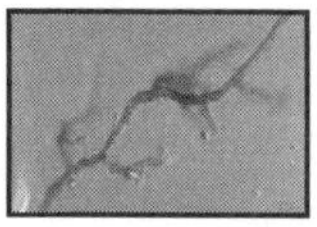

29-16x6-Protonemata.jpg

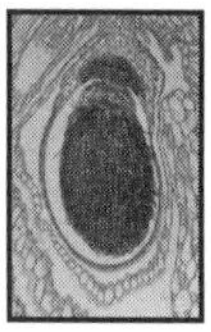

29-17-SporophyteSection.jpg

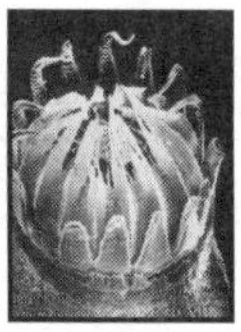

29-18-MossSporangium.jpg

29-19-SphagnumMossCollage.jpg

29-19a-PeatMossBogLake.jpg

29-19b-SphagnumMoss.jpg

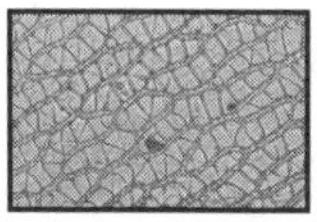

29-19c-SphagnumLeaf.jpg

29-19x-NorwayPeatMossBog.jpg

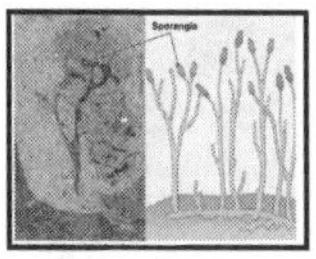

29-20-Cooksonia-L.jpg

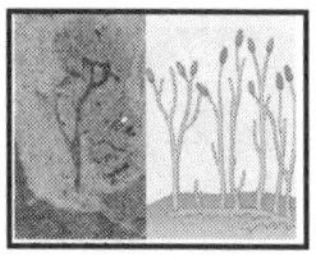

29-20-Cooksonia-NL.jpg

29-21-PteridophytesCollage.jpg

29-21a-ClubMoss.jpg

29-21b-WhiskFern.jpg

29-21c-Horsetail.jpg

29-21d-PolypodiumFern.jpg

29-21x1-Lycophyte.jpg

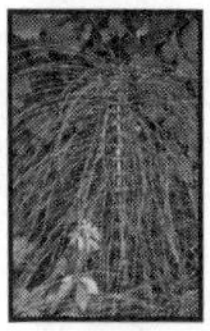

29-21x2-Horsetail.jpg

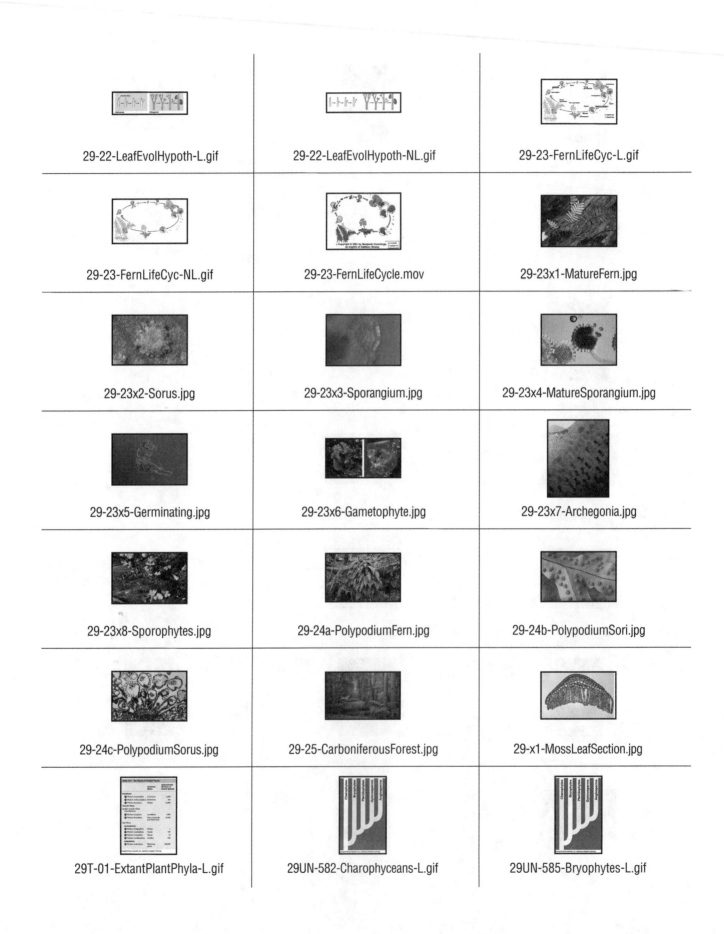

29-22-LeafEvolHypoth-L.gif

29-22-LeafEvolHypoth-NL.gif

29-23-FernLifeCyc-L.gif

29-23-FernLifeCyc-NL.gif

29-23-FernLifeCycle.mov

29-23x1-MatureFern.jpg

29-23x2-Sorus.jpg

29-23x3-Sporangium.jpg

29-23x4-MatureSporangium.jpg

29-23x5-Germinating.jpg

29-23x6-Gametophyte.jpg

29-23x7-Archegonia.jpg

29-23x8-Sporophytes.jpg

29-24a-PolypodiumFern.jpg

29-24b-PolypodiumSori.jpg

29-24c-PolypodiumSorus.jpg

29-25-CarboniferousForest.jpg

29-x1-MossLeafSection.jpg

29T-01-ExtantPlantPhyla-L.gif

29UN-582-Charophyceans-L.gif

29UN-585-Bryophytes-L.gif

29UN-590-PteridophytesL.gif

CHAPTER 30

Plant Diversity II: The Evolution of Seed Plants

Chapter Outline

Transparency Acetates

The Transparency Acetates for *Biology*, Sixth Edition, include the following images:

Figure 30.1	Three variations on gametophyte/sporophyte relationships
Figure 30.2	From ovule to seed
Figure 30.4	Hypothetical phylogeny of the seed plants
Figure 30.9	The life cycle of a pine (Layer 1)
Figure 30.9	The life cycle of a pine (Layer 2)
Figure 30.9	The life cycle of a pine (Layer 3)
Figure 30.12	Xylem cells in angiosperms
Figure 30.13	The structure of a flower
Figure 30.14	Hypothesis for the origin of the carpel from a reproductive leaf (sporophyll)
Figure 30.15	Relationship between a pea flower and a fruit (pea pod)
Table 30.1	Classification of fleshy fruits
Figure 30.17	The life cycle of an angiosperm
Table 30.2	A sampling of medicines derived from plants
Figure 30.Q7-10	Cladogram

Media for Instructors

Campbell Image Presentation Library

The Campbell Image Presentation Library CD-ROM set includes the following for your use:

- All art (available in pdf and jpeg or gif formats), photos (from the text and outside sources), and tables. Art images are also available without callouts. See the Visual Guide to the Image Library section at the end of this chapter for thumbnail versions of every image.

- A PowerPoint™ slide show of the art (with callouts), photos (both text and outside sources), and tables.

- The following video clips:

30-13-TimeLapseFlower-B.mov	Time-lapse of flower opening
30-17-TimeLapsePlant-B.mov	Time-lapse plant life history
30-18a-BeePollinator-B.mov	Pollinator/plant relationships
30-18c-BatPollinators-B.mov	Pollinator/plant relationships

- The following QuickTime animation, adapted from student media activities (also available as a Shockwave Flash .swf file):

  30-09-PineLifeCycle.mov

PowerPoint Lectures CD-ROM

The PowerPoint Lectures CD-ROM contains slides that integrate the art, photos, tables, and lecture outline from this chapter.

Campbell Biology Website (Instructor Resources)

See the insert in your copy of Campbell/Reece *Biology*, Sixth Edition, for instructions on how to access the Campbell Biology Website. The Instructor Resources section of the website includes the following:

- The art, photos, tables, PowerPoint slide shows, videos, and animations from the Campbell Image Presentation Library
- Suggested answers to the Lab Report questions from the Case Studies in the Process of Science
- The PowerPoint Lecture for this chapter
- Word files of the lecture outline for this chapter
- Photo links

Course Management Systems

The media content for this chapter is available in three course management systems: CourseCompass™, Blackboard, and WebCT. For more information, go to http://cms.aw.com. For the latest pdf instructions on how to use CourseCompass, go to **www.coursecompass.com**. In addition, a Syllabus Manager is offered on the Campbell Biology Website.

Media for Students

The Campbell Biology Website and CD-ROM include the following for your students:

- Objectives
- Chapter Review (Summary, Self-Quiz, and Essay Questions from the book; Word Roots; Key Terms linked to the Glossary)
- Activities (see list below)
- Case Studies in the Process of Science (see list below)
- Quizzes (Pre-test, Activities Quiz, Chapter Quiz, Essay Questions)
- Web Links
- News and References
- Art and videos from the Campbell Image Presentation Library
- The Campbell *Biology* Interviews (from all editions)
- Glossary with audio pronunciations
- Syllabus Manager

Student Media Activities and Case Studies in The Process of Science

Web/CD Activity 30A: *Pine Life Cycle*

Web/CD Case Study in the Process of Science: *How Are Trees Identified by Their Leaves?*

Web/CD Activity 30B: *Angiosperm Life Cycle*

Objectives

Overview of Seed Plant Evolution

1. Describe the three most important reproductive adaptations of seed plants for life on land.

Gymnosperms

2. Relate the climate changes of the Mesozoic era to the success of gymnosperms during that time.

3. List and distinguish among the four phyla of gymnosperms.

4. Describe the life history of a pine and indicate which structures are part of the gametophyte generation and which are part of the sporophyte generation.

Angiosperms (Flowering Plants)

5. Distinguish between monocots, dicots, and eudicots.

6. Explain the significance of the plant *Amborella*.

7. Identify the following floral structures and describe a function for each:

   a. sepals   d. carpels   g. stigma

   b. petals   e. filament   h. style

   c. stamens   f. anther   i. ovary

8. Define "fruit" and explain how fruits are modified in ways that help disperse seeds.

9. Diagram the generalized life cycle of an angiosperm and the development of the male and female gametophyte.

10. Explain the process and function of double fertilization.

11. Explain how animals may have influenced the evolution of terrestrial plants and vice versa.

Plants and Human Welfare

12. Describe the significance of angiosperms to human agriculture.

13. Describe the importance of plant diversity.

Key Terms

seed plants
seed
integuments
ovule
pollination
progymnosperms
sporophylls
phylum Ginkgophyta
phylum Cycadophyta
phylum Gnetophyta
phylum Coniferophyta
conifer
phylum Anthophyta
monocots

dicots
eudicots
flower
sepal
petal
stamen
carpel
filament
anther
stigma
style
ovary
fruit
pericarp

simple fruit
aggregate fruit
multiple fruit
pollen grains
ovule
embryo sac
cross-pollination
double fertilization
cotyledons
endosperm
coevolution

Word Roots

co- = with, together (*coevolution*: the mutual influence on the evolution of two different species interacting with each other and reciprocally influencing each other's adaptations)

endo- = inner (*endosperm*: a nutrient-rich tissue formed by the union of a sperm cell with two polar nuclei during double fertilization, which provides nourishment to the developing embryo in angiosperm seeds)

peri- = around; **-carp** = fruit (*pericarp*: the thickened wall of a fruit)

pro- = before; **gymno-** = naked; **-sperm** = seed (*progymnosperm*: an extinct group of plants that is probably ancestral to gymnosperms and angiosperms)

References

Raven, P. H., R. F. Evert and S. E. Eichhorn. *Biology of Plants*. 6th ed. New York: Worth Publishers, Inc., 1998.

Visual Guide to the Image Library

30-00-Seed.jpg

30-01-GametoSporophyte-L.gif

30-01-GametoSporophyte-NL.gif

30-02-OvuleToSeed-L.gif

30-02-OvuleToSeed-NL.gif

30-03-PineSeed.jpg

30-04-PhylogenySeedPlnts-L.gif

30-04-PhylogenySeedPlnts-NL.gif

30-05a-Ginkgo.jpg

30-05b-GinkgoInAutumn.jpg

30-05c-Ginkgo.jpg

30-05x1-GinkgoMaleFemale.jpg

30-05x1a-GinkgoMale.jpg

30-05x1b-GinkgoFemale.jpg

30-05x2-GinkgoSperm.jpg

30-06-Cycads.jpg

30-06a-CycadGarden.jpg

30-06b-CycadCone.jpg

30-07a-Welwitschia.jpg

30-07b-Gnetum.jpg

30-07c-Ephedra.jpg

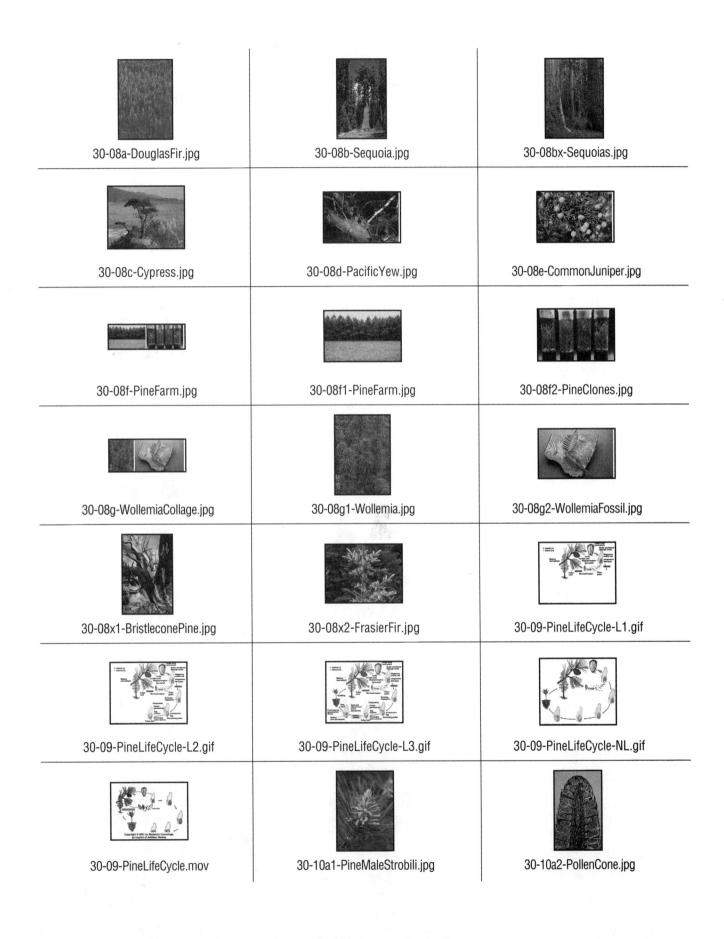

30-08a-DouglasFir.jpg

30-08b-Sequoia.jpg

30-08bx-Sequoias.jpg

30-08c-Cypress.jpg

30-08d-PacificYew.jpg

30-08e-CommonJuniper.jpg

30-08f-PineFarm.jpg

30-08f1-PineFarm.jpg

30-08f2-PineClones.jpg

30-08g-WollemiaCollage.jpg

30-08g1-Wollemia.jpg

30-08g2-WollemiaFossil.jpg

30-08x1-BristleconePine.jpg

30-08x2-FrasierFir.jpg

30-09-PineLifeCycle-L1.gif

30-09-PineLifeCycle-L2.gif

30-09-PineLifeCycle-L3.gif

30-09-PineLifeCycle-NL.gif

30-09-PineLifeCycle.mov

30-10a1-PineMaleStrobili.jpg

30-10a2-PollenCone.jpg

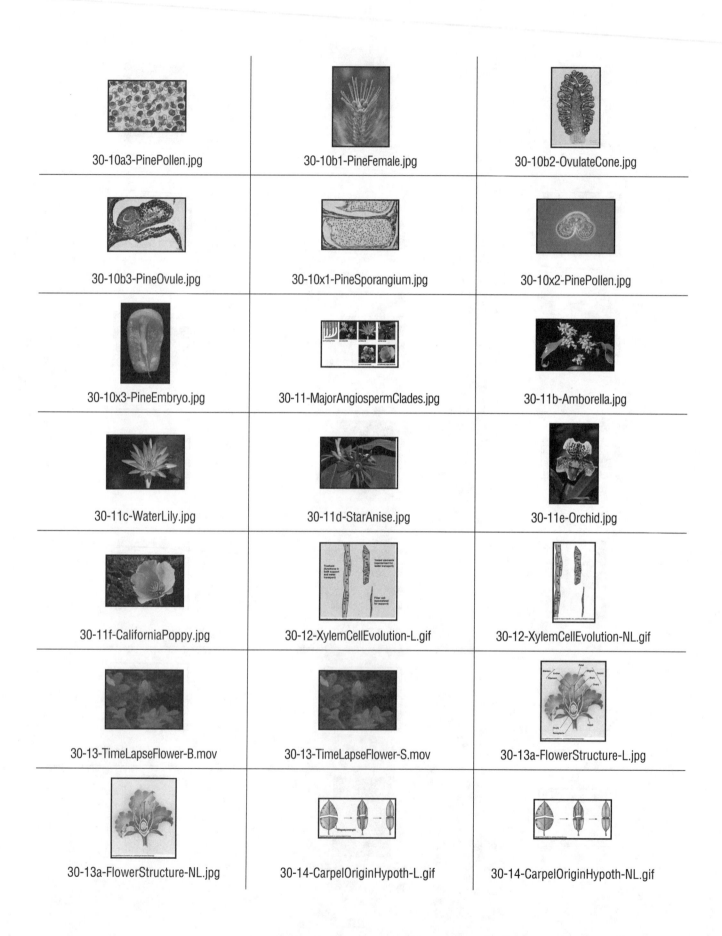

30-10a3-PinePollen.jpg

30-10b1-PineFemale.jpg

30-10b2-OvulateCone.jpg

30-10b3-PineOvule.jpg

30-10x1-PineSporangium.jpg

30-10x2-PinePollen.jpg

30-10x3-PineEmbryo.jpg

30-11-MajorAngiospermClades.jpg

30-11b-Amborella.jpg

30-11c-WaterLily.jpg

30-11d-StarAnise.jpg

30-11e-Orchid.jpg

30-11f-CaliforniaPoppy.jpg

30-12-XylemCellEvolution-L.gif

30-12-XylemCellEvolution-NL.gif

30-13-TimeLapseFlower-B.mov

30-13-TimeLapseFlower-S.mov

30-13a-FlowerStructure-L.jpg

30-13a-FlowerStructure-NL.jpg

30-14-CarpelOriginHypoth-L.gif

30-14-CarpelOriginHypoth-NL.gif

30-15-PeaFlowerFruitRel-L.jpg	30-15-PeaFlowerFruitRel-NL.jpg	30-16-DispersalCollage.jpg
30-16x1-DandelionDispersal.jpg	30-16x2-ParrotRedBerries.jpg	30-17-AngiospLifeCycle-L.gif
30-17-AngiospLifeCycle-NL.gif	30-17-TimeLapsePlant-B.mov	30-17-TimeLapsePlant-S.mov
30-18-PollinatorsCollage.jpg	30-18a-BeeOnFlower.jpg	30-18a-BeePollinator-B.mov
30-18a-BeePollinator-S.mov	30-18b-Hummingbird.jpg	30-18c-BatPollinators-B.mov
30-18c-BatPollinators-S.mov	30-18c-BatPollinatorsPhoto.jpg	30-19-Deforestation.jpg
30-19a-ClearCutting.jpg	30-19b-SlashAndBurn.jpg	30-19x-Deforestation.jpg

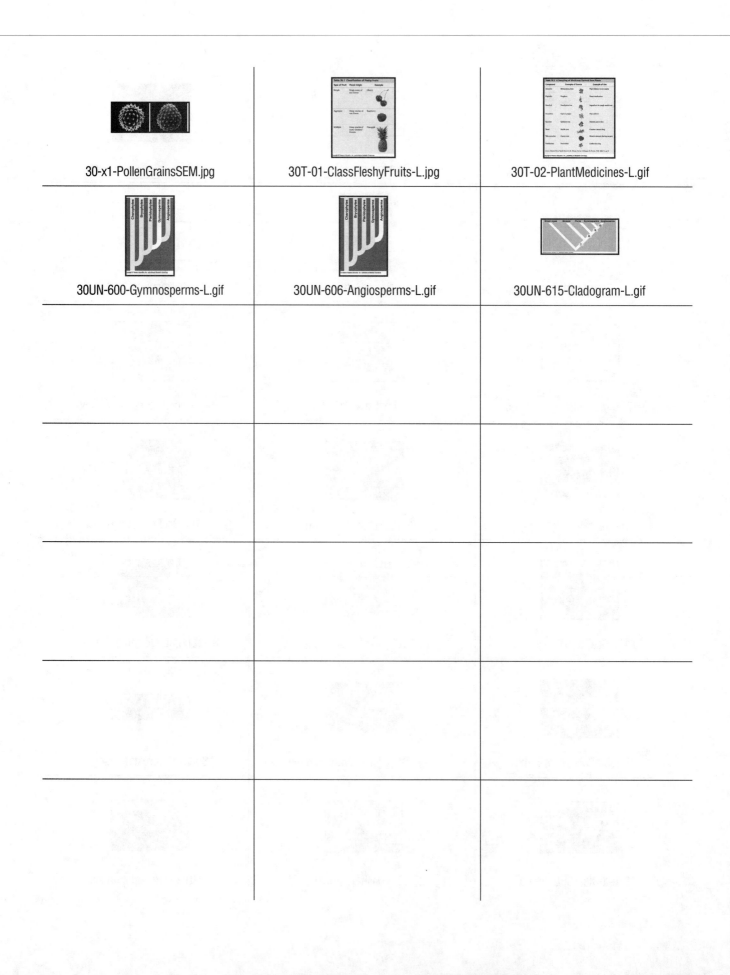

30-x1-PollenGrainsSEM.jpg

30T-01-ClassFleshyFruits-L.jpg

30T-02-PlantMedicines-L.gif

30UN-600-Gymnosperms-L.gif

30UN-606-Angiosperms-L.gif

30UN-615-Cladogram-L.gif

CHAPTER 31

Fungi

Chapter Outline

Introduction to the Fungi

Absorptive nutrition enables fungi to live as decomposers and symbionts

Extensive surface area and rapid growth adapt fungi for absorptive nutrition

Fungi disperse and reproduce by releasing spores that are produced either sexually or asexually

Many fungi have a heterokaryotic stage

Diversity of Fungi

Phylum Chytridiomycota: Chytrids may provide clues about fungal origins

Phylum Zygomycota: Zygote fungi form resistant structures during sexual reproduction

Phylum Ascomycota: Sac fungi produce sexual spores in saclike asci

Phylum Basidiomycota: Club fungi have long-lived dikaryotic mycelia

Molds, yeasts, lichens, and mycorrhizae are specialized lifestyles that evolved independently in diverse fungal phyla

Ecological Impacts of Fungi

Ecosystems depend on fungi as decomposers and symbionts

Some fungi are pathogens

Fungi are commercially important

Evolution of Fungi

Fungi colonized land with plants

Fungi and animals evolved from a common protistan ancestor

Transparency Acetates

The Transparency Acetates for *Biology*, Sixth Edition, include the following images:

Figure 31.1 Fungal mycelia

Figure 31.2 Examples of fungal hyphae

Figure 31.3	Generalized life cycle of fungi (Layer 1)
Figure 31.3	Generalized life cycle of fungi (Layer 2)
Figure 31.3	Generalized life cycle of fungi (Layer 3)
Figure 31.4	Phylogeny of fungi
Figure 31.7	The life cycle of the zygomycete *Rhizopus* (black bread mold)
Figure 31.10	The life cycle of an ascomycete
Figure 31.12	The life cycle of a mushroom-forming basidiomycete
Table 31.1	Review of fungal phyla
Figure 31.17	Anatomy of a lichen

Media for Instructors

Campbell Image Presentation Library

The Campbell Image Presentation Library CD-ROM set includes the following for your use:

- All art (available in pdf and jpeg or gif formats), photos (from the text and outside sources), and tables. Art images are also available without callouts. See the Visual Guide to the Image Library section at the end of this chapter for thumbnail versions of every image.

- A PowerPoint™ slide show of the art (with callouts), photos (both text and outside sources), and tables.

- The following video clips:

31-05PhlyctochytriumSpore-B.mov	Releasing spores from a haploid sporangium
31-05x-AllomycesSpore-S.mov	Releasing diploid zoospores from a sporangium

- The following QuickTime animation, adapted from student media activities (also available as a Shockwave Flash .swf file):

   31-03-FungusLifeCycle.mov

PowerPoint Lectures CD-ROM

The PowerPoint Lectures CD-ROM contains slides that integrate the art, photos, tables, and lecture outline from this chapter.

Campbell Biology Website (Instructor Resources)

See the insert in your copy of Campbell/Reece *Biology*, Sixth Edition, for instructions on how to access the Campbell Biology Website. The Instructor Resources section of the website includes the following:

- The art, photos, tables, PowerPoint slide shows, videos, and animations from the Campbell Image Presentation Library

- Suggested answers to the Lab Report questions from the Case Studies in the Process of Science

- The PowerPoint Lecture for this chapter
- Word files of the lecture outline for this chapter
- Photo links

Course Management Systems

The media content for this chapter is available in three course management systems: CourseCompass™, Blackboard, and WebCT. For more information, go to http://cms.aw.com. For the latest pdf instructions on how to use CourseCompass, go to **www.coursecompass.com**. In addition, a Syllabus Manager is offered on the Campbell Biology Website.

Media for Students

The Campbell Biology Website and CD-ROM include the following for your students:

- Objectives
- Chapter Review (Summary, Self-Quiz, and Essay Questions from the book; Word Roots; Key Terms linked to the Glossary)
- Activities (see list below)
- Case Studies in the Process of Science (see list below)
- Quizzes (Pre-test, Activities Quiz, Chapter Quiz, Essay Questions)
- Web Links
- News and References
- Art and videos from the Campbell Image Presentation Library
- The Campbell *Biology* Interviews (from all editions)
- Glossary with audio pronunciations
- Syllabus Manager

Student Media Activities and Case Studies in The Process of Science

Web/CD Activity 31A: *Fungal Reproduction and Nutrition*

Web/CD Activity 31B: *Fungal Life Cycles*

Web/CD Case Study in the Process of Science: *How Does the Fungus* Pilobus *Succeed as a Decomposer?*

Objectives

Introduction to the Fungi

1. List the characteristics that distinguish fungi from organisms in the other four kingdoms.
2. Explain how fungi acquire their nutrients.
3. Explain how nonmotile fungi seek new food sources and how they disperse.
4. Describe the basic body plan of a fungus.
5. Describe the processes of plasmogamy and karyogamy.

Diversity of Fungi

6. Distinguish among the groups Chytridiomycota, Zygomycota, Ascomycota, and Basidiomycota. Include a description of the sexual structure that characterizes each group and list some common examples of each.
7. Compare the structures and life cycles of molds, yeasts, lichens, and mycorrhizae.

Ecological Impacts of Fungi

8. Describe the roles of fungi in ecosystems.
9. Explain how fungi can be dangerous and costly to humans.
10. Explain how fungi are commercially important.

Evolution of Fungi

11. Describe the evolutionary relationships between the four fungal groups.
12. Describe the nature of the common ancestor of fungi and animals.

Key Terms

absorbtion	heterokaryon	conidia
exoenzymes	plasmogamy	basidium
hyphae (singular, hypha)	karyogamy	club fungus
	dikaryotic	basidiocarps
mycelium (plural, mycelia)	chytrids	mold
	zygote fungi	imperfect fungi
septa (singular, septum)	mycorrhizae	yeasts
	zygosporangium	lichen
chitin	sac fungi	soredia
coenocytic	asci (singular, ascus)	mycosis
haustoria	ascocarps	

Word Roots

-osis = a condition of (*mycosis*: the general term for a fungal infection)

coeno- = common; **-cyto** = cell (*coenocytic*: referring to a multinucleated condition resulting from the repeated division of nuclei without cytoplasmic division)

di- = two; **-karyo** = nucleus (*dikaryotic*: a mycelium with two haploid nuclei per cell, one from each parent)

exo- = out, outside (*exoenzymes*: powerful hydrolytic enzymes secreted by a fungus outside its body to digest food)

hetero- = different (*heterokaryon*: a mycelium formed by the fusion of two hyphae that have genetically different nuclei)

myco- = fungus; **rhizo-** = root (*mycorrhizae*: mutualistic associations of plant roots and fungi)

plasmo- plasm; **-gamy** = marriage (*plasmogamy*: the fusion of the cytoplasm of cells from two individuals; occurs as one stage of syngamy)

References

Motluk, A. "If the smoke don't get you the tobacco will." *New Scientist*, January 2000.

Murawski, D. A. "Fungi" *National Geographic*, volume 198, 2000.

Visual Guide to the Image Library

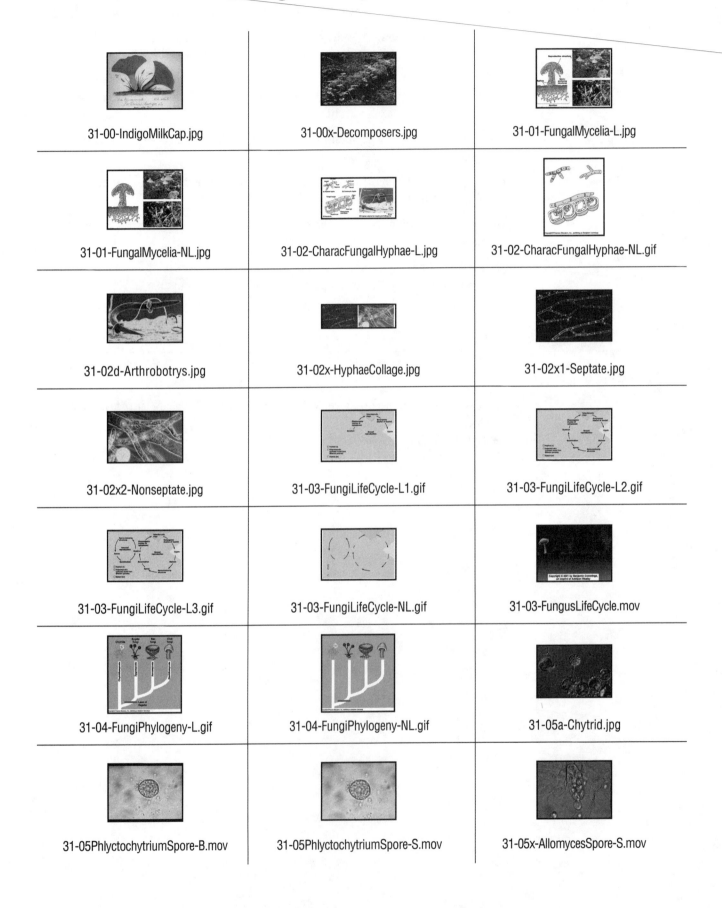

31-00-IndigoMilkCap.jpg

31-00x-Decomposers.jpg

31-01-FungalMycelia-L.jpg

31-01-FungalMycelia-NL.jpg

31-02-CharacFungalHyphae-L.jpg

31-02-CharacFungalHyphae-NL.gif

31-02d-Arthrobotrys.jpg

31-02x-HyphaeCollage.jpg

31-02x1-Septate.jpg

31-02x2-Nonseptate.jpg

31-03-FungiLifeCycle-L1.gif

31-03-FungiLifeCycle-L2.gif

31-03-FungiLifeCycle-L3.gif

31-03-FungiLifeCycle-NL.gif

31-03-FungusLifeCycle.mov

31-04-FungiPhylogeny-L.gif

31-04-FungiPhylogeny-NL.gif

31-05a-Chytrid.jpg

31-05PhlyctochytriumSpore-B.mov

31-05PhlyctochytriumSpore-S.mov

31-05x-AllomycesSpore-S.mov

31-06-Rhizophus.jpg

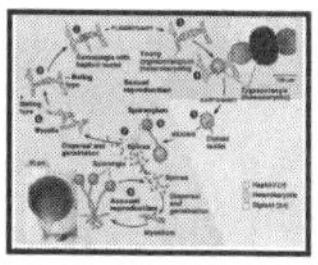

31-07-ZygomyceteLifeCyc-L.jpg

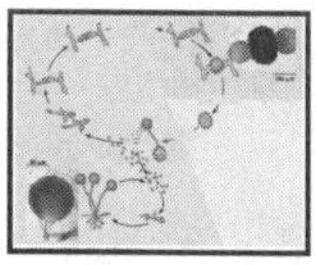

31-07-ZygomyceteLifeCyc-NL.jpg

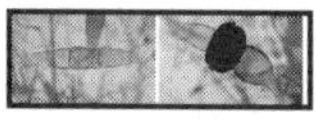

31-07x-RhizopusCollage.jpg

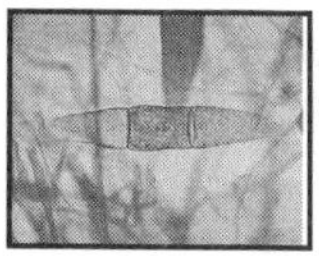

31-07x1-YoungZygosporangium.jpg

31-07x2-MatureZygosporangiu.jpg

31-08-Pilobolus.jpg

31-09-AscomycetesCollage.jpg

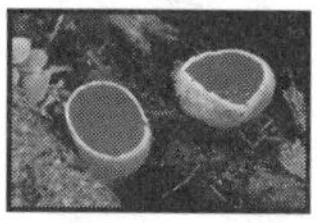

31-09a-ScarletCup.jpg

31-09b-Truffles.jpg

31-09c-Morel.jpg

31-09x1-CarbonFungus.jpg

31-09x2-Aspergillus.jpg

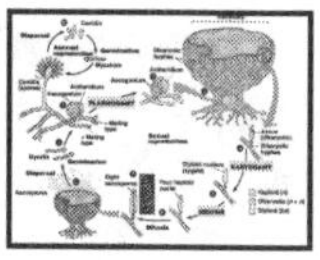

31-10-AscomycLifeCycArt-L.jpg

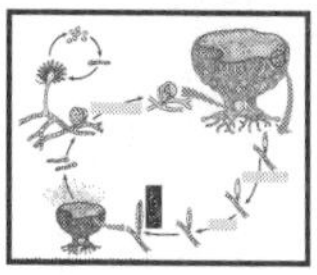

31-10-AscomycLifeCycArt-NL.jpg

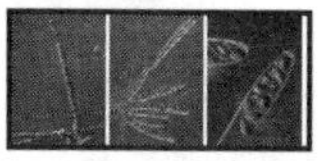

31-10x1-AscomycetesCollage.jpg

31-10x1a-AntheridialElemnts.jpg

31-10x1b-DevelopingAsci.jpg

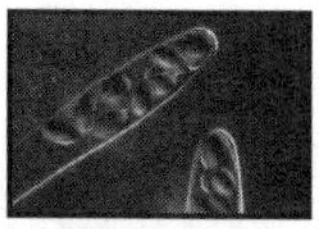

31-10x1c-MatureAsci.jpg

31-10x2-Apothecium.jpg

31-11-Basidiomycetes.jpg

31-11a-GrevillesBolete.jpg

31-11b-Trametes.jpg

31-11c-Stinkhorn.jpg

31-11x1-Coprinus.jpg

31-11x2-Geastrum.jpg

31-11x3-Tremella.jpg

31-11x4-Stinkhorn.jpg

31-11x5-Amanita.jpg

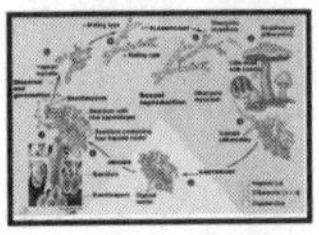

31-12-BasidiomyLifeCyc-L.jpg

31-12-BasidiomyLifeCyc-NL.jpg

31-12x-GillsBasidiaCollage.jpg

31-12xa-GillsBasidia.jpg

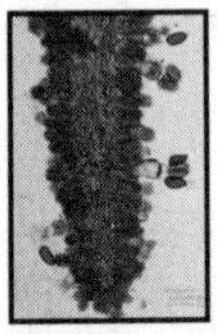

31-12xb-GillsBasidiaLM.jpg

31-13-FairyRing.jpg

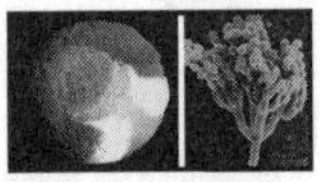

31-14-MoldyOrangeCollage.jpg

31-14a-MoldyOrange.jpg

31-14b-Penicillium.jpg

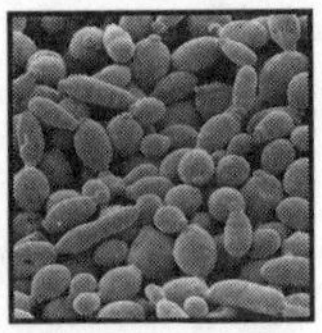

31-15-BuddingYeast.jpg

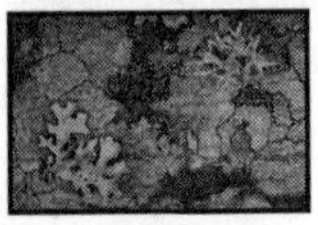

31-16-Lichens.jpg

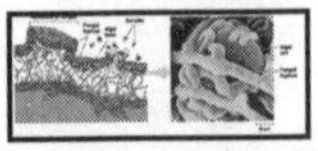

31-17-LichenAnatomy-L.jpg

31-17-LichenAnatomy-NL.jpg

31-17b-AlgaeInHyphae.jpg

31-17x-LichenAnatomy.jpg

31-18-Mycorrhizae.jpg

31-19-BenefitsMycorrhizae.jpg

31-20b-StemRust.jpg

31-20bc-FungalDiseases.jpg

31-20c-Ergot.jpg

31-20x1-Botrytis.jpg

31-20x2-PinkEarRotOnCorn.jpg

31-21-FungalAntibiotic.jpg

31-x1-SoilPlate.jpg

31T-01-FungalPhyla-L.gif

31UN-619-Chytridiomycota-L.gif

31UN-620-Zygomycota-L.gif

31UN-622-Ascomycota-L.gif

31UN-624-Basidiomycota-L.gif

CHAPTER 32

Introduction to Animal Evolution

Chapter Outline

What Is an Animal?

Structure, nutrition, and life history define animals

The animal kingdom probably evolved from a colonial, flagellated protist

Two Views of Animal Diversity

The remodeling of phylogenetic trees illustrates the process of scientific inquiry

The traditional phylogenetic tree of animals is based mainly on grades in body "plans"

Molecular systematists are moving in some branches around on the phylogenetic tree of animals

The Origins of Animal Diversity

Most animal phyla originated in a relatively brief span of geologic time

"Evo-devo" may clarify our understanding of the Cambrian diversification

Transparency Acetates

The Transparency Acetates for *Biology*, Sixth Edition, include the following images:

Media for Instructors

Campbell Image Presentation Library

The Campbell Image Presentation Library CD-ROM set includes the following for your use:

- All art (available in pdf and jpeg or gif formats), photos (from the text and outside sources), and tables. Art images are also available without callouts. See the Visual Guide to the Image Library section at the end of this chapter for thumbnail versions of every image.
- A PowerPoint™ slide show of the art (with callouts), photos (both text and outside sources), and tables.

PowerPoint Lectures CD-ROM

The PowerPoint Lectures CD-ROM contains slides that integrate the art, photos, tables, and lecture outline from this chapter.

Campbell Biology Website (Instructor Resources)

See the insert in your copy of Campbell/Reece *Biology,* Sixth Edition, for instructions on how to access the Campbell Biology Website. The Instructor Resources section of the website includes the following:

- The art, photos, tables, PowerPoint slide shows, videos, and animations from the Campbell Image Presentation Library
- Suggested answers to the Lab Report questions from the Case Studies in the Process of Science
- The PowerPoint Lecture for this chapter
- Word files of the lecture outline for this chapter
- Photo links

Course Management Systems

The media content for this chapter is available in three course management systems: CourseCompass™, Blackboard, and WebCT. For more information, go to http://cms.aw.com. For the latest pdf instructions on how to use CourseCompass, go to www.coursecompass.com. In addition, a Syllabus Manager is offered on the Campbell Biology Website.

Media for Students

The Campbell Biology Website and CD-ROM include the following for your students:

- Objectives
- Chapter Review (Summary, Self-Quiz, and Essay Questions from the book; Word Roots; Key Terms linked to the Glossary)
- Activities (see list below)
- Case Studies in the Process of Science (see list below)
- Quizzes (Pre-test, Activities Quiz, Chapter Quiz, Essay Questions)
- Web Links
- News and References
- Art and videos from the Campbell Image Presentation Library
- The Campbell *Biology* Interviews (from all editions)
- Glossary with audio pronunciations
- Syllabus Manager

Student Media Activities and Case Studies in The Process of Science

Web/CD Activity 32A: *Traditional Animal Phylogenetic Tree*

Web/CD Case Study in the Process of Science: *How Do Molecular Data Fit Traditional Phylogenies?*

Objectives

What Is an Animal?

1. List the characteristics that define animals and distinguish them from other organisms.
2. Explain how and when the first animals likely evolved.

Two Views of Animal Diversity

3. Describe the nature of the scientific evidence that is reshaping our view of the phylogenetic relationships of all forms of life. Explain how this revolution illustrates the scientific process.
4. Outline the major phylogenetic branches of the animal kingdom based on grades of organization; symmetry and embryonic germ layers; the absence or presence of a body cavity; and the protostome-deuterostome dichotomy. Distinguish between radial and bilateral symmetry.
5. Distinguish among the acoelomate, pseudocoelomate, and coelomate grades.
6. Distinguish between spiral and radial cleavage; determinant and indeterminate cleavage; and schizocoelous and enterocoelous development.

7. Compare the developmental differences between protostomes and deuterostomes, including

   a. patterns of cleavage

   b. fates of the blastopore

   c. coelom formation

8. Compare the phylogenetic tree based on grades in body plans with the emerging view of animal phylogeny based mainly on molecular biology.

The Origins of Animal Diversity

9. Describe the evidence that suggests animals may have first evolved about a billion years ago.

10. Describe the nature of the Ediacaran fossils.

11. Explain the significance of the Cambrian explosion. Describe the nature of its fossil organisms.

12. Explain and compare the three main hypotheses for what caused the Cambrian diversification of animals.

Key Terms

ingestion	bilateria	protostomes
cleavage	cephalization	deuterostomes
blastula	germ layers	spiral cleavage
gastrulation	ectoderm	determinate cleavage
gastrula	endoderm	radial cleavage
larva	archenterons	indeterminate cleavage
metamorphosis	mesoderm	schizocoelous
grade	diploblastic	enterocoelous
parazoan	triploblastic	blastopore
eumetazoan	acoelomate	Lophotrochozoa
radial symmetry	body cavity	Ecdysozoa
radiata	pseudocoelom	trocophore larva
bilateral symmetry	pseudocoelomate	lophophore
dorsal	coelomate	Ediacaran period
ventral	coelom	Cambrium explosion
anterior	Protostomia	
posterior	Deuterostomia	

Word Roots

a- = without; **-koilos** = a hollow (*acoelomate*: the condition of lacking a coelom)

arch- = ancient, beginning (*archenteron*: the endoderm-lined cavity, formed during the gastrulation process, that develops into the digestive tract of an animal)

bi- = two (*Bilateria*: members of the branch of eumetazoans possessing bilateral symmetry)

blast- = bud, sprout; **-pore** = a passage (*blastopore*: the opening of the archenteron in the gastrula that develops into the mouth in protostomes and the anus in deuterostomes)

cephal- = head (*cephalization*: an evolutionary trend toward the concentration of sensory equipment on the anterior end of the body)

deutero- = second (*deuterostome*: one of two distinct evolutionary lines of coelomates characterized by radial, indeterminate cleavage, enterocoelous formation of the coelom, and development of the anus from the blastopore)

di- = two (*diploblastic*: having two germ layers)

ecdys- = an escape (*Ecdysozoa*: one of two distinct clades within the protostomes. It includes the arthropods)

ecto- = outside; **-derm** = skin (*ectoderm*: the outermost of the three primary germ layers in animal embryos)

endo- = within (*endoderm*: the innermost of the three primary germ layers in animal embryos)

entero- = the intestine, gut (*enterocoelous*: in deuterostomes; the coelomic cavities form when mesoderm buds from the wall of the archenteron and hollows out)

gastro- = stomach, belly (*gastrulation*: the formation of a gastrula from a blastula)

in- = into; **-gest** = carried (*ingestion*: a heterotrophic mode of nutrition in which other organisms or detritus are eaten whole or in pieces)

lopho- = a crest, tuft; **-trocho** = a wheel; (*Lophotrochozoa*: one of two distinct clades within the protostomes. It includes annelids and mollusks)

meso- = middle (*mesoderm*: the middle primary germ layer of an early embryo)

meta- = boundary, turning point; **-morph** = form (*metamorphosis*: the resurgence of development in an animal larva that transforms it into a sexually mature adult)

para- = beside; **-zoan** = animal (*parazoan*: members of the subkingdom of animals consisting of the sponges)

proto- = first; **-stoma** = mouth (*protostomes*: a member of one of two distinct evolutionary lines of coelomates characterized by spiral, determinate cleavage, schizocoelous formation of the coelom, and development of the mouth from the blastopore)

pseudo- = false (*pseudocoelom*: a body cavity which is not completely lined by mesoderm)

radia- = a spoke, ray (*radiata*: members of the radially symmetrical animal phyla, including cnidarians)

schizo- = split (*schizocoelous*: the type of development found in protostomes. Initially solid masses of mesoderm split to form coelomic cavities)

tri- = three (*triploblastic*: having three germ layers)

References

Futuyma, D. J. *Evolutionary Biology.* 3rd ed. Sunderland, Massachusetts: Sinauer, 1998.

Hickman, C. P., L. S. Roberts and A. Larson. *Integrated Principles of Zoology.* 11th ed. New York, McGraw-Hill Company, 2001.

Visual Guide to the Image Library

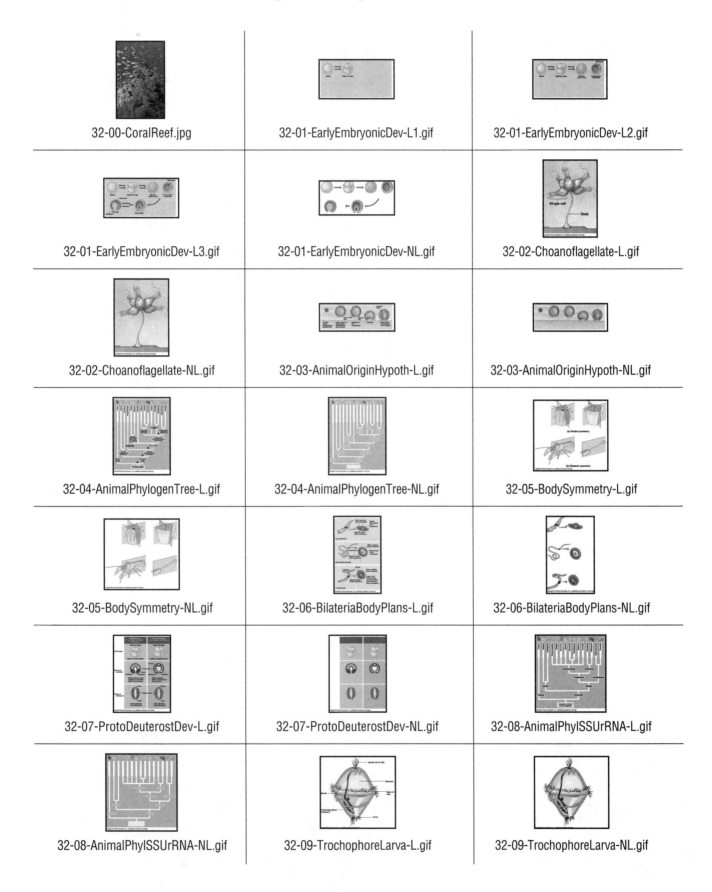

32-00-CoralReef.jpg

32-01-EarlyEmbryonicDev-L1.gif

32-01-EarlyEmbryonicDev-L2.gif

32-01-EarlyEmbryonicDev-L3.gif

32-01-EarlyEmbryonicDev-NL.gif

32-02-Choanoflagellate-L.gif

32-02-Choanoflagellate-NL.gif

32-03-AnimalOriginHypoth-L.gif

32-03-AnimalOriginHypoth-NL.gif

32-04-AnimalPhylogenTree-L.gif

32-04-AnimalPhylogenTree-NL.gif

32-05-BodySymmetry-L.gif

32-05-BodySymmetry-NL.gif

32-06-BilateriaBodyPlans-L.gif

32-06-BilateriaBodyPlans-NL.gif

32-07-ProtoDeuterostDev-L.gif

32-07-ProtoDeuterostDev-NL.gif

32-08-AnimalPhylSSUrRNA-L.gif

32-08-AnimalPhylSSUrRNA-NL.gif

32-09-TrochophoreLarva-L.gif

32-09-TrochophoreLarva-NL.gif

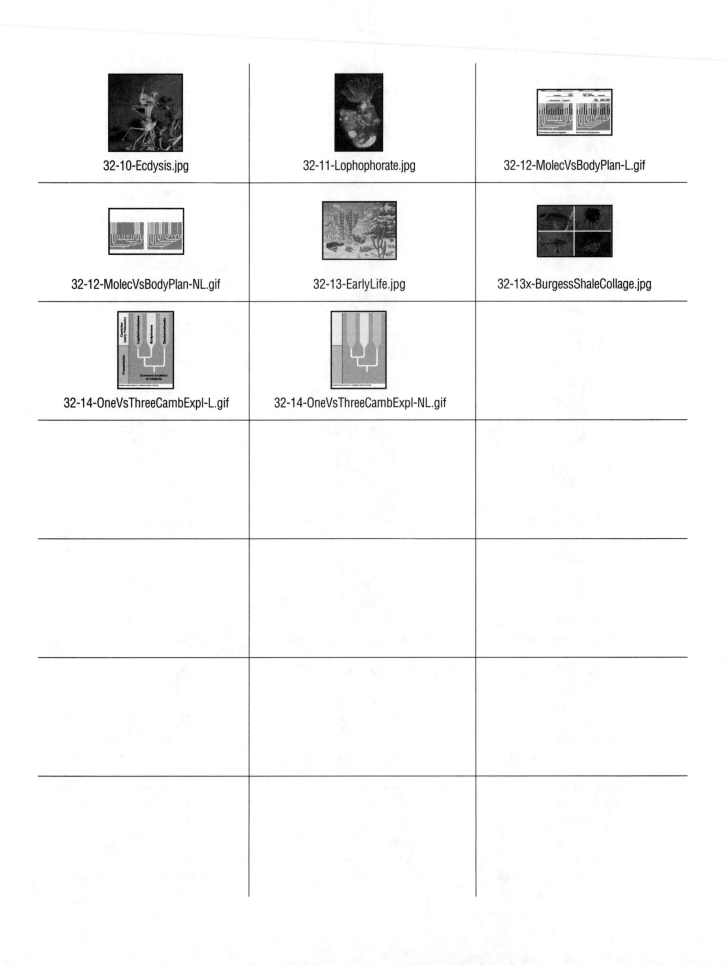

32-10-Ecdysis.jpg

32-11-Lophophorate.jpg

32-12-MolecVsBodyPlan-L.gif

32-12-MolecVsBodyPlan-NL.gif

32-13-EarlyLife.jpg

32-13x-BurgessShaleCollage.jpg

32-14-OneVsThreeCambExpl-L.gif

32-14-OneVsThreeCambExpl-NL.gif

CHAPTER 33

Invertebrates

Chapter Outline

Parazoa

Phylum Porifera: Sponges are sessile with porous bodies and choanocytes

Radiata

Phylum Cnidaria: Cnidarians have radial symmetry, a gastrovascular cavity, and cnidocytes

Phylum Ctenophora: Comb jellies possess rows of ciliary plates and adhesive colloblasts

Protostomia: Lophotrochozoa

Phylum Platyhelminthes: Flatworms are acoelomates with gastrovascular cavities

Phylum Rotifera: Rotifers are pseudocoelomates with jaws, crowns of cilia, and complete digestive tracts

The lophophorate phyla: Bryozoans, phoronids, and brachiopods are coelomates with ciliated tentacles around their mouths

Phylum Nemertea: Proboscis worms are named for their prey-capturing apparatus

Phylum Mollusca: Mollusks have a muscular foot, a visceral mass, and a mantle

Phylum Annelida: Annelids are segmented worms

Protostomia: Ecdysozoa

Phylum Nematoda: Roundworms are nonsegmented pseudocoelomates covered by tough cuticles

Arthropods are segmented coelomates with exoskeletons and jointed appendages

Deuterostomia

Phylum Echinodermata: Echinoderms have a water vascular system and secondary radial anatomy

Phylum Chordata: The chordates include two invertebrate subphyla and all vertebrates

Transparency Acetates

The Transparency Acetates for *Biology*, Sixth Edition, include the following images:

Figure 33.1	Review of animal phylogeny
Figure 33.3	Anatomy of a sponge
Figure 33.4	Polyp and medusa forms of cnidarians
Figure 33.5	A cnidocyte of a hydra
Table 33.1	Classes of Phylum Cnidaria
Figure 33.7	The life cycle of the hydrozoan *Obelia* (Layer 1)
Figure 33.7	The life cycle of the hydrozoan *Obelia* (Layer 2)
Figure 33.7	The life cycle of the hydrozoan *Obelia* (Layer 3)
Table 33.2	Classes of Phylum Platyhelminthes
Figure 33.10	Anatomy of a planarian
Figure 33.11	the life history of a blood fluke (*Schistosoma mansoni*)
Figure 33.12	Anatomy of a tapeworm
Figure 33.16	the basic body plan of mollusks
Table 33.3	Major Classes of Phylum Mollusca
Figure 33.18	The results of torsion in a gastropod
Figure 33.21	Anatomy of a clam
Figure 33.23	Anatomy of an earthworm
Table 33.4	Classes of Phylum Annelida
Figure 33.26	External anatomy of an arthropod
Table 33.5	Some Major Arthropod Classes (based on a traditional taxonomy that places all arthropods in a single phylum, Arthropoda)
Figure 33.30b	Spiders (Class Arachnida)
Figure 33.33	Anatomy of a grasshopper, an insect
Table 33.6	Some Major Orders of Insects (Anoplura—Hymenoptera)
Table 33.6	Some Major Orders of Insects (Isoptera—Trichoptera)
Figure 33.36	Three hypotheses for the origin of segmentation
Figure 33.38	Anatomy of a sea star
Table 33.7	Animal Phyla

Media for Instructors

Campbell Image Presentation Library

The Campbell Image Presentation Library CD-ROM set includes the following for your use:

- All art (available in pdf and jpeg or gif formats), photos (from the text and outside sources), and tables. Art images are also available without callouts. See the Visual Guide to the Image Library section at the end of this chapter for thumbnail versions of every image.

- A PowerPoint™ slide show of the art (with callouts), photos (both text and outside sources), and tables.
- The following video clips:

33-05-HydraEatFlea-B.mov	Time-lapse of *Hydra* ingesting a water flea
33-05-HydraSperm-B.mov	Hydra sperm
33-06b-JellySwimming-B.mov	Jellyfish swimming (large, single organism)
33-06b-ThimbleJelllies-B.mov	Thimble jellies (swarm)
33-13-Rotifer-B.mov	Rotifer
33-19b-Nudibranchs-B.mov	Nudibranchs
33-23-EarthwormLocomot-B.mov	Earthworm locomotion
33-26-LobsterMouthParts-B.mov	Close-up of working mouth parts of lobster
33-34-ButterflyEmerge-B.mov	Time-lapse of a butterfly life cycle
33-38-EchinodermTubeFeet-B.mov	Echinoderm tube feet

See also

13-01-HydraBudding-B.mov	Time-lapse of budding in hydra
21-04-CElegansCrawl-B.mov	Close-up video of *C. elegans* crawling
21-04-CElegansEmbryo-S.mov	Time-lapse *C. elegans* embryo development
50-23-Tubeworms-B.mov	Deep-sea vent communities

PowerPoint Lectures CD-ROM

The PowerPoint Lectures CD-ROM contains slides that integrate the art, photos, tables, and lecture outline from this chapter.

Campbell Biology Website (Instructor Resources)

See the insert in your copy of Campbell/Reece *Biology*, Sixth Edition, for instructions on how to access the Campbell Biology Website. The Instructor Resources section of the website includes the following:

- The art, photos, tables, PowerPoint slide shows, videos, and animations from the Campbell Image Presentation Library
- Suggested answers to the Lab Report questions from the Case Studies in the Process of Science
- The PowerPoint Lecture for this chapter
- Word files of the lecture outline for this chapter
- Photo links

Course Management Systems

The media content for this chapter is available in three course management systems: CourseCompass™, Blackboard, and WebCT. For more information, go to http://cms.aw.com. For the latest pdf instructions on how to use CourseCompass, go to **www.coursecompass.com**. In addition, a Syllabus Manager is offered on the Campbell Biolo*gy* Website.

Media for Students

The Campbell Biology Website and CD-ROM include the following for your students:

- Objectives
- Chapter Review (Summary, Self-Quiz, and Essay Questions from the book; Word Roots; Key Terms linked to the Glossary)
- Activities (see list below)
- Case Studies in the Process of Science (see list below)
- Quizzes (Pre-test, Activities Quiz, Chapter Quiz, Essay Questions)
- Web Links
- News and References
- Art and videos from the Campbell Image Presentation Library
- The Campbell *Biology* Interviews (from all editions)
- Glossary with audio pronunciations
- Syllabus Manager

Student Media Activities and Case Studies in The Process of Science

Web/CD Case Study in the Process of Science: *How Are Insect Species Identified?*

Web/CD Activity 33A: *Characteristics of Invertebrates*

Objectives

Parazoa

1. From a diagram, identify the parts of a sponge (including the spongocoel, sporocyte, epidermis, choanocyte, mesohyl, amoebocyte, osculum, and spicule) and describe the function of each.

Radiata

2. List the characteristics of the phylum Cnidaria that distinguish it from the other animal phyla.

3. Describe the two basic body plans in Cnidaria and their role in Cnidarian life cycles.

4. List the three classes of Cnidaria and distinguish among them based on life cycle and morphological characteristics.

5. List the characteristics of the phylum Ctenophora that distinguish it from the other animal phyla.

Protostomia: Lophotrochozoa

6. Distinguish between the following pairs: bilateria and urbilateria, acoelomates and coelomates, protostomes and deuterostomes, and Lophotrochozoa and Ecdysozoa.

7. List the characteristics of the phylum Platyhelminthes that distinguish it from the other animal phyla.

8. Distinguish among the four classes of Platyhelminthes and give examples of each.

9. Describe the generalized life cycle of a trematode and give an example of one fluke that parasitizes humans.

10. Describe the anatomy and generalized life cycle of a tapeworm.

11. Describe unique features of rotifers that distinguish them from other pseudocoelomates.

12. Define parthenogenesis and describe alternative forms of rotifer reproduction.

13. Define lophophore and list three lophophorate phyla.

14. List the distinguishing characteristics of the phylum Nemertea.

15. Explain the relationship between proboscis worms and flatworms.

16. List the characteristics that distinguish the phylum Mollusca from the other animal phyla.

17. Describe the basic body plan of a mollusk and explain how it has been modified in the Bivalvia, Cephalopoda, Gastropoda, and Polyplacophora.

18. Distinguish among the following four molluscan classes and give examples of each:
    a. Bivalvia
    b. Cephalopoda
    c. Gastropoda
    d. Polyplacophora

19. List the characteristics that distinguish the phylum Annelida from the other animal phyla.

20. Distinguish among the classes of Annelida and give examples of each.

21. Describe the adaptive advantage of a coelom and segmentation in annelids.

Protostomia: Ecdysozoa

22. List the characteristics of the phylum Nematoda that distinguish it from other wormlike animals.

23. Give examples of both parasitic and free-living species of nematodes.

24. List the characteristics of arthropods that distinguish them from the other animal phyla.

25. Describe advantages and disadvantages of an exoskeleton.

26. Distinguish between hemocoel and coelom.

27. Define and distinguish between the major independent arthropod lines of evolution represented by the phyla
    a. Trilobita
    b. Chelicerata
    c. Crustacea
    d. Uniramia

28. Describe the different views regarding the relationship between arthropods and annelids.

29. Describe the basic mechanism for the development of segmented bodies.

30. Describe three hypotheses that can account for the scattered distribution of segmentation in animals.

Deuterostomia

31. List the characteristics of echinoderms that distinguish them from other animal phyla.

32. Distinguish among the five classes of echinoderms and give examples of each.

33. Explain why the phylum Chordata is included in a chapter on invertebrates.

34. Describe the evolutionary relationships between echinoderms and chordates.

Key Terms

invertebrates	foot	phylum Arthropoda
spongocoel	visceral mass	phylum Trilobita
osculum	mantle	phylum Chelicerata
choanocyte	mantle cavity	phylum Uniramia
mesohyl	radula	phylum Crustacea
amoebocyte	trochophore	eurypterid
hermaphrodite	torsion	class Arachnida
gastrovascular cavity	ammonites	book lungs
polyp	metanephridium	class Diplododa
medusa	(plural,	class Chilopoda
cnidocytes	metanephridia)	class Insecta
nematocysts	arthropods	entomology
colloblasts	cuticle	Malpighian tubules
urbilateria	exoskeleton	tracheal system
planarians	molting	incomplete
complete digestive	open circulatory	metamorphosis
tract	system	complete
parthenogenesis	trilobites	metamorphosis
lophophorate animals	chelicerates	isopods
lophophore	uniramians	copepods
bryozoan	crustacean	decapod
phoronids	chelicerae	echinoderms
brachiopod	mandibles	water vascular system
closed circulatory	antennae	tube feet
system	compound eye	

Word Roots

arthro- = jointed; **-pod** = foot (*Arthropoda*: segmented coelomates with exoskeletons and jointed appendages)

arachn- = a spider class (*Arachnida*: the animal group that includes scorpions, spiders, ticks, and mites)

brachio- = the arm (*brachiopod*: also called lamp shells, these animals superficially resemble clams and other bivalve mollusks, but the two halves of the brachiopod shell are dorsal and ventral to the animal rather than lateral, as in clams)

bryo- = moss; **-zoa** = animal (*bryozoan*: colonial animals that superficially resemble mosses)

cheli- = a claw (*chelicerae*: clawlike feeding appendages characteristic of the chelicerate group)

choano- = a funnel; **-cyte** = cell (*choanocyte*: flagellated collar cells of a sponge)

cnido- = a nettle (*cnidocytes*: unique cells that function in defense and prey capture in cnidarians)

-coel = hollow (*spongocoel*: the central cavity of a sponge)

cope- = an oar (*copepods*: a group of small crustaceans that are important members of marine and freshwater plankton communities)

cuti- 5 the skin (*cuticle*: the exoskeleton of an arthropod)

deca- = ten (*decapod*: a relatively large group of crustaceans that includes lobsters, crayfish, crabs, and shrimp)

diplo- = double (*Diplopoda*: the millipede group of animals)

echino- = spiny; **-derm** = skin (*echinoderm*: sessile or slow-moving animals with a thin skin that covers an exoskeleton; the group includes sea stars, sea urchins, brittle stars, crinoids, and basket stars)

entom- = an insect; **-ology** = the study of (*entomology*: the study of insects)

eury- = broad, wide; **-pter** = a wing, a feather, a fin (*eurypterid*: mainly marine and freshwater, extinct, chelicerates; these predators, also called water scorpions, ranged up to 3 meters long)

exo- = outside (*exoskeleton*: a hard encasement on the surface of an anima.)

gastro- stomach; **-vascula** = a little vessel (*gastrovascular cavity*: the central digestive compartment, usually with a single opening that functions as both mouth and anus)

hermaphrod- = with both male and female organs (*hermaphrodite*: an individual that functions as both male and female in sexual reproduction by producing both sperm and eggs)

in- = without (*invertebrates*: an animal without a backbone)

iso- = equal (*isopods*: one of the largest groups of crustaceans, primarily marine, but including pill bugs common under logs and moist vegetation next to the ground)

lopho- = a crest, tuft; **-phora** = to carry *lophophore*: a horseshoe-shaped or circular fold of the body wall bearing ciliated tentacles that surround the mouth)

meso- = the middle; **-hyl** = matter (*mesohyl*: a gelatinous region between the two layers of cells of a sponge)

meta- = change; **-morph** = shape (*metamorphosis*: the resurgence of development in an animal larva that transforms it into a sexually mature adult)

nemato- = a thread; **-cyst** = a bag (*nematocysts*: a ciliated larva common to the life cycle of many mollusks, it is also characteristic of marine annelids and some other lophotrochozoans)

nephri- = the kidney (*metanephridium*: in annelid worms, a type of excretory tubule with internal openings called nephrostomes that collect body fluids and external openings called nephridiopores)

oscul- = a little mouth (*osculum*: a large opening in a sponge that connects the spongocoel to the environment)

partheno- = without fertilization; **-genesis** = producing (*parthenogenesis*: a type of reproduction in which females produce offspring from unfertilized eggs.

plan- = flat or wandering (*planarians*: carnivores that prey on smaller animals or feed on dead animals)

tri- = three; **-lobi** = a lobe (*trilobite*: an extinct group of arthropods with pronounced segmentation)

trocho- = a wheel (*trochophore*: a ciliated larva common to the life cycle of many mollusks, it is also characteristic of marine annelids and some other lophotrochozoans)

uni- = one; **-rami** = a branch (*uniramia*: the animal group that includes centipedes, millipedes, and insects)

ur- = earliest (*urbilateria*: the original group of bilateral animals that were relatively complex with true coeloms)

References

Hickman, C. P., L. S. Roberts and A. Larson. *Integrated Principles of Zoology.* 11th ed. New York, McGraw-Hill Company, 2001.

Johnsen, S. "Transparent Animals." *Scientific American*, February 2000.

Visual Guide to the Image Library

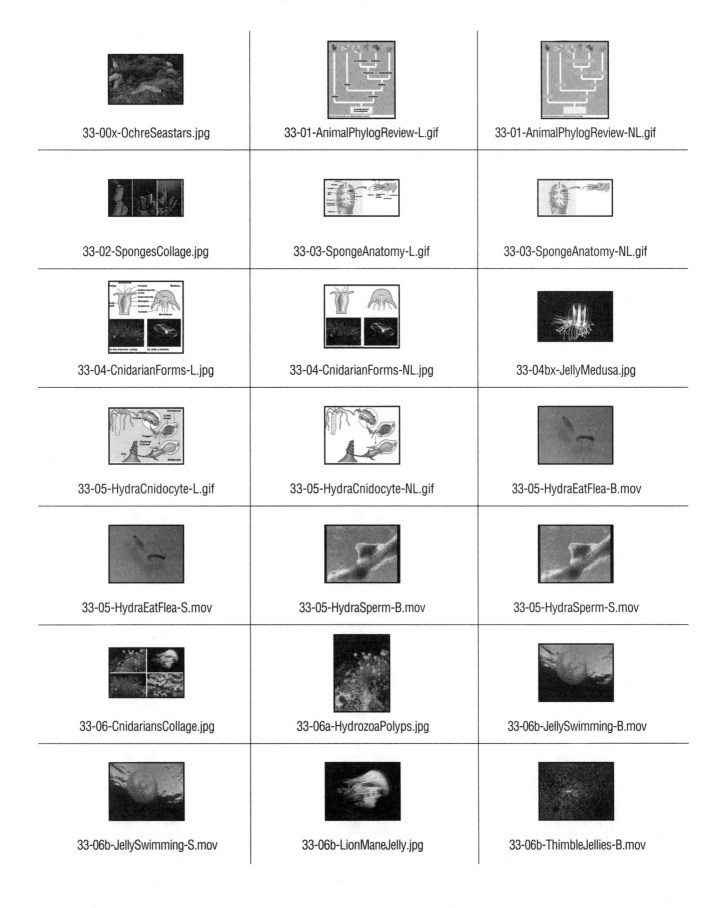

33-00x-OchreSeastars.jpg

33-01-AnimalPhylogReview-L.gif

33-01-AnimalPhylogReview-NL.gif

33-02-SpongesCollage.jpg

33-03-SpongeAnatomy-L.gif

33-03-SpongeAnatomy-NL.gif

33-04-CnidarianForms-L.jpg

33-04-CnidarianForms-NL.jpg

33-04bx-JellyMedusa.jpg

33-05-HydraCnidocyte-L.gif

33-05-HydraCnidocyte-NL.gif

33-05-HydraEatFlea-B.mov

33-05-HydraEatFlea-S.mov

33-05-HydraSperm-B.mov

33-05-HydraSperm-S.mov

33-06-CnidariansCollage.jpg

33-06a-HydrozoaPolyps.jpg

33-06b-JellySwimming-B.mov

33-06b-JellySwimming-S.mov

33-06b-LionManeJelly.jpg

33-06b-ThimbleJellies-B.mov

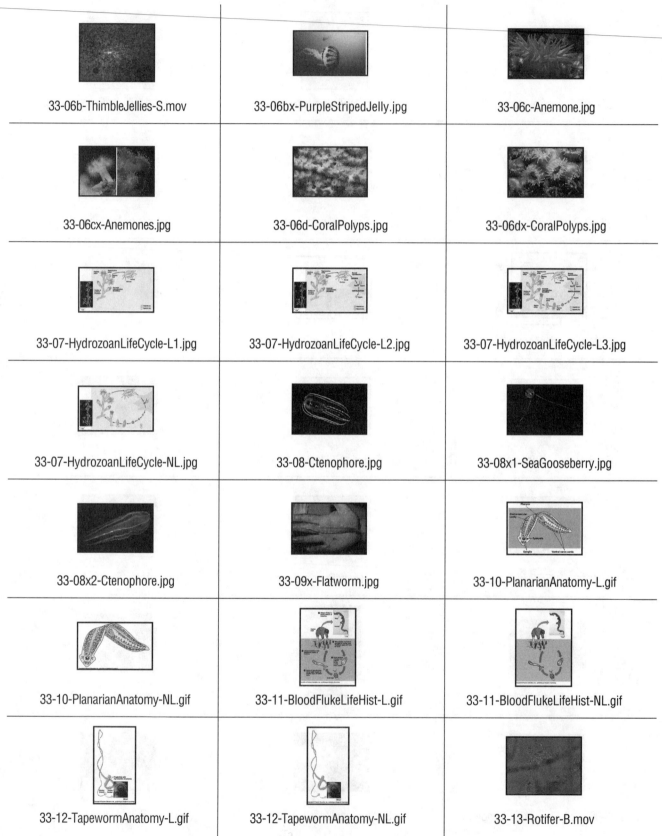

33-06b-ThimbleJellies-S.mov

33-06bx-PurpleStripedJelly.jpg

33-06c-Anemone.jpg

33-06cx-Anemones.jpg

33-06d-CoralPolyps.jpg

33-06dx-CoralPolyps.jpg

33-07-HydrozoanLifeCycle-L1.jpg

33-07-HydrozoanLifeCycle-L2.jpg

33-07-HydrozoanLifeCycle-L3.jpg

33-07-HydrozoanLifeCycle-NL.jpg

33-08-Ctenophore.jpg

33-08x1-SeaGooseberry.jpg

33-08x2-Ctenophore.jpg

33-09x-Flatworm.jpg

33-10-PlanarianAnatomy-L.gif

33-10-PlanarianAnatomy-NL.gif

33-11-BloodFlukeLifeHist-L.gif

33-11-BloodFlukeLifeHist-NL.gif

33-12-TapewormAnatomy-L.gif

33-12-TapewormAnatomy-NL.gif

33-13-Rotifer-B.mov

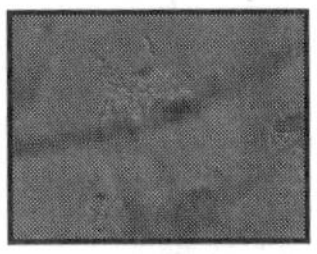

33-13-Rotifer-S.mov

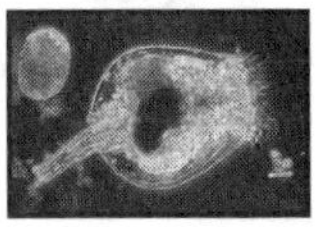

33-13-Rotifer.jpg

33-14-Lophophorates.jpg

33-14a-Bryozoans.jpg

33-14b-Brachiopods.jpg

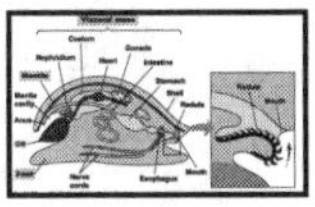

33-16-MolluskBodyPlan-L.gif

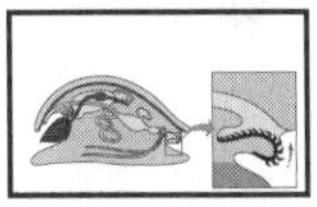

33-16-MolluskBodyPlan-NL.gif

33-17-Chiton.jpg

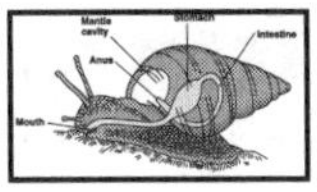

33-18-GastropodTorsion-L.gif

33-18-GastropodTorsion-NL.gif

33-18x-GardenSnail.jpg

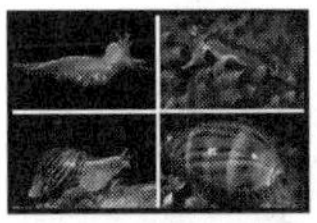

33-19-GastropodsCollage.jpg

33-19a-Nudibranch.jpg

33-19b-Nudibranch.jpg

33-19b-Nudibranchs-B.mov

33-19b-Nudibranchs-S.mov

33-19c-Snail.jpg

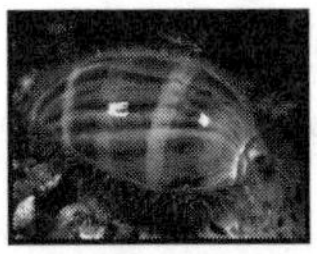

33-19d-DeerCowrie.jpg

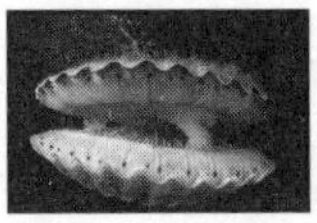

33-20-Bivalve.jpg

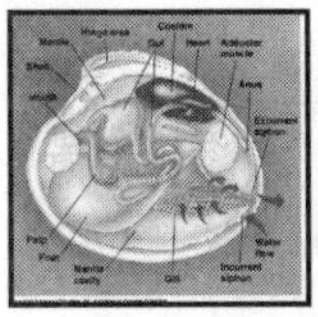

33-21-ClamAnatomy-L.jpg

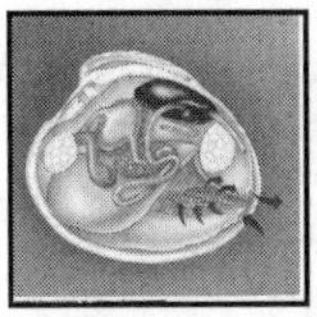

33-21-ClamAnatomy-NL.jpg

33-22-CephalopodsCollage.jpg

33-23-EarthwormAnatomy-L.jpg

33-23-EarthwormAnatomy-NL.jpg

33-23-EarthwormLocomot-B.mov

33-23-EarthwormLocomot-S.mov

33-23x-EarthwormPhoto.jpg

33-24-AnnelidsCollage.jpg

33-24b-Polychaete.jpg

33-24c-FeatherDusterWorm.jpg

33-24cx-ChristmasTreeWorm.jpg

33-24d-Leech.jpg

33-25a-FreeLivingNematode.jpg

33-25ax-NematodeCElegans.jpg

33-25b-ParasiticNematode.jpg

33-26-ArthropodExtAnatom-L.jpg

33-26-ArthropodExtAnatom-NL.jpg

33-26-LobsterMouthParts-B.mov

33-26-LobsterMouthParts-S.mov

33-27-TrilobiteFossil.jpg

33-28-HorseshoeCrabs.jpg

33-29-ArachnidsCollage.jpg

33-29c-ParasiticMites.jpg

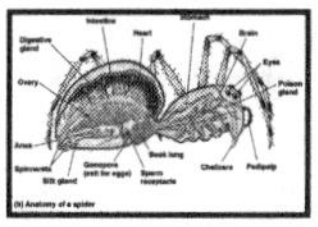

33-30b-SpiderAnatomy-L.gif

33-30b-SpiderAnatomy-NL.gif

33-30x-LycosidSpider.jpg

33-31a-Millipedes.jpg

33-32-InsectFlight.jpg

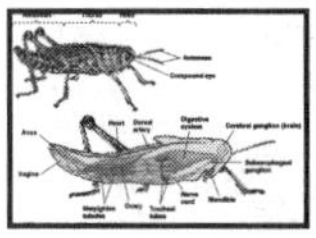

33-33-InsectAnatomy-L.gif

33-33-InsectAnatomy-NL.gif

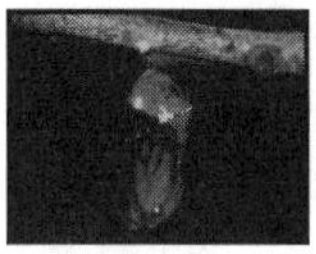

33-34-ButterflyEmerge-B.mov

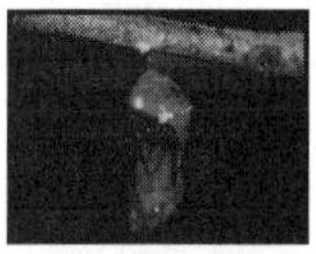

33-34-ButterflyEmerge-S.mov

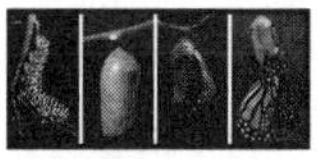

33-34-MetamorphosisButtrfly.jpg

33-35-CrustaceansCollage.jpg

33-35a-Lobster.jpg

33-35b-BandedCoralShrimp.jpg

33-35c-Barnacles.jpg

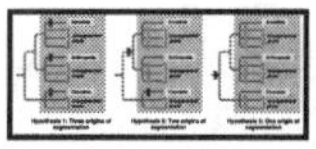

33-36-SegmentationOrigin-L.gif

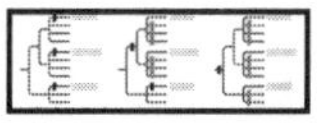

33-36-SegmentationOrigin-NL.gif

33-37-EchinodermsCollage.jpg

33-37a-SeaStar.jpg

33-37ax-Bloodstar.jpg

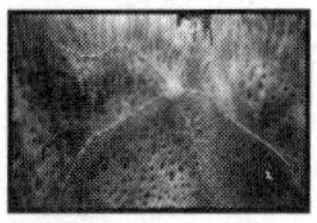

33-37c-BrittleStar.jpg

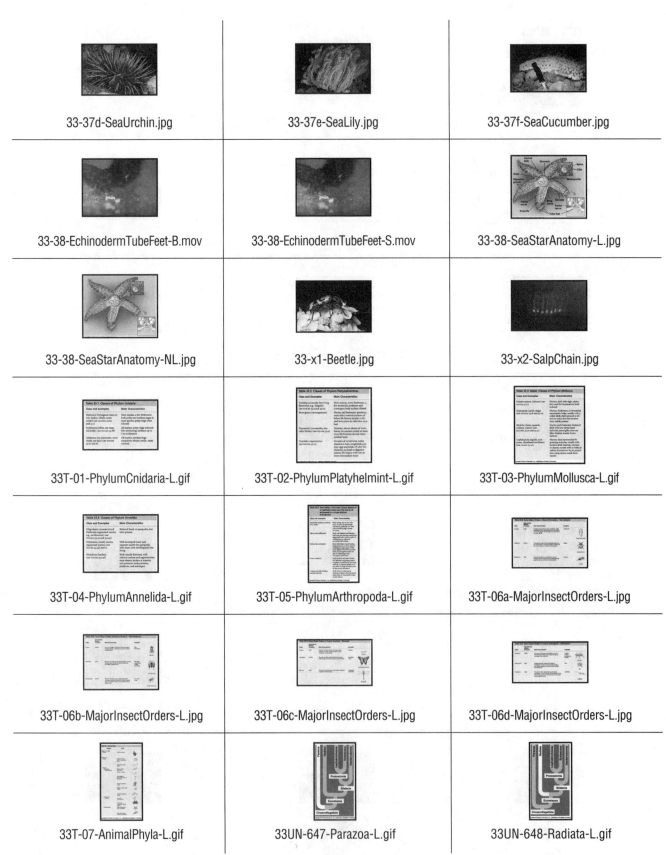

33-37d-SeaUrchin.jpg

33-37e-SeaLily.jpg

33-37f-SeaCucumber.jpg

33-38-EchinodermTubeFeet-B.mov

33-38-EchinodermTubeFeet-S.mov

33-38-SeaStarAnatomy-L.jpg

33-38-SeaStarAnatomy-NL.jpg

33-x1-Beetle.jpg

33-x2-SalpChain.jpg

33T-01-PhylumCnidaria-L.gif

33T-02-PhylumPlatyhelmint-L.gif

33T-03-PhylumMollusca-L.gif

33T-04-PhylumAnnelida-L.gif

33T-05-PhylumArthropoda-L.gif

33T-06a-MajorInsectOrders-L.jpg

33T-06b-MajorInsectOrders-L.jpg

33T-06c-MajorInsectOrders-L.jpg

33T-06d-MajorInsectOrders-L.jpg

33T-07-AnimalPhyla-L.gif

33UN-647-Parazoa-L.gif

33UN-648-Radiata-L.gif

33UN-651-Lophotrochozoa-L.gif

33UN-661-Ecdysozoa-L.gif

33UN-672-Deuterostomia-L.gif

CHAPTER 34

Vertebrate Evolution and Diversity

Chapter Outline

Transparency Acetates

The Transparency Acetates for *Biology*, Sixth Edition, include the following images:

Figure 34.1	Clades of extant chordates
Figure 34.2	Chordate characteristics
Figure 34.3	Subphylum Urochordata: a tunicate
Figure 34.4a	Subphylum Cephalochordata: the lancelet *Branchiostoma*
Figure 34.6	The neural crest, embryonic source of many unique vertebrate characters
Figure 34.7	Phylogeny of the major groups of extant vertebrates
Figure 34.10	Hypothesis for the evolution of vertebrate jaws
Figure 34.13	Anatomy of a trout, a representative ray-finned fish
Figure 34.15	The origin of tetrapods
Figure 34.16	Skeleton of *Acanthostega*, a Devonian tetrapod fish
Figure 34.19	The amniotic egg
Figure 34.20	A hypothetical phylogeny of amniotes
Figure 34.21	Taxonomic classes of amniotes
Figure 34.25	Form fits function: the avian wing and feather
Figure 34.27	*Archaeopteryx*, a Jurassic bird-reptile
Figure 34.30	The evolution of the mammalian jaw and ear bones
Figure 34.32	Evolutionary convergence of marsupial and eutherian (placental) mammals.
Table 34.1	Major Orders of Mammals (Monotremata–Primates)
Table 34.1	Major Orders of Mammals (Carnivora–Insectivora)
Figure 34.33	Hypothetical cladogram of mammals
Figure 34.35	A phylogenetic tree of primates
Figure 34.38	A timeline for some hominid species
Figure 34.41	Two hypotheses for the origin of anatomically modern humans

Media for Instructors

Campbell Image Presentation Library

The Campbell Image Presentation Library CD-ROM set includes the following for your use:

- All art, photos (text and outside sources), and tables (available in pdf and jpeg or gif formats). Art images are also available without callouts. See the Visual Guide to the Image Library section at the end of this chapter for thumbnail versions of every image.
- A PowerPoint™ slide show of the art (with callouts), photos (both text and outside sources), and tables.

- The following video clips:

34-11c-MantaRay-B.mov	Manta Ray swimming
34-26-FlappingGeese-B.mov	Flapping geese
34-26-SoaringHawk-B.mov	Soaring hawk
34-26-SwansTakeFlight-B.mov	Swans take flight
34-33-BatLicking-B.mov	Bat licking
34-37a-GibbonBrachiating-B.mov	Gibbon brachiating

See also

01-16-SeaHorses-B.mov	Sea Horses
51-19-SnakesWrestle-B.mov	Snakes wrestling

PowerPoint Lectures CD-ROM

The PowerPoint Lectures CD-ROM contains slides that integrate the art, photos, tables, and lecture outline from this chapter.

Campbell Biology Website (Instructor Resources)

See the insert in your copy of Campbell/Reece *Biology*, Sixth Edition, for instructions on how to access the Campbell Biology Website. The Instructor Resources section of the website includes the following:

- The art, photos, tables, PowerPoint slide shows, videos, and animations from the Campbell Image Presentation Library
- Suggested answers to the Lab Report questions from the Case Studies in the Process of Science
- The PowerPoint Lecture for this chapter
- Word files of the lecture outline for this chapter
- Photo links

Course Management Systems

The media content for this chapter is available in three course management systems: CourseCompass™, Blackboard, and WebCT. For more information, go to http://cms.aw.com. For the latest pdf instructions on how to use CourseCompass, go to www.coursecompass.com. In addition, a Syllabus Manager is offered on the Campbell Biology Website.

Media for Students

The Campbell Biology Website and CD-ROM include the following for your students:

- Objectives
- Chapter Review (Summary, Self-Quiz, and Essay Questions from the book; Word Roots; Key Terms linked to the Glossary)

- Activities (see list below)
- Case Studies in the Process of Science (see list below)
- Quizzes (Pre-test, Activities Quiz, Chapter Quiz, Essay Questions)
- Web Links
- News and References
- Art and videos from the Campbell Image Presentation Library
- The Campbell *Biology* Interviews (from all editions)
- Glossary with audio pronunciations
- Syllabus Manager

Student Media Activities and Case Studies in The Process of Science

Web/CD Case Study in the Process of Science: *How Does Bone Structure Shed Light on the Origin of Birds?*

Web/CD Activity 34A: *Characteristics of Chordates*

Web/CD Activity 34B: *Primate Diversity*

Web/CD Activity 34C: *Human Evolution*

Objectives

Invertebrate Chordates and the Origin of Vertebrates

1. Distinguish between the two subgroups of deuterostomes.
2. Describe the four unique characteristics of chordates.
3. Distinguish between the three subphyla of the phylum Chordata and give examples of each.
4. Describe the two-stage hypothesis for the evolution of vertebrates from invertebrates.

Introduction to the Vertebrates

5. Describe the specialized characteristics found in the subphylum Vertebrata and explain how each is beneficial to survival.
6. Define and distinguish between gnathostomes, tetrapods, and amniotes.

Jawless Vertebrates

7. Define and compare the groups Myxini, Cephalaspidomorphi, ostracoderms, conodonts, and placoderms.
8. Distinguish between agnathans and fishes.

Fishes and Amphibians

9. Describe the function and evolution of jaws.
10. Describe and distinguish between the classes Chondrichthyes and Osteichthyes, noting the main traits of each group.

11. Identify and describe the main subgroups of the class Osteichthyes.

12. Describe the early evolution of amphibians.

13. Describe the common traits of amphibians and distinguish among the three orders of living amphibians.

Amniotes

14. Describe an amniotic egg and explain its significance in the evolution of reptiles, birds, and mammals.

15. Distinguish between the two systems of classifying amniotes (synapsids, anapsids, and diapsids versus reptiles, birds, and mammals).

16. List the distinguishing characteristics of members of the class Reptilia and explain any special adaptations to the terrestrial environment.

17. Compare the interpretations of dinosaurs as ectotherms or endotherms.

18. Characterize and compare the first and second major reptilian radiations.

19. List and compare the traits of the major groups of modern reptiles.

20. List the distinguishing characteristics of members of the class Aves and explain any special adaptations for flight.

21. Summarize the evidence supporting the fact that birds evolved from reptilian ancestors.

22. List and compare the major groups of modern birds.

23. Describe the main features of mammals.

24. Describe the evolution of mammals.

25. Distinguish among monotreme, marsupial, and placental mammals.

26. Describe the adaptive radiation of mammals during the Cretaceous and early Tertiary periods.

27. Compare and contrast the four main evolutionary clades of eutherian mammals.

Primates and the Evolution of *Homo sapiens*

28. Describe the general characteristics of primates. Note the particular features associated with an arboreal existence.

29. Distinguish between the two suborders of primates and describe their early evolutionary relationship.

30. Distinguish between hominoid and hominid.

31. Name three of the most prominent misconceptions about human evolution.

32. Describe the evolutionary changes that occurred in the course of human evolution from about 35 to 5 million years ago.

33. Describe the evolution of the major features of humans.

34. Describe the global dispersion patterns during the evolution of humans.

Key Terms

vertebrate
chordate
notochord
urochordate
tunicates
lancelets
cephalochordates
somite
paedogenesis
neural crest
Craniata
gnathostomes
tetrapod
amniote
agnathan
ostracoderm
conodonts
placoderm
acanthodians
class Chondrichthyes
spiral valve
lateral line system
oviparous
ovoviviparous
viviparous
cloaca
class Osteichthyes

operculum
swim bladder
ray-finned fish
class Actinopterygii
class Actinistia
class Dipnoi
class Amphibia
order Urodela
order Anura
order Apoda
extraembryonic
  membranes
synapsids
anapsids
diapsids
lepidosaurs
archosaurs
ectotherms
dinosaurs
pterosaurs
endothermic
class Testudines
class Sphenodontia
class Squamata
class Crocodilia
theropods
ratites

carinates
passeriformes
class Mammalia
placenta
therapsids
monotremes
marsupial
eutherian mammals
Afrotheria
opposable thumb
prosimians
anthropoids
paleoanthropology
hominoid
hominid
mosaic evolution
prognathic jaws
anatomically modern
  humans
multiregional
  hypothesis
"Out of Africa"
  hypothesis
replacement
  hypothesis

Word Roots

a- = without (*agnathan*: a member of a jawless class of vertebrates represented today by the lampreys and hagfishes)

an- = without; **-apsi** = a juncture (*anapsids*: one of three groups of amniotes based on key differences between their skulls)

arch = ancient (*archosaurs*: the reptilian group which includes crocodiles, alligators, dinosaurs, and birds)

cephalo- = head (*cephalochordates*: a chordate without a backbone, represented by lancelets, tiny marine animals)

aktin- = a ray; **-pterygi** = a fin (*Actinopterygii*: the class of ray-finned fishes.)

crani- = the skull (*craniata*: The chordate subgroup that possess a cranium)

crocodil- = a crocodile (*Crocodilia*: the reptile group that includes crocodiles and alligators)

di- = two (*diapsids*: one of three groups of amniotes based on key differences between their skulls)

dino- terrible; **-saur** = lizard (*dinosaurs*: an extremely diverse group of ancient reptiles varying in body shape, size, and habitat)

endo- = inner; **therm-** = heat (*endotherm*: an animal that uses metabolic energy to maintain a constant body temperature, such as a bird or mammal)

eu- = good (*eutherian mammals*: placental mammals; those whose young complete their embryonic development within the uterus, joined to the mother by the placenta)

extra- = outside, more (*extraembryonic membranes*: four membranes that support the developing embryo in reptiles, birds, and mammals)

gnantho- = the jaw; **-stoma** = the mouth (*gnathostomes*: the vertebrate subgroup that possesses jaws)

homin- = man (*hominid*: a term that refers to mammals that are more closely related to humans than to any other living species)

lepido- = a scale (*lepidosaurs*: the reptilian group which includes lizards, snakes, and two species of New Zealand animals called tuataras)

marsupi- = a bag, pouch (*marsupial*: a mammal, such as a koala, kangaroo, or opossum, whose young complete their embryonic development inside a maternal pouch called the marsupium)

mono- = one (*monotremes*: an egg-laying mammal, represented by the platypus and echidna)

neuro- = nerve (*neural crest*: a band of cells along the border where the neural tube pinches off from the ectoderm)

noto- = the back; **-chord** = a string (*notochord*: a longitudinal, flexible rod formed from dorsal mesoderm and located between the gut and the nerve cord in all chordate embryos)

opercul- = a covering, lid (*operculum*: a protective flap that covers the gills of fishes)

osteo- = bone; **ichthy-** = fish (*Osteichthyes*: the vertebrate class of bony fishes)

ostraco- = a shell; **-derm** = skin (*ostracoderm*: an extinct agnathan; a fishlike creature encased in an armor of bony plates)

ovi- = an egg; **-parous** = bearing (*oviparous*: referring to a type of development in which young hatch from eggs laid outside the mother's body)

paedo- = a child; **-genic** = producing (*paedogenesis*: the precocious development of sexual maturity in a larva)

paleo- = ancient; **anthrop-** = man; **-ology** = the science of (*paleoanthropology*: the study of human origins and evolution)

passeri- = a sparrow; **form-** = shape (*passeriformes*: the order of perching birds)

placo- = a plate (*placoderm*: a member of an extinct class of fishlike vertebrates that had jaws and were enclosed in a tough, outer armor)

pro- = before; **-simi** = an ape (*prosimians*: a suborder of primates, the premonkeys, that probably resemble early arboreal primates)

ptero- = a wing (*pterosaurs*: winged reptiles that lived during the time of dinosaurs)

ratit- = flat-bottomed (*ratites*: the group of flightless birds)

soma- = body (*somites*: blocks of mesoderm that give rise to muscle segments in chordates)

syn- = together (*synapsids*: one of three groups of amniotes based on key differences between their skulls)

tetra- = four; **-podi** = foot (*tetrapod*: a vertebrate possessing two pairs of limbs, such as amphibians, reptiles, birds, and mammals)

tunic- = a covering (*tunicates*: members of the subphylum Urochordata)

uro- = the tail (*urochordate*: a chordate without a backbone, commonly called a tunicate, a sessile marine animal)

uro- = tail; **-del** = visible (*Urodela*: the order of salamanders that includes tetrapod amphibians with tails)

vivi- = a live (*ovoviviparous*: referring to a type of development in which young hatch from eggs that are retained in the mother's uterus) Check for completeness

References

Futuyma, D. J. *Evolutionary Biology.* 3rd ed. Sunderland, Massachusetts: Sinauer, 1998.

Hickman, C. P., L. S. Roberts and A. Larson. *Integrated Principles of Zoology.* 11th ed. New York, McGraw-Hill Company, 2001.

Levin, P. S. and M. H. Schiewe. "Preserving Salmon Biodiversity." *American Scientist*, May–June 2001.

Tattersall, I. "Once We Were Not Alone." *Scientific American,* January 2000.

Visual Guide to the Image Library

34-00-SnakeSkeleton.jpg

34-01-ExtantChordatClade-L.gif

34-01-ExtantChordatClade-NL.gif

34-02-ChordateCharacters-L.gif

34-02-ChordateCharacters-NL.gif

34-03-Tunicate-L.jpg

34-03-Tunicate-NL.jpg

34-04a-LanceletAnatomy-L.gif

34-04a-LanceletAnatomy-NL.gif

34-04b-Lancelet.jpg

34-05-EarlyVertebrates.jpg

34-06-NeuralCrest-L.gif

34-06-NeuralCrest-NL.gif

34-07-PhylogExtantVerteb-L.gif

34-07-PhylogExtantVerteb-NL.gif

34-08-Hagfish.jpg

34-09-SeaLamprey.jpg

34-09a-Lamprey.jpg

34-09b-LampreyMouth.jpg

34-10-VertebrateJawEvol-L.gif

34-10-VertebrateJawEvol-NL.gif

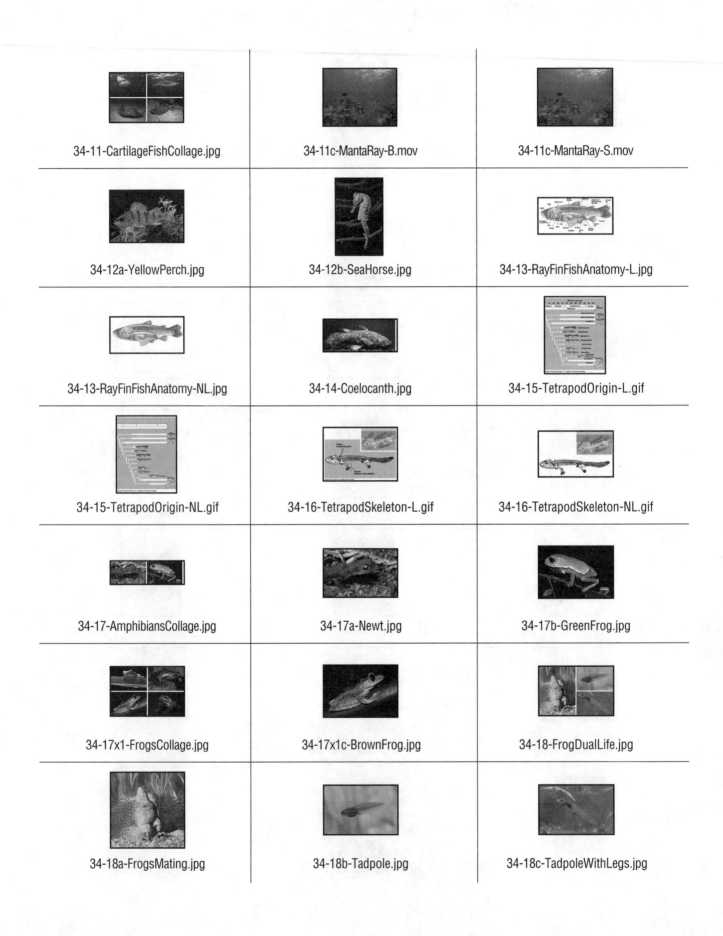

34-11-CartilageFishCollage.jpg

34-11c-MantaRay-B.mov

34-11c-MantaRay-S.mov

34-12a-YellowPerch.jpg

34-12b-SeaHorse.jpg

34-13-RayFinFishAnatomy-L.jpg

34-13-RayFinFishAnatomy-NL.jpg

34-14-Coelocanth.jpg

34-15-TetrapodOrigin-L.gif

34-15-TetrapodOrigin-NL.gif

34-16-TetrapodSkeleton-L.gif

34-16-TetrapodSkeleton-NL.gif

34-17-AmphibiansCollage.jpg

34-17a-Newt.jpg

34-17b-GreenFrog.jpg

34-17x1-FrogsCollage.jpg

34-17x1c-BrownFrog.jpg

34-18-FrogDualLife.jpg

34-18a-FrogsMating.jpg

34-18b-Tadpole.jpg

34-18c-TadpoleWithLegs.jpg

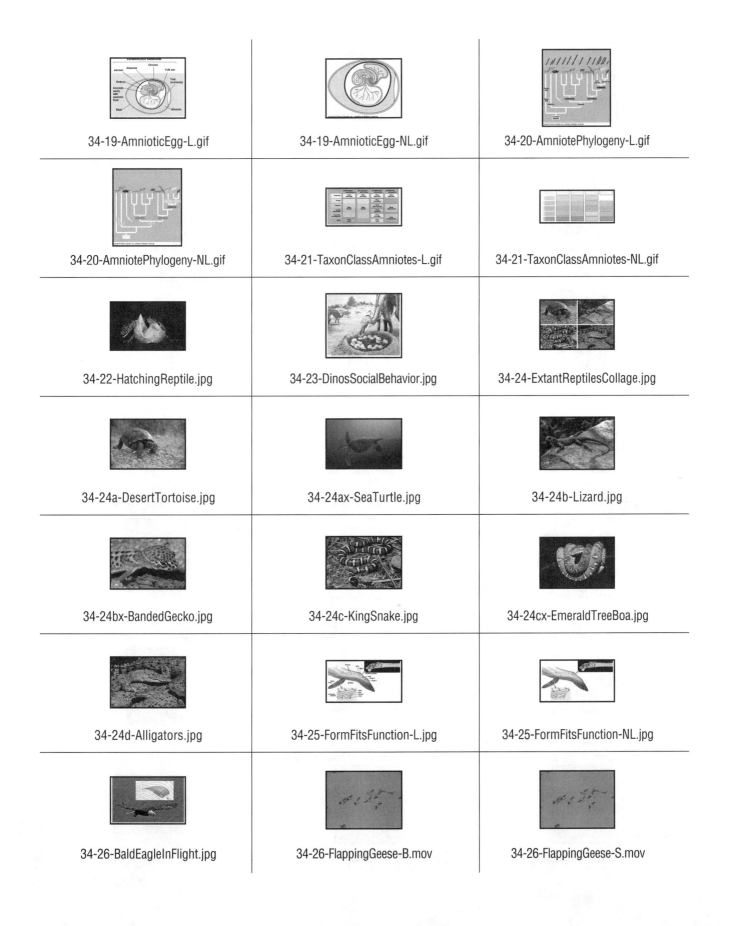

34-19-AmnioticEgg-L.gif	34-19-AmnioticEgg-NL.gif	34-20-AmniotePhylogeny-L.gif
34-20-AmniotePhylogeny-NL.gif	34-21-TaxonClassAmniotes-L.gif	34-21-TaxonClassAmniotes-NL.gif
34-22-HatchingReptile.jpg	34-23-DinosSocialBehavior.jpg	34-24-ExtantReptilesCollage.jpg
34-24a-DesertTortoise.jpg	34-24ax-SeaTurtle.jpg	34-24b-Lizard.jpg
34-24bx-BandedGecko.jpg	34-24c-KingSnake.jpg	34-24cx-EmeraldTreeBoa.jpg
34-24d-Alligators.jpg	34-25-FormFitsFunction-L.jpg	34-25-FormFitsFunction-NL.jpg
34-26-BaldEagleInFlight.jpg	34-26-FlappingGeese-B.mov	34-26-FlappingGeese-S.mov

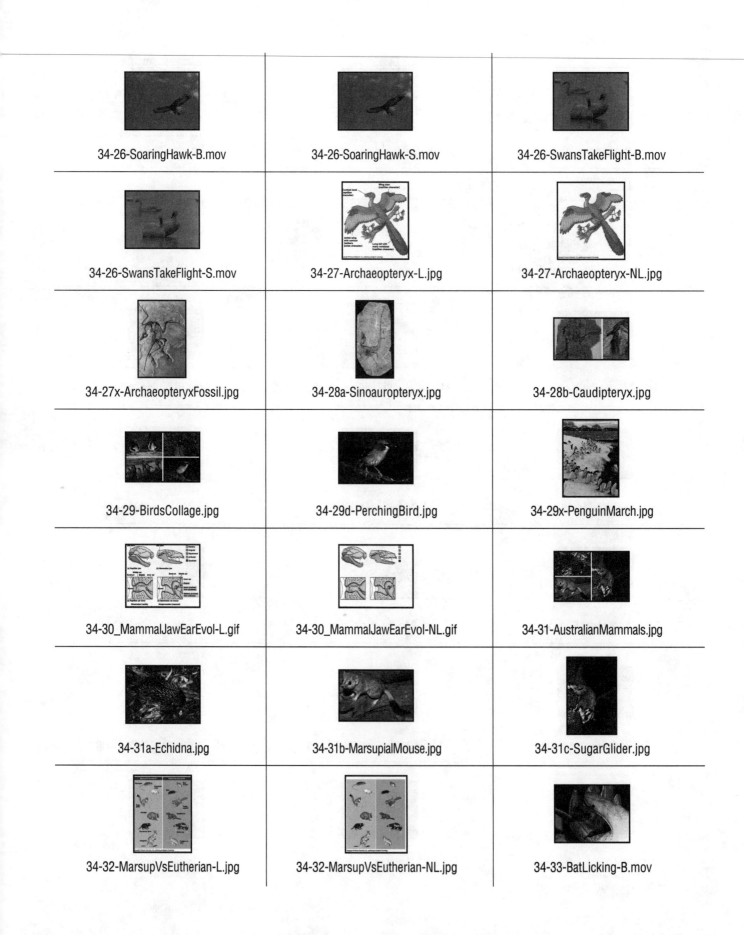

34-26-SoaringHawk-B.mov

34-26-SoaringHawk-S.mov

34-26-SwansTakeFlight-B.mov

34-26-SwansTakeFlight-S.mov

34-27-Archaeopteryx-L.jpg

34-27-Archaeopteryx-NL.jpg

34-27x-ArchaeopteryxFossil.jpg

34-28a-Sinoauropteryx.jpg

34-28b-Caudipteryx.jpg

34-29-BirdsCollage.jpg

34-29d-PerchingBird.jpg

34-29x-PenguinMarch.jpg

34-30_MammalJawEarEvol-L.gif

34-30_MammalJawEarEvol-NL.gif

34-31-AustralianMammals.jpg

34-31a-Echidna.jpg

34-31b-MarsupialMouse.jpg

34-31c-SugarGlider.jpg

34-32-MarsupVsEutherian-L.jpg

34-32-MarsupVsEutherian-NL.jpg

34-33-BatLicking-B.mov

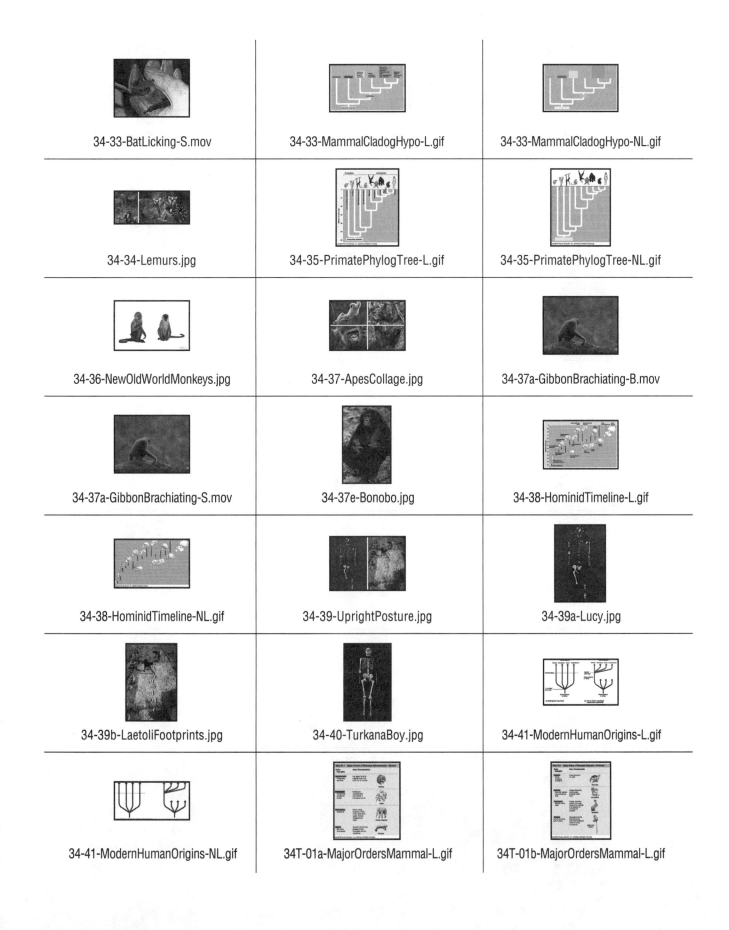

34-33-BatLicking-S.mov

34-33-MammalCladogHypo-L.gif

34-33-MammalCladogHypo-NL.gif

34-34-Lemurs.jpg

34-35-PrimatePhylogTree-L.gif

34-35-PrimatePhylogTree-NL.gif

34-36-NewOldWorldMonkeys.jpg

34-37-ApesCollage.jpg

34-37a-GibbonBrachiating-B.mov

34-37a-GibbonBrachiating-S.mov

34-37e-Bonobo.jpg

34-38-HominidTimeline-L.gif

34-38-HominidTimeline-NL.gif

34-39-UprightPosture.jpg

34-39a-Lucy.jpg

34-39b-LaetoliFootprints.jpg

34-40-TurkanaBoy.jpg

34-41-ModernHumanOrigins-L.gif

34-41-ModernHumanOrigins-NL.gif

34T-01a-MajorOrdersMammal-L.gif

34T-01b-MajorOrdersMammal-L.gif

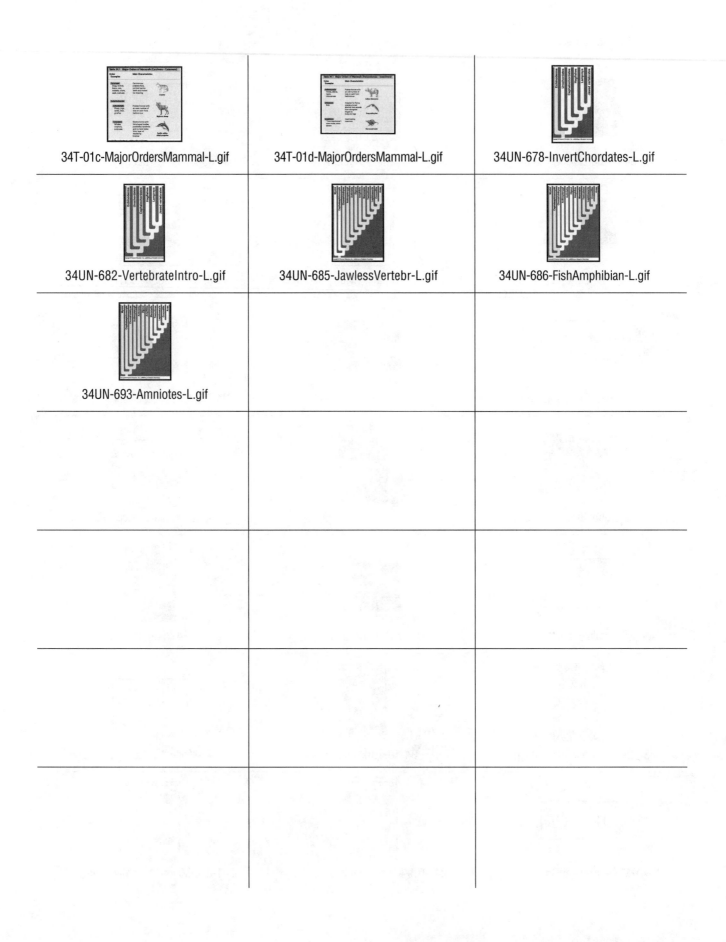

34T-01c-MajorOrdersMammal-L.gif

34T-01d-MajorOrdersMammal-L.gif

34UN-678-InvertChordates-L.gif

34UN-682-VertebrateIntro-L.gif

34UN-685-JawlessVertebr-L.gif

34UN-686-FishAmphibian-L.gif

34UN-693-Amniotes-L.gif

CHAPTER 35

Plant Structure and Growth

Chapter Outline

The Plant Body

Both genes and environment affect plant structure

Plants have three basic organs: roots, stems, and leaves

Plant organs are composed of three tissues systems: dermal, vascular, and ground

Plant tissues are composed of three basic cell types: parenchyma, collenchyma, and sclerenchyma

The Process of Plant Growth and Development

Meristems generate cells for new organs throughout the lifetime of a plant: *an overview of plant growth*

Primary growth: Apical meristems extend roots and shoots by giving rise to the primary plant body

Secondary growth: Lateral meristems add girth by producing secondary vascular tissue and periderm

Mechanisms of Plant Growth and Development

Molecular biology is revolutionizing the study of plants

Growth, morphogenesis, and differentiation produce the plant body

Growth involves both cell division and cell expansion

Morphogenesis depends on pattern formulation

Cellular differentiation depends on the control of gene expression

Clonal analysis of the shoot apex emphasizes the importance of a cell's location in its developmental fate

Phase changes mark major shifts in development

Genes controlling transcription play key roles in a meristem's change from a vegetative to a floral phase

Transparency Acetates

The Transparency Acetates for *Biology,* Sixth Edition, include the following images:

Figure 35.1   A comparison of monocots and dicots

Figure 35.2   Morphology of a flowering plant: an overview

Figure 35.5   Simple versus compound leaves

Figure 35.7   The three tissue systems

Figure 35.8   Water-conducting cells of xylem

Figure 35.9   Food-conducting cells of the phloem

Figure 35.12   Locations of major meristems: an overview of plant growth

Figure 35.13   Morphology of a winter twig

Figure 35.14   Primary growth of a root

Figure 35.19   Leaf anatomy

Figure 35.20   Production of secondary xylem and phloem by the vascular cambium

Figure 35.21   Secondary growth of a stem (Layer 1)

Figure 35.21   Secondary growth of a stem (Layer 2)

Figure 35.21   Secondary growth of a stem (Layer 3)

Figure 35.23   Anatomy of a tree trunk

Figure 35.24   A summary of primary and secondary growth in a woody stem

Figure 35.25   *Arabidopsis thaliana*

Figure 35.26   The plane and symmetry of cell division influence development of form

Figure 35.27   The preprophase band and the plane of cell division

Figure 35.28   The orientation of plant cell expansion

Figure 35.29   A hypothetical mechanism for how microtubules orient cellulose microfibrils

Figure 35.36   The ABC hypothesis for the functioning of organ identity genes in flower development

Media for Instructors

Campbell Image Presentation Library

The Campbell Image Presentation Library CD-ROM set includes the following for your use:

- All art (available in pdf and jpeg or gif formats), photos (from the text and outside sources), and tables. Art images are also available without callouts. See the Visual Guide to the Image Library section at the end of this chapter for thumbnail versions of every image.

- A PowerPoint™ slide show of the art (with callouts), photos (both text and outside sources), and tables.

- The following video clip:

  35-14-TimeLapseRoot-B.mov   Time-lapse video of root growth

PowerPoint Lectures CD-ROM

The PowerPoint Lectures CD-ROM contains slides that integrate the art, photos, tables, and lecture outline from this chapter.

Campbell Biology Website (Instructor Resources)

See the insert in your copy of Campbell/Reece *Biology*, Sixth Edition, for instructions on how to access the Campbell Biology Website. The Instructor Resources section of the website includes the following:

- The art, photos, tables, PowerPoint slide shows, videos, and animations from the Campbell Image Presentation Library
- Suggested answers to the Lab Report questions from the Case Studies in the Process of Science
- The PowerPoint Lecture for this chapter
- Word files of the lecture outline for this chapter
- Photo links

Course Management Systems

The media content for this chapter is available in three course management systems: CourseCompass™, Blackboard, and WebCT. For more information, go to http://cms.aw.com. For the latest pdf instructions on how to use CourseCompass, go to www.coursecompass.com. In addition, a Syllabus Manager is offered on the Campbell Biology Website.

Media for Students

The Campbell Biology Website and CD-ROM include the following for your students:

- Objectives
- Chapter Review (Summary, Self-Quiz, and Essay Questions from the book; Word Roots; Key Terms linked to the Glossary)
- Activities (see list below)
- Case Studies in the Process of Science (see list below)
- Quizzes (Pre-test, Activities Quiz, Chapter Quiz, Essay Questions)
- Web Links
- News and References
- Art and videos from the Campbell Image Presentation Library
- The Campbell *Biology* Interviews (from all editions)
- Glossary with audio pronunciations
- Syllabus Manager

Student Media Activities and Case Studies in The Process of Science

Web/CD Activity 35A: *Root, Stem, and Leaf Sections*
Web/CD Activity 35B: *Primary and Secondary Growth*

Objectives

The Plant Body

1. Describe several examples of a plant's structural responses to environmental change.
2. Describe the relationships between the evolution of multicellular plants and that of animals.
3. Describe and compare the three basic organs of plants. Explain how these basic organs are interdependent.
4. List the basic functions of roots. Describe and compare the structures and functions of fibrous roots, taproots, root hairs, and adventitious roots.
5. Describe the basic structure of plant stems.
6. Explain the phenomenon of apical dominance.
7. Describe the structures and functions of four types of modified shoots.
8. Describe and distinguish between the leaves of monocots and eudicots.
9. Describe and distinguish between the three tissue systems of plant organs.
10. Describe and distinguish between the three basic cell types of plant tissues.

The Process of Plant Growth and Development

11. Distinguish between plant growth and plant development.
12. Distinguish between annual, biennial, and perennial plants.
13. Explain how plants are capable of indeterminate growth.
14. Define and distinguish between primary and secondary growth.
15. Describe in detail the primary growth of the tissues of roots and shoots. Describe the specific tissue organization of leaves.
16. Describe in detail the secondary growth of the tissues of shoots and roots.

Mechanisms of Plant Growth and Development

17. Explain why *Arabidopsis* is an excellent model for the study of plant development. Describe the results of recent research on this plant's development.
18. Describe and distinguish between morphogenesis, differentiation, and growth.
19. Explain why (a) the plane and symmetry of cell division, (b) the orientation of cell expansion, and (c) cortical microtubules are important determinants of plant growth and development.
20. Explain how pattern formation is determined in plants.

21. Explain how cellular differentiation is controlled by gene expression.

22. Explain how a cell's location influences its developmental fate.

23. Define phase change and explain its importance to the development of plants.

24. Explain how a vegetative shoot tip changes into a floral meristem.

Key Terms

root system
shoot system
fibrous root
taproot
root hairs
adventitious
node
internodes
axillary bud
terminal bud
apical dominance
blade
petiole
dermal tissue
epidermis
cuticle
vascular tissue
xylem
phloem
tracheids
vessel elements
pits
xylem vessels
sieve-tube members
sieve plates
companion cell
ground tissue
pith

cortex
protoplast
parenchyma cell
collenchyma cell
sclerenchyma cell
fiber
sclereids
growth
development
annual
biennial
perennial
meristem
apical meristems
primary growth
secondary growth
lateral meristem
primary plant body
root cap
zone of cell division
quiescent center
protoderm
procambium
ground meristem
zone of elongation
zone of maturation
stele
endodermis

lateral roots
pericycle
vascular bundles
stomata
guard cell
mesophyll
secondary plant body
vascular cambium
cork cambium
ray initials
fusiform initials
periderm
lenticels
bark
morphogenesis
differentiation
asymmetrical cell
  division
preprophase band
pattern formation
positional information
polarity
phase change
meristem identity
  gene(s)
organ identity gene(s)

Word Roots

apic- = the tip; **meristo-** = divided (*apical meristems*: embryonic plant tissue on the tips of roots and in the buds of shoots that supplies cells for the plant to grow)

a- = not, without; **-symmetr** = symmetrical (*asymmetric cell division*: cell division in which one daughter cell receives more cytoplasm than the other during mitosis)

bienn- = every 2 years (*biennial*: a plant that requires two years to complete its life cycle)

coll- = glue; **-enchyma** 5 an infusion (*collenchyma cell*: a flexible plant cell type that occurs in strands or cylinders that support young parts of the plant without restraining growth)

endo- = inner; **derm-** = skin (*endodermis*: the innermost layer of the cortex in plants roots)

epi- = over (*epidermis*: the dermal tissue system in plants; the outer covering of animals.

fusi- = a spindle (*fusiform initials*: the cambrium cells within the vascular bundles; the name refers to the tapered ends of these elongated cells)

inter- = between (*internode*: the segment of a plant stem between the points where leaves are attached)

meso- = middle; **-phyll** = a leaf (*mesophyll*: the ground tissue of a leaf, sandwiched between the upper and lower epidermis and specialized for photosynthesis)

morpho- = form; **-genesis** = origin (*morphogenesis*: the development of body shape and organization during ontogeny)

perenni- = through the year (*perennial*: a plant that lives for many years)

peri- = around; **-cycle** = a circle (*pericycle*: a layer of cells just inside the endodermis of a root that may become meristematic and begin dividing again)

phloe- = the bark of a tree (*phloem*: the portion of the vascular system in plants consisting of living cells arranged into elongated tubes that transport sugar and other organic nutrients throughout the plant)

pro- = before (*procambium*: a primary meristem of roots and shoots that forms the vascular tissue)

proto- = first; **-plast** = formed, molded (*protoplast*: the contents of a plant cell exclusive of the cell wall)

quiesc- = quiet, resting (*quiescent center*: a region located within the zone of cell division in plant roots, containing meristematic cells that divide very slowly)

sclero- = hard (*sclereid*: a short, irregular sclerenchyma cell in nutshells and seed coats and scattered through the parenchyma of some plants)

trachei- = the windpipe (*tracheids*: a water-conducting and supportive element of xylem composed of long, thin cells with tapered ends and walls hardened with lignin)

trans- = across (*transpiration*: the evaporative loss of water from a plant)

vascula- = a little vessel (*vascular tissue*: plant tissue consisting of cells joined into tubes that transport water and nutrients throughout the plant body)

xyl- = wood (*xylem*: the tube-shaped, nonliving portion of the vascular system in plants that carries water and minerals from the roots to the rest of the plant)

References

Hopkins, W. G. *Introduction to Plant Physiology*. New York: John Wiley & Sons, Inc. 1995.

Raven, P. H., R. F. Evert and S. E. Eichhorn. *Biology of Plants*. 6th ed. New York: Worth Publishers, Inc., 1998.

Somerville, C. "The Twentieth Century Trajectory of Plant Biology." *Cell*, January, 2000

Visual Guide to the Image Library

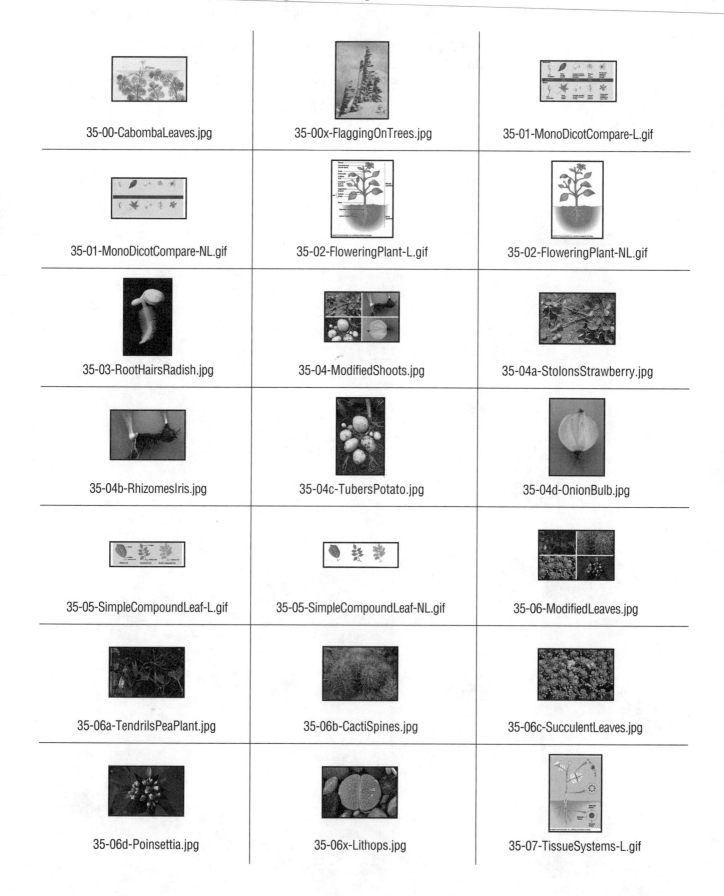

35-00-CabombaLeaves.jpg

35-00x-FlaggingOnTrees.jpg

35-01-MonoDicotCompare-L.gif

35-01-MonoDicotCompare-NL.gif

35-02-FloweringPlant-L.gif

35-02-FloweringPlant-NL.gif

35-03-RootHairsRadish.jpg

35-04-ModifiedShoots.jpg

35-04a-StolonsStrawberry.jpg

35-04b-RhizomesIris.jpg

35-04c-TubersPotato.jpg

35-04d-OnionBulb.jpg

35-05-SimpleCompoundLeaf-L.gif

35-05-SimpleCompoundLeaf-NL.gif

35-06-ModifiedLeaves.jpg

35-06a-TendrilsPeaPlant.jpg

35-06b-CactiSpines.jpg

35-06c-SucculentLeaves.jpg

35-06d-Poinsettia.jpg

35-06x-Lithops.jpg

35-07-TissueSystems-L.gif

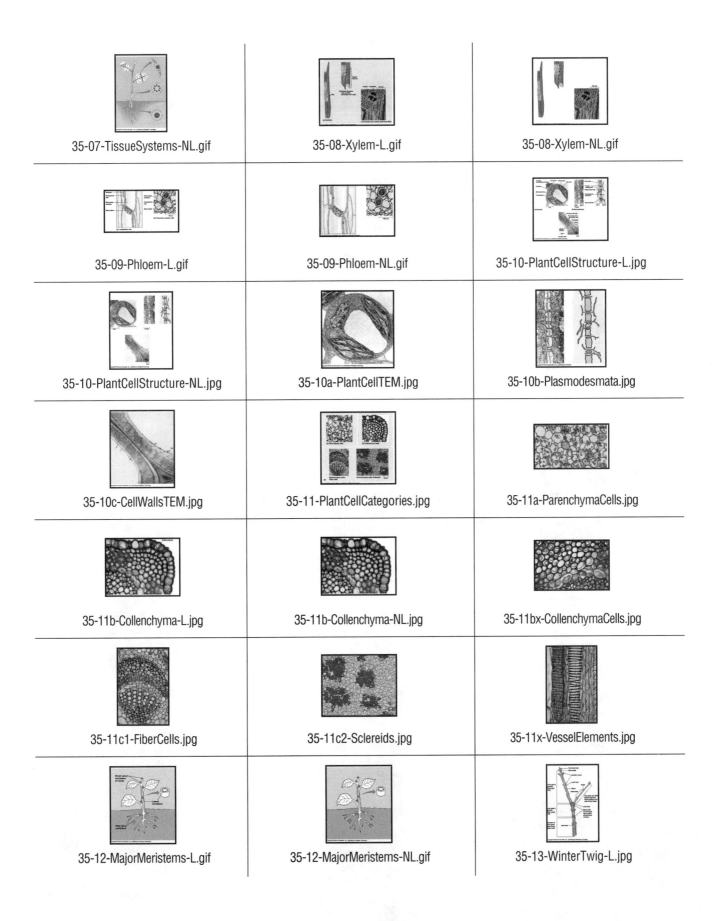

35-07-TissueSystems-NL.gif

35-08-Xylem-L.gif

35-08-Xylem-NL.gif

35-09-Phloem-L.gif

35-09-Phloem-NL.gif

35-10-PlantCellStructure-L.jpg

35-10-PlantCellStructure-NL.jpg

35-10a-PlantCellTEM.jpg

35-10b-Plasmodesmata.jpg

35-10c-CellWallsTEM.jpg

35-11-PlantCellCategories.jpg

35-11a-ParenchymaCells.jpg

35-11b-Collenchyma-L.jpg

35-11b-Collenchyma-NL.jpg

35-11bx-CollenchymaCells.jpg

35-11c1-FiberCells.jpg

35-11c2-Sclereids.jpg

35-11x-VesselElements.jpg

35-12-MajorMeristems-L.gif

35-12-MajorMeristems-NL.gif

35-13-WinterTwig-L.jpg

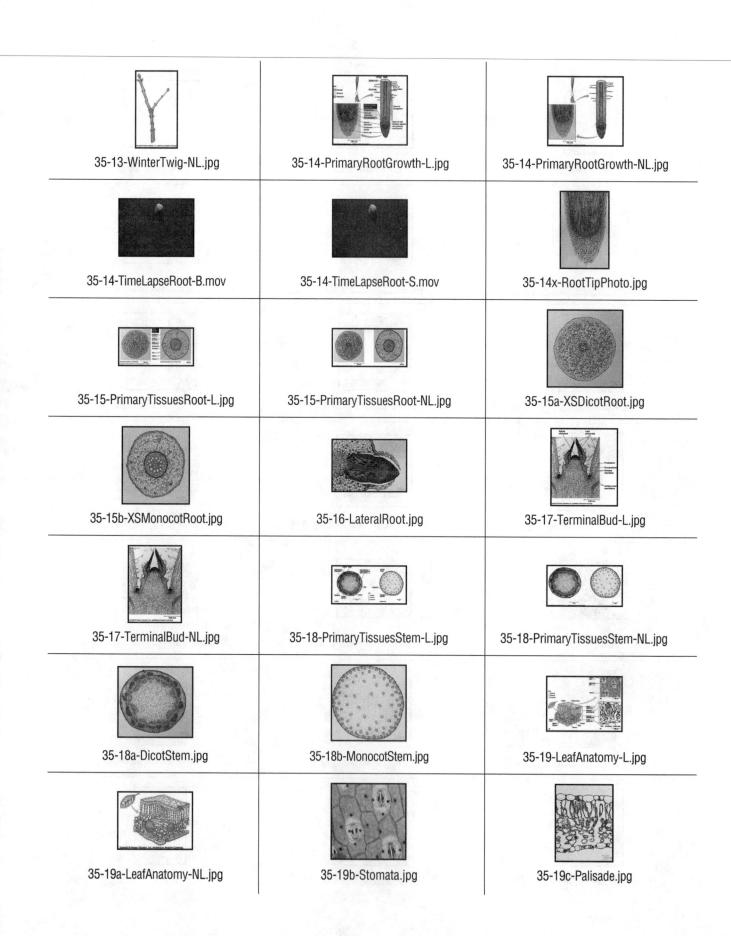

35-13-WinterTwig-NL.jpg

35-14-PrimaryRootGrowth-L.jpg

35-14-PrimaryRootGrowth-NL.jpg

35-14-TimeLapseRoot-B.mov

35-14-TimeLapseRoot-S.mov

35-14x-RootTipPhoto.jpg

35-15-PrimaryTissuesRoot-L.jpg

35-15-PrimaryTissuesRoot-NL.jpg

35-15a-XSDicotRoot.jpg

35-15b-XSMonocotRoot.jpg

35-16-LateralRoot.jpg

35-17-TerminalBud-L.jpg

35-17-TerminalBud-NL.jpg

35-18-PrimaryTissuesStem-L.jpg

35-18-PrimaryTissuesStem-NL.jpg

35-18a-DicotStem.jpg

35-18b-MonocotStem.jpg

35-19-LeafAnatomy-L.jpg

35-19a-LeafAnatomy-NL.jpg

35-19b-Stomata.jpg

35-19c-Palisade.jpg

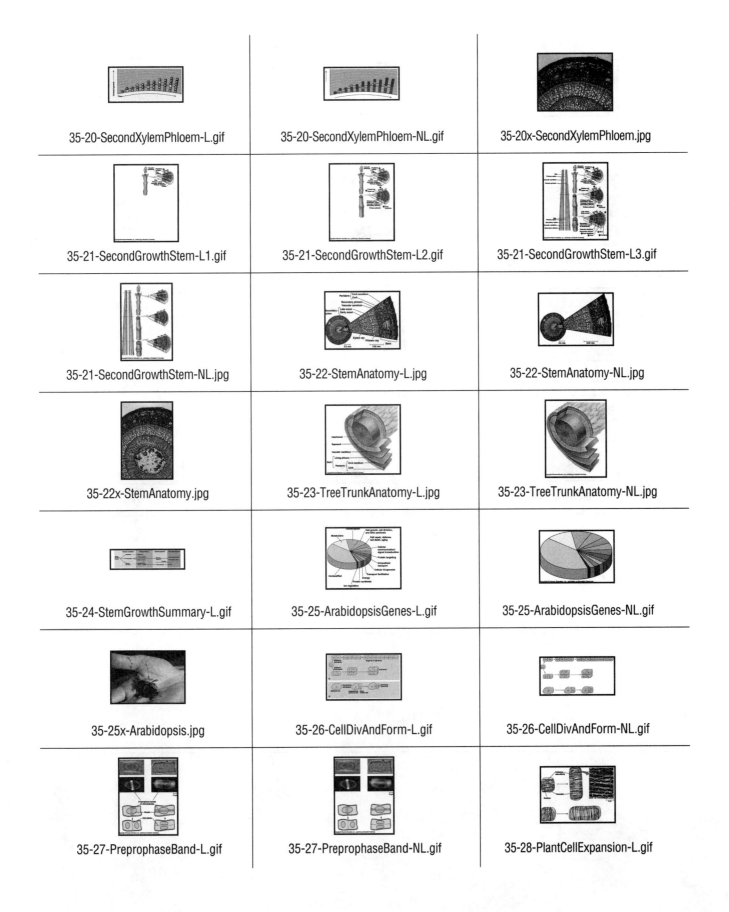

35-20-SecondXylemPhloem-L.gif

35-20-SecondXylemPhloem-NL.gif

35-20x-SecondXylemPhloem.jpg

35-21-SecondGrowthStem-L1.gif

35-21-SecondGrowthStem-L2.gif

35-21-SecondGrowthStem-L3.gif

35-21-SecondGrowthStem-NL.jpg

35-22-StemAnatomy-L.jpg

35-22-StemAnatomy-NL.jpg

35-22x-StemAnatomy.jpg

35-23-TreeTrunkAnatomy-L.jpg

35-23-TreeTrunkAnatomy-NL.jpg

35-24-StemGrowthSummary-L.gif

35-25-ArabidopsisGenes-L.gif

35-25-ArabidopsisGenes-NL.gif

35-25x-Arabidopsis.jpg

35-26-CellDivAndForm-L.gif

35-26-CellDivAndForm-NL.gif

35-27-PreprophaseBand-L.gif

35-27-PreprophaseBand-NL.gif

35-28-PlantCellExpansion-L.gif

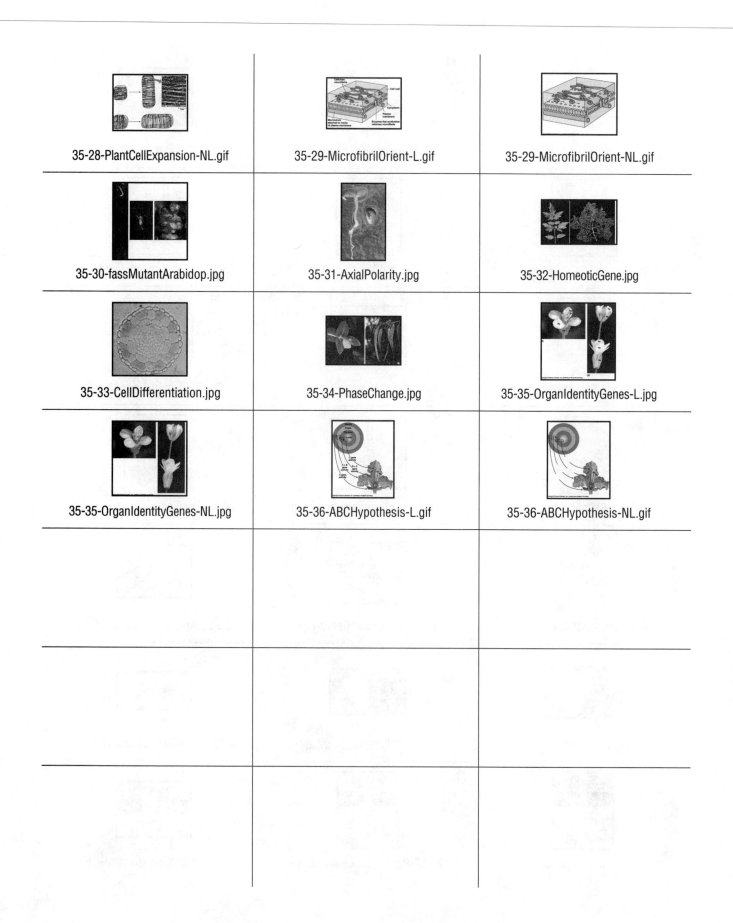

35-28-PlantCellExpansion-NL.gif

35-29-MicrofibrilOrient-L.gif

35-29-MicrofibrilOrient-NL.gif

35-30-fassMutantArabidop.jpg

35-31-AxialPolarity.jpg

35-32-HomeoticGene.jpg

35-33-CellDifferentiation.jpg

35-34-PhaseChange.jpg

35-35-OrganIdentityGenes-L.jpg

35-35-OrganIdentityGenes-NL.jpg

35-36-ABCHypothesis-L.gif

35-36-ABCHypothesis-NL.gif

Transport in Plants

Chapter Outline

Transparency Acetates

The Transparency Acetates for *Biology*, Sixth Edition, include the following images:

Figure 36.1	An overview of transport in whole plants (Layer 1)
Figure 36.1	An overview of transport in whole plants (Layer 2)
Figure 36.1	An overview of transport in whole plants (Layer 3)
Figure 36.1	An overview of transport in whole plants (Layer 4)
Figure 36.2	A chemiosmotic model of solute transport in plant cells
Figure 36.3	Water potential and water movement: a mechanical model
Figure 36.4	Water relations of plant cells
Figure 36.6	Compartments of plant cells and tissues and routes for lateral transport
Figure 36.7	Lateral transport of minerals and water in roots
Figure 36.10	The generation of transpirational pull in a leaf
Figure 36.11	Ascent of water in a tree
Figure 36.13	The control of stomatal opening and closing
Figure 36.14	A patch-clamp study of guard cell membranes
Figure 36.16	Loading of sucrose into phloem
Figure 36.17	Pressure flow in a sieve tube

Media for Instructors

Campbell Image Presentation Library

The Campbell Image Presentation Library CD-ROM set includes the following for your use:

- All art (available in pdf and jpeg or gif formats), photos (from the text and outside sources), and tables. Art images are also available without callouts. See the Visual Guide to the Image Library section at the end of this chapter for thumbnail versions of every image.

- A PowerPoint™ slide show of the art (with callouts), photos (both text and outside sources), and tables.

- The following video clip:
  See

  08-12-PlasmolyzingElodea-B.mov   *Elodea* in process of plasmolyzing

- The following QuickTime animation, adapted from student media activities (also available as a Shockwave Flash .swf file):

  36-11-CohesionOfWater.mov

PowerPoint Lectures CD-ROM

The PowerPoint Lectures CD-ROM contains slides that integrate the art, photos, tables, and lecture outline from this chapter.

Campbell Biology Website (Instructor Resources)

See the insert in your copy of Campbell/Reece *Biology*, Sixth Edition, for instructions on how to access the Campbell Biology Website. The Instructor Resources section of the website includes the following:

- The art, photos, tables, PowerPoint slide shows, videos, and animations from the Campbell Image Presentation Library
- Suggested answers to the Lab Report questions from the Case Studies in the Process of Science
- The PowerPoint Lecture for this chapter
- Word files of the lecture outline for this chapter
- Photo links

Course Management Systems

The media content for this chapter is available in three course management systems: CourseCompass™, Blackboard, and WebCT. For more information, go to http://cms.aw.com. For the latest pdf instructions on how to use CourseCompass, go to **www.coursecompass.com**. In addition, a Syllabus Manager is offered on the Campbell Biolog*y* Website.

Media for Students

The Campbell Biology Website and CD-ROM include the following for your students:

- Objectives
- Chapter Review (Summary, Self-Quiz, and Essay Questions from the book; Word Roots; Key Terms linked to the Glossary)
- Activities (see list below)
- Case Studies in the Process of Science (see list below)
- Quizzes (Pre-test, Activities Quiz, Chapter Quiz, Essay Questions)
- Web Links
- News and References
- Art and videos from the Campbell Image Presentation Library
- The Campbell *Biology* Interviews (from all editions)
- Glossary with audio pronunciations
- Syllabus Manager

Student Media Activities and Case Studies in The Process of Science

Web/CD Activity 36A: *Transport of Xylem Sap*

Web/CD Case Study in the Process of Science: *How Is Rate of Transpiration Calculated?*

Web/CD Activity 36B: *Translocation of Phloem Sap*

Objectives

An Overview of Transport Mechanisms in Plants

1. List three levels in which transport occurs in plants.

2. Compare the processes of passive and active transport. Distinguish between the two main categories of transport proteins.

3. Describe the role and importance of proton pumps in transport across plant membranes.

4. Define cotransport and chemiosmosis.

5. Define osmosis and water potential. Explain how water potential is measured.

6. Explain how solutes and pressure affect water potential.

7. Explain how the physical properties of plant cells are changed when the plant is placed into solutions that have higher, lower, or the same solute concentrations. Define flaccid, plasmolyze, turgor pressure, and turgid.

8. Explain how aquaporins affect the rate of water transport across membranes.

9. Describe the three major compartments in vacuolated plant cells, noting their interrelationships.

10. Describe the three routes available for lateral transport in plants.

11. Define bulk flow and describe the different types of forces that generate pressure.

12. Relate the structure of sieve-tube cells, vessel cells, and tracheids to their functions in bulk flow.

Absorption of Water and Minerals by Roots

13. Explain how the structure of root hairs promotes their functions. Explain how mycorrhizae facilitate the functions of roots.

14. Explain how the endodermis functions as a selective barrier between the root cortex and vascular tissue.

Transport of Xylem Sap

15. Describe the potential and limits of root pressure to move xylem sap. Define root pressure, transpiration, and guttation.

16. Explain how transpirational pull moves xylem sap up from the root tips to the leaves.

The Control of Transpiration

17. Describe the role of guard cells in photosynthesis-transpiration.

18. Explain the advantages and disadvantages of the extensive inner surface area of a leaf.

19. Explain how the transpiration-to-photosynthesis ratio is calculated and what it indicates about a plant.

20. Explain how transpiration changes the temperatures of leaves and why this is adaptive. Explain how plants with low transpiration rates compensate for higher temperatures.

21. Explain how and when stomata open and close.

22. Explain how xerophytes reduce transpiration.

Translocation of Phloem Sap

23. Define and describe the process of translocation. Trace the path of phloem sap from the primary sugar source to common sugar sinks.

24. Describe the process of sugar loading and unloading.

25. Define pressure flow. Explain the significance of this process in angiosperms.

Key Terms

transport proteins	turgor pressure	root pressure
selective channels	turgid	guttation
proton pump	aquaporin	transpiration-to-
cotransport	tonoplast	photosynthesis ratio
chemiosmosis	symplast	circadian rhythm
osmosis	apoplast	xerophytes
water potential	bulk flow	translocation
megapascal (MPa)	mycorrhizae	sugar source
tension	endodermis	sugar sink
flaccid	Casparian strip	transfer cells
plasmolyze	transpiration	

Word Roots

apo- = off, away; **-plast** = formed, molded (*apoplast*: in plants, the nonliving continuum formed by the extracellular pathway provided by the continuous matrix of cell walls)

aqua- = water; **-pori** = a pore, small opening (*aquaporin*: a transport protein in the plasma membranes of a plant or animal cell that specifically facilitates the diffusion of water across the membrane)

chemo- = chemical (*chemiosmosis*: the production of ATP using the energy of hydrogen-ion gradients across membranes to phosphorylate ADP)

circa- = a circle (*circadian rhythm*: a physiological cycle of about 24 hours, present in all eukaryotic organisms, that persists even in the absence of external cues)

co- = together; **trans-** = across; **-port** = a gate, door (*cotransport*: the coupling of the "downhill" diffusion of one substance to the "uphill" transport of another against its own concentration gradient)

endo- within, inner; **-derm** = skin (*endodermis*: the innermost of the three primary germ layers in animal embryos)

gutt- = a drop (*guttation*: the exudation of water droplets caused by root pressure in certain plants)

mega- = large, great (*megapascal*: a unit of pressure equivalent to 10 atmospheres of pressure)

myco- = a fungus; **-rhizo** = a root (*mycorrhizae*: mutualistic associations of plant roots and fungi)

osmo- = pushing (*osmosis*: the diffusion of water across a selectively permeable membrane)

sym- = with, together (*symplast*: in plants, the continuum of cytoplasm connected by plasmodesmata between cells)

turg- = swollen (*turgor pressure*: the force directed against a cell wall after the influx of water and the swelling of a walled cell due to osmosis)

xero- = dry; **-phyto** = a plant (*xerophytes*: plants adapted to arid climates)

References

Hopkins, W. G. *Introduction to Plant Physiology*. New York: John Wiley & Sons, Inc. 1995.

Raven, P. H., R. F. Evert and S. E. Eichhorn. *Biology of Plants*. 6th ed. New York: Worth Publishers, Inc., 1998.

Visual Guide to the Image Library

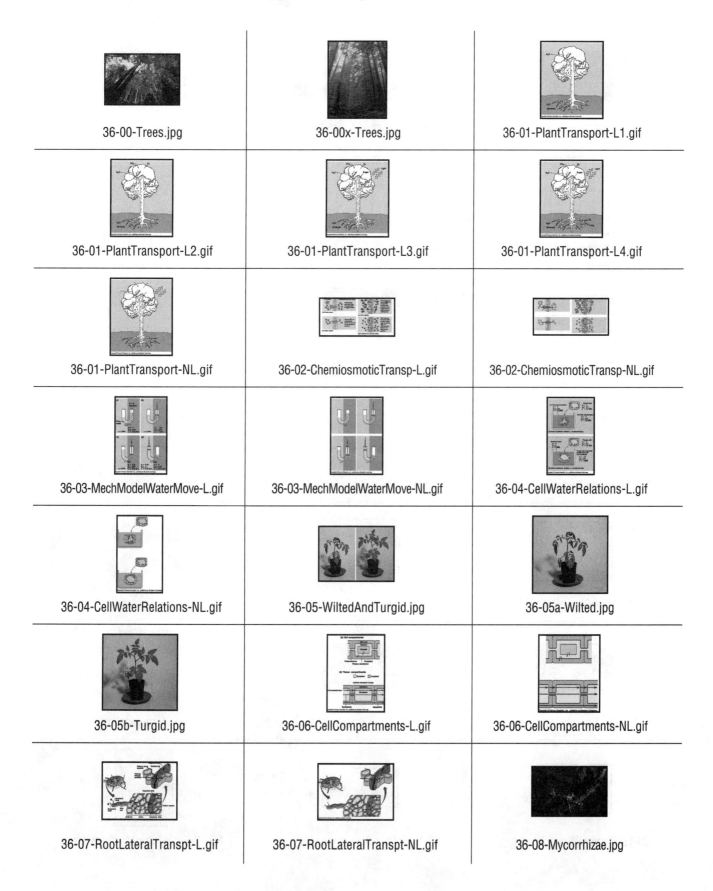

36-00-Trees.jpg

36-00x-Trees.jpg

36-01-PlantTransport-L1.gif

36-01-PlantTransport-L2.gif

36-01-PlantTransport-L3.gif

36-01-PlantTransport-L4.gif

36-01-PlantTransport-NL.gif

36-02-ChemiosmoticTransp-L.gif

36-02-ChemiosmoticTransp-NL.gif

36-03-MechModelWaterMove-L.gif

36-03-MechModelWaterMove-NL.gif

36-04-CellWaterRelations-L.gif

36-04-CellWaterRelations-NL.gif

36-05-WiltedAndTurgid.jpg

36-05a-Wilted.jpg

36-05b-Turgid.jpg

36-06-CellCompartments-L.gif

36-06-CellCompartments-NL.gif

36-07-RootLateralTranspt-L.gif

36-07-RootLateralTranspt-NL.gif

36-08-Mycorrhizae.jpg

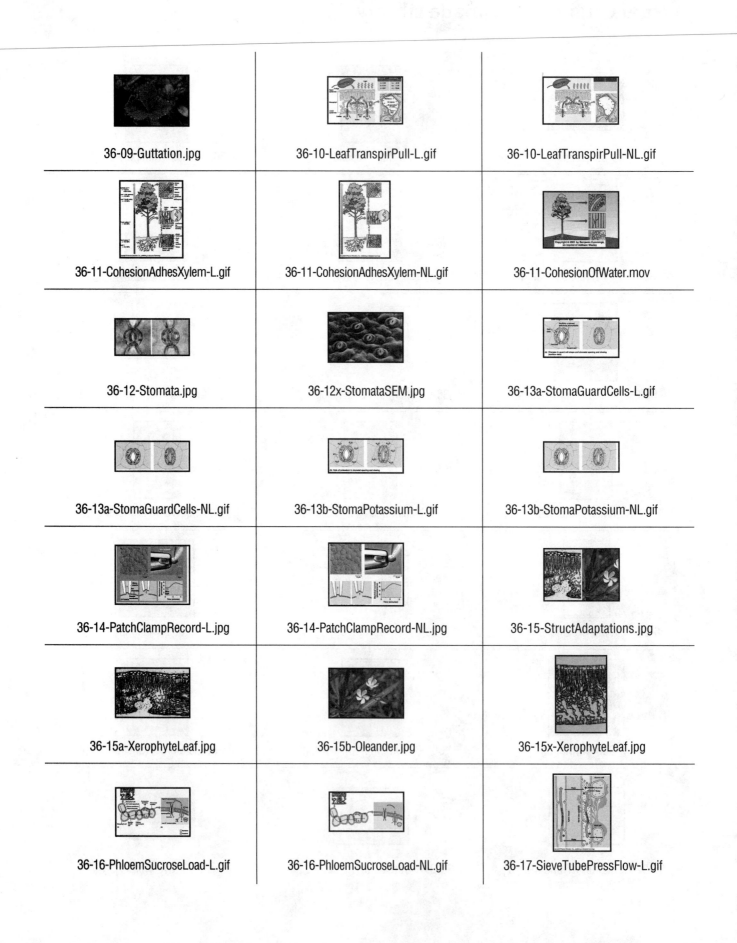

36-09-Guttation.jpg

36-10-LeafTranspirPull-L.gif

36-10-LeafTranspirPull-NL.gif

36-11-CohesionAdhesXylem-L.gif

36-11-CohesionAdhesXylem-NL.gif

36-11-CohesionOfWater.mov

36-12-Stomata.jpg

36-12x-StomataSEM.jpg

36-13a-StomaGuardCells-L.gif

36-13a-StomaGuardCells-NL.gif

36-13b-StomaPotassium-L.gif

36-13b-StomaPotassium-NL.gif

36-14-PatchClampRecord-L.jpg

36-14-PatchClampRecord-NL.jpg

36-15-StructAdaptations.jpg

36-15a-XerophyteLeaf.jpg

36-15b-Oleander.jpg

36-15x-XerophyteLeaf.jpg

36-16-PhloemSucroseLoad-L.gif

36-16-PhloemSucroseLoad-NL.gif

36-17-SieveTubePressFlow-L.gif

36-17-SieveTubePressFlow-NL.gif

36-18-TappingPhyloem.jpg

CHAPTER 37

Plant Nutrition

Chapter Outline

Nutritional Requirements of Plants

The chemical composition of plants provides clues to their nutritional requirements: *the process of science*

Plants require nine macronutrients and at least eight micronutrients

The symptoms of a mineral deficiency depend on the function and mobility of the element

The Role of Soil in Plant Nutrition

Soil characteristics are key environmental factors in terrestrial ecosystems

Soil conservation is one step toward sustainable agriculture

The Special Case of Nitrogen as a Plant Nutrient

The metabolism of soil bacteria makes nitrogen available to plants

Improving the protein yield of crops is a major goal of agricultural research

Nutritional Adaptations: Symbiosis of Plants and Soil Microbes

Symbiotic nitrogen fixation results from intricate interactions between roots and bacteria

Mycorrhizae are symbiotic associations of roots and fungi that enhance plant nutrition: *the process of science*

Mycorrhizae and root nodules may have an evolutionary relationship

Nutritional Adaptations: Parasitism and Predation by Plants

Parasitic plants extract nutrients from other plants

Carnivorous plants supplement their mineral nutrition by digesting animals

Transparency Acetates

The Transparency Acetates for *Biology*, Sixth Edition, include the following images:

Figure 37.1 The uptake of nutrients by a plant: an overview

Figure 37.2 Using hydroponic culture to identify essential nutrients

Table 37.1	Essential Nutrients in Plants
Figure 37.6	The availability of soil water and minerals
Figure 37.9	The role of soil bacteria in the nitrogen nutrition of plants (Layer 1)
Figure 37.9	The role of soil bacteria in the nitrogen nutrition of plants (Layer 2)
Figure 37.9	The role of soil bacteria in the nitrogen nutrition of plants (Layer 3)
Figure 37.11	Development of a soybean root nodule
Figure 37.13	Molecular biology of root nodule formation

Media for Instructors

Campbell Image Presentation Library

The Campbell Image Presentation Library CD-ROM set includes the following for your use:

- All art (available in pdf and jpeg or gif formats), photos (from the text and outside sources), and tables. Art images are also available without callouts. See the Visual Guide to the Image Library section at the end of this chapter for thumbnail versions of every image.
- A PowerPoint™ slide show of the art (with callouts), photos (both text and outside sources), and tables.
- The following video clip:

  37-16-SunDewTrapPrey-B.mov   Carnivorous plants trapping prey

PowerPoint Lectures CD-ROM

The PowerPoint Lectures CD-ROM contains slides that integrate the art, photos, tables, and lecture outline from this chapter.

Campbell Biology Website (Instructor Resources)

See the insert in your copy of Campbell/Reece *Biology,* Sixth Edition, for instructions on how to access the Campbell Biology Website. The Instructor Resources section of the website includes the following:

- The art, photos, tables, PowerPoint slide shows, videos, and animations from the Campbell Image Presentation Library
- Suggested answers to the Lab Report questions from the Case Studies in the Process of Science
- The PowerPoint Lecture for this chapter
- Word files of the lecture outline for this chapter
- Photo links

Course Management Systems

The media content for this chapter is available in three course management systems: CourseCompass™, Blackboard, and WebCT. For more information, go to http://cms.aw.com. For the latest pdf instructions on how to use CourseCompass, go to **www.coursecompass.com**. In addition, a Syllabus Manager is offered on the Campbell Biolog*y* Website.

Media for Students

The Campbell Biology Website and CD-ROM include the following for your students:

- Objectives
- Chapter Review (Summary, Self-Quiz, and Essay Questions from the book; Word Roots; Key Terms linked to the Glossary)
- Activities (see list below)
- Case Studies in the Process of Science (see list below)
- Quizzes (Pre-test, Activities Quiz, Chapter Quiz, Essay Questions)
- Web Links
- News and References
- Art and videos from the Campbell Image Presentation Library
- The Campbell *Biology* Interviews (from all editions)
- Glossary with audio pronunciations
- Syllabus Manager

Student Media Activities and Case Studies in The Process of Science

Web/CD Activity 37A: *How Plants Obtain Minerals from Soil*

Web/CD Case Study in the Process of Science: *How Does Acid Precipitation Affect Mineral Deficiency?*

Web/CD Activity 37B: *The Nitrogen Cycle*

Objectives

Nutritional Requirements of Plants

1. Describe the chemical composition of plants, including the
    a. percent of wet weight as water
    b. percent of dry weight as organic substances
    c. percent of dry weight as inorganic minerals

2. Explain how hydroponic culture is used to determine which minerals are essential nutrients.

3. Distinguish between macronutrient and micronutrient.

4. Recall the nine macronutrients required by plants and describe their importance in normal plant structure and metabolism.

5. List eight micronutrients required by plants and explain why plants need only minute quantities of these elements.

6. Explain how a nutrient's role and mobility determine the symptoms of a mineral deficiency.

The Role of Soil in Plant Nutrition

7. Explain how soil is formed.

8. Explain what determines the texture of topsoil and list the type of soil particles from coarsest to smallest.

9. Describe the composition of loams and explain why they are the most fertile soils.

10. Explain how humus contributes to the texture and composition of soil.

11. Explain why plants cannot extract all of the water in soil.

12. Explain how the presence of clay in soil helps prevent the leaching of mineral cations.

13. Define cation exchange, explain why it is necessary for plant nutrition, and describe how plants can stimulate the process.

14. Explain why soil management is necessary in agricultural systems but not in natural ecosystems such as forests and grasslands. Describe several examples of human mismanagement disasters.

15. List the three mineral elements that are most commonly deficient in farm soils.

16. Explain how soil pH determines the effectiveness of fertilizers and a plant's ability to absorb specific mineral nutrients.

17. Describe problems resulting from farm irrigation in arid regions and list several current approaches to solving these problems.

18. Describe precautions that can reduce wind and water erosion.

19. Explain how phytoremediation can help improve polluted environments.

The Special Case of Nitrogen as a Plant Nutrient

20. Define nitrogen fixation and write the overall equation representing the conversion of gaseous nitrogen to ammonia.

21. Describe the important role of nitrogen-fixing bacteria.

22. Recall the forms of nitrogen that plants can absorb and describe how they are used by plants.

23. Explain why it is important to improve the protein yield of crops.

24. Describe the challenges of raising crops enriched with protein.

Nutritional Adaptations: Symbiosis of Plants and Soil Microbes

25. Beginning with free-living rhizobial bacteria, describe the development of a root nodule.

26. Explain why the symbiosis between a legume and its nitrogen-fixing bacteria is considered to be mutualistic.

27. Recall the functions of leg hemoglobin and explain why its synthesis is evidence for coevolution.

28. Describe the basis for crop rotation.

29. Explain how a legume species recognizes a certain species of *Rhizobium*. Explain how that encounter leads to the development of a nodule.

30. Define mycorrhizae and explain why they are considered examples of mutualism. Explain how mycorrhizae enhance plant nutrition.

31. Explain the significance of mycorrhizae in the evolution of terrestrial plants.

32. Compare the structure and properties of ectomycorrhizae and endomycorrhizae.

33. Describe the agricultural importance of mycorrhizae.

34. Discuss the relationships between root nodule formation and mycorrhizae development.

Nutritional Adaptations: Parasitism and Predation by Plants

35. Describe the modifications for nutrition that have evolved among plants, including parasitic plants, carnivorous plants, and mycorrhizae.

Key Terms

mineral nutrient	loams	nitrogenase
essential nutrient	cation exchange	nodules
macronutrient	sustainable agriculture	bacteroids
micronutrient	phytoremediation	mycorrhizae
topsoil	nitrogen-fixing	ectomycorrhizae
humus	bacteria	endomycorrhizae
horizons	nitrogen fixation	

Word Roots

ecto- = outside; - **myco-** = a fungus; -**rhizo** = a root (*ectomycorrhizae*: a type of mycorrhizae in which the mycelium forms a dense sheath, or mantle, over the surface of the root; hyphae extend from the mantle into the soil, greatly increasing the surface area for water and mineral absorption)

endo- = inside (*endomycorrhizae*: a type of mycorrhizae that unlike ectomycorrhizae, do not have a dense mantle ensheathing the root; instead, microscopic fungal hyphae extend from the root into the soil)

macro- = large (*macronutrient*: elements required by plants and animals in relatively large amounts)

micro- = small (*micronutrient*: elements required by plants and animals in very small amounts)

-phyto = a plant (*phytoremediation*: an emerging, non-destructive technology that seeks to cheaply reclaim contaminated areas by taking advantage of the remarkable ability of some plant species to extract heavy metals and other pollutants from the soil and to concentrate them in easily harvested portions of the plant)

References

Hopkins, W. G. *Introduction to Plant Physiology.* New York: John Wiley & Sons, Inc. 1995.

Raven, P. H., R. F. Evert and S. E. Eichhorn. *Biology of Plants.* 6th ed. New York: Worth Publishers, Inc., 1998.

Visual Guide to the Image Library

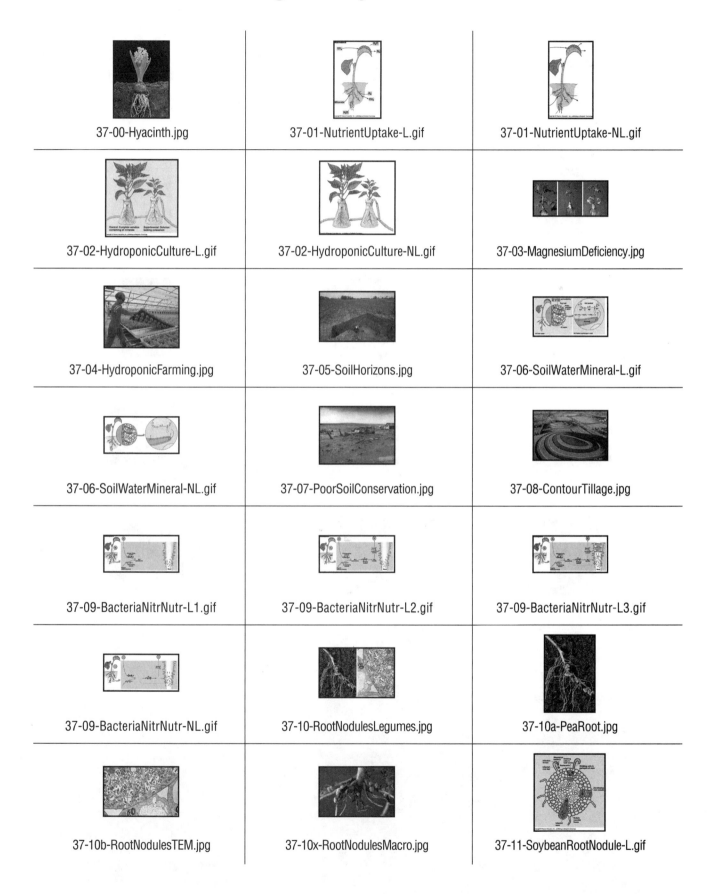

37-00-Hyacinth.jpg

37-01-NutrientUptake-L.gif

37-01-NutrientUptake-NL.gif

37-02-HydroponicCulture-L.gif

37-02-HydroponicCulture-NL.gif

37-03-MagnesiumDeficiency.jpg

37-04-HydroponicFarming.jpg

37-05-SoilHorizons.jpg

37-06-SoilWaterMineral-L.gif

37-06-SoilWaterMineral-NL.gif

37-07-PoorSoilConservation.jpg

37-08-ContourTillage.jpg

37-09-BacteriaNitrNutr-L1.gif

37-09-BacteriaNitrNutr-L2.gif

37-09-BacteriaNitrNutr-L3.gif

37-09-BacteriaNitrNutr-NL.gif

37-10-RootNodulesLegumes.jpg

37-10a-PeaRoot.jpg

37-10b-RootNodulesTEM.jpg

37-10x-RootNodulesMacro.jpg

37-11-SoybeanRootNodule-L.gif

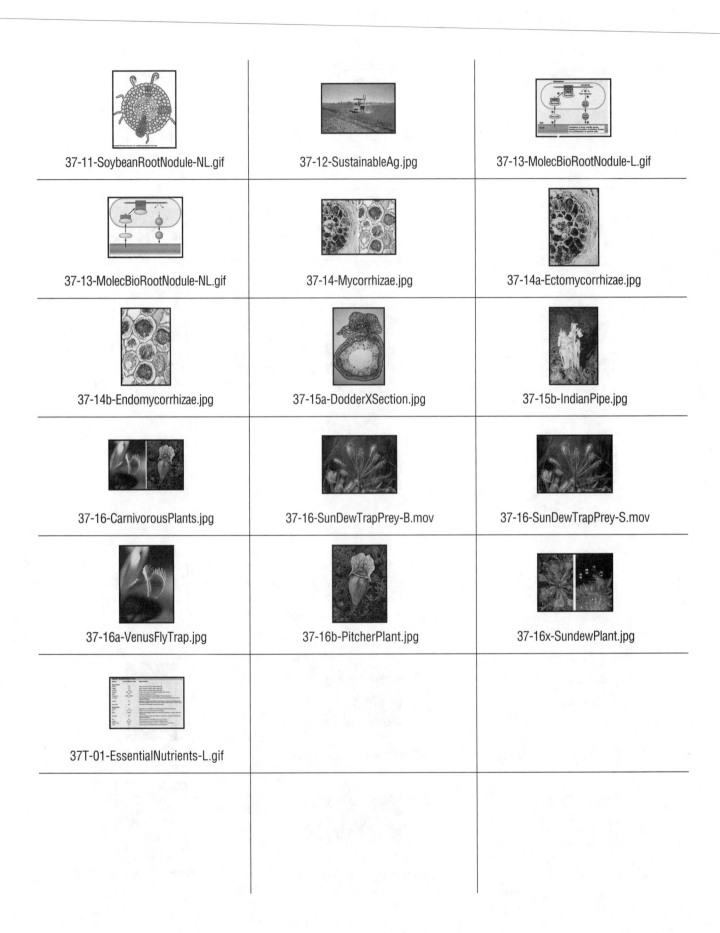

37-11-SoybeanRootNodule-NL.gif

37-12-SustainableAg.jpg

37-13-MolecBioRootNodule-L.gif

37-13-MolecBioRootNodule-NL.gif

37-14-Mycorrhizae.jpg

37-14a-Ectomycorrhizae.jpg

37-14b-Endomycorrhizae.jpg

37-15a-DodderXSection.jpg

37-15b-IndianPipe.jpg

37-16-CarnivorousPlants.jpg

37-16-SunDewTrapPrey-B.mov

37-16-SunDewTrapPrey-S.mov

37-16a-VenusFlyTrap.jpg

37-16b-PitcherPlant.jpg

37-16x-SundewPlant.jpg

37T-01-EssentialNutrients-L.gif

CHAPTER 38

Plant Reproduction and Biotechnology

Chapter Outline

Transparency Acetates

The Transparency Acetates for *Biology*, Sixth Edition, include the following images:

Figure 38.1   Simplified overview of angiosperm life cycle

Figure 38 2   Review of an idealized flower

Figure 38.4   The development of angiosperm gametophytes (pollen and embryo sacs)

Figure 38.6   "Pin" and "thrum" flower types reduce self-fertilization

Figure 38.7   Genetic basis of self-incompatibility

Figure 38.8   A possible mechanism of sporophytic self-incompatibility (Layer 1)

Figure 38.8   A possible mechanism of sporophytic self-incompatibility (Layer 2)

Figure 38.8   A possible mechanism of sporophytic self-incompatibility (Layer 3)

Figure 38.9   Growth of the pollen tube and double fertilization

Figure 38.10   The development of a dicot plant embryo

Figure 38.11   Seed structure

Figure 38.13   Mobilization of nutrients during the germination of a barley seed

Figure 38.14   Seed germination

Figure 38.17   A DNA gun

Media for Instructors

Campbell Image Presentation Library

The Campbell Image Presentation Library CD-ROM set includes the following for your use:

- All art (available in pdf and jpeg or gif formats), photos (from the text and outside sources), and tables. Art images are also available without callouts. See the Visual Guide to the Image Library section at the end of this chapter for thumbnail versions of every image.

- A PowerPoint™ slide show of the art (with callouts), photos (both text and outside sources), and tables.

- The following video clips:

  See

30-13-TimeLapseFlower-B.mov	Time-lapse of flower opening
30-17-TimeLapsePlant-B.mov	Time-lapse plant life history
30-18a-BeePollinator-B.mov	Pollinator/plant relationships
30-18c-BatPollinators-B.mov	Pollinator/plant relationships

- The following QuickTime animation, adapted from student media activities (also available as a Shockwave Flash .swf file):

  38-04-PlantFertilization.mov

  38-10-SeedDevelopment.mov

  38-12-FruitDevelopment.mov

  See also

  26-16-ClassificationSchemes.mov

PowerPoint Lectures CD-ROM

The PowerPoint Lectures CD-ROM contains slides that integrate the art, photos, tables, and lecture outline from this chapter.

Campbell Biology Website (Instructor Resources)

See the insert in your copy of Campbell/Reece *Biology*, Sixth Edition, for instructions on how to access the Campbell Biology Website. The Instructor Resources section of the website includes the following:

- The art, photos, tables, PowerPoint slide shows, videos, and animations from the Campbell Image Presentation Library
- Suggested answers to the Lab Report questions from the Case Studies in the Process of Science
- The PowerPoint Lecture for this chapter
- Word files of the lecture outline for this chapter
- Photo links

Course Management Systems

The media content for this chapter is available in three course management systems: CourseCompass™, Blackboard, and WebCT. For more information, go to http://cms.aw.com. For the latest pdf instructions on how to use CourseCompass, go to **www.coursecompass.com**. In addition, a Syllabus Manager is offered on the Campbell Biolog*y* Website.

Media for Students

The Campbell Biology Website and CD-ROM include the following for your students:

- Objectives
- Chapter Review (Summary, Self-Quiz, and Essay Questions from the book; Word Roots; Key Terms linked to the Glossary)
- Activities (see list below)
- Case Studies in the Process of Science (see list below)
- Quizzes (Pre-test, Activities Quiz, Chapter Quiz, Essay Questions)
- Web Links
- News and References
- Art and videos from the Campbell Image Presentation Library
- The Campbell *Biology* Interviews (from all editions)
- Glossary with audio pronunciations
- Syllabus Manager

Student Media Activities and Case Studies in The Process of Science

Web/CD Activity 38A: *Angiosperm Life Cycle*

Web/CD Activity 38B: *Seed and Fruit Development*

Web/CD Case Study in the Process of Science: *What Tells Desert Seeds When to Germinate?*

Web/CD Activity 38C: *Making Decisions About DNA Technology: Golden Rice*

Objectives

Sexual Reproduction

1. Outline the angiosperm life cycle.

2. List the four floral parts in their order from outside to inside the flower.

3. From a diagram of an idealized flower, correctly label the following structures and describe their function:

   a. sepals

   b. petals

   c. stamen (filament and anther)

   d. carpel (style, ovary, ovule, and stigma)

4. Describe the sequence of events that lead from pollination to fruit formation and finally germination.

5. Distinguish between (a) complete and incomplete flowers, (b) bisexual and unisexual flowers, and (c) monoecious and dioecious plant species.

6. Explain by which generation, structure, and process spores are produced.

7. Explain by which generation, structures, and processes gametes are produced.

8. Describe the development of an embryo sac and explain what happens to each of its cells.

9. Explain how pollen can be transferred between flowers.

10. Distinguish between pollination and fertilization.

11. Describe mechanisms that prevent self-pollination and explain how this contributes to genetic variation.

12. Outline the process of double fertilization and describe the function of endosperm.

13. Explain the adaptive advantage of double fertilization in angiosperms.

14. Explain how fertilization in animals is similar to that in plants.

15. Describe the fate of the ovule and ovary after double fertilization. Note where major nutrients are stored as the embryo develops.

16. Describe the development and functions of the endosperm. Distinguish between liquid endosperm and solid endosperm.

17. Describe the development of a plant embryo from the first mitotic division to the embryonic plant with rudimentary organs.

18. From a diagram, identify the following structures of a seed and recall a function for each:

    a. seed coat   d. radicle   g. endosperm

    b. embryo   e. epicotyl   h. cotyledons

    c. hypocotyl   f. plumule   i. shoot apex

19. Explain how a monocot and dicot seed differ.

20. Explain how fruit forms and ripens. List the functions of fruit.

21. Explain how selective breeding by humans has changed fruits.

22. Explain how seed dormancy can be advantageous to a plant and describe some conditions for breaking dormancy.

23. Describe variations in the process of germination, including the fate of the radicle, shoot tip, hypocotyl, epicotyl, and cotyledons.

Asexual Reproduction

24. Distinguish between sexual reproduction and vegetative reproduction.

25. Describe the natural mechanisms of vegetative reproduction in plants, including fragmentation and apomixis.

26. Explain the advantages of using both sexual and asexual reproduction.

27. Describe various methods that horticulturists use to vegetatively propagate plants from cuttings.

28. Explain how the technique of plant tissue culture can be used to clone and genetically engineer plants.

29. Describe the process of protoplast fusion and its potential agricultural impact.

Plant Biotechnology

30. Compare traditional plant-breeding techniques and genetic engineering, noting similarities and differences.

31. Explain why maize can be considered an unnatural monster.

32. Explain the need for increased crop yields within the next 20 years.

33. Describe current examples of the advantages of transgenic crops.

34. Describe some of the biological arguments for and against genetically modified crops.

Key Terms

alternation of generations	incomplete flower	coleorhiza
sporophyte	bisexual flower	coleoptile
gametophyte	unisexual flower	fruit
sepal	monoecious	pericarp
petal	dioecious	dormancy
stamen	microspore	vegetative reproduction
carpel	megaspore	fragmentation
receptacle	self-incompatibility	apomixis
anther	endosperm	callus
ovary	double fertilization	stock
ovule	seed coat	scion
pollen grains	hypocotyls	protoplast fusion
embryo sac	radicle	transgenic
complete flower	epicotyl	
	scutellum	

Word Roots

a- = without; **-pomo** = fruit (*apomixis*: the asexual production of seeds)

anth- = a flower (*anther*: the terminal pollen sac of a stamen, inside which pollen grains with male gametes form in the flower of an angiosperm)

bi- = two (*bisexual flower*: a flower equipped with both stamens and carpels)

carp- = a fruit (*carpel*: the female reproductive organ of a flower, consisting of the stigma, style, and ovary)

coleo- = a sheath; **-rhiza** = a root (*coleorhiza*: the covering of the young root of the embryo of a grass seed)

di- = two (*dioecious*: referring to a plant species that has staminate and carpellate flowers on separate plants)

dorm- = sleep (*dormancy*: a condition typified by extremely low metabolic rate and a suspension of growth and development)

endo- = within (*endosperm*: a nutrient-rich tissue formed by the union of a sperm cell with two polar nuclei during double fertilization, which provides nourishment to the developing embryo in angiosperm seeds)

epi- = on, over (*epicotyl*: the embryonic axis above the point at which the cotyledons are attached)

gamet- = a wife or husband (*gametophyte*: the multicellular haploid form in organisms undergoing alternation of generations, which mitotically produces haploid gametes that unite and grow into the sporophyte generation)

hypo- = under (*hypocotyl*: the embryonic axis below the point at which the cotyledons are attached)

mega- = large (*megaspore*: a large, haploid spore that can continue to grow to eventually produce a female gametophyte)

micro- = small (*microspore*: a small, haploid spore that can give rise to a haploid male gametophyte)

mono- = one; **- ecious** = house (*monoecious*: referring to a plant species that has both staminate and carpellate flowers on the same individual)

peri- = around; **-carp** = a fruit (*pericarp*: the thickened wall of fruit)

proto- = first; **-plast** = formed, molded (*protoplast*: the contents of a plant cell exclusive of the cell wall)

scutell- = a little shield (*scutellum*: a specialized type of cotyledon found in the grass family)

sporo- = a seed; = **-phyto** = a plant (*sporophyte*: the multicellular diploid form in organisms undergoing alternation of generations that results from a union of gametes and that meiotically produces haploid spores that grow into the gametophyte generation)

stam- = standing upright (*stamen*: the pollen-producing male reproductive organ of a flower, consisting of an anther and filament)

uni- = one (*unisexual flower*: a flower missing either stamens and carpels.

References

Hopkins, W. G. *Introduction to Plant Physiology*. New York: John Wiley & Sons, Inc. 1995.

Raven, P. H., R. F. Evert and S. E. Eichhorn. *Biology of Plants*. 6th ed. New York: Worth Publishers, Inc., 1998.

Visual Guide to the Image Library

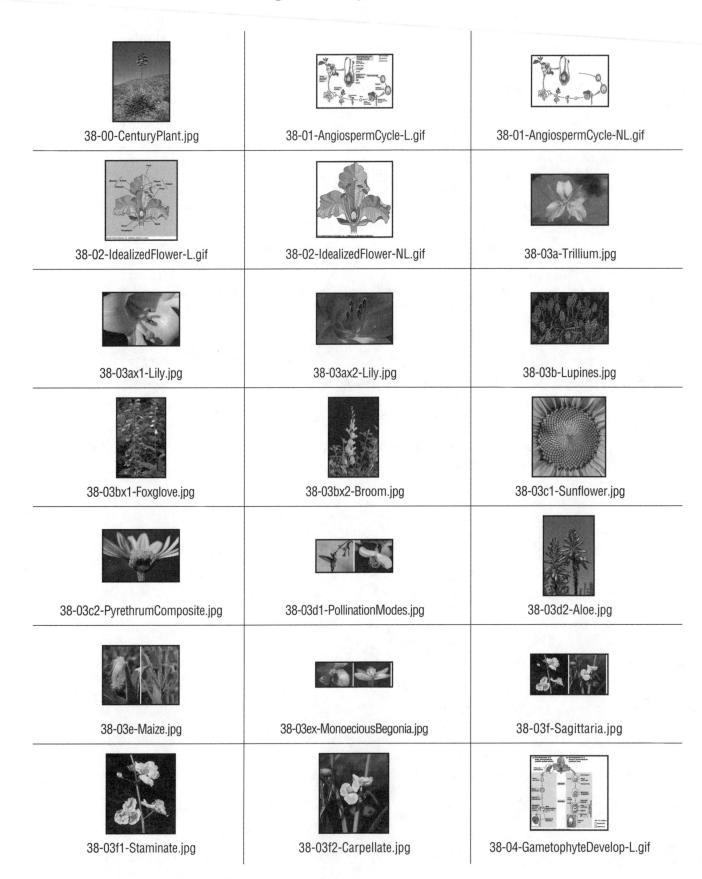

38-00-CenturyPlant.jpg

38-01-AngiospermCycle-L.gif

38-01-AngiospermCycle-NL.gif

38-02-IdealizedFlower-L.gif

38-02-IdealizedFlower-NL.gif

38-03a-Trillium.jpg

38-03ax1-Lily.jpg

38-03ax2-Lily.jpg

38-03b-Lupines.jpg

38-03bx1-Foxglove.jpg

38-03bx2-Broom.jpg

38-03c1-Sunflower.jpg

38-03c2-PyrethrumComposite.jpg

38-03d1-PollinationModes.jpg

38-03d2-Aloe.jpg

38-03e-Maize.jpg

38-03ex-MonoeciousBegonia.jpg

38-03f-Sagittaria.jpg

38-03f1-Staminate.jpg

38-03f2-Carpellate.jpg

38-04-GametophyteDevelop-L.gif

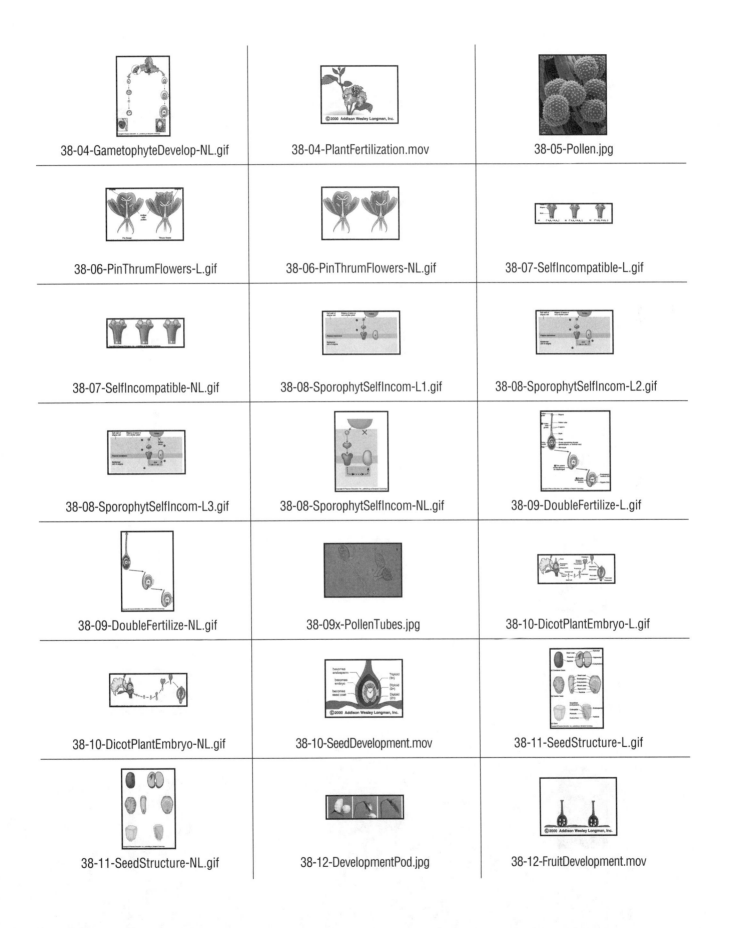

38-04-GametophyteDevelop-NL.gif

38-04-PlantFertilization.mov

38-05-Pollen.jpg

38-06-PinThrumFlowers-L.gif

38-06-PinThrumFlowers-NL.gif

38-07-SelfIncompatible-L.gif

38-07-SelfIncompatible-NL.gif

38-08-SporophytSelfIncom-L1.gif

38-08-SporophytSelfIncom-L2.gif

38-08-SporophytSelfIncom-L3.gif

38-08-SporophytSelfIncom-NL.gif

38-09-DoubleFertilize-L.gif

38-09-DoubleFertilize-NL.gif

38-09x-PollenTubes.jpg

38-10-DicotPlantEmbryo-L.gif

38-10-DicotPlantEmbryo-NL.gif

38-10-SeedDevelopment.mov

38-11-SeedStructure-L.gif

38-11-SeedStructure-NL.gif

38-12-DevelopmentPod.jpg

38-12-FruitDevelopment.mov

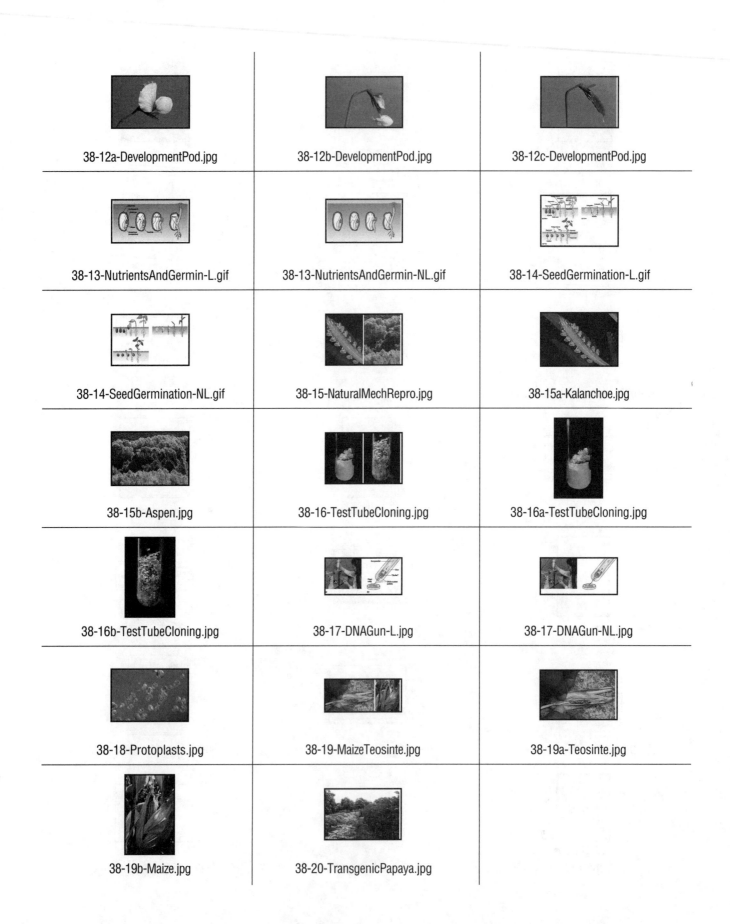

38-12a-DevelopmentPod.jpg

38-12b-DevelopmentPod.jpg

38-12c-DevelopmentPod.jpg

38-13-NutrientsAndGermin-L.gif

38-13-NutrientsAndGermin-NL.gif

38-14-SeedGermination-L.gif

38-14-SeedGermination-NL.gif

38-15-NaturalMechRepro.jpg

38-15a-Kalanchoe.jpg

38-15b-Aspen.jpg

38-16-TestTubeCloning.jpg

38-16a-TestTubeCloning.jpg

38-16b-TestTubeCloning.jpg

38-17-DNAGun-L.jpg

38-17-DNAGun-NL.jpg

38-18-Protoplasts.jpg

38-19-MaizeTeosinte.jpg

38-19a-Teosinte.jpg

38-19b-Maize.jpg

38-20-TransgenicPapaya.jpg

CHAPTER 39

Plant Responses to Internal and External Signals

Chapter Outline

Transparency Acetates

Media for Instructors

Campbell Image Presentation Library

The Campbell Image Presentation Library CD-ROM set includes the following for your use:

- All art (available in pdf and jpeg or gif formats), photos (from the text and outside sources), and tables. Art images are also available without callouts. See the Visual Guide to the Image Library section at the end of this chapter for thumbnail versions of every image.

- A PowerPoint™ slide show of the art (with callouts), photos (both text and outside sources), and tables.

- The following video clips:

39-17-PhototropismVideo-B.mov	Time-lapse of phototropism and gravitropism
39-25-Gravitropism-B.mov	Time-lapse of phototropism and gravitropism
39-27-MimosaLeaf-B.mov	Rapid leaf movements of *Mimosa*

PowerPoint Lectures CD-ROM

The PowerPoint Lectures CD-ROM contains slides that integrate the art, photos, tables, and lecture outline from this chapter.

Campbell Biology Website (Instructor Resources)

See the insert in your copy of Campbell/Reece *Biology*, Sixth Edition, for instructions on how to access the Campbell Biology Website. The Instructor Resources section of the website includes the following:

- The art, photos, tables, PowerPoint slide shows, videos, and animations from the Campbell Image Presentation Library
- Suggested answers to the Lab Report questions from the Case Studies in the Process of Science
- The PowerPoint Lecture for this chapter
- Word files of the lecture outline for this chapter
- Photo links

Course Management Systems

The media content for this chapter is available in three course management systems: CourseCompass™, Blackboard, and WebCT. For more information, go to http://cms.aw.com. For the latest pdf instructions on how to use CourseCompass, go to **www.coursecompass.com**. In addition, a Syllabus Manager is offered on the Campbell Biology Website.

Media for Students

The Campbell Biology Website and CD-ROM include the following for your students:

- Objectives
- Chapter Review (Summary, Self-Quiz, and Essay Questions from the book; Word Roots; Key Terms linked to the Glossary)
- Activities (see list below)
- Case Studies in the Process of Science (see list below)
- Quizzes (Pre-test, Activities Quiz, Chapter Quiz, Essay Questions)
- Web Links
- News and References
- Art and videos from the Campbell Image Presentation Library
- The Campbell *Biology* Interviews (from all editions)
- Glossary with audio pronunciations
- Syllabus Manager

Student Media Activities and Case Studies in The Process of Science

Web/CD Activity 39A: *Leaf Abscission*

Web/CD Case Study in the Process of Science: *How Do Plant Hormones Affect Organ Formation?*

Web/CD Activity 39B: *Flowering Lab*

Objectives

Signal Transduction and Plant Responses

1. Compare the growth of a plant in darkness to the characteristics of greening.

2. Describe the signal pathways associated with greening.

3. Describe the role of second messengers in the process of greening.

4. Describe the two main mechanisms by which a signaling pathway can activate an enzyme.

Plant Responses to Hormones

5. For each of the following scientists, describe their hypothesis, experiments, and conclusions about the mechanism of phototropism:
   a. Charles Darwin
   b. Francis Darwin
   c. Peter Boysen-Jensen
   d. F. W. Went

6. List six classes of plant hormones, describe their major functions, and note where they are produced in the plant.

7. Explain how a hormone may cause its effect on plant growth and development.

8. Describe a possible mechanism for the polar transport of auxin.

9. According to the acid-growth hypothesis, explain how auxin can initiate cell elongation.

10. Explain why 2,4-D is widely used as a weed killer.

11. Explain how the ratio of cytokinin to auxin affects cell division and cell differentiation.

12. Define apical dominance and describe the checks-and-balances control of lateral branching by auxins and cytokinins.

13. List several factors besides auxin from the terminal bud that may control apical dominance.

14. Describe how stem elongation and fruit growth depend on a synergism between auxin and gibberellins.

15. Explain the probable mechanism by which gibberellins trigger seed germination.

16. Describe how abscisic acid (ABA) helps prepare a plant for winter.

17. Describe the effects of ABA on seed dormancy and drought stress.

18. Describe the role of ethylene in the triple response to mechanical stress, apoptosis, leaf abscission, and fruit ripening.

19. Describe the functions of brassinosteroids in plants.

Plant Responses to Light

20. Define photomorphogenesis and note which colors are most important to this process.

21. Compare the roles of blue-light photoreceptors and phytochromes.

22. Define circadian rhythm and explain what happens when an organism is artificially maintained in a constant environment.

23. List some common factors that entrain biological clocks.

24. Define photoperiodism.

25. Distinguish between short-day, long-day, and day-neutral plants. Explain why these names are misleading.

26. Explain how flowering might be controlled and what is necessary for flowering to occur.

Plant Responses to Environmental Stimuli Other than Light

27. Describe how plants apparently tell up from down. Explain why roots display positive gravitropism and shoots exhibit negative gravitropism.

28. Distinguish between thigmotropism and thigmomorphogenesis.

29. Describe how motor organs can cause rapid leaf movements and sleep movements.

30. Provide a plausible explanation for how a stimulus that causes rapid leaf movement can be transmitted through the plant.

31. Describe the challenges posed by, and the responses of plants to, the following environmental stresses: drought, flooding, salt stress, heat stress, and cold stress.

Plant Defense: Responses to Herbivores and Pathogens

32. Explain how plants deter herbivores with physical and chemical defenses.

33. Describe the multiple ways that plants defend against pathogens.

Key Terms

greening	ethylene	photoperiodism
second messenger	triple response	short-day plant
hormone	apoptosis	long-day plant
tropism	brassinosteroids	day-neutral plant
phototropism	photomorphogenesis	gravitropism
auxin	action spectrum	statolith
expansins	cryptochrome	thigmomorphogenesis
cytokinins	phototropin	thigmotropism
gibberellin	zeaxanthin	action potential
abscisic acid (ABA)	circadian rhythm	heat-shock protein

canavanine

jasmonic acid

avirulent

gene-for-gene
  recognition

elicitors

oligosaccharin

phytoalexin

PR proteins

hypersensitive
  response (HR)

systemic acquired
  resistance (SAR)

salicylic acid

Word Roots

aux- = grow, enlarge (*auxins*: a class of plant hormones, including indoleacetic acid, having a variety of effects, such as phototropic response through the stimulation of cell elongation, stimulation of secondary growth, and the development of leaf traces and fruit)

circ- = a circle (*circadian rhythm*: a physiological cycle of about 24 hours, present in all eukaryotic organisms, that persists even in the absence of external cues)

crypto- = hidden; **-chromo** = color (*cryptochrome*: the name given to the unidentified blue light photoreceptor)

cyto- = cell; **-kine** = moving (*cytokinins*: a class of related plant hormones that retard aging and act in concert with auxins to stimulate cell division, influence the pathway of differentiation, and control apical dominance)

gibb- = humped (*gibberellins*: a class of related plant hormones that stimulate growth in the stem and leaves, trigger the germination of seeds and breaking of bud dormancy, and stimulate fruit development with auxin)

hyper- = excessive (*hypersensitive response*: a vigorous, localized defense response to a pathogen that is avirulent based on an *R-Avr* match)

photo- = light; **-trop** = turn, change (*phototropism*: growth of a plant shoot toward or away from light)

phyto- = a plant; **-alexi** to ward off (*phytoalexin*: an antibiotic, produced by plants, that destroys microorganisms or inhibits their growth)

stato- = standing, placed; **-lith** = a stone (*statolith*: specialized plastids that help a plant tell up from down)

thigmo- = a touch; **morpho-** = form; **-genesis** = origin (*thigmomorphogenesis*: a response in plants to chronic mechanical stimulation, resulting from increased ethylene production; an example is thickening stems in response to strong winds)

zea- = a grain; **-xantho** = yellow (*zeaxanthin*: a blue light photoreceptor involved in stomatal opening)

References

Hopkins, W. G. *Introduction to Plant Physiology.* New York: John Wiley & Sons, Inc. 1995.

Visual Guide to the Image Library

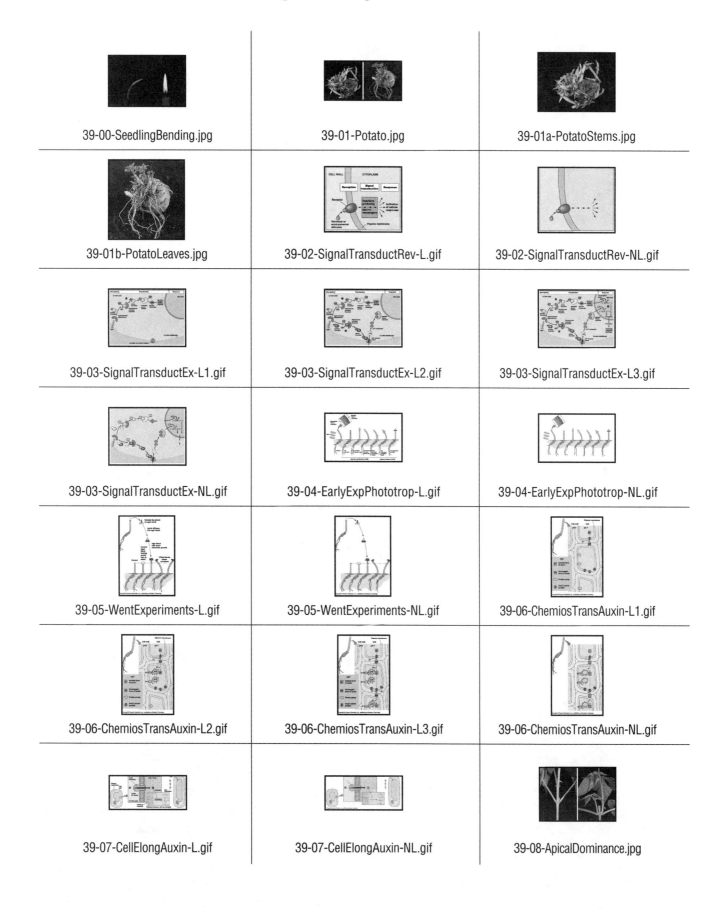

39-00-SeedlingBending.jpg

39-01-Potato.jpg

39-01a-PotatoStems.jpg

39-01b-PotatoLeaves.jpg

39-02-SignalTransductRev-L.gif

39-02-SignalTransductRev-NL.gif

39-03-SignalTransductEx-L1.gif

39-03-SignalTransductEx-L2.gif

39-03-SignalTransductEx-L3.gif

39-03-SignalTransductEx-NL.gif

39-04-EarlyExpPhototrop-L.gif

39-04-EarlyExpPhototrop-NL.gif

39-05-WentExperiments-L.gif

39-05-WentExperiments-NL.gif

39-06-ChemiosTransAuxin-L1.gif

39-06-ChemiosTransAuxin-L2.gif

39-06-ChemiosTransAuxin-L3.gif

39-06-ChemiosTransAuxin-NL.gif

39-07-CellElongAuxin-L.gif

39-07-CellElongAuxin-NL.gif

39-08-ApicalDominance.jpg

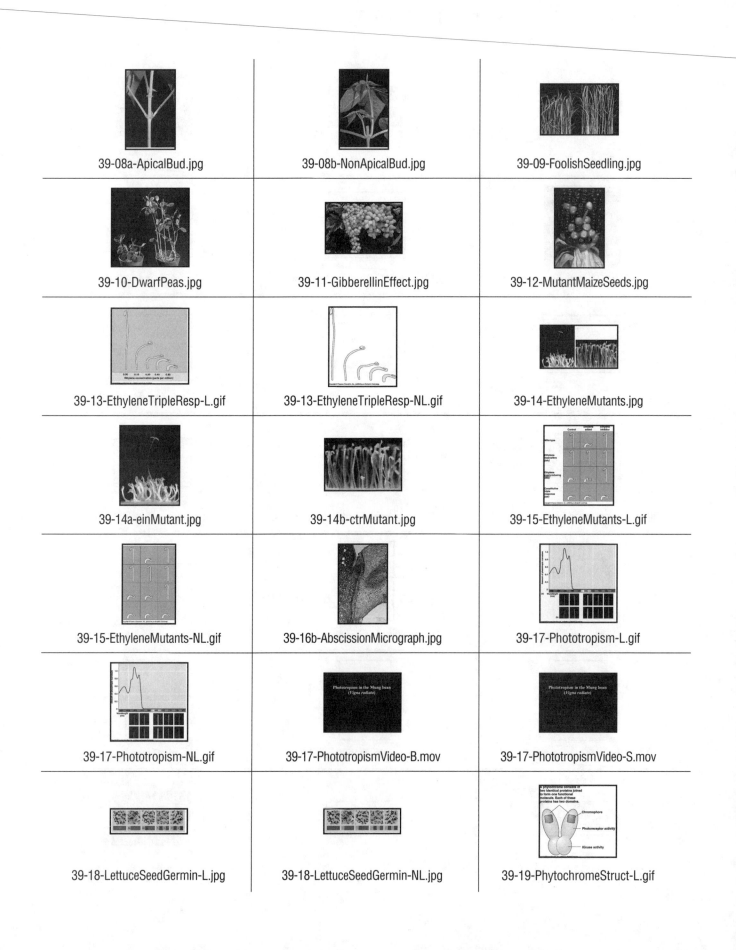

39-08a-ApicalBud.jpg

39-08b-NonApicalBud.jpg

39-09-FoolishSeedling.jpg

39-10-DwarfPeas.jpg

39-11-GibberellinEffect.jpg

39-12-MutantMaizeSeeds.jpg

39-13-EthyleneTripleResp-L.gif

39-13-EthyleneTripleResp-NL.gif

39-14-EthyleneMutants.jpg

39-14a-einMutant.jpg

39-14b-ctrMutant.jpg

39-15-EthyleneMutants-L.gif

39-15-EthyleneMutants-NL.gif

39-16b-AbscissionMicrograph.jpg

39-17-Phototropism-L.gif

39-17-Phototropism-NL.gif

39-17-PhototropismVideo-B.mov

39-17-PhototropismVideo-S.mov

39-18-LettuceSeedGermin-L.jpg

39-18-LettuceSeedGermin-NL.jpg

39-19-PhytochromeStruct-L.gif

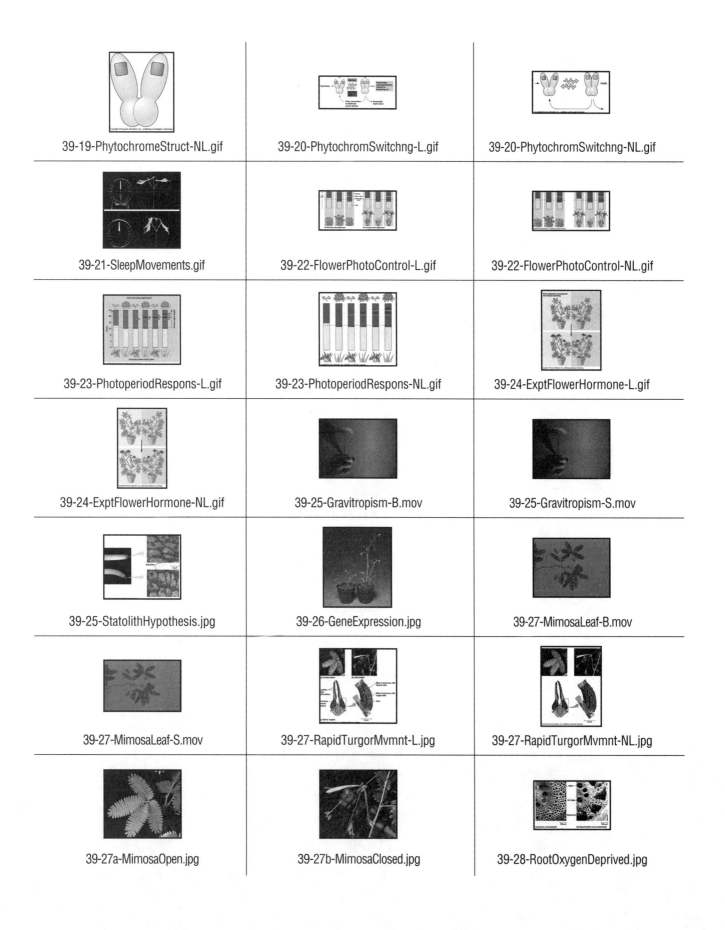

39-19-PhytochromeStruct-NL.gif

39-20-PhytochromSwitchng-L.gif

39-20-PhytochromSwitchng-NL.gif

39-21-SleepMovements.gif

39-22-FlowerPhotoControl-L.gif

39-22-FlowerPhotoControl-NL.gif

39-23-PhotoperiodRespons-L.gif

39-23-PhotoperiodRespons-NL.gif

39-24-ExptFlowerHormone-L.gif

39-24-ExptFlowerHormone-NL.gif

39-25-Gravitropism-B.mov

39-25-Gravitropism-S.mov

39-25-StatolithHypothesis.jpg

39-26-GeneExpression.jpg

39-27-MimosaLeaf-B.mov

39-27-MimosaLeaf-S.mov

39-27-RapidTurgorMvmnt-L.jpg

39-27-RapidTurgorMvmnt-NL.jpg

39-27a-MimosaOpen.jpg

39-27b-MimosaClosed.jpg

39-28-RootOxygenDeprived.jpg

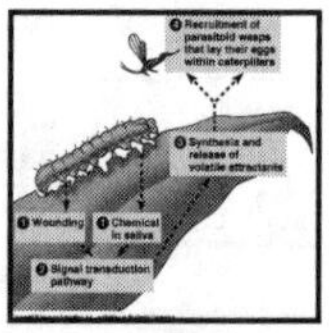

39-29-WaspRecruitment-L.gif

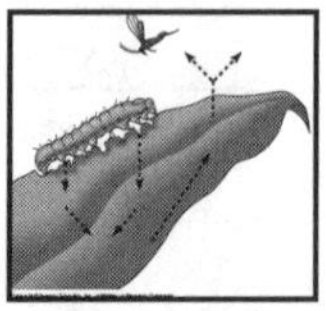

39-29-WaspRecruitment-NL.gif

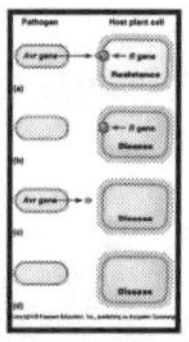

39-30-GeneForGeneResist-L.gif

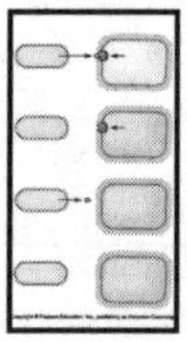

39-30-GeneForGeneResist-NL.gif

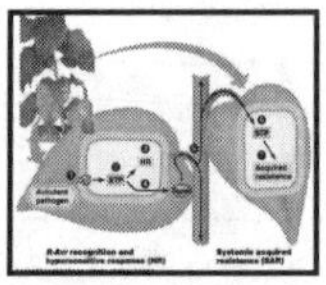

39-31-DefenseResponses-L.jpg

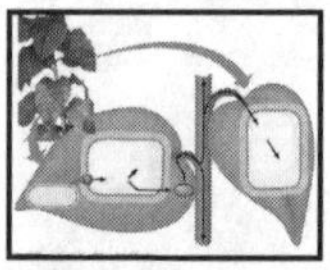

39-31-DefenseResponses-NL.jpg

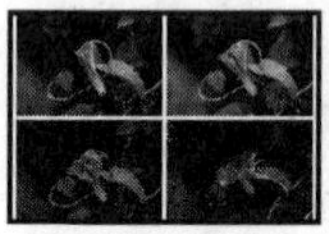

39-x1-BioClockCollage.jpg

39-x1a-BioClock1.jpg

39-x1b-BioClock2.jpg

39-x1c-BioClock3.jpg

39-x1d-BioClock4.jpg

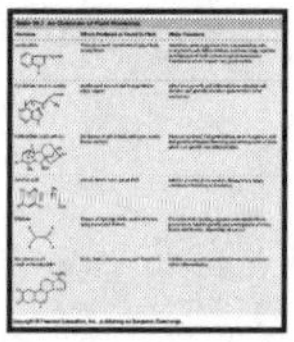

39T-01-PlantHormoneOvervw-L.gif

CHAPTER 40

An Introduction to Animal Structure and Function

Chapter Outline

Transparency Acetates

Media for Instructors

Campbell Image Presentation Library

The Campbell Image Presentation Library CD-ROM set includes the following for your use:

- All art (available in pdf and jpeg or gif formats), photos (from the text and outside sources), and tables. Art images are also available without callouts. See the Visual Guide to the Image Library section at the end of this chapter for thumbnail versions of every image.
- A PowerPoint™ slide show of the art (with callouts), photos (both text and outside sources), and tables.

PowerPoint Lectures CD-ROM

The PowerPoint Lectures CD-ROM contains slides that integrate the art, photos, tables, and lecture outline from this chapter.

Campbell Biology Website (Instructor Resources)

See the insert in your copy of Campbell/Reece *Biology*, Sixth Edition, for instructions on how to access the Campbell Biology Website. The Instructor Resources section of the website includes the following:

- The art, photos, tables, PowerPoint slide shows, videos, and animations from the Campbell Image Presentation Library
- Suggested answers to the Lab Report questions from the Case Studies in the Process of Science
- The PowerPoint Lecture for this chapter
- Word files of the lecture outline for this chapter
- Photo links

Course Management Systems

The media content for this chapter is available in three course management systems: CourseCompass™, Blackboard, and WebCT. For more information, go to http://cms.aw.com. For the latest pdf instructions on how to use CourseCompass, go to www.coursecompass.com. In addition, a Syllabus Manager is offered on the Campbell Biology Website.

Media for Students

The Campbell Biology Website and CD-ROM include the following for your students:

- Objectives
- Chapter Review (Summary, Self-Quiz, and Essay Questions from the book; Word Roots; Key Terms linked to the Glossary)
- Activities (see list below)
- Case Studies in the Process of Science (see list below)
- Quizzes (Pre-test, Activities Quiz, Chapter Quiz, Essay Questions)
- Web Links
- News and References
- Art and videos from the Campbell Image Presentation Library
- The Campbell *Biology* Interviews (from all editions)
- Glossary with audio pronunciations
- Syllabus Manager

Student Media Activities and Case Studies in The Process of Science

Web/CD Activity 40A: *Overview of Animal Tissues*

Web/CD Activity 40B: *Epithelial Tissue*

Web/CD Activity 40C: *Connective Tissue*

Web/CD Activity 40D: *Nervous Tissue*

Web/CD Activity 40E: *Muscle Tissue*

Web/CD Activity 40F: *Negative and Positive Feedback*

Web/CD Case Study in the Process of Science: *How Does Temperature Affect Metabolic Rate in* Daphnia?

Objectives

Functional Anatomy: An Overview

1. Distinguish between long-term adaptations and short-term physiological responses and list examples of each.

2. Define bioenergetics.

3. Distinguish between anatomy and physiology. Explain how functional anatomy relates to these terms.

4. Define a tissue.

5. From micrographs or diagrams, correctly identify the following animal tissues, explain how their structure relates to their functions, and note examples of each.

    a. Epithelial tissue

        i. Cuboidal

        ii. Columnar

        iii. Squamous

    b. Connective tissue

        i. Adipose

        ii. Cartilage

        iii. Bone

    c. Muscle

        i. Skeletal (striated)

        ii. Cardiac

        iii. Visceral (smooth)

    d. Nervous

6. Describe the levels of organization higher than the tissue level.

Body Plans and the External Environment

7. Explain how physical laws constrain animal form.

8. Explain how the size and shape of an animal's body affect its interactions with the environment.

Regulating the Internal Environment

9. Define homeostasis. Describe the three functional components of a homeostatic control system.

10. Distinguish between positive and negative feedback mechanisms.

Introduction to the Bioenergetics of Animals

11. Describe the basic sources of chemical energy and their fate in animal cells.

12. Define metabolic rate and explain how it can be determined for animals.

13. Distinguish between endothermic and exothermic organisms.

14. Describe the relationship between metabolic rate and body size.

15. Distinguish between basal metabolic rate and standard metabolic rate. Describe the major factors that influence energy requirements.

16. Describe the natural variations found in the energy strategies of endotherms and ectotherms.

Key Terms

anatomy	adipose tissue	organ
physiology	fibrous connective	mesentery
tissues	tissue	thoracic cavity
epithelial tissue	tendon	abdominal cavity
basement membrane	ligament	organ systems
simple epithelium	cartilage	interstitial fluid
stratified epilthelium	chondrocytes	homeostasis
cuboidal	bone	negative feedback
columnar	osteoblasts	positive feedback
squamous	osteons	metabolic rate
glandular epithelia	blood	endothermic
mucous membrane	nervous tissue	ectothermic
collagenous fibers	neuron	basal metabolic rate
elastic fibers	muscle tissue	(BMR)
reticular fibers	skeletal muscle	standard metabolic
loose connective tissue	striated muscle	rate (SMR)
fibroblast	cardiac muscle	
macrophages	smooth muscle	

Word Roots

chondro- = cartilage; **-cyte** = cell (*chondrocytes*: cartilage cells)

ecto- = outside; **-therm** = heat (*ectothermic*: organisms that do not produce enough metabolic heat to have much effect on body temperature)

endo- = inside (*endothermic*: organisms with bodies that are warmed by heat generated by metabolism; this heat is usually used to maintain a relatively stable body temperature higher than that of the external environment)

fibro- = a fiber (*fibroblast*: a type of cell in loose connective tissue that secretes the protein ingredients of the extracellular fibers)

homeo- = same; **-stasis** = standing, posture (*homeostasis*: the steady-state physiological condition of the body)

inter- = between (*interstitial fluid*: the internal environment of vertebrates, consisting of the fluid filling the space between cells)

macro- = large (*macrophage*: an amoeboid cell that moves through tissue fibers, engulfing bacteria and dead cells by phagocytosis)

osteo- = bone; **-blast** = a bud, sprout (*osteoblasts*: bone-forming cells that deposit a matrix of collagen)

References

Hickman, C. P., L. S. Roberts and A. Larson. *Integrated Principles of Zoology.* 11th ed. New York, McGraw-Hill Company, 2001.

Visual Guide to the Image Library

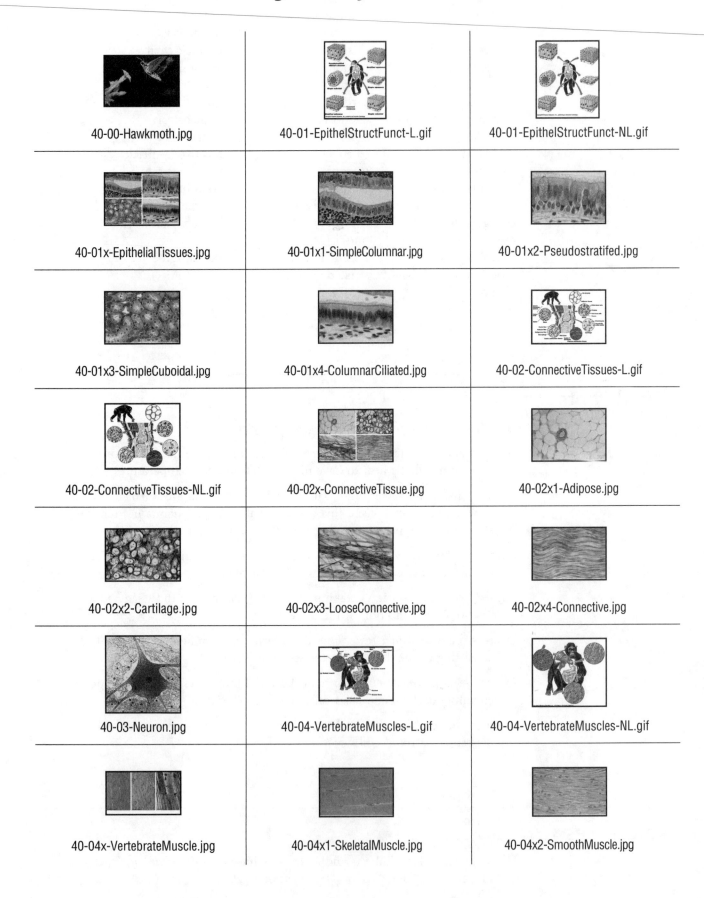

40-00-Hawkmoth.jpg

40-01-EpithelStructFunct-L.gif

40-01-EpithelStructFunct-NL.gif

40-01x-EpithelialTissues.jpg

40-01x1-SimpleColumnar.jpg

40-01x2-Pseudostratifed.jpg

40-01x3-SimpleCuboidal.jpg

40-01x4-ColumnarCiliated.jpg

40-02-ConnectiveTissues-L.gif

40-02-ConnectiveTissues-NL.gif

40-02x-ConnectiveTissue.jpg

40-02x1-Adipose.jpg

40-02x2-Cartilage.jpg

40-02x3-LooseConnective.jpg

40-02x4-Connective.jpg

40-03-Neuron.jpg

40-04-VertebrateMuscles-L.gif

40-04-VertebrateMuscles-NL.gif

40-04x-VertebrateMuscle.jpg

40-04x1-SkeletalMuscle.jpg

40-04x2-SmoothMuscle.jpg

40-04x3-CardiacMuscle.jpg

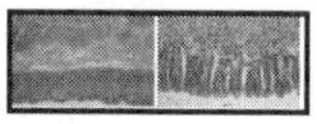

40-05x-Stomach.jpg

40-05x1-StomachLow.jpg

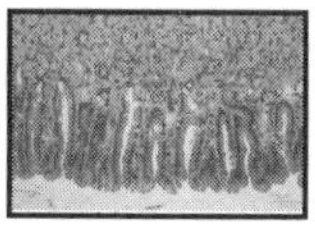

40-05x2-StomachHigh.jpg

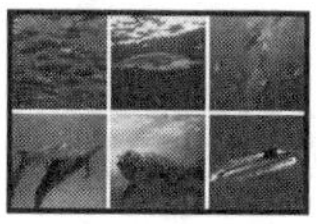

40-06-EvolutionaryConverg.jpg

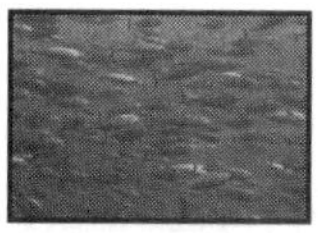

40-06a-Tuna.jpg

40-06b-SilkyShark.jpg

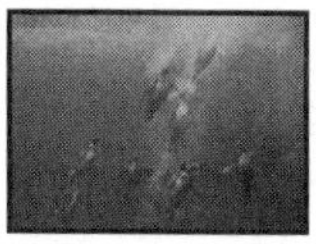

40-06c-Penguins.jpg

40-06d-Dolphins.jpg

40-06e-Seal.jpg

40-06f-Submarine.jpg

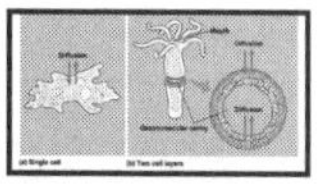

40-07-EnvironmentContact-L.gif

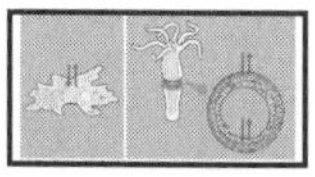

40-07-EnvironmentContact-NL.gif

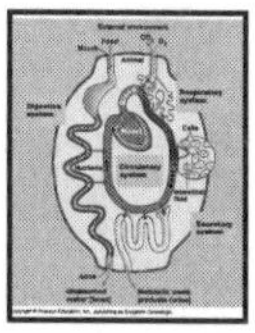

40-08-InternalSurfaces-L.gif

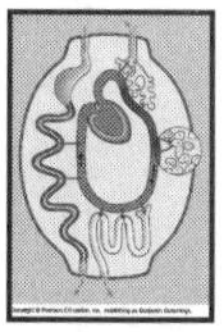

40-08-InternalSurfaces-NL.gif

40-08a-SmallIntestinePhoto.jpg

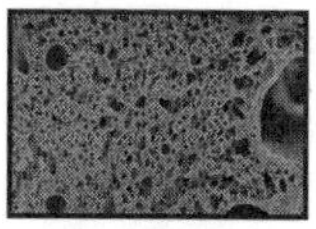

40-08b-LungPhoto.jpg

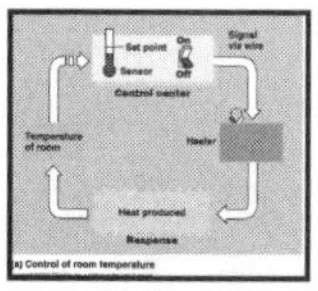

40-09a-NegFdbackRoomTemp-L.gif

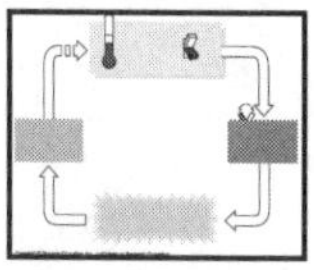

40-09a-NegFdbackRoomTemp-NL.gif

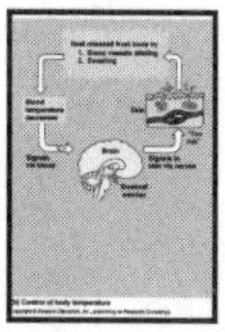

40-09b-NegFdbackBodyTemp-L1.gif

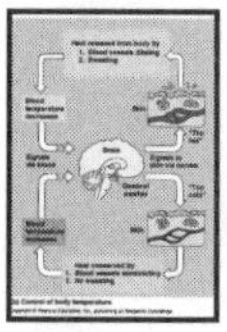

40-09b-NegFdbackBodyTemp-L2.gif

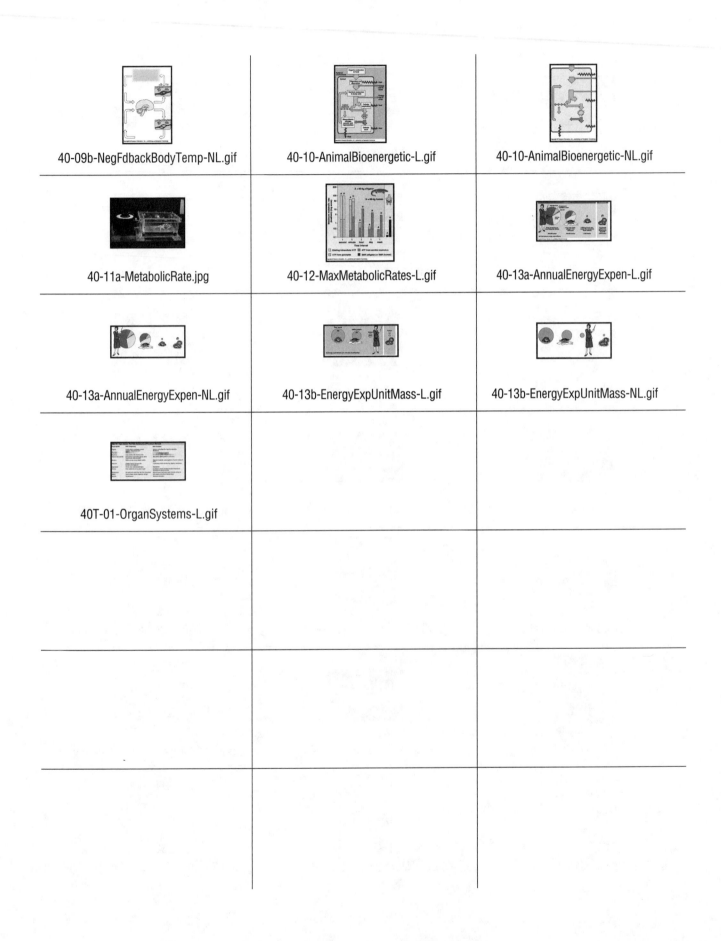

40-09b-NegFdbackBodyTemp-NL.gif

40-10-AnimalBioenergetic-L.gif

40-10-AnimalBioenergetic-NL.gif

40-11a-MetabolicRate.jpg

40-12-MaxMetabolicRates-L.gif

40-13a-AnnualEnergyExpen-L.gif

40-13a-AnnualEnergyExpen-NL.gif

40-13b-EnergyExpUnitMass-L.gif

40-13b-EnergyExpUnitMass-NL.gif

40T-01-OrganSystems-L.gif

Animal Nutrition

Chapter Outline

Transparency Acetates

The Transparency Acetates for *Biology,* Sixth Edition, include the following images:

Figure 41.1	Homeostatic regulation of cellular fuel
Figure 41.4	Essential amino acids from a vegetarian diet
Table 41.1	Vitamin Requirements of Humans: Water-Soluble Vitamins
Table 41.1	Vitamin Requirements of Humans: Fat-Soluble Vitamins
Table 41.2	Mineral Requirements of Humans
Figure 41.10	Intracellular digestion in *Paramecium*
Figure 41.11	Extracellular digestion in a gastrovascular cavity
Figure 41.12	Alimentary canals
Figure 41.13	The human digestive system
Figure 41.14	From mouth to stomach: the swallowing reflex and esophageal peristalsis (Layer 1)
Figure 41.14	From mouth to stomach: the swallowing reflex and esophageal peristalsis (Layer 2)
Figure 41.14	From mouth to stomach: the swallowing reflex and esophageal peristalsis (Layer 3)
Figure 41.15	Secretion of gastric juice
Figure 41.16	The duodenum
Figure 41.17	Enzymatic digestion in the human digestive system
Figure 41.18	Activation of protein-digesting enzymes in the small intestine
Figure 41.19	The structure of the small intestine
Figure 41.20	Dentition and diet
Figure 41.21	The digestive tracts of a carnivore (coyote) and a herbivore (koala) compared
Figure 41.22	Ruminant digestion

Media for Instructors

Campbell Image Presentation Library

The Campbell Image Presentation Library CD-ROM set includes the following for your use:

- All art (available in pdf and jpeg or gif formats), photos (from the text and outside sources), and tables. Art images are also available without callouts. See the Visual Guide to the Image Library section at the end of this chapter for thumbnail versions of every image.

- A PowerPoint™ slide show of the art (with callouts), photos (both text and outside sources), and tables.

- The following video clips:

41-09-WhaleEatSeal-B.mov   Killer whale getting baby seal

See also

07-15-ParameciumVacuole-B.mov	*Paramecium* contracting vacuole
33-05-HydraEatFlea-B.mov	Time-lapse of *Hydra* ingesting a water flea
33-26-LobsterMouthParts-B.mov	Close-up of working mouth parts of lobster

PowerPoint Lectures CD-ROM

The PowerPoint Lectures CD-ROM contains slides that integrate the art, photos, tables, and lecture outline from this chapter.

Campbell Biology Website (Instructor Resources)

See the insert in your copy of Campbell/Reece *Biology*, Sixth Edition, for instructions on how to access the Campbell Biology Website. The Instructor Resources section of the website includes the following:

- The art, photos, tables, PowerPoint slide shows, videos, and animations from the Campbell Image Presentation Library
- Suggested answers to the Lab Report questions from the Case Studies in the Process of Science
- The PowerPoint Lecture for this chapter
- Word files of the lecture outline for this chapter
- Photo links

Course Management Systems

The media content for this chapter is available in three course management systems: CourseCompass™, Blackboard, and WebCT. For more information, go to http://cms.aw.com. For the latest pdf instructions on how to use CourseCompass, go to **www.coursecompass.com**. In addition, a Syllabus Manager is offered on the Campbell Biology Website.

Media for Students

The Campbell Biology Website and CD-ROM include the following for your students:

- Objectives
- Chapter Review (Summary, Self-Quiz, and Essay Questions from the book; Word Roots; Key Terms linked to the Glossary)
- Activities (see list below)
- Case Studies in the Process of Science (see list below)
- Quizzes (Pre-test, Activities Quiz, Chapter Quiz, Essay Questions)
- Web Links

- News and References
- Art and videos from the Campbell Image Presentation Library
- The Campbell *Biology* Interviews (from all editions)
- Glossary with audio pronunciations
- Syllabus Manager

Student Media Activities and Case Studies in The Process of Science

Web/CD Activity 41A: *Digestive System Function*

Web/CD Case Study in the Process of Science: *What Role Does Amylase Play in Digestion?*

Web/CD Activity 41B: *Hormonal Control of Digestion*

Objectives

Nutritional Requirements

1. Compare the bioenergetics of animals when energy balance is positive and when it is negative.
2. Define essential nutrients and describe the four classes of essential nutrients.

Food Types and Feeding Mechanisms

3. Compare the dietary habits of herbivores, carnivores, and omnivores.
4. Compare the following types of feeders and note examples of each: suspension feeders, substrate feeders, deposit feeders, fluid feeders, and bulk feeders.

Overview of Food Processing

5. Define and compare the four main stages of food processing.
6. Compare intracellular and extracellular digestion.

The Mammalian Digestive System

7. Describe the common processes and structural components of the mammalian digestive system.
8. Compare the digestive processes of the major types of macromolecules.
9. Explain how hormones influence the digestive process.
10. Describe the major functions of the large intestine.

Evolutionary Adaptations of Vertebrate Digestive Systems

11. Relate variations in dentition and lengths of the digestive system to the feeding strategies and diets of herbivores, carnivores, and omnivores.

Key Terms

undernourishment	alimentary canals	carboxypeptidase
overnourishment	peristalsis	aminopeptidase
essential nutrients	sphincter	enteropeptidase
malnourished	salivary glands	nuclease
essential amino acids	pancreas	emulsification
essential fatty acids	liver	lipase
vitamins	gallbladder	jejunum
minerals	oral cavity	ileum
herbivore	salivary amylase	villi
carnivore	bolus	microvilli
omnivore	pharynx	lacteal
suspension-feeder	epiglottis	chylomicrons
substrate-feeder	esophagus	hepatic portal vessel
deposit-feeder	stomach	gastrin
fluid-feeder	gastric juice	enterogastrones
bulk-feeder	pepsin	secretin
ingestion	pepsinogen	cholecystokinin (CCK)
digestion	acid chyme	large intestine
enzymatic hydrolysis	pyloric sphincter	colon
absorption	small intestine	cecum
elimination	duodenum	appendix
intracellular digestion	bile	feces
extracellular digestion	trypsin	rectum
gastrovascular cavities	chymostrypsin	ruminants
complete digestive tract	dipeptidase	

Word Roots

chylo- = juice; **micro-** = small (*chylomicron*: small intracellular globules composed of fats that are mixed with cholesterol and coated with special proteins)

chymo- = juice; **-trypsi** = wearing out (*chymotrypsin*: an enzyme found in the duodenum. It is specific for peptide bonds adjacent to certain amino acids)

di- = two (*dipeptidase*: an enzyme found attached to the intestinal lining; it splits small peptides)

entero- = the intestines (*enterogastrones*: a category of hormones secreted by the wall of the duodenum)

epi- = over; **-glotti** = the tongue (*epiglottis*: a cartilaginous flap that blocks the top of the windpipe, the glottis, during swallowing)

extra- = outside (*extracellular digestion*: the breakdown of food outside cells)

gastro- = stomach; **-vascula** = a little vessel (*gastrovascular cavities*: an extensive pouch that serves as the site of extracellular digestion and a passageway to disperse materials throughout most of an animal's body)

herb- = grass; **-vora** = eat (*herbivore*: a heterotrophic animal that eats plants)

hydro- = water; **-lysis** = to loosen (*hydrolysis*: a chemical process that lyses or splits molecules by the addition of water)

intra- = inside (*intracellular digestion*: the joining of food vacuoles and lysosomes to allow chemical digestion to occur within the cytoplasm of a cell)

micro- = small; **-villi** = shaggy hair (*microvilli*: many fine, fingerlike projections of the epithelial cells in the lumen of the small intestine that increase its surface area)

omni- = all (*omnivore*: a heterotrophic animal that consumes both meat and plant material)

peri- = around; **-stalsis** = a constriction (*peristalsis*: rhythmic waves of contraction of smooth muscle that push food along the digestive tract)

References

Hickman, C. P., L. S. Roberts and A. Larson. *Integrated Principles of Zoology.* 11th ed. New York, McGraw-Hill Company, 2001.

Visual Guide to the Image Library

41-00-AnimalsEatingCollage.jpg

41-00a-FoalGrazing.jpg

41-00b-BearWithSalmon.jpg

41-00c-Stork.jpg

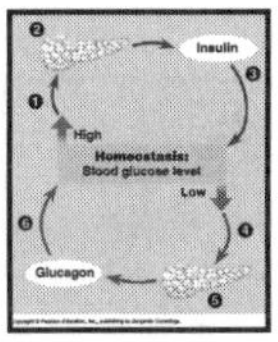

41-01-CellFuelHomeostReg-L.gif

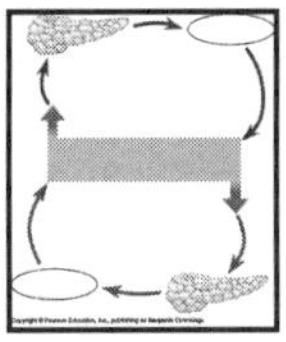

41-01-CellFuelHomeostReg-NL.gif

41-02-ObeseMouse.jpg

41-03-EssentialNutrients.jpg

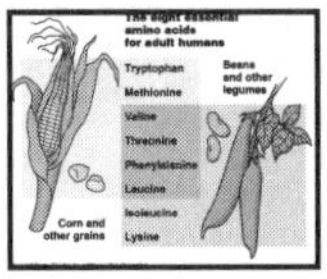

41-04-EssAminAcidVegDiet-L.gif

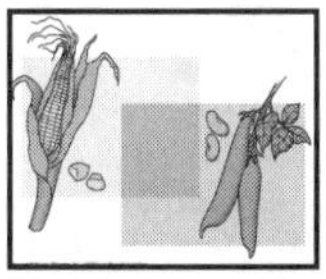

41-04-EssAminAcidVegDiet-NL.gif

41-05-MoltingAdelie.jpg

41-06-SuspensionFeeding.jpg

41-07-SubstrateFeeder.jpg

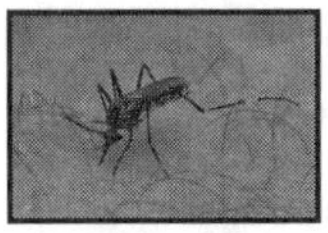

41-08-Mosquito.jpg

41-09-BulkFeeding.jpg

41-09-WhaleEatSeal-B.mov

41-09-WhaleEatSeal-S.mov

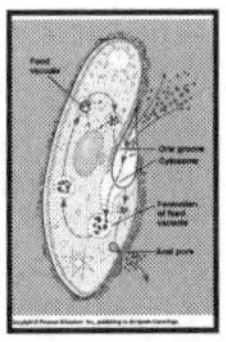

41-10-IntracellDigest-L.gif

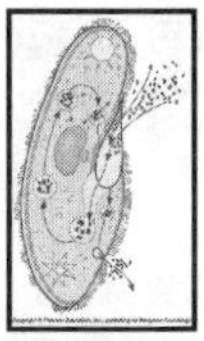

41-10-IntracellDigest-NL.gif

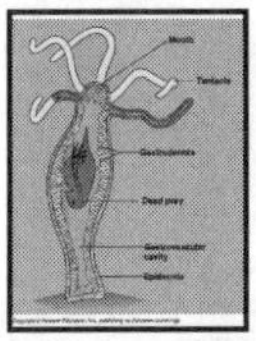

41-11-ExtraCellDigest-L.gif

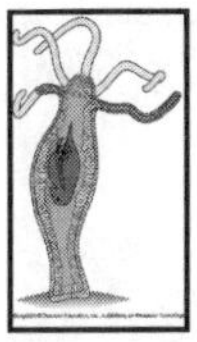

41-11-ExtraCellDigest-NL.gif

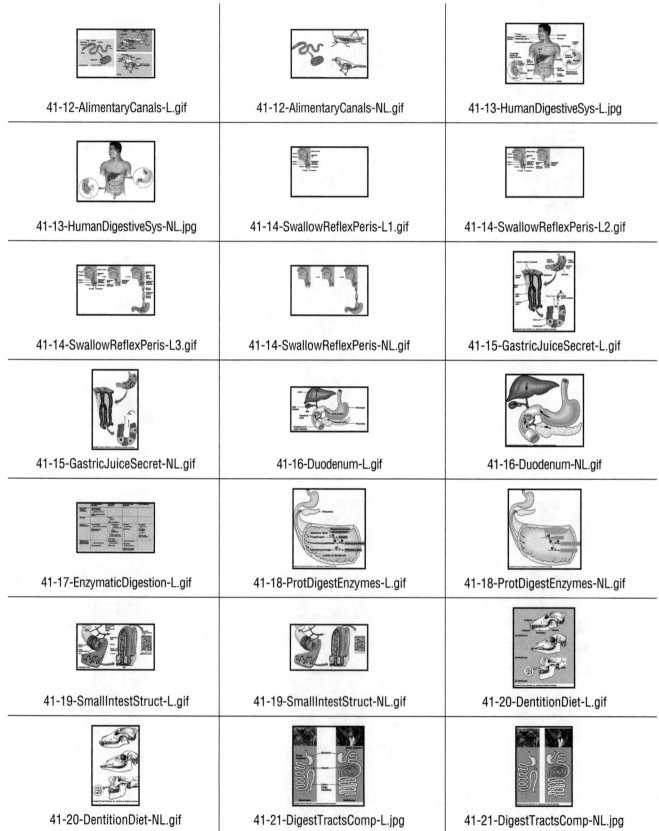

41-12-AlimentaryCanals-L.gif

41-12-AlimentaryCanals-NL.gif

41-13-HumanDigestiveSys-L.jpg

41-13-HumanDigestiveSys-NL.jpg

41-14-SwallowReflexPeris-L1.gif

41-14-SwallowReflexPeris-L2.gif

41-14-SwallowReflexPeris-L3.gif

41-14-SwallowReflexPeris-NL.gif

41-15-GastricJuiceSecret-L.gif

41-15-GastricJuiceSecret-NL.gif

41-16-Duodenum-L.gif

41-16-Duodenum-NL.gif

41-17-EnzymaticDigestion-L.gif

41-18-ProtDigestEnzymes-L.gif

41-18-ProtDigestEnzymes-NL.gif

41-19-SmallIntestStruct-L.gif

41-19-SmallIntestStruct-NL.gif

41-20-DentitionDiet-L.gif

41-20-DentitionDiet-NL.gif

41-21-DigestTractsComp-L.jpg

41-21-DigestTractsComp-NL.jpg

41-22-RuminantDigestion-L.gif

41-22-RuminantDigestion-NL.gif

41-x1-LargeIntestine.jpg

41-x2-TermiteTrichonympha.jpg

41T-01a-VitaminReqWatSol-L.gif

41T-01b-VitaminReqFatSol-L.gif

41T-02-MineralReq-L.gif

Circulation and Gas Exchange

Chapter Outline

Transparency Acetates

The Transparency Acetates for *Biology,* Sixth Edition, include the following images:

Figure 42.1	Internal transport in the cnidarian *Aurelia*
Figure 42.2	Open and closed circulatory systems
Figure 42.3	Generalized circulatory schemes of vertebrates
Figure 42.4	The mammalian cardiovascular system: an overview
Figure 42.5	The mammalian heart: a closer look
Figure 42.6	The cardiac cycle
Figure 42.7	The control of heart rhythm
Figure 42.8	The structure of blood vessels
Figure 42.9	Blood flow in veins
Figure 42.10	The interrelationship of blood flow velocity, cross-sectional area of blood vessels, and blood pressure
Figure 42.11	Measurement of blood pressure (Layer 1)
Figure 42.11	Measurement of blood pressure (Layer 2)
Figure 42.11	Measurement of blood pressure (Layer 3)
Figure 42.11	Measurement of blood pressure (Layer 4)
Figure 42.12	Blood flow in capillary beds
Figure 42.13	The movement of fluid between capillaries and the interstitial fluid
Figure 42.14	The composition of mammalian blood
Figure 42.15	Differentiation of blood cells
Figure 42.16	Blood clotting
Figure 42.18	The role of gas exchange in bioenergetics
Figure 42.19	Diversity in the structure of gills, external body surfaces functioning in gas exchange
Figure 42.20	The structure and function of fish gills
Figure 42.21	Countercurrent exchange
Figure 42.22	Tracheal systems
Figure 42.23	The mammalian respiratory system
Figure 42.24	Negative pressure breathing
Figure 42.25	The avian respiratory system
Figure 42.26	Automatic control of breathing
Figure 42.27	Loading and unloading of respiratory gases
Figure 42.28	Oxygen dissociation curves for hemoglobin
Figure 42.29	Carbon dioxide transport in the blood
Figure 42.UN1	The Process of Science: Dissociation curves for two hemoglobins

Media for Instructors

Campbell Image Presentation Library

The Campbell Image Presentation Library CD-ROM set includes the following for your use:

- All art (available in pdf and jpeg or gif formats), photos (from the text and outside sources), and tables. Art images are also available without callouts. See the Visual Guide to the Image Library section at the end of this chapter for thumbnail versions of every image.
- A PowerPoint™ slide show of the art (with callouts), photos (both text and outside sources), and tables.

PowerPoint Lectures CD-ROM

The PowerPoint Lectures CD-ROM contains slides that integrate the art, photos, tables, and lecture outline from this chapter.

Campbell Biology Website (Instructor Resources)

See the insert in your copy of Campbell/Reece *Biology*, Sixth Edition, for instructions on how to access the Campbell Biology Website. The Instructor Resources section of the website includes the following:

- The art, photos, tables, PowerPoint slide shows, videos, and animations from the Campbell Image Presentation Library
- Suggested answers to the Lab Report questions from the Case Studies in the Process of Science
- The PowerPoint Lecture for this chapter
- Word files of the lecture outline for this chapter
- Photo links

Course Management Systems

The media content for this chapter is available in three course management systems: CourseCompass™, Blackboard, and WebCT. For more information, go to http://cms.aw.com. For the latest pdf instructions on how to use CourseCompass, go to **www.coursecompass.com**. In addition, a Syllabus Manager is offered on the Campbell Biology Website.

Media for Students

The Campbell Biology Website and CD-ROM include the following for your students:

- Objectives
- Chapter Review (Summary, Self-Quiz, and Essay Questions from the book; Word Roots; Key Terms linked to the Glossary)

- Activities (see list below)
- Case Studies in the Process of Science (see list below)
- Quizzes (Pre-test, Activities Quiz, Chapter Quiz, Essay Questions)
- Web Links
- News and References
- Art and videos from the Campbell Image Presentation Library
- The Campbell *Biology* Interviews (from all editions)
- Glossary with audio pronunciations
- Syllabus Manager

Student Media Activities and Case Studies in The Process of Science

Web/CD Activity 42A: *Mammalian Cardiovascular System Structure*

Web/CD Activity 42B: *Path of Blood Flow in Mammals*

Web/CD Activity 42C: *Mammalian Cardiovascular System Function*

Web/CD Case Study in the Process of Science: *How Is Cardiovascular Fitness Measured?*

Biology Labs on Line: *HemoglobinLab*

Biology Labs on Line: *CardioLab*

Web/CD Activity 42D: *The Human Respiratory System*

Web/CD Activity 42E: *Transport of Respiratory Gases*

Objectives

Circulation in Animals

1. Describe the need for circulatory and respiratory systems due to increasing animal body size
2. Explain how a gastrovascular cavity functions in part as a circulatory system.
3. Distinguish between open and closed circulatory systems. List the three basic components common to both systems.
4. List the structural components of a vertebrate circulatory system and relate their structure to their functions.
5. Describe the general relationship between metabolic rates and the structure of the vertebrate circulatory system.
6. Distinguish between pulmonary and systemic circuits and explain the functions of each.
7. Explain the advantage of double circulation over a single circuit.
8. Using diagrams, compare and contrast the circulatory schemes of fish, amphibians, reptiles, birds, and mammals.
9. Define a cardiac cycle, distinguish between systole and diastole, and explain what causes the first and second heart sounds.
10. Define cardiac output and describe two factors that influence it.
11. List the four heart valves, describe their location, and explain their functions.

12. Define heart murmur and explain its cause.

13. Define pacemaker and describe the location of two patches of nodal tissue in the human heart.

14. Describe the origin and pathway of the action potential (cardiac impulse) in the normal human heart.

15. Explain how the pace of the SA node can be modulated by sympathetic and parasympathetic nerves, changes in temperature, physical conditioning, and exercise.

16. Relate the structures of capillaries, arteries, and veins to their functions.

17. Explain why blood flow through capillaries is substantially slower than it is through arteries and veins.

18. Define blood pressure and describe how it is measured.

19. Explain how peripheral resistance and cardiac output affect blood pressure.

20. Explain how blood returns to the heart even though it must sometimes travel from the lower extremities against gravity.

21. Explain how blood flow through capillary beds is regulated.

22. Explain how osmotic pressure and hydrostatic pressure regulate the exchange of fluid and solutes across capillaries.

23. Describe the composition of lymph and explain how the lymphatic system helps the normal functioning of the circulatory system.

24. Describe the composition and functions of plasma.

25. Relate the structure of erythrocytes to their functions.

26. List the five main types of white blood cells and generally characterize their functions.

27. Relate the structure of platelets to their functions.

28. Outline the formation of erythrocytes from stem cells to their destruction by phagocytic cells.

29. Outline the sequence of events that occur during blood clotting and explain what prevents spontaneous clotting in the absence of injury.

30. Distinguish between a heart attack and a stroke; atherosclerosis and arteriosclerosis; and low-density lipoproteins (LDLs) and high-density lipoproteins (HDLs).

31. List the factors that have been correlated with an increased risk of cardio-vascular disease.

Gas Exchange in Animals

32. Define gas exchange and distinguish between a respiratory medium and a respiratory surface.

33. Describe the general requirements for a respiratory surface and list the variety of respiratory organs that have adapted to meet them.

34. Describe respiratory adaptations of aquatic animals.

35. Describe the advantages and disadvantages of water as a respiratory medium.

36. Describe countercurrent exchange and explain why it is more efficient than the concurrent flow of water and blood.

37. Describe the advantages and disadvantages of air as a respiratory medium and explain how insect tracheal systems are adapted for efficient gas exchange in a terrestrial environment.

38. For the human respiratory system, describe the movement of air through air passageways to the alveolus, listing the structures that air must pass through on its journey.

39. Compare positive and negative pressure breathing. Explain how respiratory movements in humans ventilate the lungs.

40. Distinguish between tidal volume, vital capacity, and residual volume.

41. Explain how the respiratory system of birds is different from that in mammals.

42. Explain how breathing is controlled.

43. Define partial pressure and explain how it influences diffusion across respiratory surfaces.

44. Describe the adaptive advantage of respiratory pigments in circulatory systems. Distinguish between hemocyanin and hemoglobin.

45. Draw the Hb-oxygen dissociation curve, explain the significance of its shape, and explain how the affinity of hemoglobin for oxygen changes with oxygen concentration.

46. Describe how carbon dioxide is picked up at the tissues and deposited in the lungs.

47. Describe respiratory adaptations of diving mammals and the role of myoglobin.

Key Terms

blood	systole	white blood cell
blood vessel	diastole	platelet
heart	cardiac output	erythrocyte
blood pressure	heart rate	hemoglobin
open circulatory system	stroke volume	leukocyte
hemolymph	atrioventricular (AV) valve	pluripotent stem cell
sinuses	semilunar valves	erythropoietin
closed circulatory system	pulse	fibrinogen
cardiovascular system	heart murmur	fibrin
atrium (plural, atria)	sinoatrial (SA) node	hemophilia
ventricles	pacemaker	thrombus
artery	atrioventricular (AV) node	cardiovascular disease
vein	electrocardiogram (ECG or EKG)	heart attack
capillary	endothelium	stroke
arteriole	systolic pressure	atherosclerosis
capillary bed	peripheral resistance	arteriosclerosis
venule	diastolic pressure	hypertension
gill circulation	lymphatic system	low-density lipoproteins (LDLs)
systemic circulation	lymph	high-density lipoproteins (HDLs)
pulmocutaneous	lymph node	gas exchange
double circulation	plasma	respiratory medium
pulmonary circuit	red blood cell	respiratory surface
cardiac cycle		gills

ventilation
countercurrent
  exchange
tracheal system
lungs
larynx
vocal cords
trachea
bronchi (singular,
  bronchus)
bronchioles

alveoli (singular,
  alveolus)
breathing
positive pressure
  breathing
negative pressure
  breathing
diaphragm
tidal volume
vital capacity
residual volume

parabronchi
breathing control
  center
partial pressure
respiratory pigment
hemocyanin
dissociation curve
Bohr shift
myoglobin

Word Roots

alveol- = a cavity (*alveoli*: one of the dead-end, multilobed air sacs that constitute the gas exchange surface of the lungs)

arterio- = an artery; **-sclero** = hard (*arteriosclerosis*: a cardiovascular disease caused by the formation of hard plaques within the arteries)

atrio- = a vestibule; **-ventriculo** = ventricle (*atrioventricular node*: a region of specialized muscle tissue between the right atrium and right ventricle; it generates electrical impulses that primarily cause the ventricles to contract)

cardi- = heart; **-vascula** = a little vessel (*cardiovascular system*: the closed circulatory system characteristic of vertebrates)

counter- = opposite (*countercurrent exchange*: the opposite flow of adjacent fluids that maximizes transfer rates)

endo- = inner (*endothelium*: the innermost, simple squamous layer of cells lining the blood vessels; the only constituent structure of capillaries)

erythro- = red; **-poiet** = produce (*erythropoietin*: a hormone produced in the kidney when tissues of the body do not receive enough oxygen; this hormone stimulates the production of erythrocytes)

fibrino- = a fiber; **-gen** = produce (*fibrinogen*: the inactive form of the plasma protein that is converted to the active form fibrin, which aggregates into threads that form the framework of a blood clot)

hemo- = blood; **-philia** = loving (*hemophilia*: a human genetic disease caused by a sex-linked recessive allele, characterized by excessive bleeding following injury)

leuko- = white; **-cyte** = cell (*leukocyte*: a white blood cell)

myo- = muscle (*myoglobin*: an oxygen-storing, pigmented protein in muscle cells)

para- = beside, near (*parabronchi*: the sites of gas exchange in bird lungs. They allow air to flow past the respiratory surface in just one direction)

pluri- = more, several; **-potent** = powerful (*pluripotent stem cell*: a cell within bone marrow that is a progenitor for any kind of blood cell)

pulmo- = a lung; **-cutane** = skin (*pulmocutaneous*: the route of circulation that directs blood to the skin and lungs)

semi- = half; **-luna** = moon (*semilunar valve*: a valve located at the two exits of the heart, where the aorta leaves the left ventricle and the pulmonary artery leaves the right ventricle)

thrombo- = a clot (*thrombus*: a clump of platelets and fibrin that block the flow of blood through a blood vessel)

References

Hickman, C. P., L. S. Roberts and A. Larson. *Integrated Principles of Zoology.* 11th ed. New York, McGraw-Hill Company, 2001.

Visual Guide to the Image Library

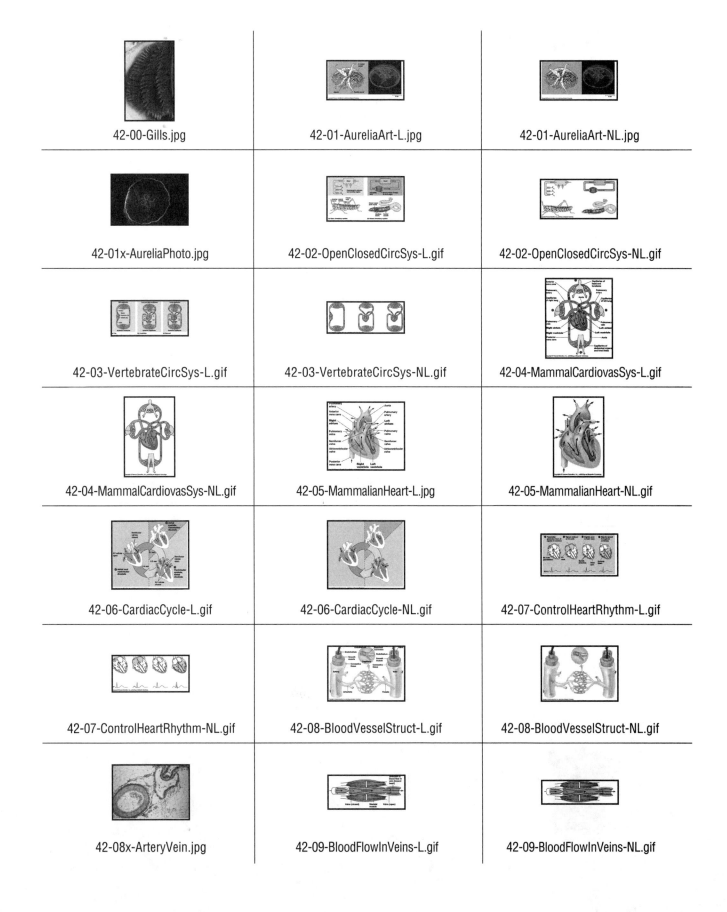

42-00-Gills.jpg

42-01-AureliaArt-L.jpg

42-01-AureliaArt-NL.jpg

42-01x-AureliaPhoto.jpg

42-02-OpenClosedCircSys-L.gif

42-02-OpenClosedCircSys-NL.gif

42-03-VertebrateCircSys-L.gif

42-03-VertebrateCircSys-NL.gif

42-04-MammalCardiovasSys-L.gif

42-04-MammalCardiovasSys-NL.gif

42-05-MammalianHeart-L.jpg

42-05-MammalianHeart-NL.gif

42-06-CardiacCycle-L.gif

42-06-CardiacCycle-NL.gif

42-07-ControlHeartRhythm-L.gif

42-07-ControlHeartRhythm-NL.gif

42-08-BloodVesselStruct-L.gif

42-08-BloodVesselStruct-NL.gif

42-08x-ArteryVein.jpg

42-09-BloodFlowInVeins-L.gif

42-09-BloodFlowInVeins-NL.gif

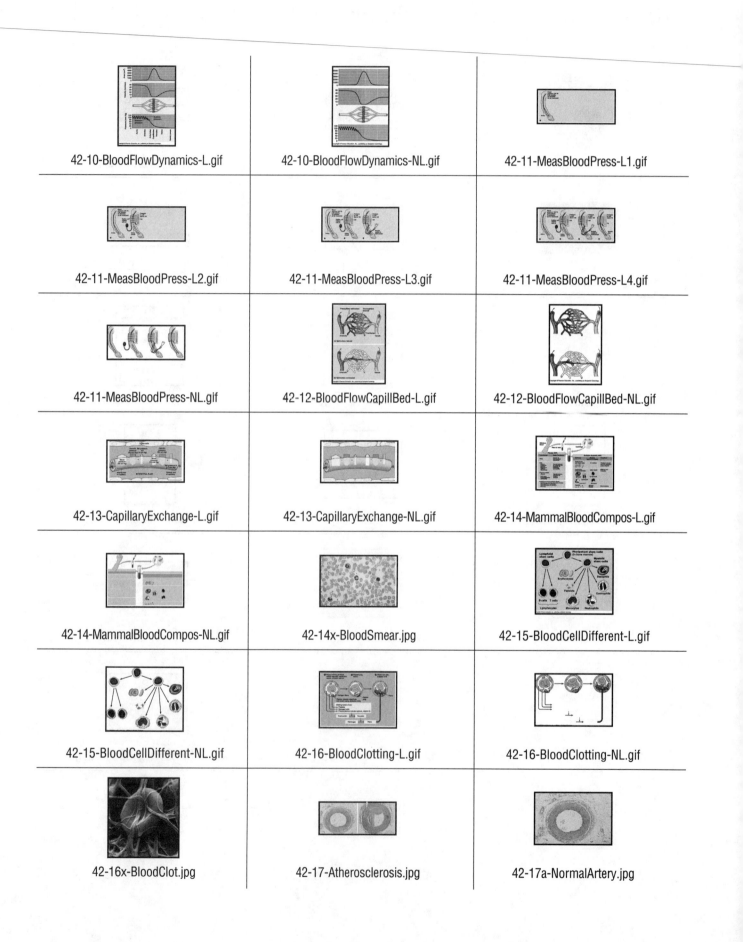

42-10-BloodFlowDynamics-L.gif

42-10-BloodFlowDynamics-NL.gif

42-11-MeasBloodPress-L1.gif

42-11-MeasBloodPress-L2.gif

42-11-MeasBloodPress-L3.gif

42-11-MeasBloodPress-L4.gif

42-11-MeasBloodPress-NL.gif

42-12-BloodFlowCapillBed-L.gif

42-12-BloodFlowCapillBed-NL.gif

42-13-CapillaryExchange-L.gif

42-13-CapillaryExchange-NL.gif

42-14-MammalBloodCompos-L.gif

42-14-MammalBloodCompos-NL.gif

42-14x-BloodSmear.jpg

42-15-BloodCellDifferent-L.gif

42-15-BloodCellDifferent-NL.gif

42-16-BloodClotting-L.gif

42-16-BloodClotting-NL.gif

42-16x-BloodClot.jpg

42-17-Atherosclerosis.jpg

42-17a-NormalArtery.jpg

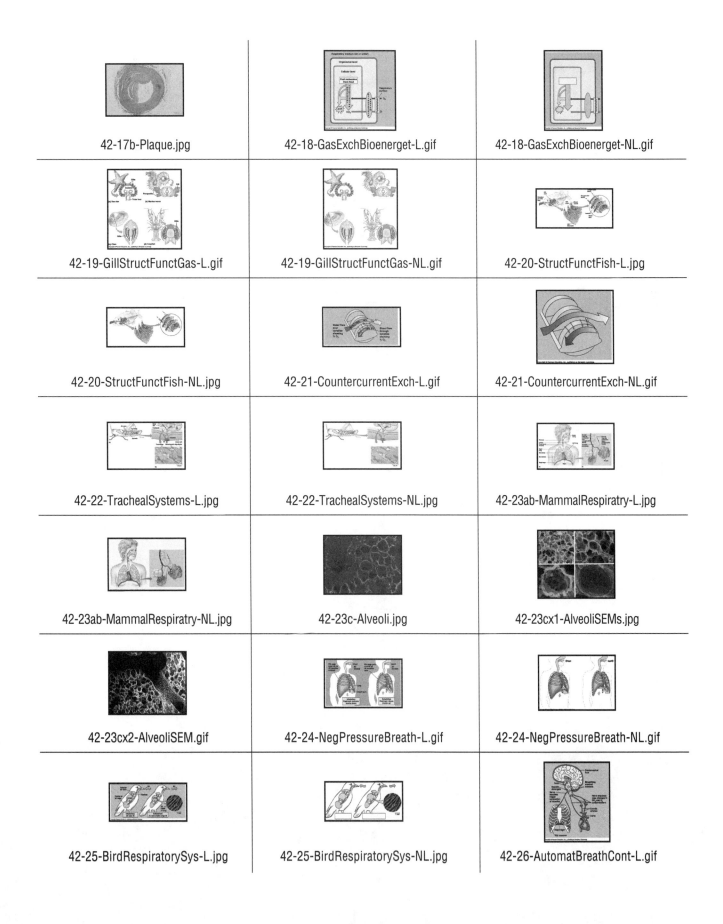

42-17b-Plaque.jpg

42-18-GasExchBioenerget-L.gif

42-18-GasExchBioenerget-NL.gif

42-19-GillStructFunctGas-L.gif

42-19-GillStructFunctGas-NL.gif

42-20-StructFunctFish-L.jpg

42-20-StructFunctFish-NL.jpg

42-21-CountercurrentExch-L.gif

42-21-CountercurrentExch-NL.gif

42-22-TrachealSystems-L.jpg

42-22-TrachealSystems-NL.jpg

42-23ab-MammalRespiratry-L.jpg

42-23ab-MammalRespiratry-NL.jpg

42-23c-Alveoli.jpg

42-23cx1-AlveoliSEMs.jpg

42-23cx2-AlveoliSEM.gif

42-24-NegPressureBreath-L.gif

42-24-NegPressureBreath-NL.gif

42-25-BirdRespiratorySys-L.jpg

42-25-BirdRespiratorySys-NL.jpg

42-26-AutomatBreathCont-L.gif

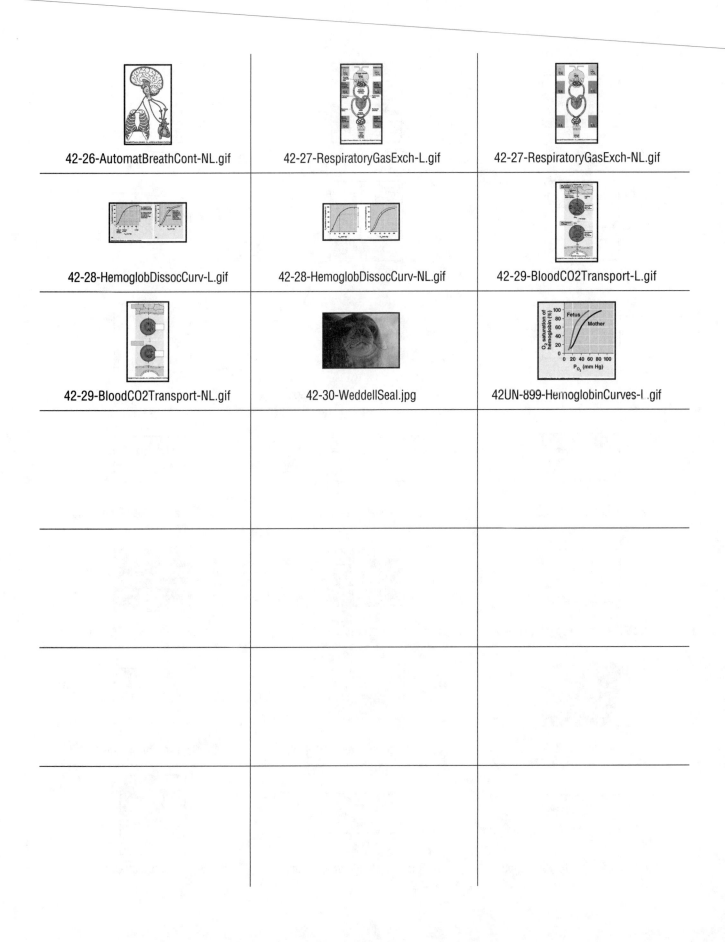

42-26-AutomatBreathCont-NL.gif	42-27-RespiratoryGasExch-L.gif	42-27-RespiratoryGasExch-NL.gif
42-28-HemoglobDissocCurv-L.gif	42-28-HemoglobDissocCurv-NL.gif	42-29-BloodCO2Transport-L.gif
42-29-BloodCO2Transport-NL.gif	42-30-WeddellSeal.jpg	42UN-899-HemoglobinCurves-L.gif

The Body's Defenses

Chapter Outline

Transparency Acetates

The Transparency Acetates for *Biology*, Sixth Edition, include the following images:

Figure 43.1	An overview of the body's defenses
Figure 43.4	The human lymphatic system
Figure 43.5	A simplified view of the inflammatory response
Figure 43.6	Clonal selection
Figure 43.7	Immunological memory
Figure 43.8	The development of lymphocytes
Figure 43.9	The interaction of T cells with MHC molecules
Figure 43.10	An overview of the immune responses (Layer 1)
Figure 43.10	An overview of the immune responses (Layer 2)
Figure 43.10	An overview of the immune responses (Layer 3)
Figure 43.10	An overview of the immune responses (Layer 4)
Figure 43.11	The central role of helper T cells: *a closer look*
Figure 43.12	The functioning of cytotoxic T cells
Figure 43.13	Humoral response to a T-dependent antigen (Layer 1)
Figure 43.13	Humoral response to a T-dependent antigen (Layer 2)
Figure 43.13	Humoral response to a T-dependent antigen (Layer 3)
Figure 43.14	Epitopes (antigenic determinants)
Figure 43.15	The structure of a typical antibody molecule
Table 43.1	The Five Classes of Immunoglobulins
Figure 43.16	Effector mechanisms of humoral immunity
Figure 43.17	The classical complement pathway, resulting in lysis of a target cell
Figure 43.18	Mast cells, IgE, and the allergic response
Figure 43.20	The stages of HIV infection

Media for Instructors

Campbell Image Presentation Library

The Campbell Image Presentation Library CD-ROM set includes the following for your use:

- All art (available in pdf and jpeg or gif formats), photos (from the text and outside sources), and tables. Art images are also available without callouts. See the Visual Guide to the Image Library section at the end of this chapter for thumbnail versions of every image.
- A PowerPoint™ slide show of the art (with callouts), photos (both text and outside sources), and tables.
- The following video clip:

  43-13-TCellReceptors-S.mov   T Cell Receptors
- The following QuickTime animations, adapted from student media activities (also available as Shockwave Flash .swf files):

43-06-RoleOfBCells.mov
43-09a-CytotoxicTCells.mov
43-09b-HelperTCells.mov
43-16-Antibodies.mov

PowerPoint Lectures CD-ROM

The PowerPoint Lectures CD-ROM contains slides that integrate the art, photos, tables, and lecture outline from this chapter.

Campbell Biology Website (Instructor Resources)

See the insert in your copy of Campbell/Reece *Biology*, Sixth Edition, for instructions on how to access the Campbell Biology Website. The Instructor Resources section of the website includes the following:

- The art, photos, tables, PowerPoint slide shows, videos, and animations from the Campbell Image Presentation Library
- Suggested answers to the Lab Report questions from the Case Studies in the Process of Science
- The PowerPoint Lecture for this chapter
- Word files of the lecture outline for this chapter
- Photo links

Course Management Systems

The media content for this chapter is available in three course management systems: CourseCompass™, Blackboard, and WebCT. For more information, go to http://cms.aw.com. For the latest pdf instructions on how to use CourseCompass, go to www.coursecompass.com. In addition, a Syllabus Manager is offered on the Campbell Biology Website.

Media for Students

The Campbell Biology Website and CD-ROM include the following for your students:

- Objectives
- Chapter Review (Summary, Self-Quiz, and Essay Questions from the book; Word Roots; Key Terms linked to the Glossary)
- Activities (see list below)
- Case Studies in the Process of Science (see list below)
- Quizzes (Pre-test, Activities Quiz, Chapter Quiz, Essay Questions)
- Web Links
- News and References
- Art and videos from the Campbell Image Presentation Library

- The Campbell *Biology* Interviews (from all editions)
- Glossary with audio pronunciations
- Syllabus Manager

Student Media Activities and Case Studies in The Process of Science

Web/CD Activity 43A: *Immune Responses*

Web/CD Activity 43B: *HIV Reproductive Cycle*

Web/CD Case Study in the Process of Science: *What Causes Infections in AIDS Patients?*

Web/CD Case Study in the Process of Science: *Why Do AIDS Rates Differ Across the U.S.?*

Objectives

Nonspecific Defenses Against Infection

1. Explain what is meant by nonspecific defense and list the nonspecific lines of defense in the vertebrate body.
2. Explain how the physical barrier of skin is reinforced by chemical defenses.
3. Define phagocytosis and list two types of phagocytic cells derived from white blood cells.
4. Explain how the function of natural killer cells differs from the function of phagocytes.
5. Describe the inflammation response, including how it is triggered.
6. Describe the factors that influence phagocytosis during the inflammation response.
7. Describe the typical sequence of cellular responses to a point of infection.
8. Describe the function of pyrogens.
9. Explain what occurs during the condition known as septic shock.
10. List and describe the roles of antimicrobial proteins.

How Specific Immunity Arises

11. Distinguish between antigens and antibodies.
12. Explain how B cells and T cells recognize specific antigens.
13. Explain how the particular structure of a lymphocyte's receptor is determined.
14. Describe the mechanism of clonal selection. Distinguish between effector cells and memory cells.
15. Distinguish between the primary and secondary immune responses.
16. Describe the cellular basis for immunological memory.
17. Outline the development of B and T lymphocytes.
18. Describe the cellular basis for self-tolerance.
19. Describe the variation found in the major histocompatibility complex (MHC) genes and their role in the rejection of tissue transplants. Explain the adaptive advantage of this variation.

20. Compare the structures and functions of cytotoxic T cells and helper T cells.

21. Compare the production and functions of class I MHC and class II MHC molecules.

Immune Responses

22. Distinguish between humoral immunity and cell-mediated immunity.

23. Describe the roles of helper T lymphocytes in both humoral and cell-mediated immunity.

24. Describe the functions of CD4, cytokines, interleukin-2, and interleukin-1.

25. Explain how class I MHC molecules expose foreign proteins that are synthesized in infected or abnormal cells.

26. Describe the functions of the proteins CD8 and perforin.

27. Explain how cytotoxic T cells and natural killer cells defend against tumors.

28. Distinguish between T-dependent antigens and T-independent antigens.

29. Explain why macrophages are regarded as the main antigen-presenting cells in the primary response but memory B cells are the main antigen-presenting cells in the secondary response.

30. Explain how antibodies interact with antigens.

31. Diagram and label the structure of an antibody and explain how this structure allows antibodies to (a) recognize and bind to antigens and (b) assist in the destruction and elimination of antigens.

32. Distinguish between the variable (V) regions and constant (C) regions of an antibody molecule.

33. Describe the production and uses of monoclonal antibodies.

34. Compare the processes of neutralization, opsonization, agglutination, and complement fixation.

35. Distinguish between the classical and alternative pathways of lysis by complement.

36. Describe the process of immune adherence.

37. Describe evidence that reveals the ability of sponges and sea stars to distinguish between self and nonself. Describe other similarities and differences between invertebrate and vertebrate immune systems.

Immunity in Health and Disease

38. Distinguish between active and passive immunity and describe examples of each.

39. For ABO blood groups, list all possible combinations for donor and recipient in blood transfusions, indicate which combinations would cause an immune response in the recipient, and state which blood type is the universal donor.

40. Explain how the immune response to Rh factor differs from the response to A and B blood antigens.

41. Describe the potential problem of Rh incompatibility between a mother and her unborn fetus and explain what precautionary measures may be taken.

42. Explain what is done medically to reduce the risk of tissue transplant rejection due to differences in the MHC. Explain what is unique about using bone marrow transplants to reduce the risk of immune rejection.

43. Describe an allergic reaction, including the roles of IgE, mast cells, and histamine.

44. Explain what causes anaphylactic shock and how it can be treated.

45. List some known autoimmune disorders and describe possible mechanisms of autoimmunity.

46. Distinguish between inborn and acquired immune dysfunction.

47. Explain how general health and mental well-being might affect the immune system.

48. Describe the infectious agent that causes AIDS and explain how it enters a susceptible cell.

49. Describe the early immune system response to HIV infection. Explain how this reaction is used to detect infected individuals.

50. Describe the progress of an HIV infection prior to the onset of AIDS. Describe the medical treatment of HIV infection and the likely prognosis for an infected individual.

51. Explain how HIV is transmitted and describe its distribution throughout the world. Note strategies that can reduce a person's risk of infection.

Key Terms

lysozyme
phagocytosis
neutrophil
monocyte
macrophage
eosinophils
natural killer (NK) cell
inflammatory response
histamine
basophils
mast cells
chemokines
pyrogen
complement system
interferons
B lymphocyte (B cell)
T lymphocyte (T cell)
antigen
antibody
antigen receptor
T cell receptor
effector cell
memory cell
clonal selection
primary immune
  response

plasma cell
secondary immune
  response
major
  histocompatibility
  complex (MHC)
class I MHC molecules
class II MHC molecules
antigen presentation
cytoxic T cells (T$_C$)
helper T cells (T$_H$)
antigen–presenting
  cells (APCs)
humoral immunity
cell-mediated immunity
CD4
cytokines
interleukin-2 (IL-2)
interleukin-1 (IL-1)
CD8
perforin
tumor antigen
T-dependent antigens
epitope
immunoglobulins (Igs)
heavy chains

light chains
monoclonal antibodies
neutralization
opsonization
agglutination
complement fixation
membrane attack
  complex (MAC)
immune adherence
active immunity
immunization
vaccination
passive immunity
ABO blood groups
Rh factor
graft versus host
  reaction
anaphylactic shock
acquired
  immunodeficiency
  syndrome (AIDS)
human
  immunodeficiency
  virus (HIV)

Word Roots

agglutinat- = glued together (*agglutination*: an antibody-mediated immune response in which bacteria or viruses are clumped together, effectively neutralized, and opsonized)

an- = without; **-aphy** = suck (*anaphylactic shock*: an acute, life threatening, allergic response)

anti- = against; **-gen** = produce (*antigen*: a foreign macromolecule that does not belong to the host organism and that elicits an immune response)

chemo- = chemistry ; **-kine** = movement (*chemokine*: a group of about 50 different proteins secreted by blood vessel endothelial cells and monocytes; these molecules bind to receptors on many types of leukocytes and induce numerous changes central to inflammation)

cyto- = cell (*cytokines*: in the vertebrate immune system, protein factors secreted by macrophages and helper T cells as regulators of neighboring cells)

epi- = over; **-topo** = place (*epitope*: a localized region on the surface of an antigen that is chemically recognized by anitobodies)

immuno- = safe, free; **-glob** = globe, sphere (*immunoglobulin*: one of the class of proteins comprising the antibodies)

inter- = between; **leuko-** = white (*interleukin-2*: a cytokine which helps B cells that have contacted antigen differentiate into antibody-secreting plasma cells)

macro- = large; **-phage** = eat (*macrophage*: an amoeboid cell that moves through tissue fibers, engulfing bacteria and dead cells by phagocytosis)

mono- = one (*monocyte*: an agranular leukocyte that is able to migrate into tissues and transform into a macrophage)

neutro- = neutral; **-phil** = loving (*neutrophil*: the most abundant type of leukocyte; neutrophils tend to self destruct as they destroy foreign invaders, limiting their lifespan to but a few days)

perfora- = bore through (*perforin*: a protein that forms pores in a target cell's membrane)

pyro- = fire (*pyrogen*: molecules which set the body's thermostat to a higher temperature; they are released by certain leukocytes)

References

Abbas, A. K. and C. A. Janeway, Jr. "Immunology: Improving on Nature in the Twenty-First Century." *Cell*, January 2000.

Laver, W. G., N. Bischofberger and R. G. Webster. "Disarming Flu Viruses." *Scientific American*, January 1999.

Weiner, D. B. and R. C. Kennedy "Genetic Vaccines." *Scientific American*, July 1999.

Visual Guide to the Image Library

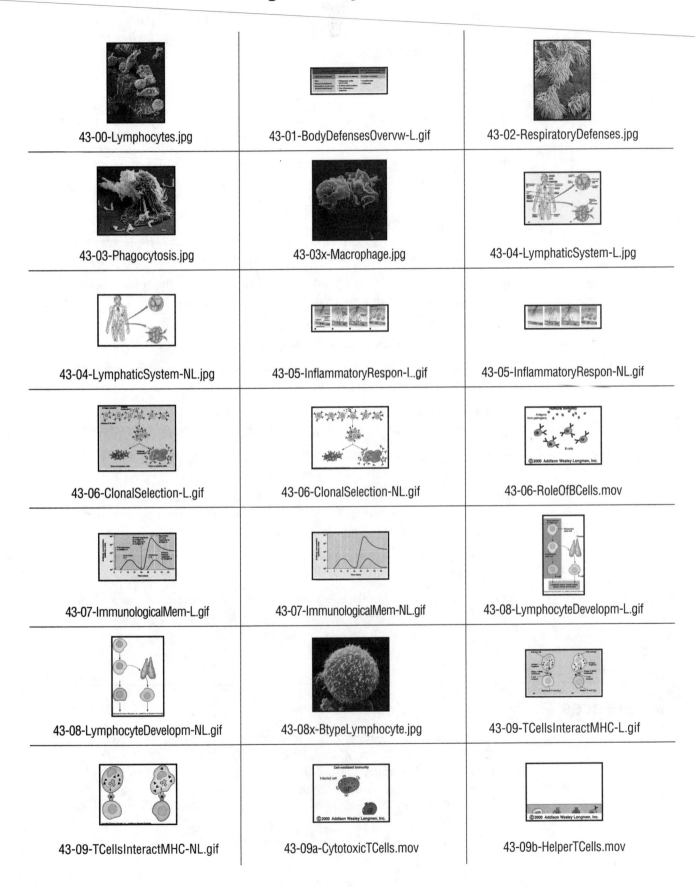

43-00-Lymphocytes.jpg

43-01-BodyDefensesOvervw-L.gif

43-02-RespiratoryDefenses.jpg

43-03-Phagocytosis.jpg

43-03x-Macrophage.jpg

43-04-LymphaticSystem-L.jpg

43-04-LymphaticSystem-NL.jpg

43-05-InflammatoryRespon-L.gif

43-05-InflammatoryRespon-NL.gif

43-06-ClonalSelection-L.gif

43-06-ClonalSelection-NL.gif

43-06-RoleOfBCells.mov

43-07-ImmunologicalMem-L.gif

43-07-ImmunologicalMem-NL.gif

43-08-LymphocyteDevelopm-L.gif

43-08-LymphocyteDevelopm-NL.gif

43-08x-BtypeLymphocyte.jpg

43-09-TCellsInteractMHC-L.gif

43-09-TCellsInteractMHC-NL.gif

43-09a-CytotoxicTCells.mov

43-09b-HelperTCells.mov

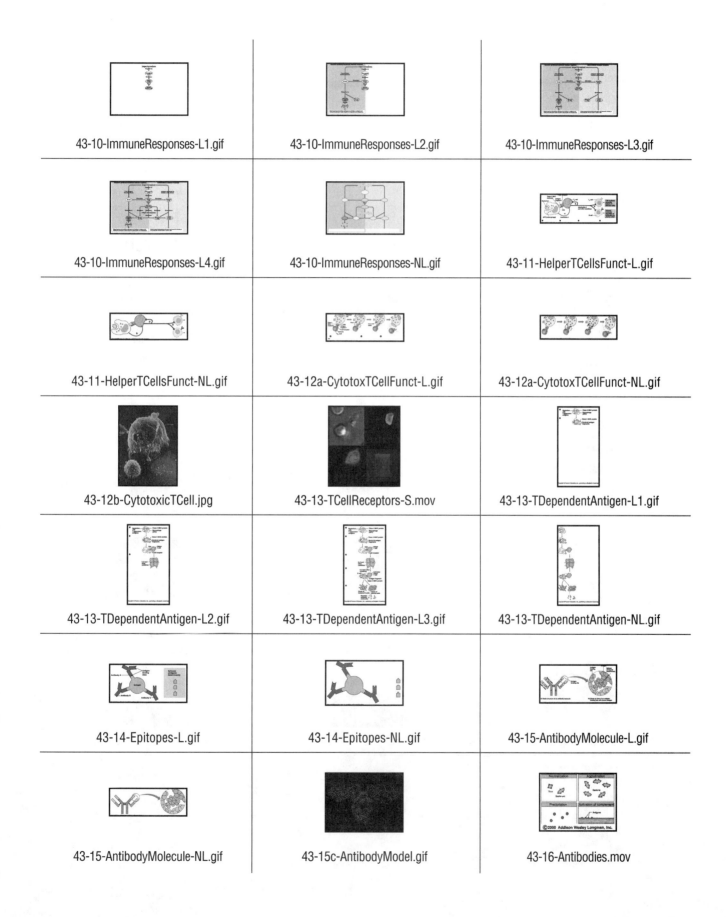

43-10-ImmuneResponses-L1.gif

43-10-ImmuneResponses-L2.gif

43-10-ImmuneResponses-L3.gif

43-10-ImmuneResponses-L4.gif

43-10-ImmuneResponses-NL.gif

43-11-HelperTCellsFunct-L.gif

43-11-HelperTCellsFunct-NL.gif

43-12a-CytotoxTCellFunct-L.gif

43-12a-CytotoxTCellFunct-NL.gif

43-12b-CytotoxicTCell.jpg

43-13-TCellReceptors-S.mov

43-13-TDependentAntigen-L1.gif

43-13-TDependentAntigen-L2.gif

43-13-TDependentAntigen-L3.gif

43-13-TDependentAntigen-NL.gif

43-14-Epitopes-L.gif

43-14-Epitopes-NL.gif

43-15-AntibodyMolecule-L.gif

43-15-AntibodyMolecule-NL.gif

43-15c-AntibodyModel.gif

43-16-Antibodies.mov

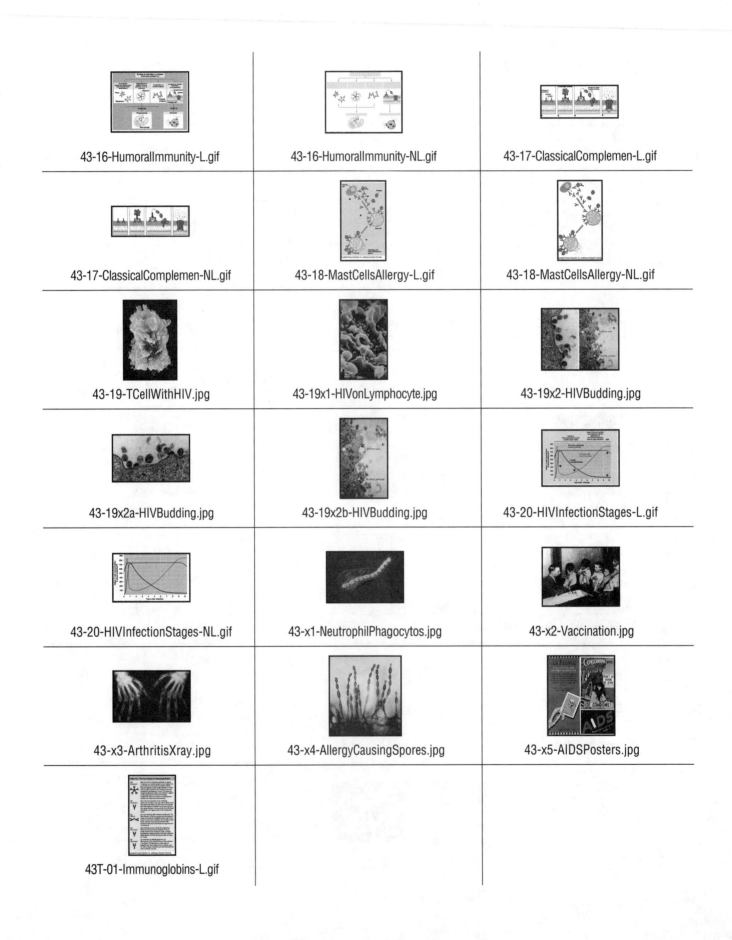

43-16-HumoralImmunity-L.gif

43-16-HumoralImmunity-NL.gif

43-17-ClassicalComplemen-L.gif

43-17-ClassicalComplemen-NL.gif

43-18-MastCellsAllergy-L.gif

43-18-MastCellsAllergy-NL.gif

43-19-TCellWithHIV.jpg

43-19x1-HIVonLymphocyte.jpg

43-19x2-HIVBudding.jpg

43-19x2a-HIVBudding.jpg

43-19x2b-HIVBudding.jpg

43-20-HIVInfectionStages-L.gif

43-20-HIVInfectionStages-NL.gif

43-x1-NeutrophilPhagocytos.jpg

43-x2-Vaccination.jpg

43-x3-ArthritisXray.jpg

43-x4-AllergyCausingSpores.jpg

43-x5-AIDSPosters.jpg

43T-01-Immunoglobins-L.gif

CHAPTER 44

Regulating the Internal Environment

Chapter Outline

Transparency Acetates

The Transparency Acetates set for Campbell, *Biology* includes the following images:

Figure 44.1   Regulators and conformers

Figure 44.2   A partial energy and material bookkeeping for ten years in the life of a young woman

Figure 44.3   Heat exchange between an organism and its environment

Figure 44.4   The relationship between body temperature and ambient (environmental) temperature in an ectotherm and an endotherm

Figure 44.5   Countercurrent heat exchangers

Figure 44.6   Skin as an organ of thermoregulation

Figure 44.8   Thermoregulation in large, active fishes

Figure 44.9   Thermoregulation in moths

Figure 44.10   The thermostat function of the hypothalamus and feedback mechanisms in human thermoregulation

Figure 44.11   Body temperature and metabolism during hibernation of Belding's ground squirrel

Figure 44.12   Salt-excreting glands in birds

Figure 44.13   Nitrogenous wastes

Figure 44.14   Osmoregulation in marine and freshwater bony fishes: a comparison

Figure 44.16   Water balance in two terrestrial mammals

Figure 44.17   Key functions of excretory systems: an overview

Figure 44.18   Protonephridia: the flame-bulb system of a planarian

Figure 44.19   Metanephridia of an earthworm

Figure 44.20   Malpighian tubules of insects

Figure 44.21   The human excretory system at four size scales

Figure 44.22   The nephron and collecting duct: regional functions of the transport epithelium

Figure 44.23   How the human kidney concentrates urine: the two-solute model (Layer 1)

Figure 44.23   How the human kidney concentrates urine: the two-solute model (Layer 2)

Figure 44.23   How the human kidney concentrates urine: the two-solute model (Layer 3)

Figure 44.24   Hormonal control of the kidney by negative feedback circuits

Media for Instructors

Campbell Image Presentation Library

The Campbell Image Presentation Library CD-ROM set includes the following for your use:

- All art (available in pdf and jpeg or gif formats), photos (from the text and outside sources), and tables. Art images are also available without callouts. See the Visual Guide to the Image Library section at the end of this chapter for thumbnail versions of every image.
- A PowerPoint™ slide show of the art (with callouts), photos (both text and outside sources), and tables.
- The following QuickTime animations, adapted from student media activities (also available as Shockwave Flash .swf files):

    44-21-NephronIntroduction.mov

    44-22a-BowmansCapsule.mov

    44-22b-LoopOfHenle.mov

    44-22c-CollectingDuct.mov

    44-24-EffectOfADH.mov

PowerPoint Lectures CD-ROM

The PowerPoint Lectures CD-ROM contains slides that integrate the art, photos, tables, and lecture outline from this chapter.

Campbell Biology Website (Instructor Resources)

See the insert in your copy of Campbell/Reece *Biology*, Sixth Edition, for instructions on how to access the Campbell Biology Website. The Instructor Resources section of the website includes the following:

- The art, photos, tables, PowerPoint slide shows, videos, and animations from the Campbell Image Presentation Library
- Suggested answers to the Lab Report questions from the Case Studies in the Process of Science
- The PowerPoint Lecture for this chapter
- Word files of the lecture outline for this chapter
- Photo links

Course Management Systems

The media content for this chapter is available in three course management systems: CourseCompass™, Blackboard, and WebCT. For more information, go to http://cms.aw.com. For the latest pdf instructions on how to use CourseCompass, go to www.coursecompass.com. In addition, a Syllabus Manager is offered on the Campbell Biology Website.

Media for Students

The Campbell Biology Website and CD-ROM include the following for your students:

- Objectives
- Chapter Review (Summary, Self-Quiz, and Essay Questions from the book; Word Roots; Key Terms linked to the Glossary)
- Activities (see list below)
- Case Studies in the Process of Science (see list below)
- Quizzes (Pre-test, Activities Quiz, Chapter Quiz, Essay Questions)
- Web Links
- News and References
- Art and videos from the Campbell Image Presentation Library
- The Campbell *Biology* Interviews (from all editions)
- Glossary with audio pronunciations
- Syllabus Manager

Student Media Activities and Case Studies in The Process of Science

Web/CD Activity 44A: *Structure of the Human Excretory System*

Web/CD Activity 44B: *Nephron Function*

Web/CD Activity 44C: *Control of Water Reabsorption*

Web/CD Case Study in the Process of Science: *What Affects Urine Production?*

Objectives

An Overview of Homeostasis

1. Distinguish between regulators and conformers.
2. Describe the special circumstances during which an animal's inputs of energy and materials exceed its outputs.
3. Compare the fractions of energy and materials used for reproduction by humans and mice.
4. Explain how homeostasis can be viewed as a set of budgets. Provide an example.

Regulation of Body Temperature

5. Describe the impact of rising temperatures on the physiology of an animal. Explain the Q_{10} effect.
6. Describe the adaptive advantages of thermoregulation.
7. Describe and compare the processes of conduction, convection, radiation, and evaporation. Explain the significance of these processes.

8. Compare the physiologies of ectotherms and endotherms, noting the advantages and disadvantages of each. Explain why the terms "cold-blooded" and "warm-blooded" can be misleading.

9. Describe the four main categories of adaptations that help animals thermoregulate. Distinguish between vasodilation and vasoconstriction.

10. Describe the thermoregulatory adaptations characteristic of animals in each of the following groups: mammals and birds; amphibians and reptiles; fishes; and invertebrates.

11. Describe the role of the hypothalamus in thermoregulation.

12. Compare the processes of acclimatization in endotherms and ectotherms.

13. Describe the specific functions of cryoprotectants and heat-shock proteins.

14. Describe the environmental conditions that induce torpor (hibernation). Note the physiological changes associated with torpor and their adaptive advantages to animals that undergo this phenomenon.

15. Describe the processes of estivation (summer torpor) and daily torpor, noting the associated physiological changes and their adaptive advantages to animals that undergo these phenomena.

Water Balance and Waste Disposal

16. Describe the ultimate function of osmoregulation. Explain how hemolymph and interstitial fluids are involved in this process.

17. Explain how transport epithelia promote osmoregulation.

18. Describe the production and elimination of ammonia. Explain the need for its elimination.

19. Compare the amounts of nitrogenous waste produced by endotherms and ectotherms, and those produced by predators and herbivores.

20. Explain how an animal's nitrogenous wastes are correlated with its phylogeny and habitat.

21. Compare the strategies to eliminate waste as ammonia, urea, or uric acid. Note which animal groups are associated with each process and why a particular strategy is most adaptive for a particular group.

22. Define osmolarity and distinguish between isotonic, hypertonic, and hypotonic solutions.

23. Compare the strategies of osmoconformers and osmoregulators. Distinguish between stenohaline and euryhaline animals.

24. Discuss the problems that marine, freshwater, and terrestrial organisms face in maintaining homeostasis and explain what osmoregulatory adaptations serve as solutions to these problems.

Excretory Systems

25. Describe the key aspects of the two-step process of urine production.

26. Describe how a flame-bulb (protonephridial) excretory system functions.

27. Explain how the metanephridial excretory tubule of annelids functions. Compare the structure to the protonephridial system.

28. Describe the Malpighian tubule excretory system of insects.

29. Using a diagram, identify and give the function of each structure in the mammalian excretory system.

30. Using a diagram, identify and describe the function of each part of the nephron.
31. Describe and show the relationships among the processes of filtration, secretion, and reabsorption.
32. Explain how the loop of Henle enhances water conservation by the kidney.
33. Describe the countercurrent mechanisms of the loop of Henle.
34. Explain how the juxtamedullary nephron can be regarded as one of the clearest examples of a structure-function relationship.
35. Describe the mechanisms involved in the regulation of the kidney.
36. Explain how the feeding habits of the South American vampire bat illustrate the versatility of the mammalian kidney.
37. Describe the structural and physiological adaptations in the kidneys of nonmammalian species that allow them those species to osmoregulate in different environments.
38. Explain the significance of the liver in maintaining homeostasis.

Key Terms

homeostasis	estivation	renal medulla
thermoregulation	daily torpor	nephron
osmoregulation	osmoregulation	glomerulus
excretion	transport epithelium	Bowman's capsule
regulator	ammonia	proximal tubule
conformers	urea	loop of Henle
budgets	uric acid	distal tubule
Q_{10} effect	osmolarity	collecting duct
conduction	osmoconformer	cortical nephrons
convection	osmoregulator	juxtamedullary
radiation	stenohaline	nephrons
evaporation	euryhaline	afferent arteriole
ectotherm	anhydrobiosis	efferent arteriole
endotherm	selective reabsorption	peritubular capillaries
vasodilation	secretion	vasa recta
vasoconstriction	filtration	antidiuretic hormone
countercurrent heat	filtrate	(ADH)
exchanger	protonephridium	juxtaglomerular
nonshivering	metanephridium	apparatus (JGA)
thermogenesis (NST)	Malphighian tubules	angiotensin II
brown fat	renal artery	aldosterone
acclimatization	renal vein	renin-angiotensin-
stress-induced proteins	ureter	aldosterone system
heat-shock proteins	urinary bladder	(RAAS)
torpor	urethra	atrial natriuretic factor
hibernation	renal cortex	(ANF)

Word Roots

an- = without; **hydro-** = water; **-bios** = life (*anyhydrobiosis*: the ability to survive in a dormant state when an organism's habitat dries up)

anti- = against; **-diure** = urinate (*antidiuretic hormone*: a hormone that helps regulate water balance)

con- = with; **-vect** = carried (*convection*: the mass movement of warmed air or liquid to or from the surface of a body or object)

counter- = opposite (*countercurrent heat exchanger*: a special arrangement of blood vessels that helps trap heat in the body core and is important in reducing heat loss in many endotherms)

-dilat = expanded (*vasodilation*: an increase in the diameter of superficial blood vessels triggered by nerve signals that relax the muscles of the vessel walls)

ecto- = outside; **-therm** = heat (*ectotherm*: an animal, such as a reptile, fish, or amphibian, that must use environmental energy and behavioral adaptations to regulate its body temperature)

endo- = inner (*endotherm*: an animal that uses metabolic energy to maintain a constant body temperature, such as a bird or mammal)

eury- = broad, wide; **-halin** = salt (*euryhaline*: organisms that can tolerate substantial changes in external osmolarity)

glomer- = a ball (*glomerulus*: a ball of capillaries surrounded by Bowman's capsule in the nephron and serving as the site of filtration in the vertebrate kidney)

homeo- = like, same; **-stasis** = standing (*homeostasis*: the steady-state physiological condition of the body)

juxta- = near to (*juxtaglomerular apparatus*: a specialized tissue located near the afferent arteriole that supplies blood to the glomerulus)

meta- = with; **-nephri** = kidney (*metanephridium*: in annelid worms, a type of excretory tubule with internal openings called nephrostomes that collect body fluids and external openings called nephridiopores)

osmo- = pushing; **-regula** = regular (*osmoregulation*: adaptations to control the water balance in organisms living in hypertonic, hypotonic, or terrestrial environments)

peri- = around (*peritubular capillaries*: the network of tiny blood vessels that surrounds the proximal and distal tubules in the kidney)

podo- = foot; **-cyte** = cell (*podocytes*: specialized cells of Bowman's capsule that are permeable to water and small solutes but not to blood cells or large molecules such as plasma proteins)

proto- = first (*protonephridium*: an excretory system, such as the flame-cell system of flatworms, consisting of a network of closed tubules having external openings called nephridiopores and lacking internal openings)

reni- = a kidney; **-angio** = a vessel; **-tens** = stretched (*renin-angiotensinaldosterone system*: a part of a complex feedback circuit that normally partners with antidiuretic hormone in osmoregulation)

steno- = narrow (*stenohaline*: organisms that cannot tolerate substantial changes in external osmolarity)

vasa- = a vessel; **-recta** = straight (*vasa recta*: the capillary system that serves the loop of Henle)

References

Hickman, C. P., L. S. Roberts and A. Larson. *Integrated Principles of Zoology.* 11th ed. New York, McGraw-Hill Company, 2001.

Visual Guide to the Image Library

44-00-WolfInSnow.jpg

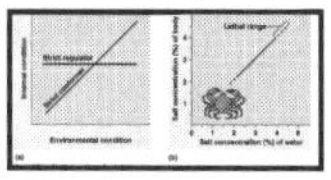

44-01-EnviroRegulat-L.gif

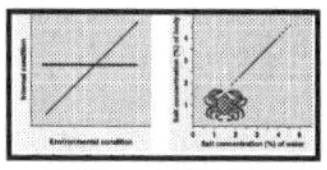

44-01-EnviroRegulat-NL.gif

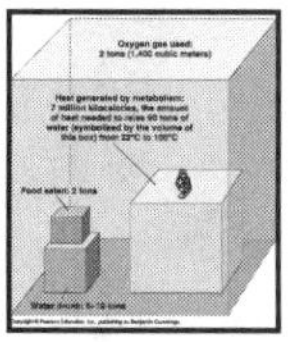

44-02-InputOutput-L.gif

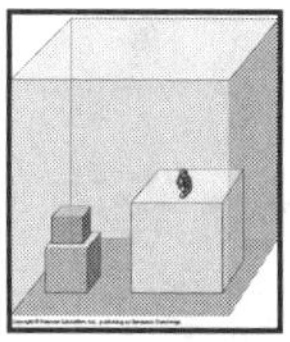

44-02-InputOutput-NL.gif

44-03-HeatExchange-L.gif

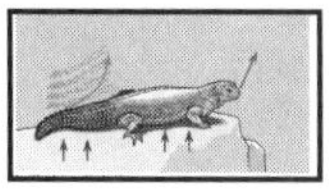

44-03-HeatExchange-NL.gif

44-03x-LizardOnRock.jpg

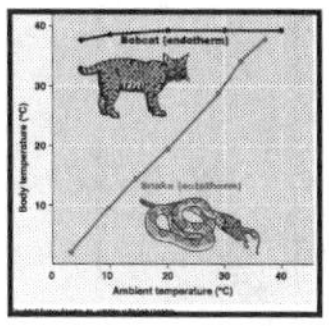

44-04-EndoEctothermTemp-L.gif

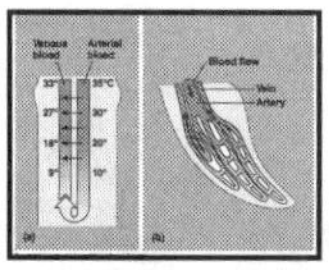

44-05-CounterCurrentHeat-L.gif

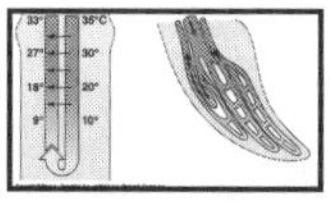

44-05-CounterCurrentHeat-NL.gif

44-05a-Puffin.jpg

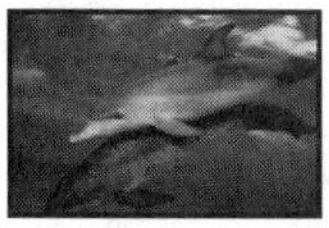

44-05b-Dolphin.jpg

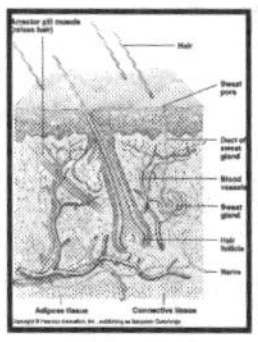

44-06-SkinThermoregOrgan-L.gif

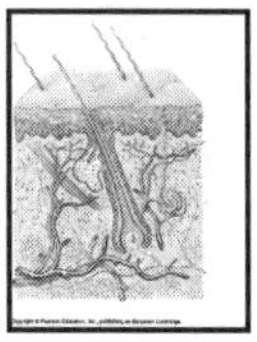

44-06-SkinThermoregOrgan-NL.gif

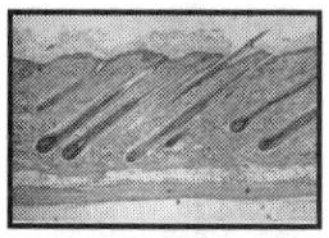

44-06x-SkinXsection.jpg

44-07x-Thermoregulation.jpg

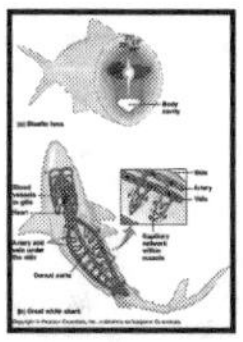

44-08-FishThermoregulat-L.gif

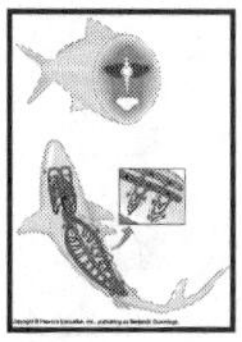

44-08-FishThermoregulat-NL.gif

44-08b-GreatWhiteShark.jpg

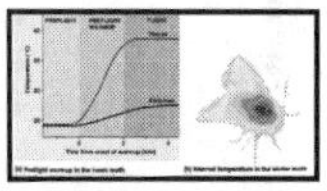

44-09-MothThermoregulat-L.jpg

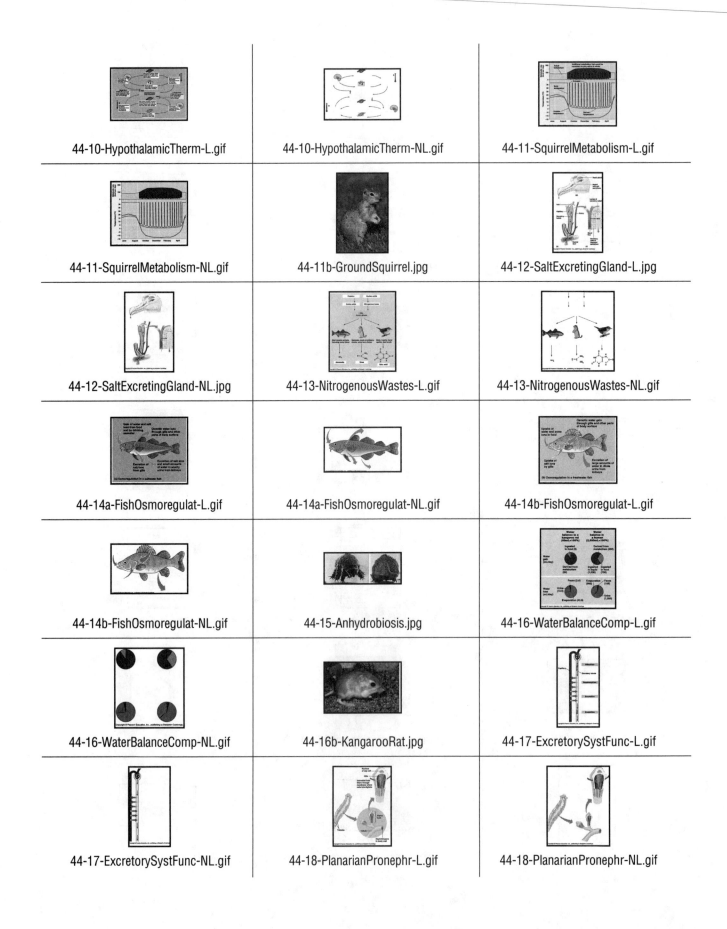

44-10-HypothalamicTherm-L.gif

44-10-HypothalamicTherm-NL.gif

44-11-SquirrelMetabolism-L.gif

44-11-SquirrelMetabolism-NL.gif

44-11b-GroundSquirrel.jpg

44-12-SaltExcretingGland-L.jpg

44-12-SaltExcretingGland-NL.jpg

44-13-NitrogenousWastes-L.gif

44-13-NitrogenousWastes-NL.gif

44-14a-FishOsmoregulat-L.gif

44-14a-FishOsmoregulat-NL.gif

44-14b-FishOsmoregulat-L.gif

44-14b-FishOsmoregulat-NL.gif

44-15-Anhydrobiosis.jpg

44-16-WaterBalanceComp-L.gif

44-16-WaterBalanceComp-NL.gif

44-16b-KangarooRat.jpg

44-17-ExcretorySystFunc-L.gif

44-17-ExcretorySystFunc-NL.gif

44-18-PlanarianPronephr-L.gif

44-18-PlanarianPronephr-NL.gif

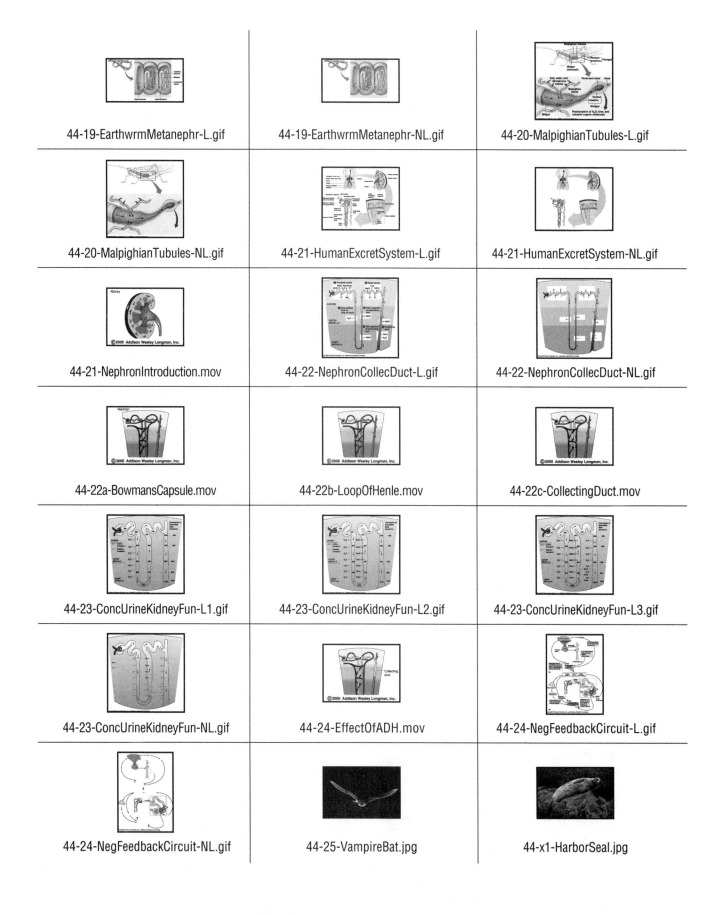

44-19-EarthwrmMetanephr-L.gif

44-19-EarthwrmMetanephr-NL.gif

44-20-MalpighianTubules-L.gif

44-20-MalpighianTubules-NL.gif

44-21-HumanExcretSystem-L.gif

44-21-HumanExcretSystem-NL.gif

44-21-NephronIntroduction.mov

44-22-NephronCollecDuct-L.gif

44-22-NephronCollecDuct-NL.gif

44-22a-BowmansCapsule.mov

44-22b-LoopOfHenle.mov

44-22c-CollectingDuct.mov

44-23-ConcUrineKidneyFun-L1.gif

44-23-ConcUrineKidneyFun-L2.gif

44-23-ConcUrineKidneyFun-L3.gif

44-23-ConcUrineKidneyFun-NL.gif

44-24-EffectOfADH.mov

44-24-NegFeedbackCircuit-L.gif

44-24-NegFeedbackCircuit-NL.gif

44-25-VampireBat.jpg

44-x1-HarborSeal.jpg

CHAPTER 45

Chemical Signals in Animals

Chapter Outline

An Introduction to Regulatory Systems

The endocrine system and the nervous system are structurally, chemically, and functionally related

Invertebrate regulatory systems clearly illustrate endocrine and nervous system interactions

Chemical Signals and Their Modes of Action

A variety of local regulators affect neighboring target cells: *the process of science*

Most chemical signals bind to plasma-membrane proteins, initiating signal-transduction pathways

Steroid hormones, thyroid hormones, and some local regulators enter target cells and bind to intracellular receptors: *the process of science*

The Vertebrate Endocrine System

The hypothalamus and pituitary integrate many functions of the vertebrate endocrine system

The pineal gland is involved in biorhythms

Thyroid hormones function in development, bioenergetics, and homeostasis

Parathyroid hormone and calcitonin balance blood calcium

Endocrine tissues of the pancreas secrete insulin and glucagon, antagonistic hormones that regulate blood glucose

The adrenal medulla and adrenal cortex help the body manage stress

Gonadal steroids regulate growth, development, reproductive cycles, and sexual behavior

Transparency Acetates

The Transparency Acetates for *Biology*, Sixth Edition, include the following images:

Media for Instructors

Campbell Image Presentation Library

The Campbell Image Presentation Library CD-ROM set includes the following for your use:

- All art (available in pdf and jpeg or gif formats), photos (from the text and outside sources), and tables. Art images are also available without callouts. See the Visual Guide to the Image Library section at the end of this chapter for thumbnail versions of every image.
- A PowerPoint™ slide show of the art (with callouts), photos (both text and outside sources), and tables.
- The following QuickTime animations, adapted from student media activities (also available as Shockwave Flash .swf files):

  45-03a-NonsteroidHormone.mov

  45-03b-SteroidHormone.mov

PowerPoint Lectures CD-ROM

The PowerPoint Lectures CD-ROM contains slides that integrate the art, photos, tables, and lecture outline from this chapter.

Campbell Biology Website (Instructor Resources)

See the insert in your copy of Campbell/Reece *Biology*, Sixth Edition, for instructions on how to access the Campbell Biology Website. The Instructor

Resources section of the website includes the following:

- The art, photos, tables, PowerPoint slide shows, videos, and animations from the Campbell Image Presentation Library
- Suggested answers to the Lab Report questions from the Case Studies in the Process of Science
- The PowerPoint Lecture for this chapter
- Word files of the lecture outline for this chapter
- Photo links

Course Management Systems

The media content for this chapter is available in three course management systems: CourseCompass^{TM}, Blackboard, and WebCT. For more information, go to http://cms.aw.com. For the latest pdf instructions on how to use CourseCompass, go to **www.coursecompass.com**. In addition, a Syllabus Manager is offered on the Campbell Biolog*y* Website.

Media for Students

The Campbell Biology Website and CD-ROM include the following for your students:

- Objectives
- Chapter Review (Summary, Self-Quiz, and Essay Questions from the book; Word Roots; Key Terms linked to the Glossary)
- Activities (see list below)
- Case Studies in the Process of Science (see list below)
- Quizzes (Pre-test, Activities Quiz, Chapter Quiz, Essay Questions)
- Web Links
- News and References
- Art and videos from the Campbell Image Presentation Library
- The Campbell *Biology* Interviews (from all editions)
- Glossary with audio pronunciations
- Syllabus Manager

Student Media Activities and Case Studies in The Process of Science

Web/CD Activity 45A: *Overview of Cell Signaling*

Web/CD Activity 45B: *Peptide Hormone Action*

Web/CD Activity 45C: *Steroid Hormone Action*

Web/CD Case Study in the Process of Science: *How Do Thyroxine and TSH Affect Metabolism?*

Web/CD Activity 45D: *Human Endocrine Glands and Hormones*

Objectives

An Introduction to Regulatory Systems

1. Compare the response times of the two major systems of internal communication: the nervous system and the endocrine system.

2. Distinguish between endocrine and exocrine glands.

3. Explain how neurosecretory cells, epinephrine, and the release of milk by a nursing mother illustrate the integration of the endocrine and nervous systems.

4. Describe several examples of the essential roles of hormones in the maintenance of homeostasis within invertebrate animals.

Chemical Signals and Their Modes of Action

5. Distinguish between the functions of local regulators and pheromones.

6. Describe the diverse functions of growth factors, nitric oxide, and prostaglandins.

7. Define a signal-transduction pathway, noting the mechanism and main components of action. Give several examples of its function.

8. Describe the nature and locations of intracellular receptors for hormones that pass easily through cell membranes. Explain how their passage compares to the signal-transduction pathway noted just above.

9. Describe several examples of different physiological reactions in animals exposed to the same hormone.

The Vertebrate Endocrine System

10. Explain how the hypothalamus and pituitary glands interact and how they coordinate the endocrine system.

11. Describe the location of the pituitary. List and explain in detail the functions of the hormones released from the anterior and posterior lobes.

12. Describe the location of the pineal gland. Explain the significance of its secretion melatonin.

13. List the hormones of the thyroid gland and explain their roles in development and metabolism. Explain the causes and symptoms of hyperthyroidism, hypothyroidism, and goiter.

14. Note the location of the parathyroid glands and describe the hormonal control of calcium homeostasis.

15. Distinguish between alpha and beta cells in the pancreas and explain how their antagonistic hormones (insulin and glucagon) regulate carbohydrate metabolism.

16. Distinguish between Type I diabetes mellitus and Type II diabetes mellitus.

17. Describe the development of the adrenal medulla. List the hormones of the adrenal medulla, describe their functions, and explain how their secretions are controlled.

18. List the hormones of the adrenal cortex, describe their functions, and explain how their secretions are controlled.

19. List the hormones of three categories of steroid hormones produced by the gonads. Describe variations in their production between the sexes. Note the functions of each category of steroid and explain how secretions are controlled.

Key Terms

hormone
target cell
endocrine system
endocrine glands
neurosecretory cells
ecdysone
brain hormone (BH)
juvenile hormone (JH)
growth factor
nitric oxide (NO)
prostaglandins (PGs)
signal-transduction
  pathway
tropic hormones
hypothalamus
pituitary gland
anterior pituitary
adenohypophysis
releasing hormone
inhibiting hormone
posterior pituitary
neurohypophysis
oxytocin
antidiuretic hormone
  (ADH)
growth hormone (GH)

insulinlike growth
  factors (IGFs)
prolactin (PRL)
follicle-stimulating
  hormone (FSH)
luteinizing hormone
  (LH)
thyroid-stimulating
  hormone (TSH)
gonadotropins
adrenocorticotropic
  hormone (ACTH)
melanocyte-
  stimulating hormone
  (MSH)
endorphin
pineal gland
melatonin
thyroid gland
triiodothyronine (T$_3$)
thyroxine (T$_4$)
calcitonin
parathyroid glands
parathyroid hormone
  (PTH)
vitamin D

pancreas
islets of Langerhans
alpha cells
glucagon
beta cell
insulin
Type I diabetes
  mellitus
Type II diabetes
  mellitus
adrenal gland
adrenal cortex
adrenal medulla
epinephrine
norepinephrine
  (noradrenaline)
catecholamines
corticosteroids
glucocorticoids
mineralocorticoids
androgens
testosterone
estrogens
progestins

Word Roots

adeno- = gland; **-hypo** = below (*adenohypophysis*: also called the anterior pituitary, this gland is positioned at the base of the hypothalamus)

andro- = male; **-gen** = produce (*androgens*: the principal male steroid hormones, such as testosterone, which stimulate the development and maintenance of the male reproductive system and secondary sex characteristics)

anti- = against; **-diure** = urinate (*antidiuretic hormone*: a hormone that helps regulate water balance)

cata- = down; **-chol** = anger (*catecholamines*: a class of compounds, including epinephrine and norepinephrine, that are synthesized from the amino acid tyrosine)

-cortico = the shell; **-tropic** = to turn or change (*adrenocorticotropic hormone*: a peptide hormone released from the anterior pituitary, it stimulates the production and secretion of steroid hormones by the adrenal cortex)

ecdys- = an escape (*ecdysone*: a steroid hormone that triggers molting in arthropods)

endo- = inside (*endorphin*: a hormone produced in the brain and anterior pituitary that inhibits pain perception)

epi- = above, over (*epinephrine*: a hormone produced as a response to stress; also called adrenaline)

gluco- = sweet (*glucagon*: a peptide hormone secreted by pancreatic endocrine cells that raises blood glucose levels; an antagonistic hormone to insulin)

lut- = yellow (*luteinizing hormone*: a gonadotropin secreted by the anterior pituitary)

melan- = black (*melatonin*: a modified amino acid hormone secreted by the pineal gland)

neuro- = nerve (*neurohypophysis*: also called the posterior pituitary, it is an extension of the brain)

oxy- = sharp, acid (*oxytocin*: a hormone that induces contractions of the uterine muscles and causes the mammary glands to eject milk during nursing)

para- = beside, near (*parathyroid glands*: four endocrine glands, embedded in the surface of the thyroid gland, that secrete parathyroid hormone and raise blood calcium levels)

pro- = before; **-lact** = milk (*prolactin*: a hormone produced by the anterior pituitary gland, it stimulates milk synthesis in mammals)

tri- = three; **-iodo** = violet (*triiodothyrodine*: one of two very similar hormones produced by the thyroid gland and derived from the amino acid tyrosine)

References

Fuchs, E., and J. A. Segre. "Stem Cells: A New Lease on Life." *Cell,* January, 2000.

Giancotti, F. G., and E. Rousilahti. "Integrin Signaling." *Science,* volume 285; 1999.

Rusting, R. "Hair: Why It Grows, Why It Stops." *Scientific American,* June 2001.

Visual Guide to the Reference Library

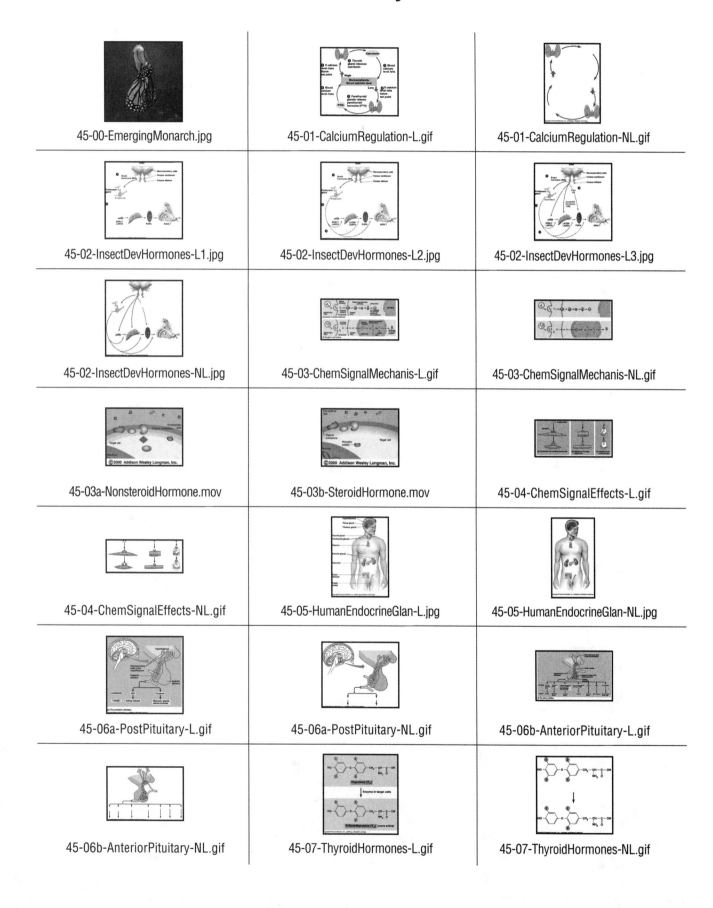

45-00-EmergingMonarch.jpg

45-01-CalciumRegulation-L.gif

45-01-CalciumRegulation-NL.gif

45-02-InsectDevHormones-L1.jpg

45-02-InsectDevHormones-L2.jpg

45-02-InsectDevHormones-L3.jpg

45-02-InsectDevHormones-NL.jpg

45-03-ChemSignalMechanis-L.gif

45-03-ChemSignalMechanis-NL.gif

45-03a-NonsteroidHormone.mov

45-03b-SteroidHormone.mov

45-04-ChemSignalEffects-L.gif

45-04-ChemSignalEffects-NL.gif

45-05-HumanEndocrineGlan-L.jpg

45-05-HumanEndocrineGlan-NL.jpg

45-06a-PostPituitary-L.gif

45-06a-PostPituitary-NL.gif

45-06b-AnteriorPituitary-L.gif

45-06b-AnteriorPituitary-NL.gif

45-07-ThyroidHormones-L.gif

45-07-ThyroidHormones-NL.gif

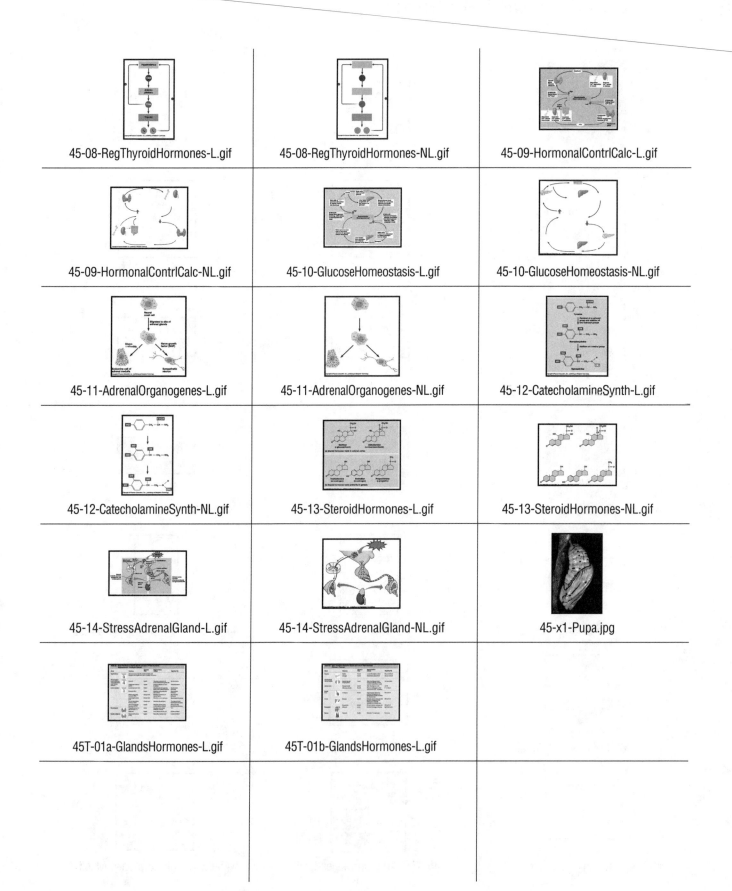

45-08-RegThyroidHormones-L.gif

45-08-RegThyroidHormones-NL.gif

45-09-HormonalContrlCalc-L.gif

45-09-HormonalContrlCalc-NL.gif

45-10-GlucoseHomeostasis-L.gif

45-10-GlucoseHomeostasis-NL.gif

45-11-AdrenalOrganogenes-L.gif

45-11-AdrenalOrganogenes-NL.gif

45-12-CatecholamineSynth-L.gif

45-12-CatecholamineSynth-NL.gif

45-13-SteroidHormones-L.gif

45-13-SteroidHormones-NL.gif

45-14-StressAdrenalGland-L.gif

45-14-StressAdrenalGland-NL.gif

45-x1-Pupa.jpg

45T-01a-GlandsHormones-L.gif

45T-01b-GlandsHormones-L.gif

CHAPTER 46

Animal Reproduction

Chapter Outline

Overview of Animal Reproduction

Both asexual and sexual reproduction occur in the animal kingdom

Diverse mechanisms of asexual reproduction enable animals to produce identical offspring rapidly

Reproductive cycles and patterns vary extensively among animals

Mechanisms of Sexual Reproduction

Internal and external fertilization both depend on mechanisms ensuring that mature sperm encounter fertile eggs of the same species

Species with internal fertilization usually produce fewer zygotes but provide more parental protection than species with external fertilization

Complex reproductive systems have evolved in many animal phyla

Mammalian Reproduction

Human reproduction involves intricate anatomy and complex behavior

Spermatogenesis and oogenesis both involve meiosis but differ in three significant ways

A complex interplay of hormones regulates reproduction

Embryonic and fetal development occur during pregnancy in humans and other eutherian (placental) mammals

Modern technology offers solutions for some reproductive problems

---

Transparency Acetates

The Transparency Acetates for *Biology*, Sixth Edition, include the following images:

Media for Instructors

Campbell Image Presentation Library

The Campbell Image Presentation Library CD-ROM set includes the following for your use:

- All art (available in pdf and jpeg or gif formats), photos (from the text and outside sources), and tables. Art images are also available without callouts. See the Visual Guide to the Image Library section at the end of this chapter for thumbnail versions of every image.

- A PowerPoint™ slide show of the art (with callouts), photos (both text and outside sources), and tables.

- The following video clips:

  46-22-UltrasoundOfFetus-B.mov   Ultrasound Imaging

  46-22x-UltrasoundOfFetus2-S.mov   Ultrasound Imaging

  See also

  13-01-HydraBudding-B.mov   Time-lapse of budding in hydra

- The following QuickTime animations, adapted from student media activities (also available as Shockwave Flash .swf files):

  46-08a-MaleReproductive.mov

  46-08b-MaleHormones.mov

  46-15a-FemaleReproductive.mov

  46-15b-Ovulation.mov

  46-15c-PostOvulation.mov

PowerPoint Lectures CD-ROM

The PowerPoint Lectures CD-ROM contains slides that integrate the art, photos, tables, and lecture outline from this chapter.

Campbell Biology Website (Instructor Resources)

See the insert in your copy of Campbell/Reece *Biology*, Sixth Edition, for instructions on how to access the Campbell Biology Website. The Instructor Resources section of the website includes the following:

- The art, photos, tables, PowerPoint slide shows, videos, and animations from the Campbell Image Presentation Library
- Suggested answers to the Lab Report questions from the Case Studies in the Process of Science
- The PowerPoint Lecture for this chapter
- Word files of the lecture outline for this chapter
- Photo links

Course Management Systems

The media content for this chapter is available in three course management systems: CourseCompass™, Blackboard, and WebCT. For more information, go to http://cms.aw.com. For the latest pdf instructions on how to use CourseCompass, go to **www.coursecompass.com**. In addition, a Syllabus Manager is offered on the Campbell Biology Website.

Media for Students

The Campbell Biology Website and CD-ROM include the following for your students:

- Objectives
- Chapter Review (Summary, Self-Quiz, and Essay Questions from the book; Word Roots; Key Terms linked to the Glossary)
- Activities (see list below)
- Case Studies in the Process of Science (see list below)
- Quizzes (Pre-test, Activities Quiz, Chapter Quiz, Essay Questions)
- Web Links
- News and References
- Art and videos from the Campbell Image Presentation Library
- The Campbell *Biology* Interviews (from all editions)
- Glossary with audio pronunciations
- Syllabus Manager

Student Media Activities and Case Studies in The Process of Science

Web/CD Activity 46A: *Reproductive System of the Human Male*

Web/CD Activity 46B: *Reproductive System of the Human Female*

Web/CD Case Study in the Process of Science: *What Might Obstruct the Male Urethra?*

Objectives

Overview of Animal Reproduction

1. Distinguish between asexual and sexual reproduction.

2. List and describe four forms of asexual reproduction.

3. Describe the adaptive advantages of asexual reproduction and the conditions that favor its occurrence.

4. Explain the advantages of periodic reproduction. Describe factors that control the timing of reproductive events.

5. Describe an example of an animal life cycle that alternates between asexual and sexual reproduction.

6. Define parthenogenesis and describe the conditions that favor its occurrence. Note examples of invertebrate and vertebrate species that use this form of reproduction.

7. Explain how hermaphroditism is advantageous in sessile or burrowing animals that might have difficulty encountering a member of the opposite sex.

8. Distinguish between protogynous and protandrous sequential hermaphroditism. Note the adaptive advantages of these reproductive systems.

Mechanisms of Sexual Reproduction

9. Describe three mechanisms that increase the probability that mature sperm will encounter fertile eggs of the same species in organisms that use external fertilization.

10. Compare reproductive systems using internal and external fertilization on the basis of the relative number of zygotes, protection of the embryos, and parental care.

11. List and describe various methods of egg and embryo protection.

12. Compare the reproductive systems of a polychaete worm, an insect, a common nonmammalian vertebrate, and a mammal.

Mammalian Reproduction

13. Using a diagram, identify and give the function of each component of the reproductive system of the human male.

14. Using a diagram, identify and give the function of each component of the reproductive system of the human female.

15. Describe the two physiological reactions common to sexual arousal in both sexes.

16. Describe the four phases of the sexual response cycle.

17. Describe spermatogenesis and the structure and function of mature sperm.

18. Describe oogenesis.

19. Describe three major differences between oogenesis and spermatogenesis.

20. Describe the influence of androgens on primary and secondary sex characteristics and behavior.

21. Compare the patterns of hormone secretion and reproductive events in male and female mammals.

22. Compare menstrual cycles and estrous cycles.

23. Describe the stages of the human menstrual cycle.

24. Explain how the menstrual cycle and ovarian cycle are synchronized in female mammals. Note in detail the functions of the particular hormones involved.

25. Describe the main features of menopause.

26. Define conception and gestation.

27. Compare the length of pregnancies in humans, rodents, dogs, cows, giraffes, and elephants. Explain the correlation between the duration of a pregnancy, the body size of the mother, and the extent of development of the young at birth.

28. Describe the changes that occur in the mother and the developing embryo during each trimester of a human pregnancy.

29. Describe the stages of parturition.

30. Describe the control of lactation.

31. Describe mechanisms that may help prevent the mother's immune system from rejecting the developing embryo.

32. List the various methods of contraception and explain how each works.

33. Describe techniques that allow us to learn about the health and genetics of a fetus.

34. Explain how and when in vitro fertilization is used.

Key Terms

asexual reproduction	prostate gland	menstruation
sexual reproduction	bulbourethral gland	estrus
gamete	penis	menstrual flow phase
zygote	baculum	proliferative phase
ovum	glans penis	secretory phase
spermatozoon	prepuce	ovarian cycle
fission	ovary	follicular phase
budding	follicle	luteal phase
gemmule	ovulation	pregnancy
fragmentation	corpus luteum	gestation
regeneration	oviduct	embryo
parthenogenesis	uterus	conception
hermaphroditism	endometrium	trimester
sequential	cervix	cleavage
hermaphroditism	vagina	blastocyst
protogynous	hymen	placenta
protandrous	vestibule	organogenesis
fertilization	labia minora	fetus
external fertilization	labia majora	human chorionic
internal fertilization	clitoris	gonadotropin (HCG)
pheromone	Bartholin's glands	parturition
gonad	mammary glands	labor
spermatheca	vasocongestion	lactation
cloaca	myotonia	contraception
testes (singular, testis)	coitus	rhythm method
seminiferous tubules	orgasm	natural family
Leydig cell	spermatogenesis	planning
scrotum	spermatogonia	barrier methods
epididymis	acrosome	condom
ejaculation	oogenesis	diaphragm
vas deferens	oogonia	birth control pills
ejaculatory duct	primary oocyte	tubal ligation
urethra	secondary oocyte	vasectomy
semen	menstrual cycle	*in vitro* fertilization
seminal vesicle	estrous cycle	

Word Roots

a- = not, without (*asexual reproduction*: a type of reproduction involving only one parent that produces genetically identical offspring)

acro- = tip; **-soma** = body (*acrosome*: an organelle at the tip of a sperm cell that helps the sperm penetrate the egg)

bacul- = a rod (*baculum*: a bone that is contained in, and helps stiffen, the penis of rodents, raccoons, walruses, and several other mammals)

blasto- = produce; **-cyst** = sac, bladder (*blastocyst*: a hollow ball of cells produced one week after fertilization in humans)

coit- = a coming together (*coitus*: the insertion of a penis into a vagina, also called sexual intercourse)

contra- = against (*contraception*: the prevention of pregnancy)

-ectomy = cut out (*vasectomy*: the cutting of each vas deferens to prevent sperm from entering the urethra)

endo- = inside (*endometrium*: the inner lining of the uterus, which is richly supplied with blood vessels)

epi- = above, over (*epididymis*: a coiled tubule located adjacent to the testes where sperm are stored)

gyno- = female (*protogynous*: a form of sequential hermaphroditism in which the female sex occurs first)

labi- = lip; **major-** = larger (*labia majora*: a pair of thick, fatty ridges that enclose and protect the labia minora and vestibule)

lact- = milk (*lactation*: the continued production of milk)

menstru- = month (*menstruation*: the shedding of portions of the endometrium during a menstrual cycle)

minor- = smaller (*labia minora*: a pair of slender skin folds that enclose and protect the vestibule)

myo- = muscle (*myotonia*: increased muscle tension)

oo- = egg; **-genesis** = producing (*oogenesis*: the process in the ovary that results in the production of female gametes)

partheno- = a virgin (*parthenogenesis*: a type of reproduction in which females produce offspring from unfertilized eggs)

partur- = giving birth (*parturition*: the expulsion of a baby from the mother, also called birth)

proto- = first; **andro-** = male (*protandrous*: form of sequential hermaphroditism in which the male sex occurs first)

-theca = a cup, case (*spermatheca*: a sac in the female reproductive system where sperm are stored)

tri- = three (*trimester*: a three month period)

vasa- = a vessel (*vasocongesition*: the filling of a tissue with blood caused by increased blood flow through the arteries of that tissue)

References

Smith, B. R. "Visualizing Human Embryos." *Scientific American*, March 1999.
Smith, R. "The Timing of Birth." *Scientific American*, March 1999.

Visual Guide to the Reference Library

46-00-FrogsMating.jpg

46-00x1-UtethesiaOrnatrix.jpg

46-00x2-BeetlesMating.jpg

46-01-AnemoneAsexRepro.jpg

46-02a-ParthenoLizardsPhoto.jpg

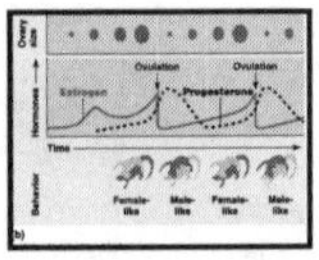

46-02b-ParthenoLizards-L.gif

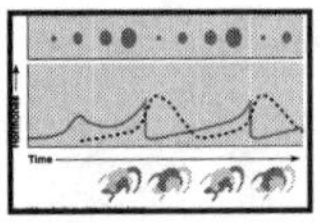

46-02b-ParthenoLizards-NL.gif

46-03-SexReversal.jpg

46-04-ExternalFertilization.jpg

46-05-InvertebrateCare.jpg

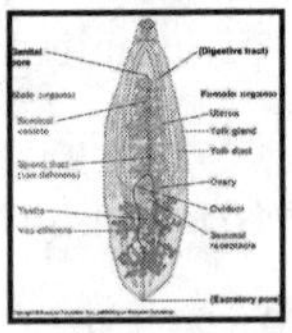

46-06-FlatwormReproAnat-L.jpg

46-06-FlatwormReproAnat-NL.jpg

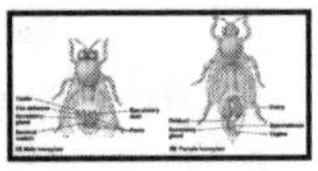

46-07-InsectReproAnatomy-L.jpg

46-07-InsectReproAnatomy-NL.jpg

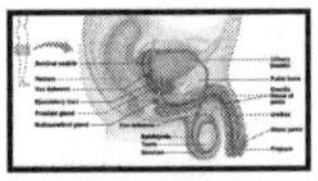

46-08a-MaleReproAnat-L.jpg

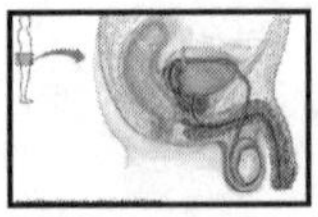

46-08a-MaleReproAnat-NL.jpg

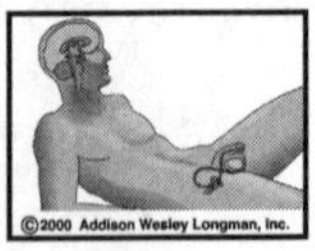

46-08a-MaleReproductive.mov

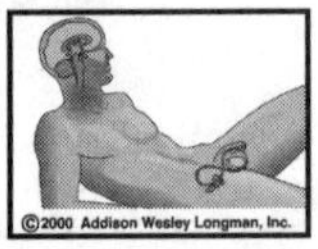

46-08b-MaleHormones.mov

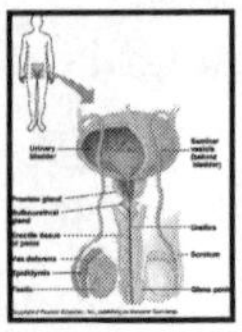

46-08b-MaleReproAnat-L.jpg

46-08b-MaleReproAnat-NL.jpg

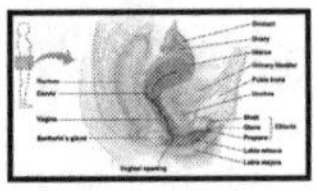

46-09a-FemaleReproAnat-L.jpg

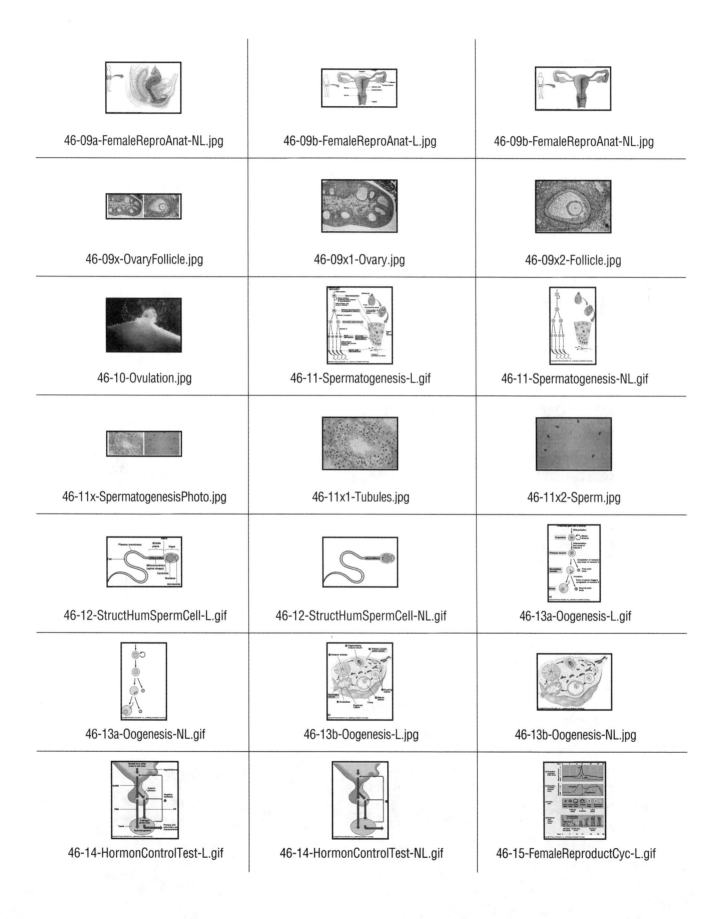

46-09a-FemaleReproAnat-NL.jpg

46-09b-FemaleReproAnat-L.jpg

46-09b-FemaleReproAnat-NL.jpg

46-09x-OvaryFollicle.jpg

46-09x1-Ovary.jpg

46-09x2-Follicle.jpg

46-10-Ovulation.jpg

46-11-Spermatogenesis-L.gif

46-11-Spermatogenesis-NL.gif

46-11x-SpermatogenesisPhoto.jpg

46-11x1-Tubules.jpg

46-11x2-Sperm.jpg

46-12-StructHumSpermCell-L.gif

46-12-StructHumSpermCell-NL.gif

46-13a-Oogenesis-L.gif

46-13a-Oogenesis-NL.gif

46-13b-Oogenesis-L.jpg

46-13b-Oogenesis-NL.jpg

46-14-HormonControlTest-L.gif

46-14-HormonControlTest-NL.gif

46-15-FemaleReproductCyc-L.gif

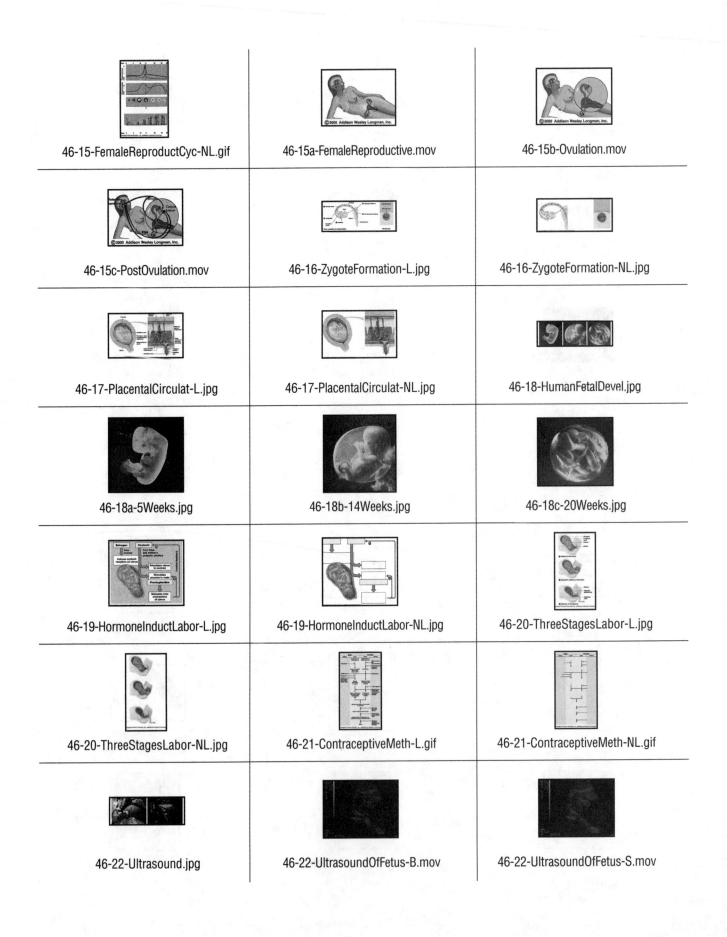

46-15-FemaleReproductCyc-NL.gif

46-15a-FemaleReproductive.mov

46-15b-Ovulation.mov

46-15c-PostOvulation.mov

46-16-ZygoteFormation-L.jpg

46-16-ZygoteFormation-NL.jpg

46-17-PlacentalCirculat-L.jpg

46-17-PlacentalCirculat-NL.jpg

46-18-HumanFetalDevel.jpg

46-18a-5Weeks.jpg

46-18b-14Weeks.jpg

46-18c-20Weeks.jpg

46-19-HormoneInductLabor-L.jpg

46-19-HormoneInductLabor-NL.jpg

46-20-ThreeStagesLabor-L.jpg

46-20-ThreeStagesLabor-NL.jpg

46-21-ContraceptiveMeth-L.gif

46-21-ContraceptiveMeth-NL.gif

46-22-Ultrasound.jpg

46-22-UltrasoundOfFetus-B.mov

46-22-UltrasoundOfFetus-S.mov

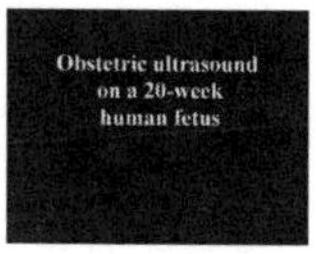

46-22x-UltrasoundOfFetus2-S.mov

46-x1-AphidBirth.jpg

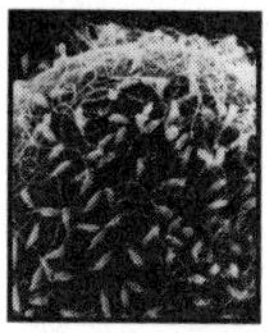

46-x2-SpermSEM.jpg

CHAPTER 47

Animal Development

Chapter Outline

The Stages of Early Embryonic Development

From egg to organism, an animal's form develops gradually: *the concept of epigenesis*

Fertilization activates the egg and brings together the nuclei of sperm and egg

Cleavage partitions the zygote into many smaller cells

Gastrulation rearranges the blastula to form a three-layered embryo with a primitive gut

In organogenesis, the organs of the animal body form from the three embryonic germ layers

Amniote embryos develop in a fluid-filled sac within a shell or uterus

The Cellular and Molecular Basis of Morphogenesis and Differentiation in Animals

Morphogenesis in animals involves specific changes in cell shape, position, and adhesion

The developmental fate of cells depends on cytoplasmic determinants and cell-cell induction: *a review*

Fate mapping can reveal cell genealogies in chordate embryos: *the process of science*

The eggs of most vertebrates contain cytoplasmic determinants that help establish the body axes and differences among cells of the early embryo

Inductive signals drive differentiation and pattern formation in vertebrates

Transparency Acetates

The Transparency Acetates for *Biology*, Sixth Edition, include the following images:

Figure 47.2   The acrosomal and cortical reactions during sea urchin fertilization

Figure 47.3   A view of CA^2 release during the coital reaction

Figure 47.4   Timeline for the fertilization of sea urchin eggs

Figure 47.5   Fertilization in mammals

Media for Instructors

Campbell Image Presentation Library

The Campbell Image Presentation Library CD-ROM set includes the following for your use:

- All art (available in pdf and jpeg or gif formats), photos (from the text and outside sources), and tables. Art images are also available without callouts. See the Visual Guide to the Image Library section at the end of this chapter for thumbnail versions of every image.
- A PowerPoint™ slide show of the art (with callouts), photos (both text and outside sources), and tables.
- The following video clip:

  47-06-SeaUrchinTimeLapse-B.mov   Sea urchin embryonic development

  47-10-XenopusDevelop-S.mov

PowerPoint Lectures CD-ROM

The PowerPoint Lectures CD-ROM contains slides that integrate the art, photos, tables, and lecture outline from this chapter.

Campbell Biology Website (Instructor Resources)

See the insert in your copy of Campbell/Reece *Biology,* Sixth Edition, for instructions on how to access the Campbell Biology Website. The Instructor Resources section of the website includes the following:

- The art, photos, tables, PowerPoint slide shows, videos, and animations from the Campbell Image Presentation Library

- Suggested answers to the Lab Report questions from the Case Studies in the Process of Science
- The PowerPoint Lecture for this chapter
- Word files of the lecture outline for this chapter
- Photo links

Course Management Systems

The media content for this chapter is available in three course management systems: CourseCompass™, Blackboard, and WebCT. For more information, go to http://cms.aw.com. For the latest pdf instructions on how to use CourseCompass, go to www.coursecompass.com. In addition, a Syllabus Manager is offered on the Campbell Biology Website.

Media for Students

The Campbell Biology Website and CD-ROM include the following for your students:

- Objectives
- Chapter Review (Summary, Self-Quiz, and Essay Questions from the book; Word Roots; Key Terms linked to the Glossary)
- Activities (see list below)
- Case Studies in the Process of Science (see list below)
- Quizzes (Pre-test, Activities Quiz, Chapter Quiz, Essay Questions)
- Web Links
- News and References
- Art and videos from the Campbell Image Presentation Library
- The Campbell *Biology* Interviews (from all editions)
- Glossary with audio pronunciations
- Syllabus Manager

Student Media Activities and Case Studies in The Process of Science

Web/CD Activity 47A: *Sea Urchin Development Video*

Web/CD Case Study in the Process of Science: *What Determines Cell Differentiation in the Sea Urchin?*

Web/CD Activity 47B: *Frog Development Video*

Objectives

The Stages of Embryonic Development in Animals

1. Compare the concepts of preformation and epigenesis.
2. List the two functions of fertilization.
3. Describe the acrosomal reaction and explain how it ensures that gametes are conspecific.
4. Describe the cortical reaction.
5. Explain how the acrosomal and cortical reactions function sequentially to prevent polyspermy.
6. Describe the changes that occur in an activated egg and explain the importance of cytoplasmic materials to egg activation.
7. Compare fertilization in a sea urchin and a mammal.
8. Describe the general process of cleavage. Explain how the distribution and abundance of yolk influence this process.
9. Explain the importance of embryo polarity during cleavage. Compare the characteristics of the animal hemisphere, vegetal hemisphere, and gray crescent in amphibian embryos.
10. Describe the formation of a morula and blastula in sea urchin, amphibian, and insect embryos. Distinguish between meroblastic cleavage and holoblastic cleavage.
11. Describe the process of gastrulation and explain its importance. Explain how this process rearranges the embryo. List adult structures derived from each of the primary tissue layers.
12. Compare gastrulation in a sea urchin and a frog.
13. Describe the formation of the notochord, neural tube, and somites in a frog.
14. Describe the significance and fate of neural crest cells.
15. List and explain the functions of the extraembryonic membranes in bird and reptile eggs.
16. Compare and contrast embryonic development in birds and mammals.

The Cellular and Molecular Basis of Morphogenesis and Differentiation in Animals

17. Describe the role of changes in cell shape and cell position during embryonic development. Explain how these cellular processes occur. Describe the process of convergent extension.
18. Describe the role of the extracellular matrix in embryonic development.
19. Describe the locations and functions of cell adhesion molecules.
20. Describe the two general principles that integrate our knowledge of the genetic and cellular mechanisms underlying differentiation.
21. Describe the process of fate mapping and the significance of fate maps.
22. Describe the two important conclusions that have resulted from the experimental manipulation of parts of embryos and the use of fate maps.
23. Explain the relationships between polarity, cytoplasmic determinants, and embryonic development.

24. Explain the process of induction and its significance in embryonic development. Explain the significance of the dorsal lip of the blastopore in the early amphibian gastrula.

25. Describe the molecular interactions associated with induction events.

26. Explain how pattern formation occurs in a developing chick limb. Explain the roles of the apical ectodermal ridge and the zone of polarizing activity.

27. Explain how a limb bud is directed to develop into either a forelimb or hind limb.

Key Terms

preformation
epigenesis
acrosomal reaction
fast block to
  polyspermy
cortical reaction
cortical granules
fertilization envelope
slow block to
  polyspermy
zona pellucida
cleavage
blastomeres
yolk
vegetal pole
animal pole
gray crescent
morula
blastocoel
blastula

meroblastic cleavage
holoblastic cleavage
gastrulation
gastrula
ectoderm
endoderm
mesoderm
invagination
archenteron
blastopore
dorsal lip
involution
yolk plug
organogenesis
notochord
neural tube
somite
amniote
blastodisc
primitive streak

extraembryonic
  membranes
yolk sac
amnion
chorion
allantois
blastocyst
inner cell mass
trophoblast
convergent extension
cell adhesion
  molecules (CAMs)
cadherins
fate maps
pattern formation
positional information
apical ectodermal ridge
  (AER)
zone of polarizing
  activity (ZPA)

Word Roots

acro- = the tip (*acrosomal reaction*: the discharge of a sperm's acrosome when the sperm approaches an egg)

arch- = ancient, beginning (*archenteron*: the endoderm-lined cavity, formed during the gastrulation process, that develops into the digestive tract of an animal)

blast- = bud, sprout; **-pore** = a passage (*blastopore*: the opening of the archenteron in the gastrula that develops into the mouth in protostomes and the anus in deuterostomes)

blasto- = produce; **-mere** = a part (*blastomere*: small cells of an early embryo)

cortex- = shell (*cortical reaction*: a series of changes in the cortex of the egg cytoplasm during fertilization)

ecto- = outside; **-derm** = skin (*ectoderm*: the outermost of the three primary germ layers in animal embryos)

endo- = within (*endoderm*: the innermost of the three primary germ layers in animal embryos)

epi- = above; **-genesis** = origin, birth (*epigenesis*: the progressive development of form in an embryo)

extra- = beyond (*extraembryonic membrane*: four membranes that support the developing embryo in reptiles, birds, and mammals)

fertil- = fruitful (*fertilization*: the union of haploid gametes to produce a diploid zygote)

gastro- = stomach, belly (*gastrulation*: the formation of a gastrula from a blastula)

holo- = whole (*holoblastic cleavage*: a type of cleavage in which there is complete division of the egg)

in- = into; **vagin-** = a sheath (*invagination*: the infolding of cells)

involut- = wrapped up (*involution*: cells rolling over the edge of a lip into the interior)

mero- = a part (*meroblastic cleavage*: a type of cleavage in which there is incomplete division of yolk-rich egg, characteristic of avian development)

meso- = middle (*mesoderm*: the middle primary germ layer of an early embryo)

morul- = a little mulberry (*morula*: a solid ball of blastomeres formed by early cleavage)

noto- = the back; **-chord 5** a string (*notochord*: a long flexible rod that runs along the dorsal axis of the body in the future position of the vertebral column.

poly- = many (*polyspermy*: fertilization by more than one sperm)

soma- = a body (*somites*: paired blocks of mesoderm just lateral to the notochord of a vertebrate embryo)

tropho- = nourish (*trophoblast*: the outer epithelium of the blastocyst, which forms the fetal part of the placenta)

zona = a belt; **pellucid-** = transparent (*zona pellucida*: the extracellular matrix of a mammalian egg)

References

Fraser, S. E., and R. M. Harland. "The Molecular Metamorphosis of Experimental Embryology." *Cell,* January 2000.

Riddle, R. D. and C. J. Tabin. "How Limbs Develop." *Scientific American,* February 1999.

Visual Guide to the Reference Library

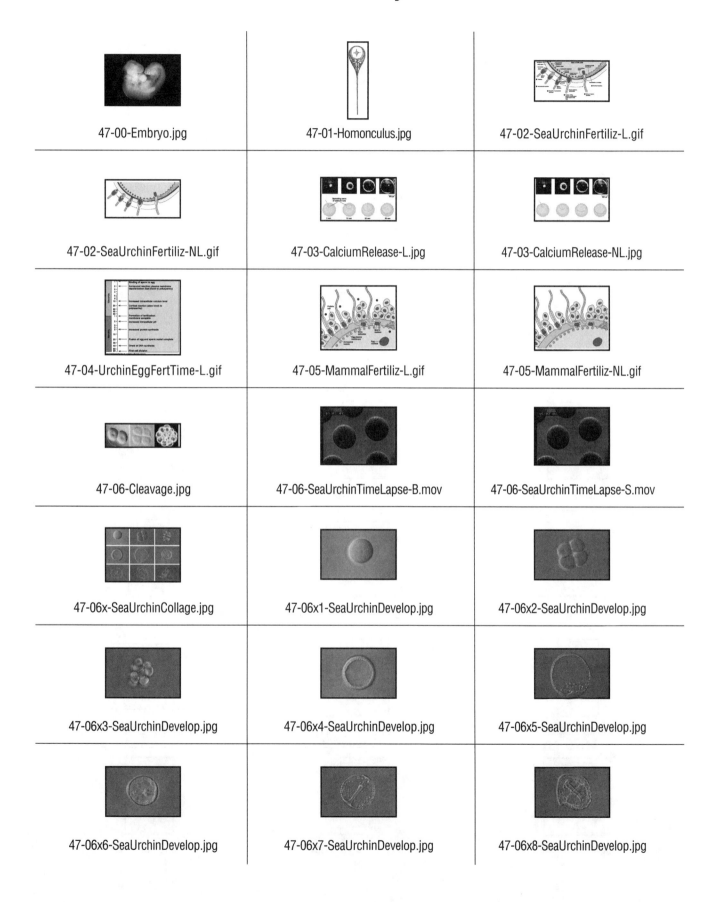

47-00-Embryo.jpg

47-01-Homonculus.jpg

47-02-SeaUrchinFertiliz-L.gif

47-02-SeaUrchinFertiliz-NL.gif

47-03-CalciumRelease-L.jpg

47-03-CalciumRelease-NL.jpg

47-04-UrchinEggFertTime-L.gif

47-05-MammalFertiliz-L.gif

47-05-MammalFertiliz-NL.gif

47-06-Cleavage.jpg

47-06-SeaUrchinTimeLapse-B.mov

47-06-SeaUrchinTimeLapse-S.mov

47-06x-SeaUrchinCollage.jpg

47-06x1-SeaUrchinDevelop.jpg

47-06x2-SeaUrchinDevelop.jpg

47-06x3-SeaUrchinDevelop.jpg

47-06x4-SeaUrchinDevelop.jpg

47-06x5-SeaUrchinDevelop.jpg

47-06x6-SeaUrchinDevelop.jpg

47-06x7-SeaUrchinDevelop.jpg

47-06x8-SeaUrchinDevelop.jpg

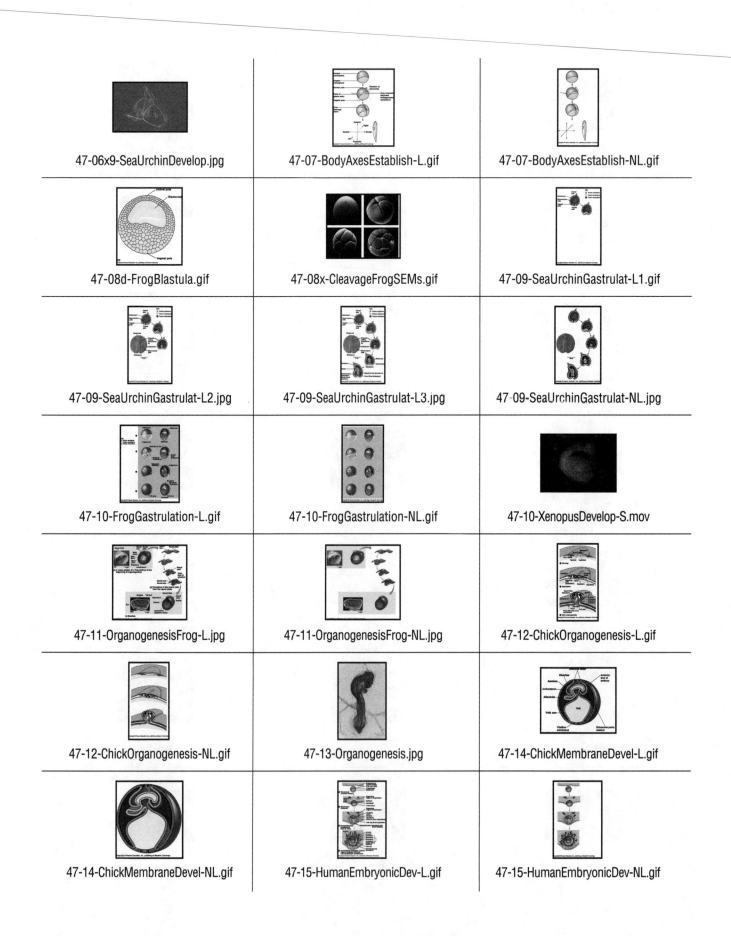

47-06x9-SeaUrchinDevelop.jpg

47-07-BodyAxesEstablish-L.gif

47-07-BodyAxesEstablish-NL.gif

47-08d-FrogBlastula.gif

47-08x-CleavageFrogSEMs.gif

47-09-SeaUrchinGastrulat-L1.gif

47-09-SeaUrchinGastrulat-L2.jpg

47-09-SeaUrchinGastrulat-L3.jpg

47-09-SeaUrchinGastrulat-NL.jpg

47-10-FrogGastrulation-L.gif

47-10-FrogGastrulation-NL.gif

47-10-XenopusDevelop-S.mov

47-11-OrganogenesisFrog-L.jpg

47-11-OrganogenesisFrog-NL.jpg

47-12-ChickOrganogenesis-L.gif

47-12-ChickOrganogenesis-NL.gif

47-13-Organogenesis.jpg

47-14-ChickMembraneDevel-L.gif

47-14-ChickMembraneDevel-NL.gif

47-15-HumanEmbryonicDev-L.gif

47-15-HumanEmbryonicDev-NL.gif

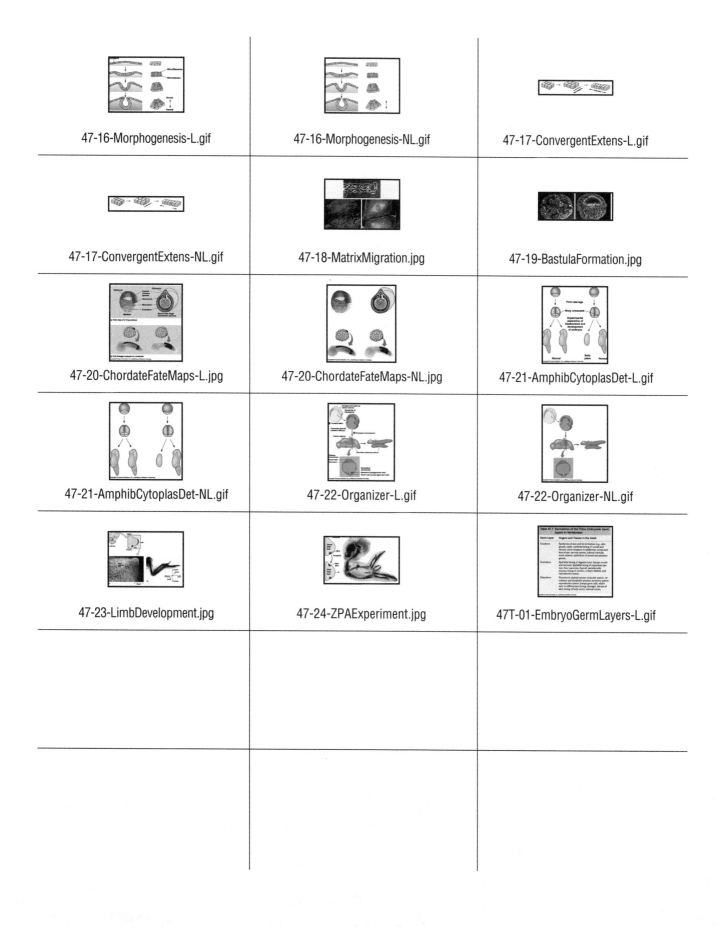

47-16-Morphogenesis-L.gif

47-16-Morphogenesis-NL.gif

47-17-ConvergentExtens-L.gif

47-17-ConvergentExtens-NL.gif

47-18-MatrixMigration.jpg

47-19-BastulaFormation.jpg

47-20-ChordateFateMaps-L.jpg

47-20-ChordateFateMaps-NL.jpg

47-21-AmphibCytoplasDet-L.gif

47-21-AmphibCytoplasDet-NL.gif

47-22-Organizer-L.gif

47-22-Organizer-NL.gif

47-23-LimbDevelopment.jpg

47-24-ZPAExperiment.jpg

47T-01-EmbryoGermLayers-L.gif

CHAPTER 48

Nervous Systems

Chapter Outline

Transparency Acetates

The Transparency Acetates for *Biology*, Sixth Edition, include the following images:

Figure 48.1	Overview of a vertebrate nervous system
Figure 48.2	Structure of a vertebrate neuron
Figure 48.3	The knee-jerk reflex
Figure 48.4	Structural diversity of neurons
Figure 48.5	Schwann cells
Figure 48.6	Measuring membrane potentials
Figure 48.7	The basis of the membrane potential
Figure 48.8	Graded potentials and the action potential in a neuron
Figure 48.9	The role of voltage-gated ion channels in the action potential (Layers 1-5)
Figure 48.10	Propagation of the action potential
Figure 48.11	Saltatory conduction
Figure 48.12	A chemical synapse
Figure 48.13	Integration of multiple synaptic inputs
Figure 48.14	Summation of postsynaptic potentials
Table 48.1	The Major Known Neurotransmitters
Figure 48.15	Diversity in nervous systems
Figure 48.16	The nervous system of a vertebrate
Figure 48.17	Functional hierarchy of the peripheral nervous system
Figure 48.18	The main roles of the parasympathetic and sympathetic nerves in regulating internal body functions
Figure 48.19	Embryonic development of the brain
Figure 48.20	The main parts of the human brain
Figure 48.21	The reticular formation
Figure 48.22b-d	Brain waves recorded by an electroencephalogram (EEG)
Figure 48.23	Activity rhythms in a nocturnal mammal
Figure 48.24	Structure and functional areas of the cerebrum
Figure 48.25	Primary motor and somatosensory areas of the human cerebral cortex
Figure 48.27	The limbic system
Figure 48.28	How do developing axons know which way to go?

Media for Instructors

Campbell Image Presentation Library

The Campbell Image Presentation Library CD-ROM set includes the following for your use:

- All art (available in pdf and jpeg or gif formats), photos (from the text and outside sources), and tables. Art images are also available without callouts. See the Visual Guide to the Image Library section at the end of this chapter for thumbnail versions of every image.
- A PowerPoint™ slide show of the art (with callouts), photos (both text and outside sources), and tables.
- The following QuickTime animations, adapted from student media activities (also available as Shockwave Flash .swf files):

  48-07-RestingPotential.mov

  48-09-ActionPotential.mov

  48-12-Synapse.mov

PowerPoint Lectures CD-ROM

The PowerPoint Lectures CD-ROM contains slides that integrate the art, photos, tables, and lecture outline from this chapter.

Campbell Biology Website (Instructor Resources)

See the insert in your copy of Campbell/Reece *Biology*, Sixth Edition, for instructions on how to access the Campbell Biology Website. The Instructor Resources section of the website includes the following:

- The art, photos, tables, PowerPoint slide shows, videos, and animations from the Campbell Image Presentation Library
- Suggested answers to the Lab Report questions from the Case Studies in the Process of Science
- The PowerPoint Lecture for this chapter
- Word files of the lecture outline for this chapter
- Photo links

Course Management Systems

The media content for this chapter is available in three course management systems: CourseCompass™, Blackboard, and WebCT. For more information, go to http://cms.aw.com. For the latest pdf instructions on how to use CourseCompass, go to www.coursecompass.com. In addition, a Syllabus Manager is offered on the Campbell Biology Website.

Media for Students

The Campbell Biology Website and CD-ROM include the following for your students:

- Objectives
- Chapter Review (Summary, Self-Quiz, and Essay Questions from the book; Word Roots; Key Terms linked to the Glossary)
- Activities (see list below)
- Case Studies in the Process of Science (see list below)
- Quizzes (Pre-test, Activities Quiz, Chapter Quiz, Essay Questions)
- Web Links
- News and References
- Art and videos from the Campbell Image Presentation Library
- The Campbell *Biology* Interviews (from all editions)
- Glossary with audio pronunciations
- Syllabus Manager

Student Media Activities and Case Studies in The Process of Science

Web/CD Activity 48A: *Neuron Structure*

Web/CD Activity 48B: *Nerve Signals: Action Potentials*

Web/CD Case Study in the Process of Science: *What Triggers Nerve Impulses?*

Web/CD Activity 48C: *Signal Transmission at a Chemical Synapse*

Objectives

An Overview of Nervous Systems

1. Compare the two coordinating systems in animals.
2. Describe the three major functions of the nervous system.
3. List and describe the major parts of a neuron and explain the function of each.
4. Define a reflex and describe the pathway of a simple reflex arc.
5. Compare the location of the cell bodies of motor neurons, interneurons, and sensory neurons. Distinguish between ganglia and nuclei.
6. Diagram and describe the three major patterns of neural circuits.
7. Describe the function and location of each type of supporting cell.

The Nature of Nerve Signals

8. Define a membrane potential and a resting potential.
9. Explain why physiologists often study the nervous systems of invertebrates.

10. Describe the factors that contribute to a membrane potential.

11. Explain why the membrane potential of a resting neuron is typically about −70 mV.

12. Explain the role of the sodium-potassium pump.

13. Distinguish between gated and ungated ion channels and between chemically-gated ion channels and voltage-gated ion channels.

14. Define a graded potential and explain how it is different from a resting potential or an action potential.

15. Describe the characteristics of an action potential. Explain the role of voltage-gated ion channels in this process.

16. Describe the two main factors that underlie the repolarizing phase of the action potential.

17. Define the refractory period.

18. Explain how the nervous system distinguishes between stronger and weaker stimuli.

19. Explain how an action potential is propagated along an axon.

20. Describe the factors that affect the speed of action potentials along an axon and describe adaptations that increase the speed of propagation.

21. Compare an electrical synapse and a chemical synapse.

22. Describe the structures of a chemical synapse and explain how they transmit an action potential from one cell to another.

23. Explain why an action potential can be transmitted in only a single direction over a neural pathway.

24. Explain how excitatory postsynaptic potentials (EPSP) and inhibitory postsynaptic potentials (IPSP) affect the postsynaptic membrane potential.

25. Define summation and distinguish between the two types. Explain how summation applies to EPSPs and IPSPs.

26. Explain the role of the axon hillock.

27. Describe the types and properties of the major neurotransmitters.

28. Describe the specific properties of the neurotransmitters acetylcholine and biogenic amines.

29. Identify and describe the functions of the four amino acids and several neuropeptides that work as neurotransmitters.

30. Describe the effects of endorphins, nitric oxide, and carbon monoxide.

The Evolution and Diversity of Nervous Systems

31. Compare and contrast the nervous systems of the following animals and explain how variations in design and complexity relate to their phylogeny, natural history, and habitat: hydra, sea star, planarian, insects, mollusks, and vertebrates.

Vertebrate Nervous Systems

32. Compare the structures and functions of the central nervous system and peripheral nervous system.

33. Distinguish between the functions of the autonomic nervous system and the somatic nervous system.

34. Describe the embryonic development of the vertebrate brain.

35. Describe the structures and functions of the following brain regions: medulla oblongata, pons, midbrain, cerebellum, thalamus, epithalamus, hypothalamus, and cerebrum.

36. Describe the specific functions of the reticular system.

37. Relate the specific regions of the cerebrum to their functions.

38. Distinguish between the functions of the left and right hemispheres of the cerebrum.

39. Describe the specific functions of the brain regions associated with language, speech, emotions, memory, and learning.

40. Distinguish between long-term depression and long-term potentiation.

41. Describe our current understanding of human consciousness.

42. Explain how research on stem cells and neural development may lead to new treatments for injuries and disease.

Key Terms

sensory receptor
sensory input
central nervous system (CNS)
motor output
effector cell
nerve
peripheral nervous system (PNS)
neuron
nerve cell
cell body
dendrite
axons
axon hillock
myelin sheath
synaptic terminals
neurotransmitter
synapse
presynaptic cell
postsynaptic cell
reflex
reflex arc
sensory neuron
motor neuron
effector cell
interneurons
ganglion (plural, ganglia)
nuclei
supporting cell
glia

astrocytes
blood-brain barrier
oligodendrocytes
Schwann cells
membrane potential
excitable cells
gated ion channel
chemically-gated ion channels
voltage-gated ion channels
hyperpolarization
depolarization
graded potential
threshold potential
action potential
refractory period
saltatory conduction
synaptic cleft
synaptic vessicles
neurotransmitter
presynaptic membrane
postsynaptic membrane
excitatory postsynaptic potential (EPSP)
inhibitory postsynaptic potential (IPSP)
summation
acetylcholine
biogenic amines
epinephrine

norepinephrine
dopamine
serotonin
gamma aminobutyric acid (GABA)
glycine
glutamate
aspartate
neuropeptides
substance P
endorphin
nerve net
cephalization
nerve cords
central canal
ventricle
cerebrospinal fluid
white matter
gray matter
cranial nerves
spinal nerve
sensory division
motor division
somatic nervous system
autonomic nervous system
sympathetic division
parasympathetic division
forebrain
midbrain

hindbrain
cerebrum
cerebral cortex
medulla oblongata
medulla
pons
reticular formation
electroencephalogram
  (EEG)
cerebellum

epithalamus
thalamus
hypothalamus
biological clock
suprachiasmatic nuclei
  (SCN)
cerebral hemispheres
basal nuclei
neocortex
corpus callosum

limbic system
short-term memory
long-term memory
long-term depression
  (LTD)
long-term potentiation
  (LTP)
growth cone

Word Roots

astro- = a star; **-cyte** = cell (*astrocytes*: glial cells that provide structural and metabolic support for neurons)

auto- = self (*autonomic nervous system*: a subdivision of the motor nervous system of vertebrates that regulates the internal environment)

bio- = life; **-genic** = producing (*biogenic amines*: neurotransmitters derived from amino acids)

cephalo- = head (*cephalization*: the clustering of sensory neurons and other nerve cells to form a small brain near the anterior end and mouth of animals with elongated, bilaterally symmetrical bodies)

dendro- = tree (*dendrite*: one of usually numerous, short, highly branched processes of a neuron that conveys nerve impulses toward the cell body)

de- = down, out (*depolarization*: an electrical state in an excitable cell whereby the inside of the cell is made less negative relative to the outside)

electro- = electricity; **-encephalo** = brain (*electroencephalogram*: a medical test that measures different patterns in the electrical activity of the brain)

endo- = within (*endorphin*: a hormone produced in the brain and anterior pituitary that inhibits pain perception)

epi- = above, over (*epithalamus*: a brain region, derived from the diencephalon, that contains several clusters of capillaries that produce cerebrospinal fluid; it is located above the thalamus.)

glia = glue (*glia*: supporting cells that are essential for the structural integrity of the nervous system and for the normal functioning of neurons)

hyper- = over, above, excessive (*hyperpolarization*: an electrical state whereby the inside of the cell is made more negative relative to the outside than at the resting membrane potential)

hypo- = below (*hypothalamus*:the ventral part of the vertebrate forebrain that functions in maintaining homeostasis, especially in coordinating the endocrine and nervous systems; it is located below the thalamus)

inter- = between (*interneurons*: an association neuron; a nerve cell within the central nervous system that forms synapses with sensory and motor neurons and integrates sensory input and motor output)

neuro- = nerve; **trans-** = across (*neurotransmitter*: a chemical messenger released from the synaptic terminal of a neuron at a chemical synapse that diffuses across the synaptic cleft and binds to and stimulates the postsynaptic cell)

oligo- = few, small (*oligodendrocytes*: glial cells that form insulating myelin sheaths around the axons of neurons in the central nervous system)

para- = near (*parasympathetic division*: one of two divisions of the autonomic nervous system)

post- = after (*postsynaptic cell*: the target cell at a synapse)

pre- = before (*presynaptic cell*: the transmitting cell at a synapse)

salta- = leap (*saltatory conduction*: rapid transmission of a nerve impulse along an axon resulting from the action potential jumping from one node of Ranvier to another, skipping the myelin-sheathed regions of membrane)

soma- = body (*somatic nervous system*: the branch of the motor division of the vertebrate peripheral nervous system composed of motor neurons that carry signals to skeletal muscles in response to external stimuli)

supra- = above, over (*suprachiasmatic nuclei*: a pair of structures in the hypothalamus of mammals that functions as a biological clock)

syn- = together (*synapse*: the locus where a neuron communicates with a postsynaptic cell in a neural pathway)

References

Damasio, A. "How the Brain Creates the Mind." *Scientific American*, May 1999.
Kempermann, G. and F. H. Gage. "New Nerve Cells for the Adult Brain." *Scientific American*, May 1999.

Visual Guide to the Image Library

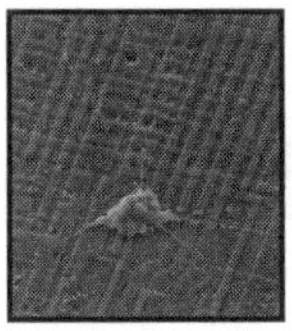

48-00-NerveCell.jpg

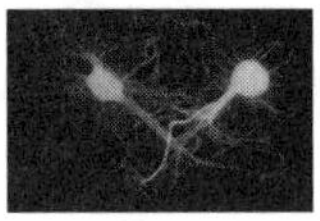

48-00x1-AplysiaNeurons.jpg

48-00x2-FrogNeuron.jpg

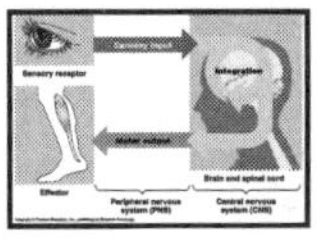

48-01-VertebNervousSys-L.gif

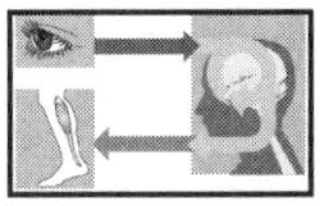

48-01-VertebNervousSys-NL.gif

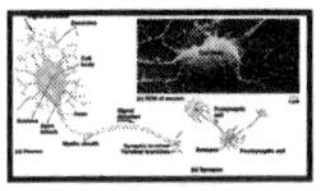

48-02-VertNeuronStruct-L.jpg

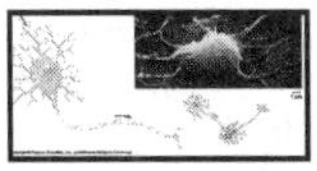

48-02-VertNeuronStruct-NL.jpg

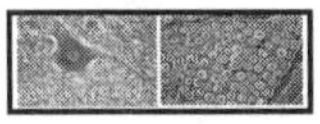

48-02x-Neurons.jpg

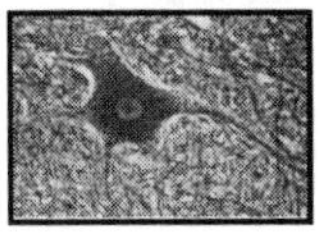

48-02x1-Neuron.jpg

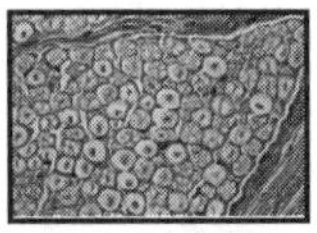

48-02x2-PeriphNerve.jpg

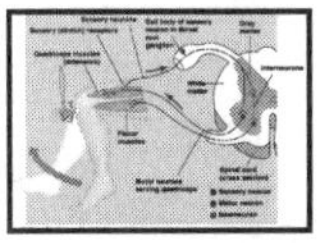

48-03-KneeJerkReflex-L.gif

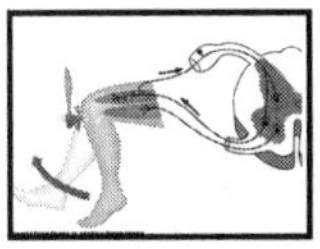

48-03-KneeJerkReflex-NL.gif

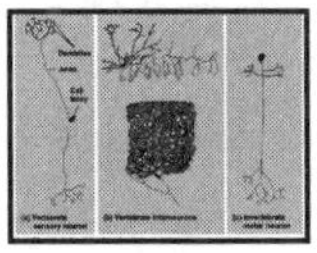

48-04-NeuronStructDiver-L.gif

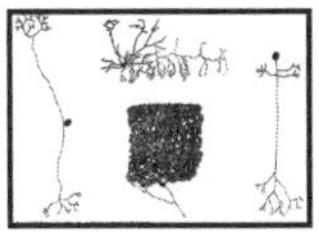

48-04-NeuronStructDiver-NL.gif

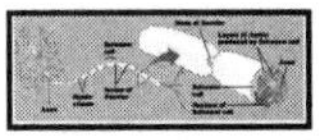

48-05-SchwannCells-L.jpg

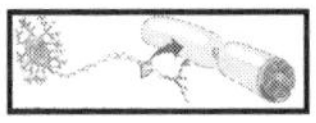

48-05-SchwannCells-NL.jpg

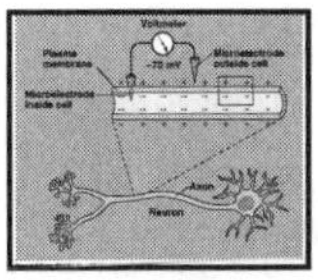

48-06a-MeasMembPotential-L.gif

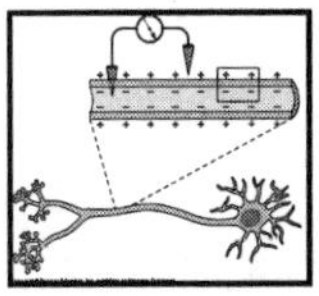

48-06a-MeasMembPotential-NL.gif

48-06b-MeasuringApparatus.jpg

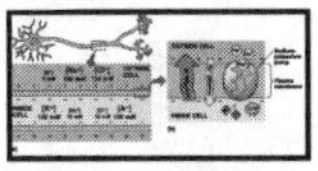

48-07-MembranePotential-L.gif

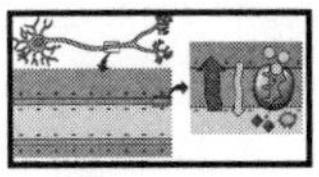

48-07-MembranePotential-NL.gif

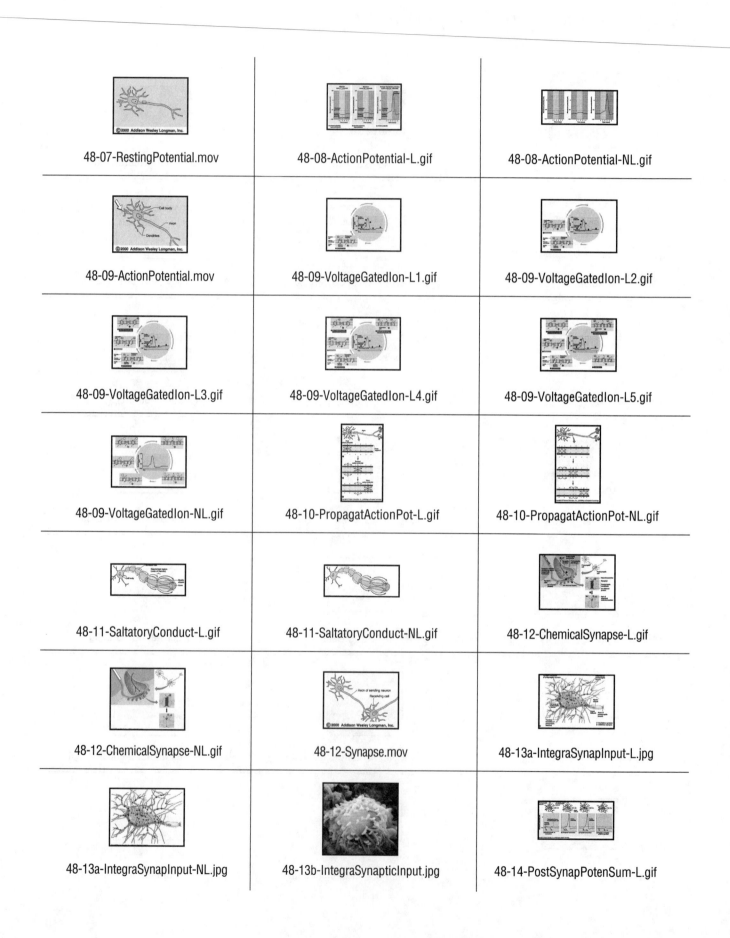

48-07-RestingPotential.mov

48-08-ActionPotential-L.gif

48-08-ActionPotential-NL.gif

48-09-ActionPotential.mov

48-09-VoltageGatedIon-L1.gif

48-09-VoltageGatedIon-L2.gif

48-09-VoltageGatedIon-L3.gif

48-09-VoltageGatedIon-L4.gif

48-09-VoltageGatedIon-L5.gif

48-09-VoltageGatedIon-NL.gif

48-10-PropagatActionPot-L.gif

48-10-PropagatActionPot-NL.gif

48-11-SaltatoryConduct-L.gif

48-11-SaltatoryConduct-NL.gif

48-12-ChemicalSynapse-L.gif

48-12-ChemicalSynapse-NL.gif

48-12-Synapse.mov

48-13a-IntegraSynapInput-L.jpg

48-13a-IntegraSynapInput-NL.jpg

48-13b-IntegraSynapticInput.jpg

48-14-PostSynapPotenSum-L.gif

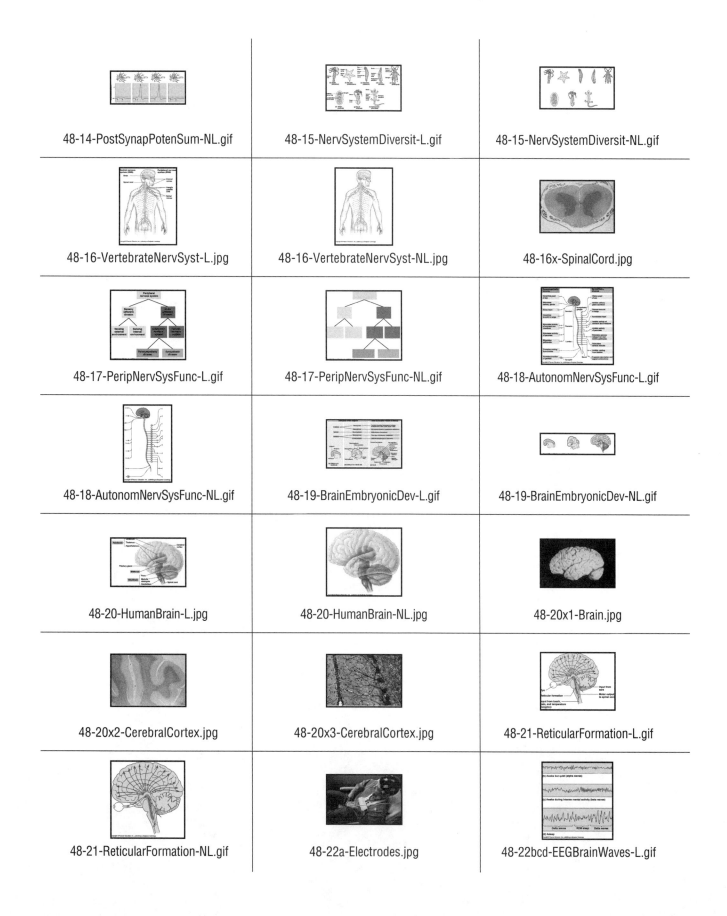

48-14-PostSynapPotenSum-NL.gif

48-15-NervSystemDiversit-L.gif

48-15-NervSystemDiversit-NL.gif

48-16-VertebrateNervSyst-L.jpg

48-16-VertebrateNervSyst-NL.jpg

48-16x-SpinalCord.jpg

48-17-PeripNervSysFunc-L.gif

48-17-PeripNervSysFunc-NL.gif

48-18-AutonomNervSysFunc-L.gif

48-18-AutonomNervSysFunc-NL.gif

48-19-BrainEmbryonicDev-L.gif

48-19-BrainEmbryonicDev-NL.gif

48-20-HumanBrain-L.jpg

48-20-HumanBrain-NL.jpg

48-20x1-Brain.jpg

48-20x2-CerebralCortex.jpg

48-20x3-CerebralCortex.jpg

48-21-ReticularFormation-L.gif

48-21-ReticularFormation-NL.gif

48-22a-Electrodes.jpg

48-22bcd-EEGBrainWaves-L.gif

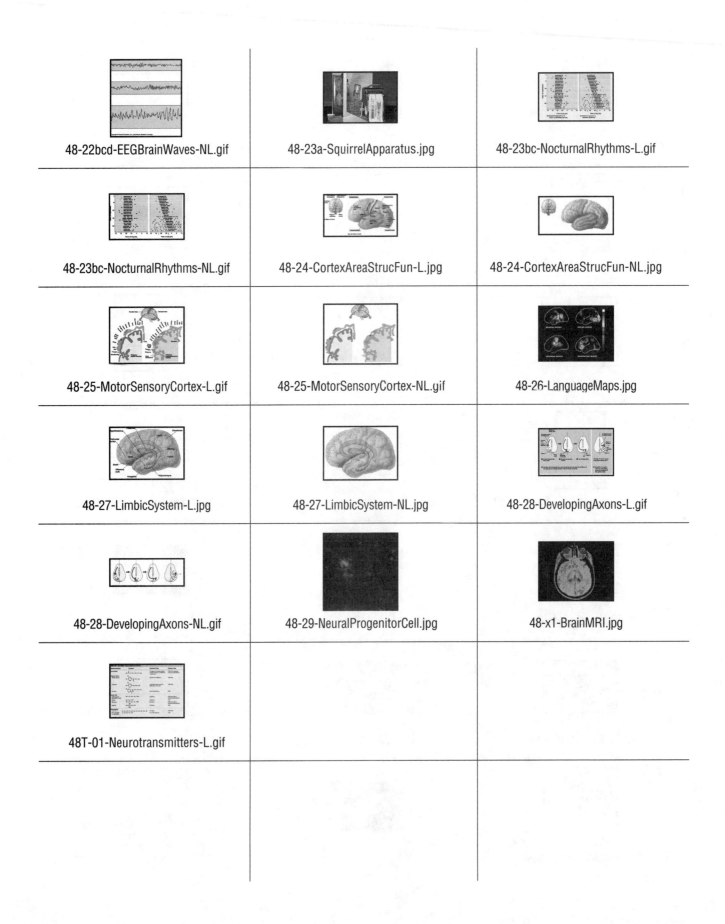

48-22bcd-EEGBrainWaves-NL.gif

48-23a-SquirrelApparatus.jpg

48-23bc-NocturnalRhythms-L.gif

48-23bc-NocturnalRhythms-NL.gif

48-24-CortexAreaStrucFun-L.jpg

48-24-CortexAreaStrucFun-NL.jpg

48-25-MotorSensoryCortex-L.gif

48-25-MotorSensoryCortex-NL.gif

48-26-LanguageMaps.jpg

48-27-LimbicSystem-L.jpg

48-27-LimbicSystem-NL.jpg

48-28-DevelopingAxons-L.gif

48-28-DevelopingAxons-NL.gif

48-29-NeuralProgenitorCell.jpg

48-x1-BrainMRI.jpg

48T-01-Neurotransmitters-L.gif

Sensory and Motor Mechanisms

Chapter Outline

Transparency Acetates

The Transparency Acetates for *Biology*, Sixth Edition, include the following images:

Figure 49.2	Sensory transduction by a taste receptor
Figure 49.3	Sensory receptors in human skin
Figure 49.4	Mechanoreception by a hair cell
Figure 49.7	Eye cups and orientation behavior of a planarian
Figure 49.8	Compound eyes
Figure 49.9	Structure of the vertebrate eye
Figure 49.10	Focusing in the mammalian eye
Figure 49.11	Photoreceptors in the vertebrate retina
Figure 49.12	Effect of light on retinal
Figure 49.13	From light reception to receptor potential: A rod cell's signal-transduction pathway
Figure 49.14	The effect of light on synapses between rod cells and bipolar cells
Figure 49.15	The vertebrate retina
Figure 49.16	Neural pathways for vision
Figure 49.17	Structure and function of the human ear
Figure 49.18	How the cochlea distinguishes pitch
Figure 49.19	Organs of balance in the inner ear
Figure 49.20	The lateral line system in a fish
Figure 49.21	The statocyst of an invertebrate
Figure 49.23	The mechanism of taste in a blowfly
Figure 49.24	Olfaction in humans
Figure 49.25	The cost of transport
Figure 49.27	Peristaltic locomotion in an earthworm
Figure 49.28a	The human skeleton
Figure 49.28b	The human skeleton
Figure 49.30	The cooperation of muscles and skeletons in movement
Figure 49.31	The structure of skeletal muscle
Figure 49.32	The sliding-filament model of muscle contraction
Figure 49.33	One hypothesis for how myosin-actin interactions generate the force for muscle contraction
Figure 49.34	Hypothetical mechanism for the control of muscle contraction
Figure 49.35	The roles of muscle fiber's sarcoplasmic reticulum and T tubules in contraction
Figure 49.36	Review of skeletal muscle contraction (Layers 1-4)
Figure 49.37	Temporal summation of muscle cell contractions
Figure 49.38	Motor units in a vertebrate muscle

Media for Instructors

Campbell Image Presentation Library

The Campbell Image Presentation Library CD-ROM set includes the following for your use:

- All art (available in pdf and jpeg or gif formats), photos (from the text and outside sources), and tables. Art images are also available without callouts. See the Visual Guide to the Image Library section at the end of this chapter for thumbnail versions of every image.

- A PowerPoint™ slide show of the art (with callouts), photos (both text and outside sources), and tables.

- The following video clips:

  See

21-04-CElegansCrawl-B.mov	Close-up video of *C. elegans* crawling
33-06b-JellySwimming-B.mov	Jellyfish swimming (large, single organism)
33-06b-ThimbleJellies-B.mov	Thimble jellies (swarm)
33-23-EarthwormLocomot-B.mov	Earthworm locomotion
33-38-EchinodermTubeFeet-B.mov	Echinoderm tube fee
34-11c-MantaRay-B.mov	Manta Ray swimming
34-26-FlappingGeese-B.mov	Flapping geese
34-26-SoaringHawk-B.mov	Soaring hawk
34-26-SwansTakeFlight-B.mov	Swans take flight
34-37a-GibbonBrachiating-B.mov	Gibbon brachiating

- The following QuickTime animations, adapted from student media activities (also available as Shockwave Flash .swf files):

  49-31-MuscleContraction.mov

PowerPoint Lectures CD-ROM

The PowerPoint Lectures CD-ROM contains slides that integrate the art, photos, tables, and lecture outline from this chapter.

Campbell Biology Website (Instructor Resources)

See the insert in your copy of Campbell/Reece *Biology*, Sixth Edition, for instructions on how to access the Campbell Biology Website. The Instructor Resources section of the website includes the following:

- The art, photos, tables, PowerPoint slide shows, videos, and animations from the Campbell Image Presentation Library

- Suggested answers to the Lab Report questions from the Case Studies in the Process of Science

- The PowerPoint Lecture for this chapter
- Word files of the lecture outline for this chapter
- Photo links

Course Management Systems

The media content for this chapter is available in three course management systems: CourseCompass™, Blackboard, and WebCT. For more information, go to http://cms.aw.com. For the latest pdf instructions on how to use CourseCompass, go to www.coursecompass.com. In addition, a Syllabus Manager is offered on the Campbell Biology Website.

Media for Students

The Campbell Biology Website and CD-ROM include the following for your students:

- Objectives
- Chapter Review (Summary, Self-Quiz, and Essay Questions from the book; Word Roots; Key Terms linked to the Glossary)
- Activities (see list below)
- Case Studies in the Process of Science (see list below)
- Quizzes (Pre-test, Activities Quiz, Chapter Quiz, Essay Questions)
- Web Links
- News and References
- Art and videos from the Campbell Image Presentation Library
- The Campbell *Biology* Interviews (from all editions)
- Glossary with audio pronunciations
- Syllabus Manager

Student Media Activities and Case Studies in The Process of Science

Web/CD Activity 49A: *Structure and Function of the Eye*

Web/CD Activity 49B: *Human Skeleton*

Web/CD Activity 49C: *Skeletal Muscle Structure*

Web/CD Activity 49D: *Muscle Contraction*

Web/CD Case Study in the Process of Science: *How Do Electrical Stimuli Affect Muscle Contraction?*

Objectives

Sensing, Acting, and Brains

1. Differentiate between sensation and perception.

Introduction to Sensory Reception

2. Explain the difference between exteroreceptors and interoreceptors.

3. Describe the four general functions of receptor cells as they convert energy stimuli into changes in membrane potentials and then transmit signals to the nervous system.

4. List and describe the energy stimulus of the five types of receptors.

Photoreceptors and Vision

5. Compare the structures of, and the processing of light by, the eye cups of *Planaria*, the compound eyes of insects, and the single-lens eyes of mollusks.

6. Using a diagram of the vertebrate eye, identify and give the function of each structure.

7. Describe the functions of the rod cells and cone cells of the vertebrate eye.

8. Explain and compare how the rods and cones of the retina transduce the stimuli into action potentials.

9. Explain how the retina assists the cerebral cortex in the processing of visual information.

Hearing and Equilibrium

10. Using a diagram of the human ear, identify and give the function of each structure.

11. Explain how the mammalian ear functions as a hearing organ.

12. Explain how the mammalian ear functions to maintain body balance and equilibrium.

13. Compare the hearing and equilibrium systems found in nonmammalian vertebrates.

14. Describe the structure and function of statocysts.

15. Explain how many insects detect sound.

Chemoreception: Taste and Smell

16. Explain how the chemoreceptors involved with taste and smell perform their functions.

Movement and Locomotion

17. List the advantages and disadvantages associated with moving through
    a. an aquatic environment
    b. a terrestrial environment
    c. air

18. Describe three functions of a skeleton.

19. Describe how hydrostatic skeletons function and explain why they are not found in large terrestrial organisms.

20. Explain how the structure of the arthropod exoskeleton provides both strength and flexibility.

21. Distinguish between an exoskeleton and an endoskeleton.
22. Explain how the skeleton combines with an antagonistic muscle arrangement to provide a mechanism for movement.
23. Explain how body proportions and posture impact physical support on land.
24. Using a diagram, identify the components of the skeletal muscle cell.
25. Explain how muscles contract.
26. Explain how muscle contraction is controlled.
27. Explain how the nervous system produces graded contractions of whole muscles.
28. Explain the adaptive advantages of slow and fast muscle fibers.
29. Distinguish among skeletal muscle, cardiac muscle, and smooth muscle.

Key Terms

sensations	lens	saccule
perception	ciliary body	semicircular canals
sensory reception	aqueous humor	lateral line system
sensory receptor	vitreous humor	statocyst
exteroreceptor	accommodation	statolith
interoreceptor	rod cell	taste buds
sensory transduction	cone cell	locomotion
receptor potential	fovea	hydrostatic skeleton
amplification	retinal	peristalsis
transmission	opsin	exoskeleton
integration	rhodopsin	chitin
sensory adaptation	bipolar cell	endoskeleton
mechanoreceptor	photopsin	skeletal muscle
muscle spindle	bipolar cell	myofibril
hair cell	ganglion cell	myofilaments
pain receptor	horizontal cell	thin filament
nociceptor	amacrine cell	thick filament
thermoreceptor	lateral inhibition	sarcomere
chemoreceptor	optic chiasm	Z lines
gustatory receptor	lateral geniculate nuclei	I band
olfactory receptor	primary visual cortex	A band
electromagnetic	outer ear	sliding-filament model
receptor	tympanic membrane	tropomyosin
photoreceptor	middle ear	troponin complex
eye cup	malleus	sarcoplasmic reticulum
compound eye	incus	T (transverse) tubules
ommatidia	stapes	tetanus
single-lens eye	oval window	motor unit
sclera	Eustachian tube	recruitment
choroid	inner ear	fast muscle fibers
conjunctiva	cochlea	slow muscle fibers
cornea	organ of Corti	myoglobin
iris	round window	cardiac muscle
pupil	pitch	intercalated discs
retina	utricle	smooth muscle

Word Roots

ama- = together (*amacrine cell*: neurons of the retina that help integrate information before it is sent to the brain)

aqua- = water (*aqueous humor*: the clear, watery aqueous humor that fills the anterior cavity of the eye)

bi- = two (*bipolar cell*: neurons that synapse with the axons of rods and cones in the retina of the eye)

chemo- = chemical (*chemoreceptor*: a receptor that transmits information about the total solute concentration in a solution or about individual kinds of molecules)

coch- = a snail (*cochlea*: the complex, coiled organ of hearing that contains the organ of Corti)

electro- = electricity (*electromagnetic receptor*: receptors of electromagnetic energy, such as visible light, electricity, and magnetism)

endo- = within (*endoskeleton*: a hard skeleton buried within the soft tissues of an animal, such as the spicules of sponges, the plates of echinoderms, and the bony skeletons of vertebrates)

exo- = outside (*exoskeleton*: a hard encasement on the surface of an animal, such as the shells of mollusks or the cuticles of arthropods, that provides protection and points of attachment for muscles)

externo- = outside (*exteroreceptor*: sensory receptors that detect stimuli outside the body, such as heat, light, pressure, and chemicals)

fovea- = a pit (*fovea*: the center of the visual field of the eye)

gusta- = taste (*gustatory receptors*: taste receptors)

hydro- = water (*hydrostatic skeleton*: a skeletal system composed of fluid held under pressure in a closed body compartment; the main skeleton of most cnidarians, flatworms, nematodes, and annelids)

inter- = between; **-cala** = insert (*intercalated discs*: specialized junctions between cardiac muscle cells which provide direct electrical coupling among cells)

interno- = inside (*interoreceptor*: sensory receptors that detect stimuli within the body, such as blood pressure and body position)

mechano- = an instrument (*mechanoreceptor*: a sensory receptor that detects physical deformations in the body's environment associated with pressure, touch, stretch, motion, and sound)

myo- = muscle; **-fibro** = fiber (*myofibril*: a fibril collectively arranged in longitudinal bundles in muscle cells; composed of thin filaments of actin and a regulatory protein and thick filaments of myosin)

noci- = harm (*nociceptor*: a class of naked dendrites in the epidermis of the skin)

olfact- = smell (*olfactory receptor*: smell receptors)

omma- = the eye (*ommatidia*: the facets of the compound eye of arthropods and some polychaete worms)

peri- = around; **-stalsis** = a constriction (*peristalsis*: rhythmic waves of contraction of smooth muscle that push food along the digestive tract)

photo- = light (*photoreceptor*: receptors of light)

rhodo- = red (*rhodopsin*: a visual pigment consisting of retinal and opsin)

sacc- = a sack (*saccule*: a chamber in the vestibule behind the oval window that participates in the sense of balance)

sarco- = flesh; **-mere** = a part (*sarcomere*: the fundamental, repeating unit of striated muscle, delimited by the Z lines)

sclero- = hard (*sclera*: a tough, white outer layer of connective tissue that forms the globe of the vertebrate eye)

semi- = half (*semicircular canals*: a three-part chamber of the inner ear that functions in maintaining equilibrium)

stato- = standing; **-lith** = a stone (*statolith*: sensory organs that contain mechanoreceptors and function in the sense of equilibrium)

tetan- = rigid, tense (*tetanus*: the maximal, sustained contraction of a skeletal muscle, caused by a very fast frequency of action potentials elicited by continual stimulation)

thermo- = heat (*thermoreceptor*: an interoreceptor stimulated by either heat or cold)

trans- = across; **-missi** = send (*transmission*: the conduction of impulses to the central nervous system)

tropo- = turn, change (*tropomyosin*: the regulatory protein that blocks the myosin binding sites on the actin molecule.)

tympan- = a drum (*tympanic membrane*: another name for the eardrum)

utric- = a leather bag (*utricle*: a chamber behind the oval window that opens into the three semicircular canals)

vitre- = glass (*vitreous humor*: the jellylike material that fills the posterior cavity of the vertebrate eye)

References

Griffin, D. R. "Return to the Magic Well: Echolocation Behavior of Bats and Response of Insect Prey" *BioScience,* July 2001.

Hickman, C. P., L. S. Roberts and A. Larson. *Integrated Principles of Zoology.* 11th ed. New York, McGraw-Hill Company, 2001.

Visual Guide to the Image Library

49-00-Bat.jpg

49-02-TasteTransduction-L.gif

49-02-TasteTransduction-NL.gif

49-03-SkinSensoryRecept-L.jpg

49-03-SkinSensoryRecept-NL.jpg

49-04-HairMechanorecept-L.gif

49-04-HairMechanorecept-NL.gif

49-05-Chemoreceptors.jpg

49-05a-FemaleBombyx.jpg

49-05b-MaleAntennaeSEM.jpg

49-06-ElectromagReceptors.jpg

49-06a-Rattlesnake.jpg

49-06b-WhaleMigration.jpg

49-06bx-BelugaPod.jpg

49-07-PlanarianOrient-L.gif

49-07-PlanarianOrient-NL.gif

49-08a-CompoundEyes.jpg

49-08b-CompoundEye-L.gif

49-08b-CompoundEye-NL.gif

49-08x1-CompoundEyeSEM.jpg

49-08x2-InsectVision.jpg

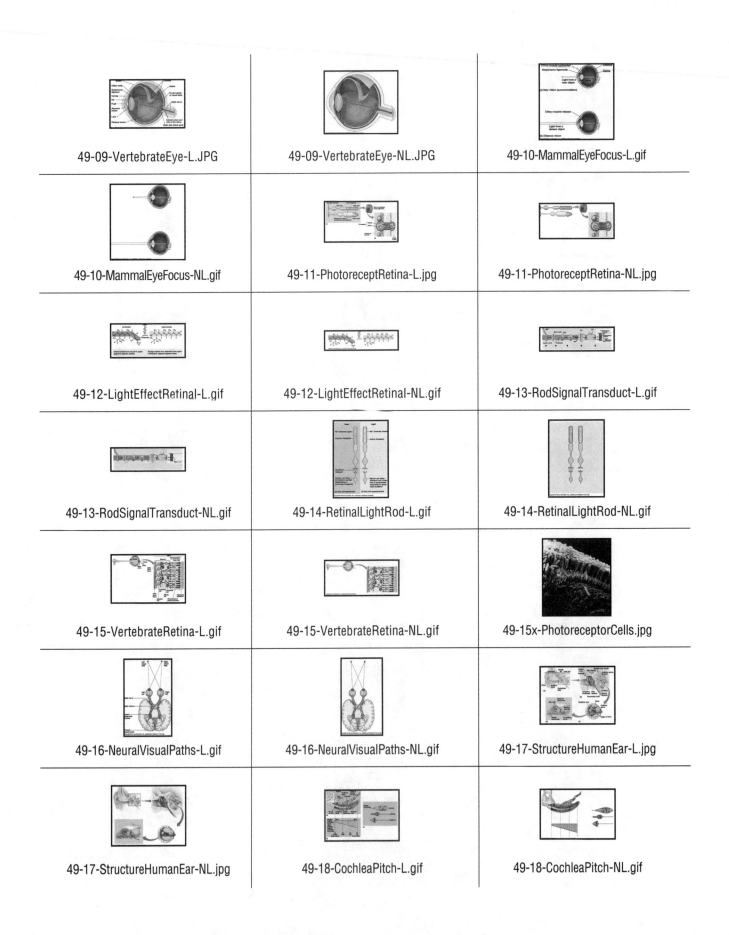

49-09-VertebrateEye-L.JPG

49-09-VertebrateEye-NL.JPG

49-10-MammalEyeFocus-L.gif

49-10-MammalEyeFocus-NL.gif

49-11-PhotoreceptRetina-L.jpg

49-11-PhotoreceptRetina-NL.jpg

49-12-LightEffectRetinal-L.gif

49-12-LightEffectRetinal-NL.gif

49-13-RodSignalTransduct-L.gif

49-13-RodSignalTransduct-NL.gif

49-14-RetinalLightRod-L.gif

49-14-RetinalLightRod-NL.gif

49-15-VertebrateRetina-L.gif

49-15-VertebrateRetina-NL.gif

49-15x-PhotoreceptorCells.jpg

49-16-NeuralVisualPaths-L.gif

49-16-NeuralVisualPaths-NL.gif

49-17-StructureHumanEar-L.jpg

49-17-StructureHumanEar-NL.jpg

49-18-CochleaPitch-L.gif

49-18-CochleaPitch-NL.gif

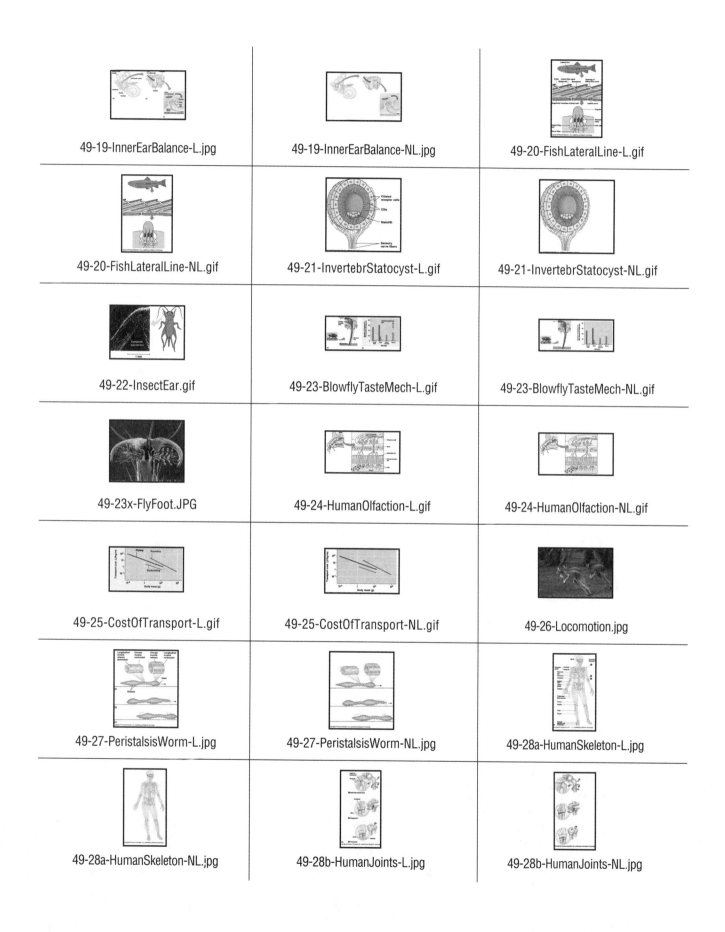

49-19-InnerEarBalance-L.jpg

49-19-InnerEarBalance-NL.jpg

49-20-FishLateralLine-L.gif

49-20-FishLateralLine-NL.gif

49-21-InvertebrStatocyst-L.gif

49-21-InvertebrStatocyst-NL.gif

49-22-InsectEar.gif

49-23-BlowflyTasteMech-L.gif

49-23-BlowflyTasteMech-NL.gif

49-23x-FlyFoot.JPG

49-24-HumanOlfaction-L.gif

49-24-HumanOlfaction-NL.gif

49-25-CostOfTransport-L.gif

49-25-CostOfTransport-NL.gif

49-26-Locomotion.jpg

49-27-PeristalsisWorm-L.jpg

49-27-PeristalsisWorm-NL.jpg

49-28a-HumanSkeleton-L.jpg

49-28a-HumanSkeleton-NL.jpg

49-28b-HumanJoints-L.jpg

49-28b-HumanJoints-NL.jpg

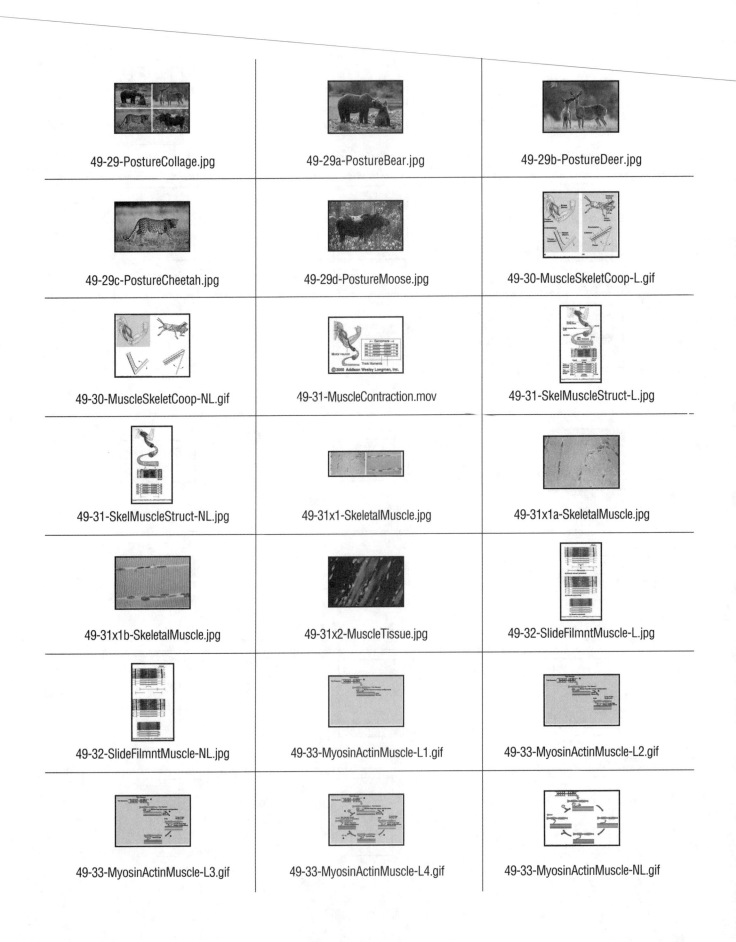

49-29-PostureCollage.jpg

49-29a-PostureBear.jpg

49-29b-PostureDeer.jpg

49-29c-PostureCheetah.jpg

49-29d-PostureMoose.jpg

49-30-MuscleSkeletCoop-L.gif

49-30-MuscleSkeletCoop-NL.gif

49-31-MuscleContraction.mov

49-31-SkelMuscleStruct-L.jpg

49-31-SkelMuscleStruct-NL.jpg

49-31x1-SkeletalMuscle.jpg

49-31x1a-SkeletalMuscle.jpg

49-31x1b-SkeletalMuscle.jpg

49-31x2-MuscleTissue.jpg

49-32-SlideFilmntMuscle-L.jpg

49-32-SlideFilmntMuscle-NL.jpg

49-33-MyosinActinMuscle-L1.gif

49-33-MyosinActinMuscle-L2.gif

49-33-MyosinActinMuscle-L3.gif

49-33-MyosinActinMuscle-L4.gif

49-33-MyosinActinMuscle-NL.gif

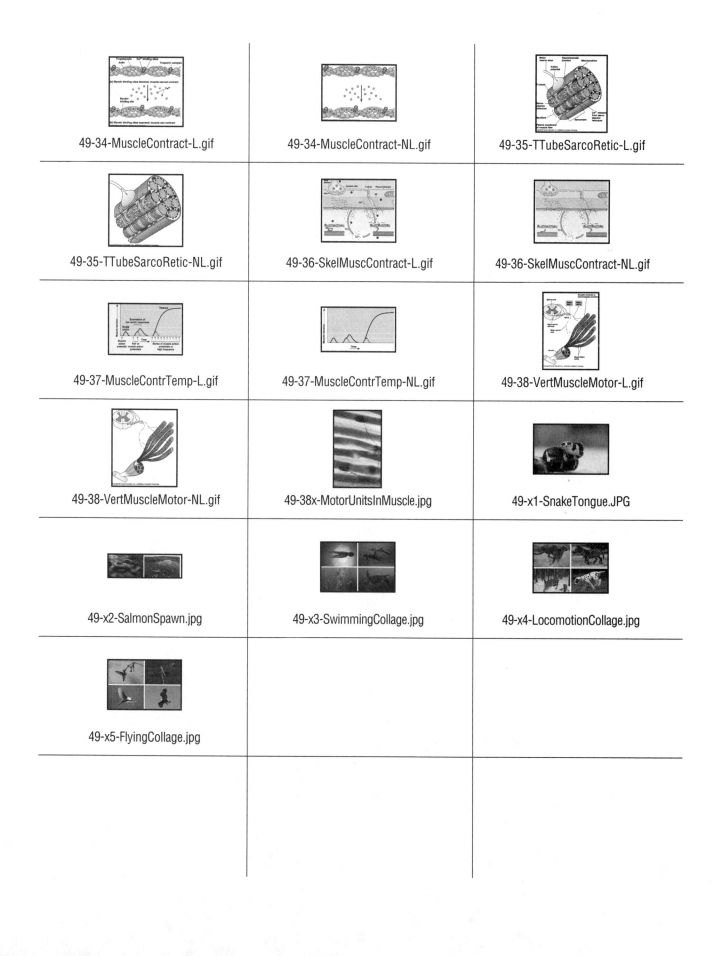

49-34-MuscleContract-L.gif

49-34-MuscleContract-NL.gif

49-35-TTubeSarcoRetic-L.gif

49-35-TTubeSarcoRetic-NL.gif

49-36-SkelMuscContract-L.gif

49-36-SkelMuscContract-NL.gif

49-37-MuscleContrTemp-L.gif

49-37-MuscleContrTemp-NL.gif

49-38-VertMuscleMotor-L.gif

49-38-VertMuscleMotor-NL.gif

49-38x-MotorUnitsInMuscle.jpg

49-x1-SnakeTongue.JPG

49-x2-SalmonSpawn.jpg

49-x3-SwimmingCollage.jpg

49-x4-LocomotionCollage.jpg

49-x5-FlyingCollage.jpg

CHAPTER 50

An Introduction to Ecology and the Biosphere

Chapter Outline

The Scope of Ecology: *the process of science*

The interactions between organisms and their environments determine the distribution and abundance of organisms

Ecology and evolutionary biology are closely related sciences

Ecological research ranges from the adaptations of individual organisms to the dynamics of the biosphere

Ecology provides a scientific context for evaluating environmental issues

Factors Affecting Distributions of Organisms

Species dispersal contributes to the distribution of organisms

Behavior and habitat selection contribute to the distribution of organisms

Biotic factors affect the distribution of organisms

Abiotic factors affect the distribution of organisms

Temperature and water are the major climatic factors determining the distribution of organisms

Aquatic and Terrestrial Biomes

Aquatic biomes occupy the largest part of the biosphere

The geographical distribution of terrestrial biomes is based mainly on regional variations in climate

The Spatial Scale of Distributions

Different factors may determine the distribution of a species on different scales

Most species have small geographical ranges

Transparency Acetates

The Transparency Acetates for *Biology,* Sixth Edition, include the following images:

Figure 50.1	Distribution and abundance of the red kangaroo in Australia, based on aerial surveys
Figure 50.4	Biogeographic realms
Figure 50.5	Flowchart of factors limiting geographic distribution
Figure 50.6	Set of transplant experiments for a hypothetical species
Figure 50.7	Spread of the African honeybee in the Americas since 1956
Figure 50.8	Expansion of the geographic range of the zebra mussel (*Dreissena polymorpha*) since near Detroit in 1988
Figure 50.9	Predator-removal experiments
Figure 50.10	A climograph for some major kinds of ecosytems (biomes) in North America
Figure 50.11	Solar radiation and latitude
Figure 50.12	What causes the seasons?
Figure 50.13	Global air circulation, precipitation, and winds
Figure 50.14	How mountains affect rainfall
Figure 50.15	Lake stratification and seasonal turnover (Layers 1-4)
Figure 50.16	Current geographic range and predicted future range for the American beach (*Fagus grandifolia*) under two climate-change scenarios
Figure 50.17	The distribution of major aquatic biomes
Figure 50.18	Zonation in a lake
Figure 50.20	Damming the Columbia River Basin
Figure 50.22	Zonation in the marine environment
Figure 50.24	The distribution of major terrestrial biomes
Figure 50.26	A hierarchy of scales for analyzing the geographic distribution of the moss *Tetraphis*
Figure 50.27	Most species have small geographic ranges

Media for Instructors

Campbell Image Presentation Library

The Campbell Image Presentation Library CD-ROM set includes the following for your use:

- All art (available in pdf and jpeg or gif formats), photos (from the text and outside sources), and tables. Art images are also available without callouts. See the Visual Guide to the Image Library section at the end of this chapter for thumbnail versions of every image.
- A PowerPoint™ slide show of the art (with callouts), photos (both text and outside sources), and tables.

- The following video clips:

50-23b-CoralReef-B.mov	Coral Reef
50-23c-Tubeworms-B.mov	Deep-sea vent communities
See also	
26-14-DeepSeaVent-B.mov	Deep-sea vent

PowerPoint Lectures CD-ROM

The PowerPoint Lectures CD-ROM contains slides that integrate the art, photos, tables, and lecture outline from this chapter.

Campbell Biology Website (Instructor Resources)

See the insert in your copy of Campbell/Reece *Biology*, Sixth Edition, for instructions on how to access the Campbell Biology Website. The Instructor Resources section of the website includes the following:

- The art, photos, tables, PowerPoint slide shows, videos, and animations from the Campbell Image Presentation Library
- Suggested answers to the Lab Report questions from the Case Studies in the Process of Science
- The PowerPoint Lecture for this chapter
- Word files of the lecture outline for this chapter
- Photo links

Course Management Systems

The media content for this chapter is available in three course management systems: CourseCompass™, Blackboard, and WebCT. For more information, go to http://cms.aw.com. For the latest pdf instructions on how to use CourseCompass, go to **www.coursecompass.com**. In addition, a Syllabus Manager is offered on the Campbell Biolog*y* Website.

Media for Students

The Campbell Biology Website and CD-ROM include the following for your students:

- Objectives
- Chapter Review (Summary, Self-Quiz, and Essay Questions from the book; Word Roots; Key Terms linked to the Glossary)
- Activities (see list below)
- Case Studies in the Process of Science (see list below)
- Quizzes (Pre-test, Activities Quiz, Chapter Quiz, Essay Questions)
- Web Links
- News and References

- Art and videos from the Campbell Image Presentation Library
- The Campbell *Biology* Interviews (from all editions)
- Glossary with audio pronunciations
- Syllabus Manager

Student Media Activities and Case Studies in The Process of Science

Web/CD Activity 50A: *Science, Technology and Society: DDT*

Web/CD Activity 50B: *Adaptations to Biotic and Abiotic Factors*

Web/CD Case Study in the Process of Science: *How Do Abiotic Factors Affect the Distribution of Organisms?*

Web/CD Activity 50C: *Aquatic Biomes*

Web/CD Activity 50D: *Terrestrial Biomes*

Objectives

The Scope of Ecology

1. Define ecology and identify the two features of organisms that ecologists try to explain. Discuss examples of experiments that examine these features.
2. Distinguish between the abiotic and biotic components of the environment.
3. Describe the relationship between ecology and evolutionary biology.
4. Distinguish among organismal ecology, population ecology, community ecology, ecosystem ecology, and landscape ecology.
5. Define the precautionary principle and illustrate its usefulness with regard to the ecological issues facing society.

Factors Affecting Distributions of Organisms

6. Describe the flowchart of inquiry used to determine what limits the geographic distribution of a particular species.
7. Describe the problem of introduced species and the specific problems posed by the introduction of African bees and zebra mussels.
8. Explain the "tens rule."
9. Explain how habitat selection can limit the range of otherwise suitable habitats.
10. Describe and illustrate biotic and abiotic factors that affect the distribution of organisms.
11. Explain how climate affects the geographic distribution of organisms.
12. Define and illustrate the concept of a microclimate.
13. Explain how the retreat of North American glaciers 16,000 years ago influenced the distribution of trees.

Aquatic and Terrestrial Biomes

14. Distinguish among the various zones found in aquatic biomes.

15. Define and compare the many types of freshwater and marine biomes.

16. Describe the characteristics of the major terrestrial biomes: tropical forest, savanna, desert, chaparral, temperate grassland, temperate forest, taiga, and tundra.

The Spatial Scale of Distributions

17. Explain why the distribution of a species is often not easily accounted for.

Key Terms

ecology	biogeography	mesotrophic
abiotic components	dispersal	wetland
biotic components	climate	estuary
ecological time	biome	intertidal zone
evolutionary time	tropics	neritic zone
organismal ecology	turnover	oceanic zone
population	microclimate	pelagic zone
population ecology	photic zone	coral reefs
community	aphotic zone	oceanic pelagic biome
community ecology	thermocline	abyssal zone
ecosystem	benthic zone	deep-sea hydrothermal
ecosystem ecology	benthos	vents
landscape ecology	detritus	canopy
landscape	littoral zone	permafrost
seascape	limnetic zone	
biosphere	profundal zone	
precautionary	oligotrophic	
principle	eutrophic	

Word Roots

a- = without; **bio-** = life (*abiotic components*: nonliving chemical and physical factors in the environment)

abyss- = deep, bottomless (*abyssal zone*: the very deep benthic communities near the bottom of the ocean; this region is characterized by continuous cold, extremely high water pressure, low nutrients, and near or total absence of light)

bentho- = the depths of the sea (*benthic zone*: the bottom surfaces of aquatic environments)

estuar- = the sea (*estuary*: the area where a freshwater stream or river merges with the ocean)

eu- = good, well; **troph-** = food, nourishment (*eutrophic*: shallow lakes with high nutrient content in the water)

geo- = the Earth (*biogeography*: the study of the past and present distribution of species)

hydro- = water; **therm-** = heat (*deep-sea hydrothermal vents*: a dark, hot, oxygen-deficient environment associated with volcanic activity; the food producers are chemoautotrophic prokaryotes)

inter- = between (*intertidal zone*: the shallow zone of the ocean where land meets water)

limn- = a lake (*limnetic zone*: the well-lit, open surface waters of a lake farther from shore)

littor- = the seashore (*littoral zone*: the shallow, well-lit waters of a lake close to shore)

oligo- = small, scant (*oligotrophic lake*: a nutrient-poor, clear, deep lake with minimum phytoplankton)

meso- = middle (*mesotrophic*: lakes with moderate amounts of nutrients and phytoplankton productivity intermediate to oligotrophic and eutrophic systems)

micro- = small (*microclimate*: very fine scale variations of climate, such as the specific climatic conditions underneath a log)

pelag- = the sea (*oceanic pelagic biome*: most of the ocean's waters far from shore, constantly mixed by ocean currents)

perman- = remaining (*permafrost*: a permanently frozen stratum below the arctic tundra)

-photo = light (*aphotic zone*: the part of the ocean beneath the photic zone, where light does not penetrate sufficiently for photosynthesis to occur)

profund- = deep (*profundal zone*: the deep aphotic region of a lake)

thermo- = heat; **-clin** = slope (*thermocline*: a narrow stratum of rapid temperature change in the ocean and in many temperate-zone lakes)

References

Enger, E. D. and B. F. Smith. *Environmental Science: A Study of Interrelationships.* 7th ed. Boston, Massachusetts, McGraw-Hill, 2000.

Herzog, H., B. Eliasson and O. Kaarstad. "Capturing Green House Gases." *Scientific American*, February 2000.

King, M. D. and D. D. Herring. "Monitoring Earth's Vital Signs." *Scientific American*, April 2000.

Visual Guide to the Image Library

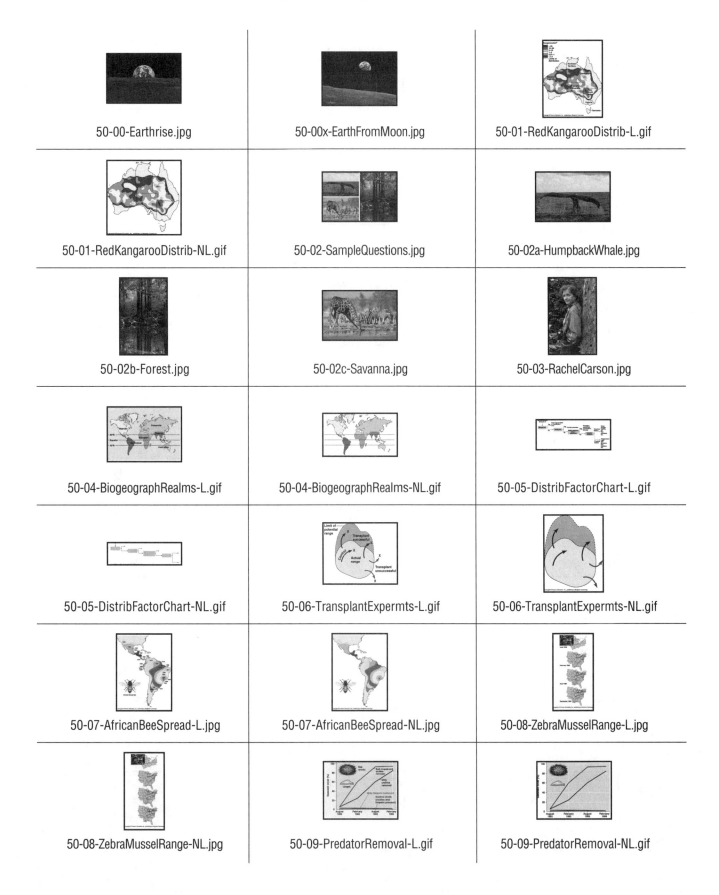

50-00-Earthrise.jpg

50-00x-EarthFromMoon.jpg

50-01-RedKangarooDistrib-L.gif

50-01-RedKangarooDistrib-NL.gif

50-02-SampleQuestions.jpg

50-02a-HumpbackWhale.jpg

50-02b-Forest.jpg

50-02c-Savanna.jpg

50-03-RachelCarson.jpg

50-04-BiogeographRealms-L.gif

50-04-BiogeographRealms-NL.gif

50-05-DistribFactorChart-L.gif

50-05-DistribFactorChart-NL.gif

50-06-TransplantExpermts-L.gif

50-06-TransplantExpermts-NL.gif

50-07-AfricanBeeSpread-L.jpg

50-07-AfricanBeeSpread-NL.jpg

50-08-ZebraMusselRange-L.jpg

50-08-ZebraMusselRange-NL.jpg

50-09-PredatorRemoval-L.gif

50-09-PredatorRemoval-NL.gif

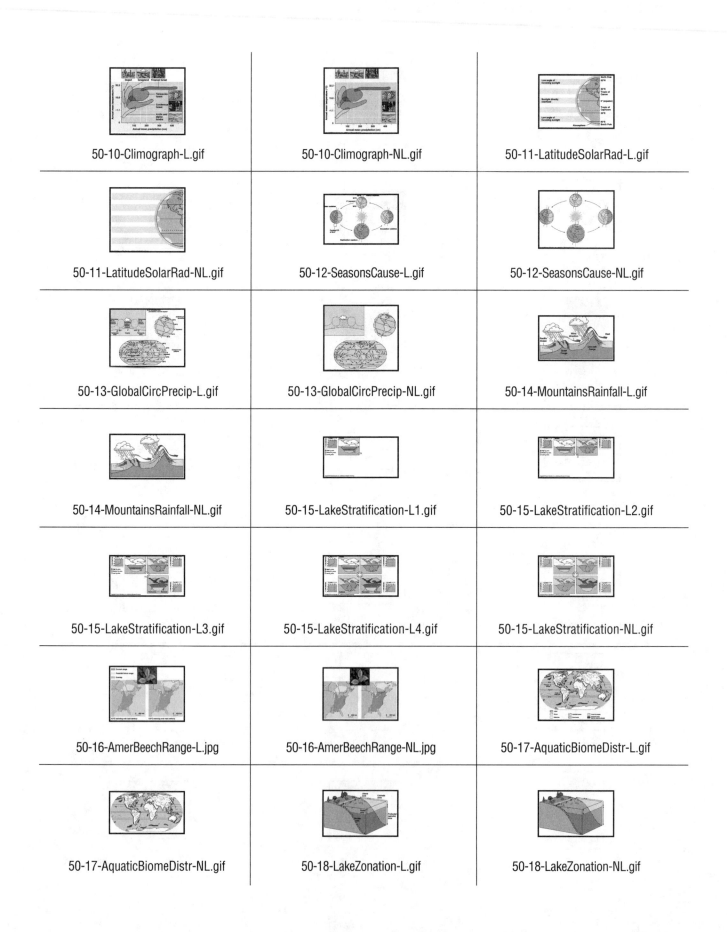

50-10-Climograph-L.gif

50-10-Climograph-NL.gif

50-11-LatitudeSolarRad-L.gif

50-11-LatitudeSolarRad-NL.gif

50-12-SeasonsCause-L.gif

50-12-SeasonsCause-NL.gif

50-13-GlobalCircPrecip-L.gif

50-13-GlobalCircPrecip-NL.gif

50-14-MountainsRainfall-L.gif

50-14-MountainsRainfall-NL.gif

50-15-LakeStratification-L1.gif

50-15-LakeStratification-L2.gif

50-15-LakeStratification-L3.gif

50-15-LakeStratification-L4.gif

50-15-LakeStratification-NL.gif

50-16-AmerBeechRange-L.jpg

50-16-AmerBeechRange-NL.jpg

50-17-AquaticBiomeDistr-L.gif

50-17-AquaticBiomeDistr-NL.gif

50-18-LakeZonation-L.gif

50-18-LakeZonation-NL.gif

50-19-Freshwater.jpg

50-19a-OligotrophicLake.jpg

50-19b-Eutrophic.jpg

50-19c-Stream.jpg

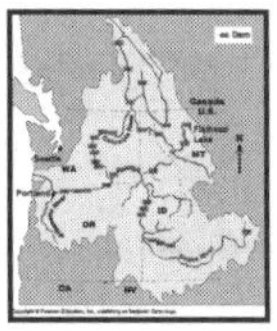

50-20-ColumbiaBasinDams-L.gif

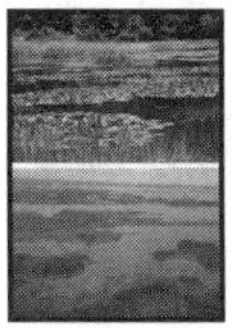

50-21-WetlandsEstuaries.jpg

50-21a-Wetlands.jpg

50-21b-Estuary.jpg

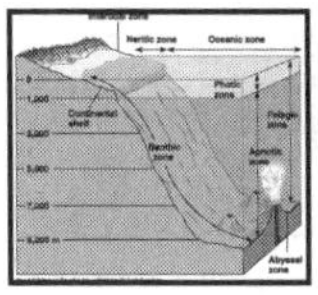

50-22-MarineZonation-L.gif

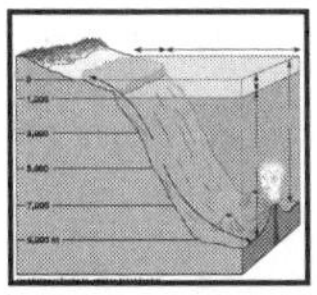

50-22-MarineZonation-NL.gif

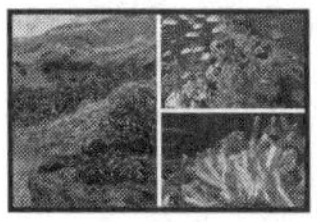

50-23-MarineBiomes.jpg

50-23a-TideZone.jpg

50-23b-CoralReef-B.mov

50-23b-CoralReef-S.mov

50-23b-CoralReef.jpg

50-23c-Benthos.jpg

50-23c-Tubeworms-B.mov

50-23c-Tubeworms-S.mov

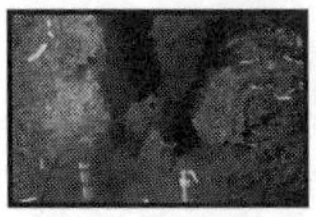

50-23x-BlackSmoker.jpg

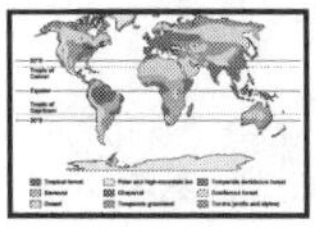

50-24-TerrestrialBiomes-L.gif

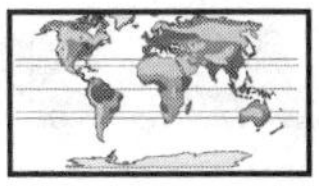

50-24-TerrestrialBiomes-NL.gif

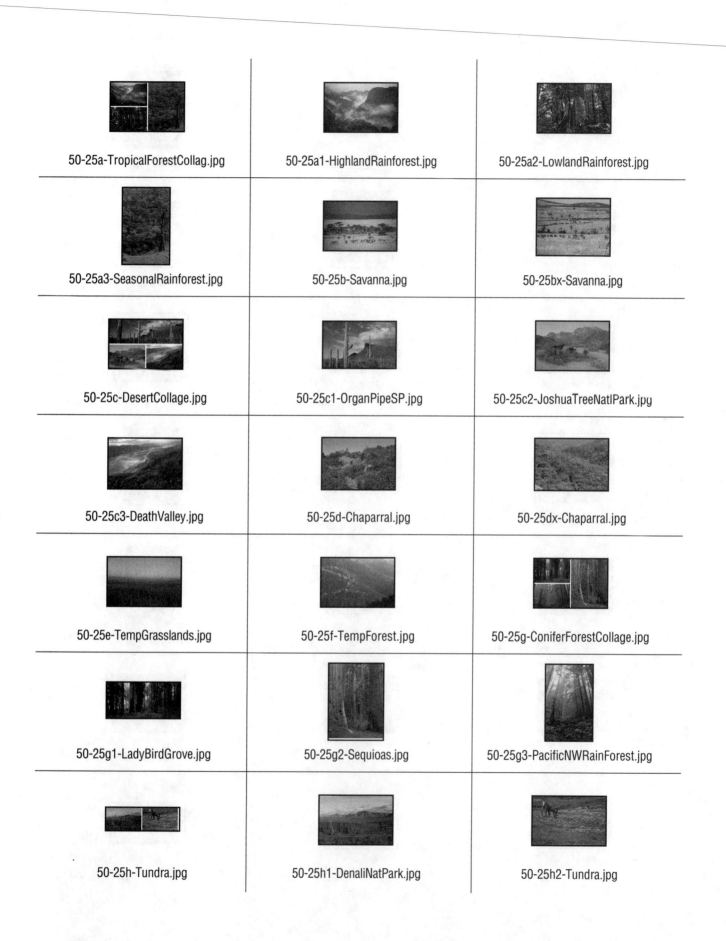

50-25a-TropicalForestCollag.jpg

50-25a1-HighlandRainforest.jpg

50-25a2-LowlandRainforest.jpg

50-25a3-SeasonalRainforest.jpg

50-25b-Savanna.jpg

50-25bx-Savanna.jpg

50-25c-DesertCollage.jpg

50-25c1-OrganPipeSP.jpg

50-25c2-JoshuaTreeNatlPark.jpg

50-25c3-DeathValley.jpg

50-25d-Chaparral.jpg

50-25dx-Chaparral.jpg

50-25e-TempGrasslands.jpg

50-25f-TempForest.jpg

50-25g-ConiferForestCollage.jpg

50-25g1-LadyBirdGrove.jpg

50-25g2-Sequioas.jpg

50-25g3-PacificNWRainForest.jpg

50-25h-Tundra.jpg

50-25h1-DenaliNatPark.jpg

50-25h2-Tundra.jpg

50-26-MossTetraphisDistr-L.gif

50-26-MossTetraphisDistr-NL.gif

50-27-SmallGeogrRange-L.jpg

50-x1-Biosphere.jpg

Behavioral Biology

Chapter Outline

Transparency Acetates

The Transparency Acetates for *Biology,* Sixth Edition, include the following images:

Figure 51.1	Genetic and environmental components of behavior: a case study
Figure 51.2	Niko Tinergen's experiments on the digger wasp's nest-locating behavior
Figure 51.3	Classic demonstration of innate behavior
Figure 51.5	The repertoire of a songbird
Figure 51.6	Female warblers prefer males with large song repertoires
Figure 51.7	Feeding by young bluegill sunfish
Figure 51.10	Two kinds of bird-song development
Figure 51.14b	Electronic surveillance of honeybees
Figure 51.15	Migration routes of the golden plover
Figure 51.16	Orientation versus navigation in juvenile and adult starlings
Figure 51.23	Courtship behavior in the three-spined stickleback
Figure 51.27	Communication in bees: one hypothesis
Figure 51.30	The coefficient of relatedness between siblings is 0.5
Figure 51.31	Kin selection and altruism in the Belding ground squirrel

Media for Instructors

Campbell Image Presentation Library

The Campbell Image Presentation Library CD-ROM set includes the following for your use:

- All art (available in pdf and jpeg or gif formats), photos (from the text and outside sources), and tables. Art images are also available without callouts. See the Visual Guide to the Image Library section at the end of this chapter for thumbnail versions of every image.
- A PowerPoint™ slide show of the art (with callouts), photos (both text and outside sources), and tables.
- The following video clips:

51-09-Ducklings-B.mov	Ducklings and their mother
51-13-ChimpCrackNut-B.mov	Chimpanzee behaviors
51-19-ChimpAgonistic-B.mov	Male chimp—aggressive display
51-19-SnakesWrestle-B.mov	Diamondback rattlesnakes
51-19-WolvesAgonistic-B.mov	Aggressive display wolves
51-23-AlbatrossCourtship-B.mov	Waved albatross
51-23-BlueFootedCourtship-B.mov	Blue-footed boobies courtship display
51-23-GiraffeCourtship-B.mov	Giraffe courtship display

PowerPoint Lectures CD-ROM

The PowerPoint Lectures CD-ROM contains slides that integrate the art, photos, tables, and lecture outline from this chapter.

Campbell Biology Website (Instructor Resources)

See the insert in your copy of Campbell/Reece *Biology*, Sixth Edition, for instructions on how to access the Campbell Biology Website. The Instructor Resources section of the website includes the following:

- The art, photos, tables, PowerPoint slide shows, videos, and animations from the Campbell Image Presentation Library
- Suggested answers to the Lab Report questions from the Case Studies in the Process of Science
- The PowerPoint Lecture for this chapter
- Word files of the lecture outline for this chapter
- Photo links

Course Management Systems

The media content for this chapter is available in three course management systems: CourseCompass™, Blackboard, and WebCT. For more information, go to http://cms.aw.com. For the latest pdf instructions on how to use CourseCompass, go to www.coursecompass.com. In addition, a Syllabus Manager is offered on the Campbell Biology Website.

Media for Students

The Campbell Biology Website and CD-ROM include the following for your students:

- Objectives
- Chapter Review (Summary, Self-Quiz, and Essay Questions from the book; Word Roots; Key Terms linked to the Glossary)
- Activities (see list below)
- Case Studies in the Process of Science (see list below)
- Quizzes (Pre-test, Activities Quiz, Chapter Quiz, Essay Questions)
- Web Links
- News and References
- Art and videos from the Campbell Image Presentation Library
- The Campbell *Biology* Interviews (from all editions)
- Glossary with audio pronunciations
- Syllabus Manager

Student Media Activities and Case Studies in The Process of Science

Web/CD Case Study in the Process of Science: *How Can Pillbug Responses to Environments Be Tested?*

Web/CD Activity 51A: *Honeybee Waggle Dance Video*

Objectives

Introduction to Behavior and Behavioral Ecology

1. Define behavior.

2. Distinguish between proximate and ultimate questions about behavior.

3. Explain how genes and the environment contribute to behavior. Explain what is unique about innate behavior.

4. Define fixed action patterns and give examples in fish and humans.

5. Explain how mayflies are threatened by an inappropriate response to an environmental stimulus.

6. Describe the evolutionary basis for behavioral ecology. Explain why these adaptations may result in suboptimal behavior.

7. Explain why it is useful to use evolutionary principles as a guide to behavioral research.

8. Explain the optimal foraging theory and illustrate it with examples.

Learning

9. Explain how learning, maturation, and habituation influence behavior.

10. Define imprinting and explain the importance of the sensitive period. Illustrate these concepts using examples from bird song.

11. Distinguish between classical conditioning and operant conditioning.

12. Define play and describe several possible adaptive advantages of this behavior.

Animal Cognition

13. Describe the ultimate bases of learning.

14. Describe and illustrate with examples kinesis, taxis, landmarks, cognitive maps, and migration.

15. Explain the problems of defining and studying consciousness.

Social Behavior and Sociobiology

16. Define sociobiology and describe the development of this field of behavior.

17. Define agonistic behavior, dominance hierarchy, and territories; give examples of each.

18. Describe the typical circumstances associated with the defense of territories.

19. Describe the advantages of courtship.

20. Explain how parental investment influences the different mating behaviors of males and females.

21. Define and distinguish between monogamous and polygamous mating relationships and between polygyny and polyandry.
22. Describe how the certainty of paternity influences the development of mating systems.
23. Describe the various modes of communication.
24. Relate an animal's mode of communication to its lifestyle.
25. Explain how honeybees communicate information about the location of sources of food.
26. Discuss why altruistic behavior might evolve.
27. Relate the coefficient of relatedness to the concept of altruism.
28. Define Hamilton's rule and the concept of kin selection.
29. Define reciprocal altruism.
30. Describe the premise of sociobiology.

Key Terms

behavior	play	promiscuous
ethology	cognition	monogamous
fixed action	cognitive ethology	polygamous
pattern(FAP)	kinesis	polygyny
sign stimulus	taxis	polyandry
behavioral ecology	landmark	signal
foraging	cognitive map	communication
optimal foraging	migration	pheromone
theory	social behavior	altruism
learning	sociobiology	inclusive fitness
maturation	agnostic behavior	coefficient of
habituation	ritual	relatedness
imprinting	reconciliation behavior	Hamilton's Rule
sensitive period	dominance hierarchy	kin selection
associative learning	territory	reciprocal altruism
classical conditioning	courtship	
operant conditioning	parental investment	

Word Roots

agon- = a contest (*agonistic behavior*: a type of behavior involving a contest of some kind that determines which competitor gains access to some resource, such as food or mates)

andro- = a man (*polyandry*: a polygamous mating system involving one female and many males)

etho- = custom, habit (*ethology*: the study of animal behavior in natural conditions)

gyno- = a woman (*polygyny*: a polygamous mating system involving one male and many females)

kine- = move (*kinesis*: a change in activity rate in response to a stimulus)

mono- = one; **-gamy** = reproduction (*monogamous*: a type of relationship in which one male mates with just one female)

poly- = many (*polygamous*: a type of relationship in which an individual of one sex mates with several of the other)

socio- = a companion (*sociobiology*: the study of social behavior based on evolutionary theory)

References

Enger, E. D. and B. F. Smith. *Environmental Science: A Study of Interrelationships.* 7th ed. Boston, Massachusetts, McGraw-Hill, 2000.

Blackmore, S. "The Power of Memes." *Scientific American*, October 2000.

Platchik, R. "The Nature of Emotions." *American Scientist*, July-August 2001.

Visual Guide to the Image Library

51-00-Warbler.jpg

51-01-BehaviorComponents-L.gif

51-01-BehaviorComponents-NL.gif

51-02-DiggerWaspBehavior-L.gif

51-02-DiggerWaspBehavior-NL.gif

51-03-InnateBehavior-L.gif

51-04-Mayflies.jpg

51-05-SongbirdRepertoire-L.gif

51-06-FemaleWarbSongPref-L.gif

51-07-SunfishFeeding-L.gif

51-08-VervetAlarm.jpg

51-09-Ducklings-B.mov

51-09-Ducklings-S.mov

51-09-LorenzAndGeese.jpg

51-09x-GeeseImprinting.jpg

51-10-BirdSongDevelopmnt-L.jpg

51-10-BirdSongDevelopmnt-NL.jpg

51-11-OperantConditioning.jpg

51-12-PlayBehavior.jpg

51-12a-CheetahsPlaying.jpg

51-12b-BearsPlaying.jpg

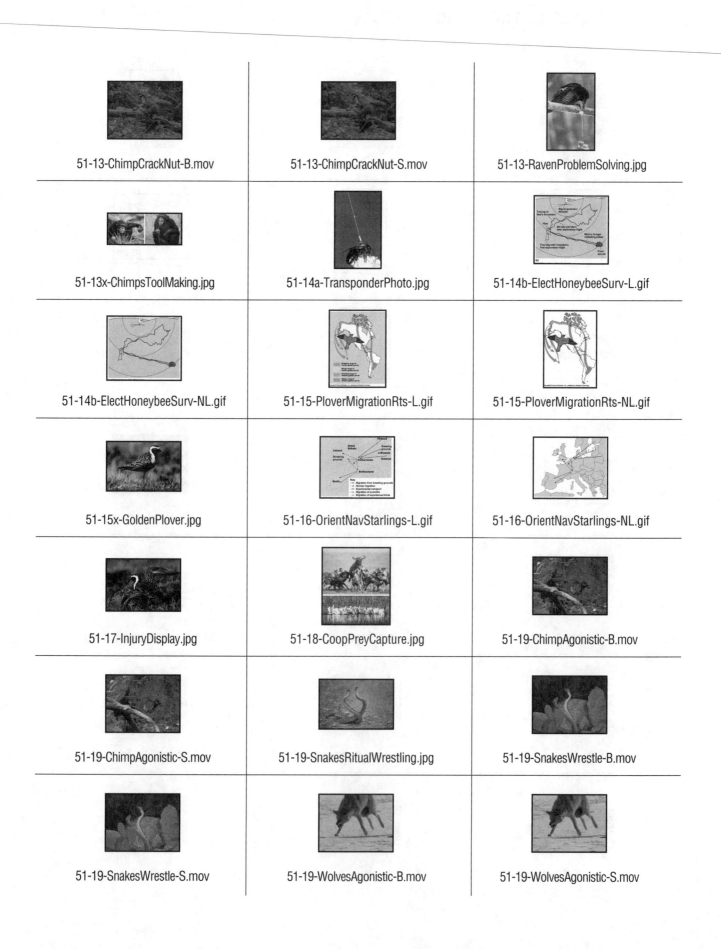

51-13-ChimpCrackNut-B.mov

51-13-ChimpCrackNut-S.mov

51-13-RavenProblemSolving.jpg

51-13x-ChimpsToolMaking.jpg

51-14a-TransponderPhoto.jpg

51-14b-ElectHoneybeeSurv-L.gif

51-14b-ElectHoneybeeSurv-NL.gif

51-15-PloverMigrationRts-L.gif

51-15-PloverMigrationRts-NL.gif

51-15x-GoldenPlover.jpg

51-16-OrientNavStarlings-L.gif

51-16-OrientNavStarlings-NL.gif

51-17-InjuryDisplay.jpg

51-18-CoopPreyCapture.jpg

51-19-ChimpAgonistic-B.mov

51-19-ChimpAgonistic-S.mov

51-19-SnakesRitualWrestling.jpg

51-19-SnakesWrestle-B.mov

51-19-SnakesWrestle-S.mov

51-19-WolvesAgonistic-B.mov

51-19-WolvesAgonistic-S.mov

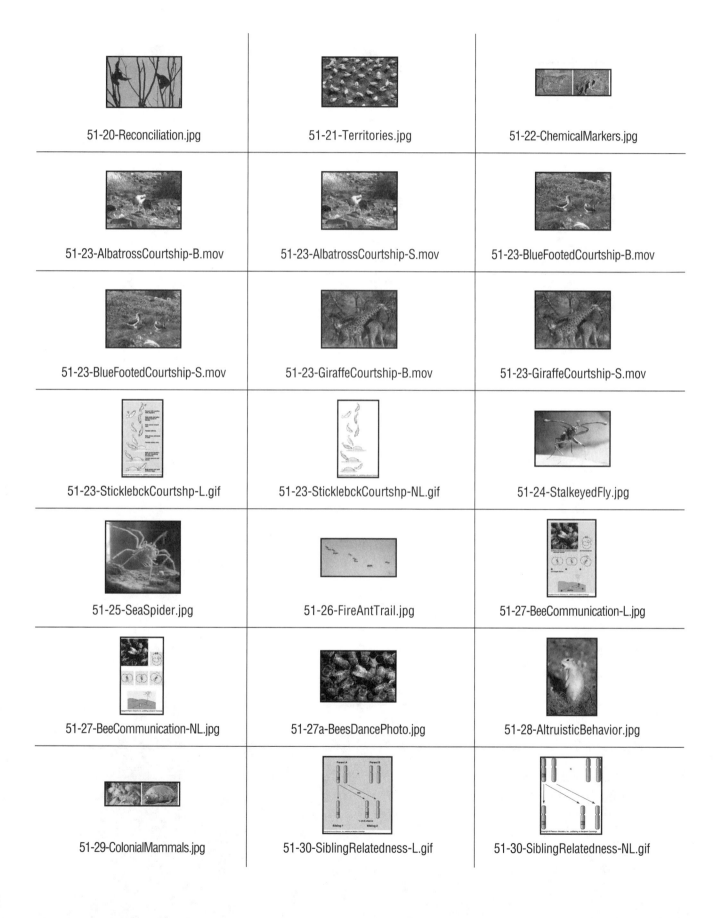

51-20-Reconciliation.jpg

51-21-Territories.jpg

51-22-ChemicalMarkers.jpg

51-23-AlbatrossCourtship-B.mov

51-23-AlbatrossCourtship-S.mov

51-23-BlueFootedCourtship-B.mov

51-23-BlueFootedCourtship-S.mov

51-23-GiraffeCourtship-B.mov

51-23-GiraffeCourtship-S.mov

51-23-SticklebckCourtshp-L.gif

51-23-SticklebckCourtshp-NL.gif

51-24-StalkeyedFly.jpg

51-25-SeaSpider.jpg

51-26-FireAntTrail.jpg

51-27-BeeCommunication-L.jpg

51-27-BeeCommunication-NL.jpg

51-27a-BeesDancePhoto.jpg

51-28-AltruisticBehavior.jpg

51-29-ColonialMammals.jpg

51-30-SiblingRelatedness-L.gif

51-30-SiblingRelatedness-NL.gif

51-31-SquirrelKinSelect-L.gif

51-31-SquirrelKinSelect-NL.gif

51-32-GenesAndCulture.jpg

51-x1-ParrotPreening.jpg

51-x2-Territoriality.jpg

CHAPTER 52

Population Ecology

Chapter Outline

Characteristics of Populations

Two important characteristics of any population are density and the spacing of individuals

Demography is the study of factors that affect the growth and decline of populations

Life Histories

Life histories are highly diverse, but they exhibit patterns in their variability

Limited resources mandate trade-offs between investments in reproduction and survival

Population Growth

The exponential model of population growth describes an idealized population in an unlimited environment

The logistic model of population growth incorporates the concept of carrying capacity

Population-Limiting Factors

Negative feedback prevents unlimited population growth

Population dynamics reflect a complex interaction of biotic and abiotic influences

Some populations have regular boom-and-bust cycles: *the process of science*

Human Population Growth

The human population has been growing almost exponentially for three centuries but cannot do so indefinitely

Estimating Earth's carrying capacity for humans is a complex problem

Transparency Acetates

The Transparency Acetates for *Biology*, Sixth Edition, include the following images:

Table 52.1	Life Table for Belding Ground Squirrels (*Spermophilus beldingi*) at Tioga Pass, in the Sierra Nevada Mountains of California
Figure 52.3	Idealized surviorship curves
Table 52.2	Reproductive Table for Belding Ground Squirrels (*Spermophilus beldingi*) at Tioga Pass, in the Sierra Nevada Mountains of California
Figure 52.5	Cost of reproduction in female red deer on the island of Rhum, in Scotland
Figure 52.6	Probability of survival over the following year for European kestrels after raising a modified brood
Figure 52.8	Population growth predicted by the exponential model
Figure 52.9	Example of exponential population growth in nature
Figure 52.10	Reduction of population growth rate with increasing population size (*N*)
Table 52.3	A Hypothetical Example of Logistic Population Growth, Where K=1,000 and r_{max} = 0.05 Per Individual Per Year
Figure 52.11	Population growth predicted by the logistic model
Figure 52.12	How well do these populations fit the logistic population growth model?
Figure 52.13	Graphic model showing how equilibrium may be determined for population density
Figure 52.14	Decreased fecundity at high population densities
Figure 52.15	Decreased survivorship at high population densities
Figure 52.16	Decline in the breeding population of the northern pintail (*Anas actua)* from 1955 to 1998
Figure 52.17	Long-term study of the moose *(Alces alces)* population of Isle Royale, Michigan
Figure 52.18	Extreme population fluctuations
Figure 52.19	Population cycles in the snowshoe hare and lynx
Figure 52.20	Human population growth
Figure 52.21	Demographic transition in Sweden and Mexico, 1750–1997
Figure 52.22	Age-structure pyramids for the human population of Kenya (growing at 2.1% per year), the United States (growing at 0.6% per year), and Italy (zero growth) for 1995
Figure 52.23	Ecological footprint in relation to available ecological capacity

Media for Instructors

Campbell Image Presentation Library

The Campbell Image Presentation Library CD-ROM set includes the following for your use:

- All art (available in pdf and jpeg or gif formats), photos (from the text and outside sources), and tables. Art images are also available without callouts. See the Visual Guide to the Image Library section at the end of this chapter for thumbnail versions of every image.

- A PowerPoint™ slide show of the art (with callouts), photos (both text and outside sources), and tables.

PowerPoint Lectures CD-ROM

The PowerPoint Lectures CD-ROM contains slides that integrate the art, photos, tables, and lecture outline from this chapter.

Campbell Biology Website (Instructor Resources)

See the insert in your copy of Campbell/Reece *Biology*, Sixth Edition, for instructions on how to access the Campbell Biology Website. The Instructor Resources section of the website includes the following:

- The art, photos, tables, PowerPoint slide shows, videos, and animations from the Campbell Image Presentation Library

- Suggested answers to the Lab Report questions from the Case Studies in the Process of Science

- The PowerPoint Lecture for this chapter

- Word files of the lecture outline for this chapter

- Photo links

Course Management Systems

The media content for this chapter is available in three course management systems: CourseCompass™, Blackboard, and WebCT. For more information, go to http://cms.aw.com. For the latest pdf instructions on how to use CourseCompass, go to www.coursecompass.com. In addition, a Syllabus Manager is offered on the Campbell Biology Website.

Media for Students

The Campbell Biology Website and CD-ROM include the following for your students:

- Objectives
- Chapter Review (Summary, Self-Quiz, and Essay Questions from the book; Word Roots; Key Terms linked to the Glossary)
- Activities (see list below)
- Case Studies in the Process of Science (see list below)
- Quizzes (Pre-test, Activities Quiz, Chapter Quiz, Essay Questions)
- Web Links
- News and References
- Art and videos from the Campbell Image Presentation Library
- The Campbell *Biology* Interviews (from all editions)
- Glossary with audio pronunciations
- Syllabus Manager

Student Media Activities and Case Studies in The Process of Science

Web/CD Activity 52A: *Techniques for Estimating Population Density and Size*

Web/CD Activity 52B: *Investigating Survivorship Curves*

Biology Labs On-Line: *PopulationEcologyLab*

Web/CD Activity 52C: *Human Population Growth*

Web/CD Activity 52D: *Analyzing Age-Structure Pyramids*

Biology Labs On-Line: *DemographyLab*

Objectives

Characteristics of Populations

1. Define the scope of population ecology.
2. Define and distinguish between density and dispersion.
3. Explain how ecologists measure the density of a species.
4. Describe conditions that may result in the clumped dispersion, uniform dispersion, and random dispersion of populations.
5. Explain how the age structure, generation time, and sex structure of a population can affect population growth.
6. Describe the characteristics of populations that exhibit Type I, Type II, and Type III survivorship curves.
7. Explain how a reproductive table is constructed and used.

Life Histories

8. Define and distinguish between semelparity and iteroparity.

9. Explain how limited resources affect life histories.

10. Give examples of the trade-off between reproduction and survival.

Population Growth

11. Compare the geometric model of population growth with the logistic model.

12. Explain how an environment's carrying capacity affects the intrinsic rate of increase of a population.

13. Distinguish between *r*-selected populations and *K*-selected populations.

14. Explain how a "stressful" environment may alter the standard *r*-selection and *K*-selection characteristics.

Population-Limiting Factors

15. Explain how density-dependent factors affect population growth.

16. Explain how density-dependent and density-independent factors may work together to control a population's growth.

17. Explain how predation can affect life history through natural selection.

18. Describe several boom-and-bust population cycles, noting possible causes and consequences of the fluctuations.

Human Population Growth

19. Describe the history of human population growth.

20. Define the demographic transition.

21. Compare the age structures of Italy, Kenya, and the United States. Describe the possible consequences for each country.

22. Describe the problems associated with estimating Earth's carrying capacity.

Key Terms

population	reproductive table	carrying capacity
density	life history	logistic population
dispersion	big-bang reproduction	growth
mark-recapture	semelparity	*K*-selection
method	repeated reproduction	*r*-selection
clumped	iteroparity	density dependent
uniform	zero population	negative feedback
random	growth (ZPG)	density independent
demography	exponential	demographic
life table	population growth	transition
cohort	intrinsic rate of	age structure
survivorship curve	increase	ecological footprint

Word Roots

co- = together (*cohort*: a group of individuals of the same age, from birth until all are dead)

demo- = people; **-graphy** = writing (*demography*: the study of statistics relating to births and deaths in populations)

itero- = to repeat (*iteroparity*: a life history in which adults produce large numbers of offspring over many years; also known as iteroparity)

semel- = once; **-parity** = to beget (*semelparity*: a life history in which adults have but a single reproductive opportunity to produce large numbers of offspring, such as the life history of the Pacific salmon; also known as "big-bang reproduction")

References

Enger, E. D. and B. F. Smith. *Environmental Science: A Study of Interrelationships.* 7th ed. Boston, Massachusetts, McGraw-Hill, 2000.

Zorpette, G. "To Save a Salmon." *Scientific American,* January 1999.

Visual Guide to the Image Library

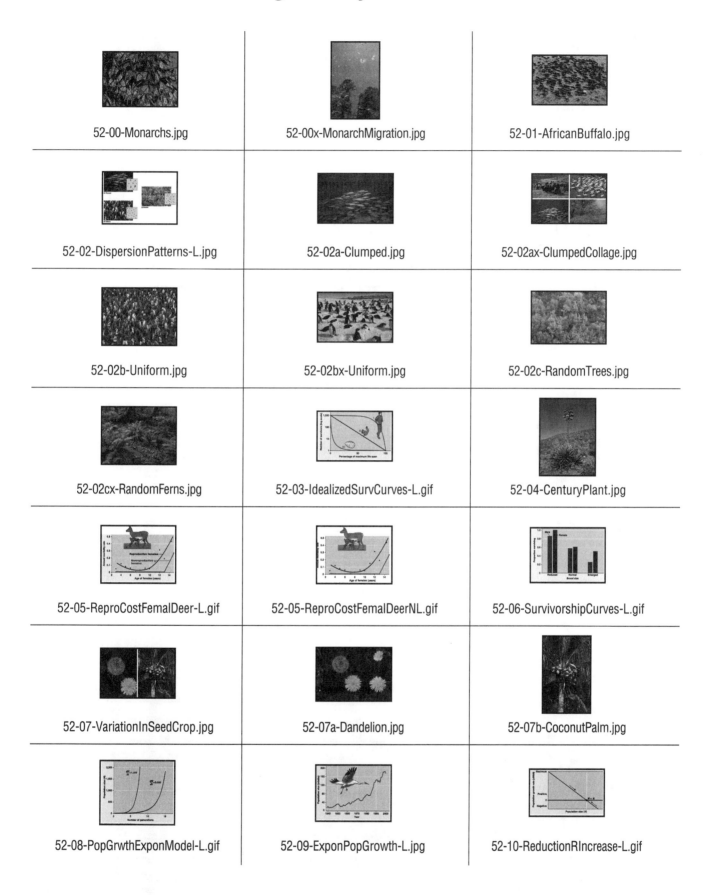

52-00-Monarchs.jpg

52-00x-MonarchMigration.jpg

52-01-AfricanBuffalo.jpg

52-02-DispersionPatterns-L.jpg

52-02a-Clumped.jpg

52-02ax-ClumpedCollage.jpg

52-02b-Uniform.jpg

52-02bx-Uniform.jpg

52-02c-RandomTrees.jpg

52-02cx-RandomFerns.jpg

52-03-IdealizedSurvCurves-L.gif

52-04-CenturyPlant.jpg

52-05-ReproCostFemalDeer-L.gif

52-05-ReproCostFemalDeerNL.gif

52-06-SurvivorshipCurves-L.gif

52-07-VariationInSeedCrop.jpg

52-07a-Dandelion.jpg

52-07b-CoconutPalm.jpg

52-08-PopGrwthExponModel-L.gif

52-09-ExponPopGrowth-L.jpg

52-10-ReductionRIncrease-L.gif

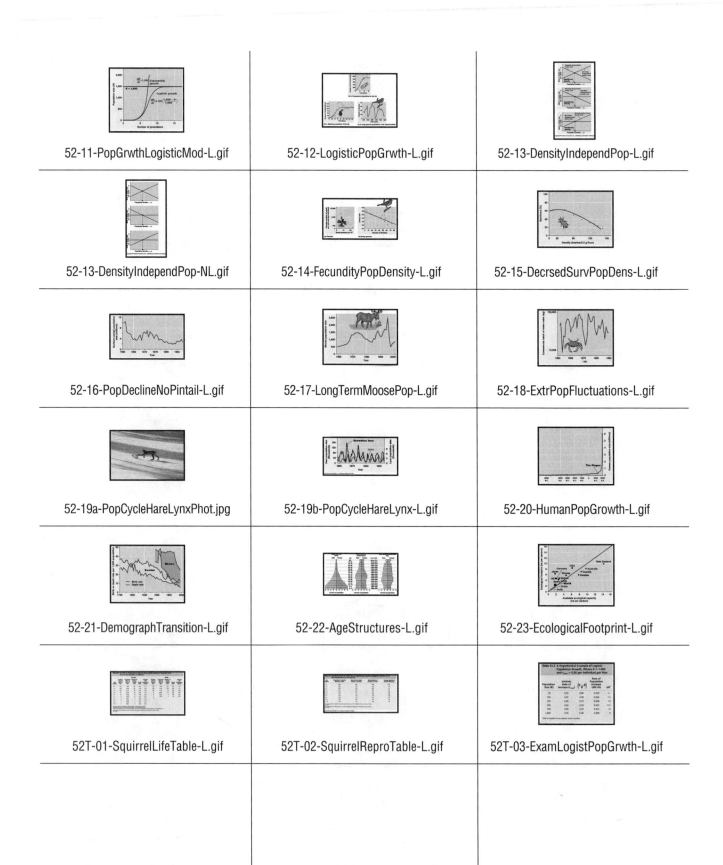

52-11-PopGrwthLogisticMod-L.gif

52-12-LogisticPopGrwth-L.gif

52-13-DensityIndependPop-L.gif

52-13-DensityIndependPop-NL.gif

52-14-FecundityPopDensity-L.gif

52-15-DecrsedSurvPopDens-L.gif

52-16-PopDeclineNoPintail-L.gif

52-17-LongTermMoosePop-L.gif

52-18-ExtrPopFluctuations-L.gif

52-19a-PopCycleHareLynxPhot.jpg

52-19b-PopCycleHareLynx-L.gif

52-20-HumanPopGrowth-L.gif

52-21-DemographTransition-L.gif

52-22-AgeStructures-L.gif

52-23-EcologicalFootprint-L.gif

52T-01-SquirrelLifeTable-L.gif

52T-02-SquirrelReproTable-L.gif

52T-03-ExamLogistPopGrwth-L.gif

Community Ecology

Chapter Outline

Transparency Acetates

The Transparency Acetates for *Biology,* Sixth Edition, include the following images:

Figure 53.1	Testing the individualistic and interactive hypotheses of communities
Table 53.1	Interspecific Interactions
Figure 53.2	Testing a competitive exclusion hypothesis in the field
Figure 53.3	Resource partitioning in a group of lizards
Figure 53.4	Character displacement: circumstantial evidence for competition in nature
Figure 53.10	Examples of terrestrial and marine food chains
Figure 53.11	An antarctic marine food web
Figure 53.12	Partial food web for the Chesapeake Bay estuary on the U.S. Atlantic coast
Figure 53.13	Test of the energetic hypothesis for the restriction on food chain length
Figure 53.14	Testing a keystone predator hypothesis
Figure 53.15	Sea otters as keystone predators in the North Pacific
Figure 53.UN1	Biomanipulation diagram
Figure 53.17	Storm disturbance to coral reef communities
Figure 53.19	A glacial retreat in southeastern Alaska
Table 53.2	The Pattern of Succession on Moraines in Glacier Bay
Figure 53.20	Change in soil nitrogen concentration during succession after glacial retreat in Glacier Bay, Alaska
Figure 53.21	Which forest is more diverse?
Figure 53.22	Relative abundance of Lepidoptera (butterflies and moths) captured in a light trap in Rothamsted, England
Figure 53.23	Geographic pattern of species richness in the land birds of North and Central America
Figure 53.24	Energy and species richness
Figure 53.25	Species-area curve for North American birds
Figure 53.26	The hypothesis of island biogeography
Figure 53.27	Number of plant species on the Galápagos Islands in relation to the area of the island

Media for Instructors

Campbell Image Presentation Library

The Campbell Image Presentation Library CD-ROM set includes the following for your use:

- All art (available in pdf and jpeg or gif formats), photos (from the text and outside sources), and tables. Art images are also available without callouts. See the Visual Guide to the Image Library section at the end of this chapter for thumbnail versions of every image.
- A PowerPoint™ slide show of the art (with callouts), photos (both text and outside sources), and tables.
- The following video clips:

  53-09-ClownfishAnemone-B.mov

  See also

01-16-SeaHorses-B.mov	Sea Horses
41-09-WhaleEatSeal-B.mov	Killer whale getting baby seal

PowerPoint Lectures CD-ROM

The PowerPoint Lectures CD-ROM contains slides that integrate the art, photos, tables, and lecture outline from this chapter.

Campbell Biology Website (Instructor Resources)

See the insert in your copy of Campbell/Reece *Biology*, Sixth Edition, for instructions on how to access the Campbell Biology Website. The Instructor Resources section of the website includes the following:

- The art, photos, tables, PowerPoint slide shows, videos, and animations from the Campbell Image Presentation Library
- Suggested answers to the Lab Report questions from the Case Studies in the Process of Science
- The PowerPoint Lecture for this chapter
- Word files of the lecture outline for this chapter
- Photo links

Course Management Systems

The media content for this chapter is available in three course management systems: CourseCompass™, Blackboard, and WebCT. For more information, go to http://cms.aw.com. For the latest pdf instructions on how to use CourseCompass, go to www.coursecompass.com. In addition, a Syllabus Manager is offered on the Campbell Biology Website.

Media for Students

The Campbell Biology Website and CD-ROM include the following for your students:

- Objectives
- Chapter Review (Summary, Self-Quiz, and Essay Questions from the book; Word Roots; Key Terms linked to the Glossary)
- Activities (see list below)
- Case Studies in the Process of Science (see list below)
- Quizzes (Pre-test, Activities Quiz, Chapter Quiz, Essay Questions)
- Web Links
- News and References
- Art and videos from the Campbell Image Presentation Library
- The Campbell *Biology* Interviews (from all editions)
- Glossary with audio pronunciations
- Syllabus Manager

Student Media Activities and Case Studies in The Process of Science

Web/CD Activity 53A: *Interspecific Interactions*

Biology Labs On-Line: *PopulationEcologyLab*

Web/CD Activity 53B: *Food Webs*

Web/CD Activity 53C: *Primary Succession*

Web/CD Case Study in the Process of Science: *How Are Impacts on Community Diversity Measured?*

Web/CD Activity 53D: *Exploring Island Biogeography*

Objectives

What Is a Community?

1. Explain the relationship between species richness and relative abundance.
2. Define and compare the individualistic hypothesis of H.A. Gleason and the interactive hypothesis of F.E. Clements with respect to communities.

Interspecific Interactions and Community Structure

3. List four possible specific interactions and explain how the relationships affect the population densities of the two species.
4. Explain how interspecific competition may affect community structure.
5. Describe the competitive exclusion principle and explain how competitive exclusion may affect community structure.

6. Define an ecological niche and restate the competitive exclusion principle using the niche concept.

7. Explain how resource partitioning can affect species diversity.

8. Define and compare predation, herbivory, and parasitism.

9. Relate some specific predatory adaptations to the properties of the prey.

10. Describe the defense mechanisms that evolved in plants to reduce predation by herbivores.

11. Explain how cryptic coloration and warning coloration aid an animal in avoiding predators.

12. Distinguish between Batesian mimicry and Müllerian mimicry.

13. Describe how predators use mimicry to obtain prey.

14. Distinguish among endoparasites, ectoparasites, and pathogens.

15. Distinguish among parasitism, mutualism, and commensalism.

16. Distinguish between a food chain and a food web. Describe the factors that transform food chains into food webs.

17. Describe two ways to simplify food webs.

18. Summarize two hypotheses that explain why food chains are relatively short.

19. Explain how dominant and keystone species exert strong control on community structure. Give several examples of each.

20. Describe and distinguish between the bottom-up and top-down models of community organization. Also describe some models that are intermediate between those two extremes.

Disturbance and Community Structure

21. Describe how disturbances affect community structure and composition. Illustrate this point with several well-studied examples.

22. Give examples of humans as widespread agents of disturbance.

23. Describe and distinguish between primary and secondary succession.

24. Describe and distinguish among facilitation, inhibition, and toleration.

25. Describe the process and pattern of succession on moraines in Glacier Bay.

Biogeographic Factors Affecting the Biodiversity of Communities

26. Describe and distinguish between species richness and relative abundance.

27. Describe the data necessary to measure biodiversity.

28. Describe and explain how species richness varies along the equatorial-polar gradient.

29. Define the species-area curve.

30. Explain how species richness on islands varies according to island size and distance from the mainland.

Key Terms

community
species richness
relative abundance
individualistic
  hypothesis
interactive hypothesis
rivet model
redundancy model
interspecific
  interactions
interspecific
  competition
competitive exclusion
  principle
ecological niche
resource partitioning
character displacement
predation
herbivory
parasitism

cryptic coloration
aposematic coloration
Batesian mimicry
Müllerian mimicry
parasite
host
endoparasites
ectoparasites
parasitoidism
mutualism
commensalism
coevolution
trophic structure
food chain
trophic level
food webs
energetic hypothesis
dynamic stability
  hypothesis
dominant species

biomass
keystone species
bottom-up model
top-down model
stability
nonequilibrium model
disturbance
ecological succession
primary succession
secondary succession
biodiversity
species richness
relative abundance
heterogeneity
species-area curve

Word Roots

crypto- = hidden, concealed (*cryptic coloration*: a type of camouflage that makes potential prey difficult to spot against its background)

ecto- = outer (*ectoparasites*: parasites that feed on the external surface of a host)

endo- = inner (*endoparasites*: parasites that live within a host)

herb- = grass; **-vora** = eat (*herbivory*: the consumption of plant material by an herbivore)

hetero- = other, different (*heterogeneity*: a measurement of biological diversity considering richness and relative abundance)

inter- = between (*interspecific competition*: competition for resources between plants, between animals, or between decomposers when resources are in short supply)

mutu- = reciprocal (*mutualism*: a symbiotic relationship in which both the host and the symbiont benefit)

References

Enger, E. D. and B. F. Smith. *Environmental Science: A Study of Interrelationships.* 7th ed. Boston, Massachusetts, McGraw-Hill, 2000.

Gibbs, W. W. "The Arctic Oil and Wildlife Refuge." *Scientific American*, May 2001.

Visual Guide to the Image Library

53-00-LionKill.jpg

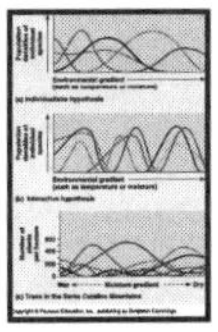

53-01-IndivInteractHypoth-L.gif

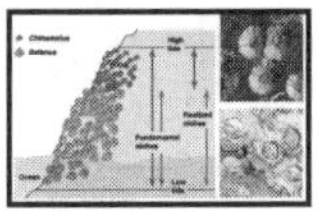

53-02-CompetExcluHypoth-L.jpg

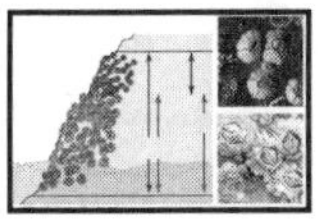

53-02-CompetExcluHypoth-NL.jpg

53-03a-ResourcePartition-L.gif

53-03a-ResourcePartition-NL.gif

53-03b-AnolisDistichus.jpg

53-03c-AnolisInsolitus.jpg

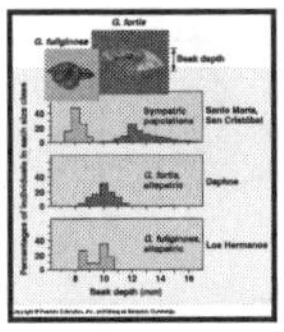

53-04-CharacDisplacement-L.gif

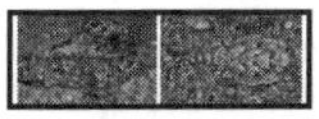

53-05-CamouflageCollage.jpg

53-05a-Poorwill.jpg

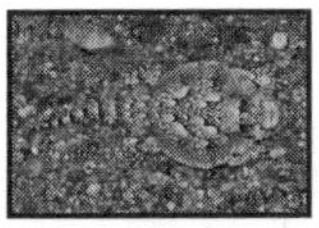

53-05b-Lizard.jpg

53-06-AposematicColoration.jpg

53-07-BatesianMimicry.jpg

53-07a-HawkmothLarva.jpg

53-07b-Snake.jpg

53-08-MllerianMimicry.jpg

53-08a-CuckooBee.jpg

53-08b-YellowJacket.jpg

53-09-ClownfishAnemone-B.mov

53-09-ClownfishAnemone-S.mov

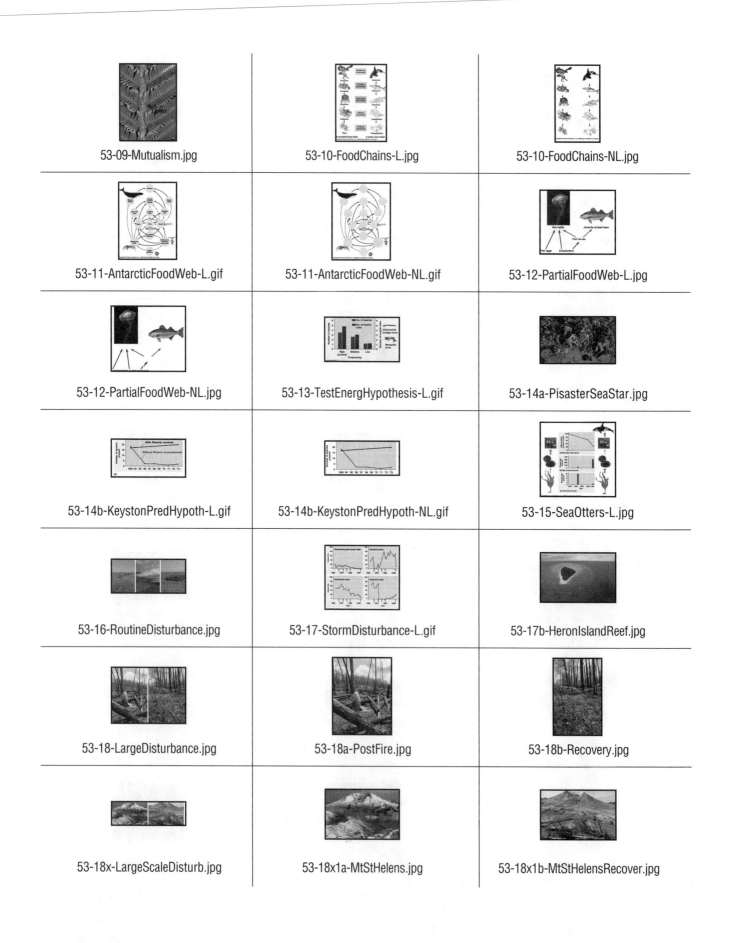

53-09-Mutualism.jpg

53-10-FoodChains-L.jpg

53-10-FoodChains-NL.jpg

53-11-AntarcticFoodWeb-L.gif

53-11-AntarcticFoodWeb-NL.gif

53-12-PartialFoodWeb-L.jpg

53-12-PartialFoodWeb-NL.jpg

53-13-TestEnergHypothesis-L.gif

53-14a-PisasterSeaStar.jpg

53-14b-KeystonPredHypoth-L.gif

53-14b-KeystonPredHypoth-NL.gif

53-15-SeaOtters-L.jpg

53-16-RoutineDisturbance.jpg

53-17-StormDisturbance-L.gif

53-17b-HeronIslandReef.jpg

53-18-LargeDisturbance.jpg

53-18a-PostFire.jpg

53-18b-Recovery.jpg

53-18x-LargeScaleDisturb.jpg

53-18x1a-MtStHelens.jpg

53-18x1b-MtStHelensRecover.jpg

53-18x2-ForestFire.jpg

53-19-GlacialRetreat-L.jpg

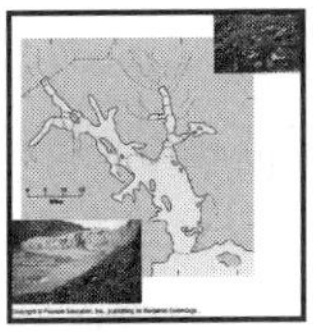

53-19-GlacialRetreat-NL.jpg

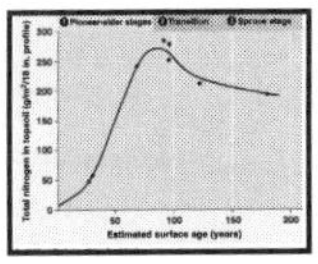

53-20-SoilNitrogenConcen-L.gif

53-20a-AldersCottonwoods.jpg

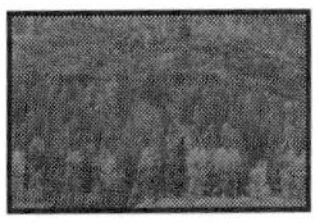

53-20b-SpruceIntoForest.jpg

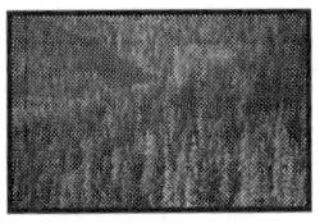

53-20c-SpruceAndHemlock.jpg

53-21-ForestDiversity-L.gif

53-21-ForestDiversity-NL.gif

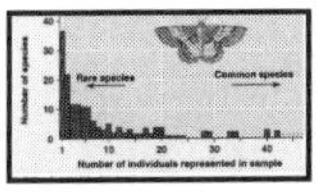

53-22-RelativeAbundance-L.jpg

53-23-SpeciesRichness-L.gif

53-23-SpeciesRichness-NL.gif

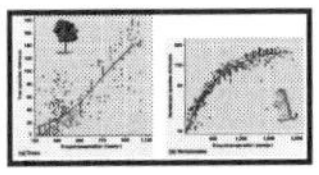

53-24-EnergySpeciesRich-L.gif

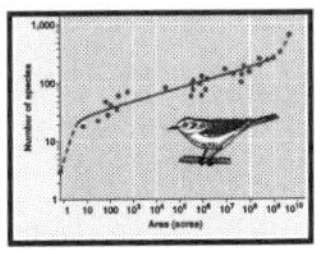

53-25-SpeciesAreaCurve-L.gif

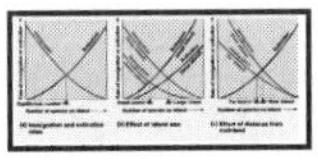

53-26-IslandBiogeography-L.gif

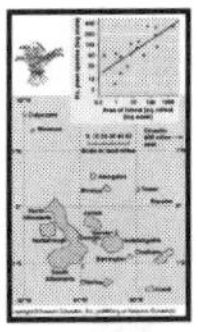

53-27-GalapagosPlantSpec-L.jpg

53-x1-DeceptiveColoration.jpg

53-x2-ParasiticNasonia.jpg

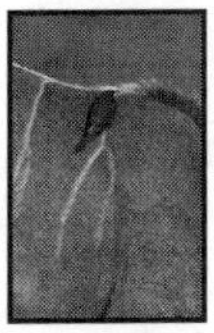

53-x3-Commensalism.jpg

53-x4-SmallScaleDisturbance.jpg

53-x5-DistinctBoundary.jpg

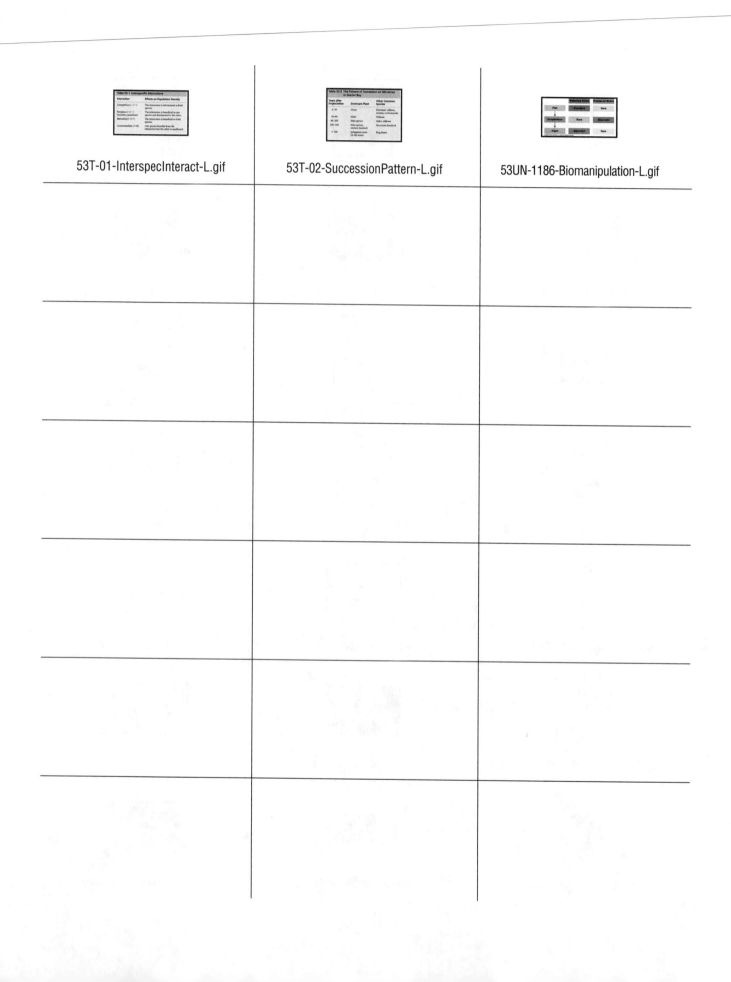

53T-01-InterspecInteract-L.gif

53T-02-SuccessionPattern-L.gif

53UN-1186-Biomanipulation-L.gif

Ecosystems

Chapter Outline

Transparency Acetates

The Transparency Acetates for *Biology*, Sixth Edition, include the following images:

Figure 54.1   An overview of ecosystem dynamics

Figure 54.3   Primary production of different ecosystems

Figure 54.5   Vertical distribution of temperature, nutrients, and production in the upper layer of the central North Pacific during summer

Figure 54.6   Experiments on nutrient limitations to phytoplankton production in coastal waters of Long Island

Table 54.1   Nutrient Enrichment Experiments for Sargasso Sea Samples

Figure 54.9   Nutrient addition experiments in a Hudson Bay salt marsh

Figure 54.10 Energy partitioning within a link of the food chain

Figure 54.11 An idealized pyramid of net production

Figure 54.12 Pyramids of biomass (standing crop)

Figure 54.13 A pyramid of numbers

Figure 54.14 Food energy available to the human population at different trophic levels

Figure 54.15 A general model of nutrient cycling

Figure 54.16 The water cycle

Figure 54.17 The carbon cycle

Figure 54.18 The nitrogen cycle

Figure 54.19 The phosphorous cycle

Figure 54.20 Review: Generalized scheme for biogeochemical cycles

Figure 54.21 Nutrient cycling in the Hubbard Brook Experimental Forest: an example of long-term ecological research

Figure 54.23 Distribution of acid precipitation in North America and Europe

Figure 54.24 We've changed our tune

Figure 54.25 Biological magnification of DDT in a food chain

Figure 54.26 The increase in atmospheric carbon dioxide and average temperatures from 1958 to 2000

Figure 54.27 Erosion of Earth's ozone shield

Media for Instructors

Campbell Image Presentation Library

The Campbell Image Presentation Library CD-ROM set includes the following for your use:

- All art (available in pdf and jpeg or gif formats), photos (from the text and outside sources), and tables. Art images are also available without callouts. See the Visual Guide to the Image Library section at the end of this chapter for thumbnail versions of every image.

- A PowerPoint™ slide show of the art (with callouts), photos (both text and outside sources), and tables.

PowerPoint Lectures CD-ROM

The PowerPoint Lectures CD-ROM contains slides that integrate the art, photos, tables, and lecture outline from this chapter.

Campbell Biology Website (Instructor Resources)

See the insert in your copy of Campbell/Reece *Biology*, Sixth Edition, for instructions on how to access the Campbell Biology Website. The Instructor Resources section of the website includes the following:

- The art, photos, tables, PowerPoint slide shows, videos, and animations from the Campbell Image Presentation Library
- Suggested answers to the Lab Report questions from the Case Studies in the Process of Science
- The PowerPoint Lecture for this chapter
- Word files of the lecture outline for this chapter
- Photo links

Course Management Systems

The media content for this chapter is available in three course management systems: CourseCompass™, Blackboard, and WebCT. For more information, go to http://cms.aw.com. For the latest pdf instructions on how to use CourseCompass, go to **www.coursecompass.com**. In addition, a Syllabus Manager is offered on the Campbell Biolog*y* Website.

Media for Students

The Campbell Biology Website and CD-ROM include the following for your students:

- Objectives
- Chapter Review (Summary, Self-Quiz, and Essay Questions from the book; Word Roots; Key Terms linked to the Glossary)
- Activities (see list below)
- Case Studies in the Process of Science (see list below)
- Quizzes (Pre-test, Activities Quiz, Chapter Quiz, Essay Questions)
- Web Links
- News and References
- Art and videos from the Campbell Image Presentation Library
- The Campbell *Biology* Interviews (from all editions)
- Glossary with audio pronunciations
- Syllabus Manager

Student Media Activities and Case Studies in The Process of Science

Web/CD Case Study in the Process of Science: *How Do Temperature and Light Affect Primary Production*

Web/CD Activity 54A: *Pyramids of Production*

Web/CD Activity 54B: *Energy Flow and Chemical Cycling*

Web/CD Activity 54C: *The Carbon Cycle*

Web/CD Activity 54D: *The Nitrogen Cycle*

Web/CD Activity 54E: *Water Pollution from Nitrates*

Web/CD Activity 54F: *The Greenhouse Effect*

Objectives

The Ecosystem Approach to Ecology

1. Describe the relationship between autotrophs and heterotrophs in an ecosystem.

2. Explain how decomposition connects all trophic levels in an ecosystem.

3. Explain how the first and second laws of thermodynamics apply to ecosystems.

Primary Production in Ecosystems

4. Explain why the amount of energy used in photosynthesis is so much less than the amount of solar energy that reaches Earth.

5. Define and compare gross primary production and net primary production.

6. Define and compare biomass and standing crop.

7. Compare primary productivity in marine, freshwater, and terrestrial ecosystems.

Secondary Production in Ecosystems

8. Explain why energy is said to flow rather than cycle within ecosystems. Use the example of insect caterpillars to illustrate energy flow.

9. Define, compare, and illustrate the concepts of production efficiency and trophic efficiency.

10. Distinguish between energy pyramids and biomass pyramids. Explain why both relationships are in the form of pyramids. Explain the special circumstances of inverted biomass pyramids.

11. Explain why food pyramids usually have only four or five trophic levels.

12. Define the pyramid of numbers.

13. Explain why worldwide agriculture could feed more people if all humans consumed only plant material.

14. Explain the green-world hypothesis. Describe six factors that keep herbivores in check.

The Cycling of Chemical Elements in Ecosystems

15. Describe the four nutrient reservoirs and the processes that transfer the elements between reservoirs.

16. Explain why it is difficult to trace elements through biogeochemical cycles.

17. Describe the hydrologic water cycle.

18. Describe the nitrogen cycle and explain the importance of nitrogen fixation to all living organisms.

19. Describe the phosphorus cycle and explain how phosphorus is recycled locally in most ecosystems.

20. Explain how decomposition affects the rate of nutrient cycling in ecosystems.

21. Describe the experiments at Hubbard Brook that revealed the key role that plants play in regulating nutrient cycles.

Human Impact on Ecosystems and the Biosphere

22. Describe how agricultural practices can interfere with nitrogen cycling.

23. Explain how "cultural eutrophication" can alter freshwater ecosystems.

24. Describe the causes and consequences of acid precipitation.

25. Explain why toxic compounds usually have the greatest effect on top-level carnivores.

26. Describe how increased atmospheric concentrations of carbon dioxide could affect Earth.

27. Describe how human interference might alter the biosphere.

Key Terms

trophic level
primary producers
heterotrophs
primary consumers
secondary consumers
tertiary consumers
detritivores
decomposers
detritus
primary production
gross primary
  production (GPP)
net primary
  production (NPP)

biomass
standing crop
limiting nutrient
eutrophication
secondary production
production efficiency
trophic efficiency
pyramid of production
biomass pyramid
turnover time
pyramid of numbers
green world hypothesis
biogeochemical cycles
nitrogen fixation

nitrification
denitrification
ammonification
long-term ecological
  research (LTER)
critical load
cultural eutrophication
acid precipitation
biological magnification
greenhouse effect

Word Roots

auto- = self; **troph-** = food, nourishment (*autotroph*: an organism that obtains organic food molecules without eating other organisms)

bio- = life; **geo-** = the Earth (*biogeochemical cycles*: the various nutrient circuits which involve both biotic and abiotic components of ecosystems)

de- = from, down, out (*denitrification*: the process of converting nitrate back to nitrogen)

detrit- = wear off; **-vora** = eat (*detritivore*: a consumer that derives its energy from nonliving organic material)

hetero- = other, different (*heterotroph*: an organism that obtains organic food molecules by eating other organisms or their by-products)

References

Enger, E. D. and B. F. Smith. *Environmental Science: A Study of Interrelationships.* 7th ed. Boston, Massachusetts, McGraw-Hill, 2000.

Karl, T. R. and K. E. Trenberth. "The Human Impact on Climate." *Scientific American,* December 1999.

Visual Guide to the Image Library

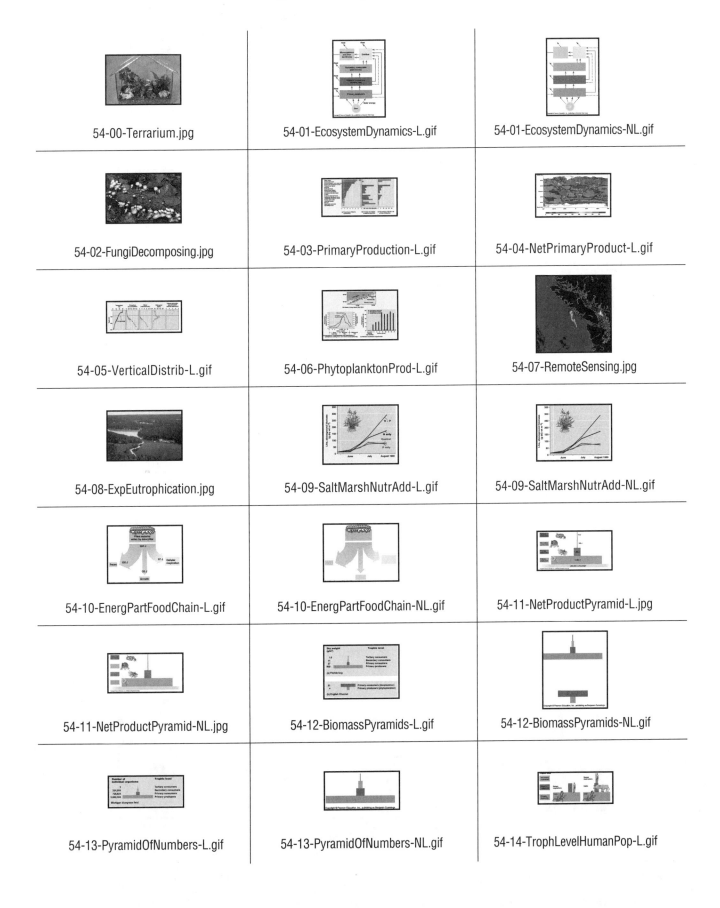

54-00-Terrarium.jpg

54-01-EcosystemDynamics-L.gif

54-01-EcosystemDynamics-NL.gif

54-02-FungiDecomposing.jpg

54-03-PrimaryProduction-L.gif

54-04-NetPrimaryProduct-L.gif

54-05-VerticalDistrib-L.gif

54-06-PhytoplanktonProd-L.gif

54-07-RemoteSensing.jpg

54-08-ExpEutrophication.jpg

54-09-SaltMarshNutrAdd-L.gif

54-09-SaltMarshNutrAdd-NL.gif

54-10-EnergPartFoodChain-L.gif

54-10-EnergPartFoodChain-NL.gif

54-11-NetProductPyramid-L.jpg

54-11-NetProductPyramid-NL.jpg

54-12-BiomassPyramids-L.gif

54-12-BiomassPyramids-NL.gif

54-13-PyramidOfNumbers-L.gif

54-13-PyramidOfNumbers-NL.gif

54-14-TrophLevelHumanPop-L.gif

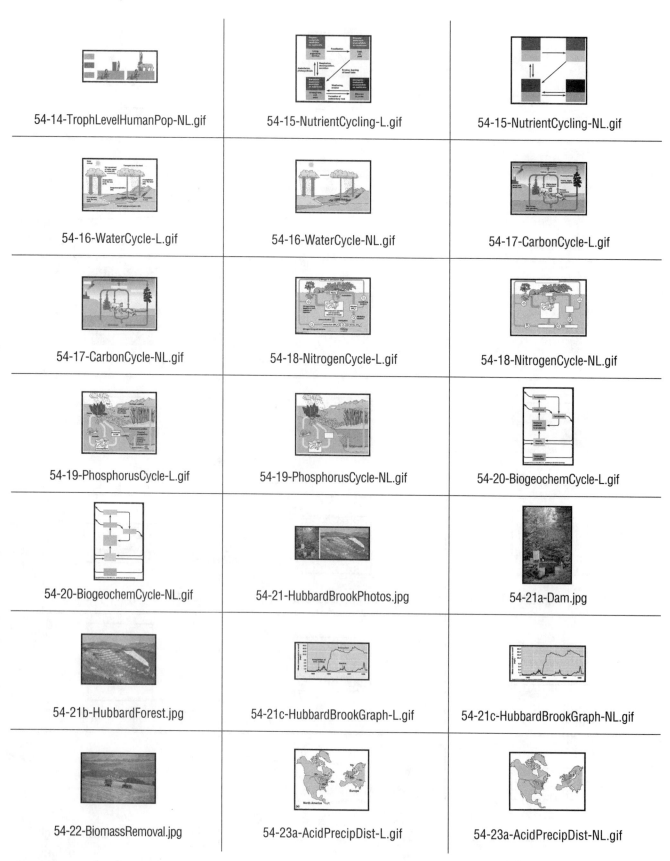

54-14-TrophLevelHumanPop-NL.gif

54-15-NutrientCycling-L.gif

54-15-NutrientCycling-NL.gif

54-16-WaterCycle-L.gif

54-16-WaterCycle-NL.gif

54-17-CarbonCycle-L.gif

54-17-CarbonCycle-NL.gif

54-18-NitrogenCycle-L.gif

54-18-NitrogenCycle-NL.gif

54-19-PhosphorusCycle-L.gif

54-19-PhosphorusCycle-NL.gif

54-20-BiogeochemCycle-L.gif

54-20-BiogeochemCycle-NL.gif

54-21-HubbardBrookPhotos.jpg

54-21a-Dam.jpg

54-21b-HubbardForest.jpg

54-21c-HubbardBrookGraph-L.gif

54-21c-HubbardBrookGraph-NL.gif

54-22-BiomassRemoval.jpg

54-23a-AcidPrecipDist-L.gif

54-23a-AcidPrecipDist-NL.gif

54-23b-PrecipPHAverages-L.jpg

54-23b-PrecipPHAverages-NL.jpg

54-24-DDTIsGoodForMe.jpg

54-25-DDTInFoodChain-L.jpg

54-25-DDTInFoodChain-NL.jpg

54-26-IncreasCarbonDiox-L.gif

54-27a-OzoneHole.gif

54-27b-OzoneLayerThicknes-L.gif

54T-01-NutrienEnrichExper-L.gif

CHAPTER 55

Conservation Biology

Chapter Outline

The Biodiversity Crisis

The three levels of biodiversity are genetic diversity, species diversity, and ecosystem diversity

Biodiversity at all three levels is vital to human welfare

The four major threats to biodiversity are habitat destruction, introduced species, overexploitation, and food-chain disruptions

Conservation at the Population and Species Levels

According to the small-population approach, a population's small size can draw it into an extinction vortex

The declining-population approach is a proactive conservation strategy for detecting, diagnosing, and halting population declines

Conserving species involves weighing conflicting demands

Conservation at the Community, Ecosystem, and Landscape Levels

Edges and corridors can strongly influence landscape biodiversity

Conservation biologists face many challenges in setting up protected areas

Nature reserves must be functional parts of landscapes

Restoring degraded areas is an increasingly important conservation effort

The goal of sustainable development is reorienting ecological research and challenging all of us to reassess our values

The future of the biosphere may depend on our biophilia

Transparency Acetates

The Transparency Acetates for *Biology*, Sixth Edition, include the following images:

Media for Instructors

Campbell Image Presentation Library

The Campbell Image Presentation Library CD-ROM set includes the following for your use:

- All art (available in pdf and jpeg or gif formats), photos (from the text and outside sources), and tables. Art images are also available without callouts. See the Visual Guide to the Image Library section at the end of this chapter for thumbnail versions of every image.
- A PowerPoint™ slide show of the art (with callouts), photos (both text and outside sources), and tables.

PowerPoint Lectures CD-ROM

The PowerPoint Lectures CD-ROM contains slides that integrate the art, photos, tables, and lecture outline from this chapter.

Campbell Biology Website (Instructor Resources)

See the insert in your copy of Campbell/Reece *Biology*, Sixth Edition, for instructions on how to access the Campbell Biology Website. The Instructor Resources section of the website includes the following:

- The art, photos, tables, PowerPoint slide shows, videos, and animations from the Campbell Image Presentation Library
- Suggested answers to the Lab Report questions from the Case Studies in the Process of Science
- The PowerPoint Lecture for this chapter
- Word files of the lecture outline for this chapter
- Photo links

Course Management Systems

The media content for this chapter is available in three course management systems: CourseCompass™, Blackboard, and WebCT. For more information, go to http://cms.aw.com. For the latest pdf instructions on how to use CourseCompass, go to www.coursecompass.com. In addition, a Syllabus Manager is offered on the Campbell Biology Website.

Media for Students

The Campbell Biology Website and CD-ROM include the following for your students:

- Objectives
- Chapter Review (Summary, Self-Quiz, and Essay Questions from the book; Word Roots; Key Terms linked to the Glossary)
- Activities (see list below)
- Case Studies in the Process of Science (see list below)
- Quizzes (Pre-test, Activities Quiz, Chapter Quiz, Essay Questions)
- Web Links
- News and References
- Art and videos from the Campbell Image Presentation Library
- The Campbell *Biology* Interviews (from all editions)
- Glossary with audio pronunciations
- Syllabus Manager

Student Media Activities and Case Studies in The Process of Science

Web/CD Activity 55A: *Madagascar and the Biodiversity Crisis*

Web/CD Activity 55B: *Introduced Species: Fire Ants*

Web/CD Case Study in the Process of Science: *How Are Potential Prairie Restoration Sites Analyzed?*

Web/CD Activity 55C: *Conservation Biology Review*

Objectives

The Biodiversity Crisis

1. Describe the three levels of biodiversity.

2. Explain why biodiversity at all levels is vital to human welfare.

3. List the four major threats to biodiversity and give an example of each.

Conservation at the Population and Species Levels

4. Define and compare the small-population approach and the declining-population approach.

5. Describe the basic steps common to the declining-population approach. Describe the case of the declining red-cockaded woodpecker to illustrate this approach.

6. Describe the conflicting demands that accompany species conservation.

Conservation at the Community, Ecosystem, and Landscape Levels

7. Explain how edges and corridors can strongly influence landscape biodiversity.

8. Define biodiversity hot spots and explain why they are important.

9. Explain why natural reserves must be functional parts of landscapes.

10. Define zoned reserves and explain why they are important.

11. Define restoration ecology and describe its goals. Explain the importance of bioremediation and the augmentation of ecosystem processes in restoration efforts.

12. Describe the process of adaptive management.

13. Describe the concept of sustainable development.

14. Explain the goals of the Sustainable Biosphere Initiative.

15. Define biophilia and explain why the concept gives some biologists hope.

Key Terms

conservation biology
biodiversity crisis
endangered species
threatened species
ecosystem services
introduced species
small-population
  approach
extinction vortex

minimum viable
  population size
  (MVP)
population viability
  analysis (PVA)
effective population size
declining-population
  approach
landscape

landscape ecology
movement corridor
biodiversity hot spot
zoned reserve
restoration ecology
bioremediation
adaptive management
Sustainable Biosphere
  Initiative

Word Root

bio- = life (*biodiversity hotspot*: a relatively small area with an exceptional concentration of species)

References

Enger, E. D. and B. F. Smith. *Environmental Science: A Study of Interrelationships.* 7th ed. Boston, Massachusetts, McGraw-Hill, 2000.

Gleick, P. H. "Making Every Drop Count." *Scientific American*, February 2001.

Visual Guide to the Image Library

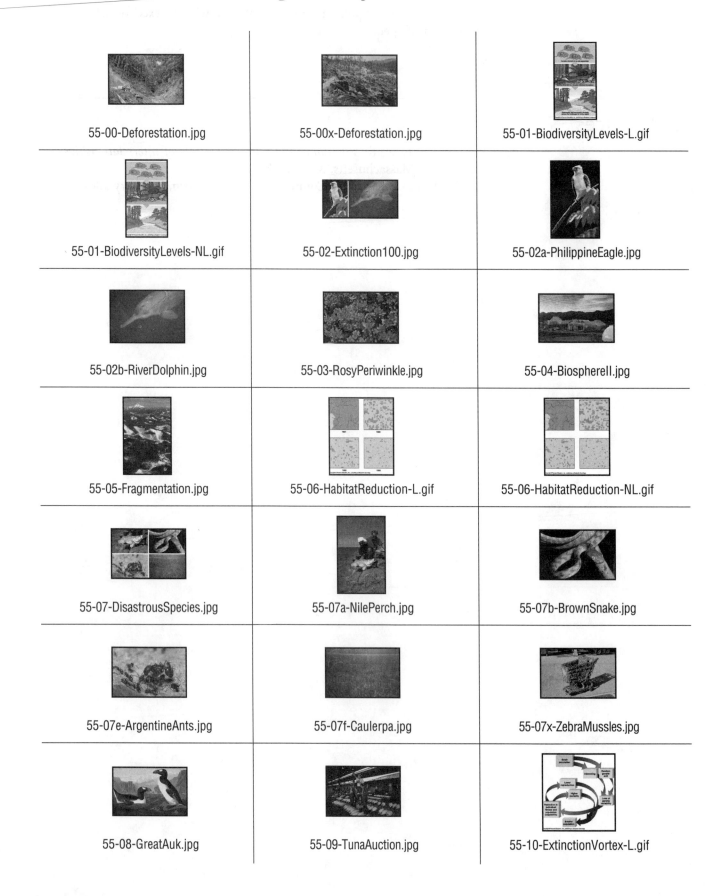

55-00-Deforestation.jpg

55-00x-Deforestation.jpg

55-01-BiodiversityLevels-L.gif

55-01-BiodiversityLevels-NL.gif

55-02-Extinction100.jpg

55-02a-PhilippineEagle.jpg

55-02b-RiverDolphin.jpg

55-03-RosyPeriwinkle.jpg

55-04-BiosphereII.jpg

55-05-Fragmentation.jpg

55-06-HabitatReduction-L.gif

55-06-HabitatReduction-NL.gif

55-07-DisastrousSpecies.jpg

55-07a-NilePerch.jpg

55-07b-BrownSnake.jpg

55-07e-ArgentineAnts.jpg

55-07f-Caulerpa.jpg

55-07x-ZebraMussles.jpg

55-08-GreatAuk.jpg

55-09-TunaAuction.jpg

55-10-ExtinctionVortex-L.gif

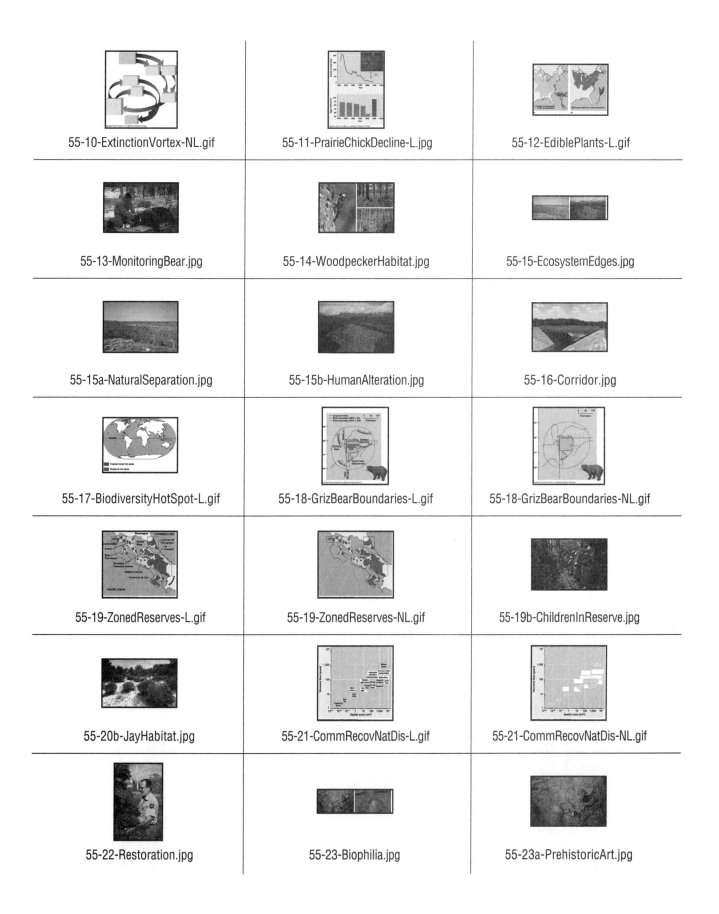

55-10-ExtinctionVortex-NL.gif

55-11-PrairieChickDecline-L.jpg

55-12-EdiblePlants-L.gif

55-13-MonitoringBear.jpg

55-14-WoodpeckerHabitat.jpg

55-15-EcosystemEdges.jpg

55-15a-NaturalSeparation.jpg

55-15b-HumanAlteration.jpg

55-16-Corridor.jpg

55-17-BiodiversityHotSpot-L.gif

55-18-GrizBearBoundaries-L.gif

55-18-GrizBearBoundaries-NL.gif

55-19-ZonedReserves-L.gif

55-19-ZonedReserves-NL.gif

55-19b-ChildrenInReserve.jpg

55-20b-JayHabitat.jpg

55-21-CommRecovNatDis-L.gif

55-21-CommRecovNatDis-NL.gif

55-22-Restoration.jpg

55-23-Biophilia.jpg

55-23a-PrehistoricArt.jpg

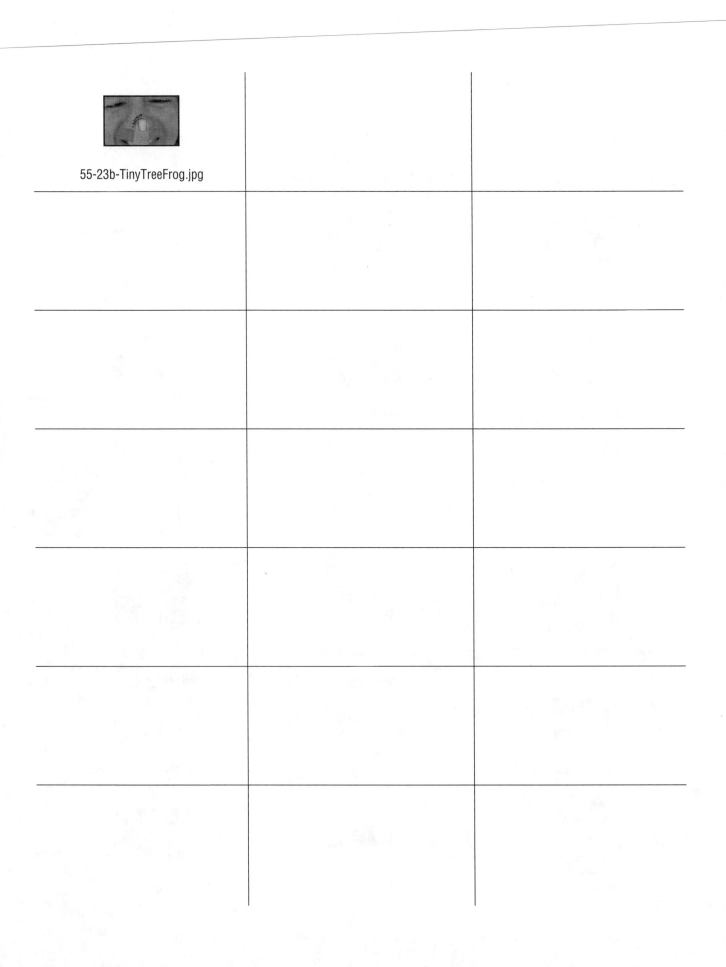

55-23b-TinyTreeFrog.jpg